Computerized Accounting with

Peachtree

2007

Jim Mazza, MBA, ABA
DeVry University

Gary Chavez, MBA
DeVry University

Paradigm PUBLISHING

Senior Developmental Editor: Tom Modl   **Proofreading:** DPS Associates
Production Editor: Amy McGuire   **Cover Design:** Leslie Anderson
Composition: Precision Graphics

Care has been taken to verify the accuracy of information presented in this book. However, the authors, editors, and publisher cannot accept responsibility for Web, e-mail, newsgroup, or chat room subject matter or content, or for consequences from application of the information in this book, and make no warranty, expressed or implied, with respect to its content.

Trademarks: Some of the product names and company names included in this book have been used for identification purposes only and may be trademarks or registered trade names of their respective manufacturers and sellers. The authors, editors, and publisher disclaim any affiliation, association, or connection with, or sponsorship or endorsement by, such owners.

Peachtree® is a trademark of Sage Software SB, Inc. Microsoft, Windows, and Internet Explorer are registered trademarks of Microsoft Corporation in the United States and other countries.

Website Image Credits: Pages 27, 452: Screen shots reprinted with permission of Sage Software SB, Inc. All rights reserved. Peachtree and the Peachtree logo are registered trademarks of Sage Software SB, Inc. **67:** Thompson's Curling Rink Equipment. **118:** Small Business Administration. **169:** D&B. **216:** Office Depot. **324:** www.annualreports.com. **360:** Inventory Control Forum. **491:** Permission granted by Institute of Management Accountants. **529:** Internal Revenue Service, United States Department of the Treasury. **572:** ©Copyright 2007, The Nasdaq Stock Market, Inc. Reprinted with permission.

We have made every effort to trace the ownership of all copyrighted material and to secure permission from copyright holders. In the event of any question arising as to the use of any material, we will be pleased to make the necessary corrections in future printings. Thanks are due to the aforementioned authors, publishers, and agents for permission to use the materials indicated.

ISBN 978-0-76383-030-4 (Text and CD-ROM)

© 2008 by Paradigm Publishing Inc., a division of EMC Corporation
875 Montreal Way
St. Paul, MN 55102
E-mail: educate@emcp.com
Web site: www.emcp.com

Printed in the United States of America

16 15 14 13 12 11 10 09 08 07   1 2 3 4 5 6 7 8 9 10

CONTENTS

Preface

Computerized Accounting with Peachtree® 2007 teaches all the key accounting software skills supported in Peachtree® Complete Accounting, Release 2007. In addition, it covers the accounting concepts associated with each chapter in substantial detail for a software textbook. The material is presented in a clear and concise manner, with a step-by-step approach to introduce new functions.

Textbook Features

Several aspects of this text are unique and will lead to better student understanding of the material while giving the instructor the flexibility needed in the classroom.

- Learning objectives focus the instruction for each chapter.
- Each accounting concept is thoroughly explained before students begin using any of Peachtree's functions.
- All of the learning objectives are presented using a step-by-step approach and illustrated by detailed screen captures.
- Definitions of key phrases and helpful hints are included in the margins to help students fully understand the learning objectives.
- Checkpoint quizzes are located at the end of each major learning objective.
- Two methods of negotiating the Peachtree environment are intermittently used throughout the text. Students can use Menu bar drop-down menus or navigation aids to work through the problems.
- Practice exercises specific to each objective (with selected answers) are provided at the end of each learning objective.
- Internet activities specific to chapter topics are included at the end of each chapter.
- Two levels of comprehensive case problems test students' knowledge of the learning objectives.
- Cooperative learning problems that focus on specific chapter issues are available in each chapter.
- A writing and decision-making problem relating to the chapter's learning objectives is included at the end of each chapter.
- Comprehensive problems to be administered at the end of chapter 7 and chapter 12 are available in the Instructor's Guide.

Chapters at a Glance

Chapter 1 – Getting Started

Chapter 1 introduces students to accounting as the language of business and to users of accounting information. The differences between computerized and manual accounting are stressed.

The chapter also explains how to open Peachtree 2007 and details the different navigation methods. In an effort to enhance the Peachtree experience, the Help feature is explained, and students are given instructions for exploring the Help feature. The Save and Backup features are also introduced.

Chapter 2 – Setting Up a Company

Chapter 2 explains the business organization types in detail, with charts illuminating the advantages and disadvantages of each. The chart of accounts and the general ledger are fully explained. There is an in-depth discussion of the differences between the cash and accrual methods of accounting, as well as an explanation of accounting periods. The account types that are used in Peachtree are thoroughly explained and the accounting definitions are detailed.

Students learn to set up a new company with easy-to-follow instructions and screen captures. Students create the chart of accounts, learn to create new accounts from scratch, and enter beginning balances in the accounts. Finally, students learn how to use the print filter and how to print documents. From this point on, the Print function is used at the end of each chapter.

Chapter 3 – Entering Transactions for a Cash Business

Chapter 3 introduces students to the meaning of transactions and how transactions affect the journal. Along with this, the treatment of debits and credits is explained. Subject matter is thoroughly discussed before students are expected to tackle the Peachtree functions—manual journal entries are demonstrated prior to having students do them using Peachtree.

Students create a new company and enter sample transactions using Peachtree. The sample manual transaction is presented prior to the computerized transaction so students are aware of the desired results. Edited transactions, recurring transactions, and memorized transactions are also introduced. Students then learn to print the financial transactions.

Chapter 4 – Accounts Receivable and Sales for a Service Business

In chapter 4, the concept of accounts receivable is revisited in some detail. The concepts of subsidiary receivable ledger accounts and the controlling accounts are introduced. In addition, the concept and procedures for accounting for uncollectible accounts is introduced and explained using the direct write-off and allowance methods.

In Peachtree, students learn to create customer accounts and enter beginning balances, reviewing account terms associated with accounts receivable. They record sales on credit and record payments to the customers' accounts. Students use the journal to write off uncollectible accounts. In addition to mastering the accounts receivable transactions, students learn to use Action Items, Event Logs, and Company Alerts.

Chapter 5 – Accounts Payable and Purchases for a Service Business

Students are introduced to the concept of accounts payable and the underlying meanings associated with accounts payable and vendors are explained. The chapter also introduces controlling accounts and the accounts payable subsidiary.

In Peachtree, students create vendor accounts and enter their beginning balances. After the accounts are created, purchase and accounts payable transactions are demonstrated. Students use the Edit (Open) feature and the Action Items once again while entering accounts payable transactions. Additionally, the Peachtree Alert feature is demonstrated and practiced.

Chapter 6 – Cash Payments and Cash Receipts

Chapter 6 deals with managing cash and cash discounts. Invoices and payments to invoices are explained in detail.

In Peachtree, students learn how to process cash payments using the cash payments module. In addition, they learn how to process cash receipts using the cash receipts module and how to apply discount terms where applicable. Another Peachtree feature introduced is the bank reconciliation. The process is demonstrated for students, who then have several chances to prepare a bank reconciliation using Peachtree.

Chapter 7 – Preparing the Financial Statements

Although introduced in chapter 2, the preparation of financial statements is covered more thoroughly in chapter 7. This chapter discusses the different types of adjusting entries, giving examples of each. In addition, it reviews financial statements and the information contained within each.

Students practice creating adjusting journal entries and preparing financial statements using Peachtree.

They learn special financial statement formatting features, including how to design unique financial statements for a given business. More importantly, students learn to change the accounting period and close the fiscal year.

Chapter 8 – Purchases of Inventory in a Merchandise Business

The two basic inventory systems and the methods for costing inventory are explained in detail. The inventory costing methods are demonstrated manually to give students a visual feel for what Peachtree will do automatically, which is to cost out inventory for a given inventory valuation method. These methods are explained using easy-to-understand examples. Additionally, there is a discussion about the results that each method provides the accountant.

In Peachtree, students create the inventory accounts and their associated subsidiary ledger accounts. Sales representatives accounts are established to allow Peachtree to track individual salespersons' inventory sales. Purchase transactions are demonstrated, and students practice the different types of transactions, including transactions involving discounts, purchase orders, and returns.

Chapter 9 – Sales of Inventory in a Merchandise Business

In this chapter students are introduced to inventory sales concepts and the perpetual inventory system. Sales tax is a part of the process of selling merchandise, so how to calculate and account for it is fully explained in this chapter. The necessary accounts and percentages are reviewed.

In Peachtree, students create the sales tax codes and accounts. After the sales tax accounts have been established, students can process sales transactions, create invoices, and add appropriate interest where applicable. Students have a chance to practice accounting for a sales return and processing a credit memo. Additionally, they have a chance to create a sales quotation and convert that quotation into a sales order.

Chapter 10 – Payroll

Chapter 10 reviews payroll concepts and introduces students to Peachtree payroll functions. Payroll concepts such as payroll periods, payroll laws and regulations, as well as the federal and state tax returns associated with payroll activities are covered. The normal payroll deductions that employees and employers are subject to are also reviewed.

In Peachtree, students use the Payroll Setup wizard to create a company's payroll system. Once the payroll system is created, students create individual employee payroll accounts. Instruction in the preparation of payroll and the printing of payroll checks follows the setup process. The payroll tax returns and payroll reports are then completed using the Print function.

Chapter 11 – Job Costing

Chapter 11 introduces students to job costing. The three basic methods for job costing—jobs only, phases, and phases with cost codes—are all demonstrated and explained.

In Peachtree, the setup for the job costing process is explored and practiced by students. This includes creating phase codes and cost codes, as well as estimating revenue and expenses. The procedures for using job costing to record and allocate purchases, payroll, and sales to specific jobs are explained and reviewed.

Chapter 12 – Fixed Assets

One of the unique features of this text is the treatment of fixed assets, since most textbooks do not include fixed assets among their topics. The concepts of depreciation and fixed assets valuation are covered. The most widely accepted depreciation methods are demonstrated for students in manual form.

In Peachtree, students will learn to create the individual fixed asset accounts and to create the appropriate supporting accounts, including the accumulated depreciation accounts. Transactions for the purchase, monthly depreciation, and disposal of assets are explained, demonstrated, and practiced. In addition, the associated depreciation reports are generated. Additionally, transactions are viewed using both the fixed asset module and the main Peachtree module to see the impact one module has on the other.

Peachtree 2007 Educational Version does not include the Fixed Assets module (FAS for Peachtree). If you do not have access to the Peachtree Fixed Assets module, fixed assets are also covered in the Appendix (see below).

Chapter 13 – Partnerships and Corporations

The differences among sole proprietorships, partnerships, and corporations are revisited. The advantages of the partnership form and the corporate form are reviewed. In the case of the corporation, the chapter introduces accounting concepts associated with stock and stockholder ownership. In addition, the treatment of dividends is also covered in some length.

Students will create partnership accounts and enter partnership transactions, as well as distribute partnership gains and losses among and between the partners. Then they will create a new company as a corporation and practice several transactions.

Appendix – Fixed Assets

This appendix is for users who do not have access to the Fixed Assets module (FAS for Peachtree). It is designed to demonstrate the depreciation and disposal of fixed assets using the main Peachtree Accounting module rather than the Fixed Assets module.

Supplements

This text comes with an Instructor's Guide CD and the Computerized Accounting Internet Resource Center.

The **Instructor's Guide CD** includes the following information:
Overview
Sample Syllabi
Teaching Hints
Solutions (Content Checks and Case Problems)
Two Comprehensive Problems
Objective Mid-term and Final Exams

The **Computerized Accounting Internet Resource Center** provides study aids, Web links, and additional course content for students.

Using the *Computerized Accounting with PEACHTREE® 2007* CD

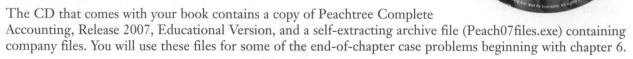

Computerized Accounting with Peachtree® 2007 teaches you how to use the latest version of Peachtree Complete Accounting to complete accounting tasks similar to those you will perform in a business environment. As you work through the book, you will apply accounting concepts and software procedures using Peachtree company files that you either create or open in a designated location on your hard drive or network.

The CD that comes with your book contains a copy of Peachtree Complete Accounting, Release 2007, Educational Version, and a self-extracting archive file (Peach07files.exe) containing company files. You will use these files for some of the end-of-chapter case problems beginning with chapter 6.

Before you begin, check with your instructor to see if Peachtree Complete Accounting and/or the company files have already been loaded in a designated location for you. If they have not, or if you are doing your work at home, take the following steps to install Peachtree and download the company files.

Installing Peachtree Complete Accounting, Release 2007, Educational Version

If you do need to install Peachtree on your workstation or you are using this book at home, simply place the CD in your CD-ROM drive, and the Peachtree installation program will automatically appear and guide you through installing the software. The educational version of Peachtree Complete Accounting has the same features and functions—except for the Fixed Assets Module (needed for chapter 12)—that the commercial version does, but is not upgradeable.

Note: During installation, enter the following serial number: 45950604.

In order to successfully install and run Peachtree Complete Accounting Release 2007, Educational Version, you will need at a minimum the following hardware and software:

- IBM Compatible 1 GHz Intel Pentium III computer for a single user; 1.8 GHz Pentium 4 for multiple concurrent users.
- Windows XP SP1 or Windows 2000 SP3. Product will not operate in a Windows Terminal Server Environment using Windows Terminal Services.
- 256MB RAM for a single user; 512MB for multiple concurrent users.
- Display settings of at least High Color (16 bit). SVGA video. 800 x 600 screen resolution with small fonts.
- 2xCD-ROM Drive.
- Mouse or compatible pointing device.
- 450MB free hard disk space.
- Printers supported by Windows XP/2000.
- Internet Explorer 6.0 or higher required. Microsoft Internet Explorer 6.0 is included on the Peachtree CD. Requires 70MB (or higher) for installation.
- Online Services require Internet access. Minimum connection speed depends on service.
- In-product demos require Macromedia® Flash™ Player.
- To use Microsoft Excel with Peachtree products, Excel 2000, 2002, or 2003 is required.

Downloading Company Files from the CD

If you are using a computer in a lab setting, we suggest that you create a separate folder on either your hard drive or in a designated network directory in which to save the Peachtree company files that you create, open, and add to while working through this book. Your instructor may have already set up a designated location for your files. Once you have either created that folder or been told where your folder is, take the following steps to extract the company files from the CD to your folder:

1. Insert the *Computerized Accounting with Peachtree 2007* CD into the CD-ROM drive.
2. At the Welcome to Peachtree Accounting window, click "Browse CD."
3. In the Exploring window that appears, on the right side, double-click *Peach07files.exe*.
4. Confirm with your instructor where your company files should be located.
5. At the WinZip Self-Extractor – Peach07files.exe dialog box, click Browse.
6. At the Browse for Folder dialog box, locate the folder where you will be storing your company files, and then click OK.
7. If the folder shown in the Unzip to folder text box is correct, click Unzip.

If you are using a computer at home, and you are the only one who is going to use that computer for the course, you can simply accept the default location in the Winzip Self-Extractor – Peach07files.exe dialog box (c:\), and click Unzip. Your files will be in a folder called Peachtree 2007 Student Data (Company Files).

Creating and Naming Company Files

As you work through the exercises in this textbook, you will create, open, and name Peachtree company files. You will learn the procedures for opening, creating, and backing up company files in chapters 1 and 2. Company files created in Peachtree take up a lot of memory. Typically, you will save your files to a computer's hard drive or a designated network directory. You may also backup and restore to flash drives. Be aware that if you use flash drives, you will need to backup at the end of each session and restore at the beginning of each session. See your instructor to determine where exactly you should save your company files.

When you create a company file, or use one of the company files that are provided with the book, you may want to customize the name so that it is readily identifiable as your version of the company. You can do this by putting an extension at the end of the company's name. The extension could be your last name and first initial. For example, suppose you were working on the Acme Laundry Company file. When the company was first created, the file would have the name Acme Laundry Company. Everyone in the class would have the same file name; as a result, you could not tell your file from any other file. To solve this problem, you could add your name to the company name as you create the company file. If your name is John Jones, for example, the new company name and file name would be: **Acme Laundry – JONESJ,** and your file would be unique. This is only a suggestion—ask your instructor for specific instructions on how to name and save files.

To customize the name of a company as you create it, enter the customized company name in the *Company Name* field of the New Company Setup – Company Information dialog box. (See pp. 38-39 of chapter 2.)

To customize the names of already-created companies downloaded from the CD, take the following steps:

1. At the Peachtree Accounting-Start Window, click *Open an existing company*.
2. Find and open the company file on which you will be working. (See pp. 23-24 of chapter 1.)
3. Click Maintain, and then click Company Information.
4. At the Maintain Company Information window, click in the *Company Name* field, and then change the company name as needed.
5. Click the OK button at the top of the window. The next time you open the company, its name will reflect the changes you made.

CHAPTER

1

GETTING
STARTED

1. Understand the differences between computerized and manual accounting

2. Open Peachtree Complete Accounting 2007

3. Use the basic Peachtree window, Custom toolbar, and the Menu bar

4. Use the Help feature

5. Open, save, and back up files

accounting The process of recording, summarizing, analyzing, and interpreting financial activities.

Accounting is the process of recording, summarizing, analyzing, and interpreting financial activities—activities that involve money. The purpose of accounting is to provide financial information that owners, managers, and other interested parties can use to make decisions about a business.

Every accounting system—simple or complex, manual or computerized—must produce a complete, ongoing record of the financial events that take place in a business and must provide periodic reports showing the results of operations and the financial condition of the business. The steps of the accounting process are recording, summarizing, analyzing, and interpreting.

- *Recording* involves preparing a written record of financial events.
- *Summarizing* involves organizing the financial data into reports at regular intervals.
- *Analyzing* involves examining the reports to determine financial success or failure.
- *Interpreting* involves using financial data to make decisions.

Accounting is often called "the language of business" because it is used to communicate information about the financial results and financial condition of businesses. Is a firm profitable? Can it pay its debts? Does it have the resources to expand? This is the kind of information that accounting provides. Users of such information include owners, managers, current and potential investors, banks and other lending institutions, tax authorities, government agencies that regulate business activities, and potential suppliers and customers.

MANUAL AND COMPUTERIZED ACCOUNTING SYSTEMS

Whether an accounting system is manual or computerized, the underlying principles of accounting are the same. What does change when using a computerized system is the method of recording data and preparing reports. Once data about financial events is entered into a computerized accounting system, the system can be used to perform many tasks automatically: print a journal, post to the ledger accounts, prepare a trial balance, and print reports and financial statements.

Peachtree Accounting is designed for small and medium-sized businesses. One of the advantages of this software is that it produces records that are very similar to those found in a manual accounting system. For example, Peachtree allows you to work with special journals for sales, purchases, cash receipts, and cash disbursements as well as a general journal. Some other computerized accounting systems, such as QuickBooks Pro, permit the use of just a single journal.

Special journals are an efficient means of recording financial data, and they make it easier to locate information that may be needed later. It is much quicker to look for a particular sale on credit in the sales journal than it is to trace through all the different transactions recorded in a single journal.

Computerized accounting systems like Peachtree save an enormous amount of time and effort for you because they do so many tasks automatically. Just as important, computerized accounting systems greatly reduce the number of errors that can occur with a manual accounting system.

A manual accounting system offers many opportunities for making errors. Data must be transferred by hand from the journals to the ledger accounts, then to the trial balance, and finally to the financial statements. Throughout this process, many calculations must be made.

With a computerized accounting system, there is still the possibility of making an error when a financial event is entered into the system. However, many computerized accounting systems have built-in checks that help you avoid errors. For example, when an entry is being made in the general journal, Peachtree alerts you if the entry contains unequal debits and credits.

Computerized accounting systems also reduce errors because they make all calculations automatically. For example, they compute the balances of the ledger accounts, the totals of the trial balance, and the subtotals and totals of the financial statements.

Note that computerized accounting systems like Peachtree do more than just the traditional tasks of journalizing, posting, preparing a trial balance, and preparing financial statements. These systems also handle many other financial activities, such as doing payroll and tax calculations, keeping records of the time and costs involved in projects, billing customers, processing credit card transactions, keeping records of fixed assets such as equipment, and keeping track of prospective customers.

Check
POINT

1. What is the purpose of accounting?
2. What are two major advantages of computerized accounting systems over manual accounting systems?

Answers
1. *The purpose of accounting is to provide financial information that owners, managers, and other interested parties can use to make decisions about a business.*
2. *Computerized accounting systems save time and effort and reduce errors.*

OBJECTIVE 2 — OPEN PEACHTREE COMPLETE ACCOUNTING 2007

Peachtree Complete Accounting 2007 includes two sample companies: Stone Arbor Landscaping and Bellwether Garden Supply. These sample companies are provided to help you become familiar with the basic functions of the software. In this chapter, we will work with Bellwether Garden Supply, a retail firm that sells goods and services.

Note: This text comes with a copy of Peachtree Complete Accounting 2007 (Educational) and assumes you will use Peachtree Complete Accounting as you work through the book. In order to be more concise, from this point on the software will be referred to as "Peachtree Accounting" or "Peachtree."

Follow the steps outlined on the following pages to begin the opening process for Peachtree Complete Accounting 2007.

Step 1:

Click the *Peachtree Complete Accounting 2007* icon from the desktop or click Start, All Programs, Peachtree Complete Accounting 2007, and again Peachtree Complete Accounting 2007 from the Start menu lists that pop up. (See figure 1–1.)

FIGURE 1-1

Peachtree Startup Menus

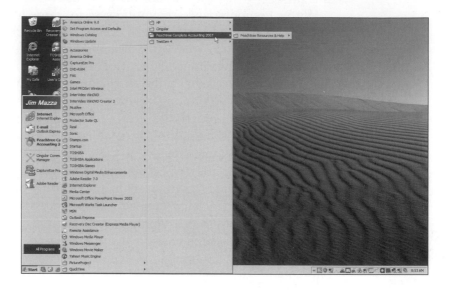

Step 2:

Click *Explore a sample company* from the Startup window, as shown in figure 1–2.

FIGURE 1-2

Peachtree Accounting Opening Window

At the Explore a Sample Company window, click *Bellwether Garden Supply*, as shown by figure 1–3. Then click <u>O</u>K.

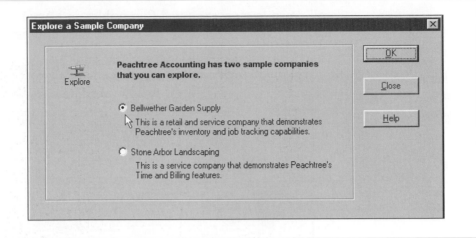

HINT

When you see a menu or button name with one of the letters underlined, that means you can activate that command by pressing at the same time the Alt key and the underlined letter on the keyboard.

A new interactive feature of Peachtree Complete Accounting 2007 called Business Status will appear. This window allows you to access many helpful options using the existing program to analyze several business aspects. Through these options, you can obtain information about Peachtree and your accounts. Peachtree also offers a number of services that can be obtained by clicking the labels found under the headings Business Status, Customers & Sales, Vendors & Purchases, Inventory & Services, Employees & Payroll, Banking, and Company.

For example, the Business Status feature provides an instant view of a firm's overall financial performance within specified areas. This section can be reached by clicking the *Business Status* tab that appears in the Peachtree opening window.

Step 4:

Click the *Business Status* tab, as shown in figure 1–4.

Follow steps 5 through 8 to explore a few of the valuable reports and graphs available in the Business Status section. The information shown is for Bellwether Garden Supply.

Step 5:

Scroll down to view the Aged Receivables and Aged Payables pie charts and Customers Who Owe Money. These are shown in figure 1–5.

FIGURE 1-5

Summary Reports and Graph from the Business Status Window

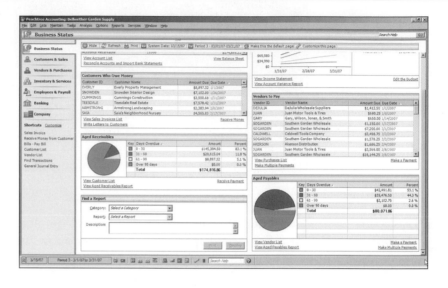

Information about any account can be reached by clicking the account name or any blue text line. For example, suppose that Bellwether Garden Supply wants information about the sales invoice that it issued to Armstrong Landscaping.

Step 6:

To access information about sales invoices to Armstrong Landscaping, scroll up to *Customers Who Owe Money* located in the Business Status section of the Peachtree opening window.

Step 7:

Click <u>Armstrong</u> in the Customer ID section, as shown in figure 1–6.

FIGURE 1-6

Armstrong Landscaping Selected from the Business Status Window

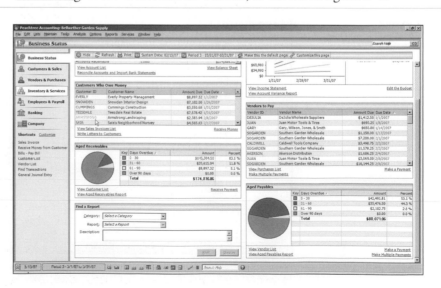

Step 8:

Review the latest invoice for Armstrong Landscaping in the Sales/Invoicing window. (See figure 1–7.) Then click Close.

FIGURE 1-7

Armstrong Landscaping Sales/Invoicing Window

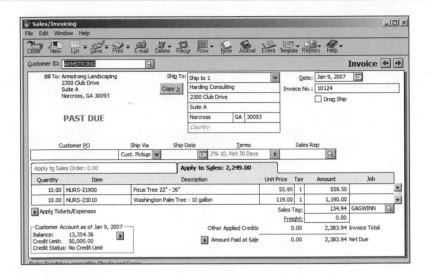

FIGURE 1-7

Armstrong Landscaping Sales/Invoicing Window

Step 9:

Click the *Company* tab, located below the Business Status tab. If your computer is connected to the Internet, you can click *Check for Peachtree Updates* to update Peachtree Complete Accounting 2007.

Step 10:

Click Check Now to update the program or Close to proceed to the next step.

Step 11:

Scroll over to *View All Financial Statements* in the Company window, as shown in figure 1–8. This is one example of the helpful features that are available to users through the Company section of the window. (**Note:** Since this data may be updated by Peachtree, your screen may be different.)

FIGURE 1-8

View All Financial Statements Company Window

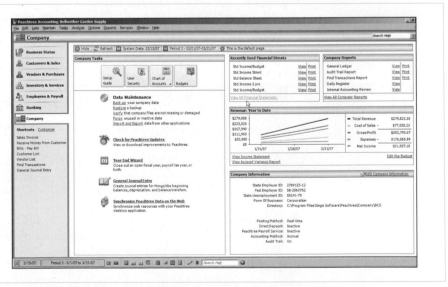

If you want to explore other features, click the hyperlinks to move between the sections of the window.

HINT

The Peachtree Business Status window can be minimized at any time by clicking Hide from the Business Status Menu bar and maximized by clicking Show from the same menu.

Step 12:

Exit Peachtree Complete Accounting 2007 by clicking File from the Menu bar, and then clicking Exit. (See figure 1–9.)

FIGURE 1-9

Exit Selected from the File Drop-Down List

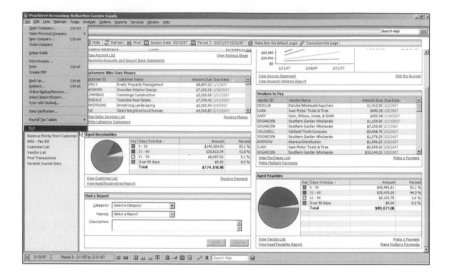

Check POINT

1. What is the major purpose of the Business Status window?
2. What are the 7 main hyperlinks in the Peachtree opening window?

Answers

1. *The Business Status window allows you to access options that provide information about the accounts of your business.*
2. *The 7 main hyperlinks are Business Status, Customers & Sales, Vendors & Purchases, Inventory & Services, Employees & Payroll, Banking, and Company.*

PRACTICE *objective* 2

1. Open Peachtree Complete Accounting 2007.

2. Click *Explore a sample company* and then *Bellwether Garden Supply.*

3. Click *Business Status* from the Peachtree opening window.

4. Access Snowden Interior Design from the Customers Who Owe Money section, review the account information, and then close the Snowden Interior Design window.

5. If you have Internet access, click *Check for Peachtree Updates* from the Peachtree Company window.

6. Close your Web browser, then close the Peachtree window.

7. Exit Peachtree Complete Accounting 2007.

OBJECTIVE 3 — USE THE PEACHTREE WINDOW AND MENU BAR

Two methods can be used for navigating within Peachtree. One method involves using the opening window icons and links, and the other method involves using the traditional pull-down menus from the Menu bar. Both methods produce the same results and are accessed from the basic Peachtree window.

BASIC PEACHTREE WINDOW

The basic Peachtree window is made up of several parts, including the Custom toolbar and the Menu bar. (See figure 1–10.)

FIGURE 1-10

Basic Peachtree Window, Business Status, and Custom Toolbar

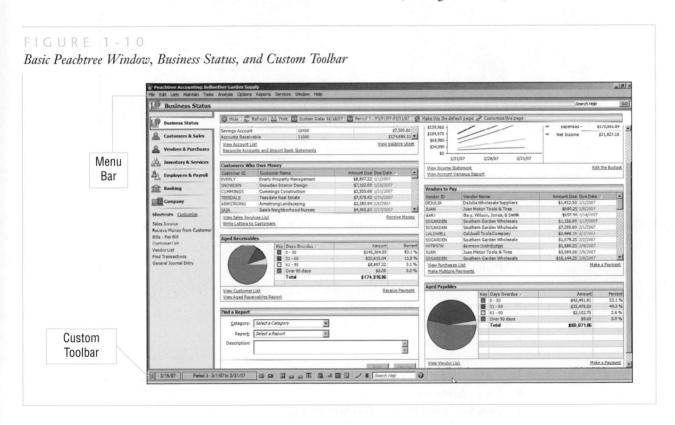

Many of the functions located in the basic Peachtree window are general Microsoft Windows functions and are implemented using typical Windows commands. For example, the Minimize/Maximize/Close buttons function in the same way for any application of the Windows operating system. In addition, the scroll bar, window sizing tools, and mouse pointer operate normally for Windows. There are, however, some features that are unique to the basic Peachtree window.

OPENING WINDOW ICONS AND LINKS

The opening window icons (pictures) help you move through the Peachtree accounting system. The Custom toolbar, located at the bottom of the basic Peachtree window, accesses several functions used on a daily basis.

If the Custom toolbar is not visible, it may be turned off. If this is the case, click Options from the Menu bar at the top of the basic Peachtree window. Then click View Custom Toolbar from the drop-down list, as shown in figure 1–11.

FIGURE 1-11

View Custom Toolbar Command Selected from Drop-Down List

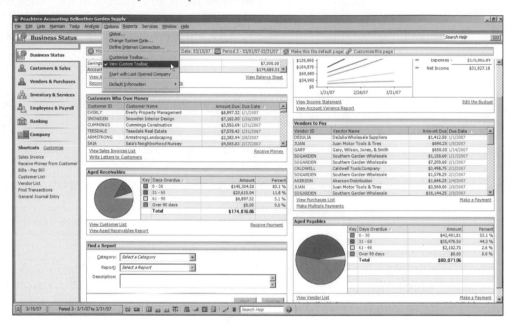

NOTE

Custom Toolbar is not available on the educational version of Peachtree.

The Custom toolbar is made up of 12 general icons:

- View Action Items
- Calculator
- Maintain Customer Records
- Maintain Vendor Records
- Maintain Employee Records
- Maintain Chart of Accounts
- Enter/View Receipts
- Enter/View Payments
- View Account Register
- Enter/View General Journal Entries
- Opens the Internal Accounting Review
- General Ledger

When you click any of these general icons, additional options appear for selection. To view other available icons, follow the steps outlined below.

Step 1:

Open Peachtree Accounting, and then open Bellwether Garden Supply by clicking *Explore a sample company* from the Peachtree Complete Accounting window.

Step 2:

Click the *Customers & Sales* tab in the basic Peachtree window. You will now see the options available in the (*Customers & Sales*) folder, as shown in figure 1–12. For each tab, you will get a similar collection of icons directing you to the various parts and functions of the program.

FIGURE 1-12

Options Available with the Customers & Sales Tab

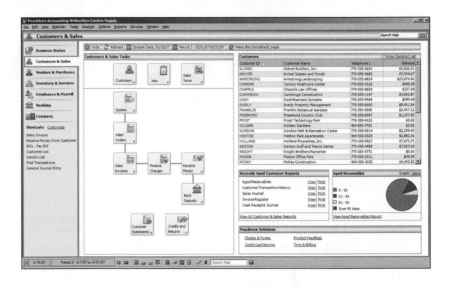

MENU BAR

The Menu bar, located at the top of the basic Peachtree window, can be used to move through Peachtree in the same way that the Custom toolbar icons are used. However, the Menu bar has 11 different general areas that can be accessed. These areas serve the following functions:

- File – Open, create, back up, and restore companies.
- Edit – Make changes and locate transactions.
- Lists – Create lists of various accounting aspects such as Customers & Sales, Vendors & Purchases, Chart of Accounts, and others.
- Maintain – Create and update the chart of accounts and accounts for customers, vendors, and inventory items.
- Tasks – Enter transactions of all types in the general journal and the special journals.
- Analysis – Use the cash, collection, payment, and financial management features.
- Options – Use to open, close, and customize toolbars. Use to change global options and to change the system date.
- Reports – Generate various reports.
- Services – Order checks, forms, and various customer support services.
- Window – Arrange the window.
- Help – Access help, a tutorial, technical support, and information about Peachtree products.

The File menu, shown in figure 1–13, is a typical Main Menu drop-down list.

FIGURE 1-13

File Menu Drop-Down List

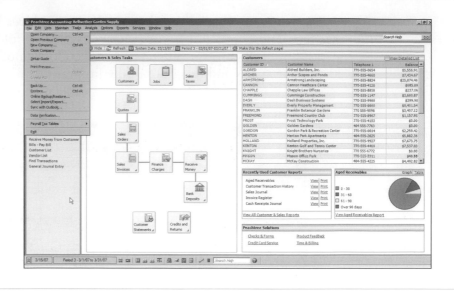

Click the screen to remove the drop-down list.

A COMPARISON OF THE TWO NAVIGATION METHODS

To understand the differences between the two navigation methods, we will assume that Bellwether Garden Supply provides a service to a customer on credit.

Opening Window

Step 1:

Click the *Customers & Sales* tab from the left side of the basic Peachtree window.

Step 2:

Click the *Customers* icon at the top of the Customers & Sales Tasks window. (See figure 1–14.)

FIGURE 1-14

Customers Selected from Customers & Sales Tasks Folder

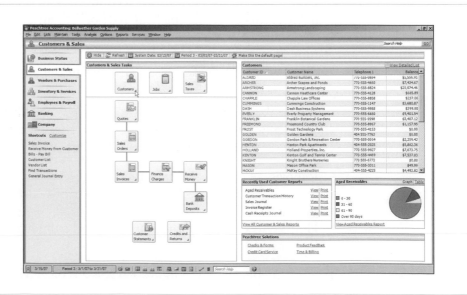

Step 3:

Click *New Customer* and review the Maintain Customers/Prospects window.

Step 4:

Click the Close button from the toolbar at the top of the Maintain Customers/Prospects window.

Menu Bar

Step 1:

Now click Maintain and then Customers/Prospects from the Menu bar, as shown in figure 1–15.

FIGURE 1-15

*Maintain Customers/
Prospects Selected from
Drop-Down List*

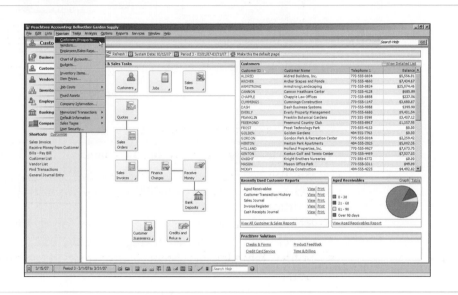

Step 2:

Review the Maintain Customers/Prospects window. Note that it is the same window as the one you reached using the Customers icon.

In this example, there is no difference in the destination reached. There is only a difference in the route taken through Peachtree Complete Accounting 2007. One route involves use of the Peachtree icons, whereas the other route involves use of the Menu bar.

GENERAL WINDOW AND SCREEN OPTIONS

Peachtree Accounting uses certain terms in connection with its particular windows and screens. These terms are explained below, using the Maintain Customers/Prospects window as a reference. (See figure 1–16.)

FIGURE 1-16

Maintain Customers/
Prospects Window with
Parts Labeled

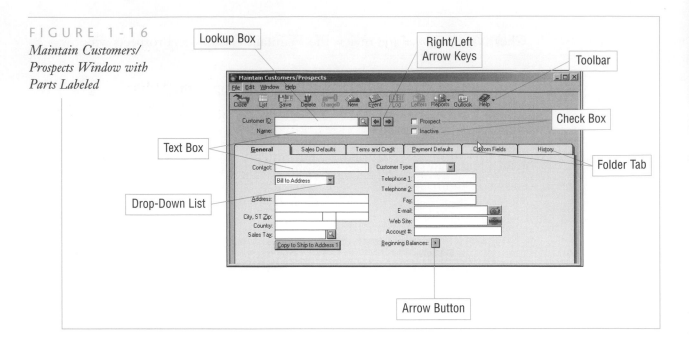

- Toolbar – Use to access the command buttons, including the Help feature.
- Lookup Box – Use the *magnifying glass* icon in this type of field to access additional records.
- Right/Left Arrow Keys – Use to move to previous or next record.
- Check Box – Select by clicking inside the box.
- Folder Tab – Use to access the information in a file folder within the system.
- Text Box – Use to enter information.
- Drop-Down List – Click the arrow to produce a list of choices.
- Arrow Button – Click to obtain additional information.
- Date Box – Use the *calendar* icon in this type of field to change dates (not shown).

Examine the Maintain Customers/Prospects window to see examples of a toolbar, lookup boxes, check boxes, folder tabs, text boxes, arrow buttons, and drop-down list arrows. Then click the Close button to close the window.

Check POINT

1. What are the two methods of navigating through Peachtree?
2. Will the results differ when different navigation methods are used?

Answers
1. The two methods are Peachtree icons and the Menu bar.
2. No, the results of the two navigation methods are the same.

1. Open Bellwether Garden Supply (if it is not already open).

2. Use the Custom toolbar to access the General Ledger. Then access the General Journal Entry. Close the window.

3. Use the Ta<u>s</u>ks drop-down menu from the Menu bar to access the <u>G</u>eneral Journal Entry window. Close the window.

4. Use the Custom toolbar to access the Maintain Vendors window. Close the window.

5. Use the <u>M</u>aintain drop-down menu from the Menu bar to access the Maintain Vendors window. Close the window.

OBJECTIVE 4 — USE THE HELP FEATURE

Peachtree Complete Accounting 2007 provides a variety of ways for you to get help. Help is available from the Menu bar and in all other windows. The Help feature provides information that allows you to work more efficiently with Peachtree. Follow the steps outlined below to use the Help feature of Peachtree.

Step 1:

Click <u>H</u>elp from the Menu bar as shown in figure 1–17.

Step 2:

Click Peachtree Accounting <u>H</u>elp from the drop-down list or press the F1 key.

FIGURE 1-17

Peachtree Accounting Help Selected

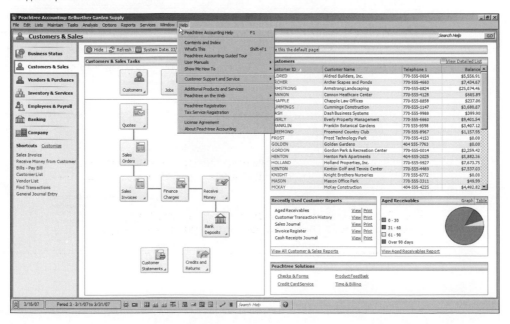

Step 3:

Review the <u>C</u>ontents tab of the Help window, which is shown in figure 1–18.

FIGURE 1-18

Contents Tab of Help Window

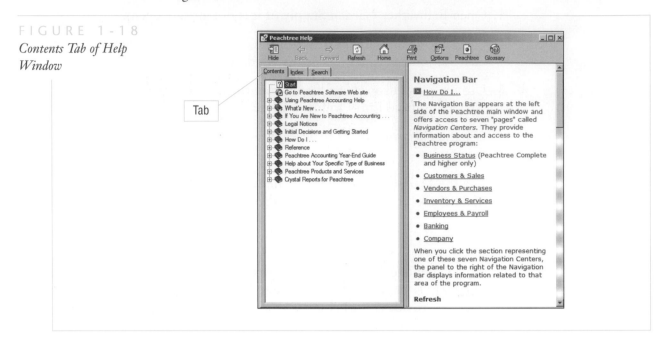

Tab

Step 4:

Click the <u>S</u>earch tab in the Help window to view the search options, as shown in figure 1–19.

FIGURE 1-19

Search Tab Selected from Help Window

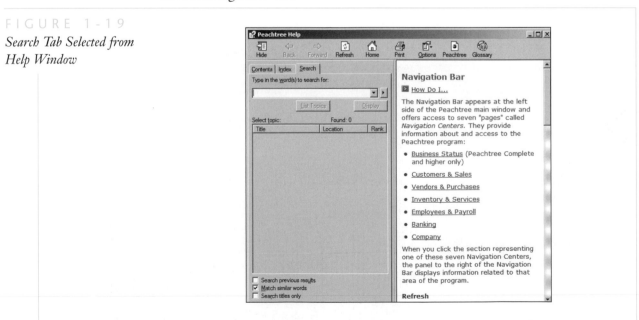

Step 5:

Key **Accounts Receivable** in the *Type in the word(s) to search for* text box.

Step 6:

Click List Topics to reveal a partial list of related topics, as shown in figure 1–20.

FIGURE 1-20

Accounts Receivable Topic List

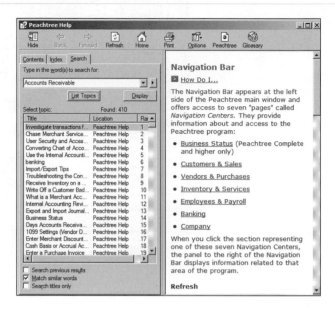

Step 7:

Select *Necessary Accounts* (Record 28) by using the scroll bar, as shown in figure 1–21.

FIGURE 1-21

Necessary Accounts Help Topic Selected

HINT

Select means to click a word or choice once with the mouse.

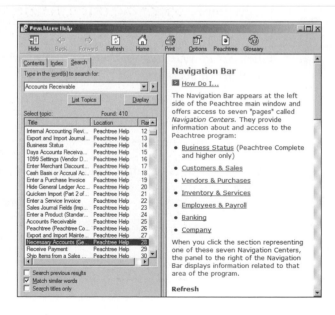

Step 8:

Double-click *Necessary Accounts* to reveal the topic information on the right side of the Help window, as shown in figure 1–22.

FIGURE 1-22

Account Information from Help Window

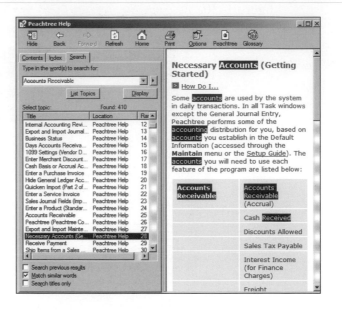

Step 9:

Scroll down the right side of the window to reveal additional topic suggestions.

Step 10:

Click *Set up your chart of accounts* to obtain information about establishing the chart of accounts.

Step 11:

Click the I<u>n</u>dex tab in the Help window.

Step 12:

Key the words **Accounts Receivable** to reveal general related topics, as shown in figure 1–23.

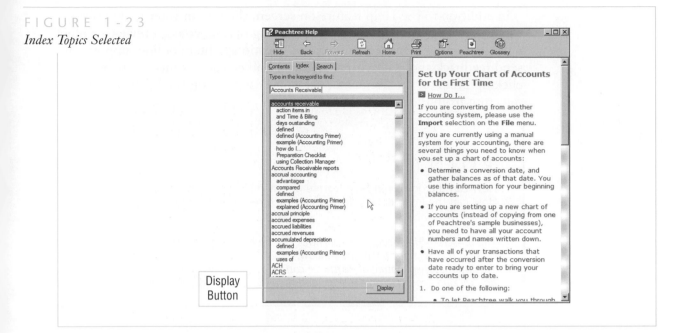

Display
Button

Step 13:

Click Display at the bottom of the Help window to reveal all of the directly related topics. This information appears in the Topics Found window, as shown in figure 1–24.

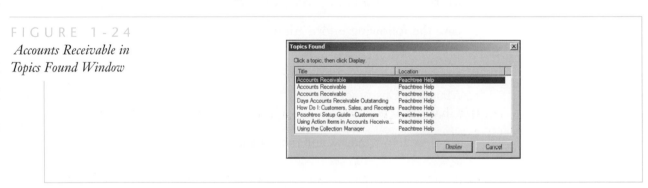

Step 14:

Click Display and view the Accounts Receivable information on the right side of the window.

Step 15:

Close the Peachtree Help window by clicking the Close button (X) in the upper right corner of the active window.
Important: Do not click the Close button (X) on the main Peachtree window because you will be closed out of Peachtree and will have to restart the program.

In addition to the Help feature on screen, there is an Internet Help feature called Peachtree on the Web. By going online, you can review product news, get answers to frequently asked questions, obtain online support, and send feedback about Peachtree features. You can access this resource by clicking Help on the Menu bar, clicking Peachtree on the Web, and then selecting from the submenu of choices.

Check POINT

1. How can the on-screen Help feature of Peachtree be accessed?
2. How can the Internet Help feature of Peachtree be accessed?

Answers

1. The on-screen Help feature of Peachtree can be accessed from the Menu bar or by clicking the Help button in any window.
2. The Internet Help feature of Peachtree can be accessed by clicking Help from the Menu bar, clicking Peachtree on the Web, and then clicking a selection from the submenu.

PRACTICE *objective* 4

1. Open Bellwether Garden Supply (if it is not already open).

2. Open the Help feature by using the Menu bar.

3. Locate the following information:

   a. Accounts Payable
   b. Maintain Vendors
   c. Maintain Customers
   d. Chart of Accounts

4. Close the Help window, and close Peachtree.

OBJECTIVE 5 — OPEN, SAVE, AND BACK UP FILES

Up to this point, we have opened the sample company by using the Explore a sample company option from the Peachtree Accounting startup window. Normally, however, a company is opened by using the Open an existing company option from the startup window or by clicking File from the Menu bar and then Open Company.

In most working environments, it is necessary to save and back up computer files. This practice reduces the risk of lost data. Anyone who works with computers and disks is aware of the potential for data loss and the problems that it can cause. The loss of financial data can be especially troublesome. For example, suppose a computer error results in the loss of the data needed to bill customers for goods sold to them. This can result in the loss of thousands of dollars of potential cash receipts. Because so much of the data you enter into an accounting system is vital, it is important that you save and back up data.

Fortunately, Peachtree makes it easy to save data. Once posted, all transactions are saved. Data that does not require posting is automatically saved when you exit Peachtree.

The backup process saves a copy of the company data which can be used to restore a company to a previous condition. This procedure usually requires saving to a hard disk, flash drive, or CD-ROM. Floppy disks can also be used for backup purposes. However, a tremendous amount of disk space is required, and several diskettes would be needed to accomplish this task.

OPENING AN EXISTING COMPANY

Follow the steps outlined below to open an existing company.

Step 1:
Start Peachtree Accounting.

Step 2:
Click *Open an existing company* from the Peachtree Accounting startup window, as shown in figure 1– 25.

FIGURE 1-25

Startup Window with Open an Existing Company Option Selected

Step 3:
Click OK at the Open an Existing Company dialog box to open Bellwether Garden Supply, as shown in figure 1–26.

FIGURE 1-26

Open an Existing Company Dialog Box

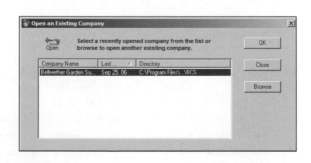

HINT

If a company has recently been opened, it will appear on the list. The company can then be opened by highlighting its name and by clicking OK. The dialog box may also have other companies listed.

To open an existing company through the File option of the Menu bar, use the following steps.

Step 4:

Click <u>F</u>ile from the Menu bar.

Step 5:

Click <u>O</u>pen Company from the drop-down list and then click OK at the Peachtree Accounting message "This will close the current company."

Step 6:

Select Bellwether Garden Supply and click <u>O</u>K in the Open Company dialog box, as shown in figure 1–27.

Open Company Dialog Box

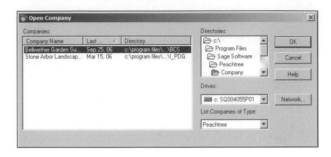

BACKING UP DATA

Frequently a user of Peachtree must back up work. Follow the steps outlined below to back up data.

Step 1:

Click <u>F</u>ile from the Menu bar.

Step 2:

Click <u>B</u>ack Up from the drop-down list. The Back Up Company dialog box appears, and offers you the option to be reminded to back up data. It also offers the option to include the company name in the name of the backup files.

Step 3:

Click the check box next to *Include company name in the backup file name*.

Step 4:

Click <u>B</u>ack Up, as shown in figure 1–28.

Back Up Company Window

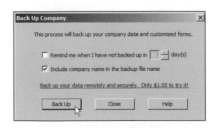

Step 5:

The Save Backup for Bellwether Garden Supply as dialog box will appear as shown in figure 1–29. If you will be backing up your company files on a flash drive, insert the flash drive into the appropriate drive. (For most computers this is the E drive.)

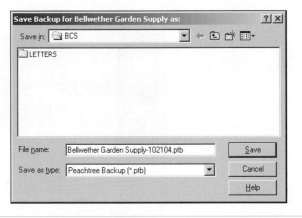

Click the down arrow next to the Save in box to select the destination where the backup is to be stored. The file name has already been entered. It consists of the company name and the date the file is being saved.

Step 6:

Click Save to save the company to the destination.

Step 7:

Click OK at the Peachtree Accounting window that indicates the file size. The progress of the backup is displayed until it is complete.

RESTORING DATA TO ITS ORIGINAL CONDITION

If it is necessary to restore data you have backed up, the process is not difficult. It can be accomplished by completing the following steps.

Step 1:

Click File from the Menu bar.

Step 2:

Click Restore.

Step 3:

At the Restore Wizard – Select Backup File dialog box, select the location of where the file was backed up by clicking the Browse button.

Step 4:
Select *Bellwether Garden Supply*. (Various dates will appear as part of the file name.) The company will now appear in the Company Name text box as shown in figure 1–30.

Step 5:
Click Next.

FIGURE 1-30

Open Backup File Dialog Box with Bellwether Garden Supply Selected

Notice the full path.

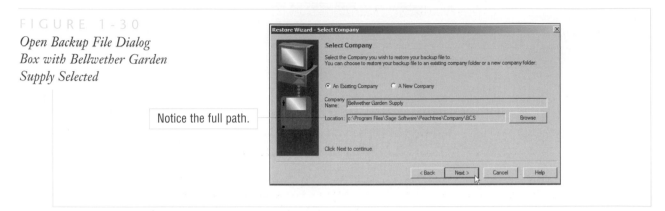

Step 6:
At the Restore Wizard – Select Company dialog box, click An Existing Company and then Browse to select the company to restore to a previous condition. Then click Next.

Step 7:
At the Restore Wizard – Restore Options dialog box, select Company Data as shown in figure 1–31, and click Next.

FIGURE 1-31

Company Data Selected from the Restore Wizard-Restore Options Window.

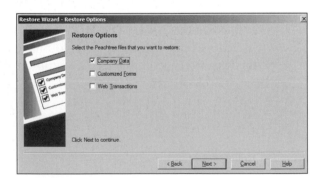

Step 8:
At the Restore Wizard – Confirmation dialog box, click Finish.

Check
POINT

1. How is data saved in Peachtree?
2. What is the purpose of the restore process?

Answers
1. *Peachtree saves all transactions that are posted. Data that does not require posting is saved when you exit Peachtree.*
2. *The restore process will overwrite the current company data with previous saved data.*

1. Open Bellwether Garden Supply using each of the two methods for opening a company file.
2. Practice the Back Up feature. (However, do not save any work unless you are instructed to do so.)
3. Close Bellwether Garden Supply.

INTERNET *Access*

Peachtree Complete Accounting makes a great deal of information accessible via the Internet. Resources of many types are available by accessing various Peachtree Web sites. The Peachtree sites can be reached by clicking *Peachtree on the Web* from the Help on the Menu bar or directly by keying the Peachtree Web site address **www.Peachtree.com** into your Web browser. The Peachtree home page is shown in figure 1–32.

FIGURE 1-32

Home Page for Peachtree Web Site

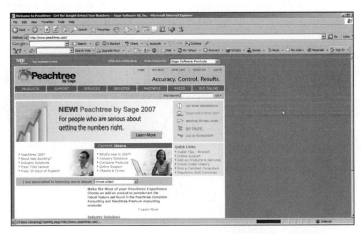

INTERNET ASSIGNMENT:

Search the Peachtree Web sites to find the following information:
1. The newest version of Peachtree Complete Accounting that is currently available
2. The benefits of using Peachtree's credit card processing service
3. What the Peachtree Passport is and why it would be helpful to a user of the software

S O F T W A R E
Command Summary

Open Start Window	Start, All <u>P</u>rograms, Peachtree Complete Accounting 2007, Peachtree Complete Accounting 2007
Open Company	<u>F</u>ile, <u>O</u>pen Company or Open an existing company, "Company Name," <u>OK</u>
Help	The Help button from any menu toolbar
Custom toolbar	<u>O</u>ptions, View Custom Toolbar
Back up	<u>F</u>ile, <u>B</u>ack Up
Restore	<u>F</u>ile, <u>R</u>estore

P R O J E C T S
and Problems

CONTENT CHECK

Multiple Choice: Choose only one response for each question.

1. Peachtree Complete Accounting _____ is discussed in this book.
   A. 8.0
   B. Plus
   C. 2007
   D. 6.0
   E. None of the above.

2. Accounting is the process of
   A. recording, summarizing, analyzing, and interpreting financial activities.
   B. journalizing, posting, and preparing financial statements.
   C. recording adjusting and closing entries.
   D. transferring data to the computer.
   E. None of the above.

3. The users of accounting information include
    A. managers.
    B. investors.
    C. lenders.
    D. government agencies.
    E. All of the above.

4. Peachtree allows users to record financial events in
    A. just a general journal.
    B. just special journals.
    C. special journals and a general journal.
    D. a single combined journal.
    E. None of the above.

5. Computerized accounting systems
    A. improve accuracy and efficiency.
    B. save time and effort.
    C. do many tasks automatically.
    D. handle many different types of financial activities.
    E. All of the above.

Short Essay Response: Provide a detailed answer for each question.

1. What is the difference between manual and computerized accounting systems?
2. Name some of the features that Peachtree Complete Accounting provides you. Explain how these features might help you in your business.
3. Explain two ways of opening Peachtree.
4. Describe the process of back up and restore.
5. Explain the two generally accepted methods of navigating through Peachtree. Is one superior to the other?
6. What benefits do you see from the Help feature of Peachtree?

CASE PROBLEMS

PROBLEM 1A
- Start Peachtree Accounting.
- Open Bellwether Garden Supply.
- Click the Customers & Sales tab from the Peachtree tab.
- Click Sales Invoices and then New Sales Invoice.
- List the names of the buttons on the toolbar of the Maintain Sales/ Inventory window. Close the window.
- Click Tasks from the Menu bar.
- Click General Journal Entry from the drop-down list.
- List the names of the buttons on the toolbar of the General Journal Entry window. Close the window.

PROBLEM 2A

- Open the Help feature by using the Menu bar.
- Click <u>C</u>ontents and Index from the drop-down list.
- Click the I<u>n</u>dex tab and key **Accounts Receivable**.
- Click the <u>D</u>isplay button.
- Click the <u>D</u>isplay button again, and note the definition of *Accounts Receivable*.
- Click the <u>S</u>earch tab.
- Key **Payroll**.
- Click <u>L</u>ist Topics.
- Double-click Payroll Setup Wizard.
- List the payroll items that the Payroll Setup Wizard establishes.
- Close the Peachtree Help window.

PROBLEM 1B

- Open Stone Arbor Landscaping.
- Click the Maintain Chart of Accounts from the Custom toolbar.
- List the names of the buttons on the toolbar of the Maintain Chart of Accounts window. Close the window.
- Click <u>R</u>eports from the Menu bar.
- Click <u>F</u>inancial Statements from the drop-down list.
- List the names of the buttons on the toolbar of the Select a Report window. Close the window.

PROBLEM 2B

- Open the Help feature by using the Menu bar.
- Click <u>C</u>ontents and Index from the drop-down list.
- Click the I<u>n</u>dex tab and key **Payroll**.
- Click the <u>D</u>isplay button.
- Click the <u>D</u>isplay button again, and note the information regarding Bonus or Commission for Hourly Employees.
- Click the <u>S</u>earch tab.
- Key **General Journal**.
- Click <u>L</u>ist Topics.
- Double-click *Record a General Journal Entry*.
- List the reasons why the general journal might be used.
- Close the Peachtree Help window.

COOPERATIVE LEARNING

1. Form into pairs and write a one-page paper comparing and contrasting manual and computerized accounting systems. Indicate which type of system you would prefer to use and why.
2. In groups of three or four students, visit some local businesses that use computerized accounting programs. List the names of the programs. How are the programs used in the daily operation of the business?

3. In groups of three or four students, visit two or three software retailers. List the names and prices of the most popular accounting software packages. Also list the main features of each package.

WRITING AND DECISION MAKING

Your employer has announced that the company will be switching from a manual accounting system to a computerized accounting system. Peachtree is considered to be the favored accounting software due to all of its accounting and financial capabilities. However, the owner would still like to know what type of services would be available once the decision has been made to switch. Therefore, you have been asked to visit the Peachtree Web site at www.Peachtree.com and prepare a summary of services available.

CHAPTER
2

SETTING UP
A COMPANY

LEARNING OBJECTIVES

1. Set up a new company in Peachtree

2. Create a chart of accounts

3. Enter beginning account balances

SOFTWARE FEATURES

- Create function

- Edit function

- Print function for the chart of accounts and general ledger

An individual company must set up its books before any transactions can be entered. Regardless of whether the company uses a manual or automated accounting system, the procedure is basically the same. The business setup process involves several steps—

- Enter company information
- Select a business organization type
- Create a chart of accounts
- Select an accounting method
- Select a posting method
- Select an accounting period

ORGANIZATION TYPES AND COMPANY INFORMATION

Businesses can operate as merchandising, service, or manufacturing organizations. **Merchandising businesses** purchase goods from wholesalers and resell them to consumers for a profit. Examples include department stores, grocery stores, and sporting goods stores.

Service businesses, including law offices, medical offices, and accounting firms, provide services to consumers for a profit. Note, however, that some service businesses also sell merchandise. A beauty shop, for example, might sell hair care products. However, its main business of styling hair generates the vast majority of its revenue.

Manufacturing businesses produce products from raw materials and sell those products to consumers for a profit. Their customers might be wholesalers or end-users. Airplane manufacturers, construction companies, and furniture makers would be considered manufacturing businesses.

Some companies are difficult to classify because of their mix of revenue from service, merchandising, and manufacturing activities. For example, restaurants provide a service, sell products, and manufacture products using raw materials. So, what type of business is a restaurant?

Each business takes on one of three basic organization types: sole proprietorship, partnership, or corporation. The organization type, or structure, that a business decides on is a result of various factors. How many owners the company will have, for example, is one factor. Another factor is expertise. Will one owner have the knowledge required to run a specific business? If yes, then the sole proprietorship form of business might be sufficient. If, however, more expertise is needed to own and operate the company, then perhaps a partnership will provide better results.

Before an owner decides on a business organization type, liability, capital formation, and tax issues must be considered. For example, some business types provide less liability protection for their owners than do others. Sole proprietorships and partnerships, for example, have unlimited liability. This means that the owners are personally liable for the debts of the business. The owners can lose their personal as well as their business assets if the business does poorly or is the guilty party in a lawsuit. Liability is just one of the important issues to consider in determining which type of organization is best for a specific business.

SOLE PROPRIETORSHIPS

A **sole proprietorship** is a business owned by one person who makes the decisions, takes all the risks, and earns all the profits. Unfortunately, the sole proprietor suffers all the losses, too. A sole proprietorship is very easy to form. One owner with a limited amount of capital can open a business. In most states, all that is needed is a business license and a mailing address. The sole proprietor is free to make all the management decisions. Small local businesses such as barbershops, hardware stores, and dry cleaning stores are examples of firms that might be sole proprietorships. In recent years, many individuals have set up small sole proprietorship firms that provide computer consulting and management consulting services.

One drawback to the sole proprietorship type of organization is that a single owner often does not have all the expertise needed to run a particular business. Individuals with specific technical skills open businesses and then realize later that those skills are not sufficient. For example, suppose a ski instructor decides to open a ski equipment shop. The ski instructor may know all about skiing and can discuss skiing with potential buyers. In other words, the ski instructor has a lot of technical knowledge about skiing and ski equipment. However, what does the ski instructor know about advertising, accounting, or finance? Frequently, a sole proprietor knows very little about basic business procedures.

Financing and capital formation also may be difficult for the sole proprietor. Because the asset base and creditworthiness of the business rests with one individual, banks and other potential lenders might be leery of lending to that person. This can be especially true in the early years of a business when there is very little credit history for potential lenders to evaluate.

The freedom to make all the decisions that a sole proprietor enjoys comes with a price—unlimited liability for the debts of the business. The owner's personal and business assets are accessible to creditors in the case of a business failure. First-year business failures can run as high as 50%, making it very risky to start a business as a sole proprietor. Table 2–1 lists the advantages and disadvantages of the sole proprietorship type of business.

TABLE 2-1
Sole Proprietorships

ADVANTAGES	DISADVANTAGES
1. Complete management control by owner 2. Ease of formation 3. Few government restrictions	1. Limited level of expertise 2. Limited amount of capital 3. Unlimited liability

PARTNERSHIPS

partnership A business owned by two or more people.

A **partnership** is a group of two or more people who enter into a business arrangement for the purpose of making a profit. The benefits of a partnership can be great. Because there are more people involved as owners, the amount of expertise brought to the business is increased. This can lead to a synergistic relationship that can help the business grow. In the United States today, 10% of all businesses are partnerships. These businesses include small local firms as well as large national firms. In fact, some large multinational accounting firms are partnerships.

Because a partnership has more than one owner, it usually has more capital and capital formation potential than a sole proprietorship. Often, businesses do not start with enough capital to succeed. The owners must borrow money so that the firm can survive and grow. Generally, the more partners involved in a business, the easier it is to borrow money.

As with a sole proprietorship, in a partnership the owners are subject to unlimited liability. Creditors can go after the personal and business assets of all partners to satisfy the debts of the firm. This can be costly if a business experiences financial difficulties.

One of the biggest drawbacks to the partnership business type is the mutual agency rule. This rule provides that each partner can bind all the other partners to an agreement. For example, suppose partner X goes to a car dealer to buy a new car in the name of the partnership and, prior to the purchase, does not tell the other partners about the purchase. The result is that all partners are liable for the purchase even though they had no prior knowledge of it. Also, even if partner X leaves the business, the remaining partners are still required to pay for the car.

Partnerships have a limited life. Any time an old partner leaves or a new partner is added, a new partnership must be formed. This creates accounting as well as relationship problems. Assets, for example, must be revalued when a new partner is added or an old partner leaves. Table 2–2 lists advantages and disadvantages of partnerships.

TABLE 2-2

Partnerships

ADVANTAGES	DISADVANTAGES
1. Ease of formation	1. Unlimited liability
2. Greater amount of expertise	2. Possible disagreements about management decisions
3. Greater potential for raising capital	3. Mutual agency rule
4. Synergistic relationship	4. Limited life

CORPORATIONS

The ownership of a corporation is divided into shares of stock. Therefore, a **corporation** is a business owned by stockholders or shareholders. A large corporation usually has many stockholders. A small corporation may have just a few stockholders. Unlike a sole proprietorship or a partnership, a corporation is considered a legal entity in and of itself. It acts as its own "person" when it comes to business transactions and holdings. In other words, the corporation acts on its own behalf. Large, well-known companies such as Ford, Sears, IBM, and Microsoft are examples of corporations that operate in the United States. The corporation type is so dominant in our economy that even though corporations make up only 20% of the businesses in the country, they receive more than 90% of the revenue.

The stockholders, or owners, of a corporation are not personally liable for its actions or debts. Stockholders can only lose what they have invested in the corporation's stock. This is known as limited liability. By issuing or selling stock, a corporation can raise needed capital more easily than can a sole proprietorship or partnership.

corporation A business owned by stockholders or shareholders.

Stockholders elect a board of directors for a corporation, which in turn hires the management. Ordinary stockholders are not directly involved in the day-to-day operations of the business. They must rely on management to work in their best interest. However, one of the duties of the board of directors is to periodically evaluate the performance of management and make changes if necessary. Management must also consult with the board of directors about financial policies.

Because a corporation is considered a separate legal entity, it is taxed like an individual. This tax reduces the amount of income available for stockholders, who are, after all, owners. Stockholders share in the earnings of the corporation by receiving dividends or by selling their stock for a profit, or capital gain. The stockholders then pay personal income tax on these dividends and capital gains. The result is double taxation: the earnings of the corporation are taxed once at the corporate level and again at the individual level when stockholders receive dividends or realize capital gains. Table 2–3 lists the advantages and disadvantages of a corporation.

HINT

The setup guide in Peachtree is a valuable resource for general accounting and company setup information.

TABLE 2-3

Corporations

ADVANTAGES	DISADVANTAGES
1. Ease of raising capital	1. More difficult and expensive to form
2. Limited liability	2. Subject to more government regulation
3. Continuous life	3. Double taxation
4. No mutual agency rule	

Check
POINT

1. What are the three main types of business organizations?
2. In what two types of business organizations do the owners have unlimited liability?

Answers
1. Sole proprietorships, partnerships, and corporations.
2. Sole proprietorships and partnerships.

OBJECTIVE 1 — SET UP A NEW COMPANY IN PEACHTREE

Several steps are necessary when setting up a new company in Peachtree. Each step must be read carefully and evaluated before you select a particular system, date, or accounting method. Follow the steps below to begin the business setup process for Bell Accounting Services.

Step 1:
Start Peachtree Complete Accounting 2007.

At the Peachtree Complete Accounting dialog box, click *Create a new company.* (See figure 2–1.)

FIGURE 2-1

Peachtree Accounting Dialog Box

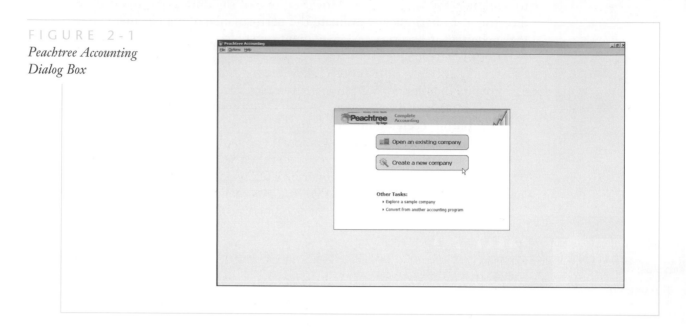

Step 3:

After reading the screen, click Next at the Create a New Company – Introduction dialog box. (See figure 2–2.)

FIGURE 2-2

Create a New Company – Introduction Dialog Box

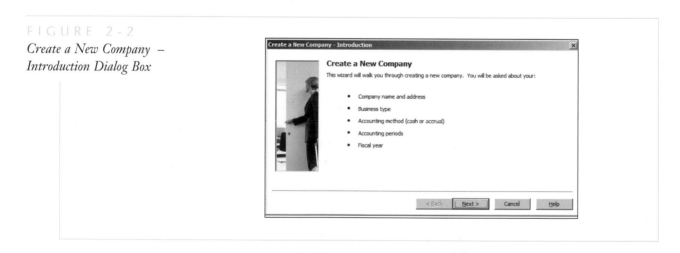

The Create a New Company – Company Information dialog box appears as shown in figure 2–3.

FIGURE 2-3

Create a New Company –
Company Information
Dialog Box

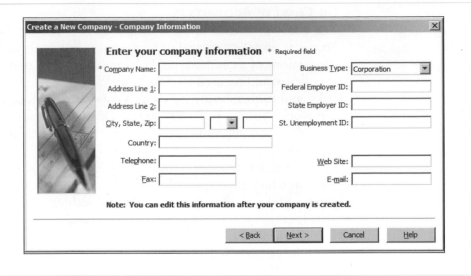

Step 4:

Complete the Create a New Company – Company Information dialog box using the following information:

Company Name:	**Bell Accounting Service**
Address Line 1:	**2128 Wood Lawn Drive**
Address Line 2:	
City, State, Zip	**Sacramento, CA 95311**
Country:	**USA**
Telephone:	**916-555-5121**
Fax:	**916-555-2155**
Business Type:	**Sole Proprietorship**
Federal Employer ID:	**95-2962961**
State Employer ID:	**06-556-01**
St. Unemployment ID:	**00564-76**

Press the Tab or Enter key after you complete each entry. Compare your entries with figure 2–4, and correct any errors before continuing. Click Next at the bottom of the dialog box when all entries are correct.

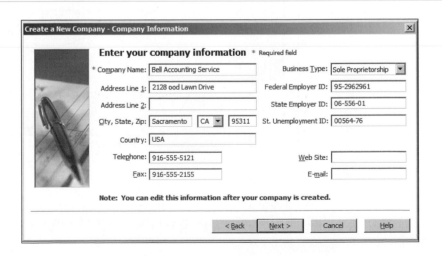

THE CHART OF ACCOUNTS

chart of accounts A listing of all the accounts used by a business.

The **chart of accounts** is a listing of all the accounts a business uses. Accounts provide a record of transactions in which each account groups all transactions of a similar type. For example, an account labeled Office Supplies would be used to classify purchases of file folders, staples, floppy disks, and rubber bands. These purchases could all be listed separately, but that would make it necessary to trace through hundreds or thousands of transactions to determine the firm's total purchases of office supplies in any period.

ledger A group of related accounts.

general ledger The main ledger of a business.

On the chart of accounts, all accounts are listed and numbered in the order in which they appear in the firm's general ledger. A **ledger** is simply a group of related accounts. The **general ledger** is the main ledger of a business. It contains the information that is used to prepare financial statements for the business.

Peachtree provides you with several methods for setting up a chart of accounts. You can—

- Use the chart of accounts of a sample company from the list provided. Several companies are included in the list. Once a particular company's chart of accounts is selected, accounts can be added, edited, or deleted.
- Copy a chart of accounts from an existing Peachtree Accounting company.
- Import a company's chart of accounts from another accounting program. QuickBooks files, for example, convert easily.
- Build the chart of accounts from scratch.

Step 5:

Click the "Use a sample business type that closely matches your company" option in the Create a New Company – Setup dialog box (figure 2–5), and then click Next.

FIGURE 2-5
Create a New Company – Setup Dialog Box

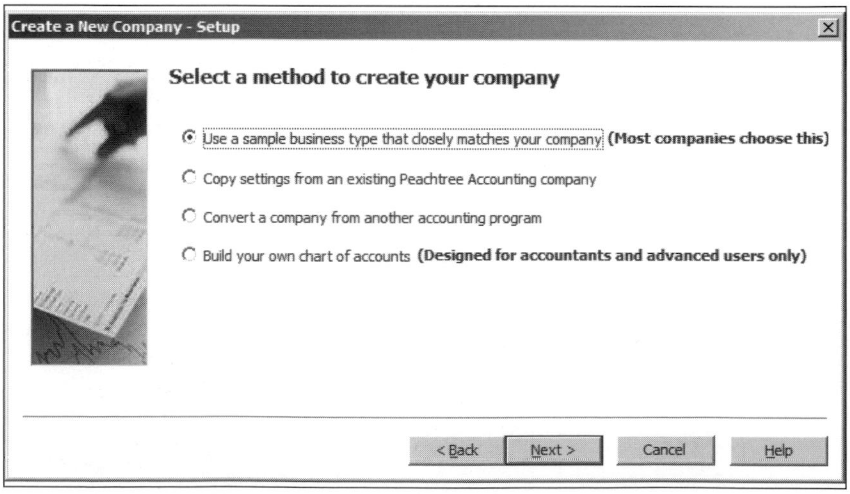

A Create a New Company – Business Type dialog box appears. Within the Select a business type text box, Service Company is highlighted (figure 2–6).

FIGURE 2-6

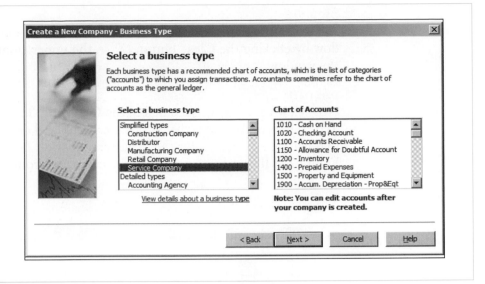

Step 6:

After reading the screen, select Detailed types and Accounting Agency.

Step 7:

Click the *View details about a business type* link below the dialog box to view
the help area.

Step 8:

Select Accounting Agency after scrolling up in the Contents box. This area
provides a brief overview of the accounting industry (figure 2–7).

FIGURE 2-7

*Accounting Agency Overview
and Related Topics*

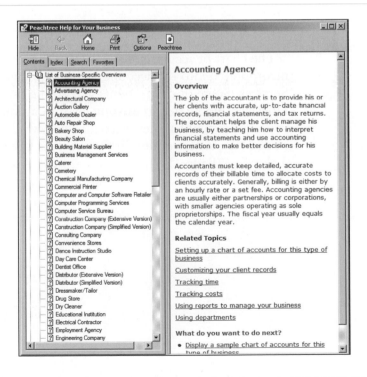

Explore the related topics listed in the Peachtree Help for Your Business
window by selecting the desired topic.

Step 9:

After reviewing the related topics for the accounting industry, close the window by clicking the Close button (X) in the upper right corner of the window.

Step 10:

Now view the chart of accounts in the Create a New Company – Business Type Chart of Accounts dialog box. Scroll up and down to see the accounts that will be established for the newly created Bell Accounting Service. Figure 2–8 illustrates a portion of the chart of accounts.

FIGURE 2-8

Accounting Company Chart of Accounts

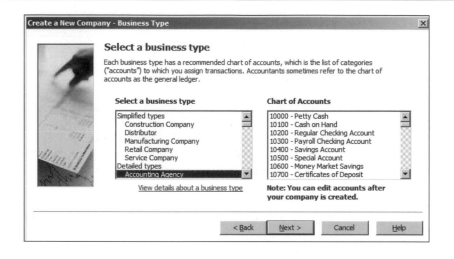

The chart of accounts selected from the sample company list will be incorporated into the accounting system being set up for Bell Accounting Services. Some of the accounts will not be used, and some will be renamed. However, modifying an existing chart of accounts saves time and effort. If you want to build all new accounts, you would click the "Build your own chart of accounts" option in the previous Create a New Company – Setup dialog box (figure 2–9).

FIGURE 2-9
*Build Your Own Company
Option Selected*

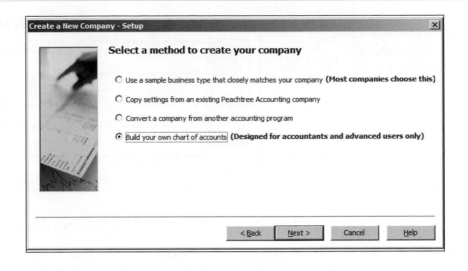

Step 11:

Click <u>N</u>ext in the Create a New Company – Business Type dialog box with Accounting Agency selected to establish the chart of accounts and move to the next step in the company setup process.

ACCOUNTING METHODS

Every business must decide on an accounting method. Some firms use the cash basis, others use the accrual basis, and still others use a hybrid of cash and accrual accounting. Peachtree allows businesses to use either cash or accrual accounting.

cash basis An accounting method in which a firm recognizes revenue when cash is received and recognizes expenses when cash is paid.

The **cash basis** requires a business to recognize (record) revenue when the related cash is received and recognize (record) expenses when the related cash is paid. Small companies with no inventory, no accounts receivable, and no accounts payable can use the cash basis. Thus, this basis is limited to small service businesses such as law offices, consulting firms, and bookkeeping firms.

accrual basis An accounting method in which a firm recognizes revenue when it is earned and recognizes expenses when they are incurred.

Generally accepted accounting principles (GAAP) require the use of the accrual basis by merchandising and manufacturing businesses. Under the **accrual basis**, a firm recognizes (records) revenue when it is earned, even if the related cash has not yet been received. Similarly, the firm recognizes (records) expenses when they are incurred, even if the related cash has not yet been paid. For example, if a customer purchases merchandise or receives services on account, generally, this transaction would be recorded using an accrual accounting method. Similarly, if a business purchases supplies on account, it would use an accrual accounting method. In addition to merchandising and manufacturing businesses, service businesses that make sales on credit must use the accrual basis.

Step 12:

At the Create a New Company – Accounting Method dialog box (figure 2–10), click Cash. This is the accounting method that Bell Accounting Service will use. **Caution: After you choose an accounting method, you CANNOT change it.** Click <u>N</u>ext.

FIGURE 2-10

Create a New Company –
Accounting Method Dialog
Box with Cash Selected

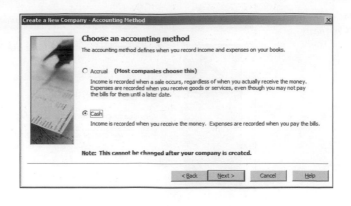

POSTING METHODS: REAL TIME OR BATCH PROCESSING

After entries are made for transactions, the information must be transferred to the appropriate ledger accounts. This process is known as **posting**. Peachtree offers two alternative posting methods: real time and batch processing.

posting The transfer of information about transactions to ledger accounts.

Real-time processing results in instant account updates. For example, when a customer in a bank makes a deposit, the teller enters the transaction and the customer generally has immediate access to those funds. However, suppose a customer sends a check to a department store, and the department store waits until the end of the day to post that payment; this would be an example of batch posting.

Step 13:

Most companies select real time as their posting method so that their accounts will be updated as each transaction is entered and saved. Click Real Time at the Create a New Company – Posting Method dialog box (figure 2–11). Then click Next.

FIGURE 2-11

Create a New Company –
Posting Method Dialog Box
with Real Time Selected

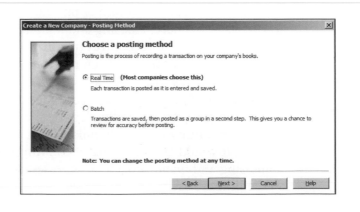

THE ACCOUNTING PERIODS

accounting period
The period of time covered by a firm's financial statements.

An **accounting period** is the time covered by a firm's financial statements. It is the period for which the firm reports its operating results—its net income or net loss. Most businesses have a yearly accounting period but prepare interim statements on a monthly or quarterly basis.

An accounting period cannot exceed one year. Many firms use the calendar year (January 1–December 31) as their accounting period. However, it is not necessary to do so. Some firms have legitimate business reasons for using an accounting period other than the calendar year. For example, many department stores end their yearly accounting period on January 31. Because so much of their yearly business occurs in December, it would be an accounting nightmare to compile all the information needed for the financial statements by December 31.

fiscal year An accounting period of one year.

A yearly accounting period is often referred to as a **fiscal year**. Peachtree uses this term as well.

Step 14:

Bell Accounting Service will use the calendar year as its accounting period. So click "12 monthly accounting periods per year" at the Create a New Company – Accounting Periods dialog box (figure 2–12), and then click Next.

FIGURE 2-12

Create a New Company – Accounting Periods Dialog Box

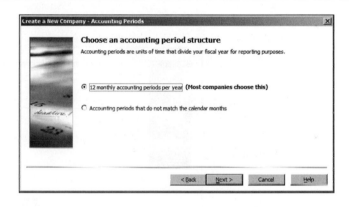

Step 15:

At the Create a New Company – Fiscal Year dialog box, follow the procedures listed below.

- Select January from the drop-down list.
- Select 2007 from the drop-down list.

Compare your entries with figure 2–13 before continuing, and then click Next.

FIGURE 2-13

Create a New Company –
Fiscal Year Dialog Box

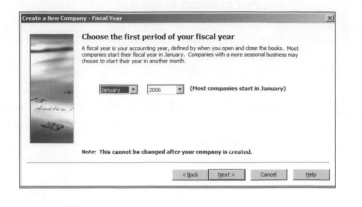

Step 16:

The Create a New Company – Finish dialog box (figure 2–14) indicates that your setup of Bell Accounting Service is complete. Click Finish.

FIGURE 2-14

Create a New Company –
Finish Dialog Box

The Peachtree Setup Guide window now appears (figure 2–15). You can access various areas of your business setup procedure by clicking one of the areas below. **Note:** If the Setup Guide does not appear, Click <u>F</u>ile and then Setup Guide.

FIGURE 2-15

Peachtree Setup Guide Window

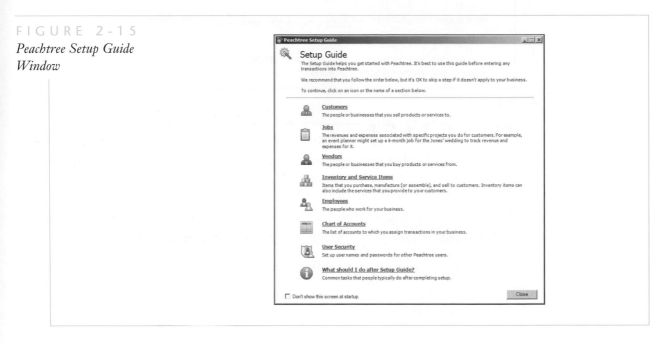

To review a specific area of the window, follow these steps:

- Click the item you want to view, for example, *Chart of Accounts*.
- Click the *General Ledger* link to get more detailed information about the general ledger.
- Click another item to browse or click the Close button (X) in the upper right corner of the Peachtree Setup Guide – Chart of Accounts window.

Important: Peachtree automatically creates the new company in the program folder on the hard drive. You may therefore open, work on, and save the company from and to the hard drive. However, in the unique circumstance you are unable to save any data to the hard drive because of your institution's policy, simply use the back up feature to save a copy of the company to an external drive such as a flash drive. When you need to open the company from the external drive, use the restore feature and it will place a copy of the company back on the hard drive. In this unique situation, you will need to back up at the end of each session and restore at the beginning of each session. The only difference with the restore process given in chapter 1 is that you will click A New Company option at the Restore Wizard – Select Company window.

Check POINT

1. Name one aspect of the company setup process that cannot be changed after it is selected.
2. When does posting occur if you select the real-time posting process?

Answers
1. The accounting method, either cash or accrual.
2. Posting occurs immediately when each transaction is entered and saved.

PRACTICE *objective* 1

Set up the following company using the procedures outlined in Objective 1. Note that the Bullfrog Maintenance Company will use the accrual accounting method and will build its own Chart of Accounts.

Company Name:	**Bullfrog Maintenance Company**
Address Line 1:	**456 Ballinger Lane**
Address Line 2:	
City, State, Zip	**Stockton, CA 95101**
Country:	**USA**
Telephone:	**209-555-2222**
Fax:	**209-555-6666**
Business Type:	**Sole Proprietorship**
Federal Employer ID:	**95-343434**
State Employer ID:	**06-3333-01**
St. Unemployment ID:	**00221-78**
Chart of Accounts:	**Build your own chart of accounts**
Accounting Method:	**Accrual**
Posting Method:	**Real Time**
Accounting Periods:	**12 monthly accounting periods**
Fiscal Year to Start:	**January 2007**

Close the Peachtree Setup Guide and click OK on the Peachtree Setup Guide dialog box.

OBJECTIVE 2 — CREATE A CHART OF ACCOUNTS

In Objective 1, you learned the company setup process. Now you will review the setup process and explore some variations to it. For example, you set up Bell Accounting Service with the cash basis as its accounting method. The company setup you will do in this section will use the accrual basis as the accounting method. Follow the steps below to set up a new company.

Step 1:

Click *File* from the main menu.

Step 2:

Select *New Company* from drop-down list (figure 2–16).

FIGURE 2-16

New Company Selected from
the File Drop-Down List

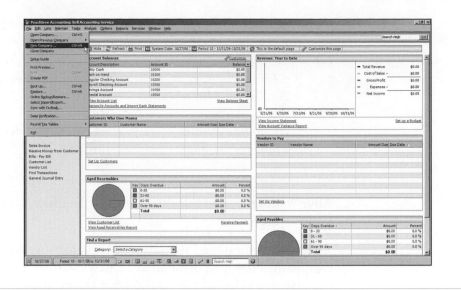

Step 3:

Click <u>N</u>ext at the Create a New Company – Introduction window.
Then carefully enter the information shown below in the Create a New
Company – Company Information dialog box. Compare your entries
with figure 2–17 before continuing.

Company Name:	**Woodward Construction Company**
Address Line 1:	**2116 Benson Way**
Address Line 2:	
City, State, Zip:	**Fresno, CA 95011**
Country:	**USA**
Telephone:	**209-555-1111**
Fax:	**209-555-5555**
Business Type:	**Sole Proprietorship**
Federal Employer ID:	**95-3458767**
State Employer ID:	**06-3363-01**
St. Unemployment ID:	**00321-78**

FIGURE 2-17

Completed Create a New
Company – Company
Information Dialog Box

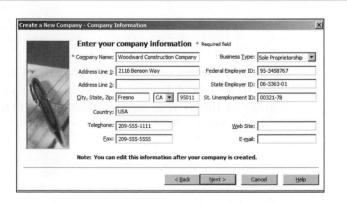

Click <u>N</u>ext. Enter the following information in the remaining dialog boxes to complete the Create a New Company Setup process, and then click <u>F</u>inish:

Chart of Accounts:	**Build your own chart of accounts**
Accounting Method:	**Accrual**
Posting Method:	**Real Time**
Accounting Periods:	**12 monthly accounting periods**
Fiscal Year to Start:	**January 2007**

After waiting for the software to create data files, close the Peachtree Setup Guide window.

You have completed the setup process for the Woodward Construction Company. Now you must create a new chart of accounts for the business because you selected the "Build your own chart of accounts" option at the Chart of Accounts setup dialog box. You will need to create all of the accounts using information that includes account ID, account description, and account type.

ACCOUNT ID

Every general ledger account must have a separate number for identification purposes. In Peachtree, this number is called the account ID. Peachtree specifies a numeric range for each account classification. For example, all asset accounts must fall within the range of 100–199, 1000–1999, or 10000–19999. The starting point for each numeric range is shown in table 2–4.

TABLE 2-4

Peachtree Numeric Ranges for Account Classification

ACCOUNT CLASSIFICATION	STARTING NUMBER FOR ACCOUNT IDs
Assets	**100, 1000, 10000**
Liabilities	**200, 2000, 20000**
Equity	**300, 3000, 30000**
Revenue	**400, 4000, 40000**
Expenses	**500, 5000, 50000**

A small business might use 100 for its Cash account and 102 for its Petty Cash account. A larger business that needs many accounts might assign 1000 or 10000 to Cash and 1020 or 10200 to Petty Cash.

All of the general ledger accounts used in Peachtree fall into the five broad classifications listed in table 2–4. The meaning of these classifications is as follows:

- *Assets* are the things a business owns.
- *Liabilities* are the debts a business owes.
- *Equity* is the difference between what a business owns and what it owes.
- *Revenue* is what a business earns when it sells goods or provides a service.
- *Expenses* are the costs a business incurs to produce revenue.

ACCOUNT DESCRIPTION

In Peachtree, every general ledger account must have an account description as well as an account ID. The account description indicates the nature of the transactions that will be recorded in the account. For example, Cash is the account description for the account that will be used to record all transactions involving the receipt and payment of cash. Other examples of account descriptions are Office Supplies, Accounts Receivable, Office Equipment, and Accounts Payable.

ACCOUNT TYPE

When creating a chart of accounts in Peachtree, it is necessary to assign an account type to each general ledger account as well as an ID and a description. The account type indicates to which group of accounts on the financial statements a particular account belongs. Having this information in the chart of accounts makes it possible for Peachtree to prepare automated financial statements at the end of each accounting period.

Peachtree uses the following 16 account types:

- *Cash.* This account type is used for any accounts that involve cash. In business, cash consists of funds on hand in the firm and funds on deposit in banks. The funds on hand include not only currency and coin but also cash equivalents such as checks and money orders received from customers. Some firms maintain just one cash account, but others have a variety of cash accounts such as Cash on Hand, Petty Cash, Regular Checking Account, Payroll Checking Account, and Money Market Savings.

- *Accounts Receivable.* The **accounts receivable** of a business are the amounts owed by its customers for goods or services sold to them on credit or on account.

accounts receivable The amounts owed to a business by its customers for goods or services sold on credit.

- *Inventory.* Inventory is the stock of goods on hand. In a merchandising business, inventory is the stock of goods that the firm has purchased for resale to customers. A manufacturing business has three kinds of inventory—raw materials, work in process, and finished goods. The inventory accounts that a business uses depend on its operations.

- *Other Current Assets.* Accounts receivable and inventory are considered **current assets**—that is, assets that will be used up or turned into cash within one year. There are also other kinds of current assets that involve much smaller amounts of money, such as office supplies and prepaid insurance. In Peachtree, any current assets besides cash, accounts receivable, and inventory are classified as other current assets.

current assets Assets that will be used up or turned into cash within one year.

- *Fixed Assets*. Physical assets that will be used by a business for more than a year are called **fixed assets**. Examples of fixed assets are equipment, trucks, buildings, and land. Fixed assets are also known as plant assets, long-term assets, and property, plant, and equipment.

- *Accumulated Depreciation*. Part of the cost of a fixed asset is allocated, or expensed, to operations during each accounting period of its useful life. This process is known as depreciation. Depreciation allows a business to match the cost of fixed assets against the revenue those assets help to produce. The accumulated depreciation represents the total depreciation expense taken in past accounting periods.

- *Other Assets*. In Peachtree, assets that are not current assets or fixed assets are classified as other assets. This category includes intangible assets such as goodwill, patents, trademarks, copyrights, and franchises. Intangible assets are assets that have no physical substance.

- *Accounts Payable*. The **accounts payable** of a business are the amounts that it owes to creditors for goods and services that it purchased on credit.

- *Other Current Liabilities*. **Current liabilities** are debts that are due for payment within one year. Accounts payable are one type of current liability. In Peachtree, all current liabilities besides accounts payable are classified as Other Current Liabilities. This category includes items such as salaries payable, taxes payable, short-term notes payable, and interest payable.

- *Long-Term Liabilities*. **Long-term liabilities** are debts that extend for more than one year. This category includes mortgages payable and long-term notes payable.

- *Equity—Doesn't Close*. In Peachtree, there are three types of equity accounts. The first type consists of accounts that do not close. These are the capital accounts of a sole proprietorship and a partnership and the capital stock accounts of a corporation.

- *Equity—Retained Earnings*. This category consists of the Retained Earnings account. At the end of each accounting period, the revenue and expense accounts are closed into Retained Earnings. The difference between the balances of the revenue and expense accounts is the net income or net loss for the period.

- *Equity—Gets Closed*. The last category of equity accounts contains the accounts that are used to record owner contributions and distributions of earnings to owners (drawings in sole proprietorships and partnerships and dividends in corporations). These equity accounts are closed at the end of the accounting period.

- *Income*. In Peachtree, the income accounts include all accounts used to record the revenue from sales of goods or services and all accounts used to record other types of income such as interest income.

- *Cost of Sales*. The accounts in this category apply to merchandising and manufacturing businesses but not to service businesses. The cost of sales is the cost of purchasing or making the goods that were sold during an accounting period. Cost of sales is also known as cost of goods sold. In a merchandising business, accounts for purchases, purchase returns and allowance, purchase discounts, and transportation charges would be categorized as cost of sales.

- *Expenses*. In Peachtree, the expense accounts include all operating expenses such as rent and salaries and other expenses such as interest.

fixed assets Physical assets that will be used by a business for more than a year.

accounts payable The amounts that a business owes to its creditors for goods or services purchased on credit.

current liabilities Debts due for payment within one year.

long-term liabilities Debts that extend for more than one year.

Step 6:

Click <u>M</u>aintain from the Menu bar and then click Chart of <u>A</u>ccounts.

For the following steps, use the Woodward Construction Company's chart of accounts shown in table 2–5. Complete the account ID, account description, and account type for all of Woodward's accounts.

TABLE 2-5
WOODWARD CONSTRUCTION COMPANY CHART OF ACCOUNTS

Account ID	Description	Account Type
100	Cash	Cash
102	Petty Cash	Cash
104	Accounts Receivable	Accounts Receivable
106	Office Supplies	Other Current Assets
108	Equipment	Fixed Assets
108.5	Accum. Depreciation-Equipment	Accumulated Depreciation
200	Accounts Payable	Accounts Payable
300	J. Woodward, Capital	Equity-doesn't close
301	J. Woodward, Equity	Equity-Retained Earnings
301.5	J. Woodward, Drawing	Equity-gets closed
400	Revenue	Income
500	Rent Expense	Expenses
502	Utilities Expense	Expenses
504	Telephone Expense	Expenses
506	Office Supplies Expense	Expenses
508	Repairs Expense	Expenses
510	Depreciation Expense-Equipment	Expenses
512	Wages and Salaries Expense	Expenses
514	Miscellaneous Expense	Expenses

Step 7:

Enter **100** in the *Account ID* field of the Maintain Chart of Accounts window to create the Woodward Construction Company's first account, the Cash account. As the numbers are entered, a drop-down lookup box appears as shown in figure 2–18.

FIGURE 2-18
Account ID: Lookup Box

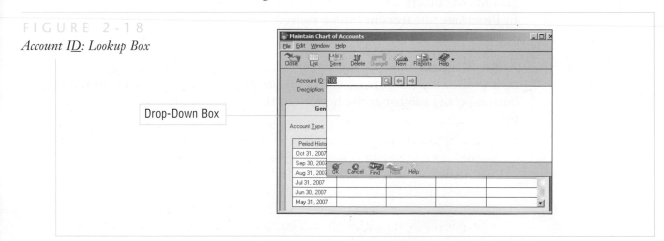

Drop-Down Box

Step 8:

Click the OK button to accept 100 as the Account ID.

Step 9:

Key **Cash** in the Description field.

Step 10:

Click *Cash* from the Account <u>T</u>ype drop-down list if it is not already showing.

Step 11:

Click the <u>S</u>ave button on the toolbar to save the account if the information is accurate. Compare the newly created account with figure 2–19.

FIGURE 2-19

Completed Cash Account

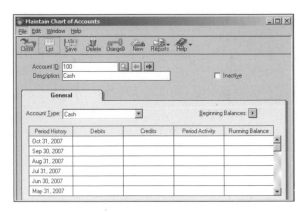

Step 12:

Repeat steps 8 through 12 until you have created all the accounts listed on the Woodward Construction Company's chart of accounts shown in table 2–5 (page 53).

Step 13:

Click the m*agnifying glass* icon next to the *Account ID* field to view a list of the accounts created. Use the scroll bar to view all the accounts.

EDITING ACCOUNTS

In Peachtree, an account can be viewed, edited, or deleted at any time.

Step 1:

At the Maintain Chart of Accounts window, click the *magnifying glass* icon next to the *Account ID* field, click *Revenue* (ID# 400), and then click the OK button on the toolbar at the bottom of the drop-down list, as shown in figure 2–20.

FIGURE 2-20

Account ID: Drop-Down List with Revenue Selected

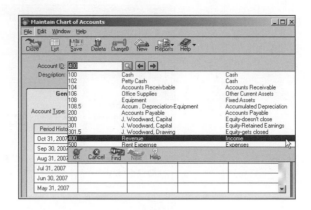

Step 2:

Any necessary changes can be made to an account by entering those changes and then clicking the Save button on the toolbar. Change the account description to *Fees Earned* and then click Save. You can also delete an account by clicking the account and then clicking the Delete button on the toolbar.

Step 3:

Review and edit any accounts as necessary, and then click the Close button on the toolbar.

HINT

The account ID and account type can also be edited during this process.

PRINTING THE CHART OF ACCOUNTS

It may be necessary to review the chart of accounts. If a company's chart of accounts is extensive, it may be impractical to view all of it on the screen. To print a chart of accounts, follow these steps.

Step 1:

Open Bell Accounting Service.

Step 2:

Click Reports from the Main Menu and then click General Ledger.

Step 3:

Click *Chart of Accounts* in the Report List section as shown in figure 2–21.

FIGURE 2-21

Select a Report — Chart of Accounts

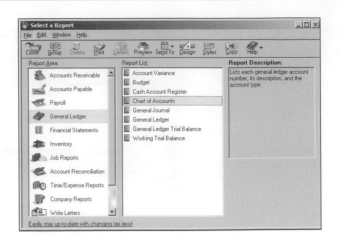

Step 4:

Click the <u>P</u>rint button on the Select a Report toolbar. Select "Do not display this message again" and click OK on the Peachtree Accounting warning box.

Step 5:

At the F<u>i</u>lter tab of the Chart of Accounts dialog box, click *General Ledger ID* from the <u>R</u>eport Order drop-down list (it may already be selected by default).

Step 6:

Enter a check mark in the box next to "Include Accounts with <u>Z</u>ero Amounts" by clicking it.

Step 7:

Click *Current Period* from the <u>A</u>s of Date drop-down list. Compare your entries with figure 2–22. If they are correct, click <u>O</u>K.

FIGURE 2-22

Print Filter Dialog Box

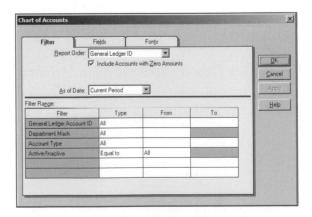

Step 8:

At the Print dialog box, click <u>A</u>ll in the Print range section. (Any pages, or combination of pages, may be printed by clicking the Pages option and entering the desired page range.) Click the number of copies desired from the Number of <u>c</u>opies box, and then click OK.

Step 9:

Compare your printed chart of accounts with figure 2–23. **Note:** The figure displays a partial view of the Chart of Accounts report.

FIGURE 2-23
Bell Accounting Services Chart of Accounts

Page: 1

Bell Accounting Service
Chart of Accounts
As of Jan 31, 2007

Filter Criteria includes: Report order is by ID. Report is printed with Accounts having Zero Amounts and in Detail Format.

Account ID	Account Description	Active?	Account Type
10000	Petty Cash	Yes	Cash
10100	Cash on Hand	Yes	Cash
10200	Regular Checking Account	Yes	Cash
10300	Payroll Checking Account	Yes	Cash
10400	Savings Account	Yes	Cash
10500	Special Account	Yes	Cash
10600	Money Market Savings	Yes	Cash
10700	Certificates of Deposit	Yes	Cash
11000	Accounts Receivable	Yes	Accounts Receivable
11400	Other Receivables	Yes	Accounts Receivable
11500	Allowance for Doubtful Acc	Yes	Accounts Receivable
12000	Inventory	Yes	Inventory
14000	Prepaid Expenses	Yes	Other Current Assets
14100	Employee Advances	Yes	Other Current Assets
14200	Notes Receivable-Current	Yes	Other Current Assets
14700	Other Current Assets	Yes	Other Current Assets
15000	Furniture and Fixtures	Yes	Fixed Assets
15100	Equipment	Yes	Fixed Assets
15200	Automobiles	Yes	Fixed Assets
15300	Other Depreciable Property	Yes	Fixed Assets
15400	Leasehold Improvements	Yes	Fixed Assets
15500	Building	Yes	Fixed Assets
15600	Building Improvements	Yes	Fixed Assets
16900	Land	Yes	Fixed Assets
17000	Accum. Depreciation - Furn	Yes	Accumulated Depreciation
17100	Accum. Depreciation - Equi	Yes	Accumulated Depreciation
17200	Accum. Depreciation - Auto	Yes	Accumulated Depreciation
17300	Accum. Depreciation - Oth	Yes	Accumulated Depreciation
17400	Accum. Depreciation - Lea	Yes	Accumulated Depreciation
17500	Accum. Depreciation - Buil	Yes	Accumulated Depreciation
17600	Accum. Depreciation - Bldg	Yes	Accumulated Depreciation
19000	Deposits	Yes	Other Assets
19100	Organization Costs	Yes	Other Assets
19150	Accum. Amortiz. - Org. Co	Yes	Other Assets
19200	Note Receivable-Noncurren	Yes	Other Assets
19900	Other Noncurrent Assets	Yes	Other Assets
20000	Accounts Payable	Yes	Accounts Payable
23000	Accrued Expenses	Yes	Other Current Liabilities
23100	Sales Tax Payable	Yes	Other Current Liabilities
23200	Wages Payable	Yes	Other Current Liabilities
23300	Deductions Payable	Yes	Other Current Liabilities
23400	Federal Payroll Taxes Paya	Yes	Other Current Liabilities
23500	FUTA Tax Payable	Yes	Other Current Liabilities
23600	State Payroll Taxes Payabl	Yes	Other Current Liabilities
23700	SUTA Payable	Yes	Other Current Liabilities
23800	Local Payroll Taxes Payabl	Yes	Other Current Liabilities
23900	Income Taxes Payable	Yes	Other Current Liabilities
24000	Other Taxes Payable	Yes	Other Current Liabilities
24100	Employee Benefits Payable	Yes	Other Current Liabilities
24200	Current Portion Long-Term	Yes	Other Current Liabilities
24400	Client Deposits	Yes	Other Current Liabilities
24800	Other Current Liabilities	Yes	Other Current Liabilities
24900	Suspense-Clearing Accoun	Yes	Other Current Liabilities
27000	Notes Payable-Noncurrent	Yes	Long Term Liabilities
27400	Other Long-Term Liabilities	Yes	Long Term Liabilities
39003	Beginning Balance Equity	Yes	Equity-doesn't close
39004	James, Capital	Yes	Equity-doesn't close
39005	Retained Earnings	Yes	Equity-Retained Earnings
39006	Owner's Contribution	Yes	Equity-gets closed
39007	Owner's Draw	Yes	Equity-gets closed
40000	Accounting Fees	Yes	Income
40200	Tax Fees	Yes	Income
40400	Consulting Fees	Yes	Income
40600	Other Income	Yes	Income

Step 10:

Click the Close button to close the Report window.

Step 11:

Open Woodward Construction Company.

Step 12:

Print a copy of the chart of accounts for Woodward Construction Company by repeating steps 2 through 8. Compare your chart of accounts to the one shown in figure 2–24.

FIGURE 2-24

Woodward Construction Company Chart of Accounts

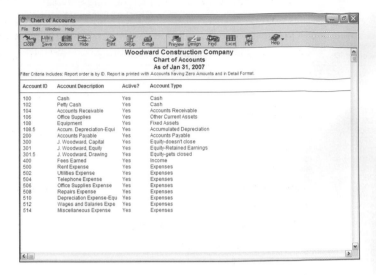

Step 13:

Click the Close button to close the Report window.

Check POINT

1. What are the three pieces of information needed to create an account in Peachtree?
2. How many account types does Peachtree support?

Answers

1. *The account ID, account description, and account type are required.*
2. *Peachtree supports 16 account types.*

PRACTICE *objective* 2

Open Bullfrog Maintenance Company and create the accounts listed in table 2–6.

TABLE 2-6
BULLFROG MAINTENANCE COMPANY CHART OF ACCOUNTS

Account ID	Description	Account Type
100	Cash	Cash
102	Petty Cash	Cash
104	Accounts Receivable	Accounts Receivable
106	Maintenance Supplies	Other Current Assets
108	Office Supplies	Other Current Assets
110	Prepaid Insurance	Other Current Assets
112	Equipment	Fixed Assets
112.5	Accum. Depreciation-Equipment	Accumulated Depreciation
200	Accounts Payable	Accounts Payable
300	J. Bull, Capital	Equity-doesn't close
301	J. Bull, Equity	Equity-Retained Earnings
301.5	J. Bull, Drawing	Equity-gets closed
400	Revenue	Income
500	Rent Expense	Expenses
502	Utilities Expense	Expenses
504	Maintenance Supplies Expense	Expenses
506	Office Supplies Expense	Expenses
508	Insurance Expense	Expenses
510	Depreciation Expense-Equipment	Expenses
512	Wages and Salaries Expense	Expenses
514	Miscellaneous Expense	Expenses

Your chart of accounts should look like figure 2–25. Print and then close the chart of accounts.

FIGURE 2-25

*Bullfrog Maintenance
Company Chart of Accounts*

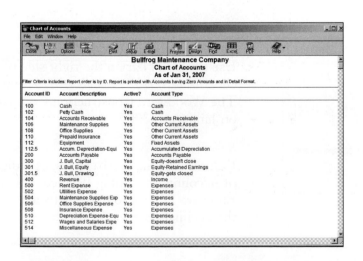

OBJECTIVE 3 — ENTER BEGINNING ACCOUNT BALANCES

Once you have created the general ledger accounts for your company, it is time to enter the beginning balances. If a company is converting to Peachtree from a manual accounting system, the normal practice is to use the ending balances from the previous month, which appear on the trial balance. For example, if a company wants to convert to Peachtree on July 1, the balances from the June 30 trial balance are used. Thus, the ending balances of the general ledger accounts as of June 30 become the beginning balances as of July 1. The **trial balance** is a listing of the general ledger accounts and their balances. It is used to prove that the general ledger is in balance.

trial balance A proof that the general ledger is in balance.

ENTERING THE BEGINNING ACCOUNT BALANCES

To enter beginning balances, follow these steps:

Step 1:

Open Woodward Construction Company.

Step 2:

Click Maintain and then click Chart of Accounts.

Step 3:

Click the Right Arrow next to Beginning Balances in the Maintain Chart of Accounts window (figure 2–26).

FIGURE 2-26

Maintain Chart of Accounts Window

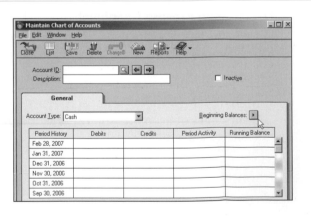

FIGURE 2-27

Select Period Dialog Box

Step 4:

Use the scroll bar on the right side of the Select Period dialog box, click *From 1/1/07 through 1/31/07* (figure 2–27), and then click OK. The Woodward Construction Company will now start its fiscal year on January 1, 2007.

Step 5:

Enter the beginning balances, as indicated in table 2–7, in the Chart of Accounts Beginning Balances window (figure 2–28). Press the Enter or Tab key to move between accounts. Remember to enter the decimal points as needed.

FIGURE 2-28
Chart of Accounts Beginning Balances Window

TABLE 2-7
WOODWARD CONSTRUCTION COMPANY BEGINNING BALANCES, JANUARY 1, 2007

Account ID	Description	Account Type	Assets, Expenses	Liabilities, Equity, Income
100	Cash	Cash	$12,000.00	
102	Petty Cash	Cash	250.00	
104	Accounts Receivable	Accounts Receivable	13,000.00	
106	Office Supplies	Other Current Asset	590.00	
108	Equipment	Fixed Assets	112,000.00	
108.5	Accum. Depreciation-Equipment	Accumulated Depreciation		$12,000.00
200	Accounts Payable	Accounts Payable		2,300.00
300	J. Woodward, Capital	Equity-doesn't close		123,540.00
301	J. Woodward, Equity	Equity-Retained Earnings		
301.5	J. Woodward, Drawing	Equity-gets closed		
400	Fees Earned	Income		
500	Rent Expense	Expenses		
502	Utilities Expense	Expenses		
504	Telephone Expense	Expenses		
506	Office Supplies Expense	Expenses		
508	Repairs Expense	Expenses		
510	Depreciation Expense-Eq.	Expenses		
512	Wages and Salaries Expense	Expenses		
514	Miscellaneous Expense	Expenses		

HINT

A new account may be added at any time while entering beginning balances by clicking the New button at the top of the Chart of Accounts Beginning Balances window.

Step 6:

When you have finished entering the balances, click the OK button to save the entries and return to the Maintain Chart of Accounts window.

Step 7:

Close the Maintain Chart of Accounts window.

HINT

Peachtree will not allow the Beginning Balances window to close unless the general ledger accounts are in balance. The trial balance at the bottom of the Chart of Accounts Beginning Balances window must show a zero (0) difference.

PRINTING THE GENERAL LEDGER WITH THE BEGINNING BALANCES

The best way to check the accuracy of the general ledger is to print a copy. You can then check the newly created accounts and their balances. Follow these steps to print a copy of the general ledger:

Step 1:

Click the *Business Status* tab on the Peachtree opening window to reveal the Find a Report access area (bottom left).

Step 2:

Select *General Ledger* from the Category drop-down list and *General Ledger* from the Report drop-down list (figure 2–29).

FIGURE 2-29

General Ledger Selected from the Find a Report Category and Report Box

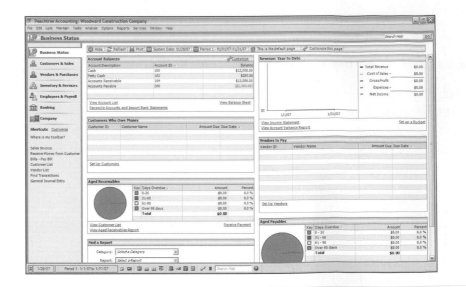

Step 3:

Click Display to display the current period's General Ledger.

The Find a Report feature enables the user to print or display a number of reports without using a filter. This feature produces reports for the current accounting period.

The *General Ledger* report will include all transactions that occurred between January 1 and January 31, 2007. This is the period for which the beginning balances were entered. The General Ledger window that now appears (figure 2–30) presents part of the ledger. Use the scroll bars to view the entire general ledger.

FIGURE 2-30
Partial General Ledger

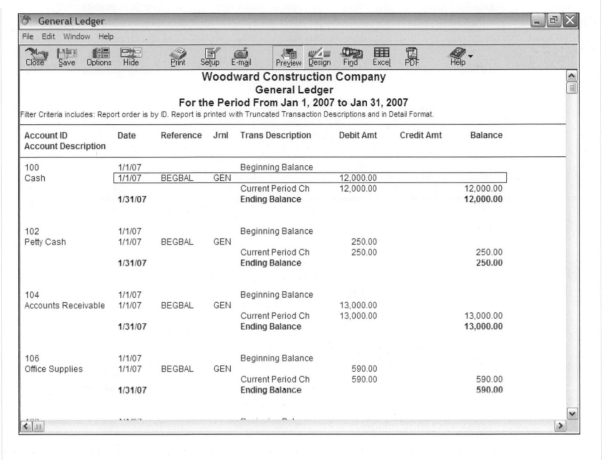

Step 4:

Click the <u>P</u>rint button on the General Ledger toolbar. At the Print dialog box, check the printing settings, and then click OK.

Step 5:

Compare your printout of the general ledger with figure 2–31.

General Ledger Printout for Woodward Construction Company

Woodward Construction Cmpany
General Ledger
For the Period From Jan 1, 2007 to Jan 31, 2007

Page: 1

Filter Criteria includes: Report order is by ID. Report is printed with Truncated Transaction Descriptions and in Detail Format.

Account ID Account Description	Date	Reference	Jrnl	Trans Description	Debit Amt	Credit Amt	Balance
100 Cash	1/1/07 1/1/07 1/31/07	BEGBAL	GEN	Beginning Balance Current Period Cha **Ending Balance**	12,000.00		12,000.00 **12,000.00**
102 Petty Cash	1/1/07 1/1/07 1/31/07	BEGBAL	GEN	Beginning Balance Current Period Cha **Ending Balance**	250.00 250.00		250.00 **250.00**
104 Accounts Receivable	1/1/07 1/1/07 1/31/07	BEGBAL	GEN	Beginning Balance Current Period Cha **Ending Balance**	13,000.00 13,000.00		13,000.00 **13,000.00**
106 Office Supplies	1/1/07 1/1/07 1/31/07	BEGBAL	GEN	Beginning Balance Current Period Cha **Ending Balance**	590.00 590.00		590.00 **590.00**
108 Equipment	1/1/07 1/1/07 1/31/07	BEGBAL	GEN	Beginning Balance Current Period Cha **Ending Balance**	112,000.00 112,000.00		112,000.00 **112,000.00**
108.5 Accum. Depreciation-	1/1/07 1/1/07 1/31/07	BEGBAL	GEN	Beginning Balance Current Period Cha **Ending Balance**		12,000.00 12,000.00	-12,000.00 **-12,000.00**
200 Accounts Payable	1/1/07 1/1/07 1/31/07	BEGBAL	GEN	Beginning Balance Current Period Cha **Ending Balance**		2,300.00 2,300.00	-2,300.00 **-2,300.00**
300 J.Woodward, Capital	1/1/07 1/1/07 1/31/07	BEGBAL	GEN	Beginning Balance Current Period Cha **Ending Balance**		123,540.00 123,540.00	-123,540.00 **-123,540.00**

Step 6:

Click the Close button from the General Ledger toolbar.

Check
POINT

1. What accounting period is usually used to enter beginning balances?
2. As with any accounting, the trial balance must be in balance. What does Peachtree do to ensure the trial balance is in balance?

Answers
1. *Either the current period or the period prior to the first period in which transactions will be entered.*
2. *Peachtree will not allow the trial balance to be saved unless it balances.*

PRACTICE *objective* 3

Open Bullfrog Maintenance Company, and enter the beginning balances of the general ledger accounts. Use the information given in table 2–8. Use the period 1/1/07 through 1/31/07 for beginning balances.

Your general ledger should look like figure 2–32.

TABLE 2-8
BULLFROG MAINTENANCE COMPANY BEGINNING BALANCES, JANUARY 1, 2007

Account ID	Description	Account Type	Assets, Expenses	Liabilities, Equity, Income
100	Cash	Cash	$14,400	
102	Petty Cash	Cash	100	
104	Accounts Receivable	Accounts Receivable		
106	Maintenance Supplies	Other Current Assets	2,300	
108	Office Supplies	Other Current Assets	490	
110	Prepaid Insurance	Other Current Assets	1,000	
112	Equipment	Fixed Assets	42,000	
112.5	Accum. Depr.-Equipment	Accumulated Depreciation		$10,000
200	Accounts Payable	Accounts Payable		
300	J. Bull, Capital	Equity-doesn't close		50,290
301	J. Bull, Equity	Equity-Retained Earnings		
301.5	J. Bull, Drawing	Equity-gets closed		
400	Revenue	Income		
500	Rent Expense	Expenses		
502	Utilities Expense	Expenses		
504	Maintenance Supplies Expense	Expenses		
506	Office Supplies Expense	Expenses		
508	Insurance Expense	Expenses		
510	Depreciation Expense-Eq.	Expenses		
512	Wages and Salaries Expense	Expenses		
514	Miscellaneous Expense	Expenses		

FIGURE 2-32

Bullfrog Maintenance Company General Ledger

Page: 1

Bullfrog Maintenance Company
General Ledger
For the Period From Jan 1, 2007 to Jan 31, 2007
Filter Criteria includes: Report order is by ID. Report is printed with Truncated Transaction Descriptions and in Detail Format.

Account ID Account Description	Date	Reference	Jrnl	Trans Description	Debit Amt	Credit Amt	Balance
100 Cash	1/1/07 1/1/07 1/31/07	BEGBAL	GEN	Beginning Balance Current Period Cha **Ending Balance**	14,400.00 14,400.00		14,400.00 **14,400.00**
102 Petty Cash	1/1/07 1/1/07 1/31/07	BEGBAL	GEN	Beginning Balance Current Period Cha **Ending Balance**	100.00 100.00		100.00 **100.00**
106 Maintenance Supplies	1/1/07 1/1/07 1/31/07	BEGBAL	GEN	Beginning Balance Current Period Cha **Ending Balance**	2,300.00 2,300.00		2,300.00 **2,300.00**
108 Office Supplies	1/1/07 1/1/07 1/31/07	BEGBAL	GEN	Beginning Balance Current Period Cha **Ending Balance**	490.00 490.00		490.00 **490.00**
110 Prepaid Insurance	1/1/07 1/1/07 1/31/07	BEGBAL	GEN	Beginning Balance Current Period Cha **Ending Balance**	1,000.00 1,000.00		1,000.00 **1,000.00**
112 Equipment	1/1/07 1/1/07 1/31/07	BEGBAL	GEN	Beginning Balance Current Period Cha **Ending Balance**	42,000.00 42,000.00		42,000.00 **42,000.00**
112.5 Accum. Depreciation-	1/1/07 1/1/07 1/31/07	BEGBAL	GEN	Beginning Balance Current Period Cha **Ending Balance**		10,000.00 10,000.00	-10,000.00 **-10,000.00**
301 J. Bull, Equity	1/1/07 1/1/07 1/31/07	BEGBAL	GEN	Beginning Balance Current Period Cha **Ending Balance**		50,290.00 50,290.00	-50,290.00 **-50,290.00**

Many small businesses in the past have been forced to close because they could not compete effectively with large businesses. Today, small businesses, through the use of creative Web sites, can add enough revenue from rapidly expanding Internet commerce to survive and flourish. Firms can increase sales by advertising and selling their products via Web pages. To see how important a Web site can be to a small company with an unusual product, visit the Thompson's Curling Rink Equipment Web page at www.thompson-broom.mb.ca/ (figure 2–33). (Curling is a game played on ice and has been an Olympic winter sport since 1998.)

FIGURE 2–33

Thompson's Curling Rink Equipment Web Page

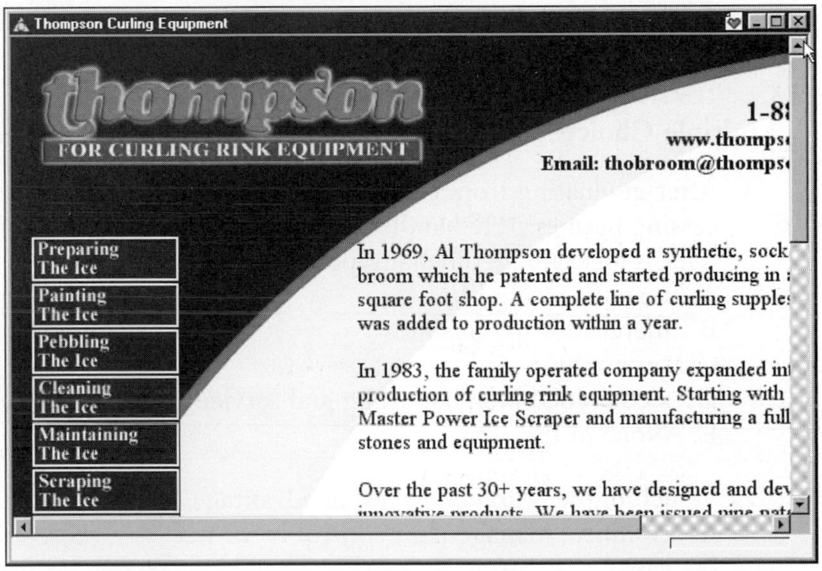

INTERNET ASSIGNMENT:

* Select a topic of interest to you that is uncommon or obscure.
* Research that topic using the Internet.
* Write a memo to your instructor indicating what information you gathered about the topic. Include the Web site address.

SOFTWARE

Command Summary

Set Up Company	Set up a new company or File, New Company, Enter Company Information, Select Chart of Accounts Option, Select Accounting Method, Select Posting Method, Set Accounting Periods, Finish
Create Chart of Accounts	Maintain, Chart of Accounts, Account ID, Description, Account Type
Enter Account Balances	Maintain, Chart of Accounts, Beginning Balances, Select Period, Enter Balances

PROJECTS

and Problems

CONTENT CHECK

Multiple Choice: Choose only one response for each question.

1. After graduating from college, a fellow student started a payroll processing business. He handles payroll work for small firms in your area. This is an example of what type of business?
   A. manufacturing business
   B. merchandising business
   C. service business
   D. a combined merchandising and service business
   E. None of the above.

2. Which of the following is *not* an advantage of a sole proprietorship?
   A. complete management control by owner
   B. ease of formation
   C. few government restrictions
   D. unlimited liability
   E. None of the above.

3. Revenue accounts would use which set of account IDs in Peachtree?
   A. 100, 1000, 10000
   B. 200, 2000, 20000
   C. 300, 3000, 30000
   D. 400, 4000, 40000
   E. 500, 5000, 50000

4. The amounts owed to a business by its customers for goods or services sold to them on credit are called
   A. accounts payable.
   B. accounts receivable.
   C. equity – retained earnings.
   D. notes payable.
   E. None of the above.

5. The financial report that lists all of a company's accounts and their balances is the
   A. general journal.
   B. general ledger.
   C. chart of accounts.
   D. account ID.
   E. None of the above.

Short Essay Response: Provide a detailed answer for each question.

1. Describe the three basic forms of business organizations. List the advantages and disadvantages of each.
2. What is the difference between the cash basis and accrual basis of accounting?
3. What are the steps required for entering beginning balances in Peachtree?
4. When setting up a new business in Peachtree, what are the six main steps in the setup process?
5. What is the difference between the two posting methods in Peachtree—real time and batch?
6. What are the three items necessary to create a new account in Peachtree? Define each.

CASE PROBLEMS

PROBLEM 1A

1. Set up a new company for GJ Professional Accounting. Use the information given below. The company you set up will be used in future chapters.

Company Name:	**GJ Professional Accounting**
Address Line 1:	**1506 East March Lane**
Address Line 2:	
City, State, Zip:	**Stockton, CA 95207**
Country:	**USA**
Telephone:	**209-555-2112**
Fax:	**209-555-1221**
Business Type:	**Sole Proprietorship**
Federal Employer ID:	**95-2962962**
State Employer ID:	**06-556-02**
St. Unemployment ID:	**00546-76**

Chart of Accounts:	**Use a sample business type that closely matches your company**
Available Charts of Accounts:	**Accounting Agency**
Accounting Method:	**Accrual**
Posting Method:	**Real Time**
Accounting Periods:	**12 monthly accounting periods**
Fiscal Year to Start:	**January 2007**

2. Edit the following accounts to reflect the information given:

Account ID	Account Description	Account Type
12000	Office Supplies	Other Current Assets
15100	Computer Equipment	Fixed Assets
39006	Garret Johnson, Capital	Equity-doesn't close
39007	Garret Johnson, Drawing	Equity-gets closed
40200	Tax Preparation Fees	Income
67500	Office Cleaning Expense	Expenses
75500	Equipment Repair Expense	Expenses

3. Enter the following beginning balances for the period from 1/1/07 through 1/31/07:

Account ID	Account Description	Account Type	Assets, Expenses	Liabilities, Equity, Income
10200	Regular Checking Account	Cash	$23,000	
11000	Accounts Receivable	Accounts Receivable	5,600	
12000	Office Supplies	Other Current Assets	1,120	
15100	Computer Equipment	Fixed Assets	4,700	
20000	Accounts Payable	Accounts Payable		$4,920
39006	Garret Johnson, Capital	Equity-doesn't close		29,500

4. Delete the following accounts:

Account ID	Description	Account Type
10000	Petty Cash	Cash
10500	Special Account	Cash
14100	Employee Advances	Other Current Assets
48000	Fee Refunds	Income
63000	Commissions and Fees Exp	Expenses

5. Print a *Chart of Accounts* report and a *General Ledger* report for the period 1/1/07 to 1/31/07.

PROBLEM 2A

1. Set up a new company for the Ramirez Construction Company. Use the information given below.

Company Name:	**Ramirez Construction Company**
Address Line 1:	**1308 Madison Avenue**
Address Line 2:	
City, State, Zip:	**Tracy, CA 95376**
Country:	**USA**
Telephone:	**209-555-7695**
Fax:	**209-555-7698**
Business Type:	**Sole Proprietorship**
Federal Employer ID:	**95-2862978**
State Employer ID:	**06-556-05**
St. Unemployment ID:	**00546-79**
Chart of Accounts:	**Build your own chart of accounts**
Accounting Method:	**Accrual**
Posting Method:	**Real Time**
Accounting Periods:	**12 monthly accounting periods**
Fiscal Year to Start:	**January 2007**

2. Create the following chart of accounts, and then enter the beginning balances for the period from 1/1/07 through 1/31/07:

RAMIREZ CONSTRUCTION COMPANY CHART OF ACCOUNTS

Account ID	Account Description	Account Type	Assets, Expenses	Liabilities, Equity, Income
100	Cash	Cash	$27,340	
104	Accounts Receivable	Accounts Receivable	13,250	
106	Office Supplies	Other Current Assets	365	
108	Construction Equipment	Fixed Assets	11,300	
108.5	Accum. Depr.-Equipment	Accumulated Depreciation		$1,800
200	Accounts Payable	Accounts Payable		2,455
300	Steve Ramirez, Capital	Equity-doesn't close		48,000
301	Steve Ramirez, Equity	Equity-Retained Earnings		
301.5	Steve Ramirez, Drawing	Equity-gets closed		
400	Revenue	Income		
500	Rent Expense	Expenses		
502	Utilities Expense	Expenses		
504	Telephone Expense	Expenses		
506	Office Supplies Expense	Expenses		
508	Repairs Expense	Expenses		
510	Depreciation Expense–Eq.	Expenses		
512	Wages and Salaries Expense	Expenses		
514	Miscellaneous Expense	Expenses		

3. Print a *Chart of Accounts* report and a *General Ledger* report for the period 1/1/07 to 1/31/07.

PROBLEM 1B

1. Set up a new company for Infinite Graphics. Use the information given below. The company you set up will be used in future chapters.

Company Name:	**Infinite Graphics**
Address Line 1:	**6051 East Sycamore Avenue**
Address Line 2:	
City, State, Zip:	**Stockton, CA 95207**
Country:	**USA**
Telephone:	**209-555-3113**
Fax:	**209-555-1331**
Business Type:	**Sole Proprietorship**
Federal Employer ID:	**95-2962984**
State Employer ID:	**06-557-03**
St. Unemployment ID:	**00546-68**
Chart of Accounts:	**Use a sample business type that closely matches your company**
Available Charts of Accounts:	**Graphic Artist**
Accounting Method:	**Accrual**
Posting Method:	**Real Time**
Accounting Periods:	**12 monthly accounting periods**
Fiscal Year to Start:	**January 2007**

2. Edit the following accounts to reflect the information given:

Account ID	Account Description	Account Type
12000	Graphing Supplies	Other Current Assets
15100	Graphing Equipment	Fixed Assets
39006	Anna Reyes, Capital	Equity-doesn't close
39007	Anna Reyes, Drawing	Equity-gets closed

3. Enter the following beginning balances for the period from 1/1/07 through 1/31/07:

Account ID	Account Description	Account Type	Assets, Expenses	Liabilities, Equity, Income
10200	Regular Checking Account	Cash	$13,000	
11000	Accounts Receivable	Accounts Receivable	2,600	
12000	Graphing Supplies	Other Current Assets	750	
15100	Graphing Equipment	Fixed Assets	7,700	
20000	Accounts Payable	Accounts Payable		$3,290
39006	Anna Reyes, Capital	Equity-doesn't close		20,760

4. Delete the following accounts:

Account ID	Account Description	Account Type
10000	Petty Cash	Cash
15500	Building	Fixed Assets
15600	Building Improvements	Fixed Assets
19100	Organization Costs	Other Assets
58500	Inventory Adjustments	Cost of Sales

5. Print a *Chart of Accounts* report and a *General Ledger* report for the period 1/1/07 to 1/31/07.

PROBLEM 2B

1. Set up a new company for Johnson Brothers Builders. Use the information given below.

Company Name:	**Johnson Brothers Builders**
Address Line 1:	**732 Alhambra Way**
Address Line 2:	
City, State, Zip:	**Tracy, CA 95376**
Country:	**USA**
Telephone:	**209-555-9567**
Fax:	**209-555-5679**
Business Type:	**Sole Proprietorship**
Federal Employer ID:	**95-2862879**
State Employer ID:	**06-566-15**
St. Unemployment ID:	**00564-97**
Chart of Accounts:	**Build your own chart of accounts**
Accounting Method:	**Accrual**
Posting Method:	**Real Time**
Accounting Periods:	**12 monthly accounting periods**
Fiscal Year to Start:	**January 2007**

2. Create the following chart of accounts, and then enter the beginning balances for the period from 1/1/07 through 1/31/07:

Account ID	Account Description	Account Type	Assets, Expenses	Liabilities, Equity, Income
100	Cash	Cash	$18,470	
104	Accounts Receivable	Accounts Receivable	4,320	
106	Construction Supplies	Other Current Assets	3,560	
108	Construction Equipment	Fixed Assets	5,300	
108.5	Accum. Depr.-Equipment	Accumulated Depreciation		$2,400
200	Accounts Payable	Accounts Payable		2,350
300	John Johnson, Capital	Equity-doesn't close		26,900
301	John Johnson, Equity	Equity-Retained Earnings		
301.5	John Johnson, Drawing	Equity-gets closed		
400	Revenue	Income		
500	Rent Expense	Expenses		
502	Utilities Expense	Expenses		
504	Telephone Expense	Expenses		
506	Construction Supplies Expense	Expenses		
508	Repairs Expense	Expenses		
510	Depreciation Expense-Eq.	Expenses		
512	Wages and Salaries Expense	Expenses		
514	Miscellaneous Expense	Expenses		

3. Print a *Chart of Accounts* report and a *General Ledger* report for the period 1/1/07 to 1/31/07.

COOPERATIVE LEARNING

1. Form into groups of three or four students, and create your own hypothetical service business. Decide on the information needed for the business setup. Summarize your ideas on paper.
2. Using the newly formed company from Cooperative Learning Exercise 1, create the chart of accounts that will be needed. Print the chart of accounts.
3. Using the newly created accounts from Cooperative Learning Exercise 2, enter beginning balances that you consider reasonable for the new business. Print the general ledger.

Assume that the owner of the company for which you work, Maria Richardson, believes in the cross training of employees. Therefore, she has informed you that next week an employee from the purchasing department will spend a day with you and observe some of the reports you work with in the accounting department. She especially wants you to explain to this employee the significance of both the chart of accounts and the general ledger and how they relate to each other. Ms. Richardson would like you to give her a memo with the information that you plan to share with the employee from the purchasing department.

C H A P T E R

3

ENTERING TRANSACTIONS

FOR A CASH BUSINESS

1. Create new accounts and enter beginning balances for a simple cash business

2. Record transactions in the general journal

3. Edit selected transactions in the general journal

4. Print the general journal and financial statements

SOFTWARE FEATURES

- General journal toolbar buttons

- General journal edit function

- General journal delete function

- General journal recurring transaction function

- General journal memorized transaction function

- Report filter and print procedures

transactions Financial events that change a firm's assets, liabilities, or owner's equity.

Transactions are financial events that change a firm's assets, liabilities, or owner's equity. Examples of transactions are selling goods on credit, purchasing office supplies for cash, paying salaries to employees, and paying an amount owed to a creditor. Every firm must record the financial effects of its transactions. Generally, the first record of a business transaction is entered in a journal.

TRANSACTIONS AND THE GENERAL JOURNAL

journal A record in which transactions are listed in order by date.

general journal A journal in which all kinds of transactions can be recorded.

source documents Business papers that provide evidence of transactions.

A **journal** is simply a chronological record of transactions—a listing of transactions in order by date. There are various types of journals, but the most basic type is the **general journal**, which can be used to record all kinds of transactions.

Peachtree's General Journal Entry window, shown in figure 3–1, is very similar to a manual general journal. In both manual and computerized accounting systems, the information needed for general journal entries normally comes from business papers such as invoices, check stubs, cash register tapes, bills, and receipts, which provide evidence of the transactions. These business papers are known as **source documents**.

FIGURE 3-1
General Journal Entry Window

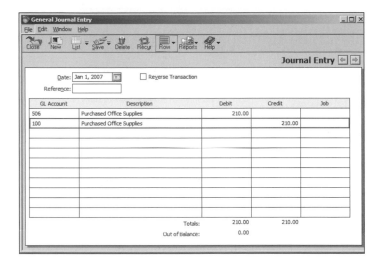

DEBITS AND CREDITS

double-entry accounting A method of accounting in which equal debits and credits are recorded for each transaction.

Debits and credits are at the heart of **double-entry accounting**. Every transaction is recorded by debiting one or more accounts and crediting one or more accounts. The total of the debits and the total of the credits recorded for the transaction must be equal.

Using source documents, the accountant analyzes each transaction to determine what accounts must be debited and credited and the amounts involved. The accountant follows the rules of debit and credit, which can be summarized as follows:

- *Asset, drawing, and expense accounts:* Record increases as debits and decreases as credits.
- *Liability, capital, and revenue accounts:* Record increases as credits and decreases as debits.

One of the great advantages of a computerized accounting system like Peachtree is that it has features that alert the accountant to unbalanced journal entries and prevent the posting of such entries to the general ledger. In a manual accounting system, entries with unequal debits and credits often go unnoticed in the general journal and are posted to the general ledger. The presence of errors is not revealed until the trial balance is prepared at the end of the month. At this point, much time and effort must be spent tracing the individual errors through the journal and ledger and recording correcting entries.

Figure 3–2 illustrates a general journal entry in Peachtree that has unequal debits and credits. A notice at the bottom of the screen indicates that the journal is out of balance and shows the difference between the debit and credit totals ($90). Peachtree will not allow an unbalanced entry such as this one to be posted.

HINT

To learn more about the general ledger, select Help from the Main Menu and Contents and Index from the drop-down list. Key "General Ledger" at the prompt.

FIGURE 3-2

General Journal Entry with Unequal Debits and Credits

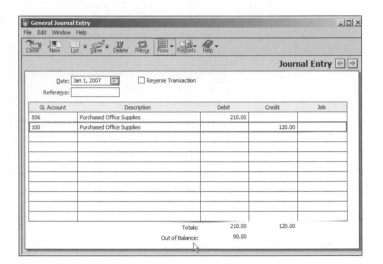

Check POINT

1. Each journal entry for a transaction must be in balance. What does that mean?
2. How does Peachtree treat a general journal entry that is not in balance?

Answers
1. *The total of the debits must equal the total of the credits.*
2. *Peachtree will not allow an unbalanced general journal entry to be posted.*

JOURNALIZING AND POSTING A SAMPLE TRANSACTION

Suppose that a business purchases office supplies for $250 in cash. The accountant's analysis of this transaction reveals that an expense (Office Supplies Expense) has increased by $250 and an asset (Cash) has decreased by $250. The accountant records this transaction by debiting Office Supplies Expense for $250 and crediting Cash for $250. (In this example, the business operates on a pure cash basis and therefore treats purchases of supplies as an expense.)

If the business has a manual accounting system, the accountant will make the necessary entry in the general journal as shown in figure 3–3.

FIGURE 3-3

General Journal Entry

	Date		Account Title	P.R.	Debit	Credit
			General Journal			**Page 1**
1	Feb.	1	Office Supplies Expense	508	250 00	
2			Cash	100		250 00
3			Purchased office supplies.			

Note: It is a good practice to provide a brief explanation.

After the general journal entry is made, the accountant posts to the appropriate general ledger accounts and records the account numbers in the posting reference (P.R.) column of the general journal. See figures 3–4 and 3–5. In the Cash account (figure 3–4), the credit entry of $250 is subtracted from the beginning debit balance of $6,500 to find the new debit balance of $6,250.

FIGURE 3-4

Cash Account

Account Cash   **Account No. 100**

	Date		Item	P.R.	Debit	Credit	Balance Debit	Balance Credit
1	Feb.	1	Beginning balance	✓			6 500 00	
2		1		GJ1		250 00	6 250 00	
3								

FIGURE 3-5

Office Supplies Expense

Account Office Supplies Expense   **Account No. 508**

	Date		Item	P.R.	Debit	Credit	Balance Debit	Balance Credit
1	Feb.	1		GJ1	250 00		250 00	
2								
3								

Once an entry is posted to the ledger accounts, a posting reference (P.R.) is recorded in the accounts to identify the source of the entry. In this example, the source of the entry is page 1 of the general journal. Therefore, GJ1 is recorded in the P.R. column of each account.

In computerized accounting systems like Peachtree, posting is done automatically by the system. Once the chart of accounts has been set up, as described in chapter 2, Peachtree can automatically transfer information from journal entries to the general ledger accounts. This feature eliminates much repetitive work and prevents many of the errors that occur in manual posting.

THE GENERAL JOURNAL AND SPECIAL JOURNALS

A very small business may record all of its transactions in the general journal, but a larger business would probably use special journals as well as the general journal. A **special journal** is a journal that is used to record a single type of transaction. Peachtree allows you to use special journals for sales, purchases, cash receipts, and cash payments. These journals increase efficiency by grouping like transactions in their own journals.

The sales journal is used to record sales of goods or services on credit. The purchase journal is used to record purchases of goods or services on credit. The cash receipts journal is used to record all cash receipts. The cash disbursements journal is used to record all cash payments.

The use of special journals does not eliminate the need for a general journal. Some transactions still require a general journal entry. For example, in Peachtree, transactions involving returns and allowances for credit sales and credit purchases must be recorded in the general journal. It is also necessary to use the general journal for correcting entries, adjusting entries, and closing entries.

In the rest of this chapter, you will establish an accounting system for a small business in Peachtree and then use the general journal functions of Peachtree. The business that you will work with—Jones Consulting—is a small service business that operates on a cash basis.

Check
POINT

1. What is the advantage of using the special journals provided by Peachtree?
2. What are the four basic types of special journals?

Answers
1. The special journals increase efficiency by grouping similar transactions.
2. Sales journal, purchase journal, cash receipts journal, and cash disbursements journal.

In chapter 2, you learned how to set up a company in Peachtree, create a chart of accounts, and enter the beginning balances of the general ledger accounts. You will now use this knowledge to establish a computerized accounting system for Jones Consulting.

SETTING UP A SIMPLE CASH BUSINESS IN PEACHTREE

Follow the steps outlined below to begin the setup process.

Step 1:

Start Peachtree Accounting.

Step 2:

At the Peachtree Accounting opening window, click *Create a new company*.

Step 3:

Click <u>N</u>ext at the bottom of the Create a New Company – Introduction dialog box.

Step 4:

Enter the information for Jones Consulting in the Create a New Company Setup – Company Information dialog box. Use the information shown in figure 3–6.

FIGURE 3-6

Create a New Company –
Company Information
Dialog Box

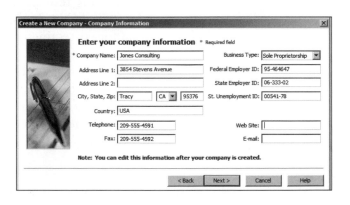

Step 5:

Click <u>N</u>ext to reveal the Create a New Company – Setup dialog box. Click the "Build your own chart of accounts" option.

Step 6:

Click <u>N</u>ext to move to the Create a New Company – Accounting Method dialog box, and then click Cash.

Step 7:

Click Next to move to the Create a New Company – Posting Method dialog box, and then click Real Time.

Step 8:

Click Next to move to the Create a New Company – Accounting Periods dialog box, click the "12 monthly accounting periods per year" option.

Step 9:

Click Next to move to the Create a New Company – Fiscal Year dialog box. Jones Consulting will use the calendar year as its fiscal year. Choose *January 2007* as the starting date of the fiscal year. (See figure 3–7.)

FIGURE 3-7

Create a New Company – Fiscal Year Dialog Box

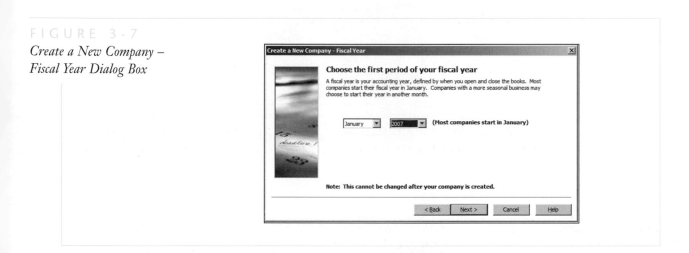

Step 10:

Click Next to move to the Create a New Company – Finish dialog box.

Step 11:

Click Finish. Wait for Peachtree to finish creating files. Then close the Peachtree Setup Guide window.

CREATING NEW ACCOUNTS AND ENTERING BEGINNING BALANCES

In chapter 2, you learned about the procedures for creating general ledger accounts and entering their beginning balances. You will now use these procedures for Jones Consulting. Follow the steps outlined below to create new accounts and enter the beginning balances for Jones Consulting.

Step 1:

Click Maintain from the Main Menu and then click Chart of Accounts.

Step 2:

Create the Cash account by keying **100** in the *Account ID* field.

Step 3:

Click OK to accept account number 100. Then key **Cash** in the *Description* field.

Step 4:

At the Account Type drop-down list, click *Cash*. Compare your entries with those shown in figure 3–8. Then click Save.

FIGURE 3-8

Completed Cash Account

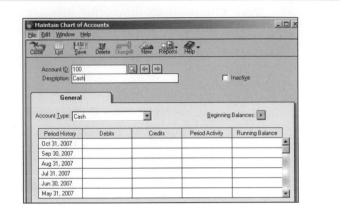

Step 5:

Click New to set up another account. Create the remainder of the general ledger accounts for Jones Consulting. Use the account IDs, account descriptions, and account types shown in table 3–1.

TABLE 3-1
JONES CONSULTING ACCOUNTS AND BEGINNING BALANCES AS OF JANUARY 1, 2007

Account ID	Account Description	Account Type	Assets, Expenses	Liabilities, Equity, Income
100	Cash	Cash	$ 98,765.00	
102	Petty Cash	Cash	100.00	
300	P. Jones, Capital	Equity-doesn't close		$ 98,865.00
301	P. Jones, Equity	Equity-Retained Earnings		
301.5	P. Jones, Drawing	Equity-gets closed		
400	Consulting Fees	Income		
500	Independent Contractor Expense	Expenses		
502	Rent Expense	Expenses		
504	Utilities Expense	Expenses		
506	Office Supplies Expense	Expenses		
508	Telephone Expense	Expenses		
510	Travel Expense	Expenses		
512	Professional Expense	Expenses		
		TOTALS	$ 98,865.00	$ 98,865.00

After creating all of the accounts listed in table 3–1, view your accounts to ensure their accuracy by clicking the *magnifying glass* icon to the right of the *Account ID* field. Click Cancel when finished.

FIGURE 3-9

Select Period Dialog Box

Step 6:

Enter the beginning balances for Jones Consulting as of December 31, 2006. To start this process, click the Right Arrow key next to <u>B</u>eginning Balances in the Maintain Chart of Accounts dialog box.

Step 7:

Click *From 12/1/06 through 12/31/06* from the Select Period dialog box, as shown in figure 3–9, and then click <u>O</u>K.

Step 8:

Enter the balances for Jones Consulting from table 3–1. Then completed Chart of Accounts Beginning Balances window is shown in figure 3–10. Press the Tab key to move from account to account.

FIGURE 3-10

Completed Chart of Accounts Beginning Balances Window

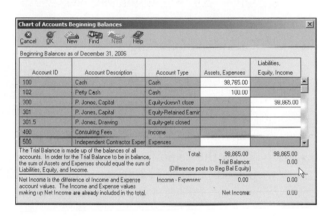

Step 9:

The totals at the bottom of the window should be equal, and the trial balance difference should be zero. This indicates that the general ledger accounts are in balance. Click the <u>O</u>K button after reviewing the Chart of Accounts Beginning Balances window.

Step 10:

Close the Maintain Chart of Accounts window.

Check
POINT

1. After you enter beginning balances in Peachtree, how can you be sure that the general ledger accounts are in balance?
2. In Peachtree, the completed chart of accounts contains what four items of information for each account?

Answers
1. *If the totals of the balances are equal and the trial balance difference is zero, the general ledger accounts are in balance.*
2. *The account ID, description, account type, and balance for each account appear in the completed chart of accounts.*

PRACTICE *objective* 1

Create a new account and enter beginning balances for Bell Accounting Service.

Step 1:

Open Bell Accounting Service. (Bell was created in chapter 2.)

Step 2:

Create the following account:

Account ID:	**39004**
Description:	**James, Capital**
Account Type:	**Equity-doesn't close**

Step 3:

Enter the beginning balances for the accounts listed in table 3–2 for the period January 1, 2007 to January 31, 2007.

TABLE 3-2
BELL ACCOUNTING SERVICE, JANUARY 1, 2007

Account ID	Account Description	Account Type	Assets, Expenses	Liabilities, Equity, Income
10100	Cash on Hand	Cash	$250	
10200	Regular Checking Account	Cash	15,000	
39004	James, Capital	Equity-doesn't close		$15,250

Step 4:

Preview the general ledger and compare it with figure 3–11.

FIGURE 3-11
Bell Accounting Service General Ledger

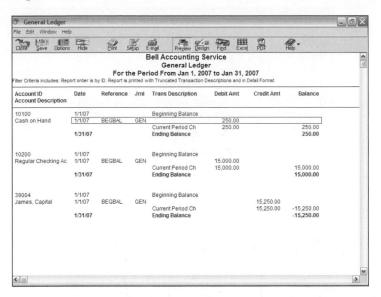

OBJECTIVE 2 — RECORD TRANSACTIONS IN THE GENERAL JOURNAL

Once you have established the general ledger accounts and their balances, you can enter transactions. The transactions presented in this section are for Jones Consulting, a simple cash business. Jones has no accounts receivable or accounts payable and owns no fixed assets. It rents a furnished office suite.

Throughout this section, the transactions of Jones Consulting are shown. You will use the general journal entry function of Peachtree to record these transactions. Follow the steps listed below to journalize the January transactions of Jones Consulting.

Step 1:

Open Jones Consulting and close the Setup Guide, if open.

Step 2:

Analyze the following transaction:

- On January 4, 2007, Jones Consulting purchased office supplies for $1,200 in cash from a local store.

   Analysis: An expense (Office Supplies Expense) has increased by $1,200 and an asset (Cash) has decreased by $1,200. Therefore, debit Office Supplies Expense for $1,200 and credit Cash for $1,200.

The manual general journal entry needed to record this transaction is shown in figure 3–12.

FIGURE 3-12
General Journal Entry

	Date		Account Title	P.R.	Debit	Credit
General Journal						Page 1
1	Jan.	4	Office Supplies Expense	506	1200 00	
2			Cash	100		1200 00
3			Purchased office supplies.			

Step 3:

Use Peachtree to record the above transaction in the general journal of Jones Consulting. Click Tas̲ks, and then click G̲eneral Journal Entry.

You can also access the general journal by clicking the General Journal Entry shortcut at the lower left of the Peachtree screen, as shown in figure 3–13. The general journal entry window appears.

FIGURE 3-13
General Journal Entry Shortcut on the Navigation Aids Toolbar

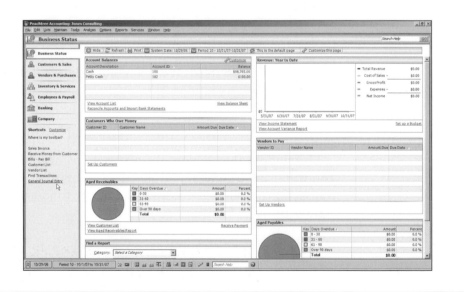

Step 4:

Enter the date of the transaction, January 4, 2007, by clicking the *calendar* icon to the right of the *D̲ate* field. Choose *January* as the month, *4* as the day, and *2007* as the year.

Step 5:

Enter the account to be debited. Click the cell under *GL Account* and then click the *magnifying glass* icon to the right of the *GL Account* field. Highlight the account *506, Office Supplies Expense*. Compare your screen with figure 3–14 and then click OK. **Note:** When using a mouse it is not necessary to click OK. Once the account is selected it is entered on the *GL Account* line.

FIGURE 3-14

*Account Drop-Down List
with Account 506 Selected*

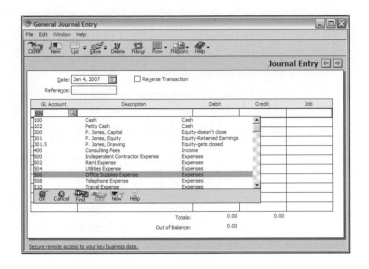

Step 6:

Key **Purchased Office Supplies** in the *Description* field. Press the Tab key and key **1,200.00** in the *Debit* field. Then tab down to the second row.

Step 7:

Enter the account to be credited. Click the *magnifying glass* icon to the right of the *GL Account* field in the second row, highlight or click the account *100*, *Cash*, and then click OK.

Step 8:

Peachtree will automatically enter the same description, *Purchased Office Supplies*, in the *Description* field. Press the Tab key and key **1,200.00** in the *Credit* field. Compare your completed general journal entry with figure 3–15.

FIGURE 3-15

*Completed General Journal
Entry—Office Supplies*

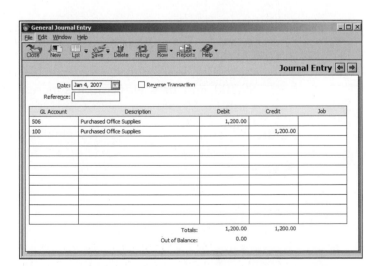

Complete the recording of the transaction by clicking the Save button from the toolbar. Peachtree then transfers the information from the general journal entry to the appropriate ledger accounts.

Use Peachtree to journalize and post the rest of the January transactions for Jones Consulting. Review the following analysis of these transactions and the general journal entries that are shown.

- On January 5, 2007, Jones decides to increase the petty cash fund from $100 to $200. He writes a check for $100 to petty cash, cashes the check, and puts the money in the petty cash box. **Analysis:** This transaction produces a shift in assets. One asset (Petty Cash) has increased by $100, and another asset (Cash) has decreased by $100. Therefore, debit Petty Cash for $100 and credit Cash for $100. (See figure 3–16.)

FIGURE 3-16

Completed General Journal Entry—Petty Cash

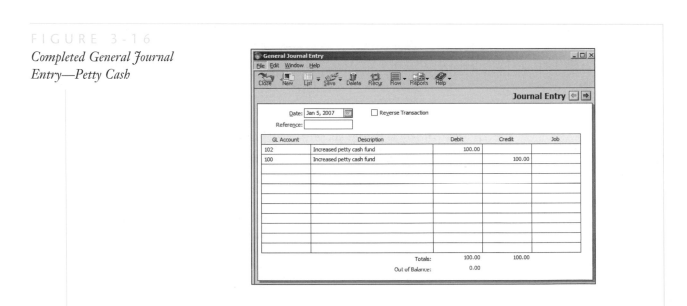

- On January 7, 2007, Jones collected fees of $9,200 for a completed consulting job. **Analysis:** Revenue (Consulting Fees) has increased by $9,200, and an asset (Cash) has increased by $9,200. Therefore, debit Cash for $9,200 and credit Consulting Fees for $9,200. (See figure 3–17.)

FIGURE 3-17

*Completed General Journal
Entry—Consulting Fees*

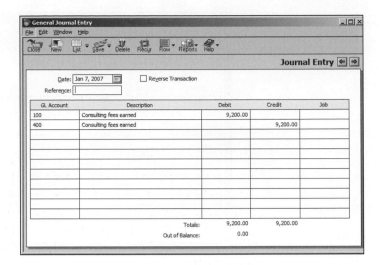

* On January 9, 2007, Jones paid the electric bill of $675. **Analysis:** An expense (Utilities Expense) has increased by $675, and an asset (Cash) has decreased by $675. Therefore, debit Utilities Expense for $675 and credit Cash for $675. (See figure 3–18.)

FIGURE 3-18

*Completed General Journal
Entry—Electric Bill*

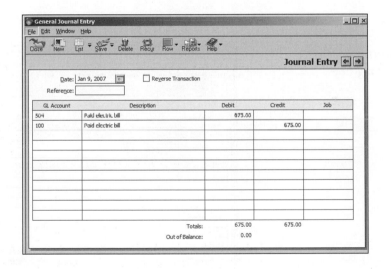

* On January 12, 2007, Jones made a trip to visit a potential client. The total cost of the gasoline, hotel, and meals was $450. **Analysis:** An expense (Travel Expense) has increased by $450, and an asset (Cash) has decreased by $450. Therefore, debit Travel Expense for $450 and credit Cash for $450. (See figure 3–19.)

FIGURE 3-19
*Completed General Journal
Entry—Business Trip*

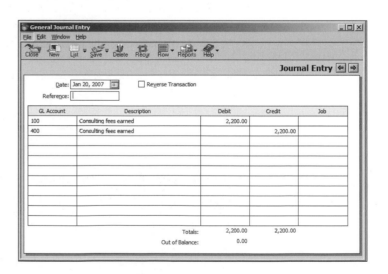

- On January 20, 2007, Jones collected fees of $2,200 after completing the first stage of a job. **Analysis:** Revenue (Consulting Fees) has increased by $2,200, and an asset (Cash) has increased by $2,200. Therefore, debit Cash for $2,200 and credit Consulting Fees for $2,200. (See figure 3–20.)

FIGURE 3-20
*Completed General Journal
Entry—Consulting Fees*

- On January 23, 2007, Jones paid $2,600 to an independent contractor who did work for the business. (An independent contractor is someone who is not an employee and does not receive a salary. Instead, this person works for a fee on a project-by-project basis.) **Analysis:** An expense (Independent Contractor Expense) has increased by $2,600, and an asset (Cash) has decreased by $2,600. Therefore, debit Independent Contractor Expense for $2,600 and credit Cash for $2,600. (See figure 3–21.)

FIGURE 3-21
Completed General Journal Entry—Contractor's Fee

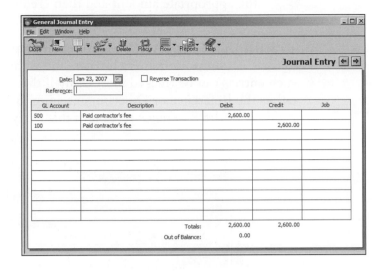

- On January 24, 2007, Jones paid $850 to a local newspaper for advertising. **Analysis:** An expense (Advertising Expense) has increased by $850, and an asset (Cash) has decreased by $850. Therefore, debit Advertising Expense for $850 and credit Cash for $850. (See figure 3–22.) Jones has no Advertising Expense account, and you must create one. Use the following information to create the account:

Account ID:	**514**
Description:	**Advertising Expense**
Account Type:	**Expenses**

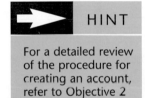

HINT

For a detailed review of the procedure for creating an account, refer to Objective 2 in Chapter 2.

FIGURE 3-22
Completed General Journal Entry—Newspaper Ads

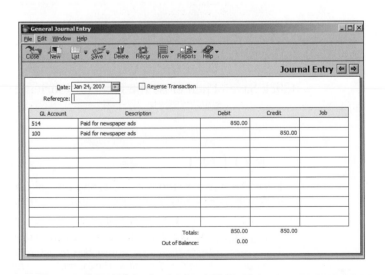

- On January 31, 2007, Jones paid month-end bills of $1,200 for rent and $350 for telephone. Jones also paid a bill of $230 for yearly dues owed to a professional organization. **Analysis:** As a result of this transaction, several expenses have increased, and the asset Cash has decreased. Therefore, debit each of the expense accounts affected for the appropriate amount and then credit Cash all at once for the total of the amounts. (See figure 3–23.)

Notice that this transaction requires a compound entry in the general journal. A **compound entry** involves more than two accounts. In Peachtree, such entries can be tracked most easily if the word *Compound* is recorded in either the Reference or Description section of the General Journal Entry window. In the Reference section of this entry, key the word **Compound**.

FIGURE 3-23
Completed General Journal Entry—Month-End Bills

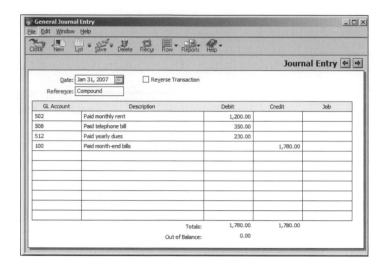

Step 11:
Click <u>S</u>ave. Then close the General Journal Entry window.

POINT

1. What are two methods for accessing the general journal in Peachtree?
2. Why is it necessary to analyze a transaction before journalizing it?

Answers
1. *The general journal can be accessed by using the Menu bar or the Custom toolbar.*
2. *It is necessary to analyze a transaction to determine the appropriate accounts and amounts to debit and credit in the journal entry for that transaction.*

Several transactions for Bell Accounting Service are listed below. Record these transactions in the general journal for the month of January 2007.

> **HINT**
>
> Remember that Bell Accounting Service uses the cash basis accounting method and will not use Accounts Receivable, Other Current Assets, Fixed Assets, and Accounts Payable type accounts.

Step 1:

Open Bell Accounting Service.

Step 2:

Journalize the following transactions.*

- On January 2, Bell purchased $2,400 of office supplies. (Because Bell uses the cash basis, it records purchases of supplies in an expense account.) Use Account 76000, Supplies Expense.
- On January 4, Bell provided accounting services for $5,200 in cash.
- On January 12, Bell paid an independent subcontractor $1,235 for maintenance services.
- On January 20, Bell paid for an employee's continuing education course (73500) for $450.
- On January 24, Bell paid advertising costs of $750. Use Account 62500, Client Promotions.
- On January 31, Bell paid the following month-end bills (*compound entry*):

Utilities	$300
Telephone	$245

* For all cash transactions, use Account 10200, Checking Account.

Step 3:

Review your journal entries for accuracy.

Step 4:

Close the General Journal Entry window.

OBJECTIVE 3 — EDIT SELECTED TRANSACTIONS IN THE GENERAL JOURNAL

Occasionally it is necessary to alter a general journal entry that contains an error. For example, if you have used the wrong date or selected a wrong account, the entry must be corrected. Peachtree has an edit function that can be used to accomplish this task. The steps outlined below illustrate the procedures for editing a general journal entry.

Step 1:

Open Jones Consulting.

Step 2:

Click Tasks, and then click General Journal Entry.

Step 3:

Click the List button at the top of the General Journal Entry toolbar. The Select General Journal List window will appear.

Step 4:

Click the first entry from the General Journal List window. That entry should be for the purchase of office supplies for $1,200. Compare your screen with figure 3–24. Click Open when the correct journal entry is highlighted.

FIGURE 3-24

Select General Journal Entry Window

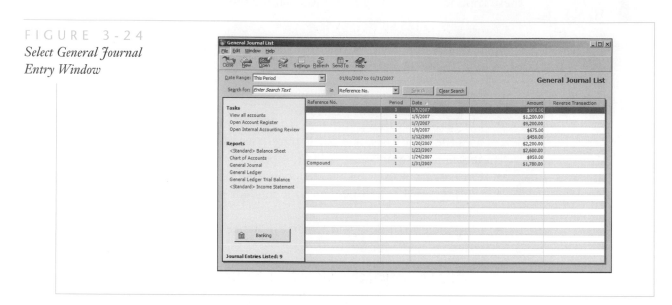

The general journal entry selected for editing is now in the active window, as shown in figure 3–25, and can be changed.

FIGURE 3-25

Selected General Journal Entry

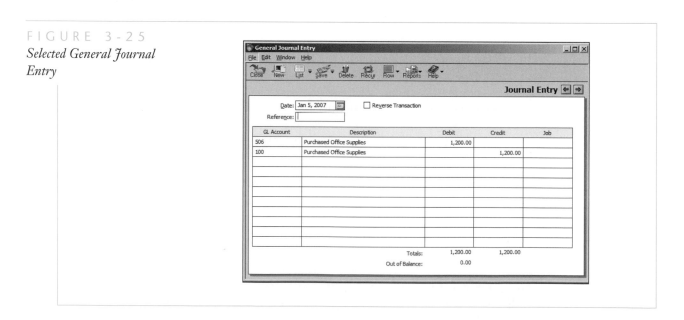

Step 5:

Assume that the accountant for Jones Consulting has entered the wrong date for the purchase of office supplies. Change the date from January 4, 2007, to January 5, 2007. Click the *calendar* icon, and then click 5 from the drop-down calendar.

Step 6:

Click Save and then Close to complete the editing process.

Step 7:

Use the Open function to review the other transactions you posted for Objective 2.

DELETING A GENERAL JOURNAL ENTRY

It may be necessary to delete an entire general journal entry. Peachtree has a function that makes this process simple.

Step 1:

Open Jones Consulting, if it is not currently open.

Step 2:

Create the following general journal entry for Jones Consulting:

- On January 23, 2007, purchased office supplies for $230 in cash. Compare the newly completed general journal entry with figure 3–26.

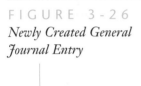

FIGURE 3-26
Newly Created General Journal Entry

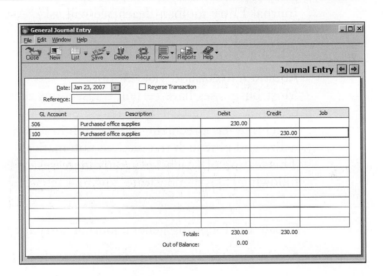

Step 3:

Click Save.

Step 4:

Retrieve the general journal entry just posted by clicking the List button on the toolbar and highlighting the desired entry as shown in figure 3–27. Then click Open (top of General Journal toolbar).

FIGURE 3-27

*Selected General Journal
Entry Highlighted*

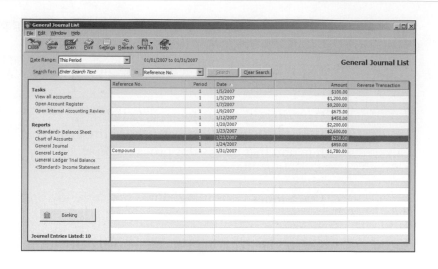

Step 5:

Assume that the accountant for Jones Consulting wants to delete the entire general journal entry created in step 2. Click the Delete button in the General Journal Entry toolbar. Peachtree will ask, "Are you sure you want to delete this transaction?" Click Yes, and the general journal entry is deleted. Close the General Journal List window.

ADDING A RECURRING TRANSACTION

Most businesses have certain transactions that recur on a regular basis. For example, payment of rent may be due on a specified day each month. Peachtree has a recurring transaction function that makes it possible to journalize and post such transactions automatically on a predetermined schedule. This feature of Peachtree greatly increases efficiency and reduces errors. The following steps demonstrate how to establish a recurring transaction.

Step 1:

Create the following general journal entry for Jones Consulting:

- On January 31, 2007, paid the monthly rent of $1,200. (See figure 3–28.)

FIGURE 3-28

*Completed General
Journal Entry*

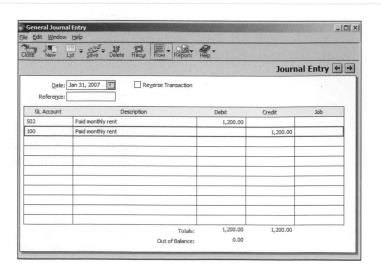

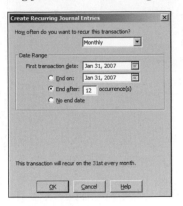

FIGURE 3-29

Create Recurring Journal Entries Dialog Box

Step 2:

Because the rent payment occurs at the same time and for the same amount each month, the transaction can be saved and automatically recalled at specific intervals by Peachtree. Click the Recur button at the top of the General Journal Entry toolbar to access the Create Recurring Journal Entries dialog box as shown in figure 3–29.

Step 3:

You can now save the journal entry for the payment of rent and designate how often it should recur. Select *Monthly* to answer "How often do you want to recur this transaction?"

Step 4:

Select *January 31, 2007* as "First transaction date." Select *End after* and key **12** for occurances, as shown in figure 3–29.

Step 5:

Click OK to save the recurring transaction and return to the General Journal Entry dialog box.

REMOVING A RECURRING TRANSACTION

Suppose that the accountant for Jones Consulting wants to remove the recurring transaction for the rent payment.

Step 1:

Click the List button on the General Journal Entry toolbar. Click the entry for the monthly rent, as shown in figure 3–30, and click Open.

FIGURE 3-30

Select General Journal List Window with Recurring Rent Transaction Chosen

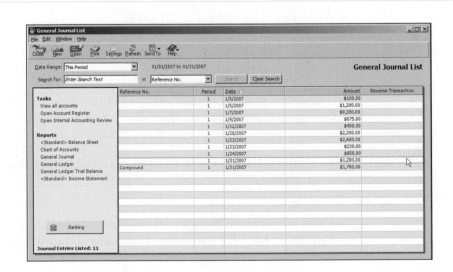

FIGURE 3-31

*Erase Recurring
Journal Entries Dialog
Box*

Step 2:

Click the Delete button on the General Journal Entry toolbar.

Step 3:

In the Delete Recurring Journal Entries dialog box, click the button next to "This transaction and <u>a</u>ll remaining," as shown in figure 3–31, and click O<u>K</u>. This selection eliminates both the current journal entry for the rent payment and all recurring entries.

Step 4:

Close the General Journal List.

ADDING A MEMORIZED TRANSACTION

Peachtree allows users to store in its memory transactions that occur often and recalls such transactions as they are needed. These transactions are known as memorized transactions.

Memorized transactions differ from recurring transactions because you must recall memorized transactions, whereas Peachtree makes recurring transactions automatically once they are established. The following steps demonstrate how to create, edit, and delete a memorized transaction.

Step 1:

Open Jones Consulting, if it is not already open.

Step 2:

Click <u>M</u>aintain, and then click <u>M</u>emorized Transactions.

Step 3:

At the Memorized Transactions submenu, click <u>G</u>eneral Journal Entries.

Create a general journal entry for the following transaction, which Jones Consulting wants to establish as a memorized transaction. The actual date of this transaction will vary from month to month.

- Paid a monthly fee of $250 to the bookkeeper, who is an independent contractor.

Step 4:

Every memorized transaction requires an identification name or number. Key **BOOKKEEPER** in the *Transaction ID* lookup box, as shown in figure 3–32. Then click OK.

FIGURE 3-32

*Transaction ID Lookup Box
with Bookkeeper Entered*

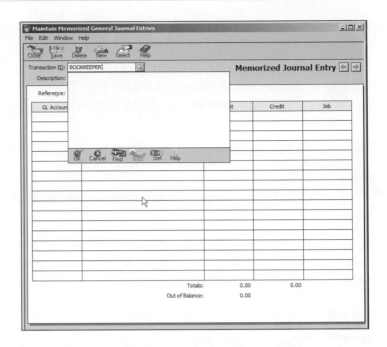

Step 5:

Key **Bookkeeper's Fee** in the *Description* field.

Step 6:

Record the remaining data as you would a regular general journal entry. Debit Independent Contractor Expense (Account 500) for $250 and credit Cash (Account 100) for $250. The completed entry for the memorized transaction is shown in figure 3–33.

FIGURE 3-33

*Completed General Journal
Entry for Memorized
Transaction*

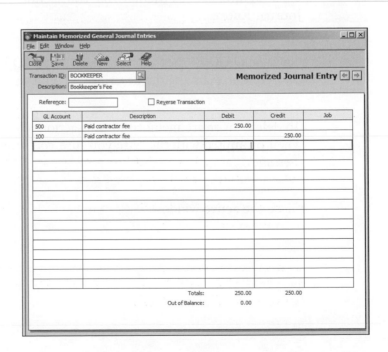

Click <u>S</u>ave and Close. The memorized transaction is now available for recall whenever it is needed.

RECALLING A MEMORIZED TRANSACTION

Suppose that Jones Consulting pays the bookkeeper's fee on January 31, 2007, and wants to recall the memorized transaction.

Step 1:

Click <u>M</u>aintain, and then click <u>M</u>emorized Transactions.

Step 2:

At the Memorized Transactions submenu, click <u>G</u>eneral Journal Entries.

Step 3:

Click the *magnifying glass* icon next to the *Transaction ID* lookup box, click *BOOKKEEPER*, and then click OK. The general journal entry for the memorized transaction appears.

Step 4:

Click the Select button from the Maintain Memorized General Journal Entries toolbar. This places the memorized transaction in the general journal entry window.

Step 5:

Key **31** in the *Date* field and press the Enter key. *Jan 31, 2007* will appear as the date. Save the completed entry, and close the general journal entry window. Close the Maintain Memorized General Journal Entries window.

EDITING OR DELETING A MEMORIZED TRANSACTION

It is possible to edit or delete existing memorized transactions.

Step 1:

Click <u>M</u>aintain, click <u>M</u>emorized Transactions, and then click <u>G</u>eneral Journal Entries.

Step 2:

Click *BOOKKEEPER* from the Transaction <u>ID</u> lookup box and edit it as desired. For example, the description could be changed and then saved.

Step 3:

To delete an entire memorized transaction, click Delete and click <u>Y</u>es when prompted with the "Are you sure you want to delete this record?" message.

Step 4:

Close the active window.

HINT

Transactions can be memorized and saved directly from the General Journal window by selecting the down arrow key to the right of the *Save* icon and selecting the Memorize option.

HINT

The date of the transaction is not memorized. It is necessary to enter the date each time the memorized transaction is used.

Check
POINT

1. What is the difference between a memorized transaction and a recurring transaction?
2. What is the purpose of the edit function for general journal entries?

Answers
1. *A memorized transaction is one that can be recalled whenever you want it. A recurring transaction is programmed to occur automatically according to a schedule chosen in advance.*
2. *The edit function allows you to make changes in any general journal entry after it has been posted.*

PRACTICE *objective* 3

Use the general journal entries that you previously recorded for Bell Accounting Service to practice the edit function. Then record recurring and memorized transactions for Bell.

Step 1:
Open Bell Accounting Service.

Step 2:
Edit the journal entry for the January 4, 2007, transaction. Change the date to January 5, 2007.

Step 3:
Create a recurring transaction for the payment of rent on January 31, 2007, for $900. (Use Account 75000, Rent or Lease Expense.) This transaction should recur monthly for 12 months.

Step 4:
Create a memorized transaction for maintenance costs of $750.00 and name it **MAINTENANCE EXPENSE**. (Use Account 69500, Maintenance and Repairs Expense.)

Step 5:
Review your work for accuracy. If any changes are necessary, use the edit function.

Step 6:
Close the active window.

OBJECTIVE 4 — PRINT THE GENERAL JOURNAL AND FINANCIAL STATEMENTS

Peachtree allows you to review and print the general journal and financial statements by using the Reports option. There are two methods for accessing the Report menu. The first method is by clicking Reports and then General Ledger from the Menu bar. The second method for accessing the

Select a Report menu is found by selecting the Business Status tab from the side toolbar and then General Ledger from the Category drop-down list and General Journal from the Report drop-down list, as shown in figure 3–34.

FIGURE 3-34

Create a Report with General Journal Selected

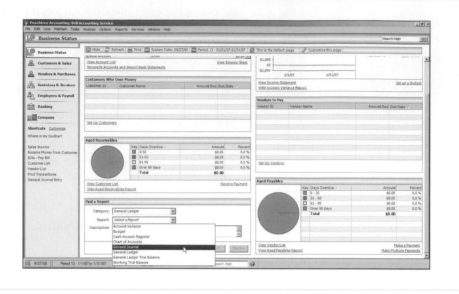

VIEWING THE GENERAL JOURNAL

Follow the steps outlined below to view and print the general journal.

Step 1:

Open Jones Consulting, if it is not already open and close the Setup Guide.

Step 2:

Click Reports from the Main Menu and then General Ledger, click *General Ledger* from the Report Area section of the Select a Report dialog box, and then click *General Journal* from the Report List section, as shown in figure 3–35.

FIGURE 3-35

Select a Report Dialog Box with General Ledger and General Journal Chosen

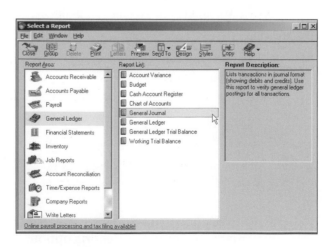

Step 3:

Click the Preview button on the Select a Report toolbar. The Filter tab appears as shown in figure 3–36.

FIGURE 3-36

Report Filter Tab for General Journal

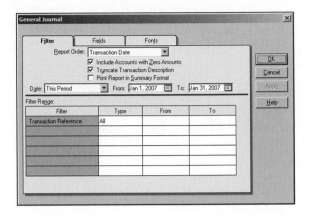

Step 4:

Click *Transaction Date* at the Report Order drop-down list. This choice means that the transactions will be listed in order by the date of occurrence.

Step 5:

Deselect (or uncheck) the check mark in the box to the left of "Include Accounts with Zero Amounts." This feature is a toggle function. It is like an on/off switch. The check mark indicates that all accounts, even those with zero balances, will be listed. Also deselect the "Truncate Transaction Description" box. This feature will shorten long descriptions on the report.

Step 6:

Click *This Period* from the Date drop-down list. In addition to the current monthly period, several other options are available including quarterly and annual periods.

Step 7:

Select the first date of the period when transactions were entered, **Jan 1, 2007**, in the *From* field, if necessary. Key the last date of the period in which transactions were entered, **Jan 31, 2007**, in the *To* field, if necessary.

Step 8:

Click *All* from the *Type* column. This choice means that all transactions that occurred during the selected period will appear in the report. Before continuing, compare your work with figure 3–37.

FIGURE 3-37

*Completed Report Filter
Dialog Box for General
Journal*

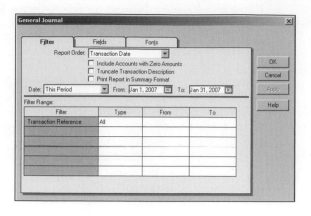

Click <u>OK</u> and view the general journal entries of Jones Consulting for
January. Then click Close.

PRINTING THE GENERAL JOURNAL

To print the general journal, follow the same procedure as you did to view
the journal entries, but in step 3, click the <u>P</u>rint button on the toolbar.
This will result in a printed copy. However, also take the following
additional steps.

Make sure that the printer is on. Then click <u>OK</u>.

Compare your printout with the one shown in figure 3–38. If you find
any errors, correct them by using the edit function as described in
Objective 3.

FIGURE 3-38
Printout of General Journal Entries

Page: 1

Jones Consulting
General Journal
For the Period From Jan 1, 2007 to Jan 31, 2007

Filter Criteria includes: Report order is by Date. Report is printed in Detail Format.

Date	Account ID	Reference	Trans Description	Debit Amt	Credit Amt
1/5/07	102		Increased petty cash fund	100.00	
	100		Increased petty cash fund		100.00
	506		Purchased Office Supplies	1,200.00	
	100		Purchased Office Supplies		1,200.00
1/7/07	100		Consulting fees earned	9,200.00	
	400		Consulting fees earned		9,200.00
1/9/07	504		Paid electric bill	675.00	
	100		Paid electric bill		675.00
1/12/07	510		Paid for business trip	450.00	
	100		Paid for business trip		450.00
1/20/07	100		Consulting fees earned	2,200.00	
	400		Consulting fees earned		2,200.00
1/23/07	500		Paid contractor's fee	2,600.00	
	100		Paid contractor's fee		2,600.00
1/24/07	514		Paid for newspaper ads	850.00	
	100		Paid for newspaper ads		850.00
1/31/07	500		Paid contractor fee	250.00	
	100		Paid contractor fee		250.00
1/31/07	502	Compound	Paid monthly rent	1,200.00	
	508		Paid telephone bill	350.00	
	512		Paid yearly dues	230.00	
	100		Paid month-end bills		1,780.00
		Total		**19,305.00**	**19,305.00**

Step 3:

Click Close to exit the General Journal Preview window, and then click Close to exit the Select a Report dialog box.

PRINTING THE FINANCIAL STATEMENTS

After all transactions for the period have been journalized and posted, the next step in the accounting process for a small cash business like Jones Consulting is to produce financial statements. For example, on January 31, 2007, the accountant for Jones used Peachtree to print an income statement, a statement of changes in financial position, and a balance sheet.

An **income statement** reports the results of operations for the period—the revenue, expenses, and net income or net loss. The **net income** or **net loss** is the difference between the revenue and expenses.

income statement A report of a firm's revenue, expenses, and net income or net loss for a period.

net income or net loss The difference between revenue and expenses.

statement of
changes in financial
position A report of a
firm's sources and uses
of working capital for
a period.

working capital The
excess of current
assets over current
liabilities.

balance sheet A
report of a firm's
assets, liabilities, and
owner's equity as of a
specific date.

A **statement of changes in financial position** shows the sources and uses of working capital for the period. **Working capital** is the excess of current assets over current liabilities.

A **balance sheet** reports the financial condition of a business on a specific date. It shows the assets, liabilities, and owner's equity of the business. A cash firm like Jones Consulting has a very simple balance sheet because it has no accounts receivable and accounts payable and no fixed assets (property and equipment).

You can print the financial statements for any given period by using the Report function of Peachtree, as outlined below.

Step 1:
Click Reports.

Step 2:
Click Financial Statements.

Step 3:
Click *<Standard> Income Stmnt* from the Report List section of the Select a Report dialog box as shown in figure 3–39.

FIGURE 3-39

*<Standard> Income Stmnt
Chosen from Select a
Report Dialog Box*

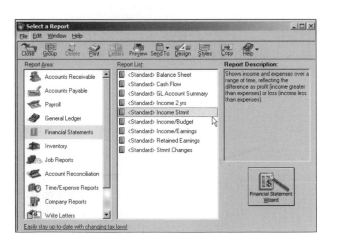

Step 4:
Click the Print button on the Select a Report toolbar.

Step 5:

Select the following in the Options folder tab for the predefined income statement:

- *Range* in the *Time Frame* field.
- *Period 1, (1/1/07)* in the *From* field and *Period 1, (1/31/07)* in the *To* field. (Only one month will be covered.)
- No check mark in the box next to "Show Zero Amounts." (This is a toggle function.)

Compare your screen to the Options dialog box shown in figure 3–40.

FIGURE 3-40

Completed Options Folder Tab for <Standard> Income Statement

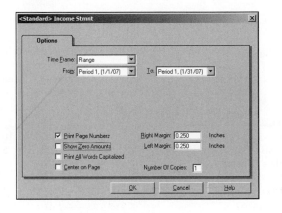

Step 6:

Click OK.

Step 7:

Make sure that the printer is on. Then click OK at the bottom of the Print dialog box.

Step 8:

Compare your income statement with the one shown in figure 3–41.

FIGURE 3-41

Completed Income Statement for Jones Consulting, January 2007

	Jones Consulting Income Statement For the One Month Ending January 31, 2007					
		Current Month			Year to Date	
Revenues						
Consulting Fees	$	11,400.00	100.00	$	11,400.00	100.00
Total Revenues		11,400.00	100.00		11,400.00	100.00
Cost of Sales						
Total Cost of Sales		0.00	0.00		0.00	0.00
Gross Profit		11,400.00	100.00		11,400.00	100.00
Expenses						
Independent Contractor Expense		2,850.00	25.00		2,850.00	25.00
Rent Expense		1,200.00	10.53		1,200.00	10.53
Utilities Expense		675.00	5.92		675.00	5.92
Office Supplies Expense		1,200.00	10.53		1,200.00	10.53
Telephone Expense		350.00	3.07		350.00	3.07
Travel Expense		450.00	3.95		450.00	3.95
Professional Expense		230.00	2.02		230.00	2.02
Advertising Expense		850.00	7.46		850.00	7.46
Total Expenses		7,805.00	68.46		7,805.00	68.46
Net Income	$	3,595.00	31.54	$	3,595.00	31.54

Step 9:

Click *<Standard> Stmnt Changes* from the Report List section of the Select a Report dialog box, as shown in figure 3–42.

FIGURE 3-42

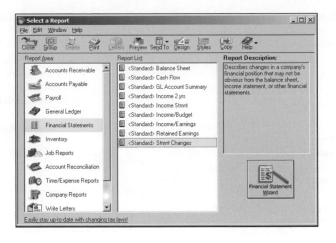

*<Standard> Stmnt
Changes Chosen from the
Select a Report Dialog Box*

Step 10:

Click the Print button, then repeat the procedures from step 5 to complete the Options folder tab for the predefined statement of changes in financial position.

Step 11:

Click OK when the Options folder tab for the predefined statement of changes in financial position is complete.

Step 12:

Click OK at the Print dialog box.

Step 13:

Compare your statement of changes in financial position with the one shown in figure 3–43.

FIGURE 3-43

Completed Statement of Changes in Financial Position for Jones Consulting, January 2007

Jones Consulting
Statement of Changes in Financial Position
For the one month ended January 31, 2007

	Current Month	Year To Date
Sources of Working Capital		
Net Income	$ 3,595.00	$ 3,595.00
Add back items not requiring working capital		
Working capital from operations	3,595.00	3,595.00
Other sources		
Total sources	3,595.00	3,595.00
Uses of working capital		
Total uses	0.00	0.00
Net change	$ 3,595.00	$ 3,595.00
Analysis of componants of changes		
Increase <Decrease> in Current Assets		
Cash	$ 3,495.00	$ 3,495.00
Petty Cash	100.00	100.00
<Increase> Decrease in Current Liabilities		
Net change	$ 3,595.00	$ 3,595.00

Step 14:
Click <*Standard*> *Balance Sheet* from the Report List section of the Select a Report dialog box.

Step 15:
Click the Print button, and then repeat the procedures from step 5 to complete the Options folder tab for the predefined balance sheet.

Step 16:
Click OK when the Options folder tab for the predefined balance sheet is complete.

Step 17:
Click OK at the Print dialog box.

Compare your balance sheet with the one shown in figure 3–44.

FIGURE 3-44

Completed Balance Sheet for Jones Consulting, January 2007

Jones Consulting
Balance Sheet
January 31, 2007

ASSETS

Current Assets		
Cash	$ 102,260.00	
Petty Cash	200.00	
Total Current Assets		102,460.00
Property and Equipment		
Total Property and Equipment		0.00
Other Assets		
Total Other Assets		0.00
Total Assets		$ 102,460.00

LIABILITIES AND CAPITAL

Current Liabilities		
Total Current Liabilities		0.00
Long-Term Liabilities		
Total Long-Term Liabilities		0.00
Total Liabilities		0.00
Capital		
P. Jones, Capital	$ 98,865.00	
Net Income	3,595.00	
Total Capital		102,460.00
Total Liabilities & Capital		$ 102,460.00

Step 19:
Click the Close button on the Select a Report toolbar.

P O I N T

1. What are the two methods used to access General Ledger report from the Report menu?
2. What three financial statements were prepared for Jones Consulting?

Answers
1. *The first method is to click Reports and then General Ledger from the Menu bar. The second method is to select General Ledger from both the Category and Report drop-down lists from the Business Status Find a Report section.*
2. *The financial statements prepared were the income statement, the statement of changes in financial position, and the balance sheet.*

PRACTICE *objective*

Print the general journal and the financial statements for Bell Accounting Service.

Step 1:

Open Bell Accounting Service.

Step 2:

Print the general journal entries for January 1–31, 2007. Compare your printout to figure 3–45.

FIGURE 3-45
Completed General Journal for Bell Accounting Service

Page: 1

Bell Accounting Service
General Journal
For the Period From Jan 1, 2007 to Jan 31, 2007
Filter Criteria includes: Report order is by Date. Report is printed in Detail Format.

Date	Account ID	Reference	Trans Description	Debit Amt	Credit Amt
1/1/07	10100	BEGBAL		250.00	
	10200			15,000.00	
	39004				15,250.00
1/2/07	76000		Purchased office supplies	2,400.00	
	10200		Purchased office supplies		2,400.00
1/5/07	10200		Provided accounting services	5,200.00	
	40000		Provided accounting services		5,200.00
1/12/07	69500		Paid for maintenance services	1,235.00	
	10200		Paid for maintenance services		1,235.00
1/20/07	65000		Paid for employee's continuing education	450.00	
	10200		Paid for employee's continuing education		450.00
1/24/07	89000		Paid advertising costs	750.00	
	10200		Paid advertising costs		750.00
1/31/07	75000		Paid monthly rent	900.00	
	10200		Paid monthly rent		900.00
1/31/07	78500	Compound	Paid utilities expense	300.00	
	79000		Paid telephone bill	245.00	
	10200		Paid month-end bills		545.00
		Total		26,730.00	26,730.00

Print the income statement for the month of January 2007. Compare your printout to figure 3–46.

FIGURE 3-46

Completed Income Statement for Bell Accounting Service

Bell Accounting Service
Income Statement
For the One Month Ending January 31, 2007

		Current Month			Year to Date	
Revenues						
Accounting Fees	$	5,200.00	100.00	$	5,200.00	100.00
Total Revenues		5,200.00	100.00		5,200.00	100.00
Cost of Sales						
Total Cost of Sales		0.00	0.00		0.00	0.00
Gross Profit		5,200.00	100.00		5,200.00	100.00
Expenses						
Employee Benefit Programs Exp		450.00	8.65		450.00	8.65
Maintenance Expense		1,235.00	23.75		1,235.00	23.75
Rent or Lease Expense		900.00	17.31		900.00	17.31
Supplies Expense		2,400.00	46.15		2,400.00	46.15
Utilities Expense		300.00	5.77		300.00	5.77
Telephone Expense		245.00	4.71		245.00	4.71
Other Expense		750.00	14.42		750.00	14.42
Total Expenses		6,280.00	120.77		6,280.00	120.77
Net Income	$	(1,080.00)	(20.77)	$	(1,080.00)	(20.77)

Print the statement of changes in financial position for the month of January 2007. Compare your printout to figure 3–47.

FIGURE 3-47

Statement of Changes in Financial Position, Bell Accounting Service

Bell Accounting Service
Statement of Changes in Financial Position
For the one month ended January 31, 2007

	Current Month	Year To Date
Sources of Working Capital		
Net Income	$ (1,080.00)	$ (1,080.00)
Add back items not requiring working capital		
Working capital from operations	(1,080.00)	(1,080.00)
Other sources		
James, Capital	15,250.00	15,250.00
Total sources	14,170.00	14,170.00
Uses of working capital		
Total uses	0.00	0.00
Net change	$ 14,170.00	$ 14,170.00
Analysis of componants of changes		
Increase <Decrease> in Current Assets		
Cash on Hand	$ 250.00	$ 250.00
Regular Checking Account	13,920.00	13,920.00
<Increase> Decrease in Current Liabilities		
Net change	$ 14,170.00	$ 14,170.00

Print the balance sheet for January 31, 2007. Compare your printout to figure 3–48.

FIGURE 3-48

Balance Sheet, Bell Accounting Service

Bell Accounting Service
Balance Sheet
January 31, 2007

ASSETS

Current Assets			
Cash on Hand	$	250.00	
Regular Checking Account		13,920.00	
Total Current Assets			14,170.00
Property and Equipment			
Total Property and Equipment			0.00
Other Assets			
Total Other Assets			0.00
Total Assets	$		14,170.00

LIABILITIES AND CAPITAL

Current Liabilities			
Total Current Liabilities			0.00
Long-Term Liabilities			
Total Long-Term Liabilities			0.00
Total Liabilities			0.00
Capital			
James, Capital	$	15,250.00	
Net Income		(1,080.00)	
Total Capital			14,170.00
Total Liabilities & Capital	$		14,170.00

Unaudited - For Management Purposes Only

Step 6:

Review the general journal and financial statements for accuracy.

Step 7:

Close the Select a Report dialog box.

..

Students and potential business owners can benefit from the information available on the Small Business Administration's Web site. For example, visitors to the site can obtain loan and statistical information for certain industries by simply completing a questionnaire on the site. The Web address for the SBA site is www.sba.gov. The home page is reproduced in figure 3–49.

FIGURE 3-49

SBA Web Site

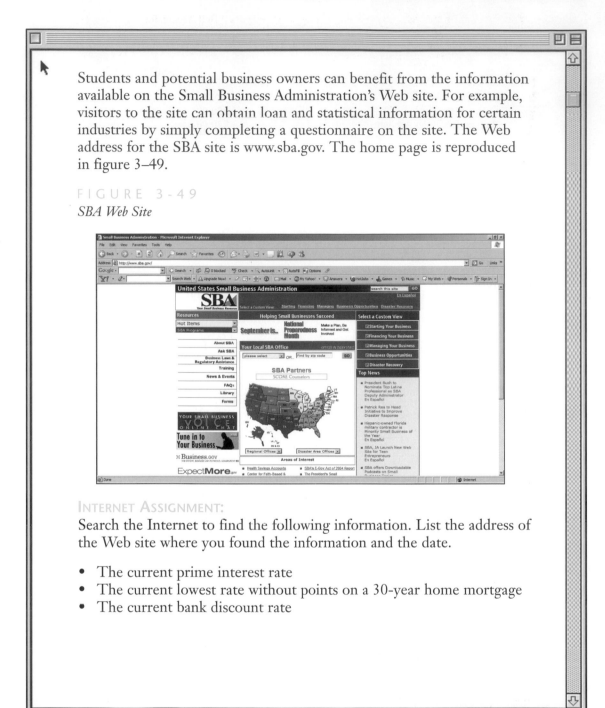

INTERNET ASSIGNMENT:

Search the Internet to find the following information. List the address of the Web site where you found the information and the date.

- The current prime interest rate
- The current lowest rate without points on a 30-year home mortgage
- The current bank discount rate

SOFTWARE
Command Summary

Create New Accounts	<u>M</u>aintain, Chart of <u>A</u>ccounts, Account I<u>D</u>, Des<u>c</u>ription, Account <u>T</u>ype
Enter Beginning Balances	<u>M</u>aintain, Chart of <u>A</u>ccounts, Beginning Balances, Select Period, Enter Balances
Journalize General Journal Transactions	Tas<u>k</u>s, <u>G</u>eneral Journal Entry, <u>S</u>ave
Edit a Selected Transaction	Tas<u>k</u>s, <u>G</u>eneral Journal Entry, L<u>i</u>st, Select Desired Transaction, <u>O</u>pen, Make Necessary Changes, <u>S</u>ave
Delete a Selected Transaction	Tas<u>k</u>s, <u>G</u>eneral Journal Entry, L<u>i</u>st, Select Desired Transaction, <u>O</u>pen, Delete
Printing or Previewing Reports	Reports, Select Category of Reports, Highlight Specific Report, <u>P</u>rint or Pre<u>v</u>iew Button, Options Screen

PROJECTS
and Problems

CONTENT CHECK

Multiple Choice: Choose only one response for each question.

1. A record in which transactions are listed in order by date is a
   A. chart of accounts.
   B. journal.
   C. ledger.
   D. trial balance.
   E. None of the above.

2. The financial statement that reports assets, liabilities, and owner's equity as of a specific date is the
   A. statement of changes in financial position.
   B. chart of accounts.
   C. balance sheet.
   D. income statement.
   E. None of the above.

3. The financial statement that shows the revenues, expenses, and net income or net loss for a period of time is known as the
   A. balance sheet.

    B. general journal.
    C. general ledger.
    D. income statement.
    E. None of the above.

4. Suppose that an accountant has recorded the wrong date in a journal entry. In Peachtree, the best way to correct the error is to
    A. use the delete function and then record the entire entry again.
    B. use the list and then open function.
    C. use the memorized transaction function.
    D. use the recurring transaction function.
    E. None of the above.

5. Which of the following functions is used to set up a journal entry that will automatically repeat in future accounting periods?
    A. add a row function
    B. open function
    C. memorized transaction function
    D. recurring transaction function
    E. None of the above.

Short Essay Response: Provide a detailed answer for each question.

1. What is the purpose of the general journal?
2. What are the steps necessary to add a new account to the chart of accounts?
3. What steps are necessary to ensure accurate posting of journal entries?
4. Under what circumstances can a business use the cash basis of accounting?
5. What is the purpose of the general ledger?
6. What information must be recorded in the general journal entry window before a transaction can be posted?

CASE PROBLEMS

PROBLEM 1A

Open GJ Professional Accounting, which was created in Problem 1A of Chapter 2.

The following transactions occurred during the month of January 2007.

Date	Transaction
Jan. 4	Paid rent of $1,500 for January. Because this payment must be made each month, set it up as a recurring transaction. Use 12 as the number of times the transaction will recur.
4	Purchased computer equipment for $2,500 in cash. (Because this business is using the accrual basis of accounting, it records purchases of equipment in an Asset account.)
4	Purchased office supplies for $375 on account. (Because this business is on the accrual basis, it records purchases of supplies in an Asset account.)

5	Paid a $340 insurance premium for the month. This is also a recurring monthly transaction. Use 12 as the number of times that it will recur. (Because this insurance covers just one month, treat it as an expense.)
6	Purchased furniture and fixtures for $2,100 on account. (Use *Account 20000, Accounts Payable.*)
10	Paid $800 for a newspaper ad that will run during the month of January. The business may run more ads in the future. Thus, create this transaction using the memorization feature. You will need to create a new account for this transaction: *60500, Advertising Expense, Expenses.*
12	Performed accounting services for Monroe Construction and received $1,800 in cash.
14	Performed accounting services for Ramirez Consultants and received $1,250 in cash.
18	The owner withdrew $500 for his personal use. (Use *Account 39007, Garrett Johnson, Drawing.*)
24	Performed accounting services for Steve's Landscaping and received $1,475 in cash.
28	Paid automobile expenses of $225 in cash.
29	Paid utilities of $325.
29	Paid the telephone bill of $135.
30	Performed accounting services for Mary's Daycare for $250 in cash.

1. Enter each of the transactions for January in the general journal. Create new accounts as needed. For all cash transactions, use *Account 10200, Regular Checking Account.*
2. Print the following reports for the month of January: *General Journal, Income Statement*, and *Balance Sheet.*

PROBLEM 2A

1. Set up a new company for Steve's Auto Detailing. Use the information given below:

Company Name:	**Steve's Auto Detailing**
Address Line 1:	**32 Sycamore Avenue**
Address Line 2:	
City, State, Zip:	**Stockton, CA 95207**
Country:	**USA**
Telephone:	**209-555-3223**
Fax:	**209-555-2332**
Business Type:	**Sole Proprietorship**
Federal Employer ID:	**09-6776754**
State Employer ID:	**098-8743-09**
St. Unemployment ID:	**00441-98**
Chart of Accounts:	**Build your own chart of accounts**
Accounting Method:	**Cash**
Posting Method:	**Real Time**

Accounting Periods: **12 monthly accounting periods**
Fiscal Year to Start: **January 2007**

2. Enter the following in the chart of accounts:

Account ID	Description	Account Type
10200	Regular Checking Account	Cash
39004	Steve Johnson, Capital	Equity-doesn't close
39005	Steve Johnson, Equity	Equity-Retained Earnings
39006	Steve Johnson, Drawing	Equity-gets closed
40000	Detailing Fees	Income
60000	Advertising Expense	Expenses
60010	Laundry Expense	Expenses
60020	Telephone Expense	Expenses
60030	Utilities Expense	Expenses
60040	Rent Expense	Expenses
60050	Detailing Supplies Expense	Expenses

3. The following transactions occurred during the month of January 2007. Enter each of the transactions in the general journal. Create new accounts as needed.

Date	Transaction
Jan. 3	The owner invested $1,500 of his personal funds in the business. (*Steve Johnson, Capital*)
3	Paid rent of $550 for January. Because this payment must be made each month, set it up as a recurring transaction. Use 12 as the number of times the transaction will recur.
3	Purchased detailing supplies for $550 in cash.
5	Set up a petty cash fund of $100. You will need to create a new account for this transaction: *10100, Petty Cash, Cash*.
5	Detailed a fleet of cars for Mavis Car Rentals and received $725 in cash. This is a recurring biweekly transaction. The number of times it will recur is 26.
11	Paid $125 for advertising flyers. Create this transaction using the memorization feature.
15	Detailing fees for the week amounted to $820 in cash.
19	The owner withdrew $425 for his personal use. (Use *Steve Johnson, Drawing*.)
19	Detailed a fleet of trucks for Baxter Trucking and received $300 in cash. This is a recurring monthly transaction. The number of times it will recur is 12.
20	Paid a telephone bill of $110.
23	Detailing fees for the week amounted to $760 in cash.
25	Paid automobile expenses of $275 in cash. You will need to create a new account for this transaction: *60060, Automobile Expense, Expenses*.
25	Paid utilities bill of $420.
31	Detailing fees for the week amounted to $960 in cash.

4. Print the following reports for the month of January: *General Ledger Trial Balance*, *General Journal*, *Income Statement*, and *Balance Sheet*.

PROBLEM 1B

Open Infinite Graphics, which was created in Chapter 2. The following transactions occurred during the month of January 2007.

Date	Transaction
Jan. 3	Paid office rent of $750 for January. Because this payment must be made each month, set it up as a recurring transaction. Use 12 as the number of times the transaction will recur.
4	Purchased graphing equipment for $3,750 on account. (Because this business is using the accrual basis of accounting, it records purchases of equipment in an Asset account. Use *Account 20000, Accounts Payable*.)
4	Purchased graphing supplies for $235 in cash. (Because this business is using the accrual basis of accounting, it records purchases of supplies in an Asset account.)
5	Paid a $120 insurance premium for the month. This is also a recurring monthly transaction. Use 12 as the number of times that it will recur. (Because this insurance covers just one month, treat it as an expense.)
6	Purchased furniture and fixtures for $2,400 on account.
11	Paid $220 for a newspaper ad that will run during the month of January. The business may run more ads in the future. Thus, create this transaction using the memorization feature.
12	Created a business logo (*Graphic Design Income*) for the ABC Nursery School and received $420 in cash.
13	Performed printing services for Gomez Consultants and received $2,400 in cash.
15	The owner withdrew $300 for her personal use. (*Anna Reyes, Drawing*)
18	Retouched photos for an advertising campaign and received $3,600 in cash.
26	Performed photo services for the *Daily News* and received $980 in cash.
28	Paid automobile expenses of $175 in cash.
28	Paid utilities bill of $260.
29	Paid a telephone bill of $178.
30	Performed illustration services for J and K Architects and received $1,425 in cash.

1. Enter each of the transactions for January in the general journal. Create new accounts as needed. For all cash transactions, use *Account 10200, Regular Checking Account*.
2. Print the following reports for the month of January: *General Ledger Trial Balance*, *General Journal*, *Income Statement*, and *Balance Sheet*.

PROBLEM 2B

1. Set up a new company for Dee's Office Cleaning. Use the information given below:

Company Name:	**Dee's Office Cleaning**
Address Line 1:	**64 West Bessie Avenue**
Address Line 2:	
City, State, Zip:	**Stockton, CA 95207**
Country:	**USA**
Telephone:	**209-555-3311**
Fax:	**209-555-1133**
Business Type:	**Sole Proprietorship**
Federal Employer ID:	**09-6776457**
State Employer ID:	**098-8734-08**
St. Unemployment ID:	**00221-87**
Chart of Accounts:	**Build your own chart of accounts**
Accounting Method:	**Cash**
Posting Method:	**Real Time**
Accounting Periods:	**12 monthly accounting periods**
Fiscal Year to Start:	**January 2007**

2. Enter the following in the chart of accounts:

Account ID	Description	Account Type
10200	Regular Checking Account	Cash
39004	Danielle Foster, Capital	Equity-doesn't close
39005	Danielle Foster, Equity	Equity-Retained Earnings
39006	Danielle Foster, Drawing	Equity-gets closed
40000	Cleaning Fees	Income
60000	Advertising Expense	Expenses
60010	Laundry Expense	Expenses
60020	Telephone Expense	Expenses
60030	Utilities Expense	Expenses
60040	Rent Expense	Expenses
60050	Cleaning Supplies Expense	Expenses

3. The following transactions occurred during the month of January 2007. Enter each of the transactions in the general journal. Create new accounts as needed.

Date	Transaction
Jan. 3	The owner invested $1,275 of her personal funds in the business. (*Danielle Foster, Capital*)
3	Paid $300 in cash for a bonding fee. You will need to create a new account for this transaction: *60060, Bond Fee Expense, Expenses.*

3	Purchased cleaning supplies for $475 in cash.
4	Established a petty cash fund of $125. You will need to create a new account for this transaction: *10100, Petty Cash, Cash*.
4	Cleaned the offices of O'Brien Car Rentals and received $220 in cash. Set this up as a recurring biweekly transaction. The number of times it will recur is 26.
5	Purchased an ad in the local newspaper for $65.
7	Performed cleaning services for the Delta Insurance Agency and received $175 in cash. Set this up as a recurring weekly transaction. The number of times it will recur is 52.
15	Cleaning fees for the week amounted to $820 in cash.
19	The owner withdrew $550 for her personal use.
21	Cleaned the offices of Baxter Trucking and received $225 in cash. Set this up as a recurring monthly transaction. The number of times it will recur is 12.
24	Paid utilities bill of $265.
27	Paid automobile expenses of $650 in cash. You will need to create a new account for this transaction: *60070, Auto Expense, Expenses*.
28	Paid a telephone bill of $130.
30	Cleaning fees for the week amounted to $460 in cash.

4. Print the following reports for the month of January: *General Journal, Income Statement*, and *Balance Sheet*.

COOPERATIVE LEARNING

1. Form groups of three or four students and create your own retail business. Decide on the business setup criteria.
2. Create 10 transactions for the newly formed business from Cooperative Learning Exercise 1. Use Peachtree to enter the transactions in the general journal. Create any new accounts as needed. Print the general ledger, general journal, chart of accounts, and balance sheet.

WRITING AND DECISION MAKING

The company for which you work, MH Design Consulting, is converting from a manual accounting system to a computerized system. You are responsible for the conversion. The owner of the company, Maria Holtzman, wants to know how you plan to use Peachtree to ensure that an accurate conversion to a computerized accounting system occurs. Therefore, in memo format, list in detail what information is needed and what decisions must be made for each screen of the New Company Setup procedure.

CHAPTER

ACCOUNTS
RECEIVABLE and SALES
FOR A SERVICE BUSINESS

1. Create subsidiary ledger accounts for customers and enter the beginning balances

2. Process accounts receivable and sales transactions

3. Create action items and event logs

4. Adjust the accounts receivable for uncollectible accounts and print reports

SOFTWARE FEATURES

- Maintain Customer Prospects toolbar buttons

- Customer defaults

- Sales and Invoicing toolbar

- Action items

- Alerts

- Accounting Behind the Screens function

Many firms sell goods and services on credit. In fact, it is often said that credit is the lifeblood of American business. Credit makes it possible for customers to obtain goods and services immediately and pay for them in the future. This arrangement is convenient for customers and usually produces higher sales for the firms that offer credit.

RECORDING ACCOUNTS RECEIVABLE

The amounts owed by customers to a business for goods or services sold to them on credit are called **accounts receivable**. Firms that sell on credit set up an asset account called Accounts Receivable in their general ledger.

When these firms make a sale on credit, they debit the amount to Accounts Receivable and credit the appropriate revenue account. Later, when they collect the amount owed by the customer, they debit (increase) Cash and credit (decrease) Accounts Receivable.

THE ACCOUNTS RECEIVABLE SUBSIDIARY LEDGER

In addition to the Accounts Receivable account in the general ledger, most businesses that sell on credit maintain a subsidiary ledger with individual accounts for their customers. This subsidiary ledger is known as the **accounts receivable ledger** or customers ledger.

A **subsidiary ledger** contains detailed information for a single general ledger account. Remember that the general ledger is a firm's main ledger. It includes the accounts that are used to prepare the financial statements. Subsidiary ledgers supplement the information in the general ledger.

The advantage of having an accounts receivable subsidiary ledger is that it provides detailed information about the transactions with credit customers and shows the balances they owe. Peachtree updates these accounts automatically when transactions are recorded and posted. As a result, management can closely monitor the status of the firm's accounts receivable.

Being able to collect its accounts receivable on time is critical to the success of a business that sells on credit. The cash from accounts receivable is needed to pay debts and operating expenses such as rent and salaries. A business may have rising sales but experience cash flow problems if it does not manage its accounts receivable properly.

Peachtree improves the efficiency of accounts receivable procedures because it allows for—
- Quick preparation of invoices (bills)
- Automatic posting of accounts receivable transactions, which eliminates the time and effort required by manual posting
- Quick preparation of a wide variety of reports, which show management the current status of the accounts receivable
- An action item feature that can be programmed to alert users to high balances, past-due amounts, and other problems with a specific customer account
- Quick preparation of contact letters and past-due notices

THE CONTROLLING ACCOUNT IN THE GENERAL LEDGER

When there is an accounts receivable subsidiary ledger, the Accounts

accounts receivable The amounts owed to a business by its customers for goods or services sold on credit.

accounts receivable ledger A subsidiary ledger that contains accounts for credit customers.

subsidiary ledger A ledger that contains detailed information for a single general ledger account.

controlling account
A general ledger account that summarizes the balances of all the accounts in a subsidiary ledger.

Receivable account in the general ledger becomes a **controlling account**. It provides a link between the general ledger and the accounts receivable subsidiary ledger because its balance is equal to the total of all the balances of the individual accounts in the subsidiary ledger.

Every subsidiary ledger must have a controlling account in the general ledger.

HANDLING UNCOLLECTIBLE ACCOUNTS

No matter how careful management is in granting credit to customers, monitoring the status of the accounts receivable, and making efforts to collect overdue balances, some accounts will become uncollectible. Events occur that are beyond the control of the seller. For example, companies may go bankrupt or have disasters occur that prevent them from paying their accounts. In those cases, the accounts must be written off or discharged. When accounts are written off, it is considered an expense of doing business.

Two methods are used to account for uncollectible accounts: the allowance method and the direct write-off method. Both will be discussed later in this chapter.

OBJECTIVE 1 — CREATE SUBSIDIARY LEDGER ACCOUNTS FOR CUSTOMERS AND ENTER THE BEGINNING BALANCES

In chapters 2 and 3, you learned how to set up general ledger accounts and enter the beginning balances. The procedure for establishing customer accounts in the accounts receivable ledger is very similar. In this chapter, you will use Peachtree to handle the accounts receivable of Woodward Construction Company.

THE MAINTAIN CUSTOMERS/PROSPECTS WINDOW

In Peachtree, certain information is needed to create an account for each customer in the accounts receivable subsidiary ledger. This information is entered into the following fields of the Maintain Customers/Prospects window. To view this window, open Woodward Construction Company, click Maintain and then Customers/Prospects. Review the following fields:

- **Customer ID**
  Peachtree requires an alphanumeric identifier for each customer's account. For example, Woodward Construction Company uses Smith-01 as the identifier for the first account in its accounts receivable subsidiary ledger. This account is for Smith's Monuments.
- **Name**
  The name given to a customer's account may be the name of the business, such as Smith's Monuments, or the name of an individual.
- **Prospect**
  Peachtree allows a firm to open accounts for potential customers as well as current customers. This feature helps salespeople keep track of potential customers. When an order is placed, Peachtree automatically activates the account of the potential customer and changes it to a current customer. A check mark is entered in the Prospect box to indicate a potential customer.

- **Inactive**

  Sometimes customers stop doing business with a company. A check mark is entered in the Inactive box to indicate this type of customer. Peachtree automatically removes the accounts of inactive customers when the fiscal year closes.

General Tab

- **Contact**

  The contact is the person whom the business calls or writes in connection with questions about orders.
- **Billing and Shipping Addresses**

  Peachtree permits the entry of separate billing and shipping addresses for a customer. In fact, Peachtree allows for several shipping addresses. If a customer has a single address for both billing and shipping, you need only enter the billing address.
- **Sales Tax**

  Retail businesses in most states and some cities and counties must charge their customers a sales tax on goods. In some areas, this tax is also levied on services. Wholesale businesses that sell to retailers do not charge sales tax because the retailers have resale certificates that exempt them from paying sales tax. If sales tax does apply, you enter the type when creating each customer's account.
- **Customer Type**

  Peachtree allows you to classify customers by type. For example, some companies have both retail and wholesale customers.
- **Telephone/Fax Numbers and E-Mail Addresses**

  Peachtree provides space for recording two telephone numbers, a fax number, and an E-mail address in each customer's account. You can e-mail a customer directly by clicking on the E-mail button to the right of the E-mail address field.
- **Web Address**

  Enter the customer's Web site address. The customer's Web site can be displayed by clicking the Internet button to the right of the Web Address field.
- **Account #**

  Enter the customer's account number.
- **Beginning Balances**

  When a business creates accounts for its customers, there may be some outstanding (unpaid) invoices. Information about these invoices is needed in order to enter the beginning balances in the accounts.

Sales Defaults Tab

- **Sales Rep**

  Some businesses assign a sales representative to each customer. The name of the sales representative is entered in the customer's account. (Peachtree's accounts receivable procedures allow a business to organize information about its sales staff and to maintain an up-to-date list of sales representatives.)
- **GL Sales Acct**

  GL Sales Acct refers to the revenue account in the general ledger that is credited when a sale is made to the customer. The number of the appropriate general ledger account is entered in the customer's account.

- **Open P.O. #**
  When a customer's account is created, it may have an open purchase order. The number of this purchase order is entered in the account.
- **Ship Via**
  Some businesses allow their customers to select a shipping method. The method chosen is entered in the customer's account.
- **Resale #**
  Sales tax authorities issue certificates to retailers that exempt them from paying sales tax on goods they buy for resale. If a customer is a retailer, the resale certificate number must be entered here.
- **Pricing Level**
  Some businesses have several different pricing levels for merchandise. For example, if a firm sells to both retailers and wholesalers, it will charge them different prices. The pricing level is entered in the customer's account.
- **Form Delivery Options**
  Businesses today use differing methods for delivering invoices. This option allows the user to check for delivery via Paper Form or E-mail, including a choice to CC Sales Reps when sending customers e-mail.

Terms and Credit Tab
- Many companies use Standard credit terms and this is an option that can be selected.
- Other terms as well as specifying discount periods, credit periods, discounts, discount percents, credit limits, and credit status can be selected.

Payment Defaults Tab
- **Cardholder's Name and Address**
  A business may want to create account information for credit card users. The cardholder's information is entered in this section.
- **City, State, Zip and Country**
  The customer's/prospect's city, state, zip, and country information are entered here.
- **Credit Card Number and Expiration Date**
  The credit card information is entered and stored here.
- **Receipt Settings**
  The payment method and the account to be debited are selected in this section. All major credit cards, as well as cash, are supported. The window's default settings are used by Peachtree if *Use receipt window settings* is checked.

Custom Fields Tab
- **Second Contact**
  In some cases, a business will want to enter the name of a second contact in a customer's account.
- **Reference**
  A business may want to enter the name of the firm or individual who referred the customer.
- **Mailing List**
  A business may want to enter information for future mailing lists.
- **Multiple Sites**
  Some customers have branch locations that should be listed in their accounts. All of the field labels in the Custom Fields tab can be changed to reflect the specific needs of the business through the customer default window.

History
- **Customer Since**
  Some businesses enter the date of the customer's first order in the customer's account.
- **Last Invoice Date**
  Some businesses enter the date of the last invoice sent to the customer.
- **Last Invoice Amt**
  Some businesses enter the amount of the last invoice sent to the customer.
- **Last Payment Date**
  Some businesses enter the date of the last payment the customer made.
- **Last Payment Amt**
  Some businesses enter the amount of the last payment the customer made.
- **Last Statement Date**
  Some businesses enter the date of the last statement sent to the customer.

Click the Close button when you have finished reviewing the fields of the Maintain Customers/Prospects window.

CREATING SUBSIDIARY LEDGER ACCOUNTS FOR THE CUSTOMERS OF A SAMPLE BUSINESS

In this section, you will create subsidiary ledger accounts for four customers of Woodward Construction Company.

List of Customers for Woodward Construction Company

Follow the steps outlined below to create subsidiary ledger accounts for the customers of Woodward Construction Company.

Name Page and General Tab

Step 1

Open Woodward Constuction Company and close Peachtree Setup Guide, if still open.

Step 2:

Click Maintain, and then click Customers/Prospects.

Step 3:

Click the General folder tab. (See figure 4–1.)

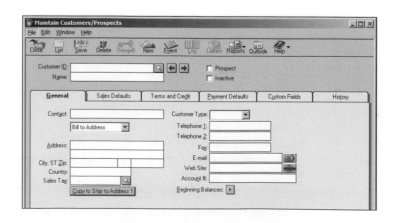

Set up the account information listed below for Smith's Monuments, the first customer of Woodward Construction Company.

Step 4:

Key **Smith-01** in the *Customer ID* field. Click the OK button at the bottom of the Customer ID drop-down list, as shown in figure 4–2.

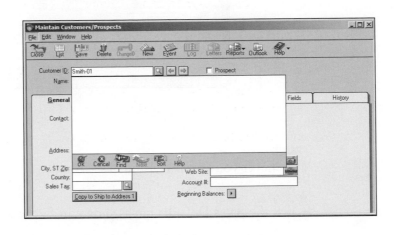

Step 5:

Key **Smith's Monuments** in the *Name* field.

Step 6:

Key **Jerome Smith** in the *Contact* field and accept *Bill to Address* from the drop-down box..

Step 7:

Key **1343 Freedom Blvd.** in the *Address* field.

Step 8:

Key **Watsonville, CA,** and **95760** in the *City, ST Zip* field.

Step 9:

Key **General** in the *Customer Type* field.

Step 10:

Key **408-555-1947** in the *Telephone 1* field.

Step 11:

Key **408-555-2121** in the *Telephone 2* field.

Step 12:

Key **408-555-4653** in the *Fax* field.

Step 13:

Key **xxx@emcp.com** in the *E-mail* field.

Step 14:

Compare your completed window with figure 4–3. Make any necessary corrections by selecting the erroneous items and reentering the information.

FIGURE 4-3

*Completed General Window
for Smith's Monuments*

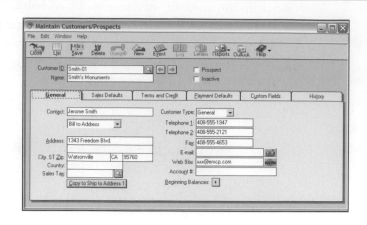

FIGURE 4-4

*Maintain Customers/Prospects
Window with Sales Defaults
Tab Selected*

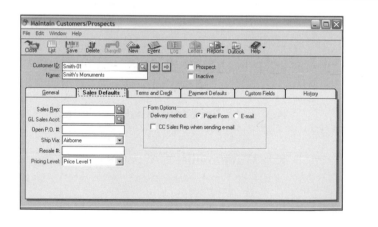

Sales Defaults Tab

Whenever you create a customer's account, you need to establish sales defaults.

Step 1:

Click the Sales Defaults tab as shown in figure 4–4.

Step 2:

Click the *magnifying glass* icon next to the GL Sales Acct drop-down list, and then click *Account 400, Fees Earned* (revenue).

Step 3:

Click *Fed-EX* in the Ship Via drop-down list.

Step 4:

Accept the default (Price Level 1) in the Pricing Level drop-down list.

Step 5:

Accept the default in the Form Delivery Options box. Compare your entries for Smith's Monuments with the entries shown in figure 4–5. Make any necessary changes.

FIGURE 4-5
Completed Sales Defaults Window for Smith's Monuments

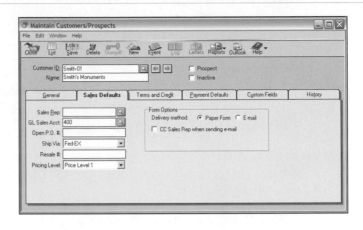

Terms and Credit Tab

Credit and discount information must be included when you create a customer's account.

Step 1:

Click the Terms and Credit tab. The Customer Terms and Credit dialog box will appear as shown in figure 4–6.

FIGURE 4-6
Terms and Credit Dialog Box

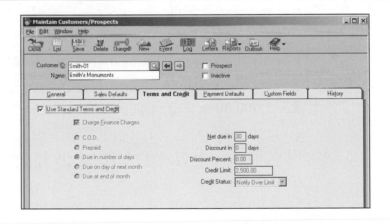

The default for the credit terms was established during the company setup process. It is currently set at Net 30 Days. Woodward offers terms set at 2% 10, net 30 days. These terms mean that the customer can pay in 10 days and receive a 2% discount or pay the net (full) amount in 30 days.

The pricing level and the credit terms relate mostly to merchandising businesses and will be explained in future chapters. The credit terms can be changed by deselecting the check mark next to Use Standard Terms and Credit and then making any necessary changes.

Step 2:

Deselect the Use Standard Terms and Credit checkmark.

Key 30 in the Net due in days box.

Key 10 in the Discount in days box.

Key 2.00 in the Discount Percent box.

There is also a default for a credit limit, which is currently set at $2,500. Whenever the recording of a sale takes a customer's balance over this limit, Peachtree sends a warning message.

Click the Save button at the top of the Maintain Customers/Prospects window.

Beginning Balances

The final phase in creating the customer accounts involves the entry of the beginning balances.

Click the General folder tab in the Maintain Customers/Prospects window.

Click the right arrow key next to *Beginning Balances*.

Key **Beginning Balance** in the *Invoice Number* field.

Key **01/01/07** in the *Date* field. (Peachtree will convert this to *Jan 1, 2007*.)

Key **5,000.00** in the *Amount* field.

Click *Account 104 (Accounts Receivable)* from the A/R Account drop-down list.

Click the Save button and then the Close button.

Create the remaining three customer accounts for Woodward Construction Company by clicking the New button at the top of the Maintain Customers/Prospects window and enter the beginning balances as of 01/01/07 using the information listed below. Use the steps that you followed for the Smith's Monuments account. When you complete your work, close and exit Woodward Construction Company.

Customer ID:	**Jones-02**
Name:	**Jones Sporting Goods**

General Tab

Contact: **Lisa Jones**

Bill to:

      Address: **2356 Main Street**

      City, ST Zip: **Salinas, CA 95660**

      Country: **USA**

Sales Tax:

Customer Type: **General**

Telephone 1:   **408-555-2122**

Telephone 2:   **408-555-2004**

Fax: **408-555-2887**

E-mail: **xxx@emcp.com**

Sales Defaults Tab

GL Sales Acct: **400**

Ship Via: **Fed-EX**

Pricing Level: **Default**

Form Delivery Options: **Default**

Terms and Credit Tab

Terms: **2% 10 Days, Net 30 Days**

Beginning Balances: **4,000.00**

Customer ID: **Barker-03**

Name: **Barker's Music**

General Tab

Contact: **George Barker**

Bill to:

      Address: **2567 McHenry Ave.**

      City, ST Zip: **Modesto, CA 95355**

      Country: **USA**

Sales Tax:

Customer Type: **General**

Telephone 1:   **209-555-9147**

Telephone 2:   **209-555-1121**

Fax: **209-555-5536**

E-mail: **xxx@emcp.com**

Sales Defaults Tab

GL Sales Acct: **400**

Ship Via: **Fed-EX**

Pricing Level: **Default**

Form Delivery Options: **Default**

Terms and Credit Tab

Terms: **2% 10 Days, Net 30 Days**

Beginning Balances: **2,000.00**

Customer ID: **Gadgets-04**

Name: **Running Gadgets**

General Tab

Contact:	Joyce Holman
Bill to:	

	Address:	3234 Airport Road
	City, ST Zip:	Watsonville, CA 95670
	Country:	USA

Sales Tax:	
Customer Type:	General
Telephone 1:	408-555-2556
Telephone 2:	408-555-5226
Fax:	408-555-9998
E-mail:	xxx@emcp.com

Sales Defaults Tab

GL Sales Acct:	400
Ship Via:	Fed-EX
Pricing Level:	Default
Form Delivery Options:	Default

Terms and Credit Tab

Terms:	2% 10 Days, Net 30 Days
Beginning Balances:	2,000.00

Check POINT

1. What is the purpose of the customer accounts in the accounts receivable subsidiary ledger?
2. Why is the Accounts Receivable account in the general ledger known as a controlling account?

Answers

1. *The accounts in the subsidiary ledger provide detailed information about transactions with customers and show the current balances owed by the individual customers.*
2. *The Accounts Receivable controlling account is a link between the general ledger and the subsidiary ledger because its balance is equal to the total of the balances in the subsidiary ledger.*

PRACTICE *objective* 1

Create subsidiary ledger accounts for the customers of the Bullfrog Maintenance Company. You set up the chart of accounts for this business in chapter 2 and recorded transactions for the firm in chapter 3.

Step 1:

Open Bullfrog Maintenance Company.

Step 2:

Create the following customer accounts. There are no beginning balances.

| Customer ID: | Honda-01 |
| Name: | Honda Center |

General Tab

Contact:	Tim Conway
Bill to:	
Address:	2122 Main Street
City, ST Zip:	Salida, CA 95111
Country:	USA
Sales Tax:	
Customer Type:	General
Telephone 1:	209-555-4934
Telephone 2:	209-555-4589
Fax:	209-555-3122
E-mail:	xxx@emcp.com

Sales Defaults Tab

GL Sales Acct:	400
Ship Via:	Fed-EX
Pricing Level:	Default
Form Delivery Options:	Default

Terms and Credit Tab

| Terms: | 2% 10 Days, Net 30 Days |
| Beginning Balances: | 0 |

| Customer ID: | Lexus-02 |
| Name: | Lexus of San Joaquin |

General Tab

Contact:	Jane Campbell
Bill to:	
Address:	2415 10th Street
City, ST Zip:	Salida, CA 95111
Country:	USA
Sales Tax:	
Customer Type:	General
Telephone 1:	209-555-6780
Telephone 2:	209-555-2400
Fax:	209-555-8987
E-mail:	xxx@emcp.com

Sales Defaults Tab

GL Sales Acct:	400
Ship Via:	Fed-EX
Pricing Level:	Default
Form Delivery Options:	Default

Terms and Credit Tab

| Terms: | 2% 10 Days, Net 30 Days |
| Beginning Balances: | 0 |

| Customer ID: | Mazda-03 |
| Name: | Curt Smith Mazda |

General Tab

Contact:		Kim Smith
Bill to:		
	Address:	2516 Main Street
	City, ST Zip:	Salida, CA 95111
	Country:	USA
Sales Tax:		
Customer Type:		General
Telephone 1:		209-555-4719
Telephone 2:		209-555-0908
Fax:		209-555-2166
E-mail:		xxx@emcp.com

Sales Defaults Tab

GL Sales Acct:	400
Ship Via:	Fed-EX
Pricing Level:	Default
Form Delivery Options:	Default

Terms and Credit Tab

Terms:	2% 10 Days, Net 30 Days
Beginning Balances:	0

Customer ID:	Mercedes-04
Name:	Valley Mercedes

General Tab

Contact:		Robert Romero
Bill to:		
	Address:	3211 Main Street
	City, ST Zip:	Salida, CA 95111
	Country:	USA
Sales Tax:		
Customer Type:		General
Telephone 1:		209-555-5678
Telephone 2:		209-555-5323
Fax:		209-555-7812
E-mail:		xxx@emcp.com

Sales Defaults Tab

GL Sales Acct:	400
Ship Via:	Fed-EX
Pricing Level:	Default
Form Delivery Options:	Default

Terms and Credit Tab

Terms:	2% 10 Days, Net 30 Days
Beginning Balances:	0

Step 3:

Close the Maintain Customers/Prospects window.

Once the customer accounts have been established, you can use Peachtree to record transactions with credit customers and post them automatically to the accounts receivable subsidiary ledger. Remember that you record a sale on credit by debiting Accounts Receivable and crediting the appropriate revenue account. You record cash collected from a credit customer by debiting Cash and crediting Accounts Receivable.

When there is an accounts receivable ledger, each sale on credit requires a debit to both the Accounts Receivable controlling account in the general ledger and the customer's account in the subsidiary ledger. Similarly, each collection of cash from a credit customer requires a credit to both the Accounts Receivable controlling account in the general ledger and the customer's account in the subsidiary ledger.

In Chapter 3, you recorded all transactions in the general journal. However, the general journal function of Peachtree does not permit the automatic posting of entries to the customer accounts. Therefore, in this chapter, you will use the sales and invoicing function of Peachtree to record credit sales and cash received on account. The sales and invoicing function, which is part of the accounts receivable module of Peachtree, permits automatic posting to both the general ledger and the accounts receivable subsidiary ledger.

RECORDING SALES ON CREDIT

A sale on credit may involve goods or services. The Woodward Construction Company is a small firm that provides construction services to local businesses and individuals. Almost all of its sales to businesses are made on credit.

On January 4, 2007, Woodward Construction Company did a small job for Smith's Monuments. The job involved 10 hours of construction work at $125 per hour. Smith issued a purchase order (PO 4567) before the job began. After it was completed, Woodward issued Invoice 1001 to bill Smith's Monuments for $1,250. Woodward's invoice has default terms of 2% 10 days, net 30 Days.

An analysis of this transaction reveals that an asset (Accounts Receivable) has increased by $1,250 and revenue has increased by $1,250. The account for Smith's Monuments has also increased by $1,250. The accountant records this transaction by debiting Accounts Receivable for $1,250 and crediting Revenue for $1,250.

When this transaction is posted, the debit part of the entry must be posted to both the Accounts Receivable controlling account in the general ledger and the Smith's Monuments account in the accounts receivable subsidiary ledger.

Use the steps outlined below to record the sale on credit that Woodward Construction Company made to Smith's Monuments.

Step 1:
Open Woodward Construction Company.

Step 2:
Click Tasks, and then click Sales/Invoicing.

Step 3:

The Sales/Invoicing window will appear, as shown in figure 4–7. Enter the information for the sale on credit that occurred on January 4, 2007.

FIGURE 4-7

Sales/Invoicing Window

HINT

If the *GL Account* field does not display as shown in figure 4-7, click Options, and then click Global. The Maintain Global Options dialog box will appear. Deselect the box that is checked next to Accounts Receivable (Quotes, Sales Orders, Invoicing, Credit Memos, Receipts). Click OK. Then close and reopen the Sales/Invoicing window.

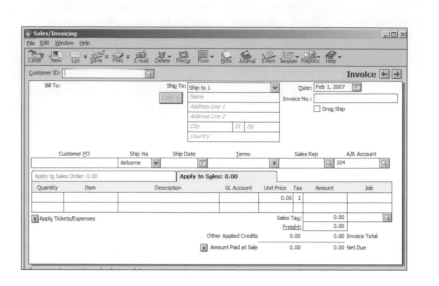

Step 4:

Click the *magnifying glass* icon next to the Customer ID drop-down list.

Step 5:

Highlight *Smith-01* from the drop-down list of customers, as shown in figure 4–8.

FIGURE 4-8

Customer ID Drop-Down List with Smith-01 Selected

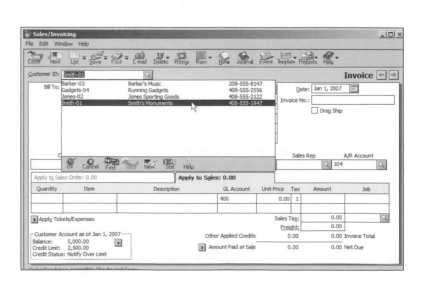

Step 6:

Click OK at the bottom of the drop-down list of customers to accept Smith-01. Peachtree automatically enters the address and billing information. (Alternatively, you could have double-clicked Smith-01.)

Step 7:

Click the *calendar* icon to the right of the *Date* field and choose *Jan 4, 2007*.

Step 8:

Key **1001** in the *Invoice No.* field.

Step 9:

Key **4567** in the *Customer PO* field.

Step 10:

Click *Hand Deliver* from the Ship Via drop down-list, as shown in figure 4–9. It is Woodward's custom to hand deliver invoices to customers whenever possible.

FIGURE 4-9

Ship Via Drop-Down List with Hand Deliver Selected

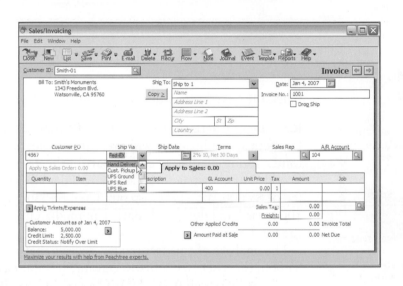

 **HINT**

In some cases, you may want to omit the quantity and unit price and enter only a total amount.

Step 11:

Key **10.00** (10 hours) in the *Quantity* field.

Step 12:

Key **10 Hours of construction services** in the *Description* field.

Step 13:

Key **125.00** in the *Unit Price* field. The total of $1,250 is automatically calculated. Leave the Tax code field at 1.

Step 14:

Review the completed Sales/Invoicing window for Smith's Monuments, as shown in figure 4–10. If your entries contain any errors, correct them.

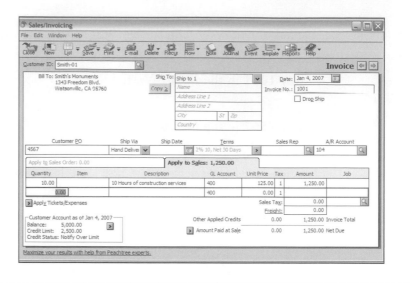

FIGURE 4-10

Completed Sales/Invoicing Window for Smith's Monuments

 NOTE

A warning stating that the customer's balance will exceed a predetermined credit limit may appear. Click Yes to continue. The default for the credit limit is set at $2,500. Peachtree is programmed to show a warning message in the event that a customer's balance goes over the credit limit.

Step 15:

Click the Save button to save the entry of the sale on credit.

RECORDING A SALE ON CREDIT AND A PARTIAL COLLECTION

On occasion, a business will present an invoice for a sale on credit to a customer and immediately collect part of the amount owed. For example, Woodward Construction Company did a job for Barker's Music for a fixed fee of $5,000. The job was completed on January 14, 2007, and Invoice 1002 was hand delivered. Barker immediately issued a check for one-half of the total due ($2,500).

The analysis of this transaction reveals that revenue has increased by $5,000, the asset Accounts Receivable has increased by $2,500, and the asset Cash has increased by $2,500. The account for Barker's Music has also increased by $2,500.

You would record this transaction by debiting Accounts Receivable for $2,500, debiting Cash for $2,500, and crediting Revenue for $5,000. The debit of $2,500 to Accounts Receivable must be posted to both the controlling account in the general ledger and the Barker's Music account in the accounts receivable subsidiary ledger.

Use the steps outlined below to record the sale on credit and the partial collection involving Barker's Music.

HINT

The system will automatically assign invoice numbers in sequence. For example, 1002 is assigned to the invoice for Barker's Music because the previous invoice for Smith's Monuments was 1001.

Step 1:

Click the *magnifying glass* icon next to the *Customer ID* field of the Sales/Invoicing window.

Step 2:

Click *Barker-03* from the drop-down list of customers.

Step 3:

Use the *calendar* icon next to the *Date* field and choose *Jan 14, 2007*.

Step 4:

Key **2356** in the *Customer PO* field. This is the number of the purchase order that was issued by Barker's Music.

Step 5:

Click *Hand Deliver* from the Ship Via drop-down list.

Step 6:

Key **Performed construction services** in the *Description* field.

Step 7:

Key **5,000.00** in the *Amount* field. Because this job was done for a fixed fee, it is not necessary to complete the *Quantity* and *Unit Price* fields.

Step 8:

Next, record the amount collected from the customer. Click the right arrow key to the right of Amount Paid at Sale (at the bottom of the window). The Receive Payment window appears as in figure 4–11.

FIGURE 4-11
Receive Payment Window

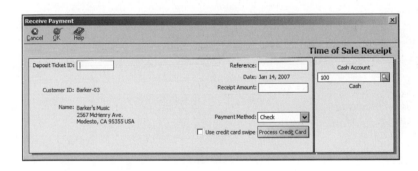

Step 9:

Key **01/14/07** in the *Deposit Ticket ID* field. This is the date of the probable bank deposit.

Step 10:

Key **1002** in the *Reference* field. This is the invoice number.

Step 11:

Key **2500.00** in the *Receipt Amount* field.

Step 12:

At the Payment Method drop-down list, click *Check*. (It should be already selected as a default.)

Step 13:

At the Cash Account drop-down list, double-click *100*.

Step 14:

Compare your work with the completed Receive Payment window, shown in figure 4–12.

FIGURE 4-12

Completed Receive Payment Window

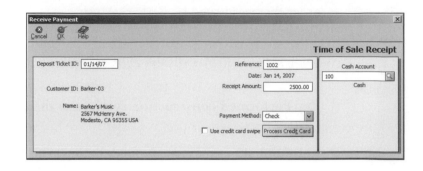

Step 15:

Click <u>O</u>K. Peachtree will automatically transfer the information about the amount collected to the Sales/Invoicing window and will calculate the net amount that is now due.

Step 16:

Review the completed Sales/Invoicing window for Barker's Music, as shown in figure 4–13.

FIGURE 4-13

Completed Sales/Invoicing Window for Barker's Music

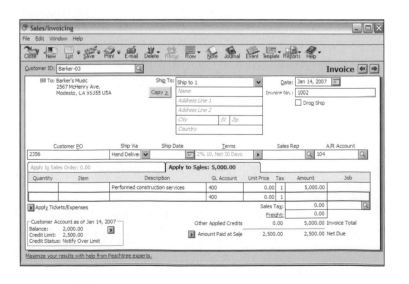

Step 17:

Click <u>S</u>ave, and then Yes to save the transaction, then close the Sales/Invoicing window.

Step 18:

Close the Sales/Invoicing window.

PRINTING CUSTOMER LEDGER REPORTS

Peachtree produces a wide variety of accounts receivable reports. The *Customer Ledgers* report is probably the most important of the accounts receivable reports. This report shows all transactions with credit customers and the balances they owe. Use the following steps to view and print the *Customer Ledgers* report.

Step 1:

Click <u>R</u>eports, and then click Accounts <u>R</u>eceivable.

Step 2:

At the Select a Report dialog box, click *Customer Ledgers* in the Report Lis<u>t</u> section, as shown in figure 4–14.

FIGURE 4-14

Accounts Receivable Report List with Customer Ledgers Selected

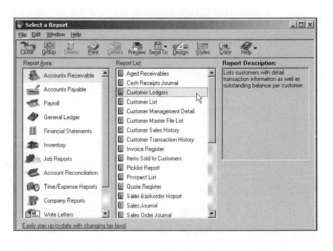

Step 3:

Click the Pre<u>v</u>iew button on the Select a Report toolbar.

Step 4:

At the Customer Ledgers window with the F<u>i</u>lter tab selected, click *This Period* from the D<u>a</u>te drop-down list, and then click <u>O</u>K.

Step 5:

Examine the *Customer Ledgers* report shown in figure 4–15. (The abbreviation *SJ* in the report stands for sales journal. The abbreviation *CRJ* stands for cash receipts journal.)

FIGURE 4-15
Customer Ledgers Report

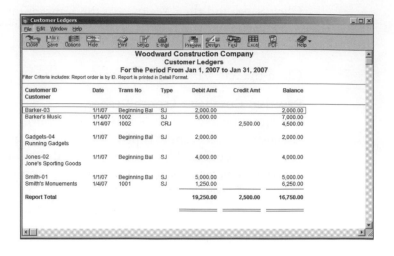

Step 6:

Click the Print button to print a copy of the *Customer Ledgers* report.

Step 7:

Close the Customer Ledgers window and the Select a Report dialog box.

PRACTICE objective 2

The Bullfrog Maintenance Company provides maintenance services to local car dealers. You previously created customer accounts for this firm.

Step 1:

Open Bullfrog Maintenance Company.

Step 2:

Record the following transactions.
- On January 2, 2007, Bullfrog Maintenance Company issued Invoice 1101 to Honda Center for 10 hours of work at a rate of $12 per hour. The invoice was sent by regular mail.
- On January 8, 2007, Bullfrog Maintenance Company issued Invoice 1102 to Lexus of San Joaquin for a fixed fee of $420, which covers monthly services. The invoice was hand delivered.
- On January 19, 2007, Bullfrog Maintenance Company issued Invoice 1103 to Curt Smith Mazda for 48 hours of work at a rate of $16 per hour. The invoice was sent by regular mail.
- On January 29, 2007, Bullfrog Maintenance Company issued Invoice 1104 to Valley Mercedes for a fixed fee of $650, which covers monthly services. The invoice was hand delivered, and the customer immediately wrote a check for one-half of the amount due.

Print the *Customer Ledgers* report. Check the accuracy of your work by comparing your report with figure 4–16.

Close the Customer Ledgers window and the Select a Report dialog box.

FIGURE 4-16

*Bullfrog Maintenance Company
Customer Ledgers Report*

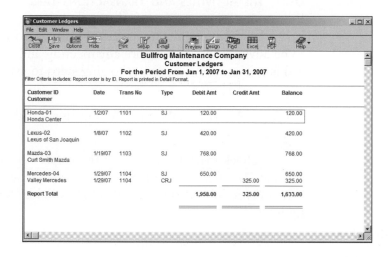

OBJECTIVE 3 — CREATE ACTION ITEMS AND EVENT LOGS

Having reliable, up-to-date information about customer accounts is one of the keys to collecting balances on time and minimizing losses from bad debts. Management must keep a close watch on the status of customer accounts and take prompt action to collect overdue amounts. The longer an amount remains overdue, the more likely it is that the account will eventually become uncollectible.

Peachtree has certain features that help management track problem customer accounts. One of these features has already been mentioned: the warning message that the system produces whenever a customer's balance exceeds the credit limit. Other features provided by Peachtree are action items and event logs.

Action items and event logs allow you to create a list of actions to be taken and program the system to display alerts on your screen before these events occur. For example, you might want to schedule meetings, telephone calls, or letters in connection with overdue balances and might want to be alerted to these events two days ahead of time. Action items and event logs can be used for other purposes besides managing customer accounts. They can also be used to schedule actions related to the vendor (creditor) accounts and to employees.

Follow the steps listed below to access the Action Items/Event Log Options.

Step 1:

Open Woodward Construction Company.

Step 2:

Click Tas_k_s from the Main Menu bar and then _A_ction Items from the drop-down list.

Step 3:

Click _O_ptions from the Action Items toolbar. The Action Items and Event Log Options window appears.

USING THE ACTIVITIES AND TRANSACTIONS TABS

Events can be set up as defaults so that they can later be displayed as action items. For example, the managers of Woodward Construction Company want to be advised two days before any meeting and one day before any telephone call is to be made. Use the following steps to establish the necessary defaults.

Step 1:

Click the Acti_v_ities tab in the Action Items and Event Log Options window.

Step 2:

Place a check mark for *Call To* in the *Display in Action Items* field. Key **1** in the *# of Days* field. Then place a check mark for *Meeting* in the *Display in Action Items* field. Key **2** in the *# of Days* field. Compare the window with figure 4–17.

FIGURE 4-17

Activities Tab

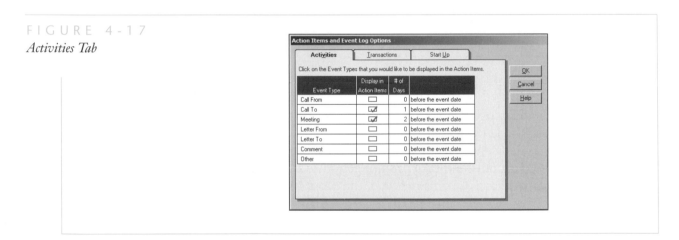

Peachtree can be programmed to generate alerts for a variety of events. For example, Woodward Construction Company wants to create events for all possible event types specified by Peachtree. Woodward also wants an advance warning for customer invoices that are due for payment. They want this warning to appear as an action item two days before payment due dates. Use the following steps to generate an alert to Woodward two days before a customer's invoice is due.

Step 1:

Click the _T_ransactions tab in the Action Items and Event Log Options window.

Step 2:

For *Customer Invoices Due*, key **2** in the *# of Days* field, as shown in figure 4–18.

FIGURE 4-18
Transactions Tab

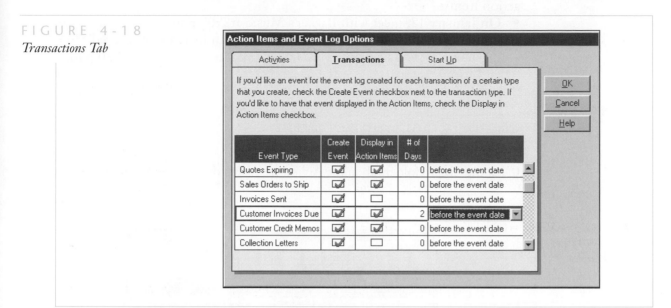

USING THE START UP TAB

You can have the action items displayed whenever you open a new company or you can have the items displayed on top of the screen.

Step 1:

Click the Start Up tab in the Action Items and Event Log Options window.

Step 2:

Place a check mark next to "Display Action Items each time a new company is opened." (See figure 4–19.)

FIGURE 4-19
Start Up Tab

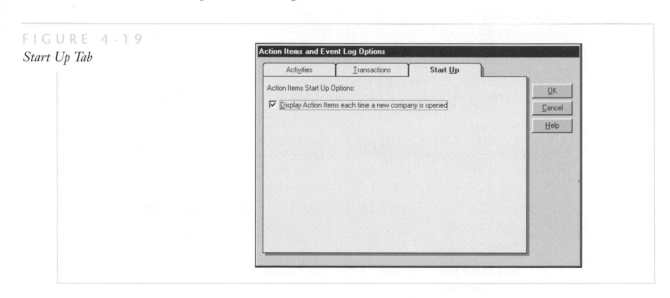

Step 3:

Click OK to accept all of the defaults that you have established.
Because the process of setting up the defaults is complete, you can now create and access events that are action items.

RECORDING ACTION ITEMS ON THE TO DO LIST

Woodward Construction Company wants to include the following events as action items:

- On January 12, meet with Barker's Music at 2:00 p.m.
- On January 13, call Running Gadgets about an increase in its credit limit.
- On January 13, meet with Smith's Monuments for lunch at 12:30 p.m.

Use the following steps to establish these events as action items.

Step 1:

Click Ta<u>s</u>ks, and then click <u>A</u>ction Items.

Step 2:

Click the To <u>D</u>o folder tab in the Action Items window, as shown in figure 4–20.

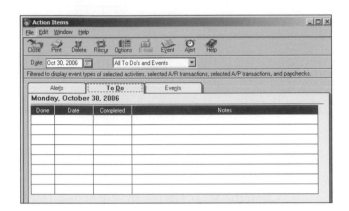

Step 3:

Key **01/12/07**, the date of the first event, in the first cell of the *Date* field in the To <u>D</u>o tab.

Step 4:

In the *Notes* field, key **Meet with Barker's Music at 2:00 p.m.**

Step 5:

Key **01/13/07,** the date of the second event, in the second cell of the *Date* field in the To <u>D</u>o tab.

Step 6:

In the *Notes* field, key **Call Running Gadgets about an increase in its credit limit**.

Step 7:

Key **01/13/07,** the date of the third event, in the next cell of the *Date* field.

Step 8:

In the *Notes* field, key **Meet with Smith's Monuments for lunch at 12:30 p.m.**

Compare your completed To Do list with the one shown in figure 4–21.

FIGURE 4-21

Completed To Do List

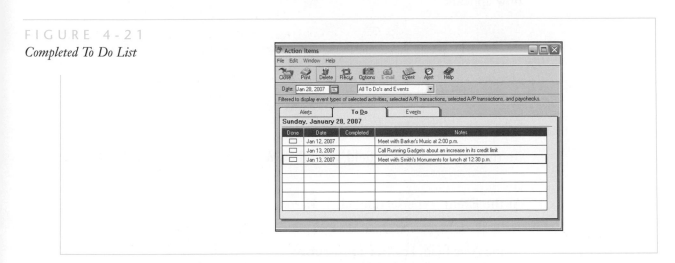

RECORDING EVENTS ON THE ACTION LIST

Some events have been programmed to appear as action items. For example, customer invoices that are due for payment will be listed as action items two days prior to their due dates. The programming of this item was accomplished when the defaults were set up. However, a business might want to add other events to its action list.

Assume that Woodward Construction Company wants to place the following additional event on its action list: Set up a meeting with Barker's Music for January 18, 2007. Advise two days ahead of time.

Step 1:

Click the Events tab as shown in figure 4–22.

FIGURE 4-22

Events Tab Selected from Action Items Window

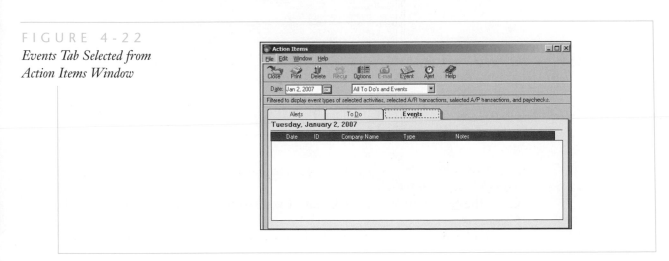

Step 2:

Click the Event button on the Action Items toolbar. The Create Event window appears.

Step 3:

At the Type drop-down list, click *Customer/Prospect*.

Step 4:

At the ID drop-down list, click the *magnifying glass* icon and then click *Barker-03*.

Step 5:

To the right of the *Date* field, click the *calendar* icon and choose *Jan 18, 2007*.

Step 6:

At the Event Type section, click *Meeting*.

Step 7:

In the *Note* field, key **Set up meeting**.

Step 8:

Place a check mark next to Display in Action Items.

Step 9:

Key **2** as the number of days. Then click *Before* in the "_____ the event date" drop-down list. (These may already be selected by default.)

Step 10:

Compare your work with the completed Create Event window shown in figure 4–23.

FIGURE 4-23
Completed Create Event Window

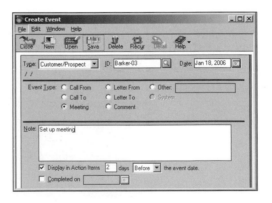

Step 11:

Click the Save button on the Create Event window toolbar, and then click Close.

Step 12:

Woodward Construction Company wants to add the following two events to its action list. Add them using steps 1 through 11:

- Call Jones Sporting Goods three days before a meeting set for January 19, 2007.
- Send a letter to Running Gadgets advising it of a change in credit terms that will take effect on January 31, 2007. Send the letter on January 26.

Step 13:

Click the Close button, and then close the Action Items window.

DISPLAYING THE EVENTS

Each of the events placed on the action list is scheduled to appear according to the number of days set before the event. For example, the first event for Woodward Construction Company—the meeting with Barker's Music on January 18—will automatically appear two days before the event in the Action Items window as the system date changes to January 16. Follow the steps outlined below to check the events listed for any date. In this case, the date to be checked is January 16, 2007.

Step 1:

Click Tas_k_s, and then _A_ction Items.

Step 2:

Click the Eve_n_ts tab.

Step 3:

At the Action Items window, in the _Date_ field, click the _calendar_ icon to choose _Jan 16, 2007._ (See figure 4–24.)

FIGURE 4-24

Action Items Window with Date Field Showing Jan 16, 2007

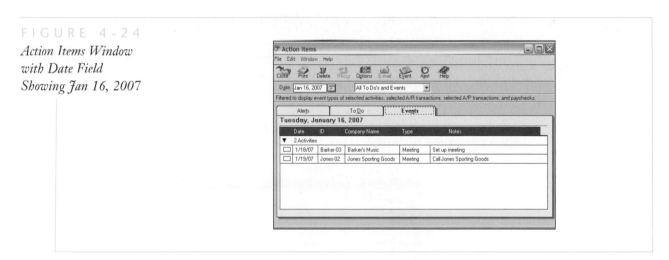

The events that are scheduled will appear in the Action Items window when Peachtree is started on January 16, 2007.

SETTING ALERTS

The Action Items window has an Alerts tab that allows you to select certain conditions for notification. For example, an alert can be set to notify you when a particular customer's balance is too high. Assume that Woodward Construction Company wants to be notified when the balance owed by Smith Monuments, Jones Sporting Goods, or Barker's Music reaches $4,000. Follow the steps outlined below to set the alert.

Step 1:
Click the Alerts tab in the Action Items window.

Step 2:
Click the Alert button on the Action Items toolbar. The Set Company Alerts window appears, as shown in figure 4–25.

FIGURE 4-25

Set Company Alerts Window

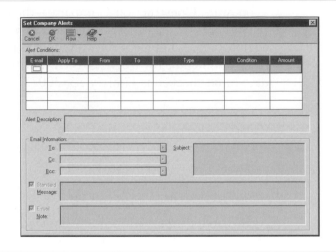

Setting an alert requires entry of information using the following steps:

Step 3:
Click inside the *Apply To* field, click the down-pointing arrow that appears, and then click *Customer*.

Step 4:
Click in the *From* field, click the *magnifying glass* icon, click *Barker-03*, and then click the OK button. (See figure 4–26.)

FIGURE 4-26

Set Company Alerts Window—From Field

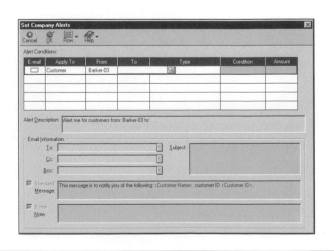

HINT

Customers can be e-mailed and alerted by selecting the E-mail box and completing the e-mail information at the bottom of the Set Company Alerts window.

Step 5:

In the *To* field, click the *magnifying glass* icon, and then click *Smith-01*. Steps 4 and 5 establish a filter for the customer who is the subject of the alert.

Step 6:

In the *Type* field, click the down-pointing arrow, and then click *Current Balance*.

Step 7:

Click in the *Condition* field, click the down-pointing arrow, and then click >=.

Step 8:

Key **4,000.00** in the *Amount* field. Compare your work with the completed window shown in figure 4–27.

FIGURE 4-27

Completed Set Company Alerts Window

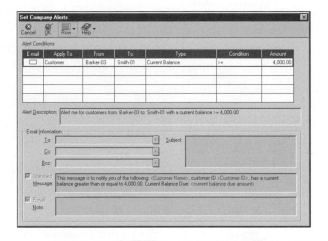

Step 9:

Click the OK button to save the alert. The alerts that were set up for Barker's Music, Jones Sporting Goods, and Smith's Monuments will now appear in the Alerts tab. (See figure 4–28.)

FIGURE 4-28

Alerts Tab with Alerts for Customers' Balances

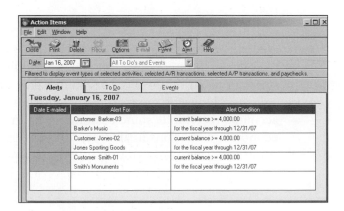

1. What is the purpose of the action items and event log options of Peachtree?
2. What is the purpose of the alert function of Peachtree?

Answers
1. *The action item and event log options allow you to create a list of actions to be taken and program the system to display alerts before these events occur.*
2. *The alert function allows you to select certain conditions for notification.*

Step 10:
Close the Action Items window.

P R A C T I C E *objective* 3

You previously established customer accounts for Bullfrog Maintenance Company. Now you will set up action items and alerts for this firm.

Step 1:
Open Bullfrog Maintenance Company.

Step 2:
Use the Start Up tab from the Action Items and Event Log Options window to check the "Display Action Items each time a new company is opened" box.

Step 3:
Record the following events as action items on the To Do list.
* On January 12, 2007, call Honda Center to discuss maintenance for its new facility.
* On January 18, 2007, meet with Lexus of San Joaquin to explain our new pricing policy.
* On January 23, 2007, call Kim Smith of Curt Smith Mazda to wish her a happy birthday.
* On January 24, 2007, call Valley Mercedes to set up a new maintenance schedule.

Step 4:
Create an alert that will notify you when the current balance owed by any of your customers reaches or exeeds $1,500.

Step 5:
Create an event in which Peachtree will tell you to call Lexus of San Joaquin two days before the meeting that is scheduled for January 18, 2007.

Step 6:
Close the Action Items window.

OBJECTIVE 4 — ADJUST THE ACCOUNTS RECEIVABLE FOR UNCOLLECTIBLE ACCOUNTS AND PRINT REPORTS

A well-run business is careful about extending credit, closely monitors the status of its customer accounts, and makes strong efforts to collect overdue balances. However, no matter how diligent a business is in managing its accounts receivable, some customer accounts will become uncollectible. Bad economic conditions in an area, bad management decisions, or new competition may cause a previously sound customer to go bankrupt.

METHODS FOR RECORDING UNCOLLECTIBLE ACCOUNTS

Two methods are available for recording uncollectible accounts. The first and simpler approach is the **direct write-off method**. With this method, the expense from an uncollectible account is recorded when the customer's account actually becomes a bad debt. At that time, you debit the loss to Uncollectible Accounts Expense and credit it to Accounts Receivable. The credit part of this entry is posted to both the Accounts Receivable controlling account in the general ledger and the customer's account in the subsidiary ledger.

The second approach to recording uncollectible accounts is the **allowance method**. At the end of each accounting period, the accountant makes an estimate of the bad debts loss that will result from the period's sales. This amount is recorded by means of an adjusting entry. You debit Uncollectible Accounts Expense and credit Allowance for Doubtful Accounts. Figure 4–29 illustrates the adjusting entry for an estimated bad debts loss of $45,000.

F I G U R E   4 - 2 9

Initial Adjustment for Estimation of Bad Debt Loss Using the Allowance Method

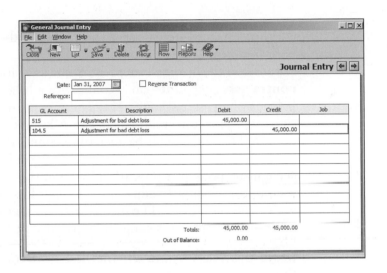

With the allowance method, when a customer's account actually becomes uncollectible, you write it off by debiting Allowance for Doubtful Accounts and crediting Accounts Receivable, as shown in figure 4–30. The credit part of this entry is posted to both the Accounts Receivable controlling account in the general ledger and the customer's account in the subsidiary ledger.

FIGURE 4-30

*Adjustment for Bad Debt
Loss against a Specific
Customer Account Using the
Allowance Method*

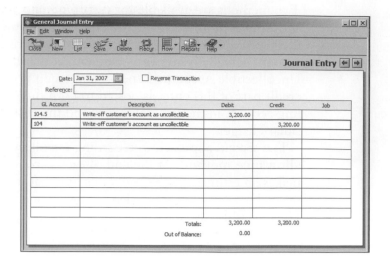

When financial statements are prepared at the end of an accounting
period, Uncollectible Accounts Expense appears as an operating
expense on the income statement. Allowance for Doubtful Accounts is a
contra asset account—an account with a balance opposite to the normal
balance of an asset account. If the allowance method is used, the balance
sheet will show the credit balance of Allowance for Doubtful Accounts
deducted from the debit balance of Accounts Receivable.

The allowance method is the approach required by generally accepted
accounting principles (GAAP). However, the direct write-off method will be
used in this chapter to adjust for bad debt loss because this chapter deals
with small businesses. The direct write-off method is used by many small
businesses because it is simple compared with the allowance method.

USING THE DIRECT WRITE-OFF METHOD TO RECORD THE WRITE-OFF OF A CUSTOMER'S ACCOUNT

In a manual accounting system, the write-off of a customer's account is
recorded in the general journal. However, in Peachtree, it is necessary to
use the accounts receivable module so that the credit part of the entry can
be posted automatically to the accounts receivable subsidiary ledger as well
as to the general ledger.

A simple journal entry is used to write off a specific accounts receivable
when it is deemed uncollectible. Therefore, no end-of-the-period adjusting
entry is required. Figure 4–31 gives an example of a general journal entry
needed to write off a bad debt loss.

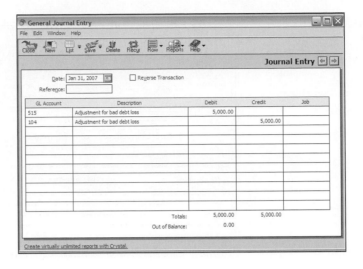

Assume that Running Gadgets has owed $2,000 to Woodward Construction Company for six months. Woodward has been unsuccessful in its efforts to collect this overdue balance. On January 29, 2007, Woodward receives a legal notice that Running Gadgets has gone bankrupt.

Woodward uses the direct write-off method for recording uncollectible accounts. Therefore, on January 29, 2007, its accountant made a journal entry to record the bad debt loss for the sale that occurred in 2006. Now you must write off the account of Running Gadgets as of January 29, 2007.

Step 1:

Open Woodward Construction Company.

Step 2:

Open the Chart of Accounts, add the account *Uncollectible Accounts Expense* to it using the information below, and then click <u>S</u>ave and Close.

Account ID:	**515**
Description:	**Uncollectible Accounts Expense**
Account Type:	**Expenses**

Step 3:

Click Tas<u>k</u>s, and then click <u>R</u>eceipts. The Receipts window will appear. (See figure 4–32.)

FIGURE 4-32

Receipts Window

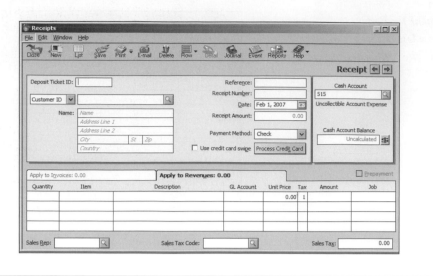

Step 4:

Key **01/29/07** in the *Deposit Ticket ID* field.

Step 5:

Click the *magnifying glass* icon and then click *Running Gadgets* from the drop-down list of customer IDs.

Step 6:

Key **Bankruptcy** in the *Reference* field.

Step 7:

Click the Journal button from the Receipts window toolbar. You will now see the Accounting Behind the Screens window.

Step 8:

Click the *magnifying glass* icon in the *Account No.* field and then click 515 *Uncollectible Accounts Expense* from the drop-down list of accounts. Normally, there is a default to Cash in the Receipts window because Cash is the account debited to record an amount received from a customer. However, because a customer's account is being written off, you must go "behind the screens" to ensure that Uncollectible Accounts Expense will be debited. See figure 4–33.

FIGURE 4-33

*Uncollectible Accounts
Expense Selected*

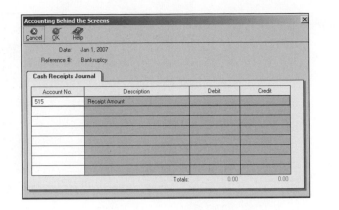

Step 9:

Click the <u>O</u>K button to confirm your choice of the account to be debited.

Step 10:

The Receipts window will reappear. At the <u>*Date*</u> field, click the *calendar* icon to choose *Jan 29, 2007,* as the date.

Step 11:

Key **Write-off** in the *Payment Method* field.

Step 12:

Click the Apply to I<u>n</u>voices tab.

Step 13:

Key **Bad debt loss** in the *Description* field.

Step 14:

Key **2,000.00** in the *Amount Paid* field.

Step 15:

Tab to the *Pay* field and notice that a check mark appears there.

Step 16:

Click the Journal button from the Receipts window toolbar. Compare the Accounting Behind the Screens window with figure 4–34, and then click the <u>O</u>K button.

FIGURE 4-34

Accounting Behind the Screens Window

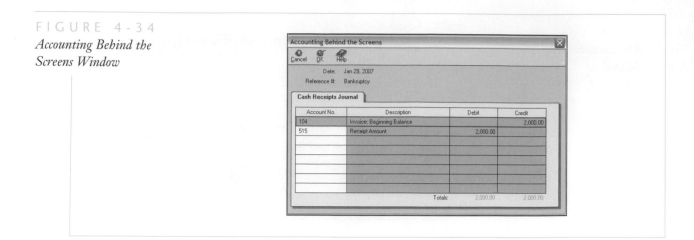

Step 17:

Compare your entries for the write-off with the completed Receipts window shown in figure 4–35.

FIGURE 4-35

Completed Receipts Window with Write-off

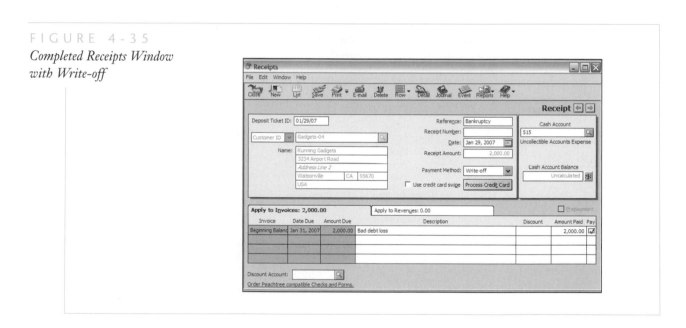

Step 18:

Click the Save button and then the Close button.

PRINTING ACCOUNTS RECEIVABLE REPORTS

Peachtree can produce several accounts receivable reports, including:

- *Aged Receivables*
- *Cash Receipts Journal*
- *Customer Ledgers*
- *Customer List*
- *Customer Master File List*
- *Customer Sales History*
- *Invoice Register*
- *Collection Letters*
- *Customer Statements*

Assume that the management of the Woodward Construction Company wants to print two of these reports: the *Customer List* and *Customer Ledgers*.

Step 1:

Click <u>R</u>eports, and then click Accounts <u>R</u>eceivable.

Step 2:

The Select a Report dialog box will appear. Click *Customer List* from the Report Lis<u>t</u> section, as shown in figure 4–36.

FIGURE 4-36

Customer List Chosen from Select a Report Dialog Box

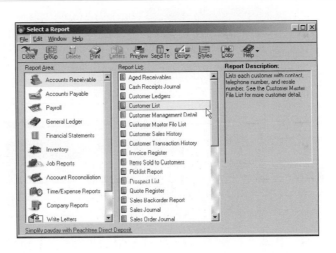

Step 3:

Click the <u>P</u>rint button on the Select a Report toolbar.

Step 4:

Click *Customer ID*, if it is not already selected, from the <u>R</u>eport Order drop-down list, as shown in figure 4–37.

FIGURE 4-37

*Customer ID Selected from
Report Order Drop-
Down List*

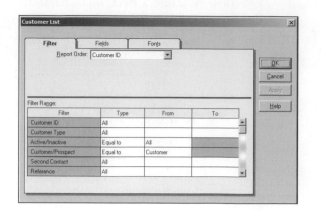

Step 5:

Click OK.

Step 6:

Complete the Print window, and click OK to print.

Step 7:

Compare your *Customer List* report with the one shown in figure 4–38.

FIGURE 4-38

Customer List for Woodward Construction Company

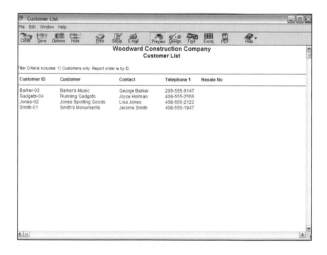

Step 8:

Use steps 2–6 to print a copy of the *Customer Ledgers*. (In step 2, select *Customer Ledgers* from the Report List section.) Compare your printed report with the one shown in figure 4–39.

FIGURE 4-39

Customer Ledgers for Woodward Construction Company

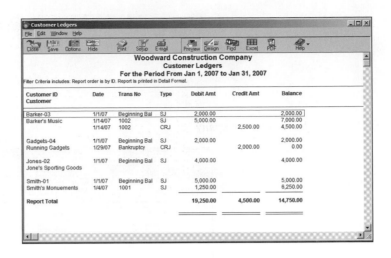

Step 9:

Close the Select a Report dialog box.

POINT

1. What two methods are used to record uncollectible accounts?
2. When a customer's balance is written off under the direct write-off, what accounts are debited and credited?

Answers

1. The two methods used to record uncollectible accounts are the direct write-off method and the allowance method.
2. When a customer's balance is written off under the direct write-off, it is necessary to debit Uncollectible Accounts Expense and credit Accounts Receivable in the general ledger. It is also necessary to credit the customer's account in the subsidiary ledger.

PRACTICE *objective* 4

Step 1

Open Bullfrog Maintenance Company.

Step 2

Add the account Uncollectible Accounts Expense using the information below.

Account ID:	**515**
Description:	**Uncollectible Accounts Expense**
Account Type:	**Expenses**

Step 3:

Write off the Honda Center account as of January 31, 2007. Honda Center has gone bankrupt. It owes $120 for Invoice 1101.

Step 4:
Print a copy of the *Customer List* report. Compare your report to the report shown in figure 4–40.

FIGURE 4-40

Customer List for Bullfrog Maintenance Company

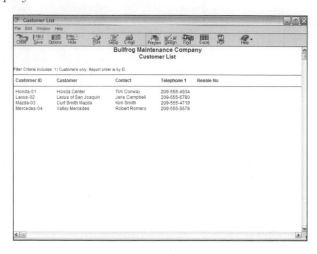

Step 5:
Print a copy of the *Customer Ledgers* report. Compare your report to the report shown in figure 4–41.

FIGURE 4-41

Customer Ledgers for Bullfrog Maintenance Company

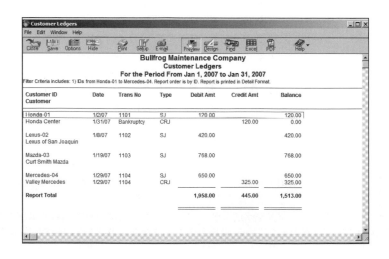

Step 6:
Close the Select a Report dialog box.

A business that offers credit to its customers can usually achieve higher sales, but it runs the risk of losses from uncollectible accounts. Therefore, such a firm must make careful decisions about extending credit to new customers. Many businesses use credit-rating agencies like Dun & Bradstreet to investigate the financial background of potential customers. Dun & Bradstreet's Web site is located at www.dnb.com. (See figure 4–42.)

FIGURE 4-42

The Dun & Bradstreet Web Site

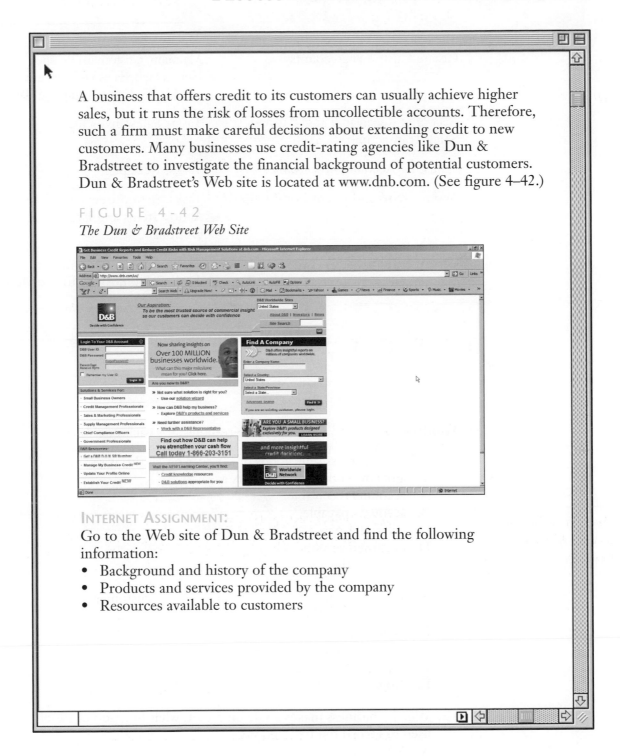

INTERNET ASSIGNMENT:

Go to the Web site of Dun & Bradstreet and find the following information:

- Background and history of the company
- Products and services provided by the company
- Resources available to customers

SOFTWARE *Command Summary*

Create Customer Accounts	Maintain, Customers/Prospects, General tab, Sales Defaults tab, Terms and Credit, Enter Beginning Balances
Accounts Receivable and Sales Transactions	Tasks, Sales/Invoicing
Adjusting Accounts Receivables	Tasks, Receipts
Action Items and Event Log Options	Tasks, Action Items, Options, Action Items and Event Log Options
Create Action Items/Alerts	Tasks, Action Items, To Do, Event Toolbar Icon, Alert Toolbar Icon

PROJECTS *and Problems*

CONTENT CHECK

Multiple Choice: Choose only one response for each question.

1. When a business sells goods or services on credit, it records the amounts owed by the customers as
   A. accounts receivable.
   B. accounts payable.
   C. prepaid expenses.
   D. unearned revenue.
   E. None of the above.

2. From a seller's perspective, sales on credit to customers affect
   A. assets and expenses.
   B. assets and revenue.
   C. liabilities and expenses.
   D. liabilities and revenue.
   E. None of the above.

3. When a business makes a sale on credit, what function of Peachtree is used to record the transaction?
   A. Action Items
   B. Purchases/Receive Inventory
   C. Receipts
   D. Sales/Invoicing
   E. None of the above

4. Which accounts receivable report shows the beginning balances of the customer accounts, all transactions with the customers during a period, and the ending balances?
   A. *Aged Receivables*
   B. *Customer Ledgers*
   C. *Invoice Register*
   D. *Sales Journal*
   E. None of the above

5. Which general ledger accounts are involved in the direct write-off of a specific customer's account?
   A. Accounts Receivable and Sales
   B. Uncollectible Accounts Expense and Accounts Receivable
   C. Allowance for Doubtful Accounts and Accounts Receivable
   D. Uncollectible Accounts Expense and Allowance for Doubtful Accounts
   E. None of the above

Short Essay Response: Provide a detailed answer for each question.

1. What are the advantages and disadvantages to a business when it sells on credit?
2. What is the purpose of the accounts receivable subsidiary ledger?
3. Under what circumstance will a resale number be required when an account is set up for a new customer?
4. Why is a default for a credit limit established when customer accounts are set up?
5. How can the Alert function be used to aid a business in collecting its accounts receivable?
6. Explain the difference between the direct write-off method and the allowance method of recording uncollectible accounts.

CASE PROBLEMS

PROBLEM 1A

Open GJ Professional Accounting. You set up this accounting services company in Chapter 2 and recorded transactions for it in Chapter 3.

The following are customers who purchase services on credit.

Customer ID:	**JM-1**
Name:	**Johnson Manufacturing**

General Tab

Contact:	**Randy Johnson**	
Bill to:		
	Address:	**4731 Eaton Avenue**
	City, ST Zip:	**Stockton, CA 95210**
	Country:	**USA**
Sales Tax:		
Customer Type:	**General**	
Telephone 1:	**209-555-4178**	
Telephone 2:	**209-555-4179**	
Fax:	**209-555-4180**	

Sales Defaults Tab

GL Sales Acct:	**40000**
Ship Via:	**Fed-EX**
Pricing Level:	**Default**
Form Delivery Options:	**Default**

Terms and Credit Tab

Terms:	**Default**
Beginning Balances:	**3,000.00**
Customer ID:	**CE-2**
Name:	**Computer Expertise**

General Tab

Contact:	Marie Jameson
Bill to:	

Address:	**475 West Lincoln Boulevard**
City, ST Zip:	**Tracy, CA 95376**
Country:	**USA**

Sales Tax:	
Customer Type:	**General**
Telephone 1:	**209-555-3820**
Telephone 2:	**209-555-3822**
Fax:	**209-555-3840**

Sales Defaults Tab

GL Sales Acct:	**40000**
Ship Via:	**Fed-EX**
Pricing Level:	**Default**
Form Delivery Options:	**Default**

Terms and Credit Tab

Terms:	**Default**
Beginning Balances	**1,600.00**
Customer ID:	**SC-3**
Name:	**Stephanie's Catering**

General Tab

Contact:	Stephanie Barron
Bill to:	

Address:	**4837 6th Street**
City, ST Zip:	**Watsonville, CA 95760**
Country:	**USA**

Sales Tax:	
Customer Type:	**General**
Telephone 1:	**209-555-2864**

Telephone 2:	**209-555-2870**
Fax:	**209-555-2875**

Sales Defaults Tab

GL Sales Acct:	**40000**
Ship Via:	**Fed-EX**
Pricing Level:	**Default**
Form Delivery Options:	**Default**

Terms and Credit Tab

Terms:	**Default**
Beginning Balances:	**1,000.00**

The following cash sales and credit sales are additional transactions that occurred during January 2007.

Date	Transaction
Jan. 3	Performed accounting services for $1,200 on credit for Johnson Manufacturing. Issued Invoice 1001.
4	Performed tax preparation services for $950 in cash.
6	Performed accounting services for $750 on credit for Computer Expertise. Issued Invoice 1002.
14	Performed accounting services for $350 on credit for Stephanie's Catering. Issued Invoice 1003. Received a check for $100 from the customer.
15	Performed consulting services for $220 in cash.
24	Performed consulting services for $825 on credit for Johnson Manufacturing. Issued Invoice 1004. Received a check for $200 from the customer.
27	Performed accounting services for $245 on credit for Computer Expertise. Issued Invoice 1005. Received a check for $100 from the customer.

1. Create a subsidiary ledger account for each credit customer and enter their beginning balance as of January 1, 2007.
2. Enter each of the transactions for January. Use the appropriate option on the Tasks menu: Sales/Invoicing or General Journal Entry. Note that this business has three different types of revenue: accounting fees, tax preparation fees, and consulting fees. Therefore, be sure that you select the number of the correct revenue account in the GL Sales Account section of the Sales/Invoicing window. (The customer accounts have been set up with a GL Sales Account default to Account 40000, Accounting Fees.)
   Hint: Enter all performances of service on credit using the Sales/Invoicing function. Enter cash sales and all other transactions using the General Journal Entry function. Use Account 10200, Regular Checking Account for all cash sales transactions.
3. Print the following reports for January: *Customer Ledgers, Sales Journal, General Journal*, and *Income Statement*.

PROBLEM 2A

Open GJ Professional Accounting.

1. Record the following events as action items on the To Do list.
   - On January 3, 2007, call Computer Expertise to discuss accounting services schedule.
   - On January 15, 2007, meet with a graphic design company, Infinite Graphics, to discuss company logo.
   - On January 17, 2007, call Johnson Manufacturing to discuss pricing policy.
   - On January 24, 2007, meet with Stephanie's Catering to set up a new accounting services schedule.
2. Create the following alert.
   - Notify you when the current balance owed by any of its customers reaches or exeeds $2,500.

PROBLEM 1B

Open Infinite Graphics. You set up this graphic services company in chapter 2 and recorded transactions for it in chapter 3.

The following are customers who purchase services on credit.

Customer ID:	**JP-1**
Name:	**Jackson Photography**

General Tab

Contact:		**Sarah Bautista**
Bill to:		
	Address:	**1374 West Bessie Avenue**
	City, ST Zip:	**Stockton, CA 95210**
	Country:	**USA**
Sales Tax:		
Customer Type:		**General**
Telephone 1:		**209-555-1478**
Telephone 2:		**209-555-1479**
Fax:		**209-555-1485**

Sales Defaults Tab

GL Sales Acct:	**40000**
Ship Via:	**Fed-EX**
Pricing Level:	**Default**
Form Delivery Options:	**Default**

Terms and Credit Tab

Terms:	**Default**
Beginning Balances	**400.00**

Customer ID:	**CC-2**
Name:	**Computer Creations**

General Tab

Contact: Lee Chang

Bill to:

	Address:	733 Madison Boulevard
	City, ST Zip:	Tracy, CA 95376
	Country:	USA

Sales Tax:

Customer Type: General

Telephone 1:   209-555-4710

Telephone 2:   209-555-4712

Fax: 209-555-4730

Sales Defaults Tab

GL Sales Acct: 40000

Ship Via: Fed-EX

Pricing Level: Default

Form Delivery Options: Default

Terms and Credit Tab

Terms: Default

Beginning Balances: 1,200.00

Customer ID: FD-3

Name: First Design

General Tab

Contact: Richard Thompson

Bill to:

	Address:	1385 12th Street
	City, ST Zip:	Stockton, CA 95210
	Country:	USA

Sales Tax:

Customer Type: General

Telephone 1:   209-555-6842

Telephone 2:   209-555-6844

Fax: 209-555-6846

Sales Defaults Tab

GL Sales Acct: 40000

Ship Via: Fed-EX

Pricing Level: Default

Form Delivery Options: Default

Terms and Credit Tab

Terms: Default

Beginning Balances   1,000.00

The following cash sales and credit sales are additional transactions that occurred during January 2007.

Date	Transaction
Jan. 3	Performed graphic design services for $775 on credit

	for Jackson Photography. Issued Invoice 1001.
4	Performed graphic design services for $850 in cash.
6	Performed graphic design services for $540 on credit for Computer Creations. Issued Invoice 1002.
12	Performed retouching services for $1,050 in cash.
15	Performed graphic design services for $1,350 on credit for Jackson Photography. Issued Invoice 1003. Received a check for $300 from the customer.
15	Performed drafting services for $320 in cash.
20	Purchased graphing supplies for $85 in cash. (Because this business is on the accrual basis, it records purchases of supplies in an asset account.)
25	Performed graphic design services for $1,325 on credit for First Design. Issued Invoice 1004. Received a check for $950 from the customer.
26	Performed retouching services for $460 on credit for Jackson Photography. Issued Invoice 1005. Received a check for $360 from the customer.
27	Performed graphic design services for $750 on credit for Computer Creations. Issued Invoice 1006.

1. Create a subsidiary ledger account for each credit customer and enter their beginning balances as of January 1, 2007.
2. Enter each of the transactions for January. Use the appropriate option on the Tasks menu: Sales/Invoicing or General Journal Entry. Note that this business has three different types of revenue: graphic design fees, retouching fees, and drafting fees. Therefore, be sure that you select the number of the correct revenue account in the GL Sales Account section of the Sales/Invoicing window. (The customer accounts have been set up with a GL Sales Account default to Account 40000, Graphic Design Fees.)
   Hint: Enter all performances of service on credit using the Sales/Invoicing function. Enter cash sales and all other transactions using the General Journal Entry function. Use Account 10200, Regular Checking Account for all cash sales transactions.
3. Print the following reports for January: *Customer Ledgers, Sales Journal, General Journal,* and *Income Statement.*

PROBLEM 2B
Open Infinite Graphics.

1. Record the following events as action items on the To Do list.
   - On January 4, 2007, call Computer Creations to discuss pricing policy.
   - On January 13, 2007, meet with Jackson Photography to discuss graphic design work.
   - On January 20, 2007, meet with First Design to discuss subcontracting work.
   - On January 27, 2007, call GJ Professional Accounting to discuss accounting services offered.
2. Create the following alert.
   - Notify you when the current balance owed by any of its customers

reaches or exceeds $2,300.

COOPERATIVE LEARNING

1. Form groups of three or four students, and assume that you are the managers of a business that sells on credit. Discuss the criteria necessary to decide whether to grant credit to a new customer.

2. As a group, prepare a list of Peachtree features that help a business to monitor its accounts receivable and locate problems that may lead to uncollectible accounts.

WRITING AND DECISION MAKING

Assume that the company for which you work has always had a policy of selling for cash. The owner, Susan Nicholson, is now considering whether to provide credit to customers. She has asked you to suggest measures that the company can take to organize, manage, and collect its accounts receivable. She has also asked that you explain to her how the controlling account in the general ledger relates to the customer accounts in the subsidiary ledger. Prepare a memo that provides Ms. Nicholson with the information she has requested.

CHAPTER

5

ACCOUNTS PAYABLE

AND PURCHASES FOR A SERVICE BUSINESS

1. Create subsidiary ledger accounts for vendors and enter the beginning balances

2. Process accounts payable and purchase transactions

3. Create action items and event logs for vendor accounts and print accounts payable reports

SOFTWARE FEATURES

- Maintain Vendor toolbar buttons

- Vendor defaults

- Purchases/Receive Inventory toolbar

- Action items

- Alerts

Most businesses make use of credit to buy the goods and ___ in their operations. Credit helps a firm to grow and to ___ efficiently. Paying cash for all purchases would make it mu___ to expand operations and take advantage of new opportuni___

RECORDING ACCOUNTS PAYABLE

The amounts that a firm owes for goods or services purchas___ called **accounts payable**. The businesses or individuals to w___ amounts are owed are known as **vendors**, **creditors**, or **supp**___

Accounts payable are short-term debts that usually extend f___ days, depending on the credit terms offered by the vendor. M___ also allow a discount if payment is made within a specified sho___ period. For example, a vendor might offer terms of 2% 10 days ___ This means that the buyer can pay in 10 days and receive a 2% ___ from the total due or pay the full amount in 30 days.

As you learned in chapter 2, businesses that buy on credit set ___ account called Accounts Payable in the general ledger. This acco___ ited for purchases of goods or services. The account debited depe___ nature of the purchase. A purchase of an asset such as office suppl___ equipment is debited to the appropriate asset account. A purchase ___ vice is usually debited to an expense account. For example, a bill f___ tricity would be debited to Utilities Expense. A purchase of merch___ resale is debited to a cost account called Purchases or debited to th___ Inventory account directly.

When a bill for a purchase on credit becomes due, a check is issu___ vendor. The payment is debited to Accounts Payable and credited t___

THE ACCOUNTS PAYABLE SUBSIDIARY LEDGER

In addition to the Accounts Payable account in the general ledger, ___ businesses that buy on credit maintain a subsidiary ledger with indiv___ accounts for their vendors. This subsidiary ledger is known as the **accounts payable ledger** or **vendors ledger**.

Remember that subsidiary ledgers supplement the information in t___ eral ledger. For example, the accounts payable ledger provides detaile___ information about all transactions with vendors and shows the balanc___ owed to them. Peachtree updates the vendor accounts automatically ___ accounts payable transactions are recorded and posted.

THE CONTROLLING ACCOUNT IN THE GENERAL LEDGER

When an accounts payable subsidiary ledger is used, the Accounts Pay___ account in the general ledger becomes a controlling account. It provid___ link between the general ledger and the accounts payable ledger. Its ___ balance is equal to the total of all the balances of the individual accoun___ the subsidiary ledger. This is similar in function to how the accounts re___ able subsidiary ledger is used as described earlier (in chapter 4).

MANAGING ACCOUNTS PAYABLE

If credit is used properly, it can be very helpful to a business. However, credit can also present a danger. Some firms take on too much debt, fin___ that their cash flow is not adequate to pay bills as they become due, and eventually go bankrupt.

accounts payable amounts that a firm owes for goods or services purchased on credit.

vendors The businesses or individuals to whom accounts payable are owed. Also called **creditors** or **suppliers**.

accounts payable ledger A subsidiary ledger that contains accounts for vendors. Also called the **vendors ledger**.

Every firm that buys on credit should have procedures in place to ensure that it—

- Pays vendors on time in order to maintain a good credit reputation.
- Takes advantage of discounts whenever they are offered.
- Keeps the total amount owed to vendors from becoming too high in relation to the firm's resources.

Peachtree assists firms in managing their accounts payable by providing a means of quickly and efficiently recording purchases and cash payments and by generating a wide variety of accounts payable reports. Peachtree produces 15 reports that can be used to closely monitor the status of the accounts payable. Another helpful feature of Peachtree is the Action Items function, which can be programmed to alert you to actions that must be taken in connection with vendor accounts.

OBJECTIVE 1 – CREATE SUBSIDIARY LEDGER ACCOUNTS FOR VENDORS AND ENTER THE BEGINNING BALANCES

In chapters 2 and 3, you learned how to set up general ledger accounts and enter the beginning balances. The procedure for establishing vendor accounts in the accounts payable ledger is very similar. In this chapter, you will use Peachtree to handle the accounts payable of the Woodward Construction Company.

Woodward is a small service business that operates on the accrual basis. In chapter 4, you established customer accounts for this firm and recorded its credit sales.

THE INFORMATION NEEDED TO CREATE THE VENDOR ACCOUNTS

In Peachtree, certain information is needed to create an account for each vendor in the accounts payable subsidiary ledger. This information, which is entered in the Maintain Vendors window (see figure 5–1), is outlined below.

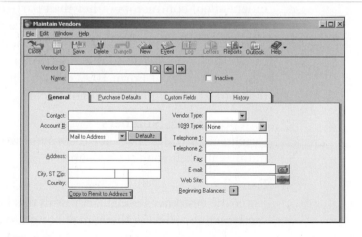

FIGURE 5-1

Maintain Vendors Blank Window with General Folder Tab Selected

- **Vendor ID**
  Peachtree requires an alphanumeric identifier for each vendor's account. The right and left arrow keys move through each Vendor ID. For example, Woodward Construction Company uses EMP-01 as the identifier for the first account in its accounts payable subsidiary ledger. This account is for EMP Management.

- **Name**
  The name given to a vendor's account may be the name of a business, such as EMP Management, or the name of an individual.

- **Inactive**
  Sometimes a company stops doing business with a vendor. A check mark is entered in the Inactive box to indicate this type of vendor. Peachtree automatically removes the accounts of inactive vendors when the fiscal year is closed.

General Tab

- **Contact**
  The contact is the person whom the business calls or writes in connection with questions about orders.

- **Account #**
  The account number is the numeric identifier the vendor has issued to the company.

- **Address**
  The address entered in the account is the one where the vendor receives checks and correspondence.

- **Vendor Type**
  Peachtree allows you to classify vendors by type. For example, many companies have vendors that provide services and vendors that provide goods. Woodward uses Expense as the type for vendors that provide services and Supplier as the type for vendors that provide goods and supplies.

- **1099 Type**
  It is necessary to issue Form 1099, a government form, to certain types of vendors. For example, some vendors are individuals who provide their services on a project-by-project basis. These individuals are considered independent contractors rather than part-time employees. By January 31 of each year, the Internal Revenue Service requires that a company issue a Form 1099 to each independent contractor for tax reasons. This form shows the amount paid to the independent contractor during the previous year. A copy of Form 1099 goes to the IRS. (If the company pays less than $650 to an independent contractor, it need not issue a Form 1099.)

- **Telephone/Fax Numbers**
  Peachtree provides space for recording two telephone numbers and a fax number in each vendor's account.

- **E-mail**
  Enter the customer's e-mail address in this field for correspondence. E-mail can be sent by clicking the E-mail button to the right of the *E-mail* field.

- **Web Address**
  Enter the customer's Web site address in this field. The customer's Web site can be displayed by clicking the Internet button to the right of the *Web Site* field.

- **Beginning Balances**
  When a business creates accounts for its vendors, there may be some outstanding (unpaid) invoices. Information about these invoices is needed to enter the beginning balances in the accounts.

- **Purchase Rep**
  The Purchase Rep is used to select the vendor's representative, if there is one.

- **Expense Acct**
  The Expense Account is the account in the general ledger that is debited when a purchase is made from a particular vendor. As noted previously, a purchase of a service such as electricity is debited to an expense account. A purchase of an asset such as office supplies is debited to an asset account. A purchase of goods for resale is debited to a cost account called Purchases or debited directly to an Inventory account. The number of the appropriate general ledger account is entered in each vendor's account.

- **Tax ID #**
  The tax identification number is the number of the resale certificate (the sales tax exemption certificate) that the vendor may have. This number is entered in the vendor's account. It is also the number used to identify a vendor on a Form 1099.

- **Ship Via**
  The vendor may have a preferred method of shipping. The method chosen should be entered in the vendor's account.

- **Terms**
  Each vendor specifies certain credit terms. For example, one vendor might offer terms of 2% 10 days, net 30 days. Another vendor might offer terms of net EOM, which means that the full amount of a bill is due at the end of the month in which the bill is issued. The terms are entered in the vendor's account. (Standard vendor terms can be established as a default when a company is set up in Peachtree. These terms can be changed as necessary for individual vendors.)

- **Form Delivery Options**
  The Form Delivery Option allows the user to deliver paper or e-mail forms. E-mail can be carbon copied (CC) to the purchase rep.

Custom Fields
- **Office Manager**
  In some cases, a business will want to enter the name of the vendor's office manager as a second contact person.

- **Account Rep**
  Some vendors assign a sales representative to each of their customers. The name of the sales representative is entered in the vendor's account.

- **Special Note**
  Any additional information about the vendor that is needed can be entered in the *Special Note* field.

History
- **Vendor Since**
  Some businesses enter the date of the first order issued to the vendor in the vendor's account.

- **Last Invoice Date**
  Some businesses enter the date of the last invoice received from the vendor.

- **Last Invoice Amt**
  Some businesses enter the amount of the last invoice received from the vendor.

- **Last Payment Date**
  Some businesses enter the date of the last payment made to the vendor.

- **Last Payment Amt**
  Some businesses enter the amount of the last payment made to the vendor.

- **Period History, Purchases, Payments Grid**
  This section gives the user running totals of purchases and payments.

CREATING SUBSIDIARY LEDGER ACCOUNTS FOR THE VENDORS OF A SAMPLE BUSINESS
In this section, you will create subsidiary ledger accounts for four vendors of the Woodward Construction Company. Start Peachtree and then open Woodward Construction Company. Then follow the steps outlined below to create a subsidiary ledger account for EMP Management.

Step 1:
Click Maintain, and then click Vendors.

Step 2:
Click the General folder tab in the Maintain Vendors window. Set up the account information for EMP Management, the first vendor of the Woodward Construction Company, by taking the following steps:

Step 3:
Key **EMP-01** in the *Vendor ID* field.

Step 4:
Click the OK button at the bottom of the Vendor ID drop-down list, as shown in figure 5–2.

FIGURE 5-2
Vendor ID Drop-Down List with EMP-01 Entered

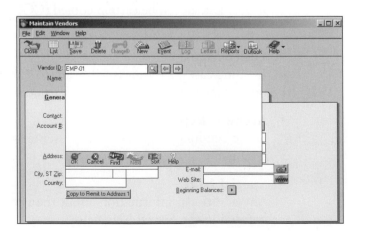

Step 5:

Key **EMP Management** in the *Name* field.

Step 6:

If there is a check mark in the Inactive box, remove it because EMP Management is an active vendor.

Step 7:

Key **Ann Elma** in the *Contact* field.

Step 8:

Key **2778** in the *Account #* field.

Step 9:

Key **1320 Washington Street** in the *Address* field.

Step 10:

Key **Watsonville, CA 95760** in the *City, ST Zip* field and **USA** in the *Country* field. (You can click the arrow key to select the state.)

Step 11:

Key **Expense** in the *Vendor Type* field.

Step 12:

At the 1099 Type drop-down list, click *None*, as shown in figure 5–3.

FIGURE 5-3

1099 Type Drop-Down List with None Selected

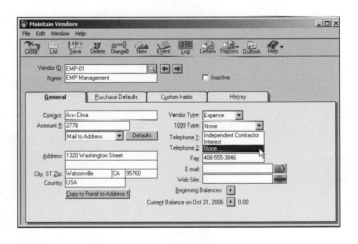

Step 13:

Key **408-555-2456** in the *Telephone 1* field.

Step 14:

Key **408-555-7890** in the *Telephone 2* field.

Step 15:

Key **408-555-3846** in the *Fax* field.

Step 16:
Compare your completed window with figure 5–4. Make any necessary corrections by selecting the erroneous items and reentering the information.

FIGURE 5-4

Completed General Tab Window with EMP Entries

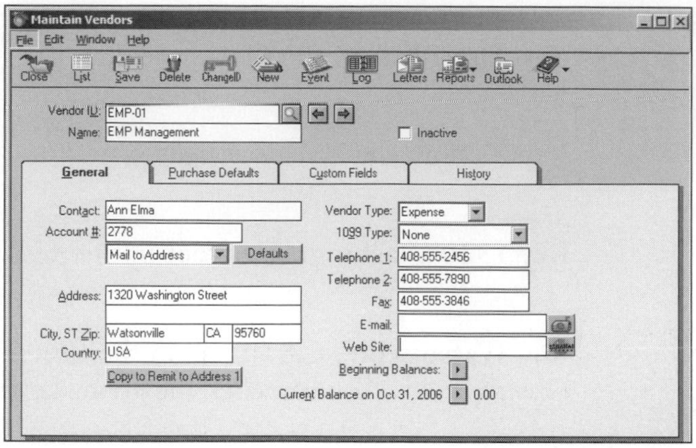

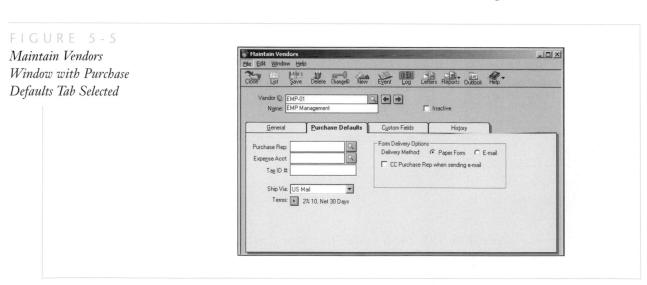

Purchase Defaults Tab
The purchase defaults must be established whenever a vendor's account is created.

Step 1:
Click the Purchase Defaults folder tab, as shown in figure 5–5.

FIGURE 5-5

Maintain Vendors Window with Purchase Defaults Tab Selected

Step 2:

Click the *magnifying glass* icon next to the *Expense Acct* field and then click *Account 500, Rent Expense*.

Step 3:

Leave the *Tax ID #* field blank.

Step 4:

At the Ship Via drop-down list, click *US Mail.*

Step 5:

Select *Paper Form* from the Form Delivery Options box.

Step 6:

Click the right arrow key next to *Terms* to reveal the Vendor Terms dialog box (figure 5–6).

As noted previously, credit terms may vary from vendor to vendor. In addition, each vendor may set a credit limit. The Vendor Terms dialog box is used to change the credit terms and credit limit whenever necessary.

Step 7:

Click the box next to Use Standard Terms to remove the check mark.

Step 8:

Click Due at end of month. These are the credit terms offered by EMP Management.

Step 9:

Key **0.00** in the *Discount %* field. Generally, only vendors of supplies or other goods allow a discount.

Step 10:

Compare your entry with the completed Vendor Terms dialog box shown in figure 5–7.

Step 11:

Click OK to accept the changes in the vendor terms.

Step 12:

Compare your work with figure 5–8. Make any necessary changes.

FIGURE 5-6

Vendor Terms Dialog Box

FIGURE 5-7

Completed Vendor Terms Dialog Box for EMP Management

FIGURE 5-8

*Completed Purchase
Defaults Window for
EMP Management*

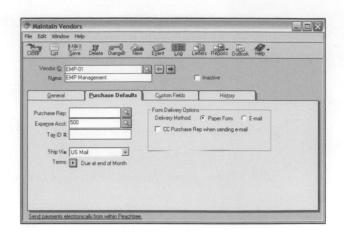

Step 13:

Click the Save button at the top of the Maintain Vendors window.

Beginning Balances

Step 1:

Click the General folder tab in the Maintain Vendors window.

Step 2:

Click the right arrow key next to Beginning Balances.

Step 3:

Click the Purchases from: EMP-01 EMP Management folder tab. Then key **Beginning Balance** in the *Invoice Number* field.

Step 4:

Key **01/01/07** in the *Date* field.

Step 5:

Key **900.00** in the *Amount* field.

Step 6:

Click *Accounts Payable (200)* from the A/P Account drop-down list, as shown in figure 5–9.

FIGURE 5-9

*Accounts Payable Selected
from the A/P Account
Drop-Down List*

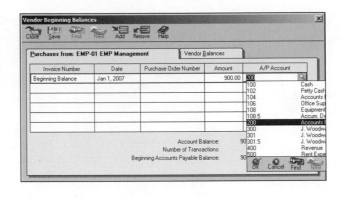

Step 7:

Compare your entries with those in figure 5–10.

FIGURE 5-10

*Completed Entries in
Vendor Beginning
Balances Window*

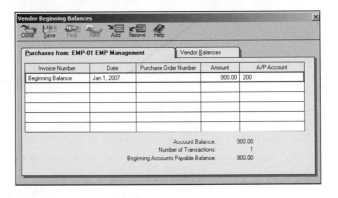

Step 8:

Click the Save button, and then click the Close button.

Step 9:

Click the History folder tab to view the current balance for the selected vendors, as shown in figure 5–11.

FIGURE 5-11

History Window

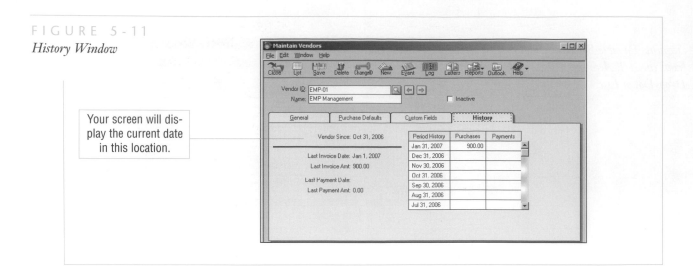

Your screen will display the current date in this location.

Create the following three vendor accounts for the Woodward Construction Company using the information given below and enter their beginning balances. Use the steps that you followed for the account of EMP Management. When you complete your work, close the Maintain Vendors window.

Vendor ID:	**MID-02**
Name:	**MID Modesto Electric**

General Tab

Contact:		**Harvey Bliss**
Account #:		**3548**
	Address:	**2356 Orangethorpe Street**
	City, ST Zip:	**Fresno, CA 95506**
	Country:	**USA**
Vendor Type:		**Expense**
1099 Type:		**None**
Telephone 1:		**209-555-6675**
Telephone 2:		**209-555-3657**
Fax:		**209-555-9008**

Purchase Defaults Tab

Expense Acct:	**502** (Utilities Expense)
Tax ID #:	
Ship Via:	**US Mail**
Terms:	**Net 30 Days (Use Standard Terms)**
Form Delivery Options:	**Default**
Beginning Balances:	**450.00**

Vendor ID:	**OFFMAX-03**
Name:	**Office Max**

General Tab

Contact:	**Bill Baker**

Account #:		27781
	Address:	2532 Oakdale Road
	City, ST Zip:	Fresno, CA 95306
	Country:	USA
Vendor Type:		Supplier
1099 Type:		None
Telephone 1:		209-555-1978
Telephone 2:		209-555-6556
Fax:		209-555-2334

Purchase Defaults Tab

Expense Acct:	106 (Office Supplies)
Tax ID #:	
Ship Via:	Fed-EX
Terms:	2% 10 days, net 30 days
Form Delivery Options:	Default
Beginning Balances:	450.00

Vendor ID:	PACBELL-04
Name:	Pacific Bell

General Tab

Contact:		Customer Service
Account #:		2379584
	Address:	3234 Airport Road
	City, ST Zip:	Watsonville, CA 95670
	Country:	USA
Vendor Type:		Expense
1099 Type:		None
Telephone 1:		209-555-2556
Telephone 2:		209-555-5226
Fax:		209-555-9998

Purchase Defaults Tab

Expense Acct:	504 (Telephone Expense)
Tax ID #:	
Ship Via:	US Mail
Terms:	Net 30 Days (Use Standard Terms)
Form Delivery Options:	Default
Beginning Balances:	500.00

Check POINT

1. What is the purpose of the vendor accounts in the accounts payable subsidiary ledger?
2. Why is the Accounts Payable account in the general ledger known as a controlling account?

Answers

1. *The accounts in the accounts payable subsidiary ledger provide detailed information about transactions with vendors and show the current balances owed to the vendors.*
2. *The Accounts Payable account is a link between the general ledger and the subsidiary ledger because its balance is equal to the total of the balances in the subsidiary ledger.*

PRACTICE *objective*

1

Create subsidiary ledger accounts for the vendors of the Bullfrog Maintenance Company. You established the chart of accounts for this business in chapter 2 and set up its customer accounts in chapter 4.

Step 1:

Open Bullfrog Maintenance Company.

Step 2:

Create the vendor accounts, and enter the beginning balances.

Vendor ID:	**ALTA-01**
Name:	**Alta Vista Business Park**

General Tab

Contact:	**Alicia Marquez**
Account #:	**398455**
Address:	**1325 Smith Road**
City, ST Zip:	**Lodi, CA 95355**
Country:	**USA**
Vendor Type:	**Expense**
1099 Type:	**None**
Telephone 1:	**209-555-4256**
Telephone 2:	**209-555-8790**
Fax:	**209-555-8346**

Purchase Defaults Tab

Expense Acct:	**500** (Rent Expense)
Tax ID #:	
Ship Via:	**US Mail**
Terms:	**Net 30 Days**
Form Delivery Options:	**Default**
Beginning Balances:	**0**

Vendor ID:	**PGE-02**
Name:	**Pacific Gas & Electric**

General Tab

Contact:	**George House**
Account #:	**345566**
Address:	**3423 Mission Street**
City, ST Zip:	**Fremont, CA 95006**
Country:	**USA**
Vendor Type:	**Expense**
1099 Type:	**None**
Telephone 1:	**209-555-9905**
Telephone 2:	**209-555-6537**
Fax:	**209-555-0008**

Purchase Defaults Tab

Expense Acct:	**502** (Utilities Expense)
Tax ID #:	
Ship Via:	**US Mail**

Terms:	Net 30 Days
Form Delivery Options:	Default
Beginning Balances:	0

| Vendor ID: | OFFDEP-03 |
| Name: | Office Depot |

General Tab

Contact:	Jim Nielson
Account #:	346557
Address:	125 Oak Road
City, ST Zip:	Fresno, CA 95306
Country:	USA
Vendor Type:	Supplier
1099 Type:	None
Telephone 1:	209-555-9178
Telephone 2:	209-555-5656
Fax:	209-555-3234

Purchase Defaults Tab

Expense Acct:	108 (Office Supplies)
Tax ID #:	
Ship Via:	Fed-EX
Terms:	2% 10 days, net 30 Days
Form Delivery Options:	Default
Beginning Balances:	0

| Vendor ID: | GTE-04 |
| Name: | General Telephone |

General Tab

Contact:	Customer Service
Account #:	3913458
Address:	32133 Tuolumne Road
City, ST Zip:	Modesto, CA 95670
Country:	USA
Vendor Type:	Expense
1099 Type:	None
Telephone 1:	209-555-2545
Telephone 2:	209-555-5245
Fax:	209-555-9945

Purchase Defaults Tab

Expense Acct:	502 (Utilities Expense)
Tax ID #:	
Ship Via:	US Mail
Terms:	Net 30 Days
Form Delivery Options:	Default
Beginning Balances:	0

Step 3:

Close the Maintain Vendors window.

OBJECTIVE 2 — PROCESS ACCOUNTS PAYABLE AND PURCHASE TRANSACTIONS

Once the vendor accounts have been established, Peachtree can be used to record purchases on credit and post them automatically to the accounts payable subsidiary ledger. Remember that each purchase is credited to Accounts Payable. The account debited may be an asset account, an expense account, or a cost account, depending on the nature of the purchase. When the bill for a purchase becomes due, the payment is debited to Accounts Payable and credited to Cash.

If there is an accounts payable ledger, each purchase requires a credit to both the Accounts Payable controlling account in the general ledger and the vendor's account in the subsidiary ledger. Similarly, each payment to a vendor requires a debit to both the Accounts Payable controlling account in the general ledger and the vendor's account in the subsidiary ledger.

It is possible to record purchases of goods and services on credit in the general journal. However, the general journal function of Peachtree does not permit the automatic posting of entries to the vendor accounts. Therefore, in this chapter, you will use the purchases function of Peachtree to record purchases of goods and services. This function, which is called Purchases/Receive Inventory, allows automatic posting to both the general ledger and the accounts payable subsidiary ledger.

RECORDING PURCHASES ON CREDIT

During January 2007, the Woodward Construction Company conducted three transactions that involved the purchase of services and one transaction that involved the purchase of supplies.

- On January 3, 2007, Woodward received a bill (Invoice 2621) from EMP Management for its monthly rent of $1,200. The bill is payable at the end of the month.

The accountant's analysis of this transaction reveals that an expense (Rent Expense) has increased by $1,200 and a liability (Accounts Payable) has increased by $1,200. The account for EMP Management has also increased by $1,200. The accountant records this transaction by debiting Rent Expense for $1,200 and crediting Accounts Payable for $1,200.

When you post this transaction, you must post the credit part of the entry to both the Accounts Payable controlling account in the general ledger and the vendor's account in the accounts payable subsidiary ledger.

Use the steps outlined below to record this purchase on credit made by the Woodward Construction Company during January 2007.

Step 1:

Open Woodward Construction Company and close the Alert Status window, if open.

Step 2:

Click Tasks, and then click Purchases/Receive Inventory.
The Purchases/Receive Inventory window will appear, as shown in figure 5–12. Enter the data for the purchase on credit that occurred on January 3, 2007.

FIGURE 5-12

*Blank Purchases/Receive
Inventory Window*

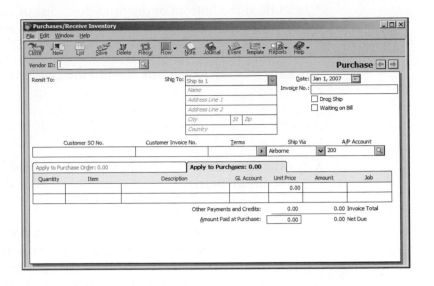

Step 3:

Click the *magnifying glass* icon next to the *Vendor ID* field.

Step 4:

Click *EMP-01* from the drop-down list of vendors, as shown in figure 5–13.

FIGURE 5-13

*Drop-Down List of
Vendors with EMP-01
Selected*

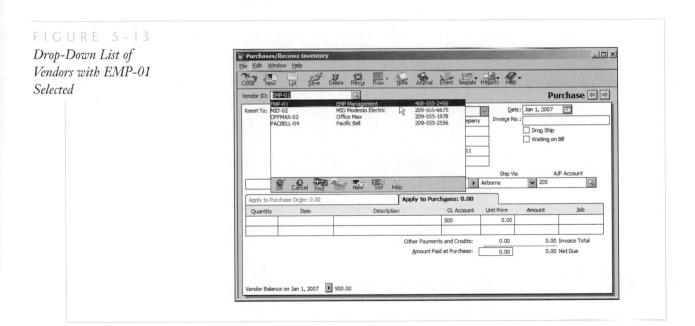

Step 5:

Click OK at the bottom of the drop-down list of vendors to accept EMP-01. Peachtree enters the name and address automatically.

Step 6:

Click the *calendar* icon to the right of the *Date* field and select *Jan 3, 2007*.

Step 7:

Key **2621** in the *Invoice No.* field.

Step 8:

Click the down arrow key below the *Ship Via* field and then click *US Mail* if it is not already selected.

FIGURE 5-14

Terms Information Dialog Box

Step 9:

The credit terms are selected when the vendor accounts are originally created. To view the terms for EMP Management, click the right arrow key in the *Terms* field. You will then see the Terms Information dialog box, as shown in figure 5–14. Click OK after viewing the terms.

Step 10:

Key **Monthly Rent** in the *Description* field.

Step 11:

Click *500 (Rent Expense)* from the drop-down list of general ledger accounts. The GL Account information should already be completed. This information was set up when the vendor account was created.

Step 12:

Key **1,200.00** in the *Amount* field.

Step 13:

Review the completed Purchases/Receive Inventory window for EMP Management, EMP as shown in figure 5–15.

FIGURE 5-15

Completed Purchases/Receive Inventory Window for EMP Management

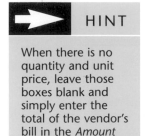

HINT

When there is no quantity and unit price, leave those boxes blank and simply enter the total of the vendor's bill in the *Amount* field.

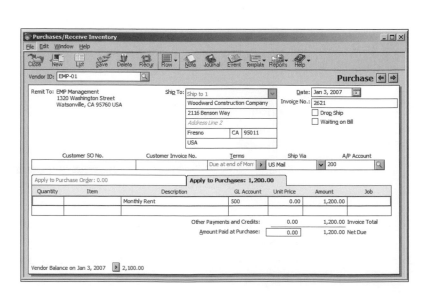

Click the Save button to save the entry of the purchase on credit.

Repeat steps 3–14 to enter the following three purchases that the Woodward Construction Company had during January 2007.

- On January 12, 2007, Woodward received a bill (Invoice 84763) of $456.75 from MID Modesto Electric for its monthly usage of electricity. The bill is payable net 30 days.

The accountant's analysis of this transaction reveals that an expense (Utilities Expense) has increased by $456.75 and a liability (Accounts Payable) has increased by $456.75. The account for MID Modesto Electric has also increased by $456.75. The accountant records this transaction by debiting Utilities Expense for $456.75 and crediting Accounts Payable for $456.75.

- On January 22, 2007, Woodward received a bill (Invoice 912867) of $565.89 from Pacific Bell for its monthly usage of telephone service. The bill is payable net 30 days.

The accountant's analysis of this transaction reveals that an expense (Telephone Expense) has increased by $565.89 and a liability (Accounts Payable) has increased by $565.89. The account for Pacific Bell has also increased by $565.89. The accountant records this transaction by debiting Telephone Expense for $565.89 and crediting Accounts Payable for $565.89.

- On January 29, 2007, Woodward received a bill (Invoice 3556) from Office Max for $1,400 of office supplies. The bill has terms of 2% 10 days, net 30 days.

The accountant's analysis of this transaction reveals that an asset (Office Supplies) has increased by $1,400 and a liability (Accounts Payable) has increased by $1,400. The account for Office Max has also increased by $1,400. The accountant records this transaction by debiting Office Supplies for $1,400 and crediting Accounts Payable for $1,400.

EDITING ACCOUNTS PAYABLE TRANSACTIONS

Accounts payable transactions can be edited as necessary after they are entered. Follow the steps outlined below to edit a particular transaction.

Click List from the toolbar at the top of the Purchases/Receive Inventory window.

At the Data Range drop-down list, click *This Period*. (It should be the default.)

Select the entry for EMP Management as shown in figure 5–16. (Notice that its window contains a Status section, which shows that the four bills recorded in January are unpaid.) Click Open from the top of the Purchase List toolbar.

FIGURE 5-16
*Select Purchase (Edit)
Window with EMP
Management Chosen*

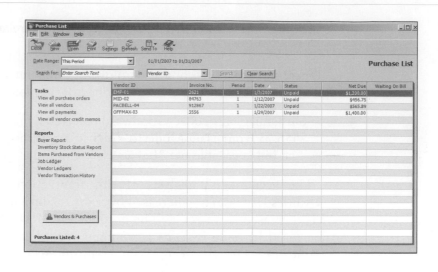

Step 4:

The entry appears in the Purchases/Receive Inventory window and can be edited if necessary. For example, if there is an error in the date, invoice number, or amount, you can change it now. When your work is complete, click Save. Then close the Purchases/Receive Inventory window.

Step 5:

Close the Purchase List window.

PRINTING THE VENDOR LEDGERS REPORT

Peachtree produces a wide variety of accounts payable reports. All of these reports will be covered to some extent throughout this text. The *Vendor Ledgers* report is probably the most important of the accounts payable reports. This report shows all transactions with the vendors and the balances owed to them. Use the following steps to view and print the *Vendor Ledgers* report.

Step 1:

Click Reports, and then click Accounts Payable.

Step 2:

At the Select a Report dialog box, in the Report List section, click *Vendor Ledgers*, as shown in figure 5–17.

FIGURE 5-17
*Accounts Payable Report
List with Vendor
Ledgers Selected*

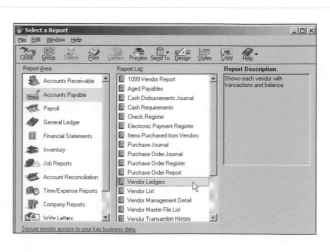

Step 3:

Click the Preview button so that you can view the *Vendor Ledgers* report.

Step 4:

At the Vendor Ledgers window, in the *Date* field, click *This Period*, and then click OK (figure 5–18).

FIGURE 5-18

Vendor Ledgers Filter Window

HINT

If you double-click *Vendor Ledgers* on any report list, the filter will be bypassed and the report will be displayed or printed without viewing the filter option.

Step 5:

Examine the *Vendor Ledgers* report, as shown in figure 5–19. Use the scroll bar to make sure that the four purchases recorded in January appear in the report. (The abbreviation *PJ* in the report stands for purchases journal.)

FIGURE 5-19

Vendor Ledgers Report

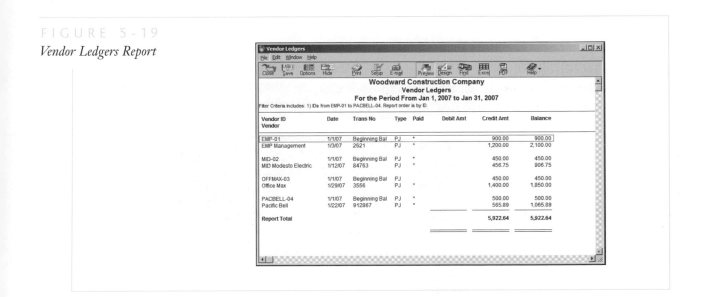

1. What is the purpose of the *Vendor Ledgers* report?
2. What function of Peachtree is used to record purchases on credit?

Answers
1. *The Vendor Ledgers report lists all transactions with vendors and the balances owed to them.*
2. *The Purchases/ Receive Inventory function of Peachtree is used to record purchases on credit.*

Step 6:

Click <u>P</u>rint to print a copy of the *Vendor Ledgers* report.

PRACTICE *objective* 2

You previously created vendor accounts for the Bullfrog Maintenance Company. Now you will record purchases on credit for this firm.

Step 1:

Open Bullfrog Maintenance Company.

Step 2:

Record the following transactions:
- On January 2, 2007, Bullfrog Maintenance Company received a bill (Invoice 012301) from Alta Vista Business Park for its monthly rent of $1,200.
- On January 10, 2007, Bullfrog Maintenance Company received a bill (Invoice 98345) of $345.89 from Pacific Gas & Electric for its monthly usage of electricity.
- On January 18, 2007, Bullfrog Maintenance Company received a bill (Invoice 55665) from Office Depot for $890 of office supplies.
- On January 27, 2007, Bullfrog Maintenance Company received a bill (Invoice 645935) of $265.98 from General Telephone for its monthly usage of telephone service.

Step 3:

Print the *Vendor Ledgers* report. Check the accuracy of your work by comparing your report to the report shown in figure 5–20.

Step 4:

Close the Select a Report dialog box.

FIGURE 5-20

Vendor Ledgers Report for Bullfrog Maintenance Company

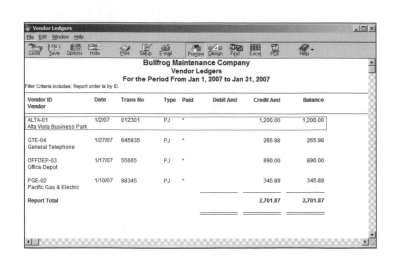

Having reliable, up-to-date information is essential to controlling a firm's accounts payable. Management must closely monitor whether payments are being made when bills become due and whether discounts are being taken.

Every business should strive to maintain a good credit reputation by paying its bills on time. Obtaining credit from new vendors and obtaining loans from banks depends in part on a firm's credit reputation. Credit rating agencies gather detailed information about the credit history of businesses and make this information available to their clients.

Businesses should also be careful to take advantage of any discounts offered by vendors. Although a 2% discount may not sound very meaningful, over a period of a year, a firm can save thousands of dollars by taking advantage of discounts on its purchases.

Peachtree provides many reports that help management to monitor a firm's accounts payable. It also provides action items and event logs to assist management in remembering and tracking telephone calls, meetings, and correspondence that are necessary in connection with vendor accounts. Take the following steps to access the Action Items/Event Log function of Peachtree.

Step 1:

Open Woodward Construction Company.

Step 2:

Select Tasks from the Main Menu and click on Action Items from the drop-down list.

Step 3:

Click Options. The Action Items and Event Log Options window will appear, as shown in figure 5–21.

FIGURE 5-21

Action Items and Event Log Options Window with Activities Tab Selected

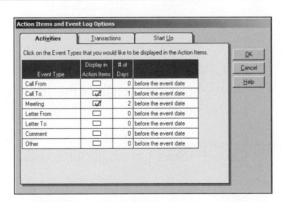

USING THE TRANSACTIONS TAB

Events can be set up as defaults so that they can later be displayed as action items. For example, the managers of the Woodward Construction Company want vendors to be paid five days ahead of the invoice due date. Use the following steps to establish the necessary default.

Step 1:

Click the Transactions tab in the Action Items and Event Log Options window.

Step 2:

Scroll down and click *Checks to Vendors* in the *Event Type* field.

Step 3:

Key **5** in the *# of Days* field, and then press Enter.

Step 4:

You will now be in the field to the right of the *# of Days* field. Click the down arrow key and then click *before the event date* if necessary.

Step 5:

Compare your entries with figure 5–22.

FIGURE 5-22

Transactions Tab
Selected from Action
Items and Event Log
Options Window

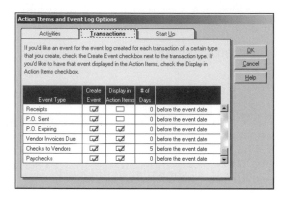

USING THE START UP TAB

In Peachtree, you can have the action items displayed whenever a new company is opened, or you can have the tips displayed on top of the screen.

Step 1:

Click the Start Up tab in the Action Items and Event Log Options window.

Step 2:

Place a check mark next to "Display Action Items each time a new company is opened" if it is not already checked.

Step 3:

Click OK to accept all the defaults that you established.

Since the process of setting up the defaults is complete, you can now create and access the events that are action items.

RECORDING ACTION ITEMS ON THE TO DO LIST

The Woodward Construction Company wants to include the following events as action items on its to do list.

- On January 19, meet with Bill Cohen at 9:00 a.m.
- On January 23, call Empire Building Supplies to set up an account.
- On January 24, have a lunch meeting at 12:30 p.m. with Jim Downs about a new job.

Use the following steps to establish these events as action items.

Step 1:

Click Ta**s**ks, and then click **A**ction Items.

Step 2:

Click the To **D**o folder tab in the Action Items window.

Step 3:

Key **01/19/07**, the date of the first event, in the first available empty *Date* field below the To **D**o tab.

Step 4:

In the *Notes* field, key **Meet with Bill Cohen at 9:00 a.m.**

Step 5:

Key **01/23/07**, the date of the second event, in the *Date* field below the To **D**o tab.

Step 6:

In the *Notes* field, key **Call Empire Building Supplies to set up an account**.

Step 7:

Key **01/24/07**, the date of the third event, in the *Date* field below the To **D**o tab.

Step 8:

In the *Notes* field, key **12:30 p.m. lunch meeting with Jim Downs about a new job**. Compare your completed to do list with figure 5–23.

FIGURE 5-23

Completed To Do List

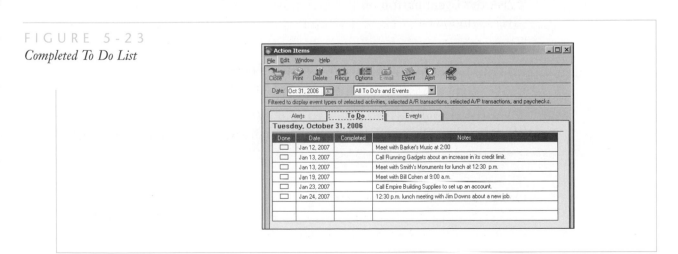

RECORDING EVENTS ON THE ACTION LIST

Some events have been programmed as default settings to appear as action items. For example, vendor invoices that are due for payment will be listed as action items five days prior to their due dates. The programming of this item was accomplished when the defaults were set up. However, a business might want to add other events to its action list.

Assume that the Woodward Construction Company wants to place the following additional event on its action list.

- Set up a meeting with EMP Management for January 18, 2007. Advise one day ahead of time.

Step 1:
Click the Events tab in the Actions Items window, as shown in figure 5–24.

FIGURE 5-24

Events Tab Selected from the Action Items Window

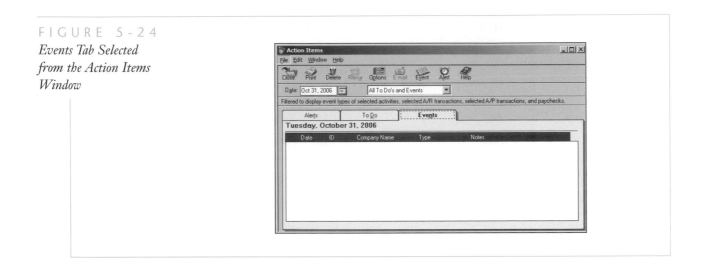

Step 2:
Click the Event button on the Action Items toolbar to view the Create Event window.

Step 3:
At the Type drop-down list, click *Vendor*, if necessary.

Step 4:
Click the *magnifying glass* icon next to the *ID* field and click *EMP-01* from the drop-down list, as shown in figure 5–25.

FIGURE 5-25
*ID Drop-Down List
with EMP-01 Selected*

Step 5:

Click the *calendar* icon and select *Jan 18, 2007* in the *Date* field.

Step 6:

At the Event Type section, click Meeting.

Step 7:

Key **Set up meeting** in the *Note* field.

Step 8:

Place a check mark next to "Display in Action Items."

Step 9:

Key **2** as the number of days. Then click the down arrow key and click *Before* if necessary.

Step 10:

Compare your work with the completed Create Event dialog box in figure 5-26.

FIGURE 5-26
Completed Create Event Window

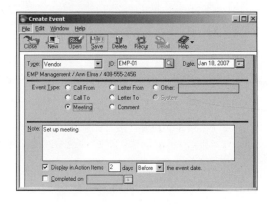

Step 11:

Click the Save button.

Step 12:

Enter the following two events that the Woodward Construction Company wants to add to its action list by repeating steps 3–11. Then close the Create Event window.

- Call Bill Cohen from MID 2 days before the January 19, 2007, meeting to discuss a new rate plan. Advise two days ahead of time.
- Send a letter on January 21, 2007, to notify Office Max about the return of a computer. Advise four days ahead of time.

DISPLAYING THE EVENTS

Each of the events placed on the action list is scheduled to appear according to the number of days set before the event. For example, the first two events for the Woodward Construction Company—the meeting with EMP Management on January 18 and the call to Jeff Gustafson on January 19—will appear as action items on January 17, one and two days, respectively, before the dates of the events. Follow the steps outlined below to check the events listed for any date. In this case, the date to be checked is January 17, 2007.

Step 1:

Click the Events tab in the Action Items window.

Step 2:

Key **01/17/07** in the *Date* field as shown in figure 5–27.

FIGURE 5-27

Date Field with
01/17/07 Entered

Step 3:
Press Enter.

The events that are scheduled will appear in the Action Items window when Peachtree is started on January 17, 2007. However, they can be viewed at any time if you do the following:

- Click Tasks, and then click Action Items.
- Click the Events folder tab.
- Enter the desired date.

Compare the action items for the date January 17, 2007, with the ones shown in figure 5–28.

FIGURE 5-28

Action Items Listed for January 17, 2007

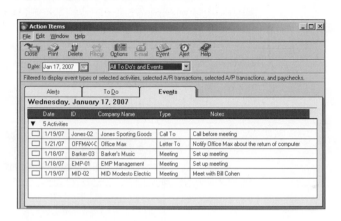

SETTING ALERTS

The Action Items window includes an Alerts tab. This tab allows you to select certain conditions for notification. For example, an alert can be set to notify you when a particular vendor's balance is too high. Assume that the Woodward Construction Company wants to be notified when the balance owed to Office Max reaches $1,850. Follow the steps outlined below to set the alert.

Step 1:

Click the Alerts folder tab in the Action Items window.

Step 2:

Click the Alert button on the Action Items toolbar as shown in figure 5–29.

FIGURE 5-29

*Alert Button on the
Action Items Toolbar*

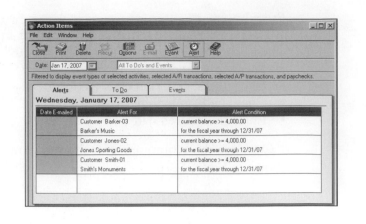

The Set Company Alerts window will appear, as shown in figure 5–30.

FIGURE 5-30

*Set Company Alerts
Window*

Setting an alert requires entry of the following information:
- Apply to (the subject of the alert such as a vendor or customer)
- From (the identifier of the first subject)
- To (the identifier of the last subject)
- Type
- Condition
- Amount

Step 3:

In the first empty box in the *Apply To* field, click the down arrow key and then click *Vendor* from the Apply To drop-down list, as shown in figure 5–31.

FIGURE 5-31

*Drop-Down List in
Apply To Field with
Vendor Selected*

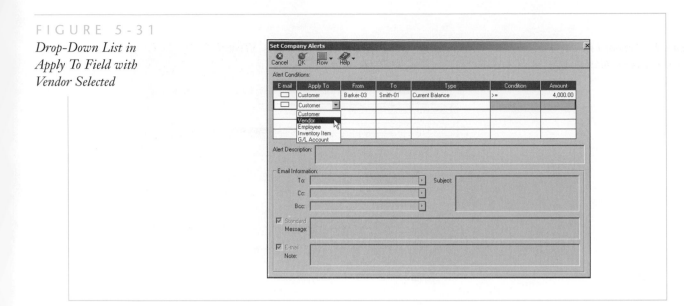

Step 4:

At the From drop-down list, select *OFFMAX-03* and then click OK. (See figure 5–32.)

FIGURE 5-32

*From Drop-Down List
with OFFMAX-03
Selected*

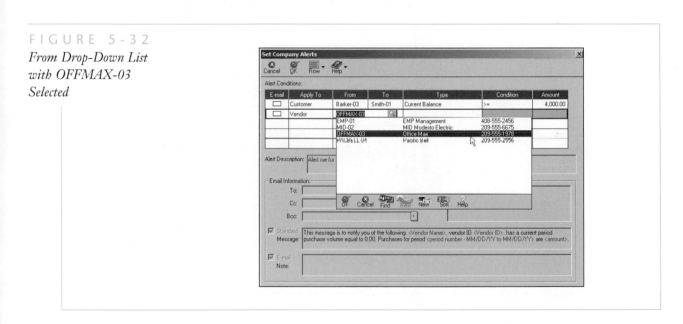

Step 5:

At the To drop-down list, select *OFFMAX-03* and then click OK.

Step 6:

At the Type drop-down list, click *Current Balance*, as shown in figure 5–33.

FIGURE 5-33

*Type Drop-Down List
with Current Balance
Selected*

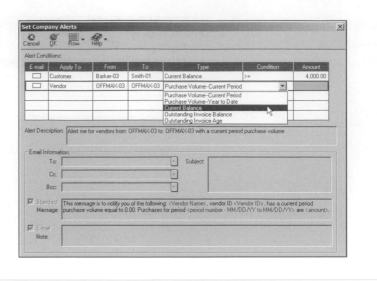

Step 7:

At the Condition drop-down list, click >=, as shown in figure 5–34.

FIGURE 5-34

*Condition Drop-Down
List with >= Selected*

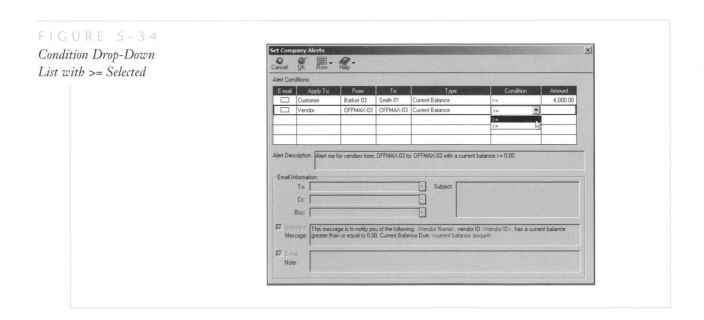

Step 8:

Key **1,850.00** in the *Amount* field. Compare your work with the completed window shown in figure 5–35.

Note: Select the Row icon on the Menu bar and select either Add or Remove to add or remove a line entry.

FIGURE 5-35

Completed Set Company
Alerts Window

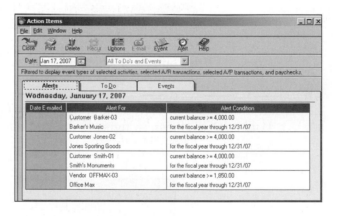

FIGURE 5-36

Alerts Folder Tab with
Alert for Vendor's Balance

Step 9:

Click <u>O</u>K to save the alert. The alert that was set up for the balance of Office Max will now appear in the Aler<u>t</u>s folder tab, as shown in figure 5–36.

Step 10:

Close the Action Items window.

PRINTING ACCOUNTS PAYABLE REPORTS

Peachtree can produce the following accounts payable reports and many others.

- *Vendor List*
- *Vendor Master File List*
- *Vendor Ledgers*
- *Purchase Order Register*

- *Purchase Journal*
- *Aged Payables*
- *1099 Forms*

Assume that the management of Woodward Construction Company wants to print two of these reports: the *Vendor List* and the *Vendor Ledgers*.

Step 1:
Click Reports, and then click Accounts Payable.

Step 2:
The Select a Report dialog box will appear. At the Report List section, click *Vendor List*, as shown in figure 5–37.

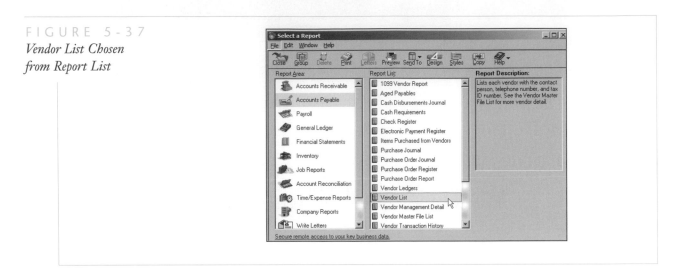

Step 3:
Click the Print button on the Select a Report toolbar.

Step 4:
At the Vendor List window, in the Report Order drop-down list, click *Vendor ID*, as shown in figure 5–38, and then click OK.

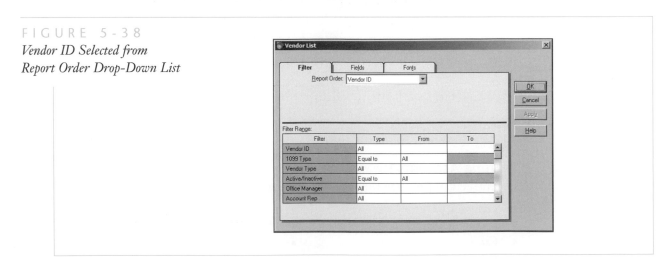

Step 5:

Complete the Print window, and then click OK to print. Compare your *Vendor List* report with the one shown in figure 5–39.

Vendor List Report for Woodward Construction Company

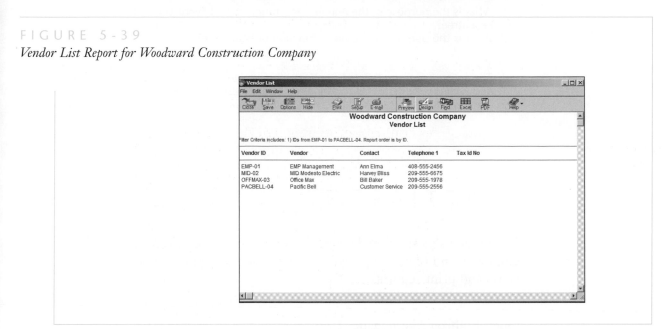

Step 6:

Repeat steps 1–5 to print a copy of the *Vendor Ledgers* report. In step 2, click *Vendor Ledgers* from the Report List area and *This Period* from the Print Filter window. Compare your printed report with the one shown in figure 5–40.

*Vendor Ledgers Report
for Woodward
Construction Company*

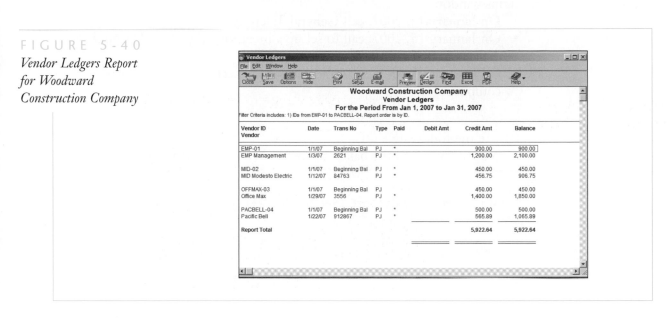

Step 7:

Close the Select a Report dialog box.

PRACTICE *objective* 3

You previously established vendor accounts for the Bullfrog Maintenance Company and recorded purchases. Now you will set up action items and alerts and print reports.

Step 1:

Open Bullfrog Maintenance Company.

Step 2:

Use the Action Items and Event Log Options dialog box and the Start Up tab to select "Display Action Items each time a new company is opened."

Step 3:

Record the following events as action items on the To Do list in the Action Items window.

- On January 14, 2007, call General Telephone about its new rate plan.
- On January 15, 2007, call to set up a meeting with Alicia Marquez of Alta Vista Business Park.
- On January 18, 2007, call Office Depot to check the price of a new computer.

Step 4:

Create the following alert.

- Notify you when the balance owed to Office Depot reaches $5,500.

Step 5:

Print the *Vendor List* report. (See figure 5–41.)

FIGURE 5-41

Vendor List Report for Bullfrog Maintenance Company

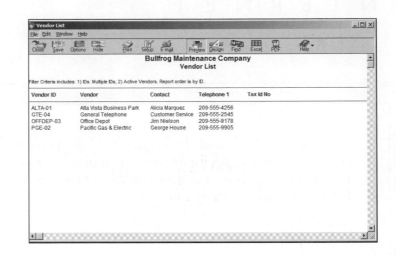

FIGURE 5-42

Vendor Ledgers Report for Bullfrog Maintenance Company

Step 6:

Print the *Vendor Ledgers* report. (See figure 5–42.)

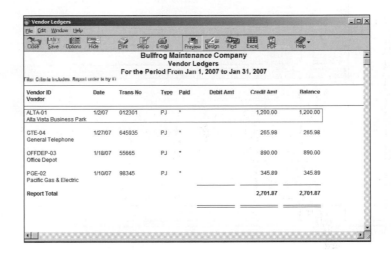

Step 7:

Close the Select a Report dialog box.

Many of the office supply businesses that have Web sites on the Internet allow you to make credit purchases. Two of the better known are Office Depot, which is located at www.officedepot.com, and Office Max, which is located at www.officemax.com.

FIGURE 5-43

Office Depot Home Page

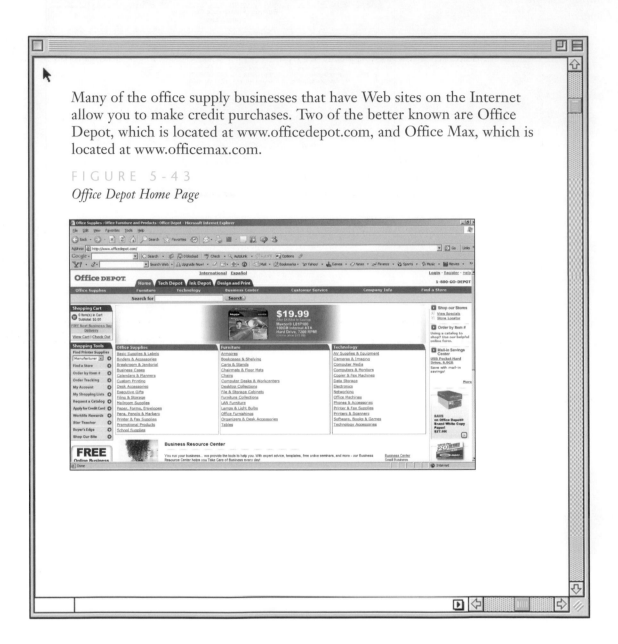

INTERNET *Access*

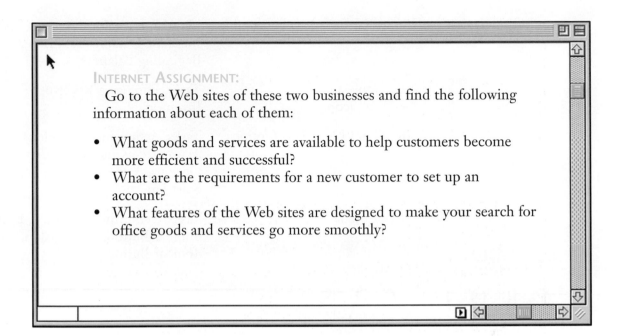

INTERNET ASSIGNMENT:

Go to the Web sites of these two businesses and find the following information about each of them:

- What goods and services are available to help customers become more efficient and successful?
- What are the requirements for a new customer to set up an account?
- What features of the Web sites are designed to make your search for office goods and services go more smoothly?

SOFTWARE
Command Summary

Create Subsidiary Vendor Account	Maintain, Vendors, General Tab, Purchase Defaults Tab, Enter Beginning Balances
Accounts Payable and Purchases Transactions	Tasks, Purchases/Receive Inventory
Action Items and Event Log Options	Tasks, Action Items, Options, Action Items and Event Log Options, Activities, Transactions, Start Up
Create Action Items	Tasks, Action Items, To Do, Event Toolbar Button, Alerts, Alert Toolbar Button

PROJECTS
and Problems

CONTENT CHECK

Multiple Choice: Choose only one response for each question.

1. Purchases made on credit are entered in the accounting records as
   A. accounts receivable.
   B. accounts payable.
   C. prepaid expense.
   D. unearned revenue.
   E. None of the above.

2. When a business purchases a service such as electricity on credit, the two types of accounts affected from the buyer's perspective are
   A. an asset account and an expense account.
   B. an asset account and a revenue account.
   C. a liability account and an expense account.
   D. a liability account and a revenue account.
   E. None of the above.

3. What function of Peachtree is used when a business buys goods or services on credit and must enter the transaction?
   A. Action Items
   B. Purchases/Receive Inventory
   C. Receipts
   D. Sales/Invoicing
   E. None of the above.

4. Which accounts payable report contains information about all transactions with vendors and the balances owed to them?
   A. *Vendor List*
   B. *Check Register*
   C. *Customer Ledgers*
   D. *Vendor Ledgers*
   E. None of the above.

5. Which general ledger account is credited to record a company's purchases on credit?
   A. Cash
   B. Accounts Payable
   C. Accounts Receivable
   D. Purchases
   E. None of the above.

Short Essay Response: Provide a detailed answer for each question.

1. What are the advantages and disadvantages to a business when it purchases goods and services on credit?
2. What is the purpose of the accounts payable subsidiary ledger?
3. How does the Accounts Payable controlling account in the general ledger relate to the accounts payable subsidiary ledger?
4. Why should a business closely monitor its accounts payable?
5. How can the Alerts function be used to aid a business in paying its bills on time?
6. Briefly explain how a purchase can be edited after it has been posted.

CASE PROBLEMS

PROBLEM 1A

Open GJ Professional Accounting. You set up this accounting services company in chapter 2 and recorded transactions for it in chapters 3 and 4. The owner has now decided to set up vendor accounts and purchase goods and services on credit.

1. Create a subsidiary ledger account for the following vendors dated 01/01/07.

Vendor ID:	**JMC-01**
Name:	**JMC Management Group**

   General Tab

Contact:	**Annette Bradley**
Account #:	**1178**
Address:	**41374 Lincoln Boulevard**
City, ST Zip:	**Stockton, CA 95210**
Country:	**USA**
Vendor Type:	**Expense**
1099 Type:	**None**

Telephone 1:	209-555-3349
Telephone 2:	209-555-3350
Fax:	209-555-3352

Purchase Defaults Tab

Expense Acct:	**75000** (Rent or Lease Expense)
Tax ID #:	
Ship Via:	**US Mail**
Terms:	**Net 30 Days**
Form Delivery Options:	**Default**
Beginning Balances:	**1,100.00**
Vendor ID:	**SW-02**
Name:	**Stockton Water District**

General Tab

Contact:	**Robert Henderson**
Account #:	**95845**
Address:	**3159 Madison Avenue**
City, ST Zip:	**Stockton, CA 95210**
Country:	**USA**
Vendor Type:	**Expense**
1099 Type:	**None**
Telephone 1:	**209-555-4738**
Telephone 2:	**209-555-4739**
Fax:	**209-555-4750**

Purchase Defaults Tab

Expense Acct:	**78500** (Utilities Expense)
Tax ID #:	
Ship Via:	**US Mail**
Terms:	**Net 30 Days**
Form Delivery Options:	**Default**
Beginning Balances:	**820.00**
Vendor ID:	**OFFMAX-03**
Name:	**Office Max**

General Tab

Contact:	**Joshua Baker**
Account #:	**61345**
Address:	**3915 Webber Lane**
City, ST Zip:	**Stockton, CA 95207**
Country:	**USA**
Vendor Type:	**Supplier**
1099 Type:	**None**
Telephone 1:	**209-555-7981**
Telephone 2:	**209-555-7985**
Fax:	**209-555-7988**

<u>Purchase Defaults Tab</u>

Expense Acct:	**12000** (Office Supplies)
Tax ID #:	
Ship Via:	**Fed-EX**
Terms:	**2% 10 days, net 30 days**
Form Delivery Options:	**Default**
Beginning Balances:	**2,400.00**
Vendor ID:	**PACBELL-04**
Name:	**Pacific Bell**

<u>General Tab</u>

Contact:		**Barbara Sinclair**
Account #:		**127648**
	Address:	**6581 East Montgomery Avenue**
	City, ST Zip:	**Stockton, CA 95207**
	Country:	**USA**
Vendor Type:		**Expense**
1099 Type:		**None**
Telephone 1:		**209-555-7890**
Telephone 2:		**209-555-7895**
Fax:		**209-555-7900**

<u>Purchase Defaults Tab</u>

Expense Acct:	**79000** (Telephone Expense)
Tax ID #:	
Ship Via:	**US Mail**
Terms:	**Net 30 Days**
Form Delivery Options:	**Default**
Beginning Balances:	**600.00**

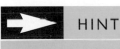

HINT

To change accounting period:
- Click Tas**k**s
- Click Sys**t**em
- Change Accounting Period
- Select 02-Feb 01, 2007 to Feb 28, 2007
- Click **OK**
- Select **N**o to query

2. Change the accounting period to *Feb 1, 2007 to Feb 28, 2007*.

3. Enter each of the transactions listed below for February 2007. Note that this business has three different sources of revenue: accounting fees, tax preparation fees, and consulting fees. Therefore, be sure that you select the number of the correct revenue account in the GL Sales Account section of the Sales/Invoicing window. (The customer accounts have been set up with a GL Sales Account default to Account 40000, Accounting Fees.) Services performed on account will be entered in the Sales/Invoicing window, and purchases on account in the Purchases/Receive Inventory window.

Date	**Transaction**
Feb. 3	Received a bill (Invoice 16475) of $1280 for monthly rent from JMC Management Group.
4	Received a bill (Invoice 62351) of $75 for monthly usage of water from Stockton Water District.
5	Performed accounting services for $420 on credit for Johnson Manufacturing. Issued Invoice 1006.

Ignore any "over balance" messages.

5	Received a bill (Invoice 51956) of $135 for monthly usage of telephone service from Pacific Bell.
8	Performed accounting services for $650 on credit for Computer Expertise. Issued Invoice 1007.
10	Purchased office supplies for $230 on credit from Office Max. Received Invoice 4891.
14	Performed accounting services for $350 on credit for Stephanie's Catering. Issued Invoice 1008. Received check # 461 for $100 from the customer.
17	Purchased office supplies for $234 on credit from Office Max. Received Invoice 5216.
24	Performed consulting services for $600 on credit, for Johnson Manufacturing. Issued Invoice 1009. Received check # 11964 for $225 from the customer.
27	Performed accounting services for $245 on credit for Computer Expertise. Issued Invoice 1010. Received check #9865 for $100 from the customer.

4. Print the following reports for February: *Vendor Ledgers, Customer Ledgers, Cash Receipts Journal*, and *General Journal*.

PROBLEM 2A

Open CC Advertising, which is located on the student data disk. The owner has decided to set up vendor accounts and purchase goods and services on credit.

1. Create a subsidiary ledger account for each of the following new vendors.

| *Vendor ID:* | **JMG-01** |
| *Name:* | **J. Madison Graphing** |

General Tab

Contact:	**John Madison**
Account #:	**2180**
Address:	**6529 West Highland Avenue**
City, ST Zip:	**Tracy, CA 95376**
Country:	**USA**
Vendor Type:	**Expense**
1099 Type:	**None**
Telephone 1:	**209-555-3349**
Telephone 2:	**209-555-3350**
Fax:	**209-555-3352**

Purchase Defaults Tab

Expense Acct:	**516** (Advertising Expense)
Tax ID #:	
Ship Via:	**US Mail**
Terms:	**Net 30 Days**
Form Delivery Options:	**Default**
Beginning Balances:	**0**
Vendor ID:	**OD-02**
Name:	**Office Depot**

General Tab

Contact:	**Brian Gentry**
Account #:	**32181**
Address:	**6529 Harding Avenue**
City, ST Zip:	**Tracy, CA 95376**
Country:	**USA**
Vendor Type:	**Supplier**
1099 Type:	**None**
Telephone 1:	**209-555-6459**
Telephone 2:	**209-555-6465**
Fax:	**209-555-6467**

Purchase Defaults Tab

Expense Acct:	**108** (Office Supplies)
Tax ID #:	
Ship Via:	**UPS Ground**
Terms:	**2% 10 days, net 30 days**
Form Delivery Options:	**Default**
Beginning Balances:	**0**

2. Enter the following events and alerts for the month of March 2007 by using the Action Items function:
   - Meet with John Madison about a design job at 10 a.m. on March 15. Advise two days ahead of time.
   - Call Office Depot on March 20 to ask about the prices of computers. Advise one day ahead of time.
   - Create an Alert to notify you when any outstanding balance to vendors reaches or exceeds $500.

3. Print a *Vendor List* report.
4. Print a list of events for the month by changing the *Date* field to Mar 31, 2007.

PROBLEM 1B

Open Infinite Graphics. You set up this graphic services company in chapter 2 and recorded transactions for it in chapters 3 and 4. The owner has now decided to set up vendor accounts and purchase goods and services on credit.

  1. Create a subsidiary ledger account for each vendor dated 01/01/07.

Vendor ID:	**JPS-01**
Name:	**Johnson Photography**

General Tab

Contact:	**Matthew Rosario**
Account #:	**3194**
Address:	**1374 West Bessie Avenue**
City, ST Zip:	**Stockton, CA 95210**
Country:	**USA**
Vendor Type:	**Expense**
1099 Type:	**None**
Telephone 1:	**209-555-4651**
Telephone 2:	**209-555-4652**
Fax:	**209-555-4658**

Purchase Defaults Tab

Expense Acct:	**76000** (Printing and Copying Expense)
Tax ID #:	
Ship Via:	**Fed-EX**
Terms:	**Net 30 Days**
Form Delivery Options:	**Default**
Beginning Balances:	**370.00**

Vendor ID:	**SD-02**
Name:	**Stockton Water District**

General Tab

Contact:	**Robert Henderson**
Account #:	**40381**
Address:	**3159 Madison Avenue**
City, ST Zip:	**Stockton, CA 95210**
Country:	**USA**
Vendor Type:	**Expense**
1099 Type:	**None**
Telephone 1:	**209-555-4738**
Telephone 2:	**209-555-4739**
Fax:	**209-555-4750**

Purchase Defaults Tab

Expense Acct:	**81500** (Utilities Expense)
Tax ID #:	
Ship Via:	**US Mail**
Terms:	**Net 30 Days**
Form Delivery Options:	**Default**

Beginning Balances:	**420.00**

Vendor ID:	**OFFMAX-03**
Name:	**Office Max**

General Tab

Contact:	**Kevin Randall**
Account #:	**395481**
Address:	**3915 Webber Lane**
City, ST Zip:	**Stockton, CA 95207**
Country:	**USA**
Vendor Type:	**Supplier**
1099 Type:	**None**
Telephone 1:	**209-555-7981**
Telephone 2:	**209-555-7985**
Fax:	**209-555-7988**

Purchase Defaults Tab

Expense Acct:	**12000** (Graphing Supplies)
Tax ID #:	
Ship Via:	**Fed-EX**
Terms:	**2% 10 days, net 30 days**
Form Delivery Options:	**Default**
Beginning Balances:	**2,200.00**

Vendor ID:	**SJR-04**
Name:	**San Joaquin Rentals**

General Tab

Contact:	**Peter Ramirez**
Account #:	**94612**
Address:	**9462 Lowell Avenue**
City, ST Zip:	**Stockton, CA 95207**
Country:	**USA**
Vendor Type:	**Expense**
1099 Type:	**None**
Telephone 1:	**209-555-6454**
Telephone 2:	**209-555-6455**
Fax:	**209-555-6460**

Purchase Defaults Tab

Expense Acct:	**78500** (Rent-Office)
Tax ID #:	
Ship Via:	**US Mail**
Terms:	**Net 30 Days**
Form Delivery Options:	**Default**
Beginning Balances:	**0**

Vendor ID:	**PACBELL-05**
Name:	**Pacific Bell**

General Tab

Contact:	**Barbara Sinclair**
Account #:	**32348**
Address:	**6581 East Montgomery Avenue**
City, ST Zip:	**Stockton, CA 95207**
Country:	**USA**
Vendor Type:	**Expense**
1099 Type:	**None**
Telephone 1:	**209-555-7890**
Telephone 2:	**209-555-7895**
Fax:	**209-555-7900**

Purchase Defaults Tab

Expense Acct:	**80000** (Telephone Expense)
Tax ID #:	
Ship Via:	**US Mail**
Terms:	**Net 30 Days**
Form Delivery Options:	**Default**
Beginning Balances:	**300.00**

HINT

To change accounting period:
• Click Tasks
• Click System
• Change Accounting Period
• Select 02-Feb 01, 2007 to Feb 28, 2007
• Click OK
• Select No to query

2. Change the accounting period to *Feb 1, 2007 to Feb 28, 2007.*
3. Enter each of the following transactions for February 2007. Note that this business has three different types of revenue: graphic design fees, retouching fees, and drafting fees. Therefore, be sure that you select the number of the correct revenue account in the GL Sales Account section of the Sales/Invoicing dialog box. (The customer accounts have been set up with a GL Sales Account default to Account 40000, Graphic Design Income.) Services performed on account will be entered in the Sales/Invoicing window, purchases on account in the Purchases/Receive Inventory window.

NOTE

Ignore any "over balance" messages.

Date	Transaction
Feb. 2	Performed graphic design services for $475 on credit for Jackson Photography. Issued Invoice 1007.
3	Received a bill (Invoice 4952) of $895 for the monthly rent from San Joaquin Rentals.
4	Received a bill of $130 (Invoice 13795) for monthly usage of telephone service from Pacific Bell.
4	Received a bill (Invoice 65429) of $234 for monthly usage of water from Stockton Water District.
5	Purchased graphing supplies for $235 on credit from Office Max. Received Invoice 4620.
8	Performed graphic design services for $320 on credit for Computer Creations. Issued Invoice 1008.

12	Purchased printing services for $450 on credit from Johnson Photography. Received Invoice 2615.
15	Performed graphic design services for $1,350 on credit for Jackson Photography. Issued Invoice 1009. Received check # 4504 for $300 from the customer.
19	Purchased graphing supplies for $135 on credit from Office Max. Received Invoice 5229.
25	Performed graphic design services for $1,325 on credit for First Design. Issued Invoice 1010. Received check # 3271 for $250 from the customer.
26	Performed retouching services for $460 on credit for Jackson Photography. Issued Invoice 1011.
27	Performed graphic design services for $750 on credit for Computer Creations. Issued Invoice 1012.

4. Print the following reports for February: *Vendor Ledgers, Customer Ledgers, Cash Receipts Journal, and General Journal.*

PROBLEM 2B

Open Ritter Insurance, which is located on the student data disk. This firm plans to purchase goods and services on credit.

1. Create a subsidiary ledger account for each of the following new vendors:

Vendor ID:	**OFFMAX-01**
Name:	**Office Max**

General Tab

Contact:		**Kevin Randall**
Account #:		**4150**
	Address:	**3915 Webber Lane**
	City, ST Zip:	**Stockton, CA 95207**
	Country:	**USA**
Vendor Type:		**Supplier**
1099 Type:		**None**
Telephone 1:		**209-555-7981**
Telephone 2:		**209-555-7985**
Fax:		**209-555-7988**

Purchase Defaults Tab

Expense Acct:	**108** (Office Supplies)
Tax ID #:	
Ship Via:	**Fed-EX**
Terms:	**2% 10 days, net 30 days**
Form Delivery Options:	**Default**
Beginning Balances:	**0**

Vendor ID:	**GJPA-02**
Name:	**GJ Professional Accounting**

General Tab

Contact:		**Jim Tyler**
Account #:		**491502**
	Address:	**1506 East March Lane**
	City, ST Zip:	**Stockton, CA 95207**
	Country:	**USA**
Vendor Type:		**Expense**
1099 Type:		**None**
Telephone 1:		**209-555-2112**
Telephone 2:		**209-555-2113**
Fax:		**209-555-1221**

Purchase Defaults Tab

Expense Acct:	**516** (Accounting Expense)
Tax ID #:	
Ship Via:	**US Mail**
Terms:	**Net 30 Days**
Form Delivery Options:	**Default**
Beginning Balances:	**0**

2. Enter the following events and alerts for March 2007 by using the Action Items function.
   - Call Office Max on March 12 to order supplies. Advise one day ahead of time.
   - Meet with Jim Tyler of GJ Professional Accounting at 9 a.m. on March 23 to discuss new accounting procedures. Advise three days ahead of time.
   - Create an Alert to notify you when any outstanding balance to vendors reaches or exceeds $700.

3. Print a *Vendor List* report.
4. Print a list of events for the month by changing the *Date* field to Mar 30, 2007.

COOPERATIVE LEARNING

1. Form into groups of three or four students, and discuss what a business can do to maintain a good credit reputation. Why is a good credit reputation important?

2. As a group, research the Small Business Administration, a government entity that helps businesses to obtain the capital they need to start or expand operations. What methods does it use to assist businesses? What are its requirements to receive assistance?

Assume that the company for which you work currently makes all purchases for cash. However, the owner, Susan Nicholson, has decided to obtain credit from vendors. She has therefore asked you to suggest measures that the company can take to organize and manage its accounts payable. She has also asked that you explain to her how the controlling account in the general ledger relates to the vendor accounts in the subsidiary ledger. Prepare a memo with the information that has been requested.

CHAPTER

CASH
PAYMENTS
AND CASH RECEIPTS

1. Process cash payments using the cash payments module

2. Process cash receipts using the cash receipts module

3. Prepare a reconciliation of the checking account

SOFTWARE FEATURES

- Receipts toolbar buttons

- Recalc feature

- Payments toolbar buttons

- Account reconciliation toolbar

- Print feature

Cash is the most essential of all assets. Without an adequate cash flow, no business can operate for long. Because cash is so important, every firm should have efficient procedures for managing its cash receipts and cash payments.

RECORDING AND MANAGING CASH

Remember that **cash** consists of the funds that a business has on hand and the funds that it has on deposit in banks. The funds on hand may include not only currency and coin but also cash equivalents such as checks and money orders received from customers.

Some firms maintain a single cash account in their general ledger. Other firms have a variety of cash accounts such as Cash on Hand, Petty Cash, Regular Checking Account, Payroll Checking Account, and Money Market Savings. If there is a single account called Cash, this account is debited whenever cash is received and credited whenever cash is paid.

You may choose to record all cash transactions in the general journal as you did in chapter 3. However, many businesses prefer to use special journals for cash receipts and cash payments. Peachtree provides such journals.

Cash is the asset that is most easily stolen, lost, or misused. Therefore, accountants recommend that businesses follow certain procedures to protect their cash. Some of these procedures are outlined below:

- Make all payments by check except for small expenditures from a petty cash fund.
- Avoid keeping large amounts of cash on the premises. Make frequent bank deposits of cash receipts.
- Use a locked safe or cash drawer to protect any cash that is on hand.
- Record cash transactions promptly.
- Reconcile the monthly bank statement with the firm's internal cash records.
- Divide responsibility. If possible, have different employees handle cash, record cash, and reconcile the bank statement.
- Peachtree allows you to quickly and efficiently issue checks, record cash receipts and cash payments, and carry out the bank reconciliation process.

OBJECTIVE 1 — PROCESS CASH PAYMENTS USING THE CASH PAYMENTS MODULE

During January 2007, Woodward Construction Company received several bills from vendors. In chapter 5, you learned how these purchases of goods and services were recorded. Now you will see how the business uses the cash payments module of Peachtree to issue checks to the vendors and record the payments.

PAYING AN INVOICE WITH A DISCOUNT

On January 29, 2007, Woodward Construction Company received Invoice 3556 from Office Max for a purchase of office supplies. The total of the invoice was $1,400 and the terms were 2% 10 days, net 30 days (2/10, net 30). On January 31, Woodward's accountant paid bills and issued a check to Office Max. Because the invoice is being paid within the discount period, Woodward is entitled to take the 2% discount offered by the vendor.

Step 1:

Open Woodward Construction Company.

Step 2:

Click Tasks, and then click Payments.

Step 3:

At the Select a Cash Account dialog box, click *Cash* from the drop-down list, as shown in figure 6–1.

Step 4:

Click OK. The Payments window will then appear, as shown in figure 6–2.

FIGURE 6-1

Select a Cash Account Dialog Box with Cash Selected

FIGURE 6-2

Blank Payments Window

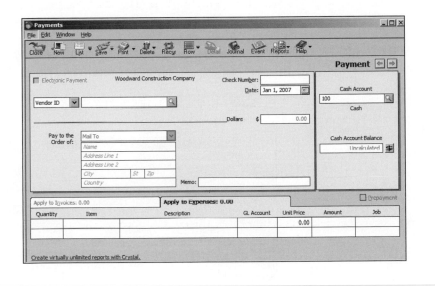

Step 5:

Click the down arrow in the first box on the left, and then click *Vendor ID* from the drop-down list as shown in figure 6–3, if it is not already selected.

FIGURE 6-3

Vendor ID Selected from
Drop-Down List

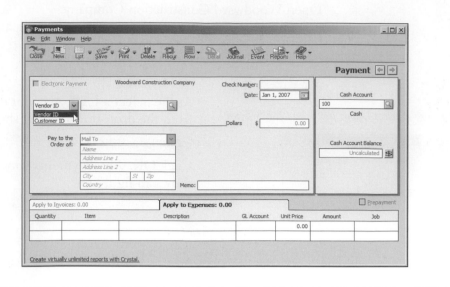

Step 6:

Click the *magnifying glass* icon and then click *OFFMAX-03* from the drop-down list of vendors, as shown in figure 6–4.

FIGURE 6-4

OFFMAX-03 Selected from
Drop-Down List of Vendors

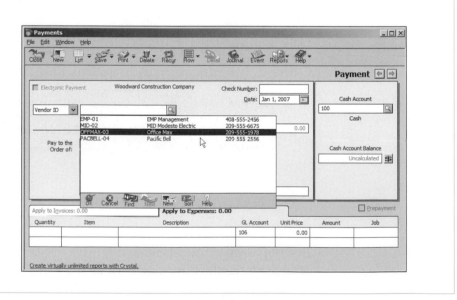

Step 7:

Click OK at the bottom of the drop-down list of vendors. Alternatively, you could simply click OFFMAX-03. The information for Office Max appears. The beginning balance of its account and the open invoice are listed near the bottom of the window, as shown in figure 6–5.

FIGURE 6-5

Account Information for Office Max Displayed

HINT

The Apply to Invoices folder tab is highlighted because there are open (unpaid) invoices for the selected vendor.

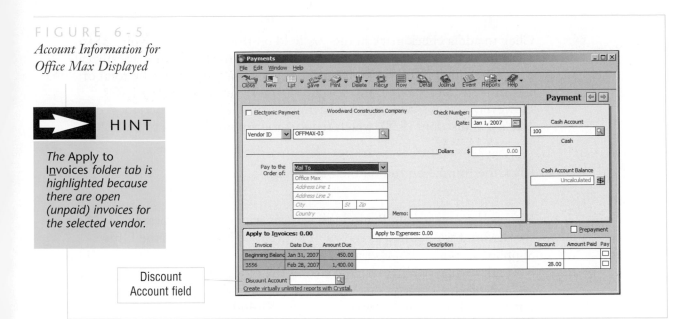

Discount Account field

Step 8:

Choose *Jan 31, 2007* in the *Date* field using the *calendar* icon.

Step 9:

Click the *magnifying glass* icon at the *Discount Account* field, which is at the lower left side of the Payments window. Click *106, Office Supplies* as shown in figure 6–6, and then click OK.

FIGURE 6-6

Office Supplies Selected from Discount Account Drop-Down List

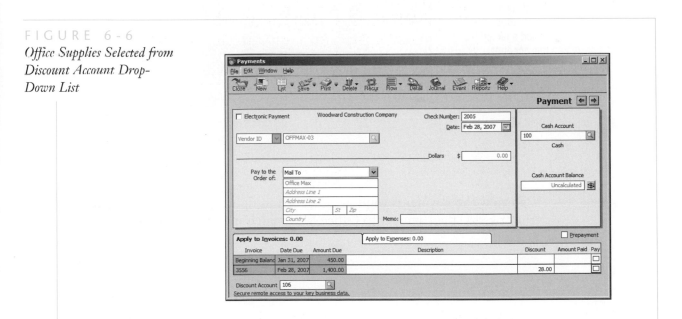

Step 10:

Click to add a check mark in the *Pay* field on the line where Invoice 3556 appears. When the check mark is entered, Peachtree will automatically calculate the amount to be paid by deducting any discount from the total of the invoice. For example, Invoice 3556 from Office Max is for $1,400. However, because Woodward is paying within the discount period, it can take a 2% discount ($28), which reduces the amount it owes to $1,372.

Step 11:

Click the Journal button on the Payments toolbar.

Step 12:

Review the Accounting Behind the Screens window that appears to see how the discount was treated as shown in figure 6–7. Notice that the Office Supplies account (106) is credited for $28, the amount of the discount. This is a logical approach because the cost of the office supplies is less than the amount originally recorded ($1,400). Remember that when the purchase was made Office Supplies was debited for $1,400. The credit of $28 reduces the recorded cost of the purchase to $1,372, the amount actually paid. Click OK.

FIGURE 6-7

Accounting Behind the Screens Window

The discount amount is applied against this account.

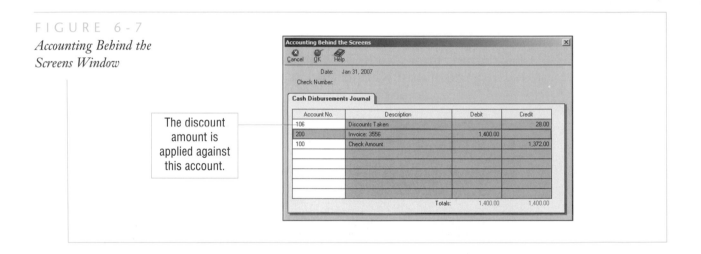

Step 13:

Review the Payments window, as shown in figure 6–8. Make sure that your entries for the payment to Office Max match the ones shown here.

FIGURE 6-8

*Payments Window with
Entries for Office Max*

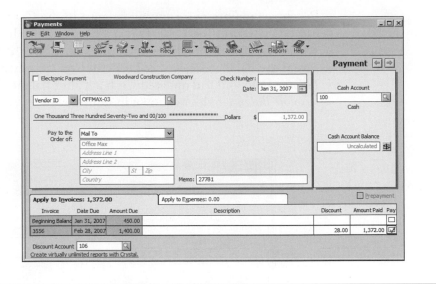

Do not key anything in the *Check Number* field. Peachtree will automatically record the check number when the check is printed. If the payment were to be made in cash rather than by check, you would key **CASH**. (In some rare circumstances, you may want to bypass the automatic check preparation feature and write a check manually. In such a case, you must key in the check number.)

Step 14:

If the number of the Cash account (100) is not already selected, click the *magnifying glass* icon next to the *Cash Account* field, and then click *100*, as shown in figure 6–9.

FIGURE 6-9

*Payments Dialog Box with
Cash Account 100 Selected*

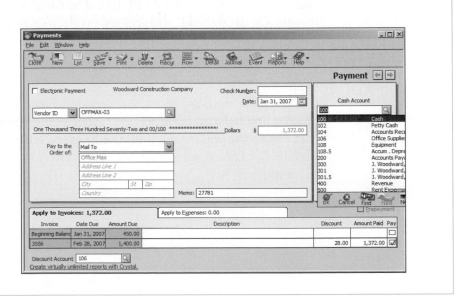

Step 15:

Peachtree maintains a running balance in the Cash account. This balance can be viewed in the *Cash Account Balance* field. However, the *Cash Account Balance* field will sometimes contain only *??????????* or *Uncalculated*. To reveal the balance, click the Recalc button ($) next to the *Cash Account Balance* field and the updated Cash account balance will appear in the *Cash Account Balance* field, as shown in figure 6–10.

FIGURE 6-10

Cash Account Balance Field Showing Current Cash Balance

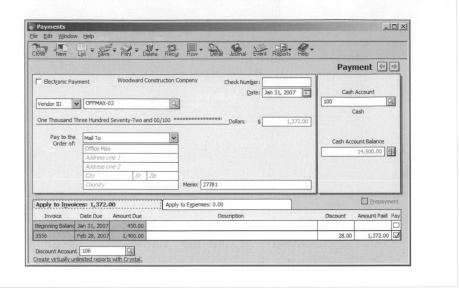

Step 16:

Click the Save button on the Payment toolbar in order to post the payment.

PAYING AN INVOICE AND A PREVIOUS BALANCE

On January 3, 2007, Woodward Construction Company received Invoice 2621 for its monthly rent of $1,200. The invoice is due at the end of the month. On January 31, the accountant decides to issue a check that will cover both Invoice 2621 and a balance of $900 owed from the previous month.

Step 1:

Use the steps outlined in the last section to pay the monthly rent and the outstanding balance owed to EMP Management. However, in this case, key check marks in the *Pay* field on the lines for both the beginning balance and Invoice 2621. Also, keep in mind that there is no discount involved in this payment.

Step 2:

Compare your entries with those shown in figure 6–11. Then click <u>S</u>ave.

FIGURE 6-11

*Completed Payments
Window with Entries for
EMP Management*

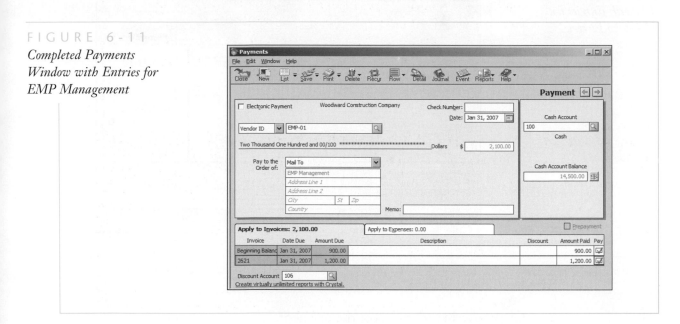

During January 2007, Woodward Construction Company received two bills. One came from MID Modesto Electric (invoice number 84763), and the other came from Pacific Bell (invoice number 912867).

Step 3:

Pay MID Modesto Electric for its monthly bill and a previous balance that Woodward owes. When you complete your work, compare your entries with those shown in figure 6–12.

Vendor ID:	**MID-02**
Date:	**Jan 31, 2007**
Cash Account:	**100**
Discount Account:	**None**
Pay:	**The beginning balance ($450) and the monthly bill ($456.75)**

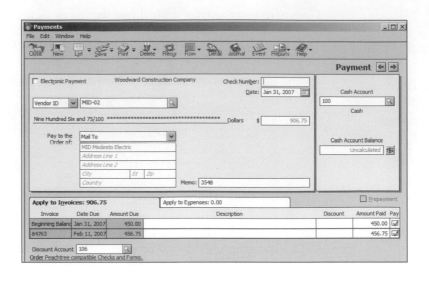

Step 4:

Click <u>S</u>ave in order to post the payment.

Step 5:

Pay Pacific Bell for its monthly bill and a previous balance that Woodward owes.
When you complete your work, compare your entries shown in figure 6–13.

Vendor ID:	**PACBELL-04**
Date:	**Jan 31, 2007**
Cash Account:	**100**
Discount Account:	**None**
Pay:	**The beginning balance ($500) and the monthly bill ($565.89)**

FIGURE 6-13

*Completed Payments
Window with Entries for
Pacific Bell*

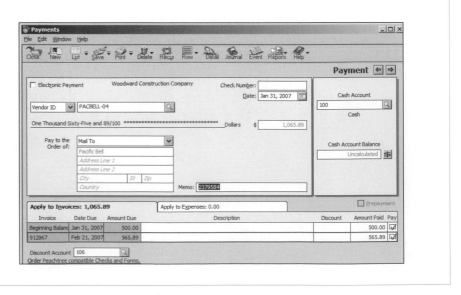

Step 6:

Click Save.

PAYING A BILL FOR A PURCHASE NOT PREVIOUSLY RECORDED

The four bills that the accountant for Woodward Construction Company has paid so far were for purchases on credit that had been recorded earlier in the month. Now assume that on January 31, 2007, the accountant is handed a bill from Apex Floor Care Service for $250. This firm has just finished polishing the floors in Woodward's office building. The bill from Apex requests immediate payment.

When a situation like this occurs, it is not necessary to first record the purchase and then record the cash payment. However, if the firm that submitted the bill is a new vendor, it is necessary to set up a vendor account for the firm.

In this particular situation, the accountant for Woodward Construction Company wants to debit the purchase to Maintenance Expense. However, the business does not have such an account in its general ledger. Therefore, the accountant must create this account before recording the purchase.

Use the steps outlined below to create the Maintenance Expense account, set up the vendor account, record the purchase, and record the cash payment.

Step 1:

Click Tasks from the Main Menu bar and Write Checks from the drop-down list, as shown in figure 6–14.

FIGURE 6-14

Write Checks Selected from the Tasks Drop-Down List

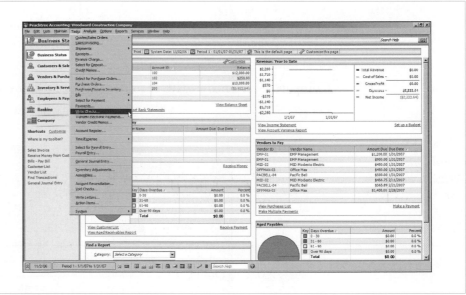

Step 2:

Click the *magnifying glass* icon next to the Expense Account box located in the lower left corner of the screen. A drop-down list appears, as shown in figure 6–15.

FIGURE 6-15

GL Account Drop-
Down List

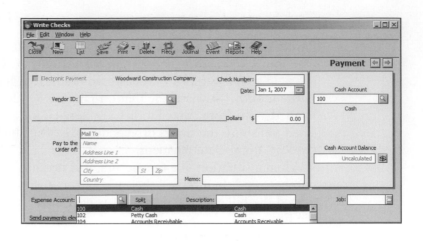

Step 3:

Click the New button at the bottom of the drop-down list of general ledger accounts.

Step 4:

At the Maintain Chart of Accounts window, key the following information to complete the setup of the new account:

Account ID:	**518**
Description:	**Maintenance Expense**
Account Type:	**Expenses**

Step 5:

Compare your entries with the ones shown in figure 6–16.

FIGURE 6-16

Completed Entries for
Maintenance Expense
Account

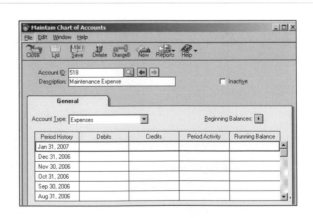

Step 6:

Click Save and then click Close to return to the Payments window.

Step 7:

We will now use the Write Checks window to set up a new vendor account. Click the *magnifying glass* icon next to the Vendor ID box to reveal the drop-down list of vendors.

Step 8:

Click the New button at the bottom of the drop-down list of vendors, as shown in figure 6–17.

FIGURE 6-17

New Button from Drop-Down List of Vendors

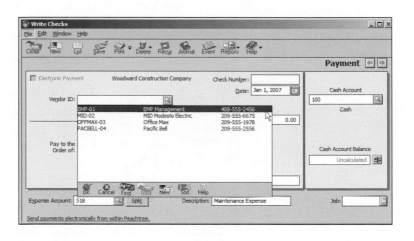

Step 9:

The Maintain Vendors window appears. Use the following information to complete the setup of a new vendor account for Apex Floor Care Service:

Vendor ID:	**APEX-05**
Name:	**Apex Floor Care Service**

General Tab

Contact:		**Tarin Land**
Account #:		**334223**
	Address:	**2310 Windham Avenue**
	City, ST Zip:	**Sacramento, CA 95670**
	Country:	**USA**
Vendor Type:		**Expense**
1099 Type:		**None**
Telephone 1:		**408-555-5634**

| Telephone 2: | 408-555-8567 |
| Fax: | 408-555-4638 |

Purchase Defaults Tab

Expense Acct:	**518** (Maintenance Expense)
Tax ID #:	
Ship Via:	**US Mail**
Terms:	**Due EOM, 0.00 Discount**
Form Delivery Options:	**Default**
Beginning Balances:	**0**

Step 10:

Compare your entries with the ones shown in figure 6–18.

FIGURE 6-18

*Completed Entries for
Vendor Account for
Apex Floor Care Service*

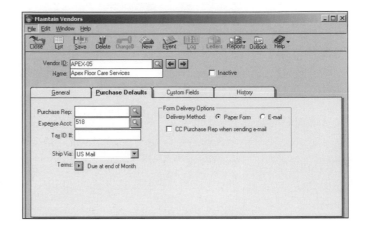

Step 11:

Click Save and then Close to return to the Write Checks window. We are now ready to actually write the check.

Step 12:

Click *APEX-05* from the drop-down list of vendors. The information for Apex Floor Care Service appears as shown in figure 6–19.

FIGURE 6-19

*Write Checks Windows
Showing Apex Floor Care
Service Information*

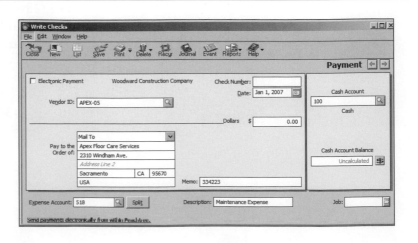

Step 13:

Click the *calendar* icon and then choose *Jan 31, 2007* in the *Date* field.

Step 14:

Key **250.00** in the *Dollars* field.

Step 15:

Click the *magnifying glass* icon and then click the number of the Cash account (*100*) in the *Cash Account* field.

Step 16:

Click account *518*, Maintenance Expense, from the drop-down list of general ledger accounts in the *Expense Account* field, if not already complete.

Step 17:

Key **Floor Care** in the *Description* field.

Step 18:

Compare your entries with the ones shown in figure 6–20.

FIGURE 6-20

Completed Write Checks Window for Apex Floor Care Service

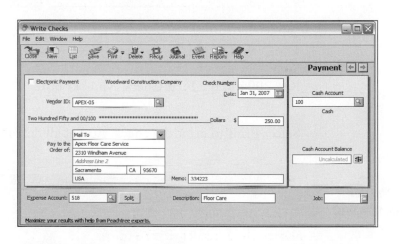

PRINTING INDIVIDUAL CHECKS

As noted previously, Peachtree allows you the option of either preparing checks automatically or preparing them manually. If you select automatic check preparation, the system will enter the check numbers in the *Check Number* field of the Payments window. With manual check preparation, you must key in the check numbers.

Woodward Construction Company uses automatic check preparation. Follow the steps outlined below to issue a check for the bill owed to the Apex Floor Care Service.

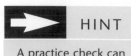
Step 1:

Click the Print button on the Write Checks toolbar. The Print Forms: Disbursement Checks dialog box appears as shown in figure 6–21.

FIGURE 6-21

Print Forms:
Disbursement Checks
Dialog Box

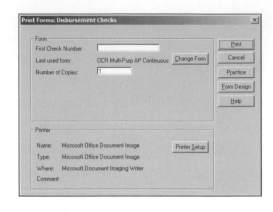

Step 2:

Key **2004** in the First Check Number box.

Step 3:

Select <u>P</u>rint to print the check. Accept all defaults as shown in figure 6–22.

FIGURE 6-22

First Check Number
Box with 2004 Entered

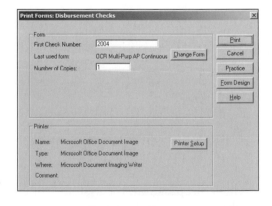

Step 4:

Compare your entries with the ones shown in figure 6–23. The check will print out on a blank sheet of paper because no blank check form was placed in the printer paper tray. It is not necessary to save. The entries are saved when the check is printed.

FIGURE 6-23
Sample of Printed Check for Apex Floor Care Service

Apex Floor Care Services

	Check Number:	2004
	Check Date:	Jan 31, 2007
	Duplicate	
	Check Amount:	$250.00

Item to be Paid - Description	Discount Taken	Amount Paid
Maintenance Expense		250.00

Check Number: 2004   Jan 31, 2007

Memo: 334223

250.00

Two Hundred Fifty and 00/100 Dollars

Apex Floor Care Services
2310 Windham Ave.
Sacramento, CA 95670
USA

Duplicate

PRINTING CHECKS PREVIOUSLY MARKED FOR PAYMENT

Woodward Construction Company needs the following checks marked for payment in January. Use the Open function for this task.

- Office Max, Check 2005
- EMP Management, Check 2006
- Pacific Bell, Check 2007
- MID Modesto Electric, Check 2008

Step 1:

Select Tasks from the Main menu bar and Payments from the drop-down list.

Step 2:

Click the List button from the Payments toolbar.

Step 3:

Click *Office Max* from the Payment List window, and then click Open.

Step 4:

Enter the check number, 2005, if not already entered.

Step 5:

Click the Print button on the Payments toolbar.

Step 6:

Click Print on the Print Forms: Disbursement Checks dialog box.

Step 7:

Follow steps 2 through 6 to print the remaining checks. Notice that the check numbers will automatically be printed in sequence after the first check number is entered. The check numbers appear in the *Check No.* field of the Payment List window, as shown in figure 6–24.

FIGURE 6-24
Payment List Window

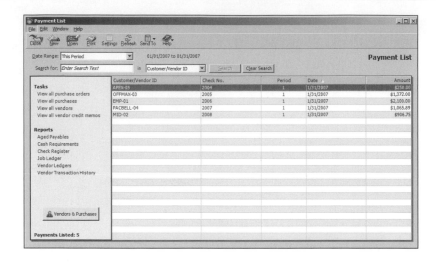

Check
POINT

1. What is the cash payments module of Peachtree used for?
2. Why is it not necessary to key anything in the *Check Number* field when Peachtree is used to issue checks?

Answers

1. *The cash payments module of Peachtree is used to record payments to vendors and issue the necessary checks.*
2. *Peachtree automatically enters a check number for the check being printed and all subsequent checks.*

Step 8:

Close the Payment List window.

PRACTICE *objective* 1

In chapter 5, you created vendor accounts for Bullfrog Maintenance Company and recorded its purchases on credit. In this chapter, you will record payments to the vendors.

Step 1:

Open Bullfrog Maintenance Company.

Step 2:

Record the following payments:

- On January 27, 2007, paid Invoice 55665 for $890, less a discount, owed to Office Depot, Check 700. (Use Office Supplies as the Discount account.)
- On January 31, 2007, paid Invoice 012301 for $1,200 owed to Alta Vista Business Park, Check 701.
- On January 31, 2007, paid a bill of $345.89 owed to Pacific Gas & Electric, Check 702.
- On January 31, 2007, paid a bill of $265.98 owed to General Telephone, Check 703.

On January 31, 2007, Bullfrog received Invoice 33223 for $650 from Happy Lawn, a new vendor. Bullfrog does not have an expense account for landscaping services. Create the necessary general ledger account.

Account ID:	**520**
Description:	**Landscaping Expense**
Account Type:	**Expenses**

Create the necessary vendor account for Happy Lawn.

Vendor ID:	**HAPPY-05**
Name:	**Happy Lawn**

General Tab

Contact:	**David Lee**
Account #:	**88997**
Address:	**3211 Williams Avenue**
City, ST Zip:	**Fresno, CA 96330**
Country:	**USA**
Vendor Type:	**Expense**
1099 Type:	**None**
Telephone 1:	**209-555-6534**
Telephone 2:	**209-555-8673**
Fax:	**209-555-8364**

Purchase Defaults Tab

Expense Acct:	**520** (Landscaping Expense)
Tax ID #:	
Ship Via:	**US Mail**
Terms:	**Due EOM, 0.00 Discount**
Form Delivery Options:	**Default**
Beginning Balances:	**0**

Record the payment of Invoice 33223 for $650 owed to Happy Lawn, Check 704.

Select List from the Payments window and review the checks and check numbers for correctness against figure 6–25.

Close the Payments window.

FIGURE 6-25

Select Payment Window

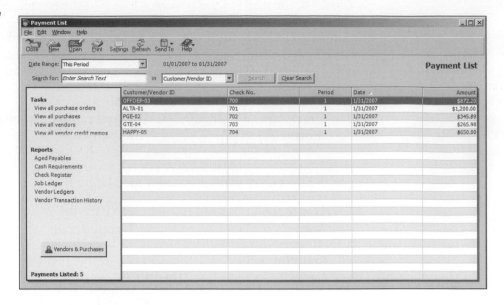

OBJECTIVE 2 — PROCESS CASH RECEIPTS USING THE CASH RECEIPTS MODULE

During January 2007, Woodward Construction Company sold services on credit to several customers. In chapter 4, you learned how these sales were recorded. Now you will see how the business uses the cash receipts module of Peachtree to issue invoices and record the amounts collected from customers.

ISSUING INVOICES

If a business wants to collect the amounts owed by customers on time, it must issue invoices promptly. Remember that an **invoice** is a bill for the goods or services sold to a customer. The invoice shows the amount that the customer owes and the credit terms as well as other information about the sale.

Peachtree allows for quick preparation of invoices. It also provides flexibility in what information is presented on invoices. For example, on January 14, 2007, Woodward Construction Company did a job for Barker's Music for a fixed fee of $5,000. Barker agreed to pay one-half of the total due ($2,500) as soon as the job was completed. Therefore, when Woodward issues Invoice 1002 for this job, the invoice must include both the total of $5,000 and the partial collection of $2,500.

invoice A bill for goods or services sold to a customer.

Step 1:

Open Woodward Construction Company. Click Tasks, and then click Sales/Invoicing.

Step 2:

Click the List button on the Sales/Invoicing toolbar.

Step 3:

Click *Barker's Music* from the Sales Invoice List window, as shown in figure 6–26.

Barker's Music Selected from Sales Invoice List Window

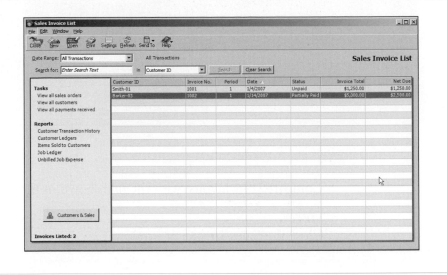

Step 4:

Click <u>O</u>pen. The invoice for Barker's Music appears, as shown in figure 6–27.

Invoice 1002 for Barker's Music

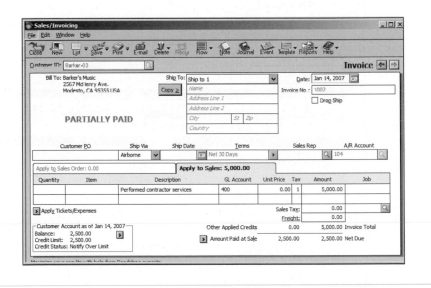

Step 5:

Click the Print button on the Sales/Invoicing toolbar.

Step 6:

The Print Forms: Invoices dialog box appears. Click <u>P</u>rint, as shown in figure 6–28.

FIGURE 6-28
*Invoice Plain Service
Selected*

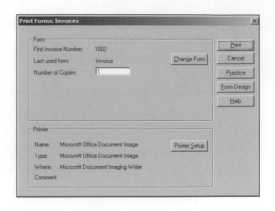

Step 7:

Compare your invoice with the one shown in figure 6–29.

Step 8:

Close the Sales/Invoicing window.

FIGURE 6-29
Printed Invoice 1002 for Barker's Music

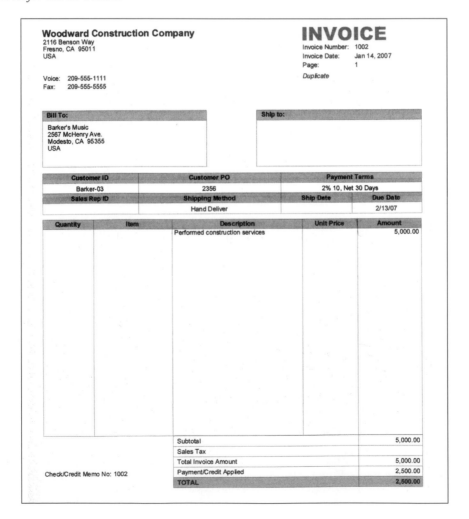

HINT

Invoices can be printed at any time. They can be printed when a job is completed or at a future date such as the end of the month. Each firm has its own billing policy.

RECORDING CASH RECEIPTS

On January 23, 2007, Woodward Construction Company received a check for $2,400 from Barker's Music. This check represents the balance owed on Invoice 1002 ($2,500) less a 2% discount on the total of the invoice ($5,000 × .02 = $100). Remember that Woodward billed Barker for $5,000 and received $2,500 immediately. Because the invoice is dated January 14, Barker has now paid the full amount due within the 10-day discount period. Thus, it is entitled to the 2% discount on the total of the invoice.

Discounts on sales are debited to an account called Sales Discount. This account is known as a contra income account because its debit balance is contrary to the normal credit balance of an income account. Woodward Construction Company does not yet have such an account in its general ledger. Therefore, use the following information to create this account using Maintain, Chart of Accounts.

Account ID:	**401**
Account Description:	**Sales Discount**
Account Type:	**Income**

After you have created the new account, you will then process a receipt of cash on account using the following steps:

Step 1:
Click Tas**k**s, and then click **R**eceipts.

Step 2:
Key **01/23/07** in the *Deposit Ticket ID* field.

Step 3:
Click the down arrow and then click *Customer ID*.

Step 4:
Click the *magnifying glass* icon and then click *Barker-03* from the drop-down list of customers, as shown in figure 6–30.

FIGURE 6-30

Barker-03 Selected from Drop-Down List of Customers

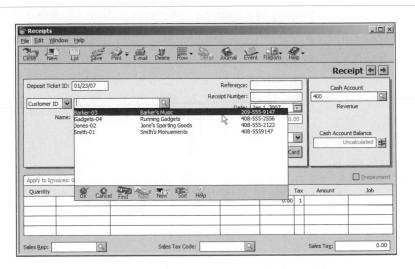

Step 5:

Key **1080** (the check number) in the *Reference* field.

Step 6:

Click the *calendar* icon and choose *Jan 23, 2007* in the *Date* field.

Step 7:

Click *Check* in the *Payment Method* field and *Cash (100)* in the *Cash Account* field.

Step 8:

Key **100.00** in the *Discount* field aligned with Invoice 1002. Press Enter.

Step 9:

2,400.00 will appear in the *Amount Paid* field. Press Enter. A check mark will appear in the *Pay* field as shown in figure 6–31.

FIGURE 6-31

Pay Field Selected for Invoice 1002

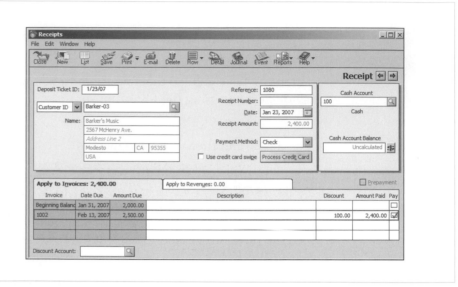

HINT

Remember that if you click the Recalc button on the Receipts toolbar, the new cash balance will appear in the *Cash Balance* field.

Step 10:

Click the Journal button on the Receipts toolbar.

Step 11:

Click in the *Account No.* field, click the *magnifying glass* icon, and then click *401*. This is the account that is used for recording sales discounts. Your screen should look like figure 6–32.

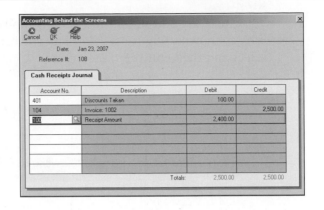

Step 12:

Click OK.

Step 13:

Compare your entries for the cash received from Barker's Music with the entries shown in figure 6–33.

FIGURE 6-33
Completed Receipts Window for Barker's Music

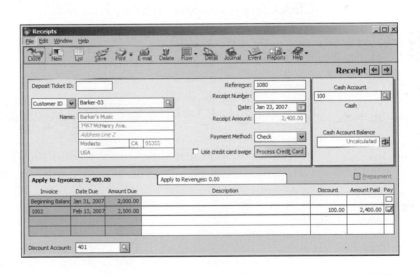

Step 14:

Click Save.

Step 15:

Click the List button on the Receipts toolbar to view the Receipt List dialog box, as shown in figure 6–34. If any corrections are needed, you can now select and then edit the transaction.

FIGURE 6-34

Receipt (Open) List Dialog Box

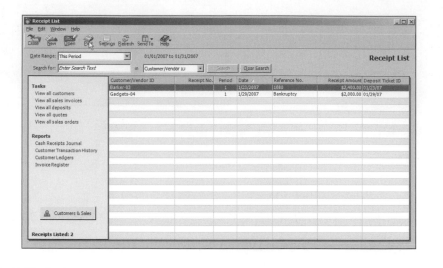

Step 16:

Click Close if no corrections are required.

Step 17:

Click Close.

Check **POINT**

1. What is an invoice?
2. The cash receipts module of Peachtree can be used for what two tasks?

Answers

1. *An invoice is a bill for goods or services sold to a customer.*
2. *The cash receipts module can be used to issue invoices and to record amounts received from customers.*

PRACTICE *objective* 2

In chapter 4, you created customer accounts for Bullfrog Maintenance Company. In this chapter, you will issue invoices and record cash received from a customer.

Step 1:

Open Bullfrog Maintenance Company.

Step 2:

Print invoices for the following customers:

- Lexus of San Joaquin, Invoice 1102
- Curt Smith Mazda, Invoice 1103
- Valley Mercedes, Invoice 1104

Your printouts should look like figures 6–35, 6–36, and 6–37.

FIGURE 6-35

Lexus of San Joaquin, Invoice 1102

Bullfrog Maintenance Company
456 Ballinger Lane
Stockton, CA 95101
USA

Voice: 209-555-2222
Fax: 209-555-6666

INVOICE

Invoice Number: 1102
Invoice Date: Jan 8, 2007
Page: 1

Duplicate

Bill To:	Ship to:
Lexus of San Joaquin 2145 10th Street Salida, CA 95111 USA	

Customer ID	Customer PO	Payment Terms	
Lexus-02		2% 10, Net 30 Days	
Sales Rep ID	Shipping Method	Ship Date	Due Date
	Hand Deliver		2/7/07

Quantity	Item	Description	Unit Price	Amount
		Monthly services		420.00

Subtotal		420.00
Sales Tax		
Total Invoice Amount		420.00
Payment/Credit Applied		
TOTAL		**420.00**

Check/Credit Memo No:

FIGURE 6-36
Curt Smith Mazda, Invoice 1103

Bullfrog Maintenance Company
456 Ballinger Lane
Stockton, CA 95101
USA

Voice: 209-555-2222
Fax: 209-555-6666

INVOICE

Invoice Number: 1103
Invoice Date: Jan 19, 2007
Page: 1

Duplicate

Bill To:	Ship to:
Curt Smith Mazda 2516 Main Street Salida, CA 95111 USA	

Customer ID	Customer PO	Payment Terms	
Mazda-03		2% 10, Net 30 Days	
Sales Rep ID	**Shipping Method**	**Ship Date**	**Due Date**
	US Mail		2/18/07

Quantity	Item	Description	Unit Price	Amount
48.00		48 hours of maintenance services	16.00	768.00
		Subtotal		768.00
		Sales Tax		
		Total Invoice Amount		768.00
Check/Credit Memo No:		Payment/Credit Applied		
		TOTAL		**768.00**

Valley Mercedes, Invoice 1104

Bullfrog Maintenance Company
456 Ballinger Lane
Stockton, CA 95101
USA

Voice: 209-555-2222
Fax: 209-555-6666

INVOICE

Invoice Number: 1104
Invoice Date: Jan 29, 2007
Page: 1

Duplicate

Bill To:

Valley Mercedes
3211 Main Street
Salida, CA 95111
USA

Ship to:

Customer ID	Customer PO	Payment Terms	
Mercedes-04		2% 10, Net 30 Days	
Sales Rep ID	**Shipping Method**	**Ship Date**	**Due Date**
	Hand Deliver		2/28/07

Quantity	Item	Description	Unit Price	Amount
		Monthly services		650.00

Subtotal		650.00
Sales Tax		
Total Invoice Amount		660.00
Payment/Credit Applied		325.00
TOTAL		**325.00**

Check/Credit Memo No: 1104

Step 3:

Bullfrog Maintenance Company does not have a Sales Discount account. Use the following information to create this general ledger account:

Account ID:	**401**
Description:	**Sales Discount**
Account Type:	**Income**

Step 4:

On January 28, 2007, received $752.64 from Curt Smith Mazda, Check 3240. This check is for Invoice 1103 ($768) less a 2% discount ($15.36). Record the transaction. (Remember to enter the sales discount account.) Make sure that *Check* and *100* are selected in the *Payment Method* and *Cash Account* fields respectively.

Print the *Customer Ledgers* report. Your printout should look like figure 6–38.

FIGURE 6-38

*Customer Ledgers for
Bullfrog Maintenance
Company*

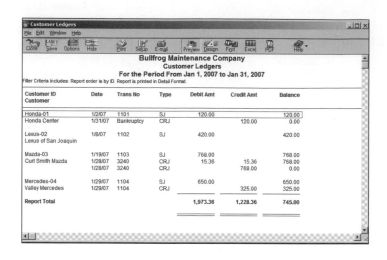

Step 6:

Close the Select a Report dialog box.

OBJECTIVE 3 — PREPARE A RECONCILIATION OF THE CHECKING ACCOUNT

bank statement A listing of all transactions that occurred in a checking account during a month and the beginning and ending balances.

Every month, a business receives a **bank statement** that shows all transactions that occurred in connection with its checking account. The bank statement lists the following information:

- The beginning balance for the period
- All deposits received by the bank and added to the balance
- Other items added to the balance such as the proceeds from promissory notes collected for the business by the bank
- All checks paid by the bank and deducted from the balance
- Other items deducted from the balance such as bank service charges
- The ending balance for the period

bank reconciliation Bringing the ending balances of the bank statement and the firm's own cash records into agreement.

A business that has efficient cash control procedures will promptly reconcile the bank statement with its own cash records, known as a **bank reconciliation**. The ending balance on the bank statement will almost always differ from the ending balance in the firm's checkbook and Cash account. The reconciliation process involves finding the factors that are causing the difference and bringing the balances into agreement.

Some of the factors that may cause a difference between the ending bank statement balance and the ending balance in a firm's cash records are as follows:

- Deposits in transit—deposits made by the firm and listed in its cash records that do not appear on the bank statement.
- Outstanding checks—checks issued by the firm and listed in its cash records that have not yet been paid by the bank.
- ATM deposits and withdrawals—deposits and withdrawals made by automatic teller machine that appear on the bank statement but may not yet be listed in the firm's cash records.
- Bank fees—service charges and other bank fees that appear on the bank statement but may not yet be listed in the firm's cash records.
- NSF checks—customer checks that were deposited but have been returned by the bank because of insufficient funds. (NSF means "non sufficient funds.")
- Errors—errors made by the bank that appear on the bank statement or errors made by the firm in its cash records.

The accountant must examine the bank statement and the firm's cash records to find the factors causing the difference between the two ending balances. The accountant then prepares a bank reconciliation statement such as the one shown below.

ACME Computer Repair
Bank Reconciliation Statement

Ending Bank Statement Balance		$36,800
Add:		
Deposits in Transit	$2,000	
Bank Errors	100	2,100
		$38,900
Deduct:		
Outstanding Checks	$4,400	
Bank Errors	200	4,600
Adjusted Bank Statement Balance		$34,300
Ending Cash Account/Checkbook Balance		$31,500
Add:		
Bank Collections	$5,000	
ATM Deposits	1,000	
Errors	300	6,300
		$37,800
Deduct:		
NSF Checks	$400	
Errors	150	
ATM Withdrawals	2,900	
Bank Fees	50	3,500
Adjusted Cash Account/Checkbook Balance		$34,300

Peachtree allows you to automate this task of preparing a bank reconciliation statement. To prepare for the bank reconciliation process for Woodward Construction Company, use the Report function of Peachtree to obtain information about the firm's cash receipts/bank deposits and checks issued.

REVIEWING/PRINTING THE CASH RECEIPTS JOURNAL

Step 1:

Open Woodward Construction Company. Click Reports, and then click Accounts Receivable.

Step 2:

The Select a Report dialog box will appear. At the Report List section, click *Cash Receipts Journal*, as shown in figure 6–39.

FIGURE 6-39

Select a Report Dialog Box with Cash Receipts Journal Chosen

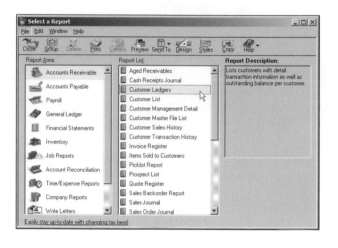

Step 3:

Click the Print button on the Select a Report toolbar.

Step 4:

Click the *Filter* folder tab in the Cash Receipts Journal window.

Step 5:

Click *Check Date* from the drop-down list in the *Report Order* field.

Step 6:

Click *100, Cash* from the drop-down list in the *Cash Account ID* field, as shown in figure 6–40. Then click OK at the bottom of the list.

FIGURE 6-40

*Account 100 Selected in
Cash Account ID Field*

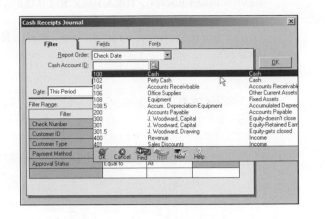

Step 7:

Click *This Period* in the *Date* field, *Jan 1, 2007* in the *From* field, and *Jan 31, 2007* in the *To* field.

Step 8:

Click <u>O</u>K. Then click OK again at the Print window.

Step 9:

Compare your printout of the Cash Receipts Journal for Woodward Construction Company with the one shown in figure 6–41.

FIGURE 6-41

*Printout of Cash
Receipts Journal*

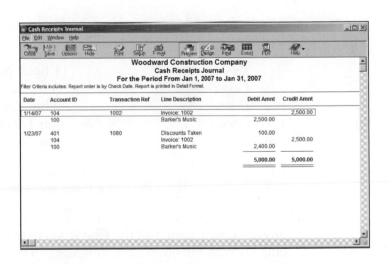

REVIEWING/PRINTING THE CHECK REGISTER

Step 1:

At the Select a Report dialog box, in the Report Area list, click *Accounts Payable*.

Step 2:

At the Report List box, click *Check Register*, as shown in figure 6–42.

FIGURE 6-42

*Report List with Check
Register Chosen*

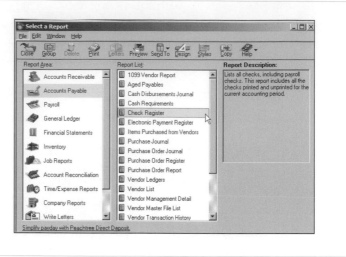

Step 3:

Click the Print button on the Select a Report toolbar.

Step 4:

Click the *Filter* folder tab in the Check Register window. Then select the following:

Report Order:	**Check Number**
Cash Account ID:	**Account 100, Cash**
Date:	**This Period**
From:	**Jan 1, 2007**
To:	**Jan 31, 2007**

Step 5:

Click OK. Then click OK at the Print window.

Step 6:

Compare your printout of the Check Register for Woodward Construction Company with the one shown in figure 6–43.

FIGURE 6-43

Printout of Check Register

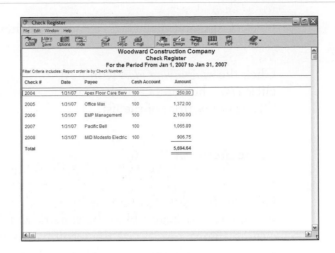

Close the Select a Report dialog box.

PREPARING THE ACCOUNT RECONCILIATION

On February 8, 2007, Woodward Construction Company received the bank statement shown in figure 6–44. This bank statement shows checks that the business issued in January and deposits that it made in January. The bank paid the checks early in February. Follow the steps outlined below to reconcile the bank statement with the firm's cash records.

FIGURE 6-44

Bank Statement for Woodward Construction Company

			Bank of California		
			2346 Center Way		
			Fresno, CA 94534		
Woodward Construction Company					
Acct: 2341121					
REGULAR CHECKING					
Previous Balance	$ 12,000.00		Statement Date: January 31, 2007		
2 Deposits (+)	4,900.00				
4 Checks (-)	4,628.75				
2 Other Deductions (-)	150.00				
Service (-)	20.00				
Ending Balance	12,101.25				
DEPOSITS					
January 14, 2007	$ 2,500.00				
January 23, 2007	2,400.00				
CHECKS (Asterisk* indicates break in check number sequence)					
January 31, 2007	2005	$ 1,372.00			
January 31, 2007	2006	2,100.00			
January 31, 2007	2008	906.75			
January 31, 2007	2004*	250.00			
January 31, 2007	Bank Fees	20.00			
OTHER DEDUCTIONS (ATM's)					
January 16, 2007	ATM	$ 50.00			
January 21, 2007	ATM	100.00			

Step 1:

Click Tasks, and then click Account Reconciliation.

Step 2:

Click the *magnifying glass* icon next to the *Account to Reconcile* field and then click *100* (the number of the Cash account) from the drop-down list. Click OK at the bottom of the list.

Step 3:

At the *Statement Date* field, choose *Jan 31, 2007*.

Step 4:

Click in the *Status* field for each check that is listed on Woodward's bank statement to display a blue check mark which designates that the check has cleared (figure 6–45). Use the scroll bar to review all the checks. Remember to check off only the cleared checks (the checks paid by the bank).

Step 5:

Compare your work with figure 6–45. Check 2007 should not be marked because it did not clear the bank.

FIGURE 6-45

Account Reconciliation Window—Cleared Checks

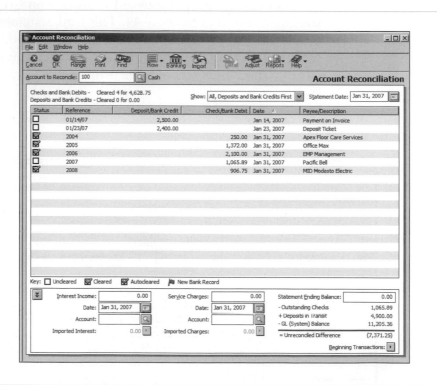

Step 6:

Click a blue check mark in the *Status* field for each of the deposits listed on the bank statement.

Step 7:

Key **12,101.25** in the *Statement Ending Balance* field at the bottom right of the screen, as shown in figure 6–46, and then press Enter.

FIGURE 6-46

Account Reconciliation Window — Statement Ending Balance

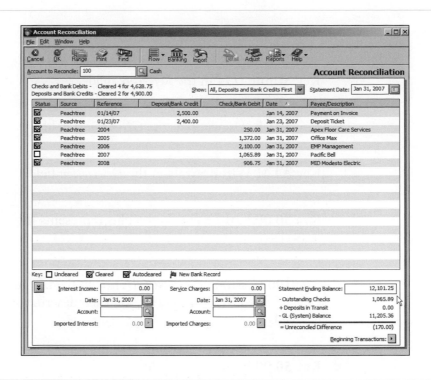

There is an unreconciled difference of *-170.00* listed at the bottom of the window. This is the difference between the bank balance and the GL (general ledger) balance. This difference results from a bank service charge ($20) and ATM withdrawals ($50 and $100) that Woodward has not yet recorded in its cash records.

Step 8:

Click the Adjust button on the Account Reconciliation toolbar to create the new account needed and enter the necessary transactions. Use the General Journal Entry window, as shown in figure 6–47.

FIGURE 6-47

General Journal Entry Window

Step 9:

Key **01/16/07** in the <u>D</u>ate field.

Step 10:

Key **Stmnt 1/31** in the *Reference* field.

Step 11:

Key **301.5** (Drawing) in the *GL Account* field.

Step 12:

Key **ATM Withdrawals** in the *Description* field.

Step 13:

Key **50.00** in the *Debit* field. This represents the ATM, personal withdrawals.

Step 14:

Key **100** (Cash) in the next *GL Account* field. The system should automatically add "ATM Withdrawals" on each description line until the entire entry is saved.

Step 15:

Key **50.00** in the *Credit* field.

Step 16:

Compare your entries with the one shown in figure 6–48.

FIGURE 6-48

General Journal Entry for ATM Withdrawls

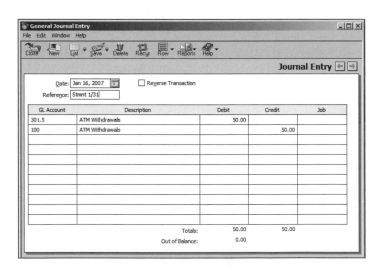

Step 17:
Click Save on the General Journal Entry toolbar.

Step 18:
Key **01/21/05** in the *Date* field and **Stmnt 1/31** in the *Reference* field.

Step 19:
Key **301.5** (Drawing) in the *GL Account* field.

Step 20:
Key **ATM Withdrawals** in the *Description* field.

Step 21:
Key **100.00** in the *Debit* field. This represents the ATM, personal withdrawals.

Step 22:
Key **100** (Cash) in the next *GL Account* field. The system should automatically add "ATM Withdrawals" on each description line until the entire entry is saved.

Step 23:
Key **100.00** in the *Credit* field.

Step 24:
Click Save and then close the General Journal Entry window.

Step 25:
Check the *Status* field to enter a blue check mark next to the ATM Withdrawals of $50.00 and $100.00 listed in the *Account Reconciliation* window.

Step 26:
Key **20.00** (Bank Service Charges) in the *Service Charges* field at the bottom of the screen.

Step 27:
Create the following account:

Account ID:	**520**
Description:	**Bank Fee Expense**
Account Type:	**Expenses**

Step 28:
Click *Account 520, Bank Fee Expense*, after clicking the magnifying glass next to the *Account* field.

Step 29:
After checking off the ATM withdrawals and entering the service charge and the account number, review figure 6–49 for accuracy.

FIGURE 6-49

*Account Reconciliation
Window with Adjustments
Cleared*

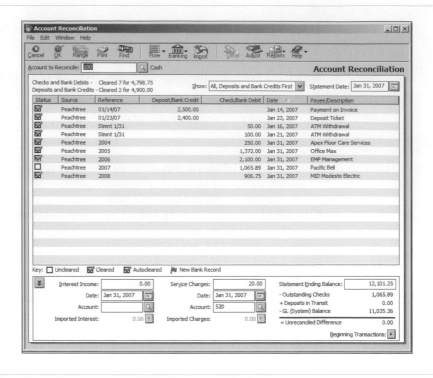

The account reconciliation is now in balance. The unreconciled difference at the bottom of the window is *0.00*.

Step 30:
Click <u>O</u>K.

PRINTING THE ACCOUNT RECONCILIATION

It is good policy to print a copy of the account reconciliation and keep it on file with the bank statement.

Step 1:
Click <u>R</u>eports, and then click Acc<u>o</u>unt Reconciliation.

Step 2:
At the Select a Report dialog box, at the Report Li<u>s</u>t section, click *Account Reconciliation*, as shown in figure 6–50.

FIGURE 6-50

*Account Reconciliation
Selected from Report List*

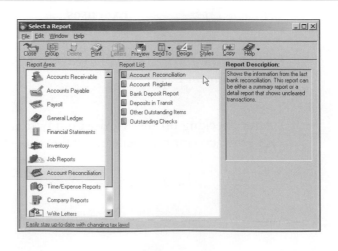

Step 3:

Click the Print button on the Select a Report toolbar.

Step 4:

Click the *Filter* folder tab and select the following information.

GL Account ID:	**100**
As Of:	**This Period**

Step 5:

Click OK. Then click OK again at the Print window.

Step 6:

Compare your printout with the one shown in figure 6–51.

FIGURE 6-51

Account Reconciliation for Woodward Construction Company

Page: 1

Woodward Construction Company
Account Reconciliation
As of Jan 31, 2007
100 - Cash
Bank Statement Date: January 31, 2007

Filter Criteria includes: Report is printed in Detail Format.

Beginning GL Balance				
Add: Cash Receipts				4,900.00
Less: Cash Disbursements				(5,694.64)
Add (Less) Other				11,830.00
Ending GL Balance				11,035.36
Ending Bank Balance				12,101.25
Add back deposits in transit				
Total deposits in transit				
(Less) outstanding checks	Jan 31, 2007	2007	(1,065.89)	
Total outstanding checks				(1,065.89)
Add (Less) Other				
Total other				
Unreconciled difference				0.00
Ending GL Balance				11,035.36

Step 7:

Close the Select a Report dialog box.

Check
POINT

1. What is the purpose of the bank reconciliation process?
2. Name six factors that can cause a difference between the bank statement balance and the Cash account/checkbook balance.

Answers
1. *The purpose of the bank reconciliation process is to bring the ending bank statement balance and the ending Cash account/checkbook balance into agreement.*
2. *Six factors that can cause a difference between the balances are deposits in transit, outstanding checks, ATM deposits and withdrawals, bank fees, NSF checks, and errors.*

PRACTICE *objective* 3

Bullfrog Maintenance Company received the bank statement shown in figure 6–52 for the month ended January 31, 2007. Use the following steps to prepare an account reconciliation.

FIGURE 6-52
Bank Reconciliation for Bullfrog Maintenance Company

| Bank of California |
| 2121 Market Street |
| San Francisco, CA 95434 |

Bullfrog Maintenance Company
   Acct: 20000897

REGULAR CHECKING

Previous Balance	$ 13,873.69	Statement Date: January 31, 2007
2 Deposits (+)	1,077.64	
3 Checks (-)	1,811.87	
2 Other Deductions (-)	150.00	
Service (-)	35.00	
Ending Balance	12,954.46	

DEPOSITS					
January 28, 2007	$ 752.64				
January 29, 2007	325.00				

CHECKS (Asterisk* indicates break in check number sequence)					
January 27, 2007	700	$ 872.20			
January 31, 2007	701	1,200.00			
January 31, 2007	703*	265.98			
January 31, 2007	Bank Fees	35.00			

OTHER DEDUCTIONS (ATM's)					
January 16, 2007	ATM	$ 50.00			
January 21, 2007	ATM	100.00			

Step 1:

Open Bullfrog Maintenance Company.

Step 2:

Print the check register. Your printout should look like figure 6–53.

FIGURE 6-53

Check Register for Bullfrog Maintenance Company

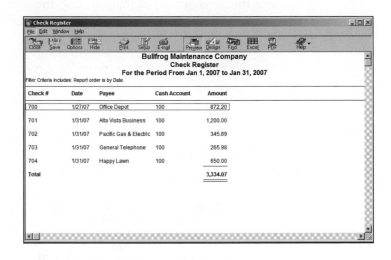

Step 3:

Print the Cash Receipts Journal. Your printout should look like figure 6–54.

FIGURE 6-54

Cash Receipts Journal for Bullfrog Maintenance Company

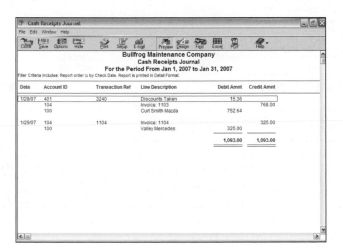

Use the following information to create the Bank Fee Expense account:

Account ID:	**522**
Description:	**Bank Fee Expense**
Account Type:	**Expenses**

Step 5:

Prepare the account reconciliation. Use the information from the check register, the cash receipts journal, and the bank statement.

Step 6:

Print the *Account Reconciliation* report. Your report should look like figure 6–55.

FIGURE 6-55

Account Reconciliation for Bullfrog Maintenance Company

Page: 1

Bullfrog Maintenance Company
Account Reconciliation
As of Jan 31, 2007
100 - Cash
Bank Statement Date: January 31, 2007

Filter Criteria includes: Report is printed in Detail Format.

Beginning GL Balance				
Add: Cash Receipts				1,077.64
Less: Cash Disbursements				(3,334.07)
Add (Less) Other				14,215.00
Ending GL Balance				11,958.57
Ending Bank Balance				12,954.46
Add back deposits in transit				
Total deposits in transit				
(Less) outstanding checks	Jan 31, 2007	702	(345.89)	
	Jan 31, 2007	704	(650.00)	
Total outstanding checks				(995.89)
Add (Less) Other				
Total other				
Unreconciled difference				0.00
Ending GL Balance				11,958.57

Step 7:

Close the Select a Report dialog box.

INTERNET *Access*

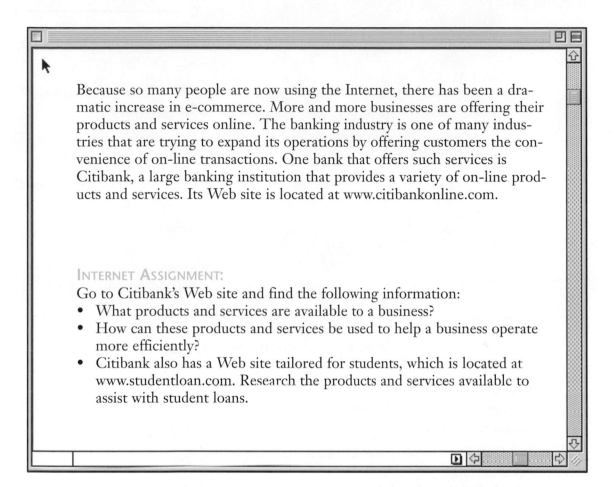

Because so many people are now using the Internet, there has been a dramatic increase in e-commerce. More and more businesses are offering their products and services online. The banking industry is one of many industries that are trying to expand its operations by offering customers the convenience of on-line transactions. One bank that offers such services is Citibank, a large banking institution that provides a variety of on-line products and services. Its Web site is located at www.citibankonline.com.

INTERNET ASSIGNMENT:

Go to Citibank's Web site and find the following information:

- What products and services are available to a business?
- How can these products and services be used to help a business operate more efficiently?
- Citibank also has a Web site tailored for students, which is located at www.studentloan.com. Research the products and services available to assist with student loans.

SOFTWARE
Command Summary

Cash Payments on Account	Tasks, Payments, Vendor ID, Apply to Invoices
Cash Payments without Invoice	Tasks, Payments, Vendor ID, Apply to Expenses
Cash Receipts on Account	Tasks, Receipts, Customer ID, Apply to Invoices
Cash Receipts without Invoice	Tasks, Receipts, Customer ID, Apply to Revenues
Prepare an Account Reconciliation	Print/Review Cash Receipts Journal, Print/Review Check Register, Tasks, Account Reconciliation, Adjust

PROJECTS
and Problems

CONTENT CHECK

Multiple Choice: Choose only one response for each question.

1. What button within the Receipts window is used to compute the new balance of the Cash account?
   A. Open
   B. Row
   C. Journal
   D. Recalculate
   E. Save

2. To verify that the correct accounts have been debited and credited, what toolbar button would you use to view the Accounting Behind the Screens window?
   A. Open
   B. Event
   C. Journal
   D. Row
   E. Save

3. Which of the following would provide information needed for the cash account reconciliation?
   A. Aged Payables
   B. Sales Journal
   C. Check Register
   D. Purchases Journal
   E. Vendor List

4. What toolbar button in the Account Reconciliation dialog box is used to enter withdrawals and other items that must be recorded to update the balance of the firm's Cash account?
   A. Range
   B. Adjust
   C. Row
   D. Open
   E. Recur

5. When a business provides a service on credit to a customer, what function of Peachtree is used to record the transaction?
   A. General Journal Entry
   B. Payments
   C. Purchases/Receive Inventory
   D. Receipts
   E. Sales/Invoicing

Short Essay Response: Provide a detailed answer for each question.

1. What are some of the procedures that a business should use to protect its cash?
2. What is the purpose of an account reconciliation?
3. What is the purpose of the Accounting Behind the Screens window?
4. What information appears on the bank statement?
5. Why do the ending balance of the bank statement and the ending balance in a firm's cash records usually differ?
6. What information from a firm's records is needed for the account reconciliation?

CASE PROBLEMS

PROBLEM 1A

Open Transnational Management Group (TMG), a business consulting firm, which you can download from the CD that comes with your book. (See "Using the *Computerized Accounting with Peachtree 2007* CD" at the beginning of this textbook for downloading instructions.)

1. TMG plans to make credit purchases from four new vendors. Create new vendor accounts for the businesses listed below.

Vendor ID:	**OPS-01**
Name:	**O'Neal Payroll Services**

General Tab

Contact:	**Annette O'Neal**
Account #:	**846357**
Address:	**7314 Sycamore Avenue**
City, ST Zip:	**Stockton, CA 95210**
Country:	**USA**
Vendor Type:	**Expense**
1099 Type:	**None**

Telephone 1:		209-555-7821
Telephone 2:		209-555-7822
Fax:		209-555-7823

Purchase Defaults Tab

Expense Account:	**78500** (Payroll Service Expense)
Tax ID #:	
Ship Via:	**US Mail**
Terms:	**Due EOM, 0.00 Discount**
Beginning Balances:	**0**

Vendor ID:	**GR-02**
Name:	**Grupe Associates**

General Tab

Contact:	**Gary Robertson**	
Account #:		**16432571**
	Address:	**4189 Holly Lane**
	City, ST Zip:	**Stockton, CA 95210**
	Country:	**USA**
Vendor Type:		**Expense**
1099 Type:		**None**
Telephone 1:		**209-555-7321**
Telephone 2:		**209-555-7322**
Fax:		**209-555-7325**

Purchase Defaults Tab

Expense Account:	**74000** (Rent or Lease Expense)
Tax ID #:	
Ship Via:	**US Mail**
Terms:	**Due EOM, 0.00 Discount**
Beginning Balances:	**0**

Vendor ID:	**OFFMAX-03**
Name:	**Office Max**

General Tab

Contact:	**Joshua Baker**	
Account #:		**15491326**
	Address:	**3915 Webber Lane**
	City, ST Zip:	**Stockton, CA 95207**
	Country:	**USA**
Vendor Type:		**Supplier**
1099 Type:		**None**
Telephone 1:		**209-555-7981**
Telephone 2:		**209-555-7985**
Fax:		**209-555-7988**

Purchase Defaults Tab

Expense Account:	**12000** (Office Supplies)
Tax ID #:	
Ship Via:	**Fed-EX**
Terms:	**2% 10 Days, Net 30 Days**
Beginning Balances:	**0**

Vendor ID:	**ATT-04**
Name:	**AT&T**

General Tab

Contact:	**George Sanchez**
Account #:	**19852637**
Address:	**6185 West Montgomery Avenue**
City, ST Zip:	**Stockton, CA 95207**
Country:	**USA**
Vendor Type:	**Expense**
1099 Type:	**None**
Telephone 1:	**209-555-5461**
Telephone 2:	**209-555-5462**
Fax:	**209-555-5463**

Purchase Defaults Tab

Expense Account:	**76000** (Telephone Expense)
Tax ID #:	
Ship Via:	**US Mail**
Terms:	**Due EOM, 0.00 Discount**
Beginning Balances:	**0**

2. TMG plans to sell its services on credit to the following three new customers. Create new customer accounts for each.

Customer ID:	**LM-01**
Name:	**Lee Manufacturing**

General Tab

Contact:	**Robert Lee**
Bill to Address	
Address:	**4639 Lincoln Boulevard**
City, ST Zip:	**Stockton, CA 95210**
Country:	**USA**
Sales Tax:	
Customer Type:	**General**
Telephone 1:	**209-555-1320**
Telephone 2:	**209-555-1321**
Fax:	**209-555-1330**

Sales Defaults Tab

GL Sales Acct:	**40000**
Ship Via:	**Fed-EX**

Pricing Level:	**Price Level 1**
Terms:	**2% 10 Days, Net 30 Days**
Beginning Balances:	**0**

Customer ID:	**CD-02**
Name:	**Computer Design**

General Tab

Contact:	**Sylvia Harrison**
Bill to Address	
Address:	**48195 East Powell**
City, ST Zip:	**Tracy, CA 95376**
Country:	**USA**
Sales Tax:	
Customer Type:	**General**
Telephone 1:	**209-555-2083**
Telephone 2:	**209-555-2084**
Fax:	**209-555-2085**

Sales Defaults Tab

GL Sales Acct:	**40000**
Ship Via:	**Fed-EX**
Pricing Level:	**Price Level 1**
Terms:	**2% 10 Days, Net 30 Days**
Beginning Balances:	**0**

Customer ID:	**BAS-03**
Name:	**Barron's Accounting Services**

General Tab

Contact:	**Armando Barron**
Bill to Address	
Address:	**44137 21st Street**
City, ST Zip:	**Watsonville, CA 95760**
Country:	**USA**
Sales Tax:	
Customer Type:	**General**
Telephone 1:	**209-555-3621**
Telephone 2:	**209-555-3622**
Fax:	**209-555-3635**

Sales Defaults Tab

GL Sales Acct:	**40000**
Ship Via:	**Fed-EX**
Pricing Level:	**Price Level 1**
Terms:	**2% 10 Days, Net 30 Days**
Beginning Balances:	**0**

3. Enter each of the transactions listed below for April 2007. Choose the appropriate option on the Tasks menu: Sales/Invoicing, Purchases/Receive Inventory, Receipts, Payments, or General Journal Entry. Use Account 49000, Fee Discount for any discounts taken by customers.

Date	Transaction
Apr. 4	Received a bill (Invoice 9582) of $1,780 for monthly rent from Grupe Associates.
5	Performed consulting services for $1,600 on credit for Lee Manufacturing. Issued Invoice 3001.
6	Received a bill (Invoice 12852) of $275 for monthly usage of telephone service from AT&T.
6	Purchased office supplies for $350 on credit from Office Max. Received Invoice 6640.
9	Performed consulting services for $980 on credit for Barron's Accounting Services. Issued Invoice 3002.
9	Performed consulting services for Computer Design for $1,800 in cash, check # 1215.
14	Received the amount due for Invoice 3001 from Lee Manufacturing, less a 2% discount, check # 3291.
15	Paid the amount due for Invoice 6640 to Office Max, less a 2% discount. Issued check # 1020. (Use Account 12000, Office Supplies as the discount account.)
18	The owner withdrew $500 for personal use.
18	Purchased payroll services for $650 on credit from O'Neal Payroll Services. Received Invoice 1593.
24	Performed consulting services for $1,300 in cash.
24	Received the full amount due for Invoice 3002 from Barron's Accounting Services, check # 3145.
25	Performed consulting services for $785 on credit for Computer Design. Issued Invoice 3003. Received check for $225 from the customer.
30	Paid $1,780 on account to Grupe Associates. Issued check # 1021.
30	Paid $275 on account to AT&T. Issued check # 1022.
30	Received the balance due (check # 1265) for Invoice 3003 from Computer Design less a 2% discount. (This customer previously made a partial payment of $225. However, the customer is entitled to take the discount of $15.70 ($785 × 2%) on the full amount of the invoice—$785.)

HINT

Enter this transaction using the General Journal Entry task feature.

HINT

Key **Cash** in the *Name* and *Reference* fields of the Receipts window.

4. Print the following reports for April: *Customer Ledgers, Cash Receipts Journal, Vendor Ledgers, Cash Disbursements Journal,* and *General Ledger Trial Balance.*

PROBLEM 2A

Open Chao and Associates, an engineering company, which you downloaded from the CD that comes with this book.

This firm received the following bank statement for the month ended June 30, 2007:

1. Prepare an account reconciliation. Bring the ending balances of the firm's bank statement and Cash account into agreement.
2. Print an *Account Reconciliation* report.

		Bank of San Joaquin
		2876 Main Street
		Tracy, CA 95376
Chao and Associates		
Account No: 87942331		
REGULAR CHECKING		
Beginning Balance	$24,000.00	**Statement Date: June 30, 2007**
2 Deposits (+)	9,900.00	
4 Checks (-)	9,257.50	
2 Other Deductions (-)	300.00	
Service Charges(-)	40.00	
Ending Balance	24,302.50	
DEPOSITS		
June 14, 2007	$5,000.00	
June 23, 2007	4,900.00	
CHECKS AND BANK FEES (Asterisk* indicates break in check number sequence)		
June 20, 2007	2000	$2,744.00
June 24, 2007	2001	4,200.00
June 28, 2007	2002	1,813.50
June 30, 2007	2004*	500.00
June 30, 2007	Bank Fees	40.00
OTHER DEDUCTIONS (ATMs)		
June 16, 2007	ATM	$ 100.00
June 21, 2007	ATM	200.00

PROBLEM 1B

Open Abelar Designs, an architectural firm, which you can download from the CD that comes with your book. (See "Using the *Computerized Accounting with Peachtree 2007* CD" at the beginning of this textbook for downloading instructions.)

1. Create new vendor accounts for the four new vendors listed below.

Vendor ID: **GPS-01**
Name: **Gentry Payroll Services**

General Tab

Contact:	**Greg Gentry**
Account #:	**659412**
Address:	**9137 Corral Drive**
City, ST Zip:	**Stockton, CA 95210**
Country:	**USA**
Vendor Type:	**Expense**
1099 Type:	**None**
Telephone 1:	**209-555-9865**
Telephone 2:	**209-555-9866**
Fax:	**209-555-9890**

Purchase Defaults Tab

Expense Account:	**78500** (Payroll Service Expense)
Tax ID #:	
Ship Via:	**US Mail**
Terms:	**Due EOM, 0.00 Discount**
Beginning Balances:	**0**

Vendor ID: **GR-02**
Name: **Grupe Associates**

General Tab

Contact:	**Gary Robertson**
Account #:	**6549763**
Address:	**4189 Holly Lane**
City, ST Zip:	**Stockton, CA 95210**
Country:	**USA**
Vendor Type:	**Expense**
1099 Type:	**None**
Telephone 1:	**209-555-7321**
Telephone 2:	**209-555-7322**
Fax:	**209-555-7325**

Purchase Defaults Tab

Expe*ns*e Account:	79000 (Rent or Lease Expense)
Ta*x* ID #:	
Ship Via:	US Mail
Terms:	Due EOM, 0.00 Discount
Beginning Balances:	0
Vendor *ID*:	OFFMAX-03
N*a*me:	Office Max

General Tab

Cont*a*ct:	Heather Brannon
Acco*u*nt #:	496782
*A*ddress:	3915 Webber Lane
City, ST *Z*ip:	Stockton, CA 95207
Country:	USA
Vendor Type:	Supplier
10*9*9 Type:	None
Telephone *1*:	209-555-7981
Telephone *2*:	209-555-7985
Fa*x*:	209-555-7988

Purchase Defaults Tab

Expe*ns*e Account:	12000 (Office Supplies)
Ta*x* ID #:	
Ship Via:	Fed-EX
Terms:	2% 10 Days, Net 30 Days
Beginning Balances:	0
Vendor *ID*:	PB-04
N*a*me:	Pacific Bell

General Tab

Cont*a*ct:	Monica Volbrecht
Acco*u*nt #:	9653294
*A*ddress:	62918 South Street
City, ST *Z*ip:	Stockton, CA 95207
Country:	USA
Vendor Type:	Expense
10*9*9 Type:	None
Telephone *1*:	209-555-7834
Telephone *2*:	209-555-7835
Fa*x*:	209-555-7840

Purchase Defaults Tab

Expe*ns*e Account:	80500 (Telephone Expense)
Ta*x* ID #:	
Ship Via:	US Mail
Terms:	Due EOM, 0.00 Discount
Beginning Balances:	0

2. Create new customer accounts for the three customers listed below.

Customer ID:	**AR-01**
Name:	**Artistic Renovation**

General Tab

Contact:	**Francisco Moreno**
Bill to Address	
Address:	**95517 Tracy Boulevard**
City, ST Zip:	**Stockton, CA 95210**
Country:	**USA**
Sales Tax:	
Customer Type:	**General**
Telephone 1:	**209-555-6497**
Telephone 2:	**209-555-6498**
Fax:	**209-555-6400**

Sales Defaults Tab

GL Sales Acct:	**40600**
Ship Via:	**Fed-EX**
Pricing Level:	**Price Level 1**
Terms:	**2% 10 Days, Net 30 Days**
Beginning Balances:	**0**

Customer ID:	**KCB-02**
Name:	**Kim's Custom Builders**

General Tab

Contact:	**Paul Kim**
Bill to Address	
Address:	**6432 West Howard Lane**
City, ST Zip:	**Tracy, CA 95376**
Country:	**USA**
Sales Tax:	
Customer Type:	**General**
Telephone 1:	**209-555-2265**
Telephone 2:	**209-555-2266**

Sales Defaults Tab

GL Sales Acct:	**40200**
Ship Via:	**Fed-EX**
Pricing Level:	**Price Level 1**
Terms:	**2% 10 Days, Net 30 Days**
Beginning Balances:	**0**

Customer ID: **WC-03**
Name: **Walsh Construction**

General Tab

Contact: **Martha Walsh**
Bill to Address

      Address: **4321 23rd Street**
      City, ST Zip: **Manteca, CA 95301**
      Country: **USA**

Sales Tax:
Customer Type: **General**
Telephone 1:   **209-555-2136**
Telephone 2:   **209-555-2137**
Fax: **209-555-2140**

Sales Defaults Tab

GL Sales Acct: **40600**
Ship Via: **Fed-EX**
Pricing Level: **Price Level 1**
Terms: **2% 10 Days, Net 30 Days**
Beginning Balances: **0**

3. Enter each of the following transactions for May 2007. Choose the appropriate option on the Tasks menu: Sales/Invoicing, Purchases/Receive Inventory, Receipts, Payments, or General Journal Entry. Use Account 49000, Fee Discount for any discounts taken by customers.

Date	Transaction
May 5	Received a bill (Invoice 10115) of $1,300 for monthly rent from Grupe Associates.
6	Performed architectural design services for $825 on credit for Artistic Renovations. Issued Invoice 4001.
7	Received a bill (Invoice 26591) of $170 for monthly usage of telephone service from Pacific Bell.
7	Purchased office supplies for $125 on credit from Office Max. Received Invoice 7281.
10	Performed architectural consulting services for $980 on credit for Kim's Custom Builders. Issued Invoice 4002.
11	Performed architectural consulting services for $1,320 in cash.
15	Received the amount due for Invoice 4001 from Artistic Renovations, less a 2% discount, check # 4521.

HINT

Key **Cash** in the *Name* and *Reference* field of the Receipts window.

HINT →

Enter this transaction using the General Journal Entry task feature.

16	Paid the amount due for Invoice 7281 to Office Max, less a 2% discount. Issued check # 231. (Use Account 12000, Office Supplies as the discount.)
18	The owner withdrew $700 for personal use.
18	Purchased payroll services for $450 on credit from Gentry Payroll Services. Received Invoice 8972.
25	Performed architectural design services for $2,340 on credit for Walsh Construction. Issued Invoice 4003.
25	Received the full amount due for Invoice 4002 from Kim's Custom Builders, check # 3238.
26	Performed architectural design services for $1,480 on credit for Artistic Renovations. Issued Invoice 4004. Received check for $480 from the customer.
30	Paid $1,300 on account to Grupe Associates. Issued check # 232.
30	Paid $170 on account to Pacific Bell. Issued check # 233.
31	Received the balance due (check # 4527) for Invoice 4004 from Artistic Renovations, less a 2% discount. (This customer previously made a partial payment of $480. However, the customer is entitled to take the discount of $29.60 ($1,480 × 2%) on the full amount of the invoice—$1,480.)

4. Print the following reports for May: *Customer Ledgers, Cash Receipts Journal, Vendor Ledgers, Cash Disbursements Journal,* and *General Ledger Trial Balance.*

		Bank of Stanislaus
		18132 West 11th Street
		Tracy, CA 95376
Hendricks Construction		
Account No: 649575321		
REGULAR CHECKING		
Beginning Balance	$36,000.00	**Statement Date: June 30, 2007**
2 Deposits (+)	14,850.00	
4 Checks (-)	13,886.25	
2 Other Deductions (-)	450.00	
Service Charges(-)	60.00	
Ending Balance	36,453.75	
DEPOSITS		
June 14, 2007	$7,500.00	
June 23, 2007	$7,350.00	
CHECKS AND BANK FEES (Asterisk* indicates break in check number sequence)					
June 20, 2007	2000	$4,116.00			
June 24, 2007	2001	6,300.00			
June 28, 2007	2002	2,720.25			
June 30, 2007	2004*	750.00			
June 30, 2007	Bank Fees	60.00			
OTHER DEDUCTIONS (ATMs)					
June 16, 2007	ATM	$ 150.00			
June 21, 2007	ATM	300.00			

PROBLEM 2B

Open Hendrick's Construction, a home building company, which you downloaded from the CD that comes with this book.

The firm received the following bank statement for the month ended June 30, 2007:

1. Prepare an account reconciliation. Bring the ending balances of the firm's bank statement and Cash account into agreement.
2. Print an *Account Reconciliation* report.

1. Form a group of three or four students. As a group, examine the Cash Manager and Collection Manager features of Peachtree. These features can be located by accessing Analysis on the main menu. Discuss how these features can be used to help a business meet its financial obligations and increase its collection of accounts receivable.

2. As a group, select a local business that you are familiar with, such as a fast-food restaurant, a supermarket, or a department store. What type of cash control problems might this business have? What procedures could this business use to protect its cash?

WRITING AND DECISION MAKING

Assume that you work for a small company that has a substantial volume of cash receipts from credit customers and cash payments to vendors. The owner, Jesse Ramirez, is thinking about buying Peachtree for her accounting system. Because you have had experience with Peachtree in a college course, she asks you to provide her with information about the Peachtree procedures for the tasks listed below. Write a memo that provides information on the following tasks:

1. Setting up customer accounts and vendor accounts
2. Recording credit sales and credit purchases
3. Recording cash receipts and cash payments on account

CHAPTER

PREPARING

THE FINANCIAL STATEMENTS

LEARNING OBJECTIVES

1. Journalize the adjusting entries

2. Prepare and print the financial statements

3. Change the accounting period

SOFTWARE FEATURES

- Print and Filter feature

- Copying Financial Statement Format feature

- Designing Reports feature, including text formatting

- Changing the Accounting Period feature

Every accounting system must keep a detailed record of the financial transactions that take place within a business. However, the ultimate purpose of an accounting system is to provide timely, reliable information that owners and managers can use to make decisions. Much of this information comes from financial statements.

How much profit did we earn? Do we have enough cash to meet our operating needs? How much do we owe to vendors? How much can we expect to receive from credit customers? The financial statements provide the answers to questions such as these.

One of the great benefits of a computerized accounting system like Peachtree is the ease with which you can produce financial statements. In manual accounting, the process of taking a trial balance of the general ledger accounts, recording adjustments, calculating the adjusted account balances, and then preparing the financial statements can be difficult and time consuming. In Peachtree, much of this work is done by the system itself.

Once adjusting entries have been recorded, Peachtree can automatically produce an income statement, a balance sheet, a statement of changes in financial position, and a statement of cash flow.

OBJECTIVE 1 – JOURNALIZE THE ADJUSTING ENTRIES

Before the financial statements are prepared at the end of a period, it is necessary to make **adjusting entries**. These types of entries are used to bring the general ledger accounts up to date so that they include previously unrecorded items that relate to the period.

In accrual accounting, all revenue must be recorded when earned and all expenses must be recorded when incurred. However, in most businesses, certain items are not recorded during a period. For example, as of January 31, 2007, Woodward Construction Company has not yet recorded the expenses for supplies used, depreciation of equipment, and unpaid salaries. Adjusting entries must be made for these items. Adjusting entries affect one balance sheet account and one income statement account.

RECORDING THE ADJUSTING ENTRY FOR SUPPLIES USED

During any accounting period, the employees of a firm constantly use paper clips, computer paper, staples, and other office supplies. Obviously, it is not practical to record the expense for supplies used on a day-to-day basis. Instead, businesses make an adjusting entry for supplies used at the end of the period.

Remember that when Woodward Construction Company purchases office supplies, it records their cost in the asset account Office Supplies. On January 31, 2007, this account has a balance of $1,962. However, when the firm takes an inventory of the office supplies on hand, it finds that they total $1,062. Thus, the firm has used $900 of office supplies during January.

On January 31, 2007, Woodward must make an adjusting entry to record the expense for the $900 of office supplies used in January. This entry appears in the general journal. It consists of a debit of $900 to Office Supplies Expense and a credit of $900 to Office Supplies.

One effect of this adjusting entry is to establish the expense for office supplies for the period. The other effect is to reduce the balance of the asset account Office Supplies to $1,062, the amount of supplies actually on hand.

adjusting entries
Entries that are used to bring the general ledger accounts up to date so that they include previously unrecorded items that relate to the period.

RECORDING THE ADJUSTING ENTRY FOR DEPRECIATION

depreciation The process of allocating the cost of a fixed asset to operations during its useful life.

Every fixed asset except land is subject to depreciation. Remember that **depreciation** is the process of allocating the cost of a fixed asset to operations during its useful life. An adjusting entry must be made to record the depreciation expense for each type of fixed asset that a business owns. Various methods are available for calculating depreciation. Some of these methods will be discussed in a later chapter.

The Woodward Construction Company owns one type of fixed asset—equipment. It depreciates the equipment at the rate of $1,000 a month. Therefore, on January 31, 2007, Woodward makes an adjusting entry to record $1,000 of depreciation expense for January. This entry consists of a debit to Depreciation Expense–Equipment and a credit to Accumulated Depreciation–Equipment.

Remember that Accumulated Depreciation–Equipment is a contra asset account. It has a credit balance, which is contrary to the normal debit balance of an asset account. Accumulated Depreciation–Equipment is used to show the total amount of depreciation taken on the equipment during its useful life.

RECORDING THE ADJUSTING ENTRY FOR UNPAID SALARIES

Often, when an accounting period ends, a business owes salaries to its employees. This situation occurs because the end of the accounting period falls in the midst of a payroll period. For example, suppose that a firm has a weekly payroll period that extends from Monday to Friday, and the employees receive their paychecks on Friday. If the accounting period ends on a Wednesday, the firm will owe unpaid salaries for three days—Monday, Tuesday, and Wednesday.

On January 31, 2007, Woodward Construction Company owes $1,400 of unpaid salaries. An adjusting entry must be made to record the expense for unpaid salaries. This entry consists of a debit of $1,400 to Wages and Salaries Expense and a credit of $1,400 to Wages and Salaries Payable.

The firm has a liability for the salaries owed to its employees. Therefore, the account credited in the adjusting entry is the liability account Wages and Salaries Payable.

USING PEACHTREE TO RECORD SAMPLE ADJUSTING ENTRIES

Follow the steps outlined below to make adjusting entries for Woodward Construction Company as of January 31, 2007. All of these entries should appear in the general journal.

Step 1:

Open Woodward Construction Company. Close the Action Items log.

Step 2:

The first adjusting entry is for $900 of office supplies used during January. Click the *General Journal Entry* from the **Shortcuts** section at the side of the basic Peachtree window, as shown in figure 7–1.

FIGURE 7-1

General Journal Entry from the Shortcuts Section

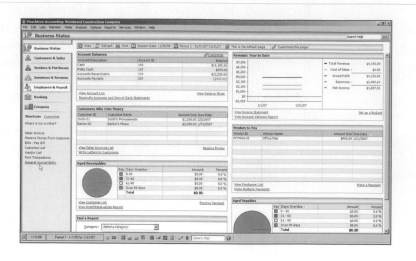

Step 3:

The General Journal Entry window will appear. Change the date to *Jan 31, 2007*.

Step 4:

Key **506** (Office Supplies Expense) in the *GL Account* field.

Step 5:

Key **Adjusting Entry** in the *Description* field.

Step 6:

Key **900.00** as the amount in the *Debit* field, and tab to the next row.

Step 7:

Key **106** (Office Supplies) in the *Account No.* field.

Step 8:

Key **900.00** in the *Credit* field.

Step 9:

Compare your work with the completed entry shown in figure 7–2. Make any necessary changes.

FIGURE 7-2

Completed Adjusting Entry for Office Supplies Used

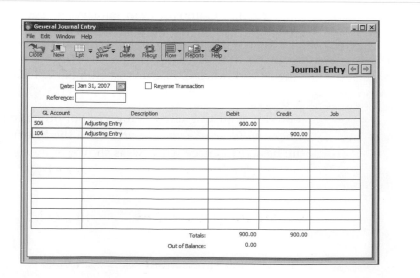

Step 10:

Click Save. **Note:** Although there are additional blank lines on which to record other adjusting entries, it is good practice to enter them separately.

Step 11:

The second adjusting entry is for $1,000 of depreciation on Woodward's equipment during January. Key **510** (Depreciation Expense–Equipment) in the *GL Account* field.

Step 12:

Key **Adjusting Entry** in the *Description* field.

Step 13:

Key **1,000.00** in the *Debit* field, and tab to the next row.

Step 14:

Key **108.5** (Accum. Depr.–Equipment) in the *GL Account* field.

Step 15:

Key **1,000.00** as the amount in the *Credit* field.

Step 16:

Check your work for accuracy by comparing it with figure 7–3. Then click Save.

FIGURE 7-3

Completed Adjusting Entry for Depreciation

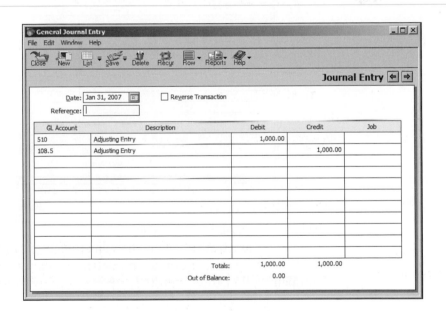

Step 17:

The third adjusting entry is for $1,400 of unpaid salaries. Key **512** (Wages and Salaries Expense) in the *GL Account* field.

Step 18:

Key **Adjusting Entry** in the *Description* field.

Step 19:

Key **1,400.00** in the *Debit* field, and tab to the next row.

Step 20:

Woodward does not have a Wages and Salaries Payable account. Therefore, use the following information to create this account.

Account ID:	**210**
Description:	**Wages and Salaries Payable**
Account Type:	**Other Current Liabilities**

Step 21:

Key **210** in the *Account No.* field.

Step 22:

Key **1,400.00** in the *Credit* field.

Step 23:

Check your work for accuracy by comparing it with figure 7–4. Then click Save and close the General Journal Entry window.

FIGURE 7-4

Completed Adjusting Entry for Unpaid Salaries

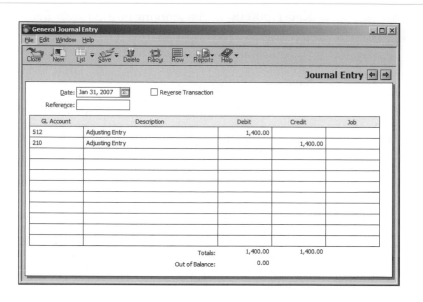

REVIEWING THE ADJUSTING ENTRIES

It is a good practice to review the adjusting entries after they have been recorded. To review the adjusting entries made for Woodward Construction Company follow these steps:

Step 1:

Click the *Business Status* icon on the Navigation Aids toolbar at the left side of the basic Peachtree window.

Step 2:

Select *General Ledger* from the Find a Report Category drop-down list, as shown in figure 7–5.

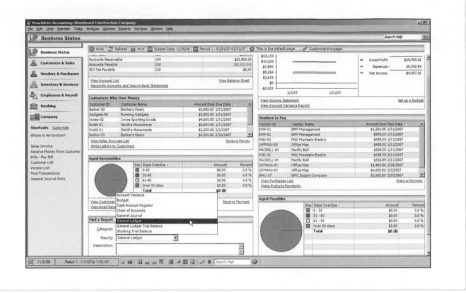

Step 3:

Select General Journal from the Find a Report Report drop-down list, as shown in figure 7–6.

FIGURE 7-6

*Completed General Journal
Filter Tab*

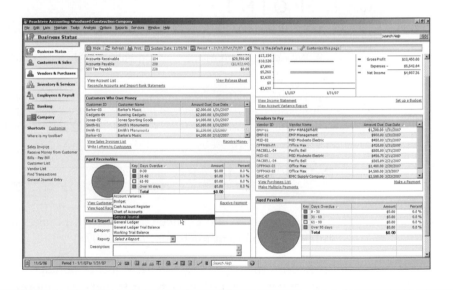

NOTE

Select Reports from the Main Menu if you wish to narrow the focus of the Report.

Step 4:

Click Display.

Step 5:

Compare your adjusting entries with the ones shown in figure 7–7. Make any necessary changes. Note that entries from previous chapters are also included in the General Journal report of January 31, 2007.

FIGURE 7-7
*Completed Adjusting Entries
in General Journal*

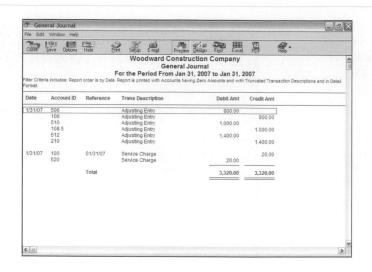

Step 6:

Close the General Journal window.

POINT

1. What three types of adjusting entries are made by Woodward Construction Company?
2. Why does a firm make adjusting entries at the end of an accounting period?

Answers

1. *Woodward makes adjusting entries for supplies used, depreciation, and unpaid salaries.*
2. *Adjusting entries are made to bring the general ledger accounts up to date so that they include previously unrecorded items that relate to the period.*

PRACTICE objective 1

Step 1:

Open Bullfrog Maintenance Company, and make the following adjusting entries for the firm for January 31, 2007:

1. Record the office supplies used during January. An inventory showed office supplies of $1,170 on hand on January 31. Subtract this amount from the balance of the Office Supplies account to find the amount of the adjustment. **Hint:** The ledger accounts and the balance sheet will provide the necessary information.
2. Record the unpaid salaries of $3,400 on January 31. There is no account for Wages and Salaries Payable. Create this account, using 210 as the Account ID. Remember, this account is of type Other Current Liabilities.
3. Record depreciation of $750 on the equipment for the month of January.

Step 2:

Compare your adjusting entries with figure 7-8.

Step 3:

Close the General Journal window.

FIGURE 7-8

Completed Adjusting Entries
in General Journal

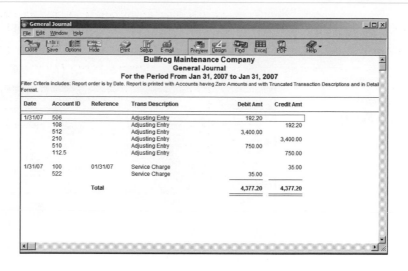

OBJECTIVE 2 — PREPARE AND PRINT THE FINANCIAL STATEMENTS

After the adjusting entries are journalized and posted, Peachtree can be used to produce the following financial statements: the income statement, the statement of changes in financial position, the balance sheet, and the statement of cash flow. You have already printed some of these reports in chapter 3; in this chapter you will learn more about how these reports are used in business, and will also learn how to customize the reports.

The **income statement** reports the results of operations for a period of time. It shows the revenue, expenses, and net income or net loss for the period. The **net income** or **net loss** is the difference between the revenue and expenses. Some people refer to the income statement as the "profit and loss statement."

The **statement of changes in financial position** reports the sources and uses of a firm's working capital for a period of time. **Working capital** is the excess of current assets over current liabilities. Working capital is a measure of a firm's ability to pay its short-term debts as they become due.

The **balance sheet** shows the financial condition of a business as of a specific date. It lists the assets, liabilities, and owner's equity of a business. The balance sheet is a detailed version of the basic accounting equation: Assets = Liabilities + Owner's Equity.

The **statement of cash flow** reports the inflows and outflows of cash from operating activities, investing activities, and financing activities that a business had during a period of time. This statement also shows the net increase or net decrease in cash for the period.

INCOME STATEMENT

Step 1:
Open Woodward Construction Company and close the Action Items log.

Step 2:
Click *Reports* from the Main Menu toolbar.

income statement A report of a firm's revenue, expenses, and net income or net loss for a period.

net income or net loss The difference between revenue and expenses.

statement of changes in financial position A report of a firm's sources and uses of working capital for a period.

working capital The excess of current assets over current liabilities.

balance sheet A report of a firm's assets, liabilities, and owner's equity as of a specific date.

statement of cash flow A report of the inflows and outflows of cash from operating activities, investing activities, and financing activities for a period.

Step 3:

Click *Financial Statements* from the <u>R</u>eports drop-down list, as shown in figure 7–9.

FIGURE 7-9

Financial Statements Selected from the Reports Drop-Down List

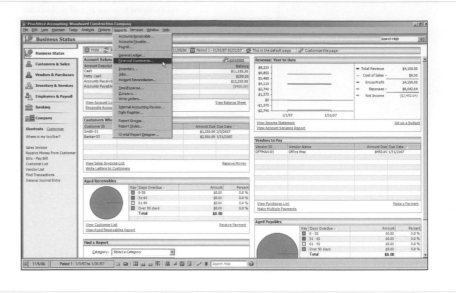

Step 4:

The Select a Report dialog box will appear. Click *<Standard> Income Stmnt* from the Report Li<u>s</u>t section, as shown in figure 7–10.

FIGURE 7-10

<Standard> Income Stmnt Chosen from Report List

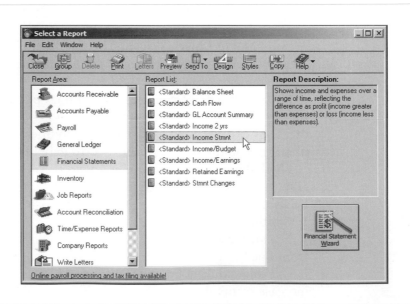

Step 5:

Click the <u>P</u>rint button on the toolbar.

Step 6:

Click *Current Period* at the *Time Fr<u>a</u>me* field of the Options folder tab.

Step 7:

Click "Show <u>Z</u>ero Amounts" to deselect it.

Step 8:

Click <u>O</u>K to print.

Step 9:

Prepare the Print dialog box as needed, and click OK when you are ready to print.

Step 10:

Compare your printout of the income statement with the one shown in figure 7–11.

FIGURE 7-11

Printout of Income Statement

Woodward Construction Company
Income Statement
For the One Month Ending January 31, 2007

	Current Month			Year to Date	
Revenues					
Revenue	$ 6,250.00	101.63	$	6,250.00	101.63
Sales Discounts	(100.00)	(1.63)		(100.00)	(1.63)
Total Revenues	6,150.00	100.00		6,150.00	100.00
Cost of Sales					
Total Cost of Sales	0.00	0.00		0.00	0.00
Gross Profit	6,150.00	100.00		6,150.00	100.00
Expenses					
Rent Expernse	1,200.00	19.51		1,200.00	19.51
Utilities Expense	456.75	7.43		456.75	7.43
Telephone Expense	565.89	9.20		565.89	9.20
Offcie Supplies Expense	900.00	14.63		900.00	14.63
Depreciation Expense-Equipment	1,000.00	16.26		1,000.00	16.26
Wages and Salaries Expense	1,400.00	22.76		1,400.00	22.76
Uncollectible Accounts Expense	2,000.00	32.52		2,000.00	32.52
Maintenance Expense	250.00	4.07		250.00	4.07
Bank Fees	20.00	0.33		20.00	0.33
Total Expenses	7,792.64	126.71		7,792.64	126.71
Net Income	$ (1,642.64)	(26.71)	$	(1,642.64)	(26.71)

STATEMENT OF CHANGES IN FINANCIAL POSITION

Step 1:
Click *<Standard> Stmnt Changes* from the Report List section of the Select a Report dialog box, as shown in figure 7–12.

FIGURE 7-12

*<Standard> Stmnt
Changes Chosen from
Report List*

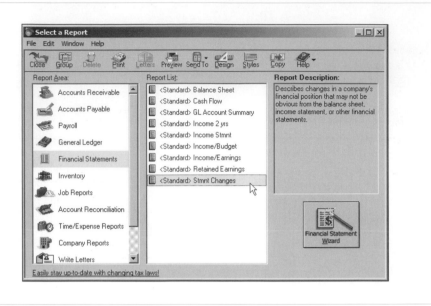

Step 2:
Click the Print button on the toolbar.

Step 3:
Click *Current Period* at the *Time Frame* field of the Options folder tab.

Step 4:
Click "Show Zero Amounts" to deselect it.

Step 5:
Click OK to print.

Step 6:
Prepare the Print dialog box as needed, and click OK when you are ready to print.

Step 7:
Compare your printout of the statement of changes in financial position with the one shown in figure 7–13.

FIGURE 7-13

Printout of Statement of Changes in Financial Position

Woodward Construction Company
Statement of Changes in Financial Position
For the one month ended January 31, 2007

	Current Month	Year To Date
Sources of Working Capital		
Net Income	$ (1,642.64)	$ (1,642.64)
Add back items not requiring working capital		
Accum . Depreciation-Equipment	13,000.00	13,000.00
Working capital from operations	11,357.36	11,357.36
Other sources		
J. Woodward, Capital	123,540.00	123,540.00
Total sources	134,897.36	134,897.36
Uses of working capital		
Equipment	(112,000.00)	(112,000.00)
Total uses	(112,000.00)	(112,000.00)
Net change	$ 22,897.36	$ 22,897.36
Analysis of componants of changes		
Increase <Decrease> in Current Assets		
Cash	$ 11,035.36	$ 11,035.36
Petty Cash	250.00	250.00
Accounts Receivbable	12,250.00	12,250.00
Office Supplies	1,062.00	1,062.00
<Increase> Decrease in Current Liabilities		
Accounts Payable	(450.00)	(450.00)
Wages and Salaries Payable	(1,400.00)	(1,400.00)
Net change	$ 22,747.36	$ 22,747.36

BALANCE SHEET

Step 1:

Click *<Standard> Balance Sheet* from the Report List section in the Select a Report dialog box, as shown in figure 7–14.

FIGURE 7-14

*<Standard> Balance Sheet
Chosen from Report List*

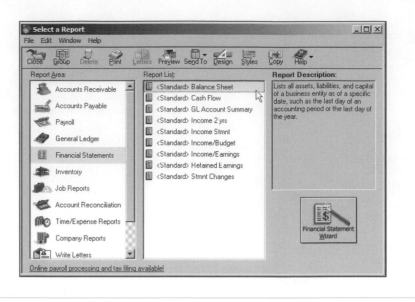

Step 2:

Click the Print button on the toolbar.

Step 3:

Click *Current Period* at the *Time Frame* field of the Options folder tab.

Step 4:

Click "Show Zero Amounts" to deselect it.

Step 5:

Click OK to print.

Step 6:

Prepare the Print dialog box as needed, and click OK when you are ready to print.

Step 7:

Compare your printout of the balance sheet with the one shown in figure 7–15.

FIGURE 7-15
Printout of Balance Sheet

Woodward Construction Company
Balance Sheet
January 31, 2007

ASSETS

Current Assets		
Cash	$ 11,035.36	
Petty Cash	250.00	
Accounts Receivable	12,250.00	
Office Supplies	1,062.00	
Total Current Assets		24,597.36
Property and Equipment		
Equipment	112,000.00	
Accum. Depreciation-Equipment	(13,000.00)	
Total Property and Equipment		99,000.00
Other Assets		
Total Other Assets		0.00
Total Assets		$ 123,597.36

LIABILITIES AND CAPITAL

Current Liabilities		
Accounts Payable	$ 450.00	
Wages Payable	1,400.00	
Total Current Liabilities		1,850.00
Long-Term Liabilities		
Total Long-Term Liabilities		0.00
Total Liabilities		1,850.00
Capital		
J. Woodward, Capital	123,540.00	
J. Woodward, Drawing	(150.00)	
Net Income	(1,642.64)	
Total Capital		121,747.36
Total Liabilities & Capital		$ 123,597.36

STATEMENT OF CASH FLOW

Step 1:

Click <Standard> Cash Flow from the Report List section of the Select a Report dialog box, as shown in figure 7–16.

FIGURE 7-16

<Standard> Cash Flow
Chosen from Report List

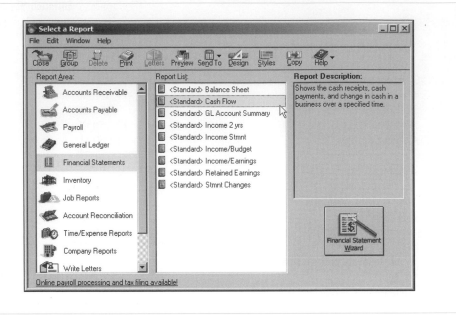

Step 2:

Click the Print button on the toolbar.

Step 3:

Click Current Period at the Time Frame field of the Options folder tab.

Step 4:

Click "Show Zero Amounts" to deselect it.

Step 5:

Click OK to print.

Step 6:

Prepare the Print dialog box as needed, and click OK when you are ready to print.

Step 7:

Compare your printout of the statement of cash flow with the one shown in figure 7–17.

FIGURE 7-17
Printout of Statement of Cash Flow

Woodward Construction Company
Statement of Cash Flow
For the one Month Ended January 31, 2007

	Current Month	Year to Date
Cash Flows from operating activities		
Net Income	$ (1,642.64)	$ (1,642.64)
Adjustments to reconcile net income to net cash provided by operating activities		
Accum. Depreciation-Equipment	13,000.00	13,000.00
Accounts Receivable	(12,250.00)	(12,250.00)
Office Supplies	(1,062.00)	(1,062.00)
Accounts Payable	450.00	450.00
Wages Payable	1,400.00	1,400.00
Total Adjustments	1,538.00	1,538.00
Net Cash provided by Operations	(104.64)	(104.64)
Cash Flows from investing activities		
Used For		
Equipment	(112,000.00)	(112,000.00)
Net cash used in investing	(112,000.00)	(112,000.00)
Cash Flows from financing activities		
Proceeds From		
J. Woodward, Capital	123,540.00	123,540.00
Used For		
J. Woodward, Drawing	(150.00)	(150.00)
Net cash used in financing	123,390.00	123,390.00
Net increase <decrease> in cash	$ 11,285.36	$ 11,285.36

Step 8:

Close the Select a Report dialog box.

COPYING ONE COMPANY'S FINANCIAL STATEMENT FORMAT FOR USE BY ANOTHER
All of the financial statements printed thus far have been selected from the standard list. However, it is possible to use the financial statement format of another company previously set up using Peachtree. For example, suppose a service company likes the format used by another similar company.

Peachtree can transfer that format. Follow the steps outlined below to use another company's financial statement format:

Step 1:
Click *Reports* from the Main Menu toolbar.

Step 2:
Click *Financial Statements* from the Reports drop-down list.

Step 3:
Click *<Standard> Balance Sheet* from the Report List section of the Select a Report dialog box.

Step 4:
Click the Copy button from the Select a Report toolbar.

Step 5:
The Copy Reports, Financial Statements & Letter Templates dialog box will appear. At the Select a Company to Copy from drop-down list, click the down arrow and then click *Bullfrog Maintenance Company*.

Step 6:
Click to check Include Standard Financial Statements located at the bottom of the window.

Step 7:
Click *<Standard> Balance Sheet*.

Step 8:
Key **Practice Balance Sheet** in the *New Name* field.

Step 9:
Compare your work with figure 7–18. Then click Copy from the Copy Reports, Financial Statements & Letter Templates toolbar.

FIGURE 7-18
Copy Reports, Financial Statements & Letter Templates Dialog Box

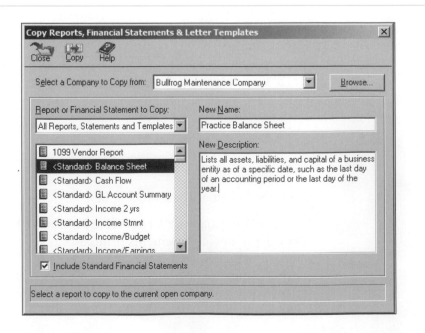

Step 10:

Click Close.

The balance sheet format of Bullfrog Maintenance Company is now available for use by Woodward Construction Company. The new Practice Balance Sheet is among the financial statement choices appearing in the Report List section of the Select a Report dialog box, as shown in figure 7–19. Any financial statement can be copied and used in the same manner as the balance sheet discussed here.

FIGURE 7-19

Practice Balance Sheet Chosen from Report List

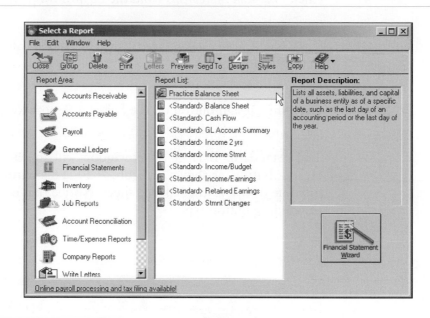

Step 11:

Close the Select a Report dialog box.

DESIGNING FINANCIAL STATEMENTS

Peachtree provides a standard, or default, financial statement format for all statements. However, some companies want to make changes to this format. Such changes may be subtle. For example, a company may want to change the font size or the typeface. The changes in format may also be substantial. Peachtree can accommodate a variety of changes.

You can make changes within each row of the financial statements. A row can have—

- Text Header
- Column Description
- Text Body
- Line Description
- Total Level
- Total Grand Total
- Text Footer

Assume that Woodward Construction Company wants to make several changes in the format of its financial statements. Follow the directions given below to make these changes.

Changing the Text Fonts

Step 1:

Click *Reports* on the Main Menu toolbar.

Step 2:

Click *Financial Statements* from the drop-down list.

Step 3:

Click *<Standard> Balance Sheet* from the Report List section of the Select a Report window.

Step 4:

Click the <u>D</u>esign button on the Select a Report toolbar.

Step 5:

The <Standard> Balance Sheet window will appear. Click the first Text-Header button, as shown in figure 7–20. This button is aligned with the first line of text of the balance sheet. Notice that each line of text has a corresponding button type.

FIGURE 7-20

Text-Header Button for First Line of Text

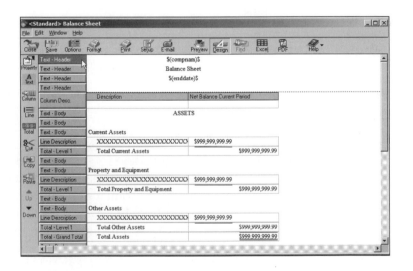

Step 6:

Click the *right* mouse button to reveal the drop-down list with text change options, as shown in figure 7–21.

FIGURE 7-21

*Drop-Down List with Text
Change Options*

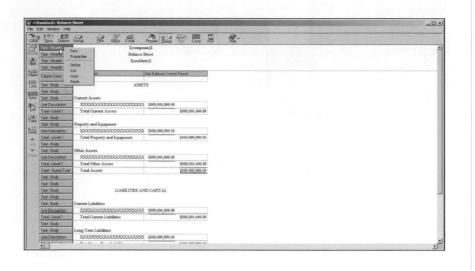

Step 7:

From the drop-down list, click the *left* mouse button to select Font.

Step 8:

At the Font dialog box, click *Arial Black* in the <u>F</u>ont section.

Step 9:

Click *11* in the <u>S</u>ize section, as shown in figure 7–22.

FIGURE 7-22

Font Dialog Box

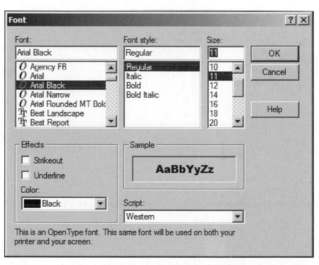

Step 10:

Click OK and then click <u>N</u>o at the Peachtree Query warning. If you click Yes, all fonts on the statement will be changed. If you click No, only the font of the specific line will be changed. Notice the change in the first line of the balance sheet shown in figure 7–23.

FIGURE 7-23

Font Style Change in First Line of Balance Sheet

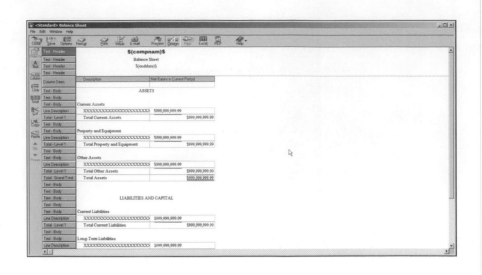

Changing the Text

Assume that Woodward Construction Company would like its balance sheet to have the title of *Special Balance Sheet*. Any change can be made in the wording of the title.

Step 1:

Click the second Text-Header button, which is aligned with the words *Balance Sheet*.

Step 2:

Click the Text button on the left side of the window to reveal the drop-down list with text change options as shown, in figure 7–24.

FIGURE 7-24

Text Drop-Down List with Text Change Options

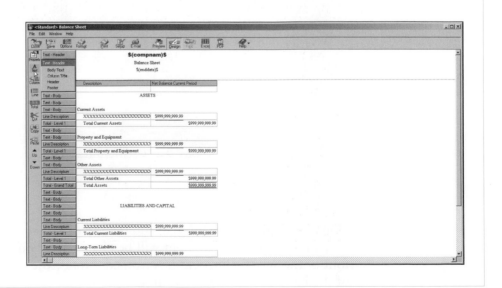

Step 3:

Click Header.

Step 4:

The Text dialog box will appear. Key **Special Balance Sheet** in the Text to Print box.

Step 5:

Click the down arrow at the *Alignment* field, and then click *Center of Column*, as shown in figure 7–25.

Step 6:

Click OK.

Notice that the new text-header *Special Balance Sheet* was inserted above the text-header *Balance Sheet*.

Step 7:

Click the third Text-Header button aligned with the words *Balance Sheet*.

Step 8:

Click the *right* mouse button to reveal the drop-down options for change list.

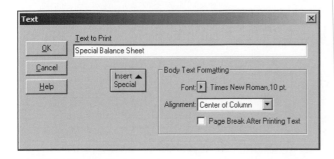

FIGURE 7-25
Completed Text Dialog Box

Step 9:

Click Delete.

Step 10:

Review the balance sheet format shown in figure 7–26. Notice the change in the header.

FIGURE 7-26
Balance Sheet Format with Change in Header

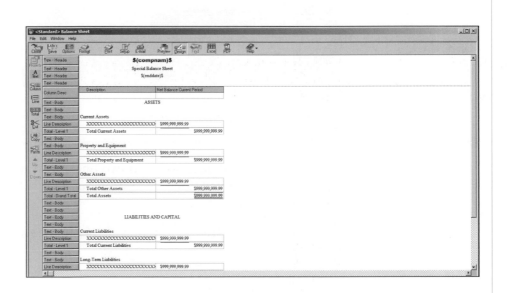

Copying a Line

A line can be copied from one place to another. Copy the header *Special Balance Sheet* to the line below.

Step 1:
Click the second Text-Header button, which is aligned with the words *Special Balance Sheet*.

Step 2:
Click the *right* mouse button to reveal the drop-down list with text change options.

Step 3:
Click Copy.

Step 4:
Click the third Text-Header button, and then click the *right* mouse button.

Step 5:
Click Paste, and a new line will appear with the words *Special Balance Sheet*, as shown in figure 7–27.

FIGURE 7-27
Copied Line

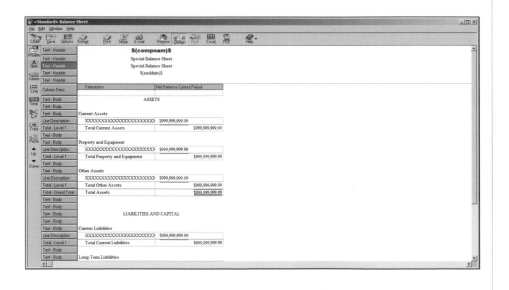

Deleting a Line

Obviously, Woodward does not need two lines that say *Special Balance Sheet*. To delete the second line, follow the steps outlined below:

Step 1:
Click the third Text-Header button, which is aligned with the second *Special Balance Sheet*.

Step 2:

Click the *right* mouse button to reveal the drop-down list with text change options.

Step 3:

Click Delete, as shown in figure 7–28.

FIGURE 7-28

Delete Selected from Text Change Options

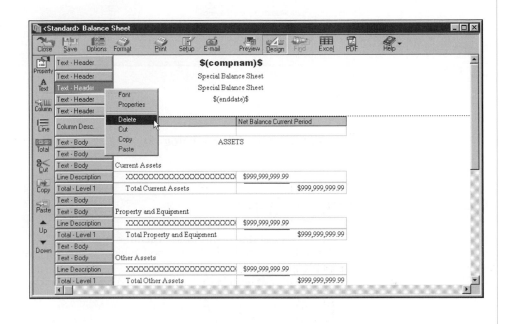

Moving rows and changing column titles can be accomplished by using the procedures outlined above.

Step 4:

Close the <Standard> Balance Sheet window.

Step 5:

Save the changes by clicking Yes at the Query box.

Step 6:

Key **Modified Balance Sheet** in the Name box of the Save As dialog box.

Step 7:

Key **Font Change** in the Description box, as shown in figure 7–29. Then click Save.

FIGURE 7-29

*Modified Balance Sheet
Save As Dialog Box*

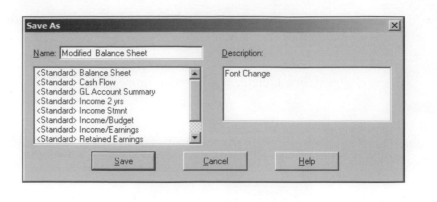

Step 8:

Close the Select a Report dialog box.

Check POINT

1. What financial statements does Peachtree produce?
2. Which button on the Select a Report toolbar is used to customize financial statements?

Answers

1. *The financial statements produced by Peachtree include the income statement, the statement of changes in financial position, the balance sheet, and the statement of cash flow.*
2. *The Design button is used to customize financial statements.*

PRACTICE *objective*   2

Step 1:

Open Bullfrog Maintenance Company.

Step 2:

Print the following financial statements:

- Income statement
- Statement of changes in financial position
- Balance sheet
- Statement of cash flow

Your printouts should look like figures 7-30, 7-31, 7-32, and 7-33.

FIGURE 7-30
Bullfrog Maintenance Company Income Statement

Bullfrog Maintenance Company
Income Statement
For the One Month Ending January 31, 2007

		Current Month			Year to Date	
Revenues						
Service Revenue	$	1,958.00	100.79	$	1,958.00	100.79
Sales Discounts		(15.36)	(0.79)		(15.36)	(0.79)
Total Revenues		1,942.64	100.00		1,942.64	100.00
Cost of Sales						
Total Cost of Sales		0.00	0.00		0.00	0.00
Gross Profit		1,942.64	100.00		1,942.64	100.00
Expenses						
Rent Expense		1,200.00	61.77		1,200.00	61.77
Utilities Expense		611.87	31.50		611.87	31.50
Office Supplies Expense		192.20	9.89		192.20	9.89
Depreciation Expense-Equipment		750.00	38.61		750.00	38.61
Wages and Salaries Expense		3,400.00	175.02		3,400.00	175.02
Uncollectible Account Expense		120.00	6.18		120.00	6.18
Landscaping Expense		650.00	33.46		650.00	33.46
Bank Fee Expense		35.00	1.80		35.00	1.80
Total Expenses		6,959.07	358.23		6,959.07	358.23
Net Income	$	(5,016.43)	(258.23)	$	(5,016.43)	(258.23)

FIGURE 7-31

Bullfrog Maintenance Company Statement of Changes in Financial Position

Bullfrog Maintenance Company
Statement of Changes in Financial Position
For the one month ended January 31, 2007

	Current Month	Year To Date
Sources of Working Capital		
Net Income	$ (5,016.43)	$ (5,016.43)
Add back items not requiring working capital		
Accum. Depreciation-Equipment	10,750.00	10,750.00
Working capital from operations	5,733.57	5,733.57
Other sources		
J. Bull, Capital	50,290.00	50,290.00
Total sources	56,023.57	56,023.57
Uses of working capital		
Equipment	(42,000.00)	(42,000.00)
Total uses	(42,000.00)	(42,000.00)
Net change	$ 14,023.57	$ 14,023.57
Analysis of componants of changes		
Increase <Decrease> in Current Assets		
Cash	$ 11,958.57	$ 11,958.57
Petty Cash	100.00	100.00
Accounts Receivable	745.00	745.00
Maintenance Supplies	2,300.00	2,300.00
Office Supplies	1,170.00	1,170.00
Prepaid Insurance	1,000.00	1,000.00
<Increase> Decrease in Current Liabilities		
Wages and Salaries Payable	(3,400.00)	(3,400.00)
Net change	$ 13,873.57	$ 13,873.57

For Management Purposes Only

FIGURE 7-32

Bullfrog Maintenance Company Balance Sheet

Bullfrog Maintenance Company
Balance Sheet
January 31, 2007

ASSETS

Current Assets		
Cash	$ 11,958.57	
Petty Cash	100.00	
Accounts Receivable	745.00	
Maintenance Supplies	2,300.00	
Office Supplies	1,170.00	
Prepaid Insurance	1,000.00	
Total Current Assets		17,273.57
Property and Equipment		
Equipment	42,000.00	
Accum. Depreciation-Equipment	(10,750.00)	
Total Property and Equipment		31,250.00
Other Assets		
Total Other Assets		0.00
Total Assets		$ 48,523.57

LIABILITIES AND CAPITAL

Current Liabilities		
Wages and Salaries Payable	$ 3,400.00	
Total Current Liabilities		3,400.00
Long-Term Liabilities		
Total Long-Term Liabilities		0.00
Total Liabilities		3,400.00
Capital		
J. Bull, Capital	50,290.00	
J. Bull, Drawing	(150.00)	
Net Income	(5,016.43)	
Total Capital		45,123.57
Total Liabilities & Capital		$ 48,523.57

Unaudited - For Management Purposes Only

FIGURE 7-33
Bullfrog Maintenance Company Statement of Cash Flow

Bullfrog Maintenance Company
Statement of Cash Flow
For the one Month Ended January 31, 2007

	Current Month	Year to Date
Cash Flows from operating activities		
Net Income	$ (5,016.43)	$ (5,016.43)
Adjustments to reconcile net income to net cash provided by operating activities		
Accum. Depreciation-Equipment	10,750.00	10,750.00
Accounts Receivable	(745.00)	(745.00)
Maintenance Supplies	(2,300.00)	(2,300.00)
Office Supplies	(1,170.00)	(1,170.00)
Prepaid Insurance	(1,000.00)	(1,000.00)
Wages Payable	3,400.00	3,400.00
Total Adjustments	8,935.00	8,935.00
Net Cash provided by Operations	3,918.57	3,918.57
Cash Flows from investing activities		
Used For		
Equipment	(42,000.00)	(42,000.00)
Net cash used in investing	(42,000.00)	(42,000.00)
Cash Flows from financing activities		
Proceeds From		
J. Bull, Capital	50,290.00	50,290.00
Used For		
J. Bull, Drawing	(150.00)	(150.00)
Net cash used in financing	50,140.00	50,140.00
Net increase <decrease> in cash	$ 12,058.57	$ 12,058.57
Summary		
Cash Balance at End of Period	$ 12,058.57	$ 12,058.57
Cash Balance at Beg of Period	0.00	0.00
Net Increase <Decrease> in Cash	$ 12,058.57	$ 12,058.57

Make the following changes to the balance sheet:

- Change the font type of the header *Bullfrog Maintenance Company* to Arial Black.
- Change the font size of the header *Bullfrog Maintenance Company* to 12.
- Add a row below the header *Balance Sheet* that will include the words *Customized Version* centered in the column.
- Save as Customized Balance Sheet.
- Print a new balance sheet when the changes are complete. Your printout should look like the partial balance sheet in figure 7–34.

FIGURE 7-34

Revised Bullfrog Maintenance Company Balance Sheet (Partial View)

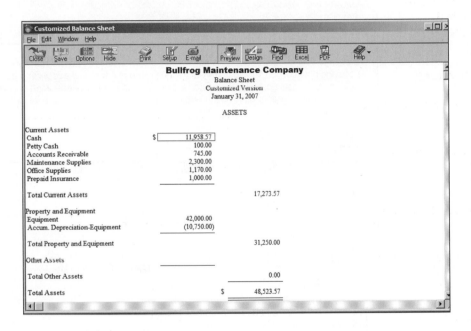

Close the Select a Report dialog box.

OBJECTIVE 3 — CHANGE THE ACCOUNTING PERIOD

Peachtree allows you to go from month to month without closing the fiscal year by changing the accounting period. This feature makes it possible to produce interim financial statements. You do not have to record the end-of-year closing entries until the fiscal year actually closes. Thus, the balances of the revenue and expense accounts continue to grow after the accounting period is changed. The same is true for the balance of the owner's drawing account.

As you saw, Woodward Construction Company has made its adjusting entries and printed its interim financial statements for January 2007. It is now time to get ready for the February entries.

CHANGING THE ACCOUNTING PERIOD

Take the following steps to change the accounting period for Woodward Construction Company:

Step 1:

Open Woodward Construction Company and close the Action Items log.

Step 2:

Click Tasks, System, and Change Accounting Period.

FIGURE 7-35

Feb 1, 2007 to Feb 28, 2007 Selected in Change Accounting Period Dialog Box

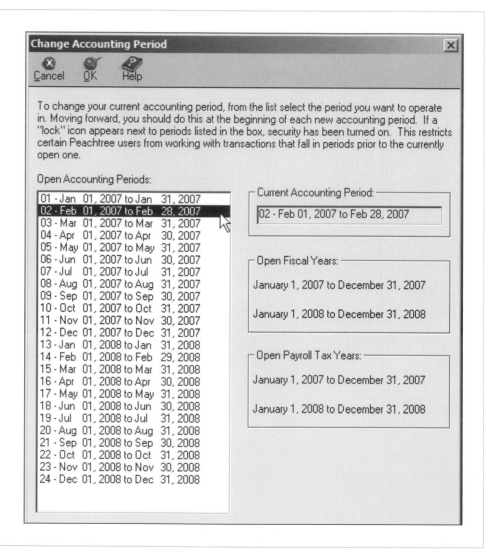

Step 3:

At the Change Accounting Period dialog box, click *02 - Feb 01, 2007 to Feb 28, 2007*, as shown in figure 7–35.

Step 4:

Click OK.

Step 5:

Click No in response to the question "Would you like to print your reports before continuing?" You printed the adjusting entries and the financial statements previously. No further entries or financial statements are needed for January 2007. Click No in response to the question "Would you like to run an Internal Accounting Review?" Woodward Construction Company is therefore ready to enter transactions for its second accounting period of the fiscal year—the month of February 2007.

POINT

1. What feature of Peachtree allows interim financial statements to be prepared?
2. Do you have to back up a company file when changing an accounting period?

Answers

1. *The Change Accounting Period feature allows the preparation of interim financial statements.*
2. *No, Peachtree maintains 25 accounting periods at any given time. Therefore, it is not necessary to back up each accounting period.*

PRACTICE *objective* 3

Step 1:

Open Bullfrog Maintenance Company.

Step 2:

Change the accounting period to Period 2. [**Note:** Do not print any reports.]

Before the Internet, investors who wanted a company's annual report had to request a copy from the firm or had to visit a library. Sometimes investors would experience a delay in receiving the annual report or would find that it was not available. Today, the Web sites of many large companies include their financial statements and other information from their annual reports. An even more convenient source of annual reports is the Report Gallery, a Web site located at www.annualreports.com (figure 7–36). This Web site contains over 2,200 annual reports.

F I G U R E 7 - 3 6
Report Gallery Web Site

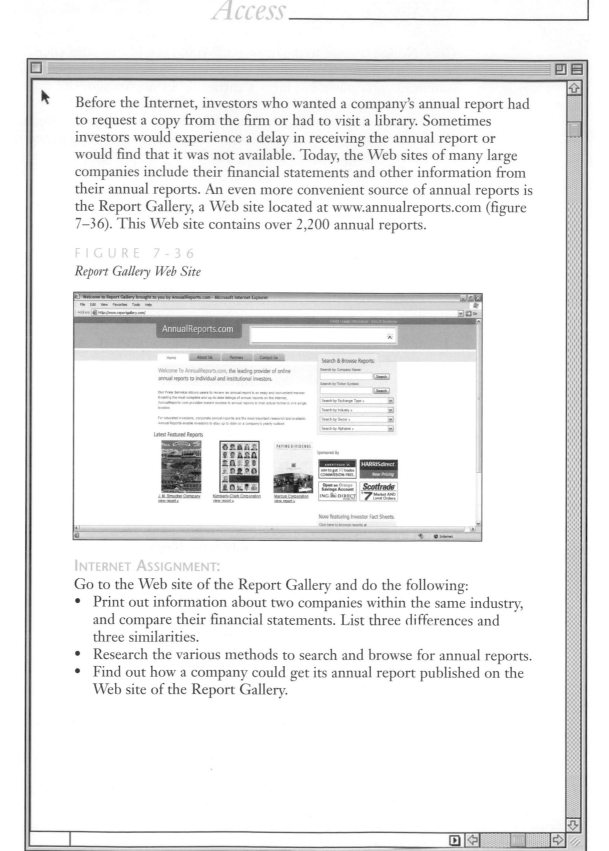

INTERNET ASSIGNMENT:
Go to the Web site of the Report Gallery and do the following:
- Print out information about two companies within the same industry, and compare their financial statements. List three differences and three similarities.
- Research the various methods to search and browse for annual reports.
- Find out how a company could get its annual report published on the Web site of the Report Gallery.

S O F T W A R E
Command Summary

Adjusting Entries	Tas<u>k</u>s, <u>G</u>eneral Journal Entry
Customizing Financial Statements	Reports, <u>F</u>inancial Statements, <u>D</u>esign
Copying Report Formats	Reports, <u>F</u>inancial Statements, <u>C</u>opy
Changing the Accounting Period	Tas<u>k</u>s, S<u>y</u>stem, Change <u>A</u>ccounting Period

P R O J E C T S
and Problems

CONTENT CHECK

Multiple Choice: Choose only one response for each question.

1. Which of the following is the basic accounting equation?
   A. Assets + Liabilities = Owner's Equity
   B. Assets = Liabilities + Owner's Equity
   C. Assets = Liabilities – Owner's Equity
   D. Assets – Owner's Equity = Liabilities
   E. None of the above.

2. The financial statement that is a detailed version of the accounting equation is the
   A. income statement.
   B. statement of changes in financial position.
   C. balance sheet.
   D. statement of cash flow.
   E. None of the above.

3. If the Office Supplies account has a balance of $2,000 at the beginning of the period and $1,200 at the end of the period, the adjusting entry would include
   A. a debit to Office Supplies and a credit to Office Supplies Expense for $1,200.
   B. a debit to Office Supplies Expense and a credit to Office Supplies for $2,000.
   C. a debit to Office Supplies Expense and a credit to Office Supplies for $800.
   D. a debit to Office Supplies and a credit to Office Supplies Expense for $800.
   E. None of the above.

4. The adjusting entry for depreciation expense would include
   A. a debit to Accumulated Depreciation and a credit to Depreciation Expense.
   B. a debit to Depreciation Expense and a credit to Accumulated Depreciation.
   C. a debit to Depreciation Expense and a credit to Revenue.
   D. a debit to Revenue and a credit to Depreciation Expense.
   E. None of the above.

5. What are the two types of accounts that appear on the income statement?
   A. expenses and liabilities
   B. expenses and capital
   C. revenue and liabilities
   D. revenue and expenses
   E. None of the above.

Short Essay Response: Provide a detailed answer for each question.

1. What information appears on the income statement?
2. What is working capital?
3. Define the balance sheet.
4. Why must businesses depreciate fixed assets such as equipment?
5. Why is it necessary to make an adjustment for supplies used at the end of an accounting period?
6. What information appears on the statement of cash flow?

CASE PROBLEMS

PROBLEM 1A

Open Transnational Management Group, which you updated in chapter 6.

1. Make the following adjusting entries for April 30, 2007:
   • Office supplies on hand on April 30, 2007, $180. Use Supplies Expense as the account to be debited.
   • Wages earned, but unpaid, as of April 30, 2007, $1,340. There is no account for Wages Payable. Create the account using 21000 and Other Current Liabilities as the Account ID and Account Type, respectively.
   • Depreciation on the equipment amounted to $1,000.
2. Print the *General Journal* and *General Ledger Trial Balance* reports.

PROBLEM 2A

Open GJ Professional Accounting, which you have already created and updated in previous chapters.

1. Change the accounting period to March 2007.
2. Print the following financial statements for the period 1/1/07 to 3/31/07:
   • Income statement
   • Statement of changes in financial position
   • Balance sheet
   • Statement of cash flow
3. Make the following changes to the Income Statement:
   • Change the Font Type of the first header "GJ Professional Accounting" to Arial Black.

- Change the Font Size of the first and second header to 11.
- Add a row below the header Income Statement to include the words "For Management Purposes Only" in the center of the column.
- Delete the Text – Footer.
- Save as Modified Income Statement.

4. Print a new Income Statement when the changes are complete.

PROBLEM 1B

Open Abelar Designs, which you updated in chapter 6.

1. Make the following adjusting entries for May 31, 2007:
   - Office supplies on hand on May 31, 2007, $25. Use Supplies Expense as the account to be debited.
   - Wages earned, but unpaid, as of May 31, 2007, $740. There is no account for Wages Payable. Create the account using 21000 and Other Current Liabilities as the Account ID and Account Type, respectively.
   - Depreciation on the equipment amounted to $150.
2. Print the *General Journal* and *General Ledger Trial Balance* reports.

PROBLEM 2B

Open Infinite Graphics, which you have already created and updated in previous chapters.

1. Change the accounting period to March 2007.
2. Print the following financial statements for the period 1/1/07 to 3/31/07:
   - Income statement
   - Statement of changes in financial position
   - Balance sheet
   - Statement of cash flow
3. Make the following changes to the Income Statement:
   - Change the Font Type of the first header "Infinite Graphics" to Arial Black.
   - Change the Font Size of the first and second header to 12.
   - Add a row below the header Income Statement to include the words "For Internal Use Only" in the center of the column.
   - Delete the Text – Footer.
   - Save as Modified Income Statement.
4. Print a new Income Statement when the changes are complete.

Cooperative Learning

1. Form a group of three or four students. As a group discuss what effects there would be on the income statement and the balance sheet if a business did not make adjustments for supplies used, depreciation, and unpaid salaries. Would expenses be overstated or understated? Net income? Assets? Liabilities?
2. As a group, open any three of the companies you have saved and customize the income statement and balance sheet to the group's liking.

Writing and Decision Making

List the different financial statements that Peachtree produces and state what information each provides. Also explain how these statements can be used to help management make wise financial decisions.

CHAPTER

PURCHASES OF INVENTORY IN
A MERCHANDISE BUSINESS

1. Understand the two basic inventory systems

2. Understand the most common inventory costing methods and create the Inventory account

3. Establish subsidiary ledger accounts for inventory items

4. Establish records for sales representatives

5. Process inventory transactions

SOFTWARE FEATURES

- Maintain inventory items

- Print the Item List

- Maintain sales rep records

- Enter purchases/inventory transactions

- Print the *Inventory Valuation* report

Chapters 2 through 7 focused on the accounting procedures of service businesses. In this chapter and succeeding chapters, the focus will be on the accounting procedures of merchandising businesses. Remember that **merchandising businesses** buy goods from manufacturers or wholesalers and resell them for a profit to consumers. Examples of merchandising businesses are department stores, grocery stores, and furniture stores.

One of the assets of a merchandising business is the stock of goods that it has on hand for resale to consumers. This stock of goods is called **inventory** or **merchandise inventory**.

OBJECTIVE 1 — UNDERSTAND THE TWO BASIC INVENTORY SYSTEMS

Two basic systems are used to keep track of inventory: the periodic inventory system and the perpetual inventory system. In the **periodic inventory system,** a count of all items in a firm's inventory is made at regular intervals, such as at the end of each accounting period, in order to determine ending inventory amounts. In the **perpetual inventory system,** the firm maintains a running balance for all inventory items.

The perpetual inventory system involves the use of inventory records that are updated throughout an accounting period as goods are purchased and sold. The periodic inventory system does not include such records. Peachtree uses the perpetual inventory system. **Note:** Both systems require a physical inventory count in order to determine discrepancies in inventory amounts.

METHODS FOR COSTING INVENTORY

The periodic and perpetual inventory systems keep track of the number of items of each type that a business has in its inventory. In addition to knowing what inventory is on hand, a business also needs to determine the dollar value of its inventory at the end of each accounting period. Various **inventory costing methods** are used for this purpose.

The three most common inventory costing methods are the average cost method, the last-in, first-out (LIFO) method, and the first-in, first-out (FIFO) method. Peachtree supports all of these inventory costing methods.

PROCESSING SALES AND INVENTORY TRANSACTIONS

Peachtree saves a great deal of time and effort for a merchandising business because it can be used to simultaneously update all records affected by a sale of goods. It increases the Sales, Sales Tax Payable, and Cost of Goods Sold accounts and decreases the Inventory account. Peachtree also adjusts the sales records for individual customers, salespeople, and inventory records for individual items of inventory.

THE RELATIONSHIP BETWEEN INVENTORY AND COST OF GOODS SOLD

The income statement of a merchandising business contains a section called Cost of Goods Sold. This section shows the cost of the merchandise that the firm sold during the accounting period. Cost of goods sold is used to determine the gross profit from sales for the period.

When the periodic inventory system is used, the calculation of cost of goods sold on the income statement involves both the beginning and ending inventory, as shown on the following page.

merchandising businesses Firms that buy goods and resell them to consumers.

inventory The stock of goods that a merchandising business has on hand for resale to consumers. Also called *merchandise inventory*.

periodic inventory system A system in which a firm's inventory is counted at regular intervals.

perpetual inventory system A system in which a firm maintains a running balance for all inventory items.

inventory costing methods Methods used to determine the dollar value of the ending inventory.

Beginning Inventory
+ Net Purchases
= Goods Available for Sale
– Ending Inventory
= Cost of Goods Sold

When the perpetual inventory system is used, there is a single Cost of Goods Sold account that includes all merchandise costs.

INVENTORY SYSTEMS

We will now take a closer look at the two basic inventory systems used by merchandising businesses—the periodic inventory system and the perpetual inventory system.

PERIODIC INVENTORY SYSTEM

Traditionally, firms that sell a wide variety of low-cost items have used the periodic inventory system. Drugstores, hardware stores, office supply stores, and grocery stores are examples of such businesses.

With the periodic inventory system, a firm does not keep a continuous record of the changes in its inventory during the accounting period. All purchases of goods are debited to the Purchases account and all sales of goods are credited to the Sales account, but no entries are made in the Inventory account. Therefore, the firm has no precise way of calculating its cost of goods sold during an accounting period.

At the end of the period, a count is made of the goods on hand. The balance of the Inventory account is then updated to show the dollar value of the ending inventory.

The periodic inventory system has several drawbacks. One drawback has already been mentioned—the lack of information about the current dollar value of the inventory during the accounting period. However, an even more serious drawback is the lack of information about the availability of any single inventory item unless a separate tracking system is used.

For example, suppose that an office supply store has a balance of 400 boxes of file folders at the beginning of a period. The store purchases another 700 boxes of file folders during the period, but this amount will not show up in the inventory count until the end of the period. Thus, if a customer orders 500 boxes of file folders, the store will not know for sure whether it has enough stock on hand to fill the order.

Today, the periodic inventory system is less widely used than it was in the past. Modern technology has made the perpetual inventory system feasible and cost efficient for businesses with a large stock of low-priced items. Computerized inventory programs, optical scanners, and the Universal Product Code (UPC) printed on packages allow such firms to maintain a continuous record of inventory transactions.

PERPETUAL INVENTORY SYSTEM

Inventory represents a major investment for a merchandising business. In fact, inventory is often the largest asset that such a firm owns.

The success of a merchandising business depends in part on careful management of its inventory. A firm wants to have an ample supply of fast-selling items available for customers, and it wants to keep its supply of slow-selling items to a minimum. Poor inventory decisions can result in lost sales because of a shortage of needed goods or because of markdowns on surplus goods that customers will only buy at reduced prices.

Because the perpetual inventory system maintains a running balance for all inventory items, it provides the information needed to effectively manage a firm's inventory. In the past, many firms considered the perpetual inventory system too time-consuming and costly. However, computerized accounting programs like Peachtree have made it possible for even very small businesses with limited staff and limited resources to use the perpetual inventory system.

The perpetual inventory system in Peachtree has the following advantages:

- It keeps detailed records for all inventory items and updates these records throughout the accounting period as transactions occur.
- It updates the Inventory and Cost of Goods Sold accounts in the general ledger throughout the accounting period. Thus, there is no need to adjust the Inventory account at the end of the period.
- The costs for inventory items are always known, and selling prices can be changed at any time. The firm can raise selling prices on items with rising costs if it wishes. It can also cut selling prices on items with weak demand.

Check
POINT

1. What are the two basic systems for keeping track of inventory?
2. Which of the two basic inventory system does Peachtree use?

Answers
1. *The periodic inventory system and the perpetual inventory system are the two basic systems for keeping track of inventory.*
2. *Peachtree uses the perpetual inventory system.*

OBJECTIVE 2 — UNDERSTAND THE MOST COMMON INVENTORY COSTING METHODS AND CREATE THE INVENTORY ACCOUNT

The inventory costing method selected by a business depends on the nature of its merchandise and other factors. Each method will produce a slightly different dollar value for the ending inventory and the cost of goods sold. As noted previously, Peachtree supports three common inventory costing methods: the average cost method; the last-in, first-out (LIFO) method; and the first-in, first-out (FIFO) method.

AVERAGE COST METHOD

average cost method
Inventory costing method in which the value of the ending inventory is based on a single cost (the average cost) assigned to all units available for sale.

The **average cost method** assigns a single cost (the average cost) to all units of an inventory item. This cost is found by dividing the total cost of the units available for sale during a period by the number of those units. The resulting figure—the average cost—is then multiplied by the number of units in the ending inventory to find the dollar value of the ending inventory.

For example, suppose that a firm had 1,090 units of a certain inventory item available for sale during a period. These units were acquired at three different prices. The total cost of the units available for sale was $12,920. The average cost was $11.85.

Beginning inventory	500 units	@	$11 =	$ 5,500
First purchase	250 units	@	$12 =	3,000
Second purchase	340 units	@	$13 =	4,420
	1,090 units			$12,920

Average cost = $12,920 ÷ 1,090 = $11.85

During the period, the firm sold 560 units of this item. Therefore, its ending inventory consists of 530 units (1,090 units – 560 units). The dollar value of the ending inventory is $6,280.50.

Ending inventory: 530 units × $11.85 (average cost) = $6,280.50

The cost of goods sold is $6,639.50.

Cost of goods available for sale	$12,920.00
Less ending inventory	6,280.50
Cost of goods sold	$ 6,639.50

LAST-IN, FIRST-OUT (LIFO) METHOD

The **last-in, first-out (LIFO) method** assumes that the last inventory items purchased are the first ones sold. This pattern may not match the actual flow of inventory items. However, the LIFO method is used for accounting purposes to value the ending inventory and need not be consistent with the physical flow of goods in a business.

Again, suppose that a firm had 1,090 units of a certain inventory item available for sale during a period. It sold 560 units, leaving 530 units in its ending inventory. Also assume the following prices for the beginning inventory and later purchases during the period.

Beginning inventory	500 units	@ $11	=	$ 5,500
First purchase	250 units	@ $12	=	3,000
Second purchase	340 units	@ $13	=	4,420
	1,090 units			$12,920

With the LIFO method, the ending inventory consists of the earliest goods because it is assumed that the first goods sold are the last ones purchased. The value of the ending inventory is therefore $5,860, as shown below. The cost of goods sold is $7,060.

Beginning inventory (earliest goods)	500 units	@ $11	=	$5,500
First purchase (next to earliest goods)	30 units	@ $12	=	360
	530 units			$5,860

Cost of goods available for sale	$12,920
Less ending inventory	5,860
Cost of goods sold	$ 7,060

FIRST-IN, FIRST-OUT (FIFO) METHOD

The **first-in, first-out (FIFO) method** assumes that the first inventory items purchased are the first ones sold. This pattern may or may not match the actual flow of inventory items in a business. However, keep in mind that an inventory costing method is selected for accounting purposes to value the ending inventory, not as a means to literally track when particular goods are purchased and sold.

Again, suppose that a firm had 1,090 units of a certain inventory item available for sale during a period, sold 560 units, and had 530 units in its ending inventory. Also assume the following prices for the beginning inventory and later purchases during the period.

LIFO method
Inventory costing method in which the value of the ending inventory is based on the assumption that the last items purchased are the first ones sold.

FIFO method
Inventory costing method in which the value of the ending inventory is based on the assumption that the first items purchased are the first ones sold.

Beginning inventory	500 units @ $11 =	$ 5,500
First purchase	250 units @ $12 =	3,000
Second purchase	340 units @ $13 =	4,420
	1,090 units	$12,920

With the FIFO method, the ending inventory consists of the latest goods because it is assumed that the first goods sold are the first ones purchased. The value of the ending inventory is therefore $6,700, as shown below. The cost of goods sold is $6,220.

Second purchase (latest goods)	340 units @ $13 =	$4,420
First purchase (next to latest goods)	190 units @ $12 =	2,280
	530 units	$6,700

Cost of goods available for sale	$12,920
Less ending inventory	6,700
Cost of goods sold	$ 6,220

A COMPARISON OF THE INVENTORY COSTING METHODS

The following table provides a summary of the results of the three inventory costing methods discussed above. In a period of rising prices, the FIFO method will produce the highest dollar value for the ending inventory and the lowest cost of goods sold. The LIFO method will produce the lowest dollar value for the ending inventory and the highest cost of goods sold. The average cost method will produce results that fall between those of FIFO and LIFO.

	FIFO Method	Average Cost Method	LIFO Method
Cost of goods available for sale	$12,920.00	$12,920.00	$12,920.00
Less ending inventory	6,700.00	6,280.50	5,860.00
Cost of goods sold	$ 6,220.00	$ 6,639.50	$ 7,060.00

Keep in mind that the higher the cost of goods sold, the lower the net income. Thus, in a period of rising prices, LIFO provides a tax advantage for a business because it results in less taxable income.

CREATING THE INVENTORY ACCOUNT

To use the inventory features of Peachtree, you must create an Inventory account in the general ledger and also create subsidiary ledger accounts for the various inventory items. For example, suppose that Woodward Construction Company, which is a service business, decides to add a merchandising operation. It will sell items such as cleaning compound, storage racks, and computer desks to its customers.

The first step for the Woodward Construction Company is to create the asset account Inventory in its general ledger. This account will serve as the controlling account for subsidiary ledger accounts that will provide detailed records of the various inventory items. Remember that a controlling account links the general ledger to a subsidiary ledger. The balance of the controlling account represents the total of all the individual balances in the subsidiary ledger.

Step 1:

Open Woodward Construction Company and close the Action Items log.

Step 2:

Click *Company* on the Navigation Aid toolbar at the left side of the basic Peachtree window.

Step 3:

Click *Chart of Accounts* at the *Company Tasks* section and click New Account, as shown in figure 8–1.

F I G U R E   8 - 1

Chart of Accounts Selected from Company Tasks Section

Step 4:

At the *Account ID* field, key **105**, and then click OK.

Step 5:

Key **Inventory** in the *Description* field.

Step 6:

At the *Account Type* field, click the down arrow key, and then click *Inventory* as shown in figure 8–2.

F I G U R E   8 - 2

Inventory Selected as Account Type

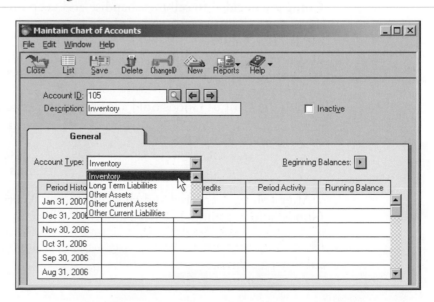

Step 7:

Compare your work with the completed information for the Inventory account as shown in figure 8–3.

FIGURE 8-3

Completed Information for Inventory Account

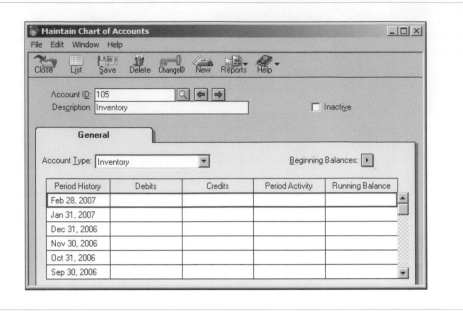

Step 8:

Click Save.

Step 9:

You will also need to create a Cost of Goods Sold account. According to standard accounting convention, this account should appear before the expense accounts on the chart of accounts. For example, cost of sales account numbers should begin with 500 and expense account numbers should begin with 600. However, keep in mind that this business began strictly as a service business and expense accounts were set up to begin with an account number of 500. Only recently has Woodward Construction Company decided to sell merchandise and keep inventory on hand. Therefore, the Cost of Goods Sold account number will be 503, the first available account number within the 500 range. This will have no adverse effect on any of the financial statements as long as Cost of Sales is chosen as the account type.

Create the Cost of Goods Sold account in the general ledger.

Account ID:	**503**
Description:	**Cost of Goods Sold**
Account Type:	**Cost of Sales**

After you have entered and checked the information for the Cost of Goods Sold account, click Save and then Close.

Check POINT

1. What are the three most common inventory costing methods?
2. What type of account is the Inventory account in the general ledger and what is its function?

Answers

1. The three most common inventory costing methods are the average cost, LIFO, and FIFO methods.
2. The Inventory account in the general ledger is an asset account. It serves as the controlling account for the subsidiary ledger accounts kept for the various inventory items.

PRACTICE *objective* 2

Step 1:

Open Bullfrog Maintenance Company.

Step 2:

Create the Inventory account for this firm.

Account ID:	**105**
Description:	**Inventory**
Account Type:	**Inventory**

Step 3:

Create the Cost of Goods Sold account.

Account ID:	**503**
Description:	**Cost of Goods Sold**
Account Type:	**Cost of Sales**

Step 4:

Close the Maintain Chart of Accounts window.

OBJECTIVE 3 — ESTABLISH SUBSIDIARY LEDGER ACCOUNTS FOR INVENTORY ITEMS

In the perpetual inventory system used by Peachtree, you must set up a subsidiary ledger account for each inventory item. This account contains detailed information about the item and allows the business to keep track of its quantity and cost. Whenever goods are purchased or sold, the subsidiary ledger accounts for the inventory items are updated.

Woodward Construction Company will start its merchandising operation with three items: cleaning compound, storage racks, and computer desks. These items will be purchased from two suppliers.

Follow the steps outlined below to establish inventory defaults and to establish subsidiary ledger accounts for the three inventory items that Woodward will initially stock.

Step 1:

Open Woodward Construction Company and close the Action Items log.

Step 2:

Click Maintain and then click Default Information from the drop-down list, as shown in figure 8–4.

FIGURE 8-4

*Default Information
Drop-Down List*

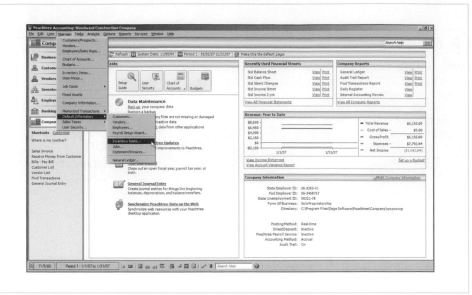

Step 3:

Click Inventory Items from the drop-down list and the Inventory Item Defaults window will appear, as shown in figure 8–5.

FIGURE 8-5

*Inventory Item Defaults
Window*

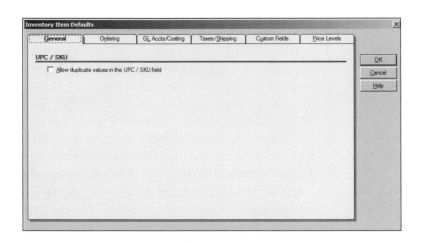

Step 4:

Select the GL Accts/Costing tab from the Inventory Item Defaults window.

Step 5:

Select account 400, Fees Earned, in the GL Sales/Inc account box aligned with Stock Item.

Step 6:

Select account 105, Inventory, in the GL Invtry/Wage account box aligned with Stock Item.

Step 7:

Select account 503, Cost of Goods Sold, in the GL Cost Sales account box aligned with Stock Item.

Step 8:

Accept the FIFO Costing default.

Step 9:

Enter account 105, Inventory, in the GL Freight Account located at the bottom of the window. Woodward adds the freight cost to inventory.

Step 10:

Review figure 8–6 for accuracy, making any necessary changes.

FIGURE 8-6

Completed GL Accts/Costing Window

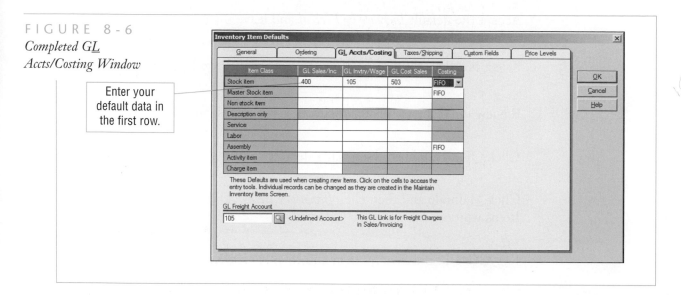

Step 11:

Select the Price Levels tab.

Step 12:

Key **Full Price** in the *Level Name* field aligned with Level 1, as shown in figure 8–7.

Step 13:

Select Checkmark Enabled in the cell aligned with Level 1, deselect all other enabled check marks, if present, as shown in figure 8–7.

FIGURE 8-7

Price Levels Completed

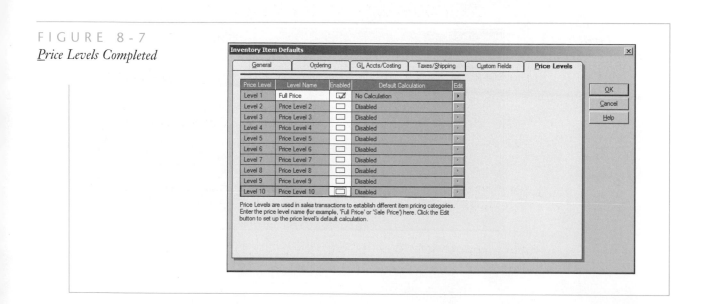

Step 14:

Select the edit button aligned with Level 1.

Step 15:

Select Last Cost from the Use drop-down list, if needed.

Step 16:

Accept the default *Increase by Percent* and leave the (%) *0*.

Step 17:

Select No Rounding at the Round Price drop-down list, if needed.

Step 18:

Review for accuracy, make any necessary changes, and click OK.

Step 19:

Click OK to establish the pricing defaults.

Step 20

Click Maintain and then click *Inventory Items*. The Maintain Inventory Items window will appear.

Step 21

Key **CC-1** in the *Item ID* field and then click OK.

Step 22

Key **Cleaning Compound** in the *Description* field.

Step 23

At the *Item Class* field, click the down arrow key, and then click *Stock item*, if needed.

Step 24:

Click the right arrow key to the right of the Full Price box.

Step 25:

Key **12.50** in the Price box aligned with Full Price, as shown in figure 8–8.

FIGURE 8-8
*Multiple Price Levels
Window Completed*

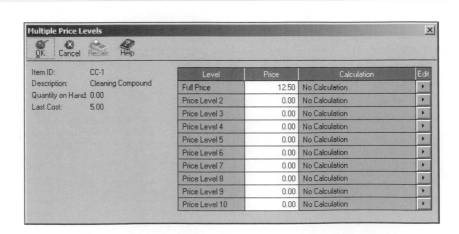

Step 26:

Click <u>O</u>K to exit the Multiple Price Levels window.

Step 27:

In the Maintain Inventory Items window, key **5.00** in the *Last Unit Cost* field.

Step 28:

Key **Retail** in the *Item Type* field.

Step 29:

Key **Each** in the *Stocking U/M* field. (**Note:** U/M stands for Units of Measure.)

Step 30:

At the *Preferred <u>V</u>endor ID* field, click the *magnifying glass* icon, and then click *APEX-05.*

FIGURE 8-9

Completed Maintain Inventory Items Window

An additional description or comment can be added if desired.

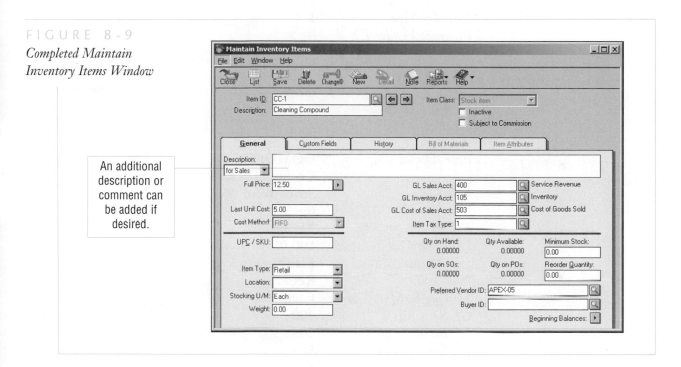

Step 31:

Compare your completed Maintain Inventory Items window with figure 8–9. Click <u>S</u>ave and then New.

Step 32:

Enter the information for the storage racks:

Item *ID*:	**STORACK-2**
Description:	**Storage Rack**
Item Class:	**Stock Item**
Description:	**for Sales**
Full Price:	**125.00**
Last Unit Cost:	**52.50**
Cost Method:	**FIFO**
Item Type:	**Retail**
Stocking U/M:	**Each**
GL Sales Acct:	**400**
GL Inventory Acct:	**105**
GL Cost of Sales Acct:	**503**
Item Ta*x* Type:	**1**
Preferred *V*endor ID:	

Step 33:

Click *S*ave and then New.

Step 34:

Enter the information for the computer desks:

Item *ID*:	**COMDESK-3**
Description:	**Computer Desk**
Item Class:	**Stock Item**
Description:	**for Sales**
Full Price:	**225.00**
Last Unit Cost:	**100.00**
Cost Method:	**FIFO**
Item Type:	**Retail**
Stocking U/M:	**Each**
GL Sales Acct:	**400**
GL Inventory Acct:	**105**
GL Cost of Sales Acct:	**503**
Item Ta*x* Type:	**1**
Preferred *V*endor ID:	

Step 35:

Click *S*ave and then Close.

PRINTING THE ITEM LIST

Peachtree provides a number of different inventory reports. One of these reports—the *Item List*—shows the quantity on hand and other information about all inventory items. Follow the steps outlined below to print the *Item List*.

Step 1:

Click *R*eports and then click *I*nventory.

At the Select a Report dialog box, in the Report List section, click *Item List*.

Click the Preview button on the Select a Report toolbar.

Click OK at the Item List window, Filter tab, as shown in figure 8–10.

FIGURE 8-10

Item List Filter

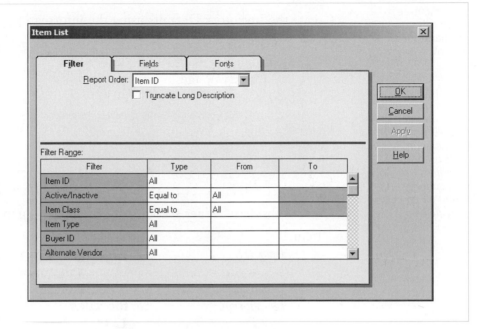

Review the *Item List* report shown in figure 8–11. The *Qty on Hand* field is blank because the firm has not yet received any goods.

FIGURE 8-11

Item List

Woodward Construction Company
Item List

Filter Criteria includes: Report order is by ID.

Item ID	Item Description	Item Class	Active?	Item Type	Qty on Hand
CC-1	Cleaning Compound	Stock item	Active	Retail	
COMDESK-3	Computer Desk	Stock item	Active	Retail	
STORACK-2	Storage Rack	Stock item	Active	Retail	

Click Close. Then close the Select a Report dialog box.

PRACTICE *objective*

3

Bullfrog Maintenance Company has decided to sell some goods to customers. It will sell carpet shampoo, mops, and water vacuums.

Step 1:
Open Bullfrog Maintenance Company.

Step 2:
Create the Inventory Defaults using the information given below:

GL Accts/Costing

GL Sales/Inc	400
GL Invtry/Wage	105
GL Cost Sales	503
Costing	FIFO
GL Freight Account	105

Price Levels

Level Name, Level 1	Full Price

Step 3:
Create subsidiary ledger accounts for the following inventory items:

Item 1

Item ID:	**CPTSHAM-1**
Description:	**Carpet Shampoo**
Item Class:	**Stock item**
Description:	**for Sales**
Full Price:	**12.00**
Last Unit Cost:	**5.00**
Cost Method:	**FIFO**
Item Type:	**Retail**
Stocking U/M:	**Gallon**
GL Sales Acct:	**400**
GL Inventory Acct:	**105**
GL Cost of Sales Acct:	**503**
Item Tax Type:	**1**
Preferred Vendor ID:	

Item 2

Item ID:	**MOP-2**
Description:	**Mops**
Item Class:	**Stock item**
Description:	**for Sales**
Full Price:	**25.00**
Last Unit Cost:	**10.00**
Cost Method:	**FIFO**
Item Type:	**Retail**
Stocking U/M:	**Each**
GL Sales Acct:	**400**
GL Inventory Acct:	**105**
GL Cost of Sales Acct:	**503**

Item Ta_x_ Type: 1
Preferred _V_endor ID:

Item 3

 Item _ID_: **WATERVAC-3**
 Description: **Water Vacuums**
 Item Class: **Stock item**
 Description: **for Sales**
 Full Price: **325.00**
 _L_ast Unit Cost: **130.00**
 _C_ost Method: **FIFO**
 Item Type: **Retail**
 Stocking U/M: **Each**
 GL Sales Acct: **400**
 GL Inventory Acct: **105**
 GL Cost of Sales Acct: **503**
 Item Ta_x_ Type: **1**
 Preferred _V_endor ID:

Step 4:

Preview the *Item List* report and compare it with figure 8–12.

FIGURE 8-12

Item List

Bullfrog Maintenance Company
Item List

Filter Criteria includes: Report order is by ID.

Item ID	Item Description	Item Class	Active?	Item Type	Qty on Hand
CPTSHAM-1	Carpet Shampoo	Stock item	Active	Retail	
MOP-2	Mops	Stock item	Active	Retail	
WATERVAC-3	Water Vacuums	Stock item	Active	Retail	

Step 5:

Close the Select a Report dialog box.

OBJECTIVE 4 — ESTABLISH RECORDS FOR SALES REPRESENTATIVES

Many merchandising businesses use sales representatives to market their goods. These sales representatives may be employees or independent contractors. Peachtree allows a firm to keep track of the sales made by its sales representatives. However, you must first set up a record for each sales representative.

Woodward Construction Company has two sales representatives, Ernest Brown and Mary Davis, who are independent contractors. Use the steps outlined below to establish records for these sales representatives. The creation of payroll records for sales representatives who are employees will be discussed in a later chapter.

Step 1:

Open Woodward Construction Company and close the Action Items log.

Step 2:

Click <u>M</u>aintain, and then click <u>E</u>mployees/Sales Reps. Click No at the Setup Payroll Wizard query. The Maintain Employees/Sales Reps window will appear. Enter the following information for Ernest Brown, a sales representative.

Step 3:

Key **EBROWN-01** in the *Employee I<u>D</u>* field.

Step 4:

Key **Ernest J. Brown** in the *N<u>a</u>me* field.

Step 5:

Click the *Sales Rep* option.

Step 6:

Key **2335 Wilson Way** in the *Address* field.

Step 7:

Key **Modesto, CA 95355** in the *City, ST <u>Z</u>ip* fields. Key **USA** in the *Country* field.

Step 8:

Key **209-555-1234** in the *Telephone <u>1</u>* field.

Step 9:

Key **887-09-9989** in the *So<u>c</u>ial Security #* field.

Step 10:

Key **Independ** for independent contractor in the *<u>T</u>ype* field.

Step 11:

Key **07/07/00** in the *Hired* field.

Step 12:

Compare your entries with the ones shown in figure 8–13.

FIGURE 8-13

Completed Maintain Employees/Sales Reps Window

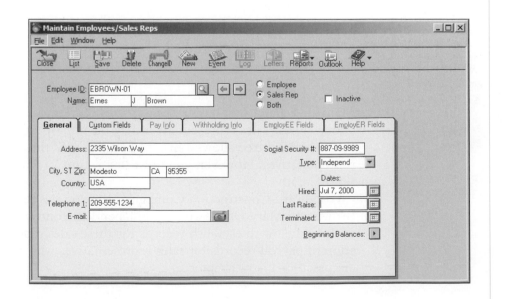

Step 13:

Click Save and then New.

Step 14:

Enter the following information for the second sales representative of Woodward Construction Company.

Employee ID:	**MDAVIS-02**
Name:	**Mary P. Davis**
Address:	**778 Kemp Road**
City, ST Zip:	**Stockton, CA 95250**
Country:	**USA**
Telephone 1:	**209-555-2468**
Social Security #:	**662-04-4434**
Type:	**Independ**
Hired:	**07/12/00**

Step 15:

Click Save and then Close.

PRACTICE *objective* 4

Check POINT

1. Why would a user of Peachtree want to set up records for its sales representatives?
2. What are the two types of sales representatives?

Answers

1. *By setting up records for its sales representatives, a user of Peachtree can keep track of each representative's sales.*
2. *Some sales representatives are employees, and others are independent contractors.*

The Bullfrog Maintenance Company has hired two sales representatives: Julio Hernandez and Isabel Guerrero.

Step 1:

Open Bullfrog Maintenance Company.

Step 2:

Establish a record for each sales representative.

Employee ID:	**JULHERND-01**
Name:	**Julio Q. Hernandez**
Address:	**1223 Westin Road**
City, ST Zip:	**Stockton, CA 95250**
Country:	**USA**
Telephone 1:	**209-555-4556**
Social Security #:	**533-45-8743**
Type:	**Independ**
Hired:	**07/18/00**

Employee ID:	**ISGUER-02**
Name:	**Isabel X. Guerrero**
Address:	**2389 Alexandria Drive**
City, ST Zip:	**Modesto, CA 95355**
Country:	**USA**
Telephone 1:	**209-555-9008**
Social Security #:	**332-09-8743**
Type:	**Independ**
Hired:	**05/26/00**

OBJECTIVE 5 — PROCESS INVENTORY TRANSACTIONS

One of the advantages of using Peachtree for a merchandising business is the ease of processing inventory transactions. Peachtree can be used to quickly and efficiently set up vendor accounts, issue purchase orders, record the receipt of inventory items, pay vendors for the items, and keep track of the quantity and cost of inventory items.

CREATING VENDOR ACCOUNTS WITH DISCOUNTS

The procedure for creating vendor accounts was covered in chapter 5. However, most of the vendors discussed there did not offer discounts. Many vendors who provide goods to merchandising businesses allow discounts for payment within a short period.

For example, Woodward Construction Company will buy its computer desks from BMC Supply Company. BMC offers credit terms of 2/10, n/30. This means that Woodward can take a 2% discount if it pays within 10 days. Otherwise, it has 30 days to pay the net (full) amount of the invoice.

Use the steps outlined below to create a vendor account for the BMC Supply Company.

Step 1:

With Woodward Construction Company open, click Maintain, and then click Vendors.

Step 2:

The Maintain Vendors dialog box will appear. Key **BMC-07** in the *Vendor ID* field.

Step 3:

Key **BMC Supply Company** in the *Name* field.

Step 4:

At the *General* folder tab, key **Jerome Jones** in the *Contact* field.

Step 5:

Key **00789** in the *Account #* field.

Step 6:

Key **2150 First Street** in the *Address* field.

Step 7:

Key **Modesto, CA 95355** in the *City, ST Zip* field. Key **USA** in the *Country* field.

Step 8:

Key **Supplier** in the *Vendor Type* field.

Step 9:

Select *None* from the *1099 Type* drop-down list.

Step 10:

Key **209-555-4444** in the *Telephone 1* field. Then check your work for accuracy by comparing it with figure 8–14.

FIGURE 8-14

Completed Entries under General Folder Tab

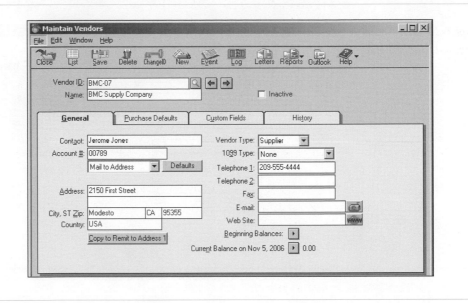

Step 11:

Click the *Purchase Defaults* folder tab.

Step 12:

Key **105** in the *Expense Acct* field.

Step 13:

Key **09-667755** in the *Tax ID #* field.

FIGURE 8-15

Vendor Terms Dialog Box

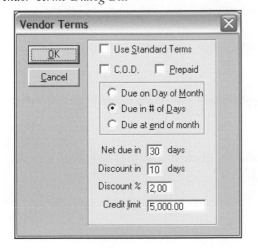

Step 14:

Click *UPS Ground* in the *Ship Via* field.

Step 15:

Click the right arrow next to *Terms* to reveal the Vendor Terms dialog box. This dialog box is used to change the credit terms offered by a vendor.

Step 16:

Deselect the check mark in the box next to *Use Standard Terms*. The default terms for vendors were set up when the company was created in Peachtree. Change the standard terms to 2/10, n/30. Confirm your entries reflect those given in figure 8–15. Click OK.

Step 17:

Accept the default, *Paper Form*, at the Form Delivery Options box.

Step 18:

Compare your work with the completed *Purchase Defaults* folder tab shown in figure 8–16.

F I G U R E   8 - 1 6

Completed Entries under Purchase Defaults Folder Tab

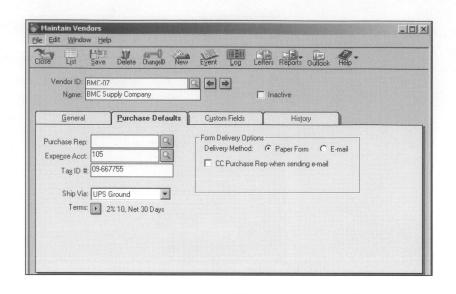

Step 19:

Click Save and then Close.

PURCHASING GOODS WITHOUT A PURCHASE ORDER

Some businesses issue a purchase order to vendors whenever they want to buy goods. Other businesses buy goods without a purchase order. Peachtree supports either method of purchasing goods.

For example, on February 3, 2007, Woodward Construction Company ordered 23 computer desks on credit from the BMC Supply Company. Woodward placed the order over the telephone and did not issue a written purchase order. BMC will send Invoice 3244 to bill Woodward for the goods.

Follow the steps outlined below to record this purchase without a purchase order.

Step 1:

Click Tasks, and then click Purchases/Receive Inventory.

Step 2:

At the Purchases/Receive Inventory window, click the *magnifying glass* icon at the *Vendor ID* field and then click *BMC-07*.

Step 3:

Change the *Date* field to *Feb. 3, 2007*.

Step 4:

Key **3244** in the *Invoice No.* field.

Step 5:

Key **23.00** in the *Quantity* field.

Step 6:

Click the *magnifying glass* icon at the *Item* field and then click *COMDESK-3*. Notice that the window is automatically completed.

Step 7:

Compare your entries with the completed Purchases/Receive Inventory window shown in figure 8–17.

FIGURE 8-17

Completed Purchases/Receive Inventory Window

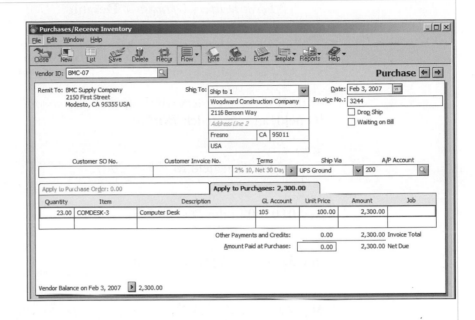

Step 8:

Click Save and then Close.

PURCHASING GOODS WITH A PURCHASE ORDER

Some businesses have a policy of issuing purchase orders to vendors for all purchases of goods and supplies. This policy helps to guard against unauthorized purchases.

Suppose that Woodward Construction Company adopts such a policy. On February 5, 2007, it decides to issue Purchase Order 010500 to the JS West Company for 30 storage racks. Follow the steps outlined below to create the necessary purchase order.

Step 1:

Set up a vendor account for the JS West Company.

Vendor ID:	**JSW-08**
Name:	**JS West Company**
Contact:	**Harry West**
Account #:	**010589**

Address:	**2121 Third Street**
City, ST Zip:	**Modesto, CA 95355**
Country:	**USA**
Vendor Type:	**Supplier**
1099 Type:	**None**
Telephone 1:	**209-555-2222**
Expense Acct:	**105**
Tax ID #:	**09-557766**
Ship Via:	**UPS Ground**
Terms:	**2/10, n/30**
Form Delivery Options:	**Default**

Step 2:

Click Tasks, and then click Purchase Orders.

Step 3:

At the Purchase Orders window, click the *magnifying glass* icon at the *Vendor ID* field, and then click *JSW-08.*

Step 4:

Change the *Date* field to *Feb. 5, 2007.*

Step 5:

Key **010500** in the *PO No.* field.

Step 6:

Key **30.00** in the *Quantity* field.

Step 7:

At the *Item* field, click the *magnifying glass* icon, and then click *STORACK-2.*

Step 8:

Compare your work with figure 8–18.

FIGURE 8-18

Completed Purchase Orders Window

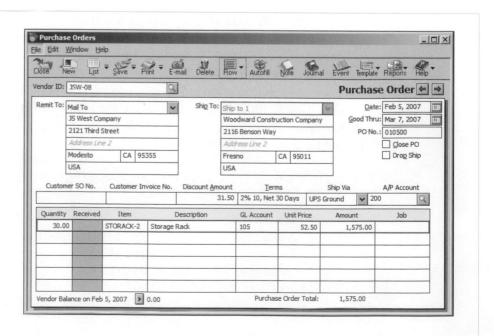

Step 9:

Click <u>S</u>ave and then Close.

RECEIVING GOODS PURCHASED WITH A PURCHASE ORDER

Remember that Woodward Construction Company issued Purchase Order 010500 to buy 30 storage racks from JS West Company. On February 10, 2007, Woodward received the goods along with Invoice 998778. Follow the steps outlined below to record the receipt of these inventory items.

Step 1:

Click Tas<u>k</u>s, and then click Pur<u>c</u>hases/Receive Inventory.

Step 2:

At the *Vendor ID* field, click the *magnifying glass* icon, and then click *JSW-08*.

Step 3:

Change the *<u>D</u>ate* field to *Feb. 10, 2007.*

Step 4:

Key **998778** in the *Invo<u>i</u>ce No.* field.

Step 5:

Click the down arrow key to the right of the folder tab label *Apply to Purchase Or<u>d</u>er No.*, and then click *PO # 010500*, as shown in figure 8–19.

FIGURE 8-19
Purchase Order Selected

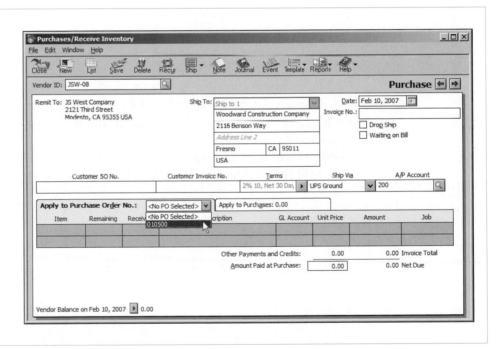

Step 6:

Key **30.00** in the *Received* field. This indicates that all the storage racks that the business ordered were received.

Compare your completed Purchases/Receive Inventory window with figure 8–20.

FIGURE 8-20

Completed Purchases/Receive Inventory Window

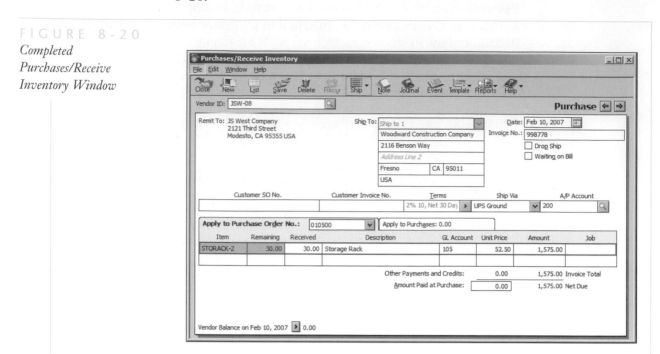

Click Save and then Close.

PAYING AN INVOICE WITH A DISCOUNT

On February 10, 2007, Woodward Construction Company issued a check for $2,254 to pay Invoice 3244 owed to the BMC Supply Company. Because Woodward paid within the 10-day discount period, it took a 2% discount ($46) from the total of the invoice ($2,300). Follow the steps outlined below to record the payment of Invoice 3244.

Click Tasks, and then click Payments.

At the Select a Cash Account dialog box, click Cash Account, 100, if needed.

At the Payments window, click the *magnifying glass* icon in the box to the right of the *Vendor ID* field box, and then click *BMC-07*.

Key **105** in the *Check Number* field.

Change the *Date* field to *Feb. 10, 2007*.

Step 6:

Click the *Apply to Invoices* folder tab, if needed.

Step 7:

Click the small box in the *Pay* field and a red check mark will appear. Notice that the discount amount is automatically calculated.

Step 8:

Key **105** in the *Discount Account* field at the bottom of the window.

Step 9:

Compare your completed entries with those shown in figure 8–21.

FIGURE 8-21

Completed Payments Window

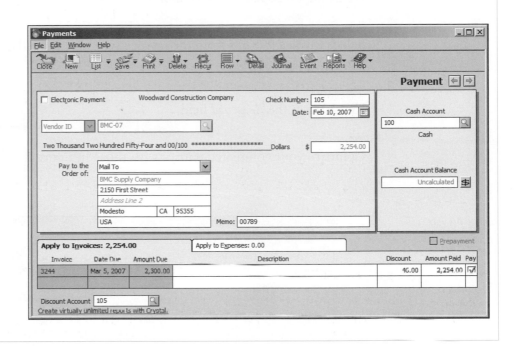

Step 10:

Click *S*ave and Close.

Step 11:

Open the payment you just created and click the *$* icon on the right side of the payment window next to the *Cash Account Balance* field to update the balance. The new balance should be $8,781.36.

Step 12:

Click Close.

RETURNING GOODS

Sometimes a business receives damaged goods or incorrect goods from a vendor. For example, assume that after Woodward Construction Company records the receipt of the 30 storage racks purchased from JS West Company, it discovers that 2 of the racks are damaged. It therefore returns these items to the vendor and sends Credit Memo 3390. The credit memo requests a credit from the vendor for the returned goods. Take the following steps to record the credit memo. **Note: You would also follow the same procedure if you were to initially receive a credit memo from the vendor.**

Step 1:

Click Tasks and then click Vendor Credit Memos.

Step 2:

At the Vendor Credit Memos window, click the *magnifying glass* icon next to the *Vendor ID* field, and then click *JSW-08*.

Step 3:

Click the *calendar* icon to select *Feb. 10, 2007* as the date.

Step 4:

Key **CM3390** in the *Credit No.* field. This is the number of the requested credit memo issued to the vendor.

Step 5:

Select Invoice 998778 from the invoice selection drop-down list in the Apply to Invoice # tab.

Step 6:

Key **2.00** in the *Returned* field.

Step 7:

Compare your completed entries with those in figure 8–22.

FIGURE 8-22

Completed Vendor Credit Memos

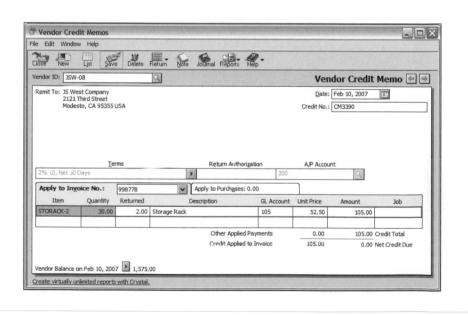

Step 8:

Click Save and then Close.

PRINTING THE INVENTORY VALUATION REPORT

One of the inventory reports that Peachtree produces shows the quantity on hand, the cost of each inventory item, and the total cost of the firm's inventory. This report is called the *Inventory Valuation* report. Follow the steps outlined below to print the *Inventory Valuation* report.

Step 1:

Click Reports, and then click Inventory.

Step 2:

At the Select a Report dialog box, in the Report List section, click *Inventory Valuation Report.*

Step 3:

Click Preview on the Select a Report toolbar.

Step 4:

Click OK at the Report Filter.

Step 5:

Compare your screen to the *Inventory Valuation* report shown in figure 8–23.

FIGURE 8-23

Inventory Valuation Report

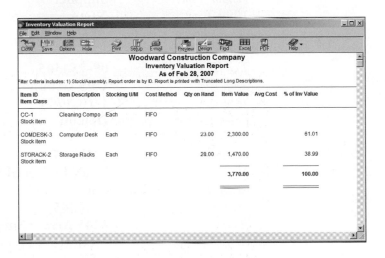

Step 6:

Click Close.

Check
POINT

1. What do the terms 2/10, n/30 on an invoice mean?
2. What does the Inventory Valuation Report show?

Answers
1. *A 2% discount can be taken if the invoice is paid within 10 days. If not, the entire net amount is due within 30 days of the invoice date.*
2. *The Inventory Valuation Report shows the quantity on hand, the cost of each inventory item, and the total cost of the firm's inventory.*

PRACTICE *objective* 5

Bullfrog Maintenance Company buys its carpet shampoo from the General Chemical Company and mops from Lou's Janitorial Supply Co.

Step 1:

Open Bullfrog Maintenance Company.

Step 2:

Create the following vendor accounts using the information provided below. Be careful to adjust vendor terms as given.

Vendor ID:	**GCC-06**
Name:	**General Chemical Company**
Contact:	**Stan Sherman**
Account #:	**09088676**
Address:	**3450 Orangeburg Drive**
City, ST Zip:	**Modesto, CA 95357**
Country:	**USA**
Vendor Type:	**Supplier**
1099 Type:	**None**
Telephone 1:	**209-555-8894**
Expense Acct:	**105**
Tax ID #:	**09-754345**
Ship Via:	**UPS Ground**
Terms:	**1/10, n/45**
Form Delivery Options:	**Default**

Vendor ID:	**LOU-07**
Name:	**Lou's Janitorial Supply Co.**
Contact:	**Lou Kim**
Account #:	**1000345**
Address:	**1245 Arrow Smith Road**
City, ST Zip:	**Modesto, CA 95353**
Country:	**USA**
Vendor Type:	**Supplier**
1099 Type:	**None**
Telephone 1:	**209-555-8445**
Expense Acct:	**105**
Tax ID #:	**09-777998**
Ship Via:	**UPS Ground**
Terms:	**3/15, n/60**
Form Delivery Options:	**Default**

Step 3:

Record the following transactions:

- On February 2, 2007, Bullfrog Maintenance Company purchased 230 gallons of carpet shampoo (CPTSHAM-1) on credit from the General Chemical Company. Bullfrog received Invoice 4556.

- On February 4, 2007, Bullfrog ordered 100 mops (MOP-2) on credit from Lou's Janitorial Supply Company. Bullfrog issued Purchase Order 010402.
- On February 10, 2007, Bullfrog received 100 mops ordered on purchase order 010402 from Lou's Janitorial Supply Company. Enclosed with the mops was Invoice 558990.
- On February 11, 2007, Bullfrog returned 10 gallons of carpet shampoo purchased from the General Chemical Company. Bullfrog received Credit Memo 890 (CM890). The original invoice was 4556.
- On February 11, 2007, Bullfrog paid Invoice 558990, less discount, to Lou's Janitorial Supply Company, check no. 705. **Note:** The *Discount Account* field should read **105**.

Step 4:

Print the *Inventory Valuation* report. Your printout should look like figure 8–24.

Step 5:

Close the Select a Report dialog box.

FIGURE 8-24

Inventory Valuation Report for Bullfrog Maintenance Company

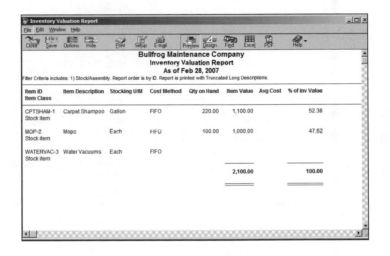

Effective inventory control is one of the most important functions of any merchandising business. To be profitable, such a firm must have enough inventory to meet customer demands, but it must avoid tying up too much cash in slow-moving items. The Internet has many sites that offer helpful advice about inventory control. One good source of information is Inventory Control Related Sites (figure 8–25), which is located at www.cris.com/~kthill/sites.htm. This group of Web sites provides many resources that can aid in inventory control.

FIGURE 8-25

Inventory Control Related Sites Web Site

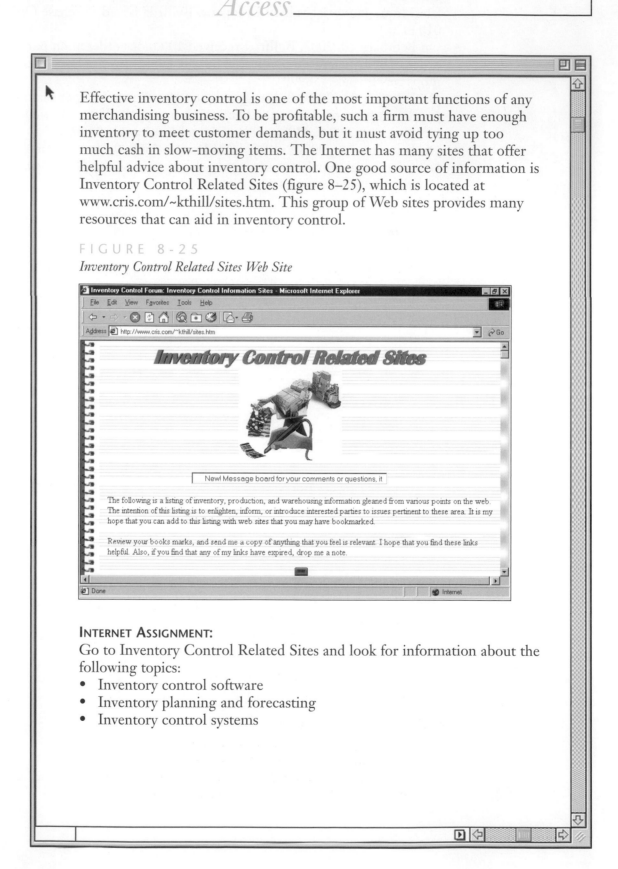

INTERNET ASSIGNMENT:

Go to Inventory Control Related Sites and look for information about the following topics:

- Inventory control software
- Inventory planning and forecasting
- Inventory control systems

SOFTWARE
Command Summary

Create Inventory Item	Maintain, Inventory Items
Print Item List	Reports, Inventory, select Item List
Create Salesperson Record	Maintain, Employees/Sales Reps
Create Vendor Account	Maintain, Vendors
Enter Purchase without Purchase Order	Tasks, Purchases/Receive Inventory
Create Purchase Order	Tasks, Purchase Orders
Pay Invoice	Tasks, Payments
Return Goods	Tasks, Vendor Credit Memos

PROJECTS
and Problems

Content Check

Multiple Choice: Choose only one response for each question.

1. Peachtree supports which of the following inventory costing methods?
   A. average cost
   B. LIFO
   C. FIFO
   D. All of the above.

2. Credit terms of 1/10, n/30 mean
   A. a 1% discount is allowed if the invoice is paid within 10 days, or the entire net amount is due within 30 days.
   B. a 1% discount is allowed if the invoice is paid within 30 days.
   C. a 10% discount is allowed if the bill is paid within 1 day of receipt, or the entire amount is due within 30 days.
   D. None of the above.

3. The perpetual inventory system involves
   A. counting goods at regular intervals.
   B. estimating the number of goods on hand.
   C. maintaining a running balance for all inventory items.
   D. estimating the cost of the goods on hand.

4. In a period of rising prices, which inventory costing method will result in the highest cost of goods sold?
   A. average cost
   B. LIFO
   C. FIFO
   D. perpetual

5. What function of Peachtree will a firm use to record the return of damaged goods to a vendor?
   A. Sales/Invoicing
   B. Receipts
   C. Vendor Credit Memos
   D. Payments

Short Essay Response: Provide a detailed answer for each question.

1. What is the difference between the perpetual inventory system and the periodic inventory system?
2. Explain each of the three most common inventory costing methods: average cost, LIFO, and FIFO.
3. Peachtree will automatically update which accounts when an inventory item is sold? Will these accounts increase or decrease?
4. Explain the steps necessary to create a new vendor account.
5. List two inventory reports that Peachtree produces. What information does each of these reports contain?
6. What advantages might a business gain by switching from the periodic inventory system to the perpetual inventory system?

CASE PROBLEMS

PROBLEM 1A

Open Kathleen's Designs, an interior decorating business, which you downloaded from the CD that comes with this book.

1. Create the Inventory account for this firm.

Account ID:	**105**
Description:	**Inventory**
Account Type:	**Inventory**

2. Create the Cost of Sales account.

Account ID:	**503**
Description:	**Cost of Goods Sold**
Account Type:	**Cost of Sales**

3. Create the following vendor accounts:

Vendor ID:	**SHGS-01**
Name:	**Sanders Home and Garden Supply**
Contact:	**Robert Sanders**

Account #:	**169135**
Address:	**23451 Main Street**
City, ST Zip:	**Modesto, CA 95355**
Country:	**USA**
Vendor Type:	**Supplier**
1099 Type:	**None**
Telephone 1:	**209-555-9756**
Expense Acct:	**105**
Tax ID #:	**09-999378**
Ship Via:	**Fed-EX**
Terms:	**2/10, n/30**

Vendor ID:	**MHS-02**
Name:	**Martin's Hobby Store**
Contact:	**Luke Martin**
Account #:	**1239437**
Address:	**2348 West Lane**
City, ST Zip:	**Modesto, CA 95355**
Country:	**USA**
Vendor Type:	**Supplier**
1099 Type:	**None**
Telephone 1:	**209-555-5623**
Expense Acct:	**105**
Tax ID #:	**09-999465**
Ship Via:	**Fed-EX**
Terms:	**5/10, n/30**

4. Create the following subsidiary ledger accounts for inventory items:

Item ID:	**STENCILS-01**
Description:	**Flower Stencils**
Item Class:	**Stock item**
Description:	**for Sales**
Price Level 1:	**15.00**
Last Unit Cost:	**5.50**
Cost Method:	**FIFO**
Item Type:	**Retail**
Stocking U/M:	**Each**
GL Sales Acct:	**401**
GL Inventory Acct:	**105**
GL Cost of Sales Acct:	**503**
Item Tax Type:	**1**
Preferred Vendor ID:	**MHS-02**

Item ID:	**PILLOWS-02**
Description:	**12-inch Pillows**
Item Class:	**Stock item**
Description:	**for Sales**

Price Level 1:	**35.00**
Last Unit Cost:	**12.50**
Cost Method:	**FIFO**
Item Type:	**Retail**
Stocking U/M:	**Each**
GL Sales Acct:	**401**
GL Inventory Acct:	**105**
GL Cost of Sales Acct:	**503**
Item Tax Type:	**1**
Preferred Vendor ID:	**SHGS-01**

5. Record the following transactions, which occurred in January 2007.

Jan. 6	Ordered 15 flower stencils from Martin's Hobby Store, using Purchase Order 100.
8	Ordered 20 pillows from Sanders Home and Garden Supply, using Purchase Order 101.
10	Received the stencils ordered, Invoice 3264.
11	Received 16 of the pillows ordered, Invoice 16425.
11	Returned 2 of the stencils, and received CM15 from the vendor.
19	Paid the balance owed to Martin's Hobby Store, less discount, Check 125. (Use 105 as the Discount Account.)
21	Paid the balance owed to Sanders Home and Garden Supply, less discount, Check 126.

6. Print the *Inventory Valuation* and *Cash Disbursements Journal* reports.

PROBLEM 2A

Open Executive Consultants, a business consulting company, which you downloaded from the CD that comes with this book.

Create records for the following sales representatives:

Employee ID:	**ACHANG-01**
Name:	**Annette Chang**
Address:	**2984 Monte Vista Lane**
City, ST Zip:	**Modesto, CA 95355**
Country:	**USA**
Telephone 1:	**209-555-6565**
Social Security #:	**888-55-5555**
Type:	**Independ**
Hired:	**05/01/03**

Employee ID:	**TWILSON-02**
Name:	**Thomas Wilson**
Address:	**21543 Holly Drive**
City, ST Zip:	**Modesto, CA 95355**
Country:	**USA**
Telephone 1:	**209-555-9564**

Social Security #:	**555-88-8888**
Type:	**Independ**
Hired:	**05/30/03**

PROBLEM 1B

Open Ana's Creations, a beauty salon, which you downloaded from the CD that comes with this book.

1. Create the Inventory account for this firm.

Account ID:	**105**
Description:	**Inventory**
Account Type:	**Inventory**

2. Create the Cost of Sales account.

Account ID:	**503**
Description:	**Cost of Goods Sold**
Account Type:	**Cost of Sales**

3. Create the following vendor account:

Vendor ID:	**BP-01**
Name:	**Beauty Products**
Contact:	**Maxine Williams**
Account #:	**16531**
Address:	**2951 Corral Hollow Road**
City, ST Zip:	**Tracy, CA 95376**
Country:	**USA**
Vendor Type:	**Supplier**
1099 Type:	**None**
Telephone 1:	**209-555-4612**
Expense Acct:	**105**
Tax ID #:	**09-912348**
Ship Via:	**Fed-EX**
Terms:	**2/10, n/30**

4. Create the following subsidiary ledger accounts for inventory items:

Item ID:	**EXSHAMPOO-01**
Description:	**Ecstasy Shampoo**
Item Class:	**Stock item**
Description:	**for Sales**
Price Level 1:	**22.00**
Last Unit Cost:	**13.50**
Cost Method:	**FIFO**
Item Type:	**Retail**
Stocking U/M:	**Each**
GL Sales Acct:	**401**

GL Inventory Acct:	**105**
GL Cost of Sales Acct:	**503**
Item Tax Type:	**1**
Preferred Vendor ID:	**BP-01**

Item ID:	**EXCONDITIONER-02**
Description:	**Ecstasy Conditioner**
Item Class:	**Stock item**
Description:	**for Sales**
Price Level 1:	**18.00**
Last Unit Cost:	**9.50**
Cost Method:	**FIFO**
Item Type:	**Retail**
Stocking U/M:	**Each**
GL Sales Acct:	**401**
GL Inventory Acct:	**105**
GL Cost of Sales Acct:	**503**
Item Tax Type:	**1**
Preferred Vendor ID:	**BP-01**

Item ID:	**HAIRGEL-03**
Description:	**Ecstasy Hair Gel**
Item Class:	**Stock item**
Description:	**for Sales**
Price Level 1:	**12.00**
Last Unit Cost:	**5.50**
Cost Method:	**FIFO**
Item Type:	**Retail**
Stocking U/M:	**Each**
GL Sales Acct:	**401**
GL Inventory Acct:	**105**
GL Cost of Sales Acct:	**503**
Item Tax Type:	**1**
Preferred Vendor ID:	**BP-01**

5. Record the following transactions, which occurred in June 2007.

June 10	Ordered 22 bottles of shampoo and 8 bottles of conditioner, using Purchase Order 200.
13	Ordered 15 bottles of hair gel, using Purchase Order 201.
13	Received 22 bottles of shampoo and 6 of the bottles of conditioner that were ordered, Invoice 1864.
15	Received 15 bottles of hair gel, Invoice 1925.
23	Paid Invoices 1864 and 1925, less discounts, Check 450. (Use 105 as the Discount Account.)

6. Print the *Inventory Valuation* and *Cash Disbursements Journal* reports.

PROBLEM 2B

Open VP Designers, a computer programming services company, which you downloaded from the CD that comes with this book.

Create records for the following sales representatives:

Employee ID:	**MANDERSON-01**
Name:	**Melody Anderson**
Address:	**19974 West Pershing Avenue**
City, ST Zip:	**Tracy, CA 95376**
Country:	**USA**
Telephone 1:	**209-555-6936**
Social Security #:	**645-55-5555**
Type:	**Independ**
Hired:	**04/02/03**

Employee ID:	**WKINCAID-02**
Name:	**William Kincaid**
Address:	**6543 Angelica Court**
City, ST Zip:	**Modesto, CA 95355**
Country:	**USA**
Telephone 1:	**209-555-9564**
Social Security #:	**544-55-9999**
Type:	**Independ**
Hired:	**04/04/03**

Cooperative Learning

1. Form groups of three or four students, and discuss how each of the inventory costing methods will affect taxable income in periods when prices are rising.
2. As a group, choose a local business such as a clothing store, a sporting goods store, or a drugstore. What inventory control problems might this business have?

Writing and Decision Making

Assume that you work for a small merchandising business that does not yet use computerized inventory procedures. The owner, Marie Ramirez, has asked you to provide information on how Peachtree can help her to manage the firm's inventory. She has specifically asked you to explain the steps necessary to set up Peachtree's inventory system, what tasks the system can handle, and what records and reports it produces. Prepare a memo providing the information that has been requested.

CHAPTER
9

SALES OF INVENTORY
IN A MERCHANDISE BUSINESS

1. Understand inventory sales concepts

2. Create sales tax accounts and codes

3. Process sales transactions and create invoices

4. Create sales orders and invoices from quotations

5. Record finance charges on overdue customer balances

6. Print inventory and sales reports

SOFTWARE FEATURES

- Sales Invoices

- Credit Memos

- Sales Quotations and Orders

- Sales Taxes

- Finance Charges

Chapter 8 focused on establishing a perpetual inventory system for a merchandising business and recording the initial purchases of goods. In this chapter, you will see how a merchandising business processes sales of inventory, sales tax, sales returns and allowances, sales discounts, and finance charges on overdue customer balances.

OBJECTIVE 1 — UNDERSTAND INVENTORY SALES CONCEPTS

Some merchandising businesses sell goods "over the counter" and record their sales transactions on a cash register. Examples of such businesses are supermarkets, drugstores, and department stores. Increasingly, these businesses are using optical scanners and electronic cash registers that transfer information about their sales to a computerized accounting system and a computerized inventory system.

Other merchandising businesses sell their goods through sales representatives who visit customers, through catalogs sent to customers, over the telephone, or through Web sites. When businesses sell through these types of channels, they usually issue invoices to their customers. Remember that an invoice is a bill for goods or services. It lists the items sold, the prices, the total owed, the credit terms, and other information about the sale. The invoice is sent to the customer with the goods or mailed after the goods are shipped.

These businesses may also issue sales quotations, sales orders, and credit memos—

- Sometimes a potential customer will ask a business to provide a form showing the prices it will charge for specified goods. In response, the business will issue a **sales quotation**.

- When a customer orders goods, a business may prepare a form that shows the items involved, the quantities, the name of the sales representative, and other information about the order. This form is called a **sales order**.

- If a customer returns damaged or incorrect goods, the business provides credit for the return. It issues a **credit memo** to the customer to show the amount of credit granted.

Peachtree allows a merchandising business to quickly and efficiently prepare invoices, sales quotations, sales orders, and credit memos. It also helps a merchandising business by automatically calculating sales tax, sales discount, and finance charges.

ACCOUNTING FOR SALES UNDER THE PERPETUAL INVENTORY SYSTEM

Suppose that a business sells goods for $500 on credit to a customer. The business must collect a 7% sales tax on all of its sales. The cost of the items sold was $300. Because the business uses the perpetual inventory system, it must make two sets of entries to record this sale.

- The business must debit Accounts Receivable for $535 (the total amount owed by the customer), credit the appropriate revenue account for $500 (the amount of revenue earned by the business), and credit Sales Tax Payable for $35 (the amount of sales tax owed).

- The business must debit Cost of Goods Sold for $300 and credit Inventory for $300. This amount is the cost of the items sold to the customer.

sales quotation A form that shows the prices a business will charge for specified goods.

sales order A form that a business may prepare to record the details of a customer's order.

credit memo A form issued to a customer to show the credit granted for a return of goods.

One of the advantages of Peachtree is that it can update all of these general ledger accounts simultaneously when you enter a sale on credit. It can also update the subsidiary ledger accounts for the customer and for the inventory items sold.

CREATING AN INCOME ACCOUNT FOR SALES OF GOODS

Businesses that sell both services and goods usually keep separate income accounts for each source of revenue. This practice provides a firm with information about how much revenue it is earning from each segment of its operations.

Woodward Construction Company currently has a single income account called Fees Earned in its general ledger. Open Woodward Construction Company, and change the description of this account to Service Revenue and use it only for the revenue earned from providing services to customers.

Account ID:	**400**
Description:	**Service Revenue**
Account Type:	**Income**

Set up a second income account called Sales Revenue in its general ledger and use it to record the revenue earned from sales of inventory.

Account ID:	**400.5**
Description:	**Sales Revenue**
Account Type:	**Income**

Because you now have two separate income accounts, it is necessary to change the GL Sales Account for each inventory item. Follow the steps outlined below to accomplish this task.

Step 1:

Click Maintain, and then Inventory Items.

Step 2:

Click the *magnifying glass* icon next to the *Item ID* field, and then click *CC-1* (Cleaning Compound).

Step 3:

Key **400.5** in the *GL Sales Acct* field, then click Save on the Maintain Inventory Items toolbar.

Step 4:

Change the GL Sales Acct to 400.5 for the other two inventory items, *Computer Desk* and *Storage Rack*. Then close the Maintain Inventory Items window.

Check
POINT

1. Name four types of forms that many merchandising businesses prepare when they sell their goods through sales representatives.
2. A merchandising business that uses the perpetual inventory system makes a sale for $1,000. The goods have a cost of $600. What entry is made in the Cost of Goods Sold account and the Inventory account?

Answers
1. *The four types of forms that many merchandising businesses prepare are the invoice, sales quotation, sales order, and credit memo.*
2. *The Cost of Goods Sold account is debited for $600 and the Inventory account is credited for $600.*

OBJECTIVE 2 — CREATE SALES TAX ACCOUNTS AND CODES

Most states and some cities and counties impose a sales tax on goods that are sold to consumers. The retail businesses that make the sales are responsible for collecting the tax and sending it to the sales tax authority at regular intervals—usually monthly or quarterly.

When a sale is recorded, the amount of sales tax owed is credited to a liability account called Sales Tax Payable. Later, when the business remits the sales tax owed for a period to the sales tax authority, it debits the Sales Tax Payable account.

Sales Tax Payable is a current liability (a short-term debt) for a business. In the Peachtree system of account classification, this account appears after Accounts Payable and is part of the group of accounts called Other Current Liabilities.

Woodward Construction Company must charge a 7% sales tax on the inventory that it sells. In California, where Woodward is located, there are several local sales tax authorities and a state sales tax authority. Woodward is under the jurisdiction of an agency called the Board of Equalization and will send the amounts of sales tax it owes to this agency.

Woodward must now create the Sales Tax Payable account in its general ledger and a vendor account for the Board of Equalization in its accounts payable ledger. Follow the steps outlined below to accomplish these tasks.

Step 1:

Create the Sales Tax Payable account in the general ledger. Use the following information:

Account ID:	**212**
Description:	**Sales Tax Payable**
Account Type:	**Other Current Liabilities**

Step 2:

Compare your work with figure 9–1, then click Save and Close.

FIGURE 9-1

Completed Entries for Sales Tax Payable Account

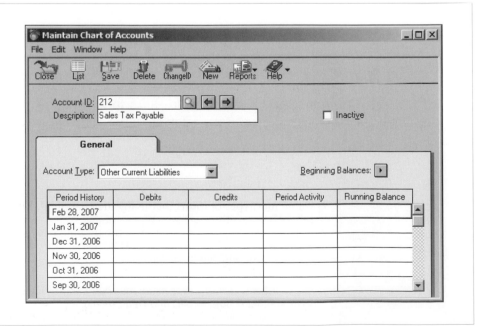

Step 3:

Create a vendor account for the Board of Equalization.

Vendor ID:	**BOARDEQUAL-06**
Name:	**Board of Equalization**
Expense Acct:	**212**
Tax ID #:	
Ship Via:	**US Mail**
Terms:	**EOM, 0.00 Discount**
Form Delivery Options:	**Default**

Step 4:

Compare your work with figure 9–2, then click Save and Close.

FIGURE 9-2

Completed Vendor Account for Board of Equalization

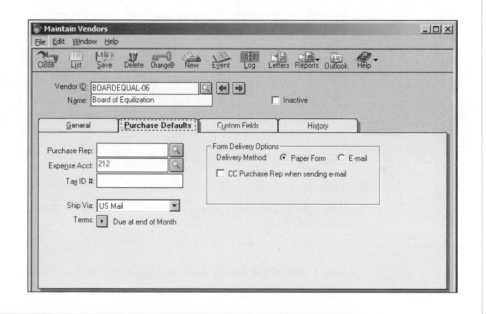

Step 5:

Click Maintain, and then click Sales Taxes, and then Sales Tax Authorities.

Step 6:

The Maintain Sales Tax Authorities window will appear. Key **CASTAX** in the *ID* field.

Step 7:

Key **California Sales Tax** in the *Description* field.

Step 8:

At the *Tax Payable To* field, click the *magnifying glass* icon, and then click **BOARDEQUAL-06.**

Step 9:

Key **212** in the *Sales Tax Payable G/L Account* field.

Step 10:

Select Single Tax Rate and key **7.00** in the % field. Your screen should now look like figure 9–3.

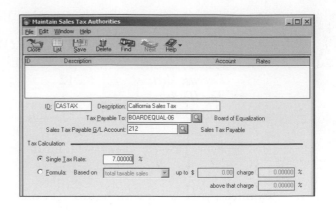

Step 11:

Click Save and then Close.

CREATE SALES TAX CODES

In addition to establishing the Sales Tax Payable account and the vendor account for the Board of Equalization, Woodward Construction Company must create sales tax codes.

Step 1:

Click Maintain, and then click Sales Taxes, and then Sales Tax Codes.

Step 2:

The Maintain Sales Tax Codes window will appear. Key **CAL** in the *Sales Tax Code* field.

Step 3:

Key **California Sales Tax** in the *Description* field.

Step 4:

Key **CASTAX** in the *ID* field, and then press Tab or Enter. Compare your work with figure 9–4.

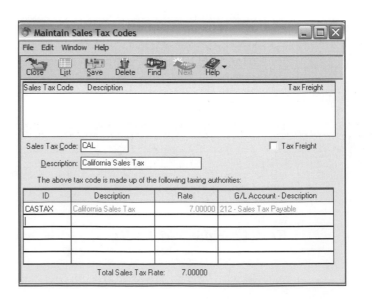

PRACTICE *objective* 2

The Bullfrog Maintenance Company must revise its general ledger accounts so that it can record sales of goods and sales tax.

Step 1:

Open Bullfrog Maintenance Company.

Step 2:

Change the description of Bullfrog's existing income account so that it now appears as follows in the chart of accounts for the general ledger.

Account ID:	**400**
Account Description:	**Service Revenue**
Account Type:	**Income**

Step 3:

Create the new income account needed to record sales of goods.

Account ID:	**400.5**
Account Description:	**Sales Revenue**
Account Type:	**Income**

Note: Because you now have two separate income accounts, it is necessary to change the GL Sales Account for each inventory item.

Step 4:

Create the Sales Tax Payable account.

Account ID:	**212**
Description:	**Sales Tax Payable**
Account Type:	**Other Current Liabilities**

Step 5:

Create a new vendor account for the Board of Equalization.

Vendor ID:	**BOARDEQUAL-08**
Name:	**Board of Equalization**
Expense Acct:	**212**
Tax ID #:	
Ship Via:	**US Mail**
Terms:	**EOM, 0.00 Discount**
Form Delivery Options:	**Default**

Step 6:

Enter the information about the sales tax authorities.

ID:	**CASTAX**
Description:	**California Sales Tax**
Tax Payable To:	**BOARDEQUAL-08**
Sales Tax Payable G/L Account:	**212**
Tax rate:	**7.00**

Step 7:

Create the sales tax codes.

Sales Tax Code:	**CAL**
Description:	**California Sales Tax**
ID:	**CASTAX**

Step 8:

Print your chart of accounts and compare it to figure 9–5.

FIGURE 9-5

Chart of Accounts for Bullfrog Maintenance Company

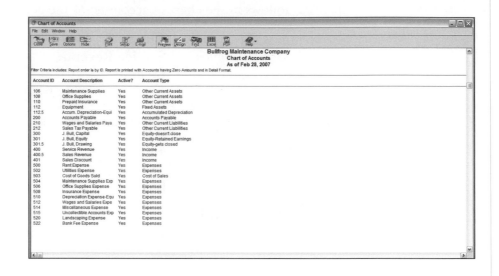

OBJECTIVE 3 — PROCESS SALES TRANSACTIONS AND CREATE INVOICES

When a merchandising business receives an order from a customer, it selects and packs the necessary goods and issues an invoice to bill the customer. The invoice may be enclosed with the goods when they are shipped to the customer, or it may be mailed separately.

Occasionally, a merchandising business will send incorrect goods to a customer or the goods will arrive in damaged condition. The customer will then return the goods and request credit or agree to keep the goods if an allowance is offered. (An allowance is a reduction in the selling price of goods.) To provide evidence of the credit granted for a return or allowance, the business issues a credit memo to the customer.

Peachtree allows a merchandising business to efficiently make accounting entries for sales on credit and sales returns and allowances and also generate the necessary invoices and credit memos.

RECORDING A SALE ON CREDIT AND CREATING THE INVOICE

Suppose that on February 17, 2007, Woodward Construction Company sells six computer desks on credit to Jim Green, who operates his own software business. The terms of the sale are 2/10, n/30.

Because Green is a new customer, it is necessary to create a customer account for him before recording the sale and issuing Invoice 11702.

Step 1:
Open Woodward Construction Company and close Action Items log.

Step 2:
Create a new customer account for Jim Green. Use the following information.

Customer ID:	**Green-11**
Name:	**Jim Green**

General Tab

Contact:	**Jim Green**
Bill to Address	
Address:	**12 Onyx Road**
City, ST Zip:	**Modesto, CA 95355**
Country:	**USA**
Sales Tax:	**CAL**
Customer Type:	**Retail**
Telephone 1:	**209-555-4845**

Sales Defaults Tab

GL Sales Acct:	**400.5**
Ship Via:	**UPS Ground**
Pricing Level:	**Full Price**
Form Delivery Options:	**Default**

Terms and Credit Tab

Terms:	**2/10, n/30**

Now record the credit sale to Jim Green and create Invoice 11702.

Step 1:
Click Tasks, and then click Sales/Invoicing.

Step 2:
The Sales/Invoicing window now appears. At the *Customer ID* field click the *magnifying glass* icon and then double-click *Green-11*.

Step 3:
Key **02/17/07** in the *Date* field.

Step 4:
Key **011705** in the *Invoice No.* field.

Step 5:
Key **6.00** in the *Quantity* field.

Step 6:

Click in the *Item* field, click the *magnifying glass* icon, and then click *COMDESK-3*.

Step 7:

Compare your completed work with figure 9–6.

FIGURE 9-6

Completed Sales/Invoicing Window

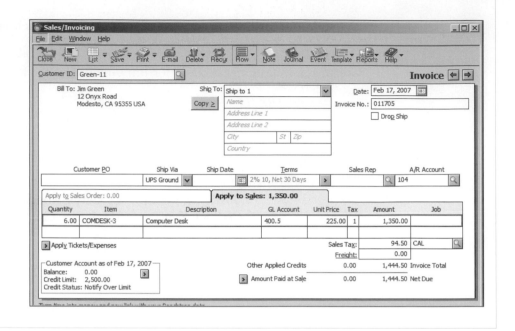

Step 8:

Click Save and then click Close.

PRINTING THE INVOICE

The sale on credit made to Jim Green has now been posted to the general ledger and the appropriate subsidiary ledgers. In the general ledger, Accounts Receivable has been debited for $1,444.50, Sales Revenue has been credited for $1,350, and Sales Tax Payable has been credited for $94.50. Also in the general ledger, Cost of Goods Sold has been debited for $600 and Inventory has been credited for $600. This amount is the cost of the six desks. Finally, the account for Jim Green in the accounts receivable subsidiary ledger has been debited for $1,444.50 and the account for the computer desks in the inventory subsidiary ledger has been credited for $600.

The next task for Woodward Construction Company is to print Invoice 011705 and send it to Jim Green. Woodward has a policy of mailing an invoice on the day the goods are shipped to the customer. Follow the steps outlined below to print Invoice 011705.

Step 1:

Click Tasks, and then click Sales/Invoicing.

Step 2:

Click the List button at the top of the Sales/Invoicing window.

Step 3:

The Sales Invoice List window will appear. Click the sale to Jim Green (Invoice 11705), as shown in figure 9–7.

FIGURE 9-7

Invoice Chosen from Sales Invoice List Window

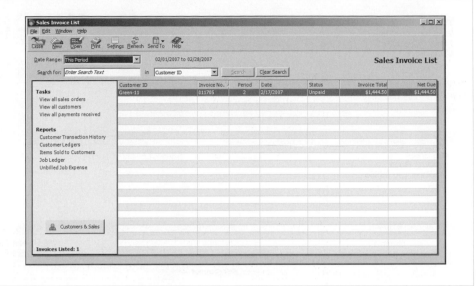

Step 4:

Click Open.

Step 5:

Click the Print button on the Sales/Invoicing toolbar.

Step 6:

Click Print at the Print Forms: Invoices dialog box, shown in figure 9–8.

FIGURE 9-8

Print Forms: Invoices Window

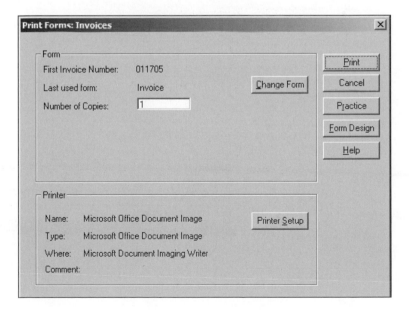

Step 7:

Compare your completed invoice with figure 9–9.

FIGURE 9-9
Invoice 11705

Woodward Construction Company
2116 Benson Way
Fresno, CA 95011
USA

Voice: 209-555-1111
Fax: 209-555-5555

INVOICE

Invoice Number: 011705
Invoice Date: Feb 17, 2007
Page: 1

Duplicate

Bill To:	Ship to:
Jim Green 12 Onyx Road Modesto, CA 95355 USA	

Customer ID	Customer PO	Payment Terms	
Green-11		2% 10, Net 30 Days	
Sales Rep ID	**Shipping Method**	**Ship Date**	**Due Date**
	UPS Ground		3/19/07

Quantity	Item	Description	Unit Price	Amount
6.00	COMDESK-3	Computer Desk	225.00	1,350.00

Subtotal		1,350.00
Sales Tax		94.50
Total Invoice Amount		1,444.50
Payment/Credit Applied		
TOTAL		**1,444.50**

Check/Credit Memo No:

Step 8:

Close the Sales/Invoicing window and the Sales Invoice List window.

RECORDING A SALES RETURN AND CREATING THE CREDIT MEMO

Suppose that on February 18, 2007, Jim Green receives the six computer desks shipped by Woodward Construction Company on February 17. Green finds that one desk is damaged and notifies Woodward that he intends to return the desk. Woodward agrees to give him a credit of $240.75 for the return. This amount includes the selling price of $225 and sales tax of $15.75.

Woodward must now record the sales return and create a credit memo. The return requires a debit of $225 to Sales Returns and Allowances, a debit of $15.75 to Sales Tax Payable, and a credit of $240.75 to Accounts Receivable. It is also necessary to record a credit of $240.75 in the subsidiary ledger account for Jim Green.

Sales returns and allowances reduce the revenue of a business. These transactions can be recorded by debiting them to the Sales Revenue account if desired. Most businesses, however, prefer to have a separate record of these transactions and therefore use a Sales Returns and Allowances account.

Follow the steps outlined below to record the desk returned by Jim Green and create the necessary credit memo.

Step 1:

Click Tasks, and then click Credit Memos.

Step 2:

At the *Customer ID* field, click the *magnifying glass* icon, and then click *Green-11*.

Step 3:

At the *Date* field, click the *calendar* icon, and choose *Feb 18, 2007*.

Step 4:

Key **CM012** (the credit memo number) in the *Credit No.* field.

Step 5:

Select Invoice 011705 from the drop-down list next to the *Apply to Invoice No.* tab.

Step 6:

Key **1.00** in the *Returned* field.

Step 7:

Key **Computer Desk** in the *Description* field, if needed.

Step 8:

Click the Journal button on the Credit Memos toolbar. The Accounting Behind the Screens window will appear, as shown in figure 9–10.

FIGURE 9-10

*Accounting Behind the
Screens Window*

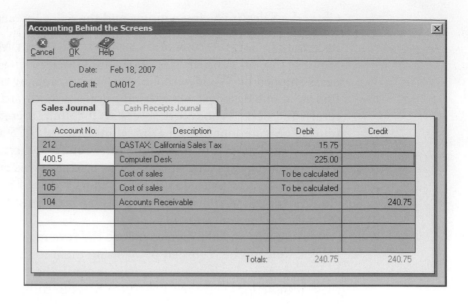

Because Woodward does not yet have a Sales Returns and Allowances account, this window shows that the Sales Revenue account (400.5) is being decreased to record the return. It is therefore necessary to create a Sales Returns and Allowances account in Woodward's general ledger.

Step 9:

Click the *magnifying glass* icon in the second row of the *Account No.* field, and then click the New button at the bottom of the window.

Step 10:

Use the following information to create the Sales Returns and Allowances account.

Account ID:	**404**
Description:	**Sales Returns and Allowances**
Account Type:	**Income**

Step 11:

Compare your work with figure 9–11. Click Save and then Close.

FIGURE 9-11

*Account 404 Added to
Maintain Chart of Accounts
Window*

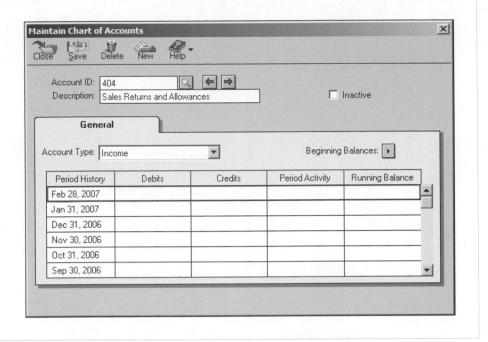

Notice that account 404 will now appear in the Account No. field. **Note:**
Peachtree automatically updates Cost of Goods Sold and Inventory for
returned items. However, you may still need to manually adjust for the cost
of damaged or defective inventory that cannot be placed back in stock.

Step 12:
Click OK to close the Accounting Behind the Screens window.

PRINTING THE CREDIT MEMO
Follow the steps outlined below to print the credit memo that the
Woodward Construction Company must send to Jim Green.

Step 1:
Click the Print button on the Credit Memos toolbar.

Step 2:
At the Print Forms: Credit Memos dialog box, click Print, as shown in
figure 9–12.

FIGURE 9-12

*Print Forms: Credit Memos
Window*

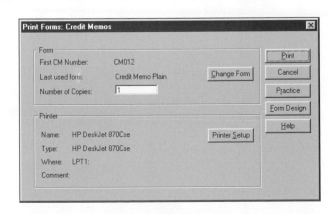

Compare your completed credit memo with figure 9–13.

FIGURE 9-13
Credit Memo 012

Woodward Construction Company
2116 Benson Way
Fresno, CA 95011
USA

Voice: 209-555-1111
Fax: 209-555-5555

CREDIT MEMO

Credit Memo Number: CM 012
Credit Date: Feb 18, 2007
Page: 1
Duplicate

Credit To:

Jim Green
12 Onyx Road
Modesto, CA 95355
USA

Customer ID	Customer PO	Sales Rep ID
JGRN-11		

Quantity	Item	Description	Unit Price	Amount
1.00	COMDESK-3	Computer Desk	225.00	225.00

	Subtotal		225.00
	Sales Tax		15.75
	Freight		
Invoice No: 011705	**TOTAL**		**240.75**

Step 4:

Click Close to close the Credit Memos window.

RECORDING A SALES DISCOUNT WHEN A CUSTOMER PAYS AN INVOICE

Suppose that on February 20, 2007, Woodward Construction Company receives a check for $1,174.86 from Jim Green. This check is in payment of Invoice 011705 ($1,444.50) less Credit Memo 012 ($240.75) and less a discount ($28.89).

The date of the invoice is February 17 and the credit terms are 2/10, n/30. Therefore, Green is paying within the 10-day discount period and is entitled to take a 2% discount on the balance due (the total of the invoice less the total of the credit memo).

When the Woodward Construction Company receives the check from Jim Green, it must debit Cash for $1174.86 (the amount received), debit Sales Discount for $28.89 (the amount of the discount taken), and credit Accounts Receivable for $1,203.75 (the total amount owed by the customer). Woodward must also credit the customer account of Jim Green for $1,203.75.

Follow the steps outlined below to record the payment Woodward Construction Company has received from Jim Green for Invoice 011705 less Credit Memo 012 and less a discount.

Step 1:

Click Tasks, and then click Receipts.

Step 2:

Select *Check* from the *Payment Method* drop-down list and *100 (Cash)* from the *Cash Account* drop-down list.

Step 3:

At the *Deposit ticket ID* field, key **02/20/07**.

Step 4:

At the *Customer ID* field of the Receipts window, click the *magnifying glass* icon, and then double-click *Green-11*, as shown in figure 9–14.

FIGURE 9-14
*Green-11 (Jim Green)
Selected from Drop-Down List*

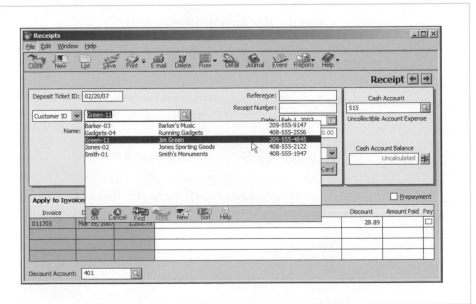

Step 5:

Key **011705** (the number of the invoice) in the *Reference* field.

Step 6:

At the *Date* field, click the *calendar* icon and choose *Feb 20, 2007.*

Step 7:

Click the box in the *Pay* field for the invoice as shown in figure 9–15. Notice that the *Receipt Amount* field indicates that the amount paid should be $1,174.86. Note also at the bottom of the Receipts window that 401, Sales Discounts, is used as the Discount Account.

FIGURE 9-15

Pay Boxes Selected

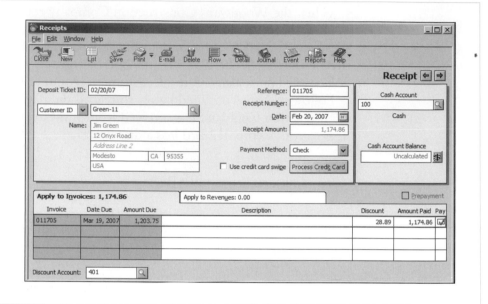

Step 8:

Click *Save.*

Step 9:

Close the Receipts window.

POINT

1. What document does a business issue in connection with a sales return or allowance?
2. When entering a sales return using the Credit Memo, is the number entered in the *Quantity* field a positive or negative number?

Answers
1. A business issues a credit memo as evidence that it is granting credit to a customer for a return or allowance.
2. You must enter a positive number in the Quantity field for a sales return.

PRACTICE *objective* 3

On February 11, 2007, Bullfrog Maintenance Company sold 20 mops on credit to George Johnson, a new customer. Bullfrog issued Invoice 021101 with credit terms of 3/10, n/30.

Step 1:
Open Bullfrog Maintenance Company.

Step 2:
Create a new customer account for George Johnson. Use the following information.

General Tab
Customer ID:	**Johnson-05**
Name:	**George Johnson**
Contact:	**George Johnson**
Bill to Address	
Address:	**1342 Rose Marie Lane**
City, ST Zip:	**Modesto, CA 95355**
Country:	**USA**
Sales Tax:	**CAL**
Customer Type:	**Retail**
Telephone 1:	**209-555-4982**

Sales Defaults Tab
GL Sales Acct:	**400.5**
Ship Via:	**UPS Ground**
Pricing Level:	**Full Price**
Form Delivery Options	**Default**

Terms and Credit Tab
Terms:	**3/10, n/30**

Step 3:
Use the Sales/Invoicing feature to record the sale and create Invoice 021101.

Step 4:
Print the invoice. Your invoice should look like figure 9–16.

FIGURE 9-16

Invoice 021101

Bullfrog Maintenance Company
456 Ballinger Lane
Stockton, CA 95101
USA

Voice: 209-555-2222
Fax: 209-555-6666

INVOICE

Invoice Number: 021101
Invoice Date: Feb 11, 2007
Page: 1

Duplicate

Bill To:	Ship to:
George Johnson 1342 Rose Marie Lane Modesto, CA 95355 USA	

Customer ID	Customer PO	Payment Terms	
Johnson-05		3% 10, Net 30 Days	
Sales Rep ID	**Shipping Method**	**Ship Date**	**Due Date**
	UPS Ground		3/13/07

Quantity	Item	Description	Unit Price	Amount
20.00	MOP-2	Mops	25.00	500.00

	Subtotal	500.00
	Sales Tax	35.00
	Total Invoice Amount	535.00
Check/Credit Memo No:	Payment/Credit Applied	
	TOTAL	**535.00**

Step 5:

On February 12, 2007, Johnson returned two mops. Bullfrog issued CM2001 (Credit Memo 2001).

Create the Sales Returns and Allowances account. Use the following information.

Account ID:	**404**
Description:	**Sales Returns and Allowances**
Account Type:	**Income**

Step 6:

Create the credit memo, and then print the credit memo. Your credit memo should look like figure 9–17.

FIGURE 9-17

Credit Memo CM2001

Bullfrog Maintenance Company
456 Ballinger Lane
Stockton, CA 95101
USA

Voice: 209-555-2222
Fax: 209-555-6666

CREDIT MEMO

Credit Memo Number: CM2001
Credit Date: Feb 12, 2007
Page: 1
Duplicate

Credit To:

George Johnson
1342 Rose Marie Lane
Modesto, CA 95355
USA

Customer ID	Customer PO	Sales Rep ID
Johnson-05		

Quantity	Item	Description	Unit Price	Amount
2.00	MOP-2	Mops	25.00	50.00

Subtotal		50.00
Sales Tax		3.50
Freight		
TOTAL		**53.50**

Invoice No: 021101

Some businesses have a policy of requesting a price quotation or bid before they buy goods from a new supplier. Usually, these businesses obtain quotations from several competing suppliers and then compare the prices and credit terms offered.

Peachtree allows you to easily create quotations for potential customers. It also permits you to maintain a list of potential customers who have requested quotations and to convert quotations into sales orders or invoices if the potential customers end up placing orders.

CREATING THE QUOTATION

Suppose that Mary Davis, one of the sales representatives for Woodward Construction Company, visits Smith's Monuments. She finds that the management of this firm is interested in buying 10 computer desks but wants a price quotation. Thus, on February 10, 2007, Woodward issues Quotation 2345. The prices quoted are good until February 25, 2007.

Follow the steps outlined below to create the quotation for Smith's Monuments.

Step 1:

Open Woodward Construction Company and close the Action Items log.

Step 2:

Click Tasks, click Quotes/Sales Orders, and then click Quotes.

Step 3:

At the Quotes window, in the *Customer ID* field, click the *magnifying glass* icon, and then click *Smith-01*.

Step 4:

At the *Date* field, click the *calendar* icon, and then choose *Feb 10, 2007*.

Step 5:

At the *Good Thru* field, click the *calendar* icon, and choose *Feb 25, 2007*.

Step 6:

Key **2345** in the *Quote No.* field.

Step 7:

At the *Sales Rep ID* field, click the *magnifying glass* icon, and then click *MDAVIS-02*.

Step 8:

Key **10.00** in the *Quantity* field.

Step 9:

Click in the *Item* field, click the *magnifying glass* icon, and then click *COMDESK-3*.

Step 10:

At the *Sales Tax* field at the bottom of the Quotes screen, click the *magnifying glass* icon, and then click *CAL*. Compare your work with figure 9–18.

FIGURE 9-18

Completed Quotes Dialog Box

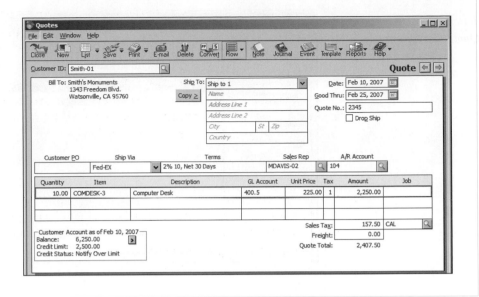

Step 11:

Click Save and then click Close.

CONVERTING A QUOTATION INTO A SALES ORDER OR AN INVOICE

If a customer places an order after a quotation is issued, Peachtree makes it possible to quickly convert the quotation into a sales order or an invoice. Some firms need a sales order because they use it for the internal processing of the customer's order—the removal of the necessary goods from inventory and the packing and shipping of the goods. When the goods are sent to the customer, the sales order is converted into an invoice.

Other firms do not use a sales order and immediately convert the quotation into an invoice. Woodward Construction Company follows this policy.

Suppose that on February 15, 2007, Smith's Monuments accepts Quotation 2345. Woodward must now use the quotation to create an invoice. Follow the steps outlined below to accomplish this task.

Step 1:

Click Tasks, click Quotes/Sales Orders, and then click Quotes.

Step 2:

The Quotes window appears. Click the List button on the Quotes toolbar.

Step 3:

The Quote List dialog box will appear. Click the quotation 2345 issued to Smith's Monuments, as shown in figure 9–19.

FIGURE 9-19

Quotation 2345 Chosen from the Quote List Dialog Box

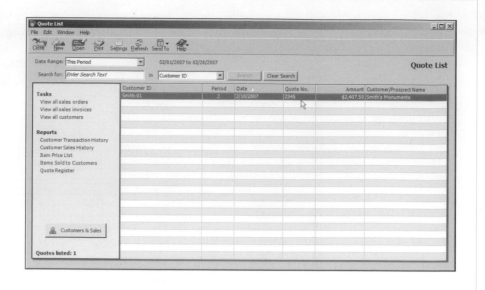

Step 4:

Click <u>O</u>pen and Quotation 2345 will appear in the active Quotes window.

Step 5:

At the *Date* field, click the *calendar* icon, and choose *Feb 15, 2007*.

Step 6:

Click the Conver<u>t</u> button on the Quotes toolbar.

Step 7:

Click the Sale/<u>I</u>nvoice button in the Convert Quote dialog box.

Step 8:

Key **011706** in the *Invoice #* field, as shown in figure 9–20.

FIGURE 9-20

Convert Quote Dialog Box

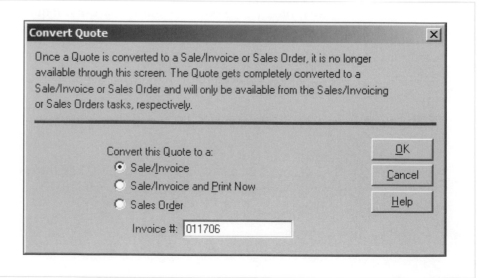

Step 9:

Click <u>O</u>K.

Step 10:

Click Yes to override the customer's credit limit. The quotation has now been converted to an invoice. The invoice can be printed or edited by using the Sales/Invoicing function.

Step 11:

Close the Quotes window.

Check POINT

1. What is the purpose of a quotation?
2. What is the purpose of a sales order?

Answers

1. *A quotation shows a potential customer the prices that a firm will charge for specified goods.*
2. *A sales order is used by a firm in the internal processing of a customer's order.*

PRACTICE objective

On February 2, 2007, Isabel Guerrero, a sales representative for Bullfrog Maintenance Company, gave Quotation 5432 for 20 mops to Valley Mercedes. This firm intends to use the mops and not resell them. Therefore, sales tax must be collected. The quotation was good until February 15, 2007. Valley Mercedes accepted the quotation on February 4, 2007.

Step 1:

Open Bullfrog Maintenance Company.

Step 2:

Create Quotation 5432 for Valley Mercedes.

Step 3:

Convert the quotation into Invoice 011100 on February 4, 2007.

Step 4:

Print the invoice. Your invoice should look like figure 9–21.

FIGURE 9-21
Invoice 011100

Bullfrog Maintenance Company
456 Ballinger Lane
Stockton, CA 95101
USA

Voice: 209-555-2222
Fax: 209-555-6666

INVOICE

Invoice Number: 011100
Invoice Date: Feb 4, 2007
Page: 1

Duplicate

Bill To:

Valley Mercedes
3211 Main Street
Salida, CA 95111
USA

Ship to:

Customer ID	Customer PO	Payment Terms	
Mercedes-04		2% 10, Net 30 Days	
Sales Rep ID	**Shipping Method**	**Ship Date**	**Due Date**
	Fed-EX		3/6/07

Quantity	Item	Description	Unit Price	Amount
20.00	MOP-2	Mops	25.00	500.00

Subtotal	500.00
Sales Tax	35.00
Total Invoice Amount	535.00
Payment/Credit Applied	
TOTAL	**535.00**

Check/Credit Memo No:

OBJECTIVE 5 — RECORD FINANCE CHARGES ON OVERDUE CUSTOMER BALANCES

statement of account
A form that a business sends each month to show all transactions with a customer and the balance owed by the customer.

In addition to issuing invoices whenever goods are sold to a customer, many firms send a monthly **statement of account** to the customer. This statement lists all transactions with the customer during the period—sales on credit, returns, and cash received on account. Most important, this statement shows the balance owed at the end of the period.

Some businesses have a policy of imposing a finance charge when customers do not pay their bills within a specified period of time. This policy is intended to discourage customers from allowing their balances to become overdue. If the firm has a policy of adding a finance charge to overdue balances, the finance charge appears on the statement of account.

Peachtree allows you to set defaults for a finance charge so that the charge is automatically calculated and recorded whenever customer accounts have overdue balances.

CREATING THE DEFAULTS FOR FINANCE CHARGES

Remember that Woodward Construction Company offers credit terms of 2/10, n/30 to its customers. Suppose that Woodward decides to add an 8% finance charge to invoices that are more than 30 days overdue. Woodward must create the necessary defaults, as outlined below. However, before that, Woodward must establish an Interest Income account in its general ledger. This account will be used to record the income received from finance charges. Interest Income will be credited for all finance charges.

Step 1:
Open Woodward Construction Company and close Action Item log.

Step 2:
Create the following account in the general ledger.

Account ID:	**450**
Description:	**Interest Income**
Account Type:	**Income**

Step 3:
Click Maintain, click Default Information, and then click Customers.

Step 4:
Click the Finance Charges tab from the Customer Defaults dialog box.

Step 5:
Click the box next to *Charge finance charges* in order to insert a check mark.

Step 6:
Key **30** in the *On invoices…days overdue* field.

Step 7:
Key **10,000.00** in the *up to* field.

Step 8:
Key **8.00** in the *Annual interest rate* field.

Step 9:
Click the box next to *Charge interest on finance charges* to insert a check mark. This indicates that the system should calculate interest on any accumulated finance charges.

Step 10:

Key **450** in the *Finance Charge GL Account* field. Compare your work with figure 9–22.

Completed Finance Charges Entries in Customer Defaults Dialog Box

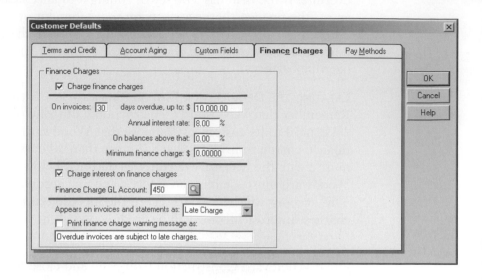

Step 11:

Click <u>O</u>K to accept the finance charge defaults.

CREATING THE FINANCE CHARGE REPORT

Suppose that Woodward Construction Company has one overdue account on March 31, 2007. A report can be generated showing the finance charges imposed on the customer's account. This report can be printed or viewed on the screen. Follow the steps outlined below to view the finance charge report for Smith's Monuments.

Step 1:

Click <u>C</u>ustomer/Prospects from the <u>M</u>aintain drop-down list on the main menu.

Step 2:

Click the magnifying glass icon next to the *Customer <u>I</u>D* field; select *Smith-01* and click OK.

Step 3:

Select the Terms and Cre<u>d</u>it Tab and check Charge <u>F</u>inance Charges to insert a check mark and close.

Step 4:

Click Tas<u>k</u>s, and then click <u>F</u>inance Charge.

Step 5:

The Calculate Finance Charges dialog box appears. At the *Starting Customer* field, click the *magnifying glass* icon, and then click *Smith-01*.

Step 6:

At the *Ending Customer* field, click the *magnifying glass* icon, and then click *Smith-01*.

Step 7:

At the *<u>D</u>ate* field, click the *calendar* icon, and then choose *Mar 31, 2007*. Compare your work with figure 9–23.

FIGURE 9-23
*Calculate Finance Charges
Window*

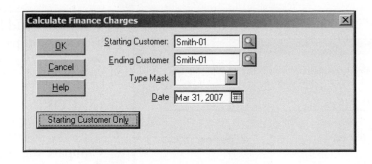

Step 8:
Click OK.

Step 9:
The Apply Finance Charges dialog box now appears. Click the No button in the Apply Finance Charges section. (You would click Yes if adding finance charges to a statement of account.)

Step 10:
Click the Screen button in the Report Destination section.

Step 11:
Click the No button in the Print Calculation Sheet section. Compare your work with figure 9–24.

FIGURE 9-24
*Completed Apply Finance
Charges Window*

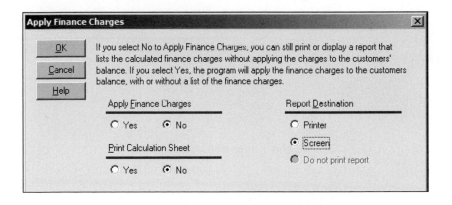

Step 12:
Click OK.

Step 13:
The Finance Charge Report Selection dialog box now appears. Click the Detail button in the Report Style section.

FIGURE 9-25

Completed Finance Charge Report Selection Window

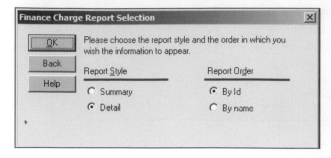

Step 14:
Click the By Id button in the Report Order section. Compare your work with figure 9–25.

Step 15:
Click OK.

Step 16:
Compare the report on your screen with figure 9–26.

FIGURE 9-26

Completed Finance Charge Report

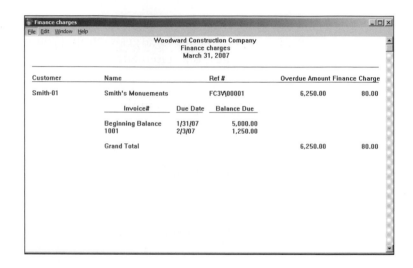

Step 17:
Close the *Finance charges* report.

Check POINT

1. Why do some businesses impose finance charges on customer accounts?
2. What account is used to record finance charges?

Answers
1. *Some businesses impose finance charges to discourage customers from allowing their balances to become overdue.*
2. *The account used to record finance charges is Interest Income.*

Bullfrog Maintenance Company wants to add a finance charge to all customer balances that are more than 45 days overdue. The interest rate will be 9.5% on invoices up to $15,000. Interest will also be calculated on finance charges.

Step 1:

Open Bullfrog Maintenance Company.

Step 2:

Create the following account in the general ledger.

Account *ID*:	**450**
Description:	**Interest Income**
Account *Type*:	**Income**

Step 3:

Create the customer finance charge defaults.

Step 4:

Print a report showing the finance charges on the open invoices for Valley Mercedes as of April 30, 2007. Your report should look like figure 9–27.

FIGURE 9-27

Finance Charges Report for Valley Mercedes

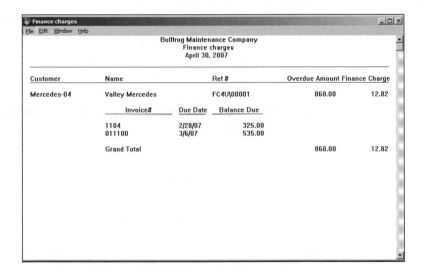

OBJECTIVE 6 — PRINT INVENTORY AND SALES REPORTS

Peachtree provides a variety of inventory and sales reports for merchandising businesses. The information from these reports can help management to answer the following types of questions: What items are selling well and what items are selling poorly? Do we have too much stock of the slow-selling items? If we want to close out some of the slow-selling items, how much can we reduce the prices for those items and still make a profit?

CREATING INVENTORY REPORTS

Peachtree offers the following inventory reports to merchandising businesses. These reports offer a wide range of information that can be used to plan and control inventory.

- The *Inventory Valuation Report* shows the value (cost) of the current inventory.
- The *Inventory Adjustment Journal* lists all inventory adjustments that were made.
- The *Item Costing Report* lists the cost, receipts, and sales for each inventory item.
- The *Cost of Goods Sold Journal* shows the cost of all inventory items sold during a period.
- The *Item Master List* gives detailed information about all inventory items.
- The *Item Price List* gives the various prices and the quantity on hand of all inventory items.
- The *Physical Inventory List* is used to compare the actual inventory on hand with the reported inventory.
- The *Inventory Profitability Report* shows the units sold and profitability of inventory items.

Woodward Construction Company wants to see the *Cost of Goods Sold Journal* for the month of February 2007. Follow the steps outlined below to generate this inventory report.

Step 1:

Open Woodward Construction Company and close Action Item log.

Step 2:

Click Reports, and then click Inventory.

Step 3:

At the Select a Report dialog box, in the Report List section, click *Cost of Goods Sold Journal*.

Step 4:

Click the Preview button on the Select a Report toolbar.

Step 5:

Click OK at the *Cost of Goods Sold Journal* filter dialog box.

Step 6:

Compare your journal with the one shown in figure 9–28.

FIGURE 9-28
Cost of Goods Sold Journal

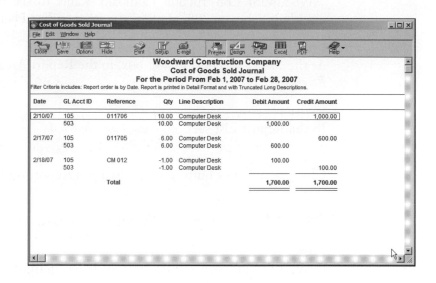

Step 7:
Click Close.

CREATING SALES REPORTS

As we have discussed, Peachtree helps a merchandising business by making it easy to produce a variety of sales-related documents that are needed in the firm's operations:

- Quotations for potential customers
- Sales orders
- Invoices
- Credit memos
- Statements of account
- Collection letters for overdue accounts

Peachtree also provides many different sales reports for merchandising businesses. Some of these reports are described below.

- The *Customer List* shows the names and contact information of all customers.
- The *Prospect List* shows the names and contact information of all prospects.
- The *Invoice Register* is a list of all invoices that have been issued to customers.
- The *Quote Register* is a list of all outstanding price quotations.
- The *Sales Journal* shows all sales on credit made during a period.
- The *Sales Rep Report* is a list of sales made by each sales representative.
- The *Customer Ledgers* include the accounts for all credit customers.
- The *Sales Tax Codes* is a list of all sales tax codes used by the business.
- The *Sales Order Register, Journal*, and *Report* show information about all sales orders issued.
- The *Customer Sales History* is a list of the transactions with each customer.

Woodward Construction Company wants to see the *Sales Journal* for the month of February 2007. Follow the steps outlined below to create this report.

Step 1:

At the Select a Report dialog box, in the Report Area section, click *Accounts Receivable*.

Step 2:

In the Report List section, click *Sales Journal*.

Step 3:

Click the Preview button on the Select a Report toolbar.

Step 4:

Click OK at the Sales Journal filter dialog box.

Step 5:

Compare your journal with the one shown in figure 9–29.

FIGURE 9-29

Sales Journal

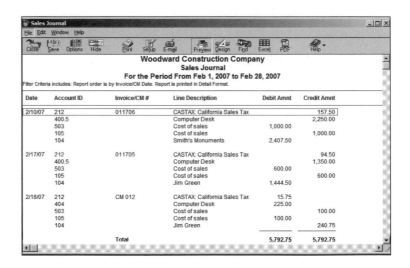

Step 6:

Click Close, then close the Select a Report dialog box.

Check POINT

1. What does the *Cost of Goods Sold Journal* show?
2. What does the *Sales Journal* show?

Answers
1. The Cost of Goods Sold Journal shows the cost of all inventory items sold during a period.
2. The Sales Journal shows all sales on credit made during a period.

PRACTICE *objective*

Step 1:

Open Bullfrog Maintenance Company.

Step 2:

Print the following reports for the month of February:

- *Sales Journal*
- *Cost of Goods Sold Journal*

Your printouts should look like figures 9–30 and 9–31, respectively.

FIGURE 9-30

Sales Journal for Bullfrog Maintenance Company

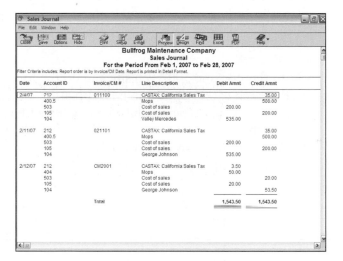

FIGURE 9-31

Cost of Goods Sold Journal for Bullfrog Maintenance Company

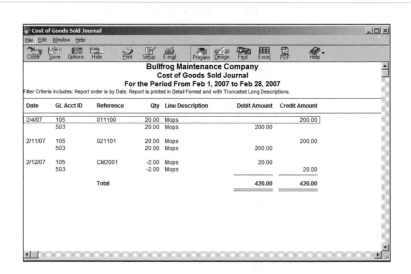

INTERNET *Access*

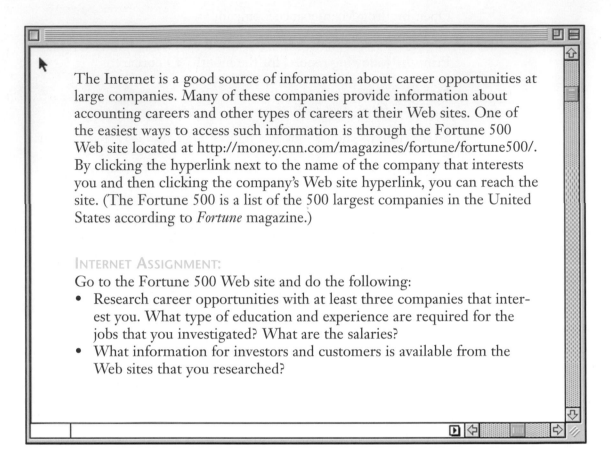

The Internet is a good source of information about career opportunities at large companies. Many of these companies provide information about accounting careers and other types of careers at their Web sites. One of the easiest ways to access such information is through the Fortune 500 Web site located at http://money.cnn.com/magazines/fortune/fortune500/. By clicking the hyperlink next to the name of the company that interests you and then clicking the company's Web site hyperlink, you can reach the site. (The Fortune 500 is a list of the 500 largest companies in the United States according to *Fortune* magazine.)

INTERNET ASSIGNMENT:

Go to the Fortune 500 Web site and do the following:
- Research career opportunities with at least three companies that interest you. What type of education and experience are required for the jobs that you investigated? What are the salaries?
- What information for investors and customers is available from the Web sites that you researched?

SOFTWARE
Command Summary

Create Sales Tax Authority	Maintain, Sales Taxes, Sales Tax Authorities
Create Sales Tax Codes	Maintain, Sales Taxes, Sales Tax Codes
Create Sales Invoice	Tasks, Sales/Invoicing
Print Sales Invoice	Tasks, Sales/Invoicing, Print
Create a Credit Memo	Tasks, Credit Memos
Collect on an Invoice	Tasks, Receipts, Apply to Invoices
Create a Quotation	Tasks, Quotes/Sales Orders, Quotes
Convert a Quotation to a Sales Order or Invoice	Tasks, Quotes/Sales Orders, Quotes, Convert
Create Finance Charge Defaults	Maintain, Default Information, Customers, Finance Charges
Create a Finance Charge Report	Tasks, Finance Charge
Create Inventory Reports	Reports, Inventory, select a report from the list
Create Sales Reports	Reports, Accounts Receivable, select a report from the list

PROJECTS
and Problems

Content Check

Multiple Choice: Choose only one response for each question.

1. The Sales Revenue account is what type of account?
   A. Cost of Sales
   B. Income
   C. Inventory
   D. Asset

2. A business that uses the perpetual inventory system sells goods for $450. The goods cost $200. When recording the sale, the business must
   A. debit Inventory and credit Cost of Goods Sold for $450.
   B. debit Cost of Goods Sold and credit Inventory for $450.
   C. debit Inventory and credit Cost of Goods Sold for $200.
   D. debit Cost of Goods Sold and credit Inventory for $200.

3. When a customer returns damaged goods, what form must be prepared for sales returns and allowances?
   A. Sales Invoice
   B. Sales Order
   C. Credit Memo
   D. Sales Quote

4. Which inventory report lists the quantity on hand and price for each inventory item?
   A. *Inventory Adjustments Journal*
   B. *Inventory Profitability Report*
   C. *Inventory Valuation Report*
   D. *Item Price List*

5. What type of account is Sales Tax Payable?
   A. Inventory
   B. Income
   C. Expense
   D. Liability

Short-Essay Response: Provide a detailed answer for each question.

1. Why would a business want to keep separate accounts for recording sales of services and sales of goods?
2. What is the purpose of each of the following: the sales quotation, the invoice, and the statement of account?
3. Why would a business establish a separate account for recording sales returns and allowances rather than just debiting them to the Sales Revenue account?
4. Why do some businesses impose a finance charge when customers do not pay their invoices on time?
5. How is a finance charge entered in a firm's accounting records?
6. What effect does a sale on credit have on the following accounts: Accounts Receivable, Sales Revenue, Cost of Goods Sold, and Inventory? (Does each account increase or decrease?)

PROBLEM 1A

Open Kathleen's Designs, an interior decoration business, which you updated in chapter 8.

1. Create the following general ledger accounts:

   Account ID: **212**
   Description: **Sales Tax Payable**
   Account Type: **Other Current Liabilities**

   Account ID: **404**
   Description: **Sales Returns and Allowances**
   Account Type: **Income**

   Account ID: **406**
   Description: **Sales Discount**
   Account Type: **Income**

2. Create a new vendor account:

   Vendor ID: **BOARDEQUAL-16**
   Name: **Board of Equalization**
   Expense Acct: **212**
   Terms: **EOM, 0.00 Discount**

3. Enter the information about the sales tax authorities:

   ID: **CASTAX**
   Description: **California Sales Tax**
   Tax Payable To: **BOARDEQUAL-16**
   Sales Tax Payable G/L Account: **212**
   Tax rate: **7.00**

4. Create the sales tax codes:

   Sales Tax Code: **CAL**
   Description: **California Sales Tax**
   ID: **CASTAX**

5. Set the Default Information for Inventory Item Defaults, Price Levels to reflect Enabled with a Level 1 Name of Full Price.

6. Create the following new customer accounts:

   General Tab
   Customer ID: **RM-01**
   Name: **Richard Marquez**
   Contact: **Richard Marquez**
   Bill to Address
        Address: **1785 Thornton Road**
        City, ST Zip: **Modesto, CA 95355**
        Country: **USA**

*Sales Ta**x**:*	**CAL**
*Customer **T**ype:*	**Retail**
*Telephone **1**:*	**209-555-3692**

Sales Defaults Tab

GL Sales Acct:	**401**
Ship Via:	**UPS Ground**
Pricing Level:	**Full Price**
Form Delivery Options:	**Default**

Terms and Credit Tab

Terms:	**3.5/10, n/30**

General Tab

*Customer I**D**:*	**SM-02**
*N**a**me:*	**Sandra McGuire**
*Cont**a**ct:*	**Sandra McGuire**
Bill to Address	
Address:	**14958 Lower Stockton Road**
*City, ST **Z**ip:*	**Modesto, CA 95355**
Country:	**USA**
*Sales Ta**x**:*	**CAL**
*Customer **T**ype:*	**Retail**
*Telephone **1**:*	**209-555-8462**

Sales Defaults Tab

GL Sales Acct:	**401**
Ship Via:	**UPS Ground**
Pricing Level:	**Full Price**
Form Delivery Options:	**Default**

Terms and Credit Tab

Terms:	**3/10, n/30**

General Tab

*Customer I**D**:*	**LA-03**
*N**a**me:*	**Luis Abelar**
*Cont**a**ct:*	**Luis Abelar**
Bill to Address	
Address:	**19485 Eaton Avenue**
*City, ST **Z**ip:*	**Stockton, CA 95210**
Country:	**USA**
*Sales Ta**x**:*	**CAL**
*Customer **T**ype:*	**Retail**
*Telephone **1**:*	**209-555-5286**

Sales Defaults Tab

GL Sales Acct:	**401**
Ship Via:	**UPS Ground**
Pricing Level:	**Full Price**
Form Delivery Options:	**Default**

Terms and Credit Tab
Terms: **3/10, n/30**

7. Record the following transactions for the month of January 2007.
   Jan. 11   Sold 8 flower stencils and 4 pillows on credit to
               Richard Marquez, Invoice 649.
        12   Sold 3 pillows on credit to Sandra McGuire,
               Invoice 650.
        14   Sandra McGuire returned 1 of the pillows. Issued
               Credit Memo 011 (CM011) to her.
        15   Sold 4 flower stencils and 6 pillows on credit to Luis
               Abelar, Invoice 651.
        18   Richard Marquez paid Invoice 649, less discount,
               check #1473.
        20   Luis Abelar paid Invoice 651, less discount, check
               #2003.
        29   Sandra McGuire paid Invoice 650, check #1146.
8. Print the *Customer Ledgers* and *Cost of Goods Sold Journal*.

PROBLEM 2A

Executive Consultants, a business consulting company, prepared the following quotations for two prospective clients during the month of June 2007. The prices were negotiated by the firm's sales representatives: Annette Chang and Thomas Wilson.

1. Open Executive Consultants, which you updated in chapter 8.
2. Create the following general ledger account:

Account ID:	**212**
Description:	**Sales Tax Payable**
Account Type:	**Other Current Liabilities**

3. Create a new vendor account:

Vendor ID:	**BOARDEQUAL-16**
Name:	**Board of Equalization**
Expense Acct:	**212**
Terms:	**EOM, 0.00 Discount**

4. Enter the information about the sales tax authorities:

ID:	**CASTAX**
Description:	**California Sales Tax**
Tax Payable To:	**BOARDEQUAL-16**
Sales Tax Payable G/L Account:	**212**
Tax rate:	**7.00**

5. Create the sales tax code:

Sales Tax Code:	**CAL**
Description:	**California Sales Tax**
ID:	**CASTAX**

HINT

Click the Journal button to review the Accounting Behind the Screens Window. Make sure Sales Returns and Allowances, account 404, is debited for the return amount.

HINT

Click the Journal button to review the Accounting Behind the Screens Window. Make sure Sales Discount, account 406, is debited for the discount amount.

6. Set the Default Information for Inventory Item Defaults, Price Levels to reflect Enabled with a Level 1 Name of Full Price.

7. Create the new following customer accounts:

General Tab

Customer ID:	**KD-01**
Name:	**Kathleen's Designs**
Contact:	**Kathleen Rosario**
Bill to Address	
Address:	**1748 West Fair Oaks**
City, ST Zip:	**Modesto, CA 95355**
Country:	**USA**
Sales Tax:	**CAL**
Customer Type:	**Retail**
Telephone 1:	**209-555-6925**

Sales Defaults Tab

GL Sales Acct:	**400**
Ship Via:	**UPS Ground**
Pricing Level:	**Full Price**
Form Delivery Options:	**Default**

Terms and Credit Tab

Terms:	**3/10, n/30**

General Tab

Customer ID:	**HD-02**
Name:	**Hendricks' Construction**
Contact:	**Randy Hendricks**
Bill to Address	
Address:	**6529 Rose Marie Lane**
City, ST Zip:	**Stockton, CA 95207**
Country:	**USA**
Sales Tax:	**CAL**
Customer Type:	**Retail**
Telephone 1:	**209-555-6523**

Sales Defaults Tab

GL Sales Acct:	**400**
Ship Via:	**UPS Ground**
Pricing Level:	**Full Price**
Form Delivery Options:	**Default**

Terms and Credit Tab

Terms:	**3/10, n/30**

HINT

As these are non-inventory items, enter the number of hours in the *Quantity* field and the hourly rate in the *Unit Price* field, then click the Journal icon to make sure the proper income account has been credited.

8. Create the following quotations as of the dates specified.

June 1   Annette Chang gave Quotation 1472 for 7 hours of training at $90 per hour to Kathleen's Designs. The quotation was good until June 10, 2007.

5   Thomas Wilson gave Quotation 1473 for 5 hours of consulting service at $75 per hour to Hendricks' Construction. The quotation was good until June 18, 2007.

9. Convert both quotations to invoices as of the dates specified.

    June 9   Kathleen's Designs has accepted the quotation. Issued Invoice 3262.

         18   Hendrick's Construction has accepted 4 of the 5 hours for which the quotation was prepared. Issued Invoice 3485.

10. Print the invoice for each company.

PROBLEM 1B

Open Ana's Creations, a beauty salon, which you updated in chapter 8.

1. Create the following general ledger accounts:

Account ID:	**212**
Description:	**Sales Tax Payable**
Account Type:	**Other Current Liabilities**

Account ID:	**404**
Description:	**Sales Returns and Allowances**
Account Type:	**Income**

Account ID:	**406**
Description:	**Sales Discount**
Account Type:	**Income**

2. Create a new vendor account:

Vendor ID:	**BOARDEQUAL-16**
Name:	**Board of Equalization**
Expense Acct:	**212**
Terms:	**EOM, 0.00 Discount**

3. Enter the information about the sales tax authorities:

ID:	**CASTAX**
Description:	**California Sales Tax**
Tax Payable To:	**BOARDEQUAL-16**
Sales Tax Payable G/L Account:	**212**
Tax rate:	**7.00**

4. Create the sales tax codes:

Sales Tax Code:	**CAL**
Description:	**California Sales Tax**
ID:	**CASTAX**

5. Set the Default Information for Inventory Item Defaults, Price Levels to reflect Enabled with a Level 1 Name of Full Price.

6. Create the following new customer accounts:

General Tab

Customer ID:	**NJ-01**
Name:	**Natalie Jones**
Contact:	**Natalie Jones**
Bill to Address	
Address:	**6154 Lower Sacramento Road**
City, ST Zip:	**Stockton, CA 95207**
Country:	**USA**
Sales Tax:	**CAL**
Customer Type:	**Retail**
Telephone 1:	**209-555-6493**

Sales Defaults Tab

GL Sales Acct:	**401**
Ship Via:	**UPS Ground**
Pricing Level:	**Full Price**
Form Delivery Options:	**Default**

Terms and Credit Tab

Terms:	**2/10, n/30**

General Tab

Customer ID:	**RG-02**
Name:	**Raquel Gannon**
Contact:	**Raquel Gannon**
Bill to Address	
Address:	**16419 Country Club**
City, ST Zip:	**Modesto, CA 95355**
Country:	**USA**
Sales Tax:	**CAL**
Customer Type:	**Retail**
Telephone 1:	**209-555-5915**

Sales Defaults Tab

GL Sales Acct:	**401**
Ship Via:	**UPS Ground**
Pricing Level:	**Full Price**
Form Delivery Options:	**Default**

Terms and Credit Tab

Terms:	**2/10, n/30**

General Tab

Customer ID:	**RC-03**
Name:	**Richard Chang**
Contact:	**Richard Chang**
Bill to Address	
Address:	**1518 West Schulte Road**
City, ST Zip:	**Modesto, CA 95355**
Country:	**USA**

Sales Tax:	**CAL**
Customer Type:	**Retail**
Telephone 1:	**209-555-5639**

Sales Defaults Tab

GL Sales Acct:	**401**
Ship Via:	**UPS Ground**
Pricing Level:	**Full Price**
Form Delivery Options:	**Default**

Terms and Credit Tab

Terms:	**2/10, n/30**

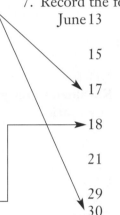

HINT

Click the Journal button to review the Accounting Behind the Screens Window. Make sure Sales Discount, account 406, is debited for the discount amount.

HINT

Click the Journal button to review the Accounting Behind the Screens Window. Make sure Sales Returns and Allowances, account 404, is debited for the return amount.

7. Record the following transactions for the month of June 2007.

June 13	Sold 2 bottles of shampoo and 1 bottle of conditioner on credit to Natalie Jones, Invoice 964.
15	Sold 2 bottles of shampoo and 2 bottles of hair gel on credit to Raquel Gannon, Invoice 965.
17	Natalie Jones paid Invoice 964, less discount, check #7906.
18	Raquel Gannon returned 1 bottle of hair gel. Issued Credit Memo 014 (CM014) to her.
21	Sold 2 bottles of shampoo and 1 bottle of hair gel on credit to Richard Chang, Invoice 966.
29	Raquel Gannon paid Invoice 965, check #1321.
30	Richard Chang paid Invoice 966, less discount, check #4320.

8. Print the *Customer Ledgers* and *Cost of Goods Sold Journal.*

PROBLEM 2B

VP Designers, a computer programming services company, prepared the following quotations for two of its prospective clients during the month of April 2007. The prices were negotiated by the firm's sales representatives: Melody Anderson and William Kincaid.

1. Open VP Designers which you updated in chapter 8.
2. Create the following general ledger account:

Account ID:	**212**
Description:	**Sales Tax Payable**
Account Type:	**Other Current Liabilities**

3. Create the new vendor account:

Vendor ID:	**BOARDEQUAL-16**
Name:	**Board of Equalization**
Expense Acct:	**212**
Terms:	**EOM, 0.00 Discount**

4. Enter the information about the sales tax authorities:

ID:	**CASTAX**
Description:	**California Sales Tax**
Tax Payable To:	**BOARDEQUAL-16**
Sales Tax Payable G/L Account:	212
Tax rate:	7.00

5. Create the sales tax codes:

Sales Tax Code:	**CAL**
Description:	**California Sales Tax**
ID:	**CASTAX**

6. Set the Default Information for Inventory Item Defaults, Price Levels to reflect Enabled with a Level 1 Name of Full Price.

7. Create the new following customer accounts:

General Tab

Customer ID:	**KD-01**
Name:	**Kathleen's Designs**
Contact:	**Kathleen Rosario**
Bill to Address	
Address:	**1748 West Fair Oaks**
City, ST Zip:	**Modesto, CA 95355**
Country:	**USA**
Sales Tax:	**CAL**
Customer Type:	**Retail**
Telephone 1:	**209-555-6925**

Sales Defaults Tab

GL Sales Acct:	**400**
Ship Via:	**UPS Ground**
Pricing Level:	**Full Price**
Form Delivery Options:	**Default**

Terms and Credit Tab

Terms:	**3/10, n/30**

General Tab

Customer ID:	**GJ-02**
Name:	**GJ Professional Accounting**
Contact:	**Cynthia Flores**
Bill to Address	
Address:	**1506 East March Lane**
City, ST Zip:	**Stockton, CA 95207**
Country:	**USA**
Sales Tax:	**CAL**
Customer Type:	**Retail**
Telephone 1:	**209-555-2112**

Sales Defaults Tab

GL Sales Acct:	**400**
Ship Via:	**UPS Ground**
Pricing Level:	**Full Price**
Form Delivery Options:	**Default**

Terms and Credit Tab

Terms:	**3/10, n/30**

8. Create the quotations as of the dates specified.

HINT

As these are non-inventory items, enter the number of hours in the *Quantity* field and the hourly rate in the *Unit Price* field, then click the Journal button to make sure the proper income account has been credited.

April 10   Melody Anderson gave Quotation 1578 for 12 hours of design services at $65 per hour to Kathleen's Designs. The quotation was good until April 20, 2007.

    15   William Kincaid gave Quotation 1579 for 6 hours of consulting service at $90 per hour to GJ Professional Accounting. The quotation was good until April 25, 2007.

9. Convert both quotations to invoices as of the dates specified.

April 18   Kathleen's Designs has accepted the quotation. Issued Invoice 64651.

    25   GJ Professional Accounting has accepted the quotation. Issued Invoice 64761.

10. Print the invoice for each company.

Cooperative Learning

1. Form groups of three or four students, and determine the factors to be taken into consideration when establishing credit terms for each customer.
2. As a group, discuss what factors a business should consider when deciding whether to impose a finance charge on customers who do not pay invoices on time.

Writing and Decision Making

Assume that the owner of the company for which you work, Marie Ramirez, is concerned about the increasing level of sales returns that she has noticed on the financial statements during the last six months. She has asked you for reasons why this may be occurring and for ideas about how the level of sales returns can be reduced. She would also like to know how the inventory reports could be used to investigate the problem. Prepare a memo with the information that has been requested.

CHAPTER

PAYROLL

1. Understand general payroll concepts

2. Create a payroll system using Peachtree's Payroll Setup Wizard

3. Maintain the payroll system

4. Prepare a payroll and print payroll checks

5. Print payroll tax returns and payroll reports

SOFTWARE FEATURES

- Establish a Payroll System

- Set Employee Defaults

- Prepare a Payroll

- Print Payroll Checks

- Print Tax Returns

- Print Payroll Reports

People are very aware of payroll because of the checks they receive from their employers. However, issuing payroll checks is just one part of the payroll work that a business must do. For even a small firm with just a few employees, managing a payroll can be difficult and time-consuming.

The payroll activities of a business fall into six basic areas:
- Calculating the earnings and deductions of employees and issuing payroll checks
- Keeping records of the time that employees work and their earnings and deductions
- Calculating the payroll taxes owed by the employer
- Depositing the taxes deducted from employee earnings and the payroll taxes owed by the employer
- Preparing payroll tax returns that must be sent to federal, state, and sometimes local tax agencies
- Making entries for payroll in the accounting records

Obviously, it is important that payroll calculations, records, and tax returns be prepared with great accuracy. It is also important to do all the necessary work on time. Employees expect to receive their payroll checks promptly, and government agencies require that tax deposits and tax returns be submitted according to strict schedules. Failure to meet these schedules can result in financial penalties.

Peachtree allows a business to handle its payroll work quickly and efficiently. Once the payroll system is set up, most operations are done automatically when the information for a payroll period is entered.

OBJECTIVE 1 — UNDERSTAND GENERAL PAYROLL CONCEPTS

Preparing a payroll can be a complex process because many laws and government regulations affect it. Federal, state, and local tax agencies publish annual guides for employers that specify the requirements for keeping payroll records, withholding taxes from employee earnings, calculating the employer's payroll taxes, depositing all taxes owed, and filing tax returns.

PAYROLL PERIODS

payroll period The time period for which earnings and deductions are calculated.

Every business must establish a payroll period. The **payroll period** is the time period for which earnings and deductions are calculated. This period may be weekly, biweekly (every other week), semimonthly (on the 15th and the last day of each month), or monthly. Some large businesses use different payroll periods for different types of employees. For example, they may pay their factory workers on a weekly basis but pay their office staff on a monthly basis.

PAY PLANS

pay plan The method used to calculate an employee's earnings.

Employees are paid according to various pay plans. The **pay plan** is the method used to calculate an employee's earnings. The most common pay plans are the hourly rate plan, the salary plan, the commission plan, the salary-commission plan, and the piece-rate plan.

- With the *hourly rate* plan, an employee receives a fixed amount for each hour worked, such as $9 an hour.

- With the *salary* plan, an employee receives a fixed amount for the payroll period, such as $500 a week.
- With the *commission* plan, an employee involved with sales receives a percentage of his or her sales, such as 5% of sales.
- With the *salary-commission* plan, an employee receives a fixed amount for the payroll period plus a percentage of his or her sales, such as $400 a week plus 2% of sales.
- With the *piece-rate* plan, an employee receives a fixed amount for each item produced, such as $2 for each circuit board assembled. This plan is used in some factories.

PAYROLL LAWS AND REGULATIONS

Many laws and regulations govern payroll work. The most important of these laws and regulations are briefly described below.

- The *Fair Labor Standards Act* is a federal law that covers many employers. This law requires that employers pay at least the federal minimum wage and pay overtime to most employees when they work more than 40 hours in a workweek. The overtime rate must be at least 1½ times the regular hourly rate. Managerial and supervisory employees are exempt from the overtime pay requirement.
- Some states and cities have their own *minimum wage laws*, which may set a higher minimum wage than the federal government.
- The *Current Tax Payment Act* requires employers to withhold federal income tax from the earnings of their employees.
- The *Federal Insurance Contributions Act (FICA)* requires employers to withhold Social Security tax and Medicare tax from the earnings of their employees and pay a matching amount themselves.
- The *Federal Unemployment Tax Act (FUTA)* requires employers to pay a tax that is intended to provide jobless benefits to employees who are temporarily out of work.
- Each state has its own *State Unemployment Tax Act (SUTA)*. In most cases, these laws impose a tax on just the employer. However, a few states also require a contribution from employees.
- Many states and some cities and counties have their own *income tax laws* and require employers to withhold this tax from employee earnings.
- Some states have *disability insurance laws*. For example, California requires employers to withhold a state disability insurance (SDI) tax from employee earnings. This tax is used to pay benefits to employees who temporarily cannot work because of illness or injury.

FEDERAL AND STATE TAX RETURNS

The federal government requires employers to file a variety of tax returns. Some of the most important of these returns are as follows.

- *Form 941*, Employer's Quarterly Federal Tax Return, is prepared after the end of each quarter. It shows the wages paid during the quarter and the federal income tax and FICA taxes owed.

- *Form 940*, Employer's Annual Federal Unemployment Tax Return, is prepared after the end of each year. It shows the wages paid during the year and the FUTA tax liability for the year.
- *Form W-2*, Wage and Tax Statement, is prepared for each employee after the end of each year. This multiple-copy form shows the wages earned by the employee during the year and the federal and state taxes withheld. Copies of this form go to the employee and to federal and state tax agencies.
- *Form W-3*, Transmittal of Wage and Tax Statements, is prepared after the end of each year. This form shows the total wages paid to employees during the year and the federal taxes withheld from employee earnings.
- *Form 1099* is prepared for each independent contractor after the end of each year. This multiple-copy form shows the fees paid to the independent contractor during the year. Copies of Form 1099 go to the independent contractor and to federal and some state tax agencies. Remember that an independent contractor does work for a business on a project-by-project basis and is not an employee. As a result, the business does not withhold taxes from the fees paid to an independent contractor. This person is responsible for paying his or her taxes directly to federal and state tax agencies.
- *Form 8109*, Federal Tax Deposit Coupon, is prepared when a deposit of federal taxes is made by check in a bank or other depositary institution. This form shows the amount being deposited. If a business makes deposits by means of electronic funds transfer, Form 8109 is not used. The schedule for making federal tax deposits depends on the amounts owed. (**Note:** This form is not currently included in Peachtree.)

You can prepare and print all of the federal payroll reports and statements mentioned above (except Form 8109) by clicking Reports and then either Accounts Payable or Payroll.

State tax agencies also require employers to file tax returns. These forms vary from state to state, as do the schedules for filing the forms and making tax deposits.

REQUIRED AND VOLUNTARY DEDUCTIONS

As you have seen, federal, state, and sometimes local laws require that employers deduct certain taxes from employee earnings. For example, Woodward Construction Company, which is located in California, must withhold the following taxes from the earnings of its employees: federal income, Social Security, Medicare, state income, and State Disability Insurance (SDI).

In addition to these required deductions, some businesses allow voluntary deductions for items such as medical insurance, life insurance, and a retirement savings plan [a 401(k) plan].

ACCOUNTING ENTRIES FOR PAYROLL

Businesses use a number of liability and expense accounts to record payroll transactions. Taxes withheld from employee earnings and taxes owed by the employer are debts of a business until they are deposited. Therefore, they are recorded in current liability accounts.

- When the payroll is calculated, the total of the employee earnings is debited to Wages and Salaries Expense and the amounts withheld for the various taxes are credited to individual liability accounts such as Federal Income Tax Payable, FICA—Social Security Tax Payable, FICA—Medicare Tax Payable, State Income Tax Payable, and SDI Tax Payable.
- When the employer's payroll taxes are calculated, the total of the taxes is debited to Payroll Taxes Expense and the amounts of the various taxes owed are credited to individual liability accounts such as FICA—Social Security Tax Payable, FICA—Medicare Tax Payable, FUTA Tax Payable, and SUTA Tax Payable.
- When a business pays the taxes it owes, it debits the appropriate liability accounts and credits Cash.

FEATURES OF THE PEACHTREE PAYROLL SYSTEM

The Peachtree payroll system allows a business to set up and maintain an earnings record for each employee, calculate earnings and deductions, calculate the employer's payroll taxes, prepare payroll tax returns for government agencies, prepare payroll reports for management, and make the necessary accounting entries for payroll.

Peachtree Complete Accounting 2007 has a special feature called the Payroll Setup Wizard, which will help you to establish the payroll system. Version 2007 also has enhanced Internet access to federal and state tax publications and tax forms. This feature helps employers to stay informed about changes in tax rates, schedules for making deposits, and schedules for filing tax returns.

POINT

1. What are the different types of payroll periods?
2. What three federal taxes must employers withhold from employee earnings?

Answers
1. *Payroll periods may be weekly, biweekly, semimonthly, or monthly.*
2. *The three federal taxes that employers must withhold are federal income tax, Social Security tax, and Medicare tax.*

OBJECTIVE 2 — CREATE A PAYROLL SYSTEM USING PEACHTREE'S PAYROLL SETUP WIZARD

The Payroll Setup Wizard in Peachtree Complete Accounting 2007 provides you with step-by-step guidance for establishing your payroll system. At the start of this process, you must select the appropriate payroll tax percentages and create several new general ledger accounts.

Assume that the Woodward Construction Company decides to establish a payroll system using Peachtree as of February 1, 2007. Follow the steps outlined below to create the new payroll system.

Step 1:
Open Woodward Construction Company and close the Action Items log.

Step 2:

Click Options from the main menu and Default Information and Payroll Setup Wizard from the drop-down list.

Step 3:

Click *Payroll Setup Wizard* from the *Peachtree Payroll Solutions* window, as shown in figure 10–1.

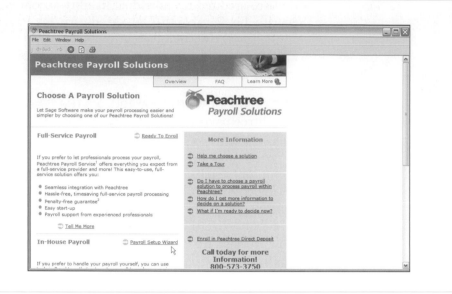

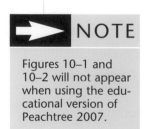

HINT

You can also access the Payroll Setup Wizard by clicking Maintain, Default Information, and Payroll Setup Wizard.

Step 4:

Click "Payroll Tax Table Information Will Be Manually Maintained" from the Payroll Setup Wizard – Peachtree Payroll Tax Update Service opening screen, as shown in figure 10–2. Click Next to continue.

NOTE

Figures 10–1 and 10–2 will not appear when using the educational version of Peachtree 2007.

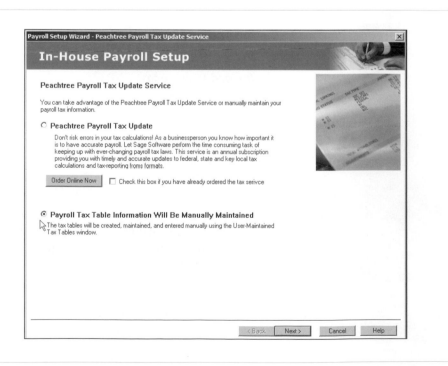

Step 5:

Click *CA* from the drop-down list in the *State...* field. (*CA* stands for California, the state where Woodward is located.) Key **5.00** in the *Unemployment Percent for Your Company* field. Your completed work should match figure 10–3.

FIGURE 10-3

Initial Payroll Setup Dialog Box

HINT

The tax tables change periodically and must be updated. Contact the Peachtree Web site, www.peachtree.com, for updated information.

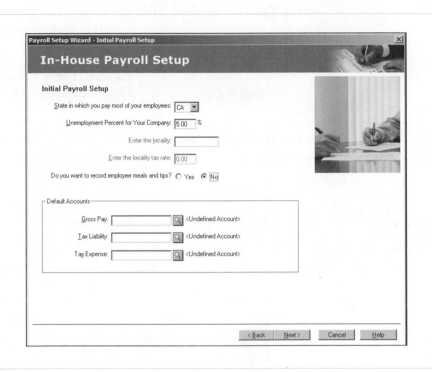

Step 6:

The Default Accounts section is at the bottom of the screen. At the *Gross Pay* field, click the *magnifying glass* icon, and then click *512* (Wages and Salaries Expense).

Step 7:

At the *Tax Liability* field, click the *magnifying glass* icon, click the New button, and create the following general ledger account.

Account ID:	**218**
Description:	**Payroll Taxes Payable**
Account Type:	**Other Current Liabilities**

Step 8:

At the *Tax Expense* field, click the *magnifying glass* icon, click the New button, and then create the following general ledger account.

Account ID:	**513**
Description:	**Payroll Taxes Expense**
Account Type:	**Expenses**

Step 9:

Compare your completed work with figure 10–4 and click *N*ext.

FIGURE 10-4
Completed Default Accounts Dialog Box

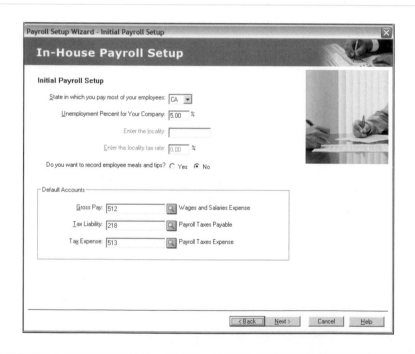

Step 10:

At the 401(k) Setup dialog box, click the *401(k) Not offered* button, as shown in figure 10–5.

FIGURE 10-5

Payroll Setup Wizard –
401(k) Setup Information
Dialog Box

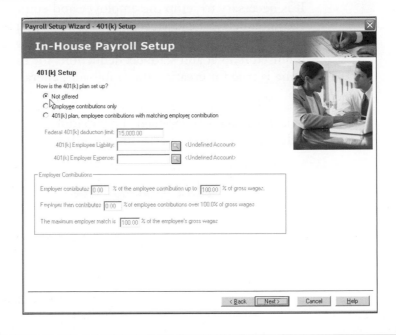

HINT

Although vacation
time is not being
tracked at this time,
this feature can be
added in the future.

Woodward Construction Company is not offering a 401(k) plan to its
employees at this time. [Remember that a 401(k) plan is a retirement savings
plan.] This feature can be added in the future.

Step 11:

Click <u>N</u>ext. At the Vacation and Sick Time Tracking Setup dialog box, click
the *Vacation time not tracked* button in the Vacation Time Tracking section at
the top.

Step 12:

In the same dialog box, click the *Sick time not tracked* button at the bottom
of the screen, as shown in figure 10–6.

FIGURE 10-6

Payroll Setup Wizard –
Vacation and Sick Time
Tracking Setup Dialog Box

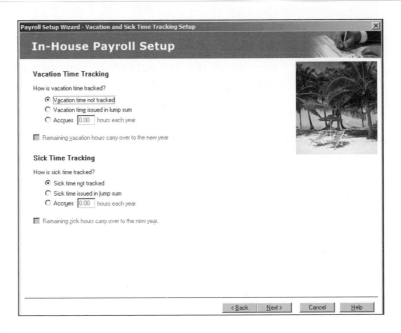

HINT

Sick time can be
tracked and accu-
mulated by using
the different options
shown in figure
10–6.

Step 13:

Click <u>N</u>ext. At the Payroll Setup Complete screen, click Finish.

It is necessary to setup the employee and employer individual payroll accounts before Peachtree can be used to complete a payroll. This requires using the general ledger accounts for gross pay and deductions, including required federal and state tax deductions for each individual employee. The same is true for creating the employer general ledger accounts.

Step 14:

Select <u>M</u>aintain and <u>D</u>efault Information, from the Peachtree main menu. Select <u>E</u>mployees from the drop-down list.

FIGURE 10-7

EmployEE Fields Folder Tab Selected

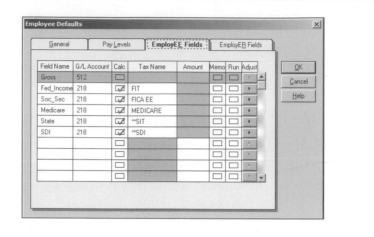

HINT

The liability account that was set up as the default for recording payroll taxes owed (Account 218) may be changed to more accurately track the different liabilities. An individual liability account for each type of tax can be established. This process will be demonstrated later in the chapter.

Step 15:

At the Employee Defaults dialog box, click the *EmployEE Fields* folder tab, as shown in figure 10–7. This screen shows the general ledger accounts that were established as defaults for recording employee earnings (gross pay) and deductions, notably 512 (Wages and Salaries Expense) and 218 (Payroll Taxes Payable).

Step 16:

Click the *EmployER Fields* folder tab in the Employee Defaults dialog box, as shown in figure 10–8. This screen shows the general ledger accounts that were established as defaults for recording the employer's payroll taxes, notably 218 (Payroll Taxes Payable) and 513 (Payroll Taxes Expense).

FIGURE 10-8

EmployER Fields Folder Tab Selected

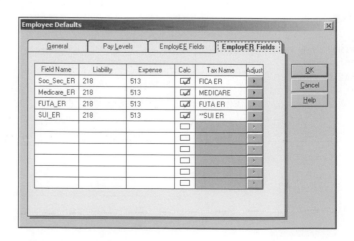

1. Where can Peachtree users find updated tax tables?
2. What account will be used to record gross pay?

Answers
1. *Updated tax tables are available from Peachtree's Web site at www.peachtree.com.*
2. *Wages and Salaries Expense will be used to record gross pay.*

Step 17:

Click <u>O</u>K to accept the Employee Defaults.

This concludes the payroll setup process. Note that changes can be made to the payroll defaults at any time by clicking <u>M</u>aintain on the main menu bar, clicking <u>D</u>efault Information, and then clicking <u>E</u>mployees.

P R A C T I C E *objective* 2

Step 1:

Open Bullfrog Maintenance Company.

Step 2:

Use the Payroll Setup Wizard to establish the payroll system for Bullfrog.

Step 3:

Use the following information to set up the payroll system.

State:	**CA**
Unemployment rate:	**5.00**
Gross Pay Acct:	**512**

Step 4:

Create the following general ledger accounts for recording payroll taxes.

Account ID:	**218**
Description:	**Payroll Taxes Payable**
Account Type:	**Other Current Liabilities**

Account ID:	**513**
Description:	**Payroll Taxes Expense**
Account Type:	**Expenses**

Step 5:

Accept all remaining defaults, and then click <u>F</u>inish.

OBJECTIVE 3 — MAINTAIN THE PAYROLL SYSTEM

Maintaining the payroll system usually involves updating accounts and updating employee information. Let us look first at the procedures for changing accounts that have been established as defaults.

CREATING ADDITIONAL DEFAULT ACCOUNTS

Suppose that Woodward Construction Company is not happy with the default accounts that it established with the Payroll Setup Wizard. Instead of having a single liability account called Payroll Taxes Payable, Woodward wants to create separate liability accounts to keep track of the different types of employee withholding taxes and employer payroll taxes.

Step 1:

Open Woodward Construction Company and close the Action Items log.

Step 2:

Click Maintain, click Default Information, and then click Employees.

Step 3:

At the Employee Defaults window, click the *EmployEE Fields* folder tab, as shown in figure 10–9.

FIGURE 10-9

Employee Defaults Window with EmployEE Fields Folder Tab Selected

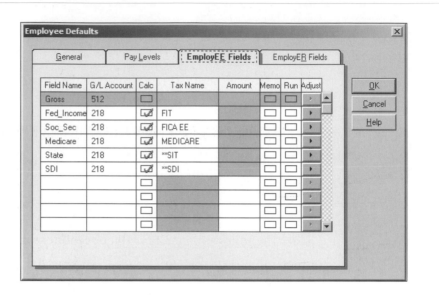

Step 4:

Up to this point, Payroll Taxes Payable (Account 218) was Woodward's default account for all the employee withholding taxes. Click in the *Fed_Income* row of the *G/L Account* column and then click the *magnifying glass* icon to create new accounts as the defaults in the following fields. Note that all of these accounts are considered "Other Current Liabilities."

a. In the *Fed_Income* field, change Account 218 to—

Account ID:	**220**
Description:	**Federal Income Tax Payable**
Account Type:	**Other Current Liabilities**

b. In the *Soc_Sec* field, change Account 218 to—

Account ID:	**222**
Description:	**Social Security Tax Payable**
Account Type:	**Other Current Liabilities**

c. In the *Medicare* field change Account 218 to—

Account ID:	**224**
Description:	**Medicare Tax Payable**
Account Type:	**Other Current Liabilities**

d. In the *State* field, change Account 218 to—

Account ID:	**226**
Description:	**State Income Tax Payable**
Account Type:	**Other Current Liabilities**

e. In the *SDI* field, change Account 218 to—

Account ID:	**228**
Description:	**SDI Tax Payable**
Account Type:	**Other Current Liabilities**

Step 5:

Review the new defaults in the *EmployEE Fields* folder tab, as shown in figure 10–10. Make any necessary changes.

FIGURE 10-10
New Accounts for Employee Defaults

These specific G/L accounts were created.

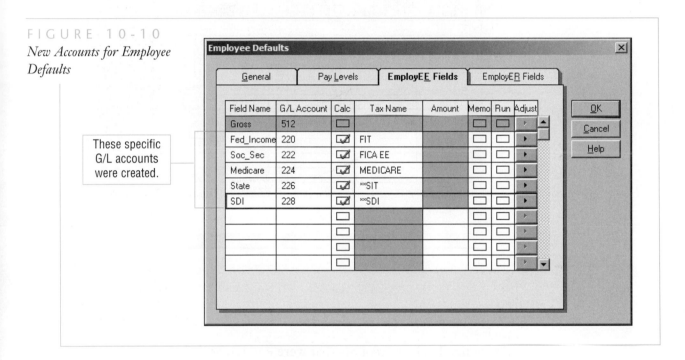

Step 6:

Click the *EmployER Fields* folder tab.

Step 7:

Change the defaults for the liability accounts to be used in recording the employer's payroll taxes. Create new accounts as follows.

a. In the *Soc_Sec_ER* field, change Account 218 to 222.
b. In the *Medicare_ER* field, change Account 218 to 224.
c. In the *FUTA_ER* field, change Account 218 to:

Account ID:	**230**
Description:	**FUTA Tax Payable**
Account Type:	**Other Current Liabilities**

d. In the *SUI_ER* field, change Account 218 to:

Account ID:	**232**
Description:	**SUTA Tax Payable**
Account Type:	**Other Current Liabilities**

Step 8:
Compare your entries with figure 10–11, and make any necessary changes.
Note: The educational version may include the SETT_ER Field Name.
Select the line with the Field Name, right click mouse and delete that Field
Name.

FIGURE 10-11
*New Accounts for Employer
Defaults*

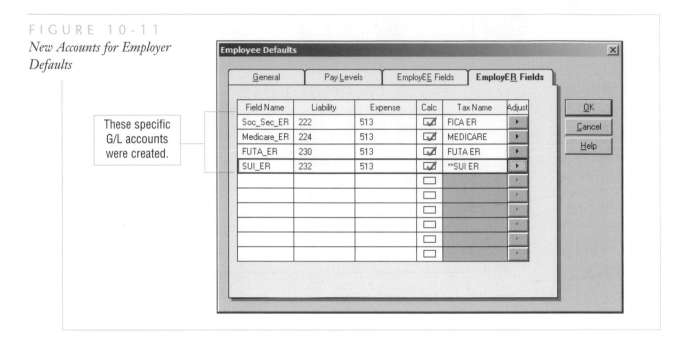

These specific
G/L accounts
were created.

Step 9:
Click <u>O</u>K to accept the new defaults.

The general ledger accounts that were entered as defaults are now the
accounts that Peachtree will use during the payroll process. Two of these
accounts, FICA—Social Security Tax Payable and FICA—Medicare Tax
Payable, are used to record both employee taxes and employer payroll taxes.
That is why they were listed in the employee and employer fields.
(Remember that the Federal Insurance Contributions Act requires employers
to match the Social Security tax and Medicare tax paid by their employees.)

CREATING THE EMPLOYEE RECORDS
In the Peachtree payroll system, an individual record must be set up for
each employee. This record includes general information, withholding
information, and pay information for the employee. The withholding information is needed to calculate the federal, state, and local income tax owed
by the employee. The pay information specifies the payroll period

(frequency), the pay plan (pay method) used for the employee, and the employee's pay rate.

Follow the steps outlined below to establish employee records for the four employees of Woodward Construction Company. This firm has a weekly payroll period and uses the hourly rate plan and the salary plan. The hourly employees have a 40-hour workweek.

Step 1:

Click Maintain, and then click Employees/Sales Reps.

Step 2:

The Maintain Employees/Sales Reps window will appear, with the *General* folder tab selected, as shown in figure 10–12.

FIGURE 10-12
General Folder Tab Selected

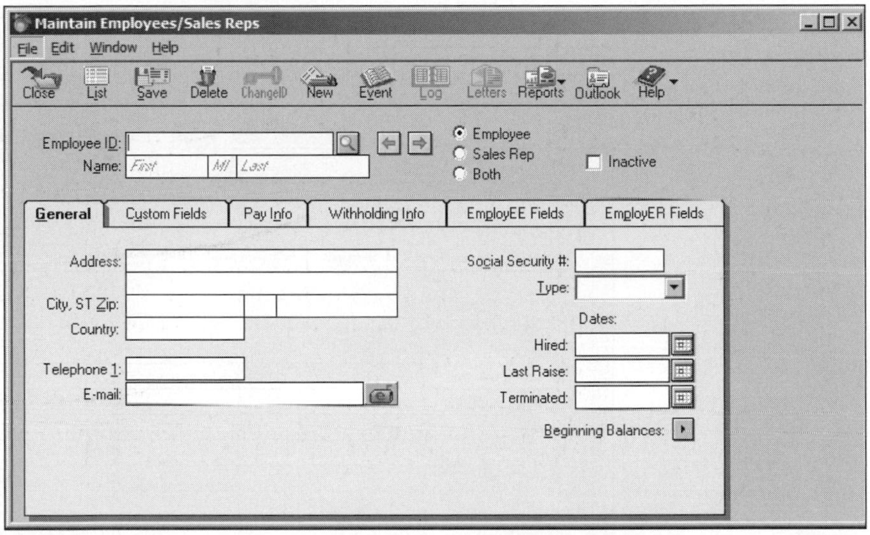

Enter the information for the first employee—George Clark.

Employee ID:	**GEOCLARK-03**
Name:	**George Clark**

General Tab

Address:	**126 New Castle Road**
City, ST, Zip:	**Modesto, CA 95355**
Country:	**USA**
Telephone 1:	**209-555-0332**
Social Security #:	**559-30-6523**
Type:	**Salary**

Dates

Hired:	**Dec 30, 2000**
Last Raise:	**Jan 31, 2004**
Terminated:	

Step 3:

Click the *Withholding Info* tab and enter the following information:

Withholding Info Tab

Federal Filing Status:	**Single**	*Allow:* **2**	*Additional Withholding:* **0.00**
State Filing Status:	**Single**	*Allow:* **2**	*Additional Withholding:* **0.00**
		State: **CA**	
Local Filing Status:	**Single**		

Step 4:

Compare your completed Maintain Employees/Sales Reps window *Witholding Info* folder tab to the one shown in figure 10–13, and make any necessary corrections.

FIGURE 10-13

Completed Withholding Info Tab

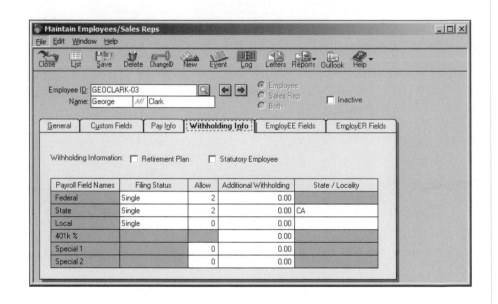

Step 5:

Click the *Pay Info* folder tab. Then enter the following information:

Pay Info Tab

Pay Method:	**Salary**
Frequency:	**Weekly**
Hourly Billing Rate:	**25.00**
Salary:	**1,000.00**

Step 6:

Compare your Maintain Employees/Sales Reps window *Pay Info* folder tab to the one shown in figure 10–14 and make any necessary corrections. Then click Save to save the new employee information for George Clark.

FIGURE 10-14

Completed Pay Information

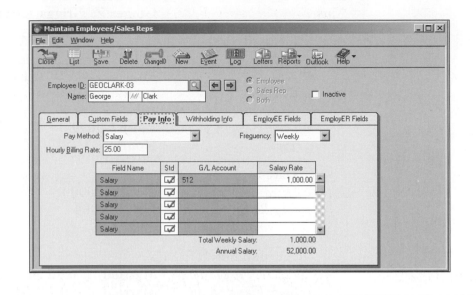

Step 7:

Enter the information for the remaining three employees of Woodward Construction Company.

| *Employee ID:* | **SAMJONES-04** |
| *Name:* | **Samuel P. Jones** |

General Tab

Address:	**413 Mill River Drive**
City, ST, Zip:	**Modesto, CA 95351**
Country:	**USA**
Telephone 1:	**209-555-3032**
Social Security #:	**562-90-9866**
Type:	**Hourly**

Dates

Hired:	**Jan 6, 2004**
Last Raise:	
Terminated:	

Withholding Info Tab

Federal Filing Status:	**Married** *Allow:* **2** *Additional Withholding:* **0.00**
State Filing Status:	**Married** *Allow:* **2** *Additional Withholding:* **0.00**
	State: **CA**
Local Filing Status:	**Married**

Pay Info Tab

Pay Method:	**Hourly—Hours per Pay Period**
Frequency:	**Weekly**
Hours per Pay Period:	**40.00**
Hourly Billing Rate:	**24.00**
Regular:	**15.00**
Overtime:	**22.50**

| Employee ID: | **GINGRIGGS-05** |
| Name: | **Ginger Z. Griggs** |

General Tab

Address:	**11121 Ceres Avenue**
City, ST, Zip:	**Modesto, CA 95351**
Country:	**USA**
Telephone 1:	**209-555-2334**
Social Security #:	**544-87-9099**
Type:	**Hourly**

Dates

Hired:	**Oct 20, 2000**
Last Raise:	**Jan 30, 2004**
Terminated:	

Withholding Info Tab

Federal Filing Status:	**Married** *Allow:* **2** *Additional Withholding:* **0.00**
State Filing Status:	**Married** *Allow:* **2** *Additional Withholding:* **0.00**
	State: **CA**
Local Filing Status:	**Married**

Pay Info

Pay Method:	**Hourly—Hours per Pay Period**
Frequency:	**Weekly**
Hours per Pay Period:	**40.00**
Hourly Billing Rate:	**24.50**
Regular:	**14.50**
Overtime:	**21.75**

| Employee ID: | **STEBROWN-06** |
| Name: | **Steven Brown** |

General Tab

Address:	**554 Boston Way**
City, ST, Zip:	**Modesto, CA 95351**
Country:	**USA**
Telephone 1:	**209-555-2344**
Social Security #:	**545-09-0009**
Type:	**Salary**

Dates

Hired:	**Dec 30, 2000**
Last Raise:	**Jan 30, 2004**
Terminated:	

Withholding Info Tab

Federal Filing Status:	**Single** *Allow:* **2** *Additional Withholding:* **0.00**
State Filing Status:	**Single** *Allow:* **2** *Additional Withholding:* **0.00**
	State: **CA**
Local Filing Status:	**Single**

Pay Info

Pay Method:	**Salary**
Frequency:	**Weekly**
Hourly Billing Rate:	**30.00**
Salary:	**1,200.00**

Step 8:
Click <u>S</u>ave. Then close the Maintain Employees/Sales Reps window.

PRACTICE *objective*   3

Step 1:
Open Bullfrog Maintenance Company.

Step 2:
Make the following changes in the employee and employer defaults. Create new accounts as necessary.

EmployEE Fields
In the *Fed_Income* field, change Account 218 to:

Account I<u>D</u>:	**220**
Des<u>c</u>ription:	**Federal Income Tax Payable**
Account <u>T</u>ype:	**Other Current Liabilities**

In the *Soc_Sec* field, change Account 218 to:

Account I<u>D</u>:	**222**
Des<u>c</u>ription:	**Social Security Tax Payable**
Account <u>T</u>ype:	**Other Current Liabilities**

In the *Medicare* field, change Account 218 to:

Account I<u>D</u>:	**224**
Des<u>c</u>ription:	**Medicare Tax Payable**
Account <u>T</u>ype:	**Other Current Liabilities**

In the *State* field, change Account 218 to:

Account I<u>D</u>:	**226**
Des<u>c</u>ription:	**State Income Tax Payable**
Account <u>T</u>ype:	**Other Current Liabilities**

In the *SDI* field, change Account 218 to:

Account I<u>D</u>:	**228**
Des<u>c</u>ription:	**SDI Tax Payable**
Account <u>T</u>ype:	**Other Current Liabilities**

Check
POINT

1. What three types of information are entered when establishing an employee record?
2. Why does a firm need withholding information for each employee?

Answers

1. *The three types of information used to establish employee records are general information, withholding information, and pay information.*
2. *Withholding information is needed to calculate the income tax owed by each employee.*

EmployER Fields

In the *Soc_Sec_ER* field, change Account 218 to Account 222.
In the *Medicare_ER* field, change Account 218 to Account 224.
In the *FUTA_ER* field, change Account 218 to:

Account ID:	**230**
Description:	**FUTA Tax Payable**
Account Type:	**Other Current Liabilities**

In the *SUI_ER* field, change Account 218 to:

Account ID:	**232**
Description:	**SUTA Tax Payable**
Account Type:	**Other Current Liabilities**

Step 3:

Set up employee records for the following three employees:

Employee ID:	**HENCARVER-03**
Name:	**Henry Carver**

General Tab

Address:	**2799 Rodeo Drive**
City, ST, Zip:	**Stockton, CA 95501**
Country:	**USA**
Telephone 1:	**209-555-0098**
Social Security #:	**344-58-9088**
Type:	**Hourly**

Dates

Hired:	**Jan 6, 2004**
Last Raise:	
Terminated:	

Withholding Info Tab

Federal Filing Status:	**Single**	*Allow:* **1**	*Additional Withholding:* **0.00**		
State Filing Status:	**Single**	*Allow:* **1**	*Additional Withholding:* **0.00**		
		State: **CA**			
Local Filing Status:	**Single**				

Pay Info

Pay Method:	**Hourly—Hours per Pay Period**
Frequency:	**Weekly**
Hours per Pay Period:	**40.00**
Hourly Billing Rate:	**20.00**
Regular:	**12.00**
Overtime:	**18.00**

| Employee ID: | **JAMSTEWART-04** |
| Name: | **James Stewart** |

General Tab

Address:	**1221 Grant Avenue**
City, ST, Zip:	**Lodi, CA 95331**
Country:	**USA**
Telephone 1:	**209-555-9867**
Social Security #:	**599-09-3343**
Type:	**Hourly**

Dates

Hired:	**Oct 20, 2000**
Last Raise:	**Jan 30, 2004**
Terminated:	

Withholding Info Tab

Federal Filing Status:	**Married** *Allow:* **2** *Additional Withholding:* **0.00**
State Filing Status:	**Married** *Allow:* **2** *Additional Withholding:* **0.00**
	State: **CA**
Local Filing Status:	**Married**

Pay Info

Pay Method:	**Hourly—Hours per Pay Period**
Frequency:	**Weekly**
Hours per Pay Period:	**40.00**
Hourly Billing Rate:	**21.50**
Regular:	**11.50**
Overtime:	**16.75**

| Employee ID: | **STASMITH-05** |
| Name: | **Stanley Smith** |

General Tab

Address:	**5233 Ireland Way**
City, ST, Zip:	**Galt, CA 95001**
Country:	**USA**
Telephone 1:	**209-555-3422**
Social Security #:	**523-88-7654**
Type:	**Salary**

Dates

Hired:	**Dec 30, 2000**
Last Raise:	**Jan 30, 2004**
Terminated:	

Withholding Information Tab

Federal Filing Status:	**Single** *Allow:* **2** *Additional Withholding:* **0.00**
State Filing Status:	**Single** *Allow:* **2** *Additional Withholding:* **0.00**
	State: **CA**
Local Filing Status:	**Single**

Pay Info

Pay Method:	**Salary**
Frequency:	**Weekly**
Hourly Billing Rate:	**40.00**
Salary Rate:	**1,600.00**

Step 4:

Close the Maintain Employees/Sales Reps window.

OBJECTIVE 4 — PREPARE A PAYROLL AND PRINT PAYROLL CHECKS

Once you have set up the Peachtree payroll system and established a record for each employee, it is possible to prepare the payroll. Usually, this process requires entry of the hours worked by employees who are on the hourly rate plan and entry of the overtime earned by any employee.

After you have entered the necessary information about hours worked and overtime, Peachtree will calculate the earnings and deductions of each employee for the payroll period and print a payroll check. The total amount earned by the employee is his or her gross pay. The amount remaining after all deductions is the employee's **net pay**. This is the amount that will appear on the employee's payroll check.

net pay The amount received by employees after deductions are made from their gross pay.

PAYROLL TAX TABLES

When Peachtree is initially installed, a generic tax table is also installed. In most cases, Peachtree will not be able to calculate automatically or accurately federal, state, and most local payroll taxes during the payroll process using this generic table. In order to calculate actual and accurate payroll tax amounts, you should subscribe to the Peachtree Payroll Tax Service and install the most current Tax Service update. Information pertaining to Peachtree Payroll Tax Service can be obtained at www.peachtree.com/taxservice.

For educational purposes a modified tax table has been created that will allow you to complete the payroll process. This tax table was created because the Peachtree problems with which you are practicing have fiscal years for which no payroll tax tables have yet been established. Remember that this tax table should be used for educational purposes only. To install the modified tax table, follow the steps below.

Step 1:

Click the Windows Start button, click All Programs, click Accessories, and then click Windows Explorer.

Step 2:

In the left window of Windows Explorer, double-click the folder to which you extracted your student files from the Student CD.

Step 3:

In the right window of Windows Explorer, click the file *TAXTABLE.DAT* (64KB, DAT File, 1/22/07) and click the Copy button on the shortcut menu. Note that the shortcut menu will appear when you right-click on the file.

Step 4:

In the left window of Windows Explorer, double-click the *Peachtree* program folder or the folder where you are saving your company files, double-click the *Company* folder, click *wooconco* (Woodward Construction Company), and then click Paste.

Step 5:

At the Confirm File Replace query message, click <u>Y</u>es. (**Note:** You can only copy the file Taxtable if no companies are currently open.)

PREPARING THE PAYROLL WITH NO OVERTIME

Suppose that there was no overtime for the employees of Woodward Construction Company during the weekly payroll period ended February 27, 2007. Follow the steps outlined below to prepare this payroll.

Step 1:

Open Woodward Construction Company and close the Action Item log.

Step 2:

Click Employees & Payroll from the Navigation Aids at the side of the main window.

Step 3:

Click the *Pay Employees* icon and "Enter Payroll for Multiple Employees," as shown in figure 10–15.

FIGURE 10-15

Enter Payroll for Multiple Employees from Pay Employees Icon

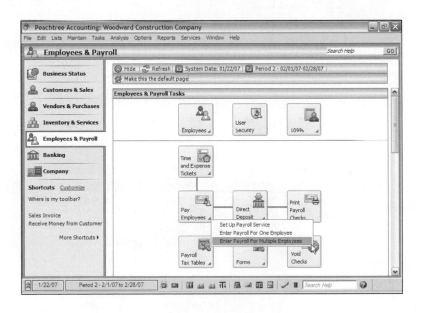

Step 4:

The Select Employees – Filter Selection dialog box will appear. At the *Pay End Date* field, click the *calendar* icon, and then choose the date *Feb 27, 2007*.

Step 5:

In the Include <u>P</u>ay Frequencies section, click Weekly only and deselect the other frequency options.

Step 6:

In the In<u>c</u>lude Pay Methods section, click Hourly and Salary, if needed.

Step 7:

In the Include <u>E</u>mployees section, click All Employees and All Type. Your completed dialog box should look like figure 10–16.

FIGURE 10-16
Completed Select Employees-Filter Selection Dialog Box

Step 8:

Click <u>O</u>K.

Step 9:

The Select Employees to Pay window will appear. In the *Check Date* field, click the *calendar* icon, and then choose *Feb 28, 2007*. This is the date that will appear on the payroll checks.

Step 10:

At the *Pay End Date* field, click the *calendar* icon, and then choose *Feb 27, 2007*. This is the ending date of the payroll period.

Step 11:

At the *Cash Acct* field, click the *magnifying glass* icon, and then click *100*, if needed.

Step 12:

Review the Select Employees to Pay window to be sure that all employees for Woodward Construction Company are included in the payroll. Compare your work with figure 10–17.

FIGURE 10-17
Completed Select Employees to Pay Dialog Box

Ensure that the payroll check date is correct.

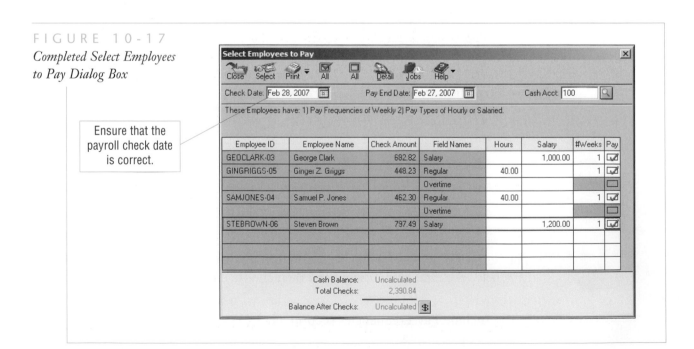

PRINTING THE PAYROLL CHECKS

Before you attempt to print the payroll checks, be sure that there are check marks in all the Pay boxes at the right of the Select Employees to Pay screen. If a particular individual is not to be paid for the payroll period, no check mark should appear in the Pay box for that employee. Follow these steps to print checks.

Step 1:
Click Print on the toolbar at the top of the Select Employees to Pay window.

Step 2:
At the Print Forms: Payroll Checks dialog box, in the *First check number* field, key **2005**, as shown in figure 10–18.

FIGURE 10-18

Completed Select Employees to Pay Dialog Box

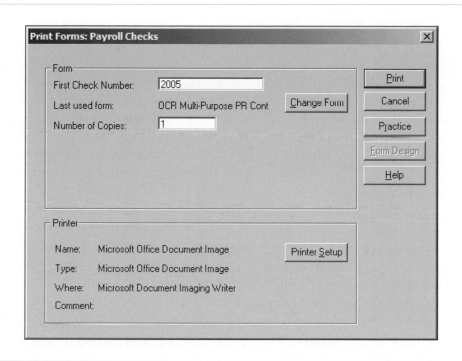

Note: Be sure that the printer is attached and turned on. The checks will print on any plain paper in the printer. Several types of preprinted check forms are available through Peachtree. Refer to the Peachtree Web site (www.peachtree.com) to locate a source for preprinted check forms.

Step 3:
Click **P**rint.

Step 4:
Review your checks. The first one should look like figure 10–19. If there are errors, click **N**o in the Peachtree Accounting query screen and repeat the printing process from step 1 above. Go to step 5 if your checks are correct.

FIGURE 10-19

Check for George Clark of Woodward Construction Company

	This Check	Year to Date			
George Clark			Employee ID: GEOCLARK-03		
			Social Sec # 559-30-6523		
Gross	1,000.00	1,000.00		Total	
Fed_Income	-178.72	-178.72	Salary	1,000.00	
Soc_Sec	-62.00	-62.00			
Medicare	-14.50	-14.50			
State	-51.96	-51.96			
SDI	-10.00	-10.00			

Net Check: $682.82   Total   1,000.00

Pay Period Beginning: 2/21/07   Check Date: 2/28/07
Pay Period Ending: 2/27/07   Weeks in Pay Period: 1

Check Number: 2005   Feb 28, 2007

682.82

Six Hundred Eighty-Two and 82/100 Dollars

George Clark
126 New Castle Road
Modesto, CA 95355
USA

Step 5:

Click <u>Y</u>es in the Peachtree Accounting query screen and the check numbers (2005–2007) will be assigned. The payroll is then posted.

PREPARING THE PAYROLL WITH OVERTIME

During the weekly payroll period ended February 27, 2007, none of the employees of Woodward Construction Company worked overtime. However, during the payroll period ended March 6, 2007, Ginger Griggs worked 50 hours rather than the normal 40 hours. She is paid according to the hourly rate plan.

Follow the steps outlined below to prepare the March 6 payroll for Woodward Construction Company.

Step 1:

Click Payroll & Employees from the Navigation Aids toolbar, if needed.

Step 2:

Click the *Pay Employees* icon and "Enter Payroll for One Employee" from the *Employees & Payroll* tasks section, as shown in figure 10–20.

Payroll Entry Selected from Payroll Folder

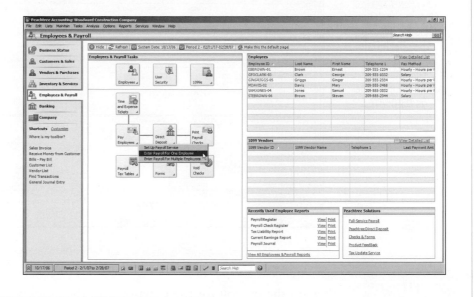

Step 3:

Click OK to acknowledge the Peachtree payroll tax registration information, if applicable.

Step 4:

At the Payroll Entry window, at the *Date* field, click the *calendar* icon and choose *Mar 7, 2007*.

Step 5:

At the *Employee ID* field, click the *magnifying glass* icon, and then double-click *GINGRIGGS-05*. The Hours Worked and Taxes-Benefits-Liabilities fields should display their data.

Step 6:

At the *Pay Period Ends* field, click the *calendar* icon, and choose *Mar 6, 2007*.

Step 7:

Key **1** in the *Weeks in Pay Period* field, if needed.

Step 8:

In the Hours Worked section, key **40.00** in the *Regular* field and **10.00** in the *Overtime* field. Compare your completed entry with the one shown in figure 10–21. Then click Save. (Do not print a check unless your instructor tells you to.)

FIGURE 10-21
*Completed Payroll Entry for
Ginger Z. Griggs*

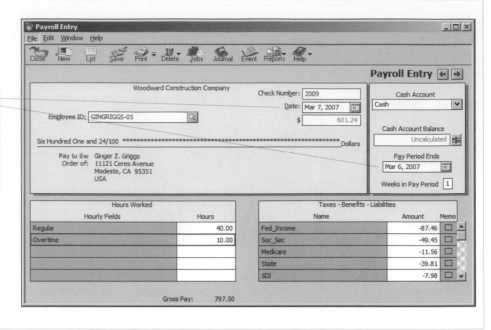

Always check your dates for accuracy. The check Date field is 03/07/07 while the Pay Period Ends date is 03/06/07.

HINT

If you make an error, use the Open function to retrieve the entry. Make any necessary corrections and post when it is complete.

Step 9:
Prepare the payroll for the remainder of the employees as you did in the March 6 period for Ginger Z. Griggs, excluding overtime (do not print checks):

• George Clark
• Samuel Jones
• Steven Brown

Step 10:
Close the Payroll Entry window.

PRINTING PAYROLL CHECKS AT A LATER DATE

Sometimes payroll checks are printed after the payroll is prepared. Use the following procedure to print the checks for the March 14 payroll of Woodward Construction Company. The date on the checks will be March 7, 2007.

Step 1:
Click Tasks from the main menu toolbar, if needed.

Step 2:
Click *Payroll Entry* from the drop-down list.

Step 3:
Click OK to acknowledge the Peachtree payroll tax registration information, if applicable.

Step 4:
Click List on the Payroll Entry toolbar.

Step 5:
At the Paycheck List window, click the down arrow at the *Date Range* field and then click *Prd 3: 3/1/07 – 3/31/07*.

Step 6:

Click *Ginger Z. Griggs*, as shown in figure 10–22.

FIGURE 10-22

Ginger Z. Griggs Selected from the Select Payroll Entry Window

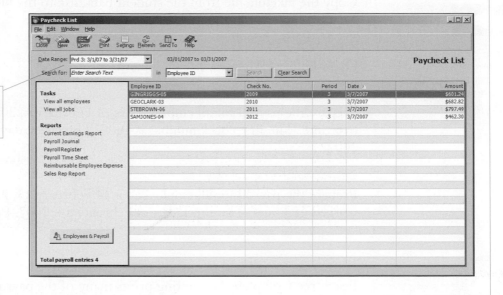

Be sure to have Prd 3: 3/1/07 - 3/31/07 selected.

Step 7:

Click Open.

Step 8:

Click Print on the Payroll Entry toolbar.

Step 9:

Click Print in the Print Forms: Payroll Checks dialog box. The first check number should be 2009.

Step 10:

Repeat steps 3 through 8 to print checks for the remaining employees who have not been assigned a check number.

Step 11:

Close the Payroll Entry window.

Check
POINT

1. What is net pay?
2. Is it necessary to print payroll checks when the payroll is prepared?

Answers

1. *Net pay is the amount remaining after deductions are made from an employee's gross pay.*
2. *No, payroll checks can be printed at a later date.*

NOTE

You must not have a company open in order to copy the sample taxtable file properly.

Step 1:

Copy the taxtable file from the student data disk to the bulmaico (Bullfrog Maintenance Company) folder.

Step 2:

Open Bullfrog Maintenance Company.

Step 3:

Prepare the payroll for all employees as of February 6, 2007. There was no overtime. The first check number is 1000. The check date is February 7, 2007.

Step 4:

Prepare the payroll for all employees as of February 13, 2007. Henry Carver worked 45 hours. The check date is February 14, 2007. Print the checks.

OBJECTIVE 5 — PRINT PAYROLL TAX RETURNS AND PAYROLL REPORTS

Peachtree Complete Accounting prints many of the payroll tax returns that must be sent to federal and state tax agencies. Among the federal tax returns produced are Forms 940, 941, W-2, W-3, and 1099. In addition, Peachtree prepares a variety of payroll reports for management. The following is a partial list of the available payroll reports for management.

- The *Current Earnings* report lists each employee's earnings and deductions.
- The *Payroll Journal* lists payroll transactions in a journal format.
- The *Payroll Tax Report* lists the payroll deductions.
- The *Quarterly Earnings Report* lists the quarterly earnings of all employees.
- The *Tax Liability Report* lists the employer's liabilities for payroll taxes.
- The *Yearly Earnings Report* lists the annual earnings of all employees.

Follow the steps outlined below to print the *Current Earnings Report*.

Step 1:

Open Woodward Construction Company and close Action Items log.

Step 2:

Click Reports, and then click Payroll.

Step 3:

At the Select a Report dialog box, at the Report List section, click *Current Earnings Report*.

Click Print on the Select a Report toolbar.

At the Current Earnings Report window, with the *Filter* folder tab selected, click *Range* in the *Date* field.

At the *From* field, click the *calendar* icon to choose *Feb 1, 2007*. At the *To* field, choose *Mar 31, 2007*, as shown in figure 10–23.

FIGURE 10-23

Current Earnings Report Filter Screen

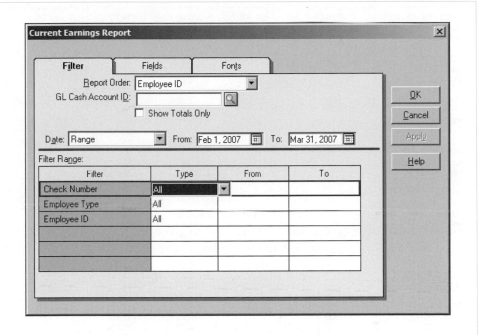

HINT

The tax amounts shown in the *Current Earnings* report will vary depending on the tax tables that were loaded. This payroll was prepared with the modified tax table that is included on the student data disk.

Click OK.

Review the *Current Earnings Report* shown in figure 10–24. Notice that this report shows the gross pay, deductions, and net pay for each employee.

FIGURE 10-24
Current Earnings Report

Page: 1

Woodward Construction Company
Current Earnings Report
For the Period From Feb 1, 2007 to Mar 31, 2007

Filter Criteria includes: Report order is by Employee ID. Report is printed in Detail Format.

Employee ID Employee SS No	Date Reference	Amount	Gross State FUTA_ER	Fed_Income SDI SUI_ER	Soc_Sec Soc_Sec_ER	Medicare Medicare_ER
GEOCLARK-03 George Clark 559-30-6523	2/28/07 2005	682.82	1,000.00 -51.96 -8.00	-178.72 -10.00 -30.00	-62.00 -62.00	-14.50 -14.50
GEOCLARK-03 George Clark 559-30-6523	3/7/07 2010	682.82	1,000.00 -51.96 -8.00	-178.72 -10.00 -30.00	-62.00 -62.00	-14.50 -14.50
Total 2/1/07 thru 3/31/07		1,365.64	2,000.00 -103.92 -16.00	-357.44 -20.00 -60.00	-124.00 -124.00	-29.00 -29.00
Report Date Total for George Clark		1,365.64	2,000.00 -103.92 -16.00	-357.44 -20.00 -60.00	-124.00 -124.00	-29.00 -29.00
YTD Total for George Clark		1,365.64	2,000.00 -103.92 -16.00	-357.44 -20.00 -60.00	-124.00 -124.00	-29.00 -29.00
GINGRIGGS-05 Ginger Z. Griggs 544-87-9099	2/28/07 2006	448.23	580.00 -26.76 -4.64	-54.84 -5.80 -17.40	-35.96 -35.96	-8.41 -8.41
GINGRIGGS-05 Ginger Z. Griggs 544-87-9099	3/7/07 2009	601.24	797.50 -39.81 -6.38	-87.46 -7.98 -23.93	-49.45 -49.45	-11.56 -11.56
Total 2/1/07 thru 3/31/07		1,049.47	1,377.50 -66.57 -11.02	-142.30 -13.78 -41.33	-85.41 -85.41	-19.97 -19.97
Report Date Total for Ginger Z. Griggs		1,049.47	1,377.50 -66.57 -11.02	-142.30 -13.78 -41.33	-85.41 -85.41	-19.97 -19.97
YTD Total for Ginger Z. Griggs		1,049.47	1,377.50 -66.57 -11.02	-142.30 -13.78 -41.33	-85.41 -85.41	-19.97 -19.97
SAMJONES-04 Samuel P. Jones 562-90-9866	2/28/07 2007	462.30	600.00 -27.96 -4.80	-57.84 -6.00 -18.00	-37.20 -37.20	-8.70 -8.70
SAMJONES-04 Samuel P. Jones 562-90-9866	3/7/07 2012	462.30	600.00 -27.96 -4.80	-57.84 -6.00 -18.00	-37.20 -37.20	-8.70 -8.70
Total 2/1/07 thru 3/31/07		924.60	1,200.00 -55.92 -9.60	-115.68 -12.00 -36.00	-74.40 -74.40	-17.40 -17.40

FIGURE 10-24
Continued

Page: 2

Woodward Construction Company
Current Earnings Report
For the Period From Feb 1, 2007 to Mar 31, 2007

Filter Criteria includes: Report order is by Employee ID. Report is printed in Detail Format.

Employee ID Employee SS No	Date Reference	Amount	Gross State FUTA_ER	Fed_Income SDI SUI_ER	Soc_Sec Soc_Sec_ER	Medicare Medicare_ER
Report Date Total for Samuel P. Jones		924.60	1,200.00 -55.92 -9.60	-115.68 -12.00 -36.00	-74.40 -74.40	-17.40 -17.40
YTD Total for Samuel P. Jones		924.60	1,200.00 -55.92 -9.60	-115.68 -12.00 -36.00	-74.40 -74.40	-17.40 -17.40
STEBROWN-06 Steven Brown 545-09-0009	2/28/07 2008	797.49	1,200.00 -63.96 -9.60	-234.75 -12.00 -36.00	-74.40 -74.40	-17.40 -17.40
STEBROWN-06 Steven Brown 545-09-0009	3/7/07 2011	797.49	1,200.00 -63.96 -9.60	-234.75 -12.00 -36.00	-74.40 -74.40	-17.40 -17.40
Total 2/1/07 thru 3/31/07		1,594.98	2,400.00 -127.92 -19.20	-469.50 -24.00 -72.00	-148.80 -148.80	-34.80 -34.80
Report Date Total for Steven Brown		1,594.98	2,400.00 -127.92 -19.20	-469.50 -24.00 -72.00	-148.80 -148.80	-34.80 -34.80
YTD Total for Steven Brown		1,594.98	2,400.00 -127.92 -19.20	-469.50 -24.00 -72.00	-148.80 -148.80	-34.80 -34.80
Summary Total 2/1/07 thru 3/31/07		4,934.69	6,977.50 -354.33 -55.82	-1,084.92 -69.78 -209.33	-432.61 -432.61	-101.17 -101.17
Report Date Final Total 2/1/07 thru 3/31/07		4,934.69	6,977.50 -354.33 -55.82	-1,084.92 -69.78 -209.33	-432.61 -432.61	-101.17 -101.17
Final YTD Total		4,934.69	6,977.50 -354.33 -55.82	-1,084.92 -69.78 -209.33	-432.61 -432.61	-101.17 -101.17

Check POINT

1. Name five types of federal tax returns that Peachtree can produce.
2. What information is shown in the *Current Earnings* report?

Answers

1. *Forms 940, 941, W-2, W-3, and 1099 are among the federal tax returns that Peachtree can produce.*
2. *The Current Earnings report shows the gross pay, deductions, and net pay for each employee.*

Step 9:
Click Close.

PRACTICE *objective*   5

Step 1:
Open Bullfrog Maintenance Company.

Step 2:
Print the *Current Earnings* report. Your printout should look like figure 10–25.

FIGURE 10-25

Current Earnings Report—Bullfrog Maintenance Company

Bullfrog Maintenance Company
Current Earnings Report
For the Period From Feb 1, 2007 to Feb 28, 2007

Filter Criteria includes: Report order is by Employee ID. Report is printed in Detail Format.

Employee ID Employee SS No	Date Reference	Amount	Gross State FUTA_ER	Fed_Income SDI SUI_ER	Soc_Sec Soc_Sec_ER	Medicare Medicare_ER
HENCARVER-03 Henry Carver 344-58-9088	2/7/07 1000	360.43	480.00 -20.76 -3.84	-57.29 -4.80 -14.40	-29.76 -29.76	-6.96 -6.96
HENCARVER-03 Henry Carver 344-58-9088	2/14/07 1003	423.02	570.00 -26.16 -4.56	-71.51 -5.70 -17.10	-35.34 -35.34	-8.27 -8.27
Total 2/1/07 thru 2/28/07		783.45	1,050.00 -46.92 -8.40	-128.80 -10.50 -31.50	-65.10 -65.10	-15.23 -15.23
Report Date Total for Henry Carver		783.45	1,050.00 -46.92 -8.40	-128.80 -10.50 -31.50	-65.10 -65.10	-15.23 -15.23
YTD Total for Henry Carver		783.45	1,050.00 -46.92 -8.40	-128.80 -10.50 -31.50	-65.10 -65.10	-15.23 -15.23
JAMSTEWART-04 James Stewart 599-09-3343	2/7/07 1001	363.81	460.00 -19.56 -3.68	-36.84 -4.60 -13.80	-28.52 -28.52	-6.67 -6.67
JAMSTEWART-04 James Stewart 599-09-3343	2/14/07 1004	363.81	460.00 -19.56 -3.68	-36.84 -4.60 -13.80	-28.52 -28.52	-6.67 -6.67
Total 2/1/07 thru 2/28/07		727.62	920.00 -39.12 -7.36	-73.68 -9.20 -27.60	-57.04 -57.04	-13.34 -13.34
Report Date Total for James Stewart		727.62	920.00 -39.12 -7.36	-73.68 -9.20 -27.60	-57.04 -57.04	-13.34 -13.34
YTD Total for James Stewart		727.62	920.00 -39.12 -7.36	-73.68 -9.20 -27.60	-57.04 -57.04	-13.34 -13.34
STASMITH-05 Stanley Smith 523-88-7654	2/7/07 1002	1,014.89	1,600.00 -87.96 -12.80	-358.75 -16.00 -48.00	-99.20 -99.20	-23.20 -23.20
STASMITH-05 Stanley Smith 523-88-7654	2/14/07 1005	1,014.89	1,600.00 -87.96 -12.80	-358.75 -16.00 -48.00	-99.20 -99.20	-23.20 -23.20
Total 2/1/07 thru 2/28/07		2,029.78	3,200.00 -175.92 -25.60	-717.50 -32.00 -96.00	-198.40 -198.40	-46.40 -46.40

F I G U R E   1 0 - 2 5
Continued

Page: 2

Bullfrog Maintenance Company
Current Earnings Report
For the Period From Feb 1, 2007 to Feb 28, 2007
Filter Criteria includes: Report order is by Employee ID. Report is printed in Detail Format.

Employee ID Employee SS No	Date Reference	Amount	Gross State FUTA_ER	Fed_Income SDI SUI_ER	Soc_Sec Soc_Sec_ER	Medicare Medicare_ER
Report Date Total for Stanley Smith		2,029.78	3,200.00 -175.92 -25.60	-717.50 -32.00 -96.00	-198.40 -198.40	-46.40 -46.40
YTD Total for Stanley Smith		2,029.78	3,200.00 -175.92 -25.60	-717.50 -32.00 -96.00	-198.40 -198.40	-46.40 -46.40
Summary Total 2/1/07 thru 2/28/07		3,540.85	5,170.00 -261.96 -41.36	-919.98 -51.70 -155.10	-320.54 -320.54	-74.97 -74.97
Report Date Final Total 2/1/07 thru 2/28/07		3,540.85	5,170.00 -261.96 -41.36	-919.98 -51.70 -155.10	-320.54 -320.54	-74.97 -74.97
Final YTD Total		3,540.85	5,170.00 -261.96 -41.36	-919.98 -51.70 -155.10	-320.54 -320.54	-74.97 -74.97

Peachtree's Web site has many online services and support to aid you in using Peachtree effectively. One particular area of the Web site that is very important for accurate payroll tax calculations is the Peachtree Tax Service located at www.peachtree.com/taxservice (figure 10–26).

FIGURE 10-26

Peachtree Tax Service Web Site

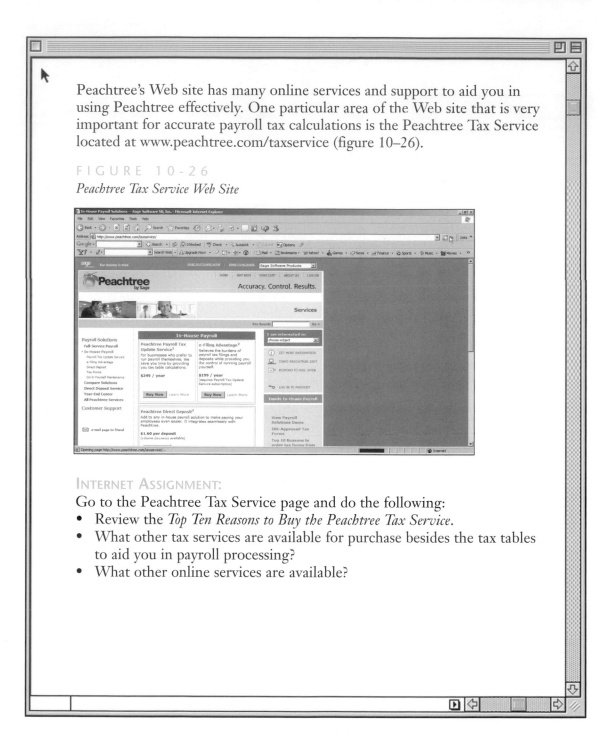

INTERNET ASSIGNMENT:

Go to the Peachtree Tax Service page and do the following:

• Review the *Top Ten Reasons to Buy the Peachtree Tax Service*.
• What other tax services are available for purchase besides the tax tables to aid you in payroll processing?
• What other online services are available?

SOFTWARE
Command Summary

Establish a Payroll	<u>M</u>aintain, <u>D</u>efault Information, <u>P</u>ayroll Setup Wizard
Set Employee Defaults	<u>M</u>aintain, <u>D</u>efault Information, <u>E</u>mployees
Create an Employee Record	<u>M</u>aintain, <u>E</u>mployees/Sales Reps
Prepare a Payroll (Group)	Tas<u>k</u>s, Select for <u>P</u>ayroll Entry
Prepare a Payroll (Individual)	Tas<u>k</u>s, Payroll <u>E</u>ntry
Preview/Print Payroll Reports	<u>R</u>eports, Pa<u>y</u>roll, select a report

PROJECTS
and Problems

Content Check
Multiple Choice: Choose only one response for each question.

1. The act that requires that employers pay the federal minimum wage and overtime to most employees when they work more than 40 hours a workweek is
   A. Current Tax Payment Act.
   B. Fair Labor Standards Act.
   C. Federal Insurance Contributions Act.
   D. Federal Unemployment Tax Act.

2. Which form is prepared at the end of the year to show the total earnings by independent contractors?
   A. Form 941
   B. Form W-2
   C. Form W-3
   D. Form 1099

3. Payroll taxes deducted from employee's earnings are recorded in what type of account?
   A. Assets
   B. Accounts Payable
   C. Long Term Liabilities
   D. Other Current Liabilities

4. FICA – Social Security Tax and FICA – Medicare Tax are paid by the
   A. employee.
   B. employer.
   C. both the employee and employer.
   D. local taxing authority.

5. The payroll report which lists each employee's earnings and deductions is the
   A. *Current Earnings Report.*
   B. *Payroll Journal.*
   C. *Payroll Tax Report.*
   D. *Tax Liability Report.*

Short-Essay Response: Provide a detailed answer for each question.
1. What are the six basic areas of payroll activities?
2. List and explain the five various pay plans.
3. List and explain the payroll reports available through Peachtree.
4. What are the six federal tax returns that employers are required to file?
5. What are the various required and voluntary deductions to be withheld from employees' earnings?
6. What is the purpose of the Payroll Setup Wizard?

NOTE

It is not necessary to copy the taxtable file into the Baxter's Solutions company folder because the company was created with the appropriate taxtable file.

CASE PROBLEMS

PROBLEM 1A

Open Baxter's Solutions, an employment staffing service, which you downloaded from the CD that comes with this book.

1. Use the Payroll Setup Wizard to establish the payroll system for Baxter's Solutions.
   Use the following information to set up the payroll system:

State:	**CA**
Unemployment percent:	**5.00**
Gross Pay Acct:	**512**

   Create the following general ledger accounts for recording payroll taxes.

Account ID:	**218**
Description:	**Payroll Taxes Payable**
Account Type:	**Other Current Liabilities**

Account ID:	**513**
Description:	**Payroll Taxes Expense**
Account Type:	**Expenses**

   Accept all remaining defaults.

2. Make the following changes in the employee and employer defaults. Create new accounts as necessary.

EmployEE Fields

In the *Fed_Income* field, change Account 218 to:

Account ID:	**220**
Description:	**Federal Income Tax Payable**
Account Type:	**Other Current Liabilities**

In the *Soc_Sec* field, change Account 218 to:

Account ID:	**222**
Description:	**Social Security Tax Payable**
Account Type:	**Other Current Liabilities**

In the *Medicare* field, change Account 218 to:

Account ID:	**224**
Description:	**Medicare Tax Payable**
Account Type:	**Other Current Liabilities**

In the *State* field, change Account 218 to:

Account ID:	**226**
Description:	**State Income Tax Payable**
Account Type:	**Other Current Liabilities**

In the *SDI* field, change Account 218 to:

Account ID:	**228**
Description:	**SDI Tax Payable**
Account Type:	**Other Current Liabilities**

EmployER Fields

In the *Soc_Sec_ER* field, change Account 218 to Account 222.
In the *Medicare_ER* field, change Account 218 to Account 224.
In the *FUTA_ER* field, change Account 218 to:

Account ID:	**230**
Description:	**FUTA Tax Payable**
Account Type:	**Other Current Liabilities**

In the *SUI_ER* field, change Account 218 to:

Account ID:	**232**
Description:	**SUTA Tax Payable**
Account Type:	**Other Current Liabilities**

3. Set up employee records for the following three employees:

Employee ID:	**BENCARTER-01**
Name:	**Benjamin Carter**

    General Tab

Address:	**2982 West Chrisman Boulevard**

City, ST, Zip:	Stockton, CA 95501
Country:	USA
Telephone 1:	209-555-0251
Social Security #:	654-46-2509
Type:	Hourly

Dates

Hired:	Jan 6, 2004
Last Raise:	
Terminated:	

Withholding Info Tab

Federal Filing Status:	**Single**	*Allow:* **1**	*Additional Withholding:* **0.00**
State Filing Status:	**Single**	*Allow:* **1**	*Additional Withholding:* **0.00**
		State: **CA**	
Local Filing Status:	**Single**		

Pay Info

Pay Method:	**Hourly—Hours per Pay Period**
Frequency:	**Weekly**
Hours per Pay Period:	**40.00**
Hourly Billing Rate:	**20.00**
Hourly Rate:	**10.00**
Overtime:	**15.00**

Employee ID:	**CINDYSOL-02**
Name:	**Cynthia Solario**

General Tab

Address:	**1651 Central Avenue**
City, ST, Zip:	**Tracy, CA 95376**
Country:	**USA**
Telephone 1:	**209-555-4852**
Social Security #:	**568-16-2137**
Type:	**Hourly**

Dates

Hired:	**Jan 20, 2004**
Last Raise:	
Terminated:	

Withholding Info Tab

Federal Filing Status:	**Married**	*Allow:* **2**	*Additional Withholding:* **0.00**
State Filing Status:	**Married**	*Allow:* **2**	*Additional Withholding:* **0.00**
		State: **CA**	
Local Filing Status:	**Single**		

Pay Info

Pay Method:	**Hourly—Hours per Pay Period**
Frequency:	**Weekly**
Hours per Pay Period:	**40.00**

Hourly Billing Rate:	22.50
Hourly Rate:	12.00
Overtime:	18.00

| Employee ID: | VICTORMOR-03 |
| Name: | Victor Moreno |

General Tab
Address:	5549 Ramona Drive
City, ST, Zip:	Tracy, CA 95376
Country:	USA
Telephone 1:	209-555-4652
Social Security #:	558-91-4852
Type:	Salary

Dates
Hired:	Jan 8, 2004
Last Raise:	
Terminated:	

Withholding Info Tab
Federal Filing Status:	**Single** *Allow:* **2**	*Additional Withholding:* **0.00**
State Filing Status:	**Single** *Allow:* **2**	*Additional Withholding:* **0.00**
	State: **CA**	
Local Filing Status:	**Single**	

Pay Info
Pay Method:	Salary
Frequency:	Weekly
Hourly Billing Rate:	50.00
Salary Rate:	1,600.00

4. Print the *Chart of Accounts* and *Employee List*.
5. Close Baxter's Solutions.

PROBLEM 2A
Open Baxter's Solutions, which you updated in Problem 1A.

1. Prepare the payroll for all employees as of March 6, 2007. There was no overtime. The first check number is 1500. The check date is March 7, 2007.
2. Prepare the payroll for all employees as of March 13, 2007. Cynthia Solario worked 46 hours this pay period. The check date is March 14, 2007.
3. Print the *Current Earnings* report and *Payroll Register*.
4. Close Baxter's Solutions.

PROBLEM 1B
Open CompNet, a computer networking design company, which you downloaded from the CD that came with this book.

NOTE

Use Account 100, Regular Checking Account as the payroll cash account.

1. Use the Payroll Setup Wizard to establish the payroll system for CompNet.

   Use the following information to set up the payroll system:

State:	**CA**
Unemployment Percent:	**5.00**
Gross Pay Acct:	**512**

   NOTE

   It is not necessary to copy the taxtable file into the CompNet company folder because the company was created with the appropriate taxtable file.

   Create the following general ledger accounts for recording payroll taxes:

Account ID:	**218**
Description:	**Payroll Taxes Payable**
Account Type:	**Other Current Liabilities**

Account ID:	**513**
Description:	**Payroll Taxes Expense**
Account Type:	**Expenses**

   Accept all the remaining defaults.

2. Make the following changes in the employee and employer defaults. Create new accounts as necessary.

   EmployEE Fields

   In the *Fed_Income* field, change Account 218 to:

Account ID:	**220**
Description:	**Federal Income Tax Payable**
Account Type:	**Other Current Liabilities**

   In the *Soc_Sec* field, change Account 218 to:

Account ID:	**222**
Description:	**Social Security Tax Payable**
Account Type:	**Other Current Liabilities**

   In the *Medicare* field, change Account 218 to:

Account ID:	**224**
Description:	**Medicare Tax Payable**
Account Type:	**Other Current Liabilities**

   In the *State* field, change Account 218 to:

Account ID:	**226**
Description:	**State Income Tax Payable**
Account Type:	**Other Current Liabilities**

   In the *SDI* field, change Account 218 to:

Account ID:	**228**
Description:	**SDI Tax Payable**
Account Type:	**Other Current Liabilities**

EmployER Fields

In the *Soc_Sec_ER* field, change Account 218 to Account 222.
In the *Medicare_ER* field, change Account 218 to Account 224.
In the *FUTA_ER* field, change Account 218 to:

Account ID:	**230**
Description:	**FUTA Tax Payable**
Account Type:	**Other Current Liabilities**

In the *SUI_ER* field, change Account 218 to:

Account ID:	**232**
Description:	**SUTA Tax Payable**
Account Type:	**Other Current Liabilities**

3. Set up employee records for the following three employees:

Employee ID:	**MARIACASE-01**
Name:	**Maria Case**

General Tab

Address:	**2256 East Madison Way**
City, ST, Zip:	**Stockton, CA 95210**
Country:	**USA**
Telephone 1:	**209-555-9526**
Social Security #:	**665-58-4259**
Type:	**Hourly**

Dates

Hired:	**Jan 30, 2005**
Last Raise:	
Terminated:	

Withholding Info Tab

Federal Filing Status:	**Single**	*Allow:* **2**	*Additional Withholding:* **0.00**
State Filing Status:	**Single**	*Allow:* **2**	*Additional Withholding:* **0.00**
	State: **CA**		
Local Filing Status:	**Single**		

Pay Info

Pay Method:	**Hourly—Hours per Pay Period**
Frequency:	**Weekly**
Hours per Pay Period:	**40.00**
Hourly Billing Rate:	**30.00**
Hourly Rate:	**10.00**
Overtime:	**15.00**

Employee *ID*: **JOHNWHITE-02**
Name: **Jonathan White**

General Tab
Address: **5219 South Grant Line**
City, ST, Zip: **Stockton, CA 95207**
Country: **USA**
Telephone 1: **209-555-9635**
Social Security #: **559-52-4825**
Type: **Hourly**

Dates
Hired: **Jan 28, 2005**
Last Raise:
Terminated:

Withholding Info Tab
Federal Filing Status: **Married** *Allow:* **2** *Additional Withholding:* **0.00**
State Filing Status: **Married** *Allow:* **2** *Additional Withholding:* **0.00**
State: **CA**
Local Filing Status: **Married**

Pay Info
Pay Method: **Hourly—Hours per Pay Period**
Frequency: **Weekly**
Hours per Pay Period: **40.00**
Hourly Billing Rate: **24.00**
Hourly Rate: **14.00**
Overtime: **21.00**

Employee *ID*: **ALCHAVEZ-03**
Name: **Albert Chavez**

General Tab
Address: **425 East Main Street**
City, ST, Zip: **Tracy, CA 95376**
Country: **USA**
Telephone 1: **209-555-5236**
Social Security #: **559-64-8745**
Type: **Salary**

Dates
Hired: **Jan 10, 2005**
Last Raise:
Terminated:

Withholding Info Tab
Federal Filing Status: **Married** *Allow:* **5** *Additional Withholding:* **0.00**
State Filing Status: **Married** *Allow:* **5** *Additional Withholding:* **0.00**
State: **CA**
Local Filing Status: **Married**

Pay Info

Pay Method:	**Salary**
Frequency:	**Weekly**
Hourly Billing Rate:	**50.00**
Salary Rate:	**1,500.00**

4. Print the *Chart of Accounts* and *Employee List*.
5. Close CompNet.

Problem 2B

Open CompNet, which you updated in Problem 1B.

NOTE

Use Account 100, Regular Checking Account as the payroll cash account.

1. Prepare the payroll for all employees as of February 7, 2007. There was no overtime. The first check number is 2200. The check date is February 8, 2007.
2. Prepare the payroll for all employees as of February 14, 2007. Maria Case worked 44 hours this pay period. The check date is February 15, 2007.
3. Print the *Current Earnings* report and *Payroll Register*.

Cooperative Learning

1. Form groups of three or four students, and research the available job market in your area. Determine the factors that are taken into consideration when determining wages and salaries for particular positions.
2. As a group, research jobs that will be in high demand in the future. What skills and training will be required for the jobs of the future? Are you currently acquiring these skills?

Writing and Decision Making

Assume that the owner of the company for which you work, Steve Randolph, is deciding whether to stop outsourcing of payroll and prepare it internally using Peachtree. One of the concerns he has is the time factor that will be required to both initially set up the payroll system, and then prepare the periodic payroll. He also wants to know what are the costs and benefits of using Peachtree to prepare the payroll. Prepare a memo with the information that has been requested.

C H A P T E R

11

JOB COSTING

1. Understand the general concepts of job costing

2. Set up a project for job costing

3. Create phase codes and cost codes and enter estimated revenue and expenses

4. Use the job costing system to record purchases, payroll, and sales

5. Create and print job cost reports

SOFTWARE FEATURES

- Set Up Jobs

- Enter Estimated Expenses and Revenue

- Create Phase Codes and Cost Codes

- Maintain Jobs

- Enter the Costs of Materials and Labor

- Enter Revenue

- Print Job Cost Reports

The work of some manufacturing businesses and service businesses is divided into a series of separate jobs (projects). For example, a printing firm may produce 5,000 catalogs for one customer and 20,000 sales brochures for another customer. A computer-consulting firm may design a Web site for one customer and plan an internal network for another customer.

For businesses such as these, it is important to be able to determine all the costs associated with completing a job. Otherwise, it is difficult to price the job properly and earn a satisfactory profit.

Having detailed information about job costs also helps management to assess the efficiency of the firm's operations. Keeping job costs under control is a necessity if a firm is to be able to offer competitive prices and obtain new business.

OBJECTIVE 1 — UNDERSTAND THE GENERAL CONCEPTS OF JOB COSTING

job costs The costs of the materials, labor, and other items required for completion of a job.

job costing Tracking of all costs associated with a job and totaling those costs at the end of the project.

Job costs are the costs of the materials, labor, and other items required for completion of a particular job. The process of **job costing** involves tracking all costs associated with a project and totaling these costs at the end of the project.

JOB COSTING PROCEDURES

When planning jobs, many businesses break them into a series of phases. Each phase represents a different stage of the project. For example, the first phase of a construction job might be preparing blueprints. The second phase might be excavating the site and putting in the foundation. Often, such jobs are covered by a contract with the customer, and payments are tied to the completion of each phase.

In some cases, however, a job is small and will last for only a short period of time. Therefore, the job is not divided into phases.

If a job does consist of phases, businesses will need to record the costs for each phase. When a phase is completed, the business can bill the customer for any revenue earned.

THE PEACHTREE JOB COSTING SYSTEM

Peachtree allows you to assign a job identifier to each project and track the revenue and expenses of many projects at the same time. For example, Woodward Construction Company usually has several jobs in production simultaneously and must be able to record financial information for each job. In this way, management can evaluate the expenses incurred and the revenue received as each job moves through the production process.

Peachtree supports three methods of job costing:

1. The Jobs Only Method is used for projects that are not divided into phases and do not require cost codes. The jobs that fall into this category are usually small jobs.
2. The Jobs with Phases Method is used for projects that will be completed in phases.
3. The Jobs with Phases and Cost Codes Method is used for projects that are divided into phases and require cost codes.

The method chosen depends on the types of jobs that a business has as well as the amount of information that management wants about each job.

Check POINT

1. What are job costs?
2. What are the three methods of job costing that Peachtree supports?

Answers
1. Job costs are the costs of materials, labor, and other items required for completion of a particular job.
2. The three methods are the Jobs Only Method, the Jobs with Phases Method, and the Jobs with Phases and Cost Codes Method.

OBJECTIVE 2 — SET UP A PROJECT FOR JOB COSTING

Suppose that Smith's Monuments hires Woodward Construction Company to build a fence around its parking area. Woodward estimates that its revenue from this project will be $5,240 and its expenses will be $3,150. Because this is a small project, Woodward will use Peachtree's Jobs Only Method to track the costs of materials and labor and record the revenue. Use the following steps to track the costs of this job.

Step 1:

Open Woodward Construction Company and close the Action Items log.

Step 2:

Click Maintain, click Job Costs, and then click Jobs.

Step 3:

The Maintain Jobs window will appear. Key **Smith Fence-Job 1** in the *Job ID* field. Then click OK.

Step 4:

Key **Smith Fence Job** in the *Description* field.

Step 5:

Click the General folder tab, and key **George Clark** in the *Supervisor* field.

Step 6:

At the *For Customer* field, click the *magnifying glass* icon, and then click *Smith-01*, as shown in figure 11–1.

FIGURE 11-1

Smith-01 Selected from Customer List

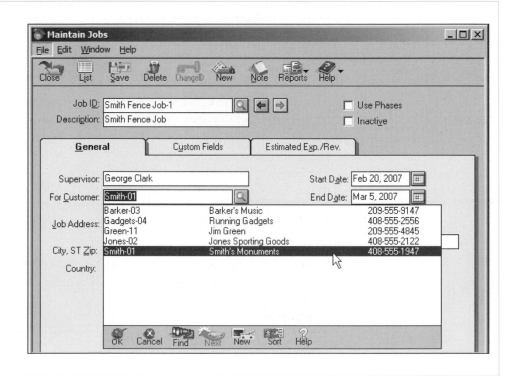

Step 7:

At the *Start Date* field, key **2/20/07**.

Step 8:

At the *End Date* field, key **3/5/07**. (This is the estimated date of completion.)

Step 9:

Key **Fence** in the *Job Type* field.

Step 10:

Key **0** in the *Percent Complete* field, if needed.

Step 11:

Compare your work with figure 11–2. Make any necessary corrections. Then click Save.

FIGURE 11-2

Completed Maintain Jobs Window

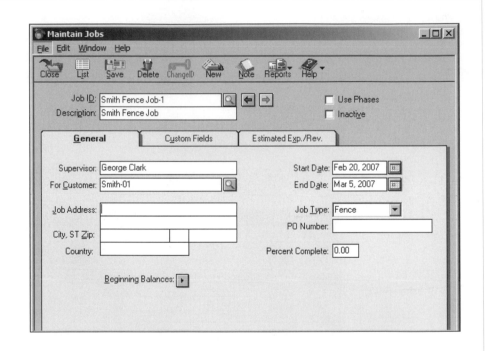

Step 12:

Click the Estimated Exp./Rev. folder tab, as shown in figure 11–3.

FIGURE 11-3

Estimated Exp./Rev. Folder
Tab Selected

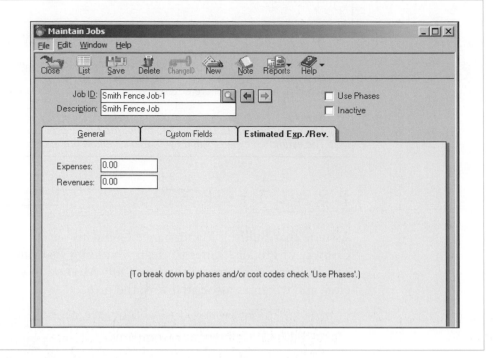

Step 13:

Key **3,150.00** in the *Expenses* field and **5,240.00** in the *Revenues* field, as shown in figure 11–4.

FIGURE 11-4

Entries for Estimated
Expenses and Revenues

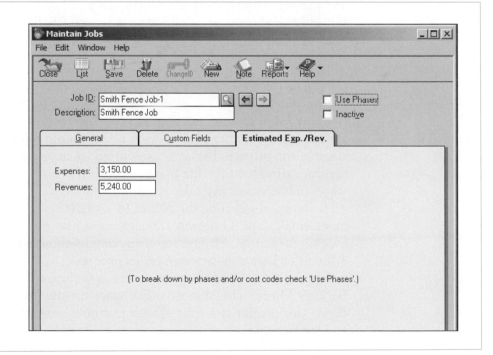

Step 14:

Click <u>S</u>ave and then Close.

PRACTICE *objective* 2

Assume that Bullfrog Maintenance Company accepts a job from Tim Conway of Honda Center to clean a building that suffered some fire damage. Bullfrog wants to use the Jobs Only Method to keep track of the revenue and expenses associated with the project.

Step 1:
Open Bullfrog Maintenance Company.

Step 2:
Set up the project of Honda Center for job costing. The revenue is expected to be $15,000, and the expenses are expected to be $8,900. The job identifier is Honda Fire-Job 1. The estimated starting date is February 10, 2007, and the estimated ending date is February 28, 2007. The job type is Clean Up and the percentage of completion is zero (0). Stanley Smith will supervise the project.

OBJECTIVE 3 — CREATE PHASE CODES AND COST CODES AND ENTER ESTIMATED REVENUE AND EXPENSES

In many cases, it is not possible to track the costs of a job effectively unless the job is divided into phases. Each phase should represent a significant stage of the project. This approach provides management with useful information throughout the life of a project. If there are cost overruns at any stage, management can take action immediately.

However, in planning the phases of a job, it is important not to create too many small steps. Otherwise, management may be overwhelmed with too much information. Having too many details about a job actually makes it difficult to keep a close watch on its progress.

Suppose that Woodward Construction Company accepts a job from Barker's Music to build more office space for the firm. Woodward decides to divide this project into four phases: planning/permits, excavation, building, and landscaping.

The identifier for the job is Barker Office-Job 2. The revenue is expected to be $500,000, and the expenses are expected to be $225,000. The estimated starting date is February 15, 2007, and the estimated ending date is December 30, 2007.

The first task for Woodward is to set up the project for job costing. Then it must create phase codes and cost codes. Finally, Woodward must enter the estimated revenue and expenses for each phase of the job.

SETTING UP A PROJECT FOR JOB COSTING

Follow the steps outlined below to set up the project to build new office space for Barker's Music in the job costing system of the Woodward Construction Company.

Step 1:
Open Woodward Construction Company and close the Action Items log.

Step 2:
Click <u>M</u>aintain, click <u>J</u>ob Costs, and then click <u>J</u>obs.

Step 3:
Key **Barker Office-Job 2** in the *Job ID* field. Then click OK.

Step 4:
Key **Barker Office Job** in the *Description* field.

Step 5:
Click the <u>G</u>eneral folder tab, and key **George Clark** in the *Supervisor* field.

Step 6:
At the *For <u>C</u>ustomer* field, click the *magnifying glass* icon, and then click *Barker-03*.

Step 7:
At the *Start D<u>a</u>te* field, click the *calendar* icon and select *Feb 15, 2007*.

Step 8:
At the *End D<u>a</u>te* field, click the *calendar* icon and select *Dec 30, 2007*.

Step 9:
Check the box next to *Use Phases*, as shown in figure 11–5.

FIGURE 11-5

Maintain Jobs Window with Use Phases Selected

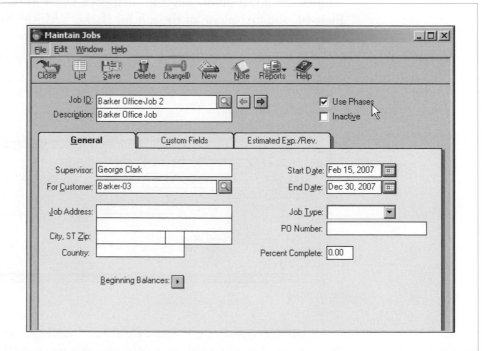

Step 10:

Key **Const** in the *Job Type* field.

Step 11:

Key **0** in the *Percent Complete* field, if needed.

Step 12:

Click <u>S</u>ave and then Close.

CREATING THE PHASE CODES FOR A JOB

The next task for Woodward Construction Company is to establish the phases and phase codes for the job that it will do for Barker's Music.

Step 1:

Click <u>M</u>aintain, click <u>J</u>ob Costs, and then click <u>P</u>hases.

Step 2:

The Maintain Phases window will appear. Key **Plan-01** in the *Phase I<u>D</u>* field. Then click OK.

Step 3:

Key **Planning and Permits** in the *Description* field.

Step 4:

Under the <u>G</u>eneral folder tab, there is a *Cost Type* field. Peachtree supports five different cost types:

- Labor
- Materials
- Equipment
- Subcontractors
- Other

Click the down-arrow key and then click *Other* as the cost type shown for Plan-01, the first phase of the job for Barker's Music. See figure 11–6.

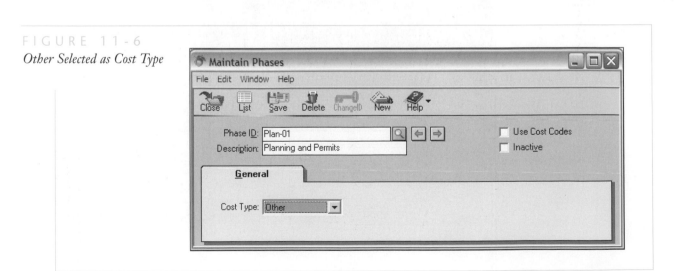

FIGURE 11-6

Other Selected as Cost Type

Step 5:

Click Save.

Step 6:

Create the following additional phases for the job for Barker's Music. (The building phase will be established in the next section.)

Phase ID	Description	Cost Type
Excav–02	Excavation	Subcontractors
Lands–04	Landscaping	Subcontractors

Step 7:

Review your work, make any necessary corrections, then save each entry. Then click Save and then Close.

CREATING THE COST CODES FOR A JOB

The cost codes provide additional information for management. These codes help management to track several cost areas for any phase of a job. For example, in the building phase of the project that Woodward Construction Company is doing for Barker's Music, management wants to track the cost of materials and the cost of labor. Follow the steps outlined below to create the necessary cost codes.

Step 1:

Click Maintain, click Job Costs, and then click Phases.

Step 2:

Key **Build–03** in the *Phase ID* field. Then click OK.

Step 3:

Key **Building** in the *Description* field.

Step 4:

Check the box next to *Use Cost Codes*, as shown in figure 11–7.

FIGURE 11-7

Use Cost Codes Selected

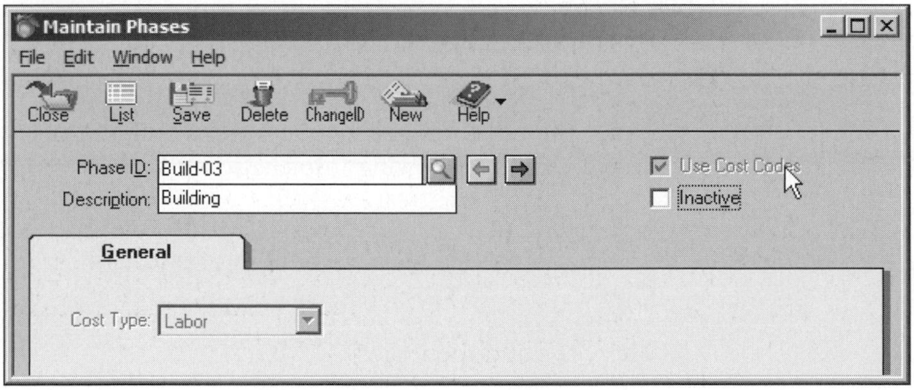

Step 5:

Click Save and then Close.

Step 6:

Click <u>M</u>aintain, click <u>J</u>ob Costs, and then click <u>C</u>ost Codes.

Woodward Construction Company will use Buildlab-10 as the identifier for the labor costs in the building phase and Buildmat-11 as the identifier for the materials costs.

Step 7:

At the Maintain Cost Codes window, key **Buildlab-10** in the *Cost I<u>D</u>* field. Then click OK.

Step 8:

Key **Building Labor** in the *Description* field.

Step 9:

Click the down-arrow at the *Cost Type* field, and then click *Labor* as shown in figure 11–8, if needed.

FIGURE 11-8

Completed Maintain Cost Codes Window

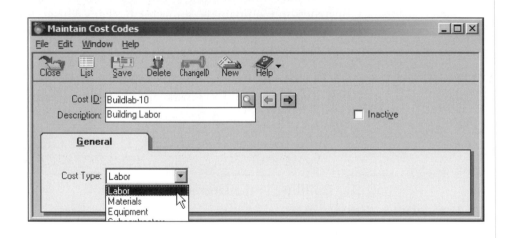

Step 10:

Click <u>S</u>ave.

Step 11:

Create the remaining cost code for the building phase of the job for Barker's Music. Use the following information:

Cost ID	Description	Cost Type
Buildmat-11	Building Materials	Materials

Step 12:

Click <u>S</u>ave and then Close.

ENTERING ESTIMATED REVENUE AND EXPENSES

Peachtree allows you to enter the estimated expenses and revenue for a project into the job costing system. For example, Woodward Construction Company will enter expense and revenue amounts for each phase of the project that it is doing for Barker's Music.

Step 1:

Click Maintain, click Job Costs, and then click Jobs.

Step 2:

The Maintain Jobs window will appear. At the *Job ID* field, click the *magnifying glass* icon, and then click *Barker Office-Job 2*.

Step 3:

Click the Estimated Exp./Rev. folder tab.

Step 4:

Click in the *Phase ID* field, click the *magnifying glass* icon, and then click *Plan-01*, as shown in figure 11–9.

FIGURE 11-9

Plan-01 Selected in Phase ID Field

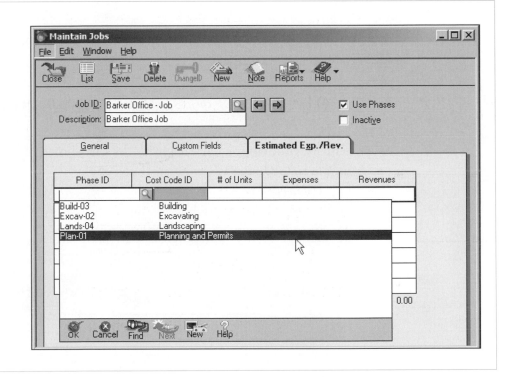

Step 5:

Key **5,000.00** in the *Expenses* field and **12,000.00** in the *Revenues* field.

Step 6:

In the second row of the *Phase ID* field, click the *magnifying glass* icon, and then click *Excav-02*.

Step 7:

Key **30,000.00** in the *Expenses* field and **55,000.00** in the *Revenues* field.

Step 8:

In the third row of the *Phase ID* field, click the *magnifying glass* icon, and then click *Lands-04*.

Step 9:

Key **20,000.00** in the *Expenses* field and **40,000.00** in the *Revenues* field.

HINT

The *Cost Code ID* field is disabled because these phases do not use cost codes.

Step 10:

In the fourth row of the *Phase ID* field, click the *magnifying glass* icon, and then click *Build-03*. Notice that the *Cost Code ID* field is now enabled.

Step 11:

At the *Cost Code ID* field, click the *magnifying glass* icon, and then click *Buildlab-10*.

Step 12:

Key **100,000.00** in the *Expenses* field and **203,000.00** in the *Revenues* field.

Step 13:

In the fifth row of the *Phase ID* field, click the *magnifying glass* icon and then click *Build-03*.

Step 14:

At the *Cost Code ID* field, click the *magnifying glass* icon, and then click *Buildmat-11*.

Step 15:

Key **70,000.00** in the *Expenses* field and **190,000.00** in the *Revenues* field.

Step 16:

Compare your completed entry with the one shown in figure 11–10. Make any necessary changes.

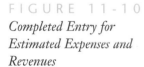

FIGURE 11-10

Completed Entry for Estimated Expenses and Revenues

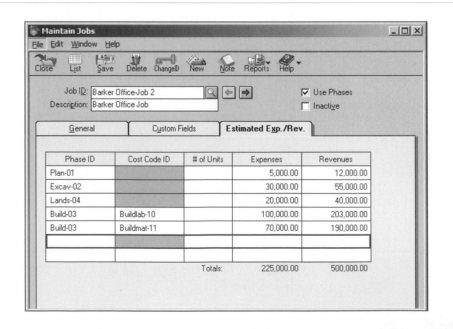

Step 17:

Click Save and then Close.

Step 18:

Close Woodward Construction Company.

Check
POINT

1. What are the five cost types supported by Peachtree?
2. What is the purpose of the cost codes?

Answers
1. The five cost types are Labor, Materials, Equipment, Subcontractors, and Other.
2. The cost codes help management to track several cost areas for any phase of a job.

PRACTICE *objective* 3

Assume that Bullfrog Maintenance Company accepts a job from Valley Mercedes to develop a maintenance system that can be used at five other Mercedes dealerships throughout the area.

Step 1:
Open Bullfrog Maintenance Company.

Step 2:
Set up the project of Valley Mercedes for job costing. The job identifier is Valley System-Job 2, the description is Mercedes Maintenance Job, and the job type is *Maint* (for Maintenance). The estimated starting date is February 20, 2007, and the estimated ending date is April 30, 2007. Stanley Smith will supervise the project.

Bullfrog estimates that this project will generate revenue of $45,500 and have expenses of $22,000. Bullfrog wants to track the costs of the project by using the following three phases: Planning, Implementation, and Feedback.

Step 3:
Create the following phases for the project:

Phase ID	Description	Cost Type
Plan-01	Planning	Other
Feed-03	Feedback	Subcontractors
Impl-02	Implementation	Use cost codes (shown below)

Step 4:
Create the following cost codes for the implementation phase (Impl-02):

Cost ID	Description	Cost Type
Implmat-11	Implementation Materials	Materials
Impllab-10	Implementation Labor	Labor

Step 5:
Enter the estimated revenue and expenses for each phase of the project:

Phase	Expenses	Revenue
Planning	$ 2,000	$ 4,000
Feedback	2,500	5,000
Implementation Labor	8,000	25,000
Implementation Materials	9,500	11,500
Totals	$22,000	$45,500

HINT

Use Maintain, Job Costs, Jobs.

Compare your work with the Maintain Jobs window shown in figure 11–11. Make any necessary changes. Notice the totals at the bottom of your screen.

FIGURE 11-11

Completed Maintain Jobs Window

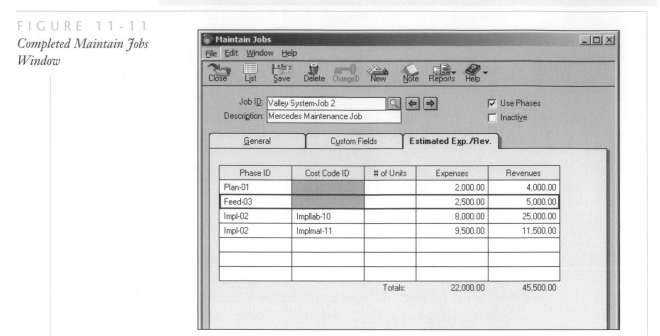

Step 7:
Click Save and Close.

OBJECTIVE 4 — USE THE JOB COSTING SYSTEM TO RECORD PURCHASES, PAYROLL, AND SALES

The Peachtree job costing system allows you to record the actual expenses incurred and the actual revenue received as a project moves through production. Remember that the estimated expenses and revenue are entered at the beginning of the project. Management is therefore able to compare estimated and actual amounts for every phase of the project.

Labor costs can easily be allocated to jobs if employees keep track of the hours that they spend on each job. Similarly, the costs of materials and other items purchased specifically for jobs can easily be allocated. However, it is more difficult to allocate the costs of materials and other items that are purchased for the firm's inventory and later used for jobs.

RECORDING THE COST OF PURCHASES

Suppose that Woodward Construction Company receives Invoice 1009 from the BMC Supply Company on February 21, 2007. This invoice is for 5,000 feet of lumber to be used in the fence being built for Smith's Monuments and 500 gallons of white paint to be placed in the firm's inventory. The price of the lumber is $0.50 per foot and the price of the paint is $2 per gallon.

The cost of the lumber, which will be used only for the Smith job, is immediately charged to that job. However, the cost of the paint is charged to inventory. Later, when some of the paint is used for the Smith job, the cost of that paint will be allocated to the job.

Step 1:

Open Woodward Construction Company and close the Action Items log.

Step 2:

Click Tasks and then click Purchases/Receive Inventory.

Step 3:

At the Purchases/Receive Inventory window, in the *Vendor ID* field, click the *magnifying glass* icon, and then click *BMC-07*.

Step 4:

At the *Date* field, click the *calendar* icon and select *Feb 21, 2007*.

Step 5:

Key **1009** in the *Invoice No.* field.

Step 6:

Key **5,000.00** in the *Quantity* field.

Step 7:

At the *Item* field, click the *magnifying glass* icon, and then click *New* at the bottom of the drop-down list.

Step 8:

Create the following inventory items. Click Save after each item is entered.

Non-stock Item (purchased for a job)

Item ID:	**BOARD-4**
Description:	**Lumber**
Item Class:	**Non-stock item**
Full Price:	**1.50**
Last Unit Cost:	**0.50**
Stocking U/M:	**Foot**
GL Sales Acct:	**400.5**
GL Salary/Wages Acct:	**512**
GL Cost of Sales Acct:	**503**
Item Tax Type:	**2 (Exempt)**
Preferred VendorID:	**BMC-07**

Stock Item (purchased for inventory)

Item ID:	**PAINTWH-5**
Description:	**White Paint**
Item Class:	**Stock item**
Full Price:	**3.50**
Last Unit Cost:	**2.00**
Cost Method:	**FIFO**
Stocking U/M:	**Gallon**
GL Sales Acct:	**400.5**
GL Inventory Acct:	**105**

GL Cost of Sales Acct:	503
Item Tax Type:	2 (Exempt)
Preferred Vendor ID:	BMC-07

Step 9:

Click Close to return to the Purchases/Receive Inventory window.

Step 10:

At the *Item* field of the Purchases/Receive Inventory window, click the *magnifying glass* icon, and then click *BOARD-4*.

Step 11:

At the *GL Account* field, click *105*.

Step 12:

Key **0.50** in the *Unit Price* field.

Step 13:

At the *Job* field at the bottom right of the screen, click the folder icon, click *Smith Fence-Job 1*, as shown in figure 11–12.

FIGURE 11-12

Smith Fence-Job 1 Selected from Drop-Down List

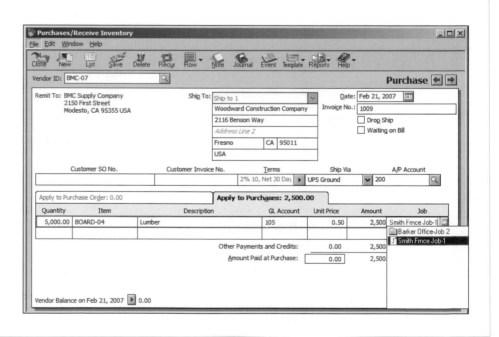

Step 14:

Key **500.00** on the second row in the *Quantity* field.

Step 15:

At the *Item* field, click the *magnifying glass* icon, and then click *PAINTWH-5*. Compare your entries with those shown in figure 11–13.

FIGURE 11-13

Completed Purchases/Receive Inventory

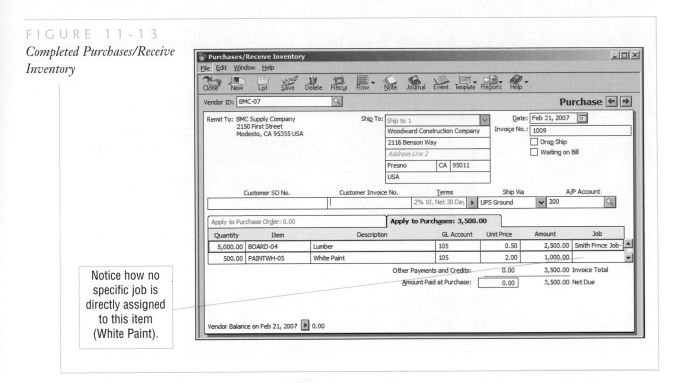

Notice how no specific job is directly assigned to this item (White Paint).

Step 16:
Click Save and then Close.

ALLOCATING THE COST OF INVENTORY ITEMS TO JOBS

Assume that Woodward Construction Company withdraws 40 gallons of white paint from its inventory on February 23, 2007. This paint will be used for the fence that Woodward is building for Smith's Monuments. Because the purchase of the paint was originally charged to Inventory, Woodward must now allocate the cost of the 40 gallons to the Smith job. Like the lumber used in the fence, this paint is part of the materials for the job.

Step 1:
Click Ta*sks*, and then click I*n*ventory Adjustments.

Step 2:
At the *Item ID* field, click the *magnifying glass* icon, and then click *PAINTWH-5*.

Step 3:
Key **2/23/07** in the *Date* field.

Step 4:
At the *Job* field, click the folder icon, and then click *Smith Fence-Job 1.*

Step 5:
At the *GL Source Acct* field, key **105**.

Step 6:
Key **–40.00** in the *Adjust Quantity By* field. (Be sure to key this amount as a negative number.)

Step 7:

Key **Used for Smith Fence Job** in the *Reason to Adjust* field. Compare your completed entries with those shown in figure 11–14.

FIGURE 11-14

Completed Inventory Adjustments Window

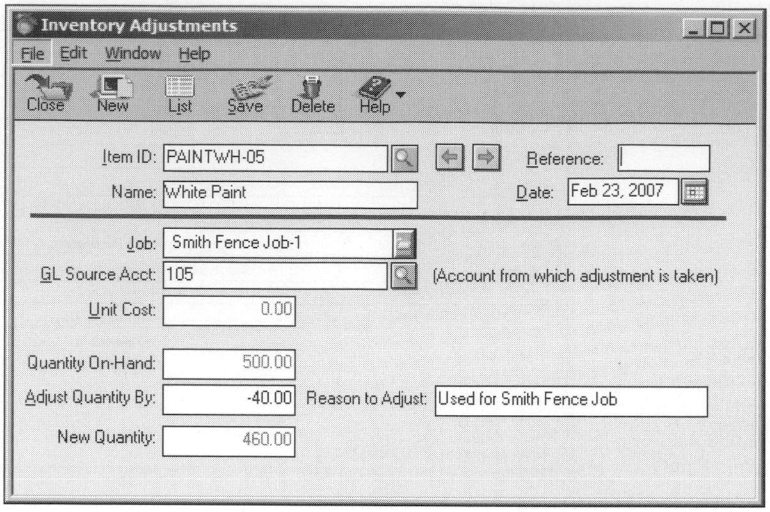

Step 8:

Click Save and then Close.

ALLOCATING LABOR COSTS TO JOBS

On February 28, 2007, Woodward Construction Company records the labor costs related to the job it is doing for Smith's Monuments. These labor costs consist of one week of salary for George Clark ($1,000) and 40 hours of wages for Samuel Jones at $15 per hour ($15 × 40 = $600).

Step 1:

Click Tasks and then click Payroll Entry.

Step 2:

The Payroll Entry window will appear. At the *Employee ID* field, click the *magnifying glass* icon, and then click *GEOCLARK-03*.

Step 3:

At the *Date* field, click the *calendar* icon and select *Feb 28, 2007*.

Step 4:

At the *Pay Period Ends* field, click the *calendar* icon and select *Feb 28, 2007*.

Step 5:

Click the Jobs button at the top of the Payroll Entry toolbar. A dialog box called Labor Distribution to Jobs will appear, as shown in figure 11–15.

FIGURE 11-15
Labor Distribution to Jobs Dialog Box

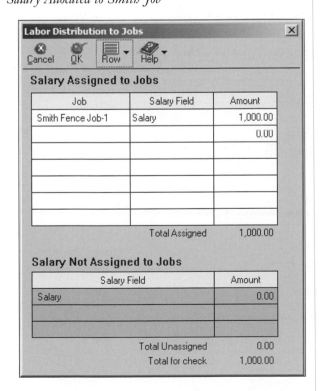

FIGURE 11-16
Salary Allocated to Smith Job

Step 6:
Click the Row button and then the Add button from the menu at the top of the Labor Distribution to Jobs dialog box. A new row will then appear.

Step 7:
Click the *Job* field on the newly created top row, then click the *folder* icon.

Step 8:
Select *Smith Fence-Job 1* by clicking.

Step 9:
Key **1,000.00** in the *Amount* field on the newly created row, then press Enter. Notice that *1,000.00* appears on that row only, as shown in figure 11–16. All of George Clark's salary has now been allocated to the Smith job.

Step 10:
Click OK to save, and then Save.

Step 11:
At the *Employee ID* field, click the *magnifying glass* icon, and then click *SAMJONES-04*.

Step 12:
At the *Date* field, click the *calendar* icon and then select *Feb 28, 2007*, if needed.

Step 13:
At the *Pay Period Ends* field, click the *calendar* icon and select *Feb 28, 2007*, if needed.

Step 14:
Click the Jobs button at the top of the Payroll Entry toolbar. The Labor Distribution to Jobs dialog box will appear.

Step 15:
Click the Row button and the Add button at the top of the Labor Distri-bution to Jobs dialog box. A new row will then appear.

Step 16:
Click the *Job* field on the newly created row, then click the *folder* icon.

Step 17:
Click *Smith Fence-Job 1*.

Step 18:
Key **40.00** in the *Hours* field in the newly created row, then press Enter. Note that the total amount of *$600.00* is automatically entered ($15 per hour × 40 hours).

Click OK.

At the Payroll Entry window, click Save and then Close.

RECORDING THE REVENUE RECEIVED FROM JOBS

Suppose that Woodward Construction Company completes the fence that it is building for Smith's Monuments on February 28, 2007. Woodward receives a check for $5,240 from Smith.

The effect of this transaction is to increase the revenue earned from construction services (Sales Revenue) and to increase the asset Cash. Therefore, Woodward must debit Cash and credit Service Revenue. You make this entry using the Receipts function of Peachtree. Because the transaction involves revenue for a job, you also use Peachtree to record the amount received in the job costing system.

Click Tasks and then click Receipts.

At the Receipts window, key **02/28/07** in the *Deposit Ticket ID* field.

At the *Customer ID* field, click the *magnifying glass* icon, and then click *Smith-01*.

Key **Fence Job** in the *Reference* field.

At the *Date* field, click the *calendar* icon and select *Feb 28, 2007*.

Select Check from the Payment Method drop-down list, if needed.

Click the Apply to Revenues folder tab.

Key **Fence Job** in the *Description* field.

At the *GL Account* field, key **400.5**. Then click OK.

Key **5,240.00** in the *Amount* field.

At the *Job* field, click the *folder* icon, and then click *Smith Fence-Job 1*, as shown in figure 11–17.

HINT

If the *GL Account* field does not display on the Apply to Revenues tab, click Options on the Main Menu toolbar, and then click Global. The Maintain Global Options dialog box will appear. Deselect the box that is checked next to "Accounts Receivable (Quotes, Sales Orders, Sales/Invoicing, Credit Memos, Receipts)," then click Ok. Close and then reopen the Receipts window.

FIGURE 11-17
Smith Fence-Job 1 Selected

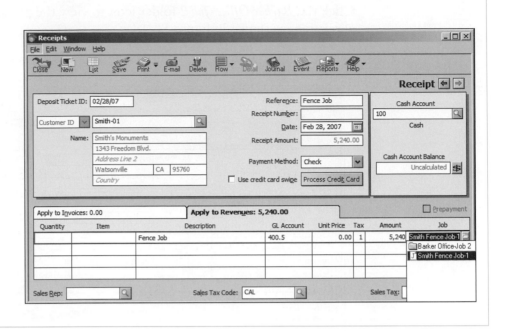

Step 12:

Click Save and then Close.

TRACKING COSTS AND REVENUE FOR JOB PHASES

The job that Woodward Construction Company did for Smith's Monuments was a simple one. However, the job for Barker's Music is more complex and was therefore divided into four phases: planning/permits, excavation, building, and landscaping. The building phase was further divided by assigning cost codes for materials and labor.

One of the advantages of the Peachtree job costing system is that you can use it to track costs and revenue for each phase of a project as the project moves through production. The phase codes and cost codes make this possible.

Suppose that Woodward Construction Company wants to access the phase codes and cost codes for the Barker job. We will use the Purchases function to accomplish this task, but it is also possible to use the Payroll and Sales functions.

Step 1:

Click Tasks, and then click Purchases/Receive Inventory.

Step 2:

At the Purchases/Receive Inventory window, click in the *Job* field, and then click the *folder* icon.

Step 3:

Click the *Barker Office-Job 2* folder icon to view the phases available for cost allocation, as shown in figure 11–18.

FIGURE 11-18
Phases Available for Barker Office Job

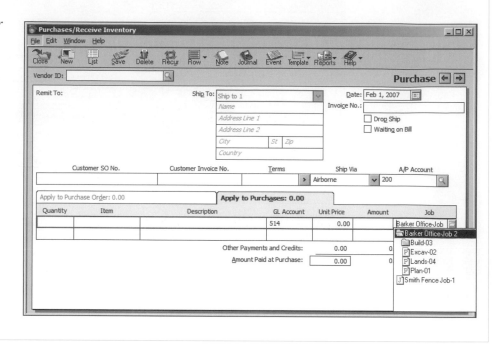

Step 4:

Click the *Build-03* folder icon to reveal the cost codes for the building phase of the Barker job, as shown in figure 11–19.

FIGURE 11-19
Cost Codes Available for Barker Office Job

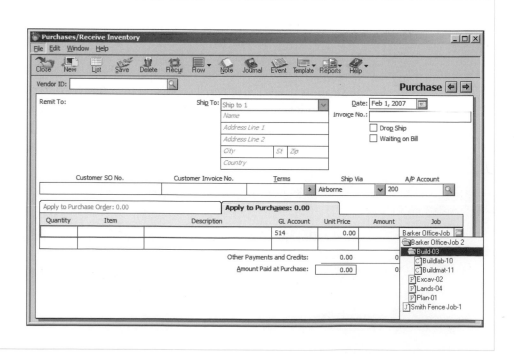

Step 5:

Do *not* click Save. Click Close to exit the Purchases/Receive Inventory window.

Check
POINT

1. When inventory items are used for a job, what happens to the cost of those items?
2. Why must employees keep track of the hours they spend on each job?

Answers
1. The cost of inventory items that are used for a job must be allocated to the job.
2. Keeping track of the hours spent on each job makes it possible to allocate labor costs.

PRACTICE *objective* 4

On February 12, 2007, Bullfrog Maintenance Company began the cleanup job for Honda Center. It purchased 1,400 gallons of a floor care product on credit from Lou's Janitorial Supply Company at a cost of $4.56 per gallon (Invoice 596781). This product will be used only for the Honda Center job. In addition, Bullfrog will use 20 gallons of carpet shampoo, CPTSHAM-1. The carpet shampoo will be taken from Bullfrog's inventory.

On February 21, 2007, Bullfrog completed the job for Honda Center and recorded the following labor costs: one week's salary for Stanley Smith and 40 hours of wages for James Stewart. On February 28, 2007, Bullfrog received $15,000 from Honda Center for the job.

Step 1:

Open Bullfrog Maintenance Company.

Step 2:

Create the following inventory item:

Item I<u>D</u>:	**FLOCARE-4**
Description:	**Floor Care Product**
Item Class:	**Non-stock item**
Full Price:	**9.50**
<u>L</u>ast Unit Cost:	**4.56**
Stocking U/M:	**Gallon**
GL Sales Acc<u>t</u>:	**400.5**
GL Salary/Wages Acc<u>t</u>:	**512**
GL Cost of Sales Acc<u>t</u>:	**503**
Item Ta<u>x</u> Type:	**2 (Exempt)**
Preferred <u>V</u>endor ID:	**LOU-07**

Step 3:

Enter the purchase of the floor care product. Key **105** at the *GL Account* field and **4.56** at the *Unit Price* field. Compare your entries with figure 11–20.

FIGURE 11-20

Completed Purchases/Receive Inventory

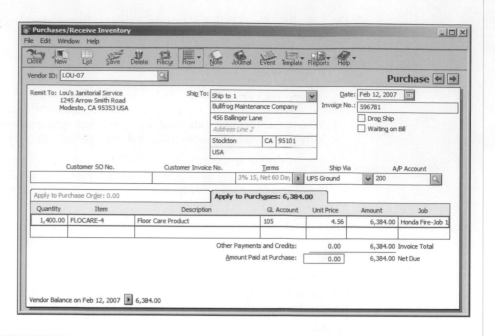

Make the necessary inventory adjustment for the carpet shampoo and allo-cate its cost to the Honda Center job. Compare your Inventory Adjustments window with figure 11–21.

FIGURE 11-21

Completed Inventory Adjustments Window

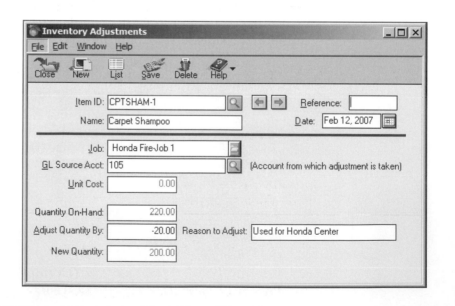

Step 5:

Allocate the labor costs to the Honda Center job.

Step 6:

Enter the service revenue received from the Honda Center job, Reference 66362.

Step 7:

Close the active window.

OBJECTIVE 5 — CREATE AND PRINT JOB COST REPORTS

The Peachtree job costing system produces many reports. Management can use the information in these reports to review estimated expenses and revenue for jobs, compare these amounts to the actual expenses and revenue, monitor profitability, and keep track of the progress of each job. Among the reports available from the Peachtree job costing system are the following:

- *Cost Code List*
- *Estimated Job Expenses*
- *Estimated Job Revenue*
- *Job Costs by Type*
- *Job Estimates*
- *Job Ledger*
- *Job List*
- *Job Master File List*
- *Job Profitability Report*
- *Job Register*
- *Phase List*
- *Unbilled Job Expense*

PREPARING THE JOB PROFITABILITY REPORT

Suppose that Woodward Construction Company wants to create the *Job Profitability* Report for the month of February 2007. This report will show the actual expenses, revenue, and profit for the job that Woodward completed for Smith's Monuments—building a fence around a parking area.

Step 1:

Open Woodward Construction Company and close the Action Item Log, if still open.

Step 2:

Click Reports, and then click Jobs.

Step 3:

The Select a Report dialog box will appear. Click *Job Profitability Report* from the Report List section.

Step 4:

Click Preview on the Select a Report toolbar.

Step 5:

In the *Time Frame* field, click *Range*. In the *From* field, select *Feb 1, 2007*, and in the *To* field, select *Feb 28, 2007*.

Step 6:

Click OK in the Job Profitability Report Filter window.

Step 7:

Review the *Job Profitability Report* and compare it to the one shown in figure 11–22.

FIGURE 11-22

Job Profitability Report

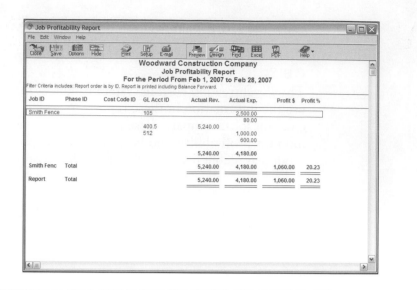

Step 8:

Click Close.

PREPARING THE ESTIMATED JOB EXPENSES REPORT

Suppose that the Woodward Construction Company now wants to create the *Estimated Job Expenses* report for the month of February 2005. This report will show the estimated expenses for current and completed jobs.

Step 1:

Click <u>R</u>eports, and then click <u>J</u>obs.

Step 2:

At the Select a Report dialog box, click *Estimated Job Expenses* from the Report Lis<u>t</u> section.

Step 3:

Click Pre<u>v</u>iew on the Select a Report toolbar.

Step 4:

In the <u>D</u>ate field, click *Exact Date*, and in the *As of* field, select *Feb 28, 2007*.

Step 5:

Click <u>O</u>K in the Estimated Job Expenses window.

Step 6:

Review the *Estimated Job Expenses* report and compare it to the partial report shown in figure 11–23.

FIGURE 11-23
Partial Estimated Job Expenses Report

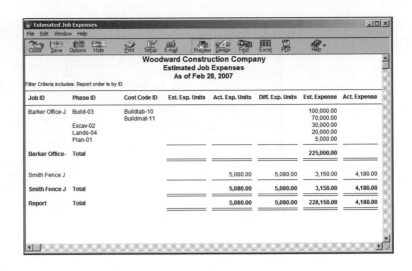

Step 7:
Click Close.

POINT

1. Name two reports available from the Peachtree job costing system.
2. What information about a job is shown in the *Job Profitability* report?

Answers
1. Answers will vary.
2. This report shows the actual expenses, revenue, and profit for a job.

PRACTICE *objective* **5**

Bullfrog Maintenance Company wants to prepare several job cost reports for the month of February 2007.

Step 1:
Open Bullfrog Maintenance Company.

Step 2:
Prepare and print the *Job Profitability* report and *Estimated Job Expenses* report. Your printouts should look like figures 11–24 and 11–25, respectively.

FIGURE 11-24

Job Profitability Report – Bullfrog Maintenance Company

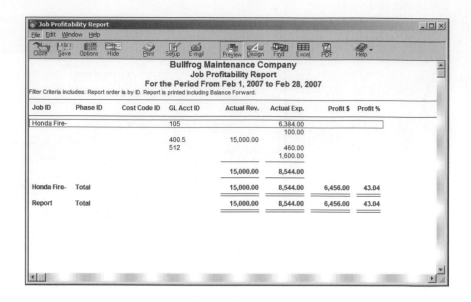

FIGURE 11-25

Partial Estimated Job Expenses Report – Bullfrog Maintenance Company

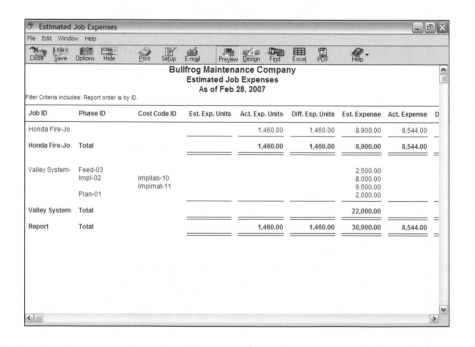

Job costing is generally considered part of *management accounting* or *managerial accounting*. This area of accounting provides information that the managers of a business use for planning, control, and decision-making. Accountants who are involved in this area are known as *management accountants*. Many such accountants belong to a professional organization called the Institute of Management Accountants (IMA). The Institute of Management Accountants' Web site is at http://www.imanet.org (figure 11–26).

FIGURE 11-26
Institute of Management Accountants Web Home Page

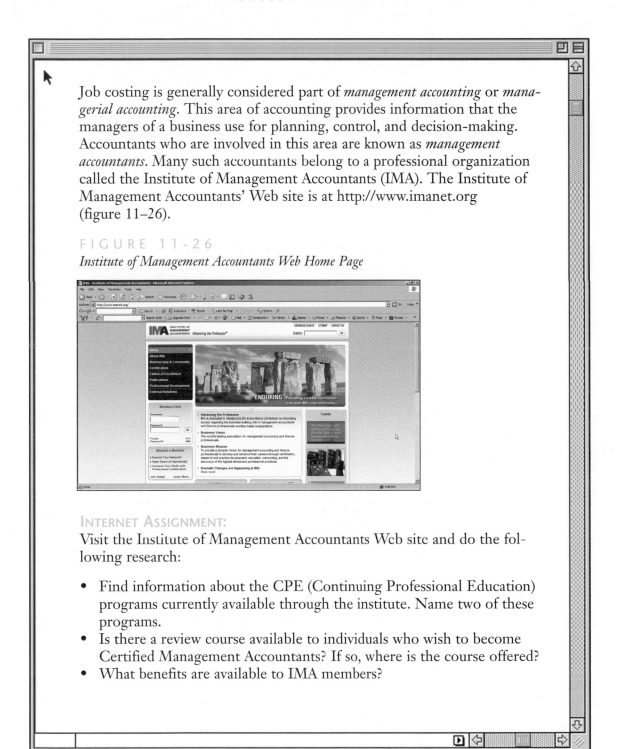

INTERNET ASSIGNMENT:

Visit the Institute of Management Accountants Web site and do the following research:

- Find information about the CPE (Continuing Professional Education) programs currently available through the institute. Name two of these programs.
- Is there a review course available to individuals who wish to become Certified Management Accountants? If so, where is the course offered?
- What benefits are available to IMA members?

SOFTWARE
Command Summary

Set up a Job for Costing	<u>M</u>aintain, <u>J</u>ob Costs, <u>J</u>obs, and enter job information
Estimated Expenses and Revenue	Same as Set up a Job for Costing, then click Estimated Ex<u>p</u>./Rev. folder tab and enter data
Create Phase Codes	<u>M</u>aintain, <u>J</u>ob Costs, <u>P</u>hases, enter information, select the cost type
Create Cost Codes	<u>M</u>aintain, <u>J</u>ob Costs, <u>C</u>ost Codes, enter information, select the cost type
Enter Purchases	Tas<u>k</u>s, Pur<u>c</u>hases/Receive Inventory, Job, select a job, a phase, and a cost code
Allocate the Cost of Inventory Items to Jobs	Tas<u>k</u>s, <u>I</u>nventory Adjustments, Item ID, <u>A</u>djust Quantity By
Allocate the Cost of Labor to Jobs	Tas<u>k</u>s, Payroll <u>E</u>ntry, Employee ID, <u>J</u>obs, Add, select a job, a phase, and a cost code, enter the salary/hourly information
Enter the Revenue from Jobs	Tas<u>k</u>s, <u>S</u>ales/Invoicing, Job, select a job, a phase, and a cost code
Print Job Cost Reports	<u>R</u>eports, <u>J</u>obs, select a report from the report list, <u>P</u>rint

PROJECTS
and Problems

CONTENT CHECK

Multiple Choice: Choose only one response for each question.

1. Which of the following methods for tracking job costs does Peachtree support?

   A. Jobs Only
   B. Jobs with Phases
   C. Jobs with Phases and Cost Codes
   D. All of the above.

2. When managers want maximum detail in their cost reports, they
   should use
   A. Phases.
   B. Cost Types.
   C. Cost Codes.
   D. All of the above.

3. What are job costs?
   A. The costs incurred in operating a business.
   B. The revenue and expenses connected with inventory adjustments.
   C. The materials, labor, and other items required to complete a job.
   D. None of the above.

4. The Peachtree job costing system tracks
   A. the estimated revenue and expenses for each job.
   B. the actual revenue and expenses for each job.
   C. the profit for each job.
   D. All of the above.

5. Which of the following job cost reports would management consult to
   see how much money the business made from a completed job?
   A. *Estimated Job Expenses* report
   B. *Job Profitability Report*
   C. *Estimated Job Revenue* report
   D. *Job Register*

Short-Essay Response: Provide a detailed answer for each question.

1. What is the purpose of job costing? Why would the information from a
   job costing system help managers to make decisions?
2. Peachtree supports several levels of detail for job costing. Name two
   situations in which it would be helpful for management to have cost
   information for the various phases of a job.
3. Suppose a construction company will complete a job over several
   months. What factors would management consider when deciding
   whether to divide this job into phases?
4. Why is the *Job Profitability* report helpful to a user of Peachtree?
5. What are the steps necessary to set up a project for job costing?
6. List and explain the five different cost types used in Peachtree.

CASE PROBLEMS

PROBLEM 1A

Robertson Construction Company accepted a job from Jerome Parks of the
Parkview Apartments to repair an apartment that had been damaged by
renters. Robertson wants to use the Jobs Only Method to keep track of the
revenue and expenses associated with the project. The revenue is expected
to be $50,000, and the expenses are expected to be $30,000. The job identifier is Park Repair-Job 1. The estimated starting date is January 10, 2007,
and the estimated ending date is January 30, 2007. The percentage of completion is zero (0). Barbara Williams will supervise the project.

1. Open Robertson Construction, which you downloaded from the CD that comes with this book.
2. Create a customer account for Parkview Apartments.

Customer ID:	**Park-99**
Name:	**Parkview Apartments**

General Tab

Contact:	**Jerome Parks**
Bill to:	
Address:	**3455 Mission Street**
City, ST, Zip:	**Modesto, CA 95355**
Country:	**USA**
Sales Tax:	**CAL**
Customer Type:	**Building**
Telephone 1:	**209-555-1234**
Telephone 2:	
Fax:	
E-mail:	
Beginning Balance:	**0**

Sales Defaults Tab

GL Sales Account:	**400**

3. Set up the project for job costing.
4. On January 10, 2007, Robertson Construction Company purchased the following non-stock items to be used exclusively in the job for the Parkview Apartments: 1,000 feet of lumber at $1.50 per foot and one sink for $250. Robertson also purchased 2,400 feet of vinyl flooring at $4.50 per foot for its inventory. All items were purchased on credit from Steve's Supply Warehouse (Invoice 1220). Use the following information to create inventory records for the items.

Non-stock Item

Item ID:	**BOARD-5**
Description:	**Lumber**
Item Class:	**Non-stock item**
Full Price:	**2.50**
Last Unit Cost:	**1.50**
Stocking U/M:	**Foot**
GL Sales Acct:	**400**
GL Salary/Wages Acct:	**512**
GL Cost of Sales Acct:	**503**
Item Tax Type:	**2 (Exempt)**
Preferred Vendor ID:	**STEVES-01**

Non-stock Item

Item ID:	**SINK-12**
Description:	**Sink**
Item Class:	**Non-stock item**

Full Price:	425.00
Last Unit Cost:	250.00
Stocking U/M:	Each
GL Sales Acct:	400
GL Salary/Wages Acct:	512
GL Cost of Sales Acct:	503
Item Tax Type:	2 (Exempt)
Preferred Vendor ID:	STEVES-01

Stock Item

Item ID:	VFLOOR-15
Description:	Vinyl Flooring
Item Class:	Stock item
Full Price:	7.50
Last Unit Cost:	4.50
Cost Method:	Average
Stocking U/M:	Foot
GL Sales Acct:	400
GL Inventory Acct:	105
GL Cost of Sales Acct:	503
Item Tax Type:	2 (Exempt)
Preferred Vendor ID:	STEVES-01

> **HINT**
>
> Remember to change the *GL Account* field to *105* when entering purchases for non-stock items.

5. Enter the purchases.
6. Robertson used 500 feet of vinyl flooring for the Parkview job. Allocate the cost of this flooring to the job, January 15, 2007.
7. Barbara Williams worked 40 hours on the Parkview job, and Michael Anderson worked 40 hours. Allocate these employees' labor costs ending January 21, 2007 to the job. The check date is January 22, 2007.
8. Print the following reports for the month of January 2007: *Job Ledger* and *Estimated Job Expenses*.

PROBLEM 2A

Robertson Construction Company accepted a job from Palmdale Offices to build a new office building. The estimated starting date is February 1, 2007, and the estimated ending date is March 1, 2007. Michael Anderson will supervise the project. The job identifier is Palm Office-Job 2. The percentage complete is zero.

Robertson has decided to create phases and cost codes to better track the revenue and expenses associated with this project. It has decided on the following phases and cost types.

Phases:

Phase ID	Description	Cost Type
Plan-01	Planning	Other
Land-03	Landscaping	Labor
Building-02	Building	Use cost codes on next page

Use the cost codes shown below.

Cost Codes:

Cost ID	Description	Cost Type
BUILDMAT-111	Building Materials	Materials
BUILDLAB-110	Building Labor	Labor

1. Open Robertson Construction Company.
2. Create a customer account for Palmdale Offices.

Customer ID:	**Palm-100**
Name:	**Palmdale Offices**

General Tab:

Contact:	**Jerry Bromberg**
Bill to:	
Address:	**4315 South First Street**
City, ST, Zip:	**Modesto, CA 95355**
Country:	**USA**
Sales Tax:	**CAL**
Customer Type:	**Building**
Telephone 1:	**209-555-2143**
Telephone 2:	
Fax:	
E-mail:	
Beginning Balance:	**0**

Sales Defaults Tab

GL Sales Account:	**400**

3. Set up the project for job costing.
4. Create the phases and cost codes.
5. Print the following reports: *Phase List* and *Cost Code List*.

PROBLEM 1B

Abelar Construction Company accepted a job from the city of Lodi to repair a storm drain that had been damaged by heavy rains. Abclar wants to use the Jobs Only Method to keep track of the revenue and expenses associated with the project. The revenue is expected to be $15,000, and the expenses are expected to be $8,000. The job identifier is Lodi Drain–Job 1. The estimated starting date is January 5, 2007, and the estimated ending date is March 31, 2007. The percentage of completion is zero (0). Alfred Martinez will supervise the project.

1. Open Abelar Construction Company, which you downloaded from the CD that comes with this book.
2. Create a customer account for the city of Lodi.

Customer ID:	**Lodi-89**
Name:	**City of Lodi**

General Tab

Contact:		**James Wright**
Bill to:		
	Address:	**34 Main Street**
	City, ST, Zip:	**Lodi, CA 95290**
	Country:	**USA**
Sales Tax:		**CAL**
Customer Type:		**Building**
Telephone 1:		**209-555-3423**
Telephone 2:		
Fax:		
E-mail:		
Beginning Balance:		**0**

Sales Defaults Tab

GL Sales Account:	**400**

3   Set up the project for job costing.

4. On January 10, 2007, the Abelar Construction Company purchased the following non-stock items to be used exclusively in the job for the city of Lodi: 350 feet of 24-inch culvert pipe at $15 per foot and one drain assembly for $500. Abelar also purchased 400 feet of copper wire at $0.75 per foot for its inventory. All items were purchased on credit from the Construction Supply Warehouse (Invoice 2009). Use the following information to create inventory records for the items.

Non-stock Item

Item ID:	**CULVERT-9**
Description:	**24-Inch Culvert Pipe**
Item Class:	**Non-stock item**
Full Price:	**25.00**
Last Unit Cost:	**15.00**
Stocking U/M:	**Foot**
GL Sales Acct:	**400**
GL Salary/Wages Acct:	**512**
GL Cost of Sales Acct:	**503**
Item Tax Type:	**2 (Exempt)**
Preferred Vendor ID:	**CSW-01**

Non-stock Item

Item ID:	**DRAIN-16**
Description:	**Drain Assembly**
Item Class:	**Non-stock item**
Full Price:	**950.00**
Last Unit Cost:	**500.00**
Stocking U/M:	**Each**
GL Sales Acct:	**400**
GL Salary/Wages Acct:	**512**

GL Cost of Sales Acct:	**503**
Item Tax Type:	**2 (Exempt)**
Preferred Vendor ID:	**CSW-01**

Stock Item

Item ID:	**COPWIRE-20**
Description:	**Copper Wire**
Item Class:	**Stock item**
Full Price:	**2.00**
Last Unit Cost:	**0.75**
Cost Method:	**Average**
Stocking U/M:	**Foot**
Item Tax Type:	**2 (Exempt)**
GL Sales Acct:	**400**
GL Inventory Acct:	**105**
GL Cost of Sales Acct:	**503**
Preferred Vendor ID:	**CSW-01**

HINT

Remember to change the *GL Account* field to *105* when entering purchases for non-stock items.

5. Enter the purchases.
6. Abelar used 200 feet of copper wire for the Lodi job. Allocate the cost of this wire to the job, January 15, 2007.
7. Alfred Martinez worked 40 hours on the Lodi job, and Peter Monroe worked 40 hours. Allocate these employees' labor costs ending January 14, 2007 to the job. The check date is January 15, 2007.
8. Print the following reports for the month of January 2007: *Job Ledger* and *Estimated Job Expenses*.

PROBLEM 2B

Abelar Construction Company accepted a job from Jeremy Lyons to build a new septic tank for a house he is renovating. The estimated starting date is January 11, 2007, and the estimated ending date is February 28, 2007. Alfred Martinez will supervise the project. The job identifier is Lyons Tank-Job 2. The percentage of the job completed is zero.

Abelar has decided to create phases and cost codes to better track the revenue and expenses associated with this project. It has decided on the following phases and cost types:

Phases:

Phase ID	Description	Cost Type
Plan-01	Planning/Permits	Other
Excav-02	Excavation	Labor
Build-03	Building	Use the cost codes shown below

Cost Codes:

Cost ID	Description	Cost Type
BUILDMAT-111	Building Materials	Materials
BUILDLAB-110	Building Labor	Labor

1. Open Abelar Construction Company.
2. Create a customer account for Lyons Renovation.

Customer ID:	**Lyons-90**
Name:	**Lyons Renovation**

General Tab:

Contact:	**Jeremy Lyons**
Bill to:	
Address:	**1278 Boston Street**
City, ST, Zip:	**Modesto, CA 95357**
Country:	**USA**
Sales Tax:	**CAL**
Customer Type:	**Building**
Telephone 1:	**209-555-4312**
Telephone 2:	
Fax:	
E-mail:	
Beginning Balance:	**0**

Sales Defaults Tab

GL Sales Account:	**400**

3. Set up the project for job costing.
4. Create the phases and cost codes.
5. Print the following reports: *Phase List* and *Cost Code List*.

COOPERATIVE LEARNING

1. Form groups of three or four students and visit a local construction company to discuss its use of job costing. If possible, determine the level of detail the managers would like to see in the job cost information. For example, do they want to see the information broken down by phase and cost type?
2. In groups of three or four students, visit a meeting of the local chapter of the Institute of Management Accountants. Find out what types of jobs are available to management accountants in the area. Also find out what courses are necessary for students who want to become management accountants. The local telephone directory should have a listing for the IMA. If not, revisit its Web site to gain information about local IMA chapters.

WRITING AND DECISION MAKING

Assume that you work for a construction company and have been given the job of project manager for a $40,000,000 shopping mall that will take several years to complete. Your supervisor wants some insight about how a job costing system operates. In memo format, briefly explain the possible ways that costs can be broken down so that you can closely monitor them throughout the job, recognize revenue and expenses in a timely manner, and determine the profitability of the project.

CHAPTER

12

FIXED ASSETS

LEARNING OBJECTIVES

1. Understand fixed assets and depreciation

2. Create subsidiary ledger records for individual fixed assets

3. Calculate and record the depreciation of fixed assets

4. Make entries to record the disposal of fixed assets

5. Prepare reports showing fixed assets and depreciation

* *Peachtree 2007 Educational Version does not include the Fixed Assets module.*

If you are using the Educational Version of Peachtree 2007 that is packaged with this textbook (not the full version of Peachtree Complete Accounting 2007), use the appendix that follows Chapter 13 to learn how to perform computerized accounting for fixed assets without using the Peachtree Fixed Assets module.

SOFTWARE FEATURES*

- Set Up Subsidiary Ledger Records for Fixed Assets

- Select a Depreciation Method

- Calculate and Record Depreciation

- Record the Disposal of Fixed Assets

- Prepare Fixed Asset Reports

Remember that assets are divided into several groups. One group consists of **current assets:** cash, assets that will be turned into cash within one year, and assets that will be used up within one year. Current assets include cash, petty cash, accounts receivable, merchandise inventory, supplies, and prepaid insurance.

Another group consists of **fixed assets.** These assets have the following characteristics:

- They have an expected life of more than one year.
- They are intended for use in the business and not for resale to customers.
- They are tangible, which means that they have a physical substance.

Examples of fixed assets are land, buildings, furniture, office equipment, factory machines, automobiles, and trucks. Fixed assets are also known as *plant assets*, *capital assets*, and *property, plant, and equipment*.

In addition to current assets and fixed assets, some businesses have intangible assets and natural resources. **Intangible assets** are long-term assets that have no physical substance, such as patents, trademarks, copyrights, and franchises. **Natural resources** are long-term assets that are removed from the ground, such as oil, natural gas, coal, and timber.

OBJECTIVE 1—UNDERSTAND FIXED ASSETS AND DEPRECIATION

A business must set up a general ledger account for each broad class of fixed assets that it owns. It might have general ledger accounts for land, land improvements, buildings, office furniture, office equipment, factory machines, and trucks. These accounts include all items in a class. For example, the Office Furniture account covers desks, chairs, sofas, file cabinets, and bookshelves. The Office Equipment account covers computers, printers, fax machines, copying machines, and telephone systems.

Because the general ledger accounts for fixed assets involve broad classes, most businesses also maintain records for the individual assets. These records form a subsidiary ledger called the **fixed asset ledger.**

RECORDING THE COST OF FIXED ASSETS

When a fixed asset is purchased, the cost is debited to the appropriate general ledger account and entered in the appropriate subsidiary record. The total cost of a fixed asset may be greater than the price paid for the asset. For example:

- The cost of land includes not only the price but also any amounts paid for real estate commissions, legal fees, taxes, removal of old structures, draining, and grading.
- Newly acquired land may require improvements such as sidewalks, fences, and outdoor lighting. (The cost of these items is debited to an account called Land Improvements rather than to the Land account.)
- The cost of a new building includes not only the amount paid for construction but also any fees paid for the planning work of architects and engineers, for permits and inspections, and for insurance during construction.
- The cost of machinery and equipment includes not only the price of the item but also any amounts paid for freight, taxes, installation, and insurance during delivery and installation.

---

current assets Cash, assets that will be turned into cash within one year, and assets that will be used up within one year.

fixed assets Assets that have an expected life of more than one year, will be used in the business, and are tangible.

intangible assets Long-term assets that have no physical substance.

natural resources Long-term assets that are removed from the ground.

fixed asset ledger A subsidiary ledger that contains records for individual fixed assets.

RECORDING DEPRECIATION

Remember that **depreciation** is the process of allocating the cost of a fixed asset to operations during its estimated useful life. Because fixed assets help to produce revenue for a business, their cost must gradually be recorded as an expense while they are being used. This procedure allows the business to match its revenue and expenses.

All fixed assets except land are subject to depreciation. Land is not depreciated because it is considered to have an indefinite useful life. The other fixed assets have limited lives.

Because land is not subject to depreciation, when land and a building are purchased together for one price, this amount must be divided. One portion is debited to the Land account, and the other portion is debited to the Building account. Similarly, land improvements, which are subject to depreciation, are recorded in a separate account, not in the Land account.

Depreciation is an operating expense for a business. It is recorded as part of the adjusting entries for each accounting period. The adjustment for each class of fixed assets consists of a debit to a depreciation expense account and a credit to an accumulated depreciation account. For example, the depreciation for office equipment is recorded by debiting Depreciation Expense–Office Equipment and crediting Accumulated Depreciation–Office Equipment.

Notice that the account used for the credit part of the entry is not the asset account Office Equipment. Instead, it is Accumulated Depreciation–Office Equipment, a contra asset account. As long as the business owns the office equipment, the asset account shows the cost and the contra asset account shows all depreciation taken. On the balance sheet, both amounts are reported and the balance of the contra asset account is subtracted from the balance of the asset account. The difference between the two balances is the **book value** of the fixed asset.

Cost of Fixed Asset – Accumulated Depreciation = Book Value

Each class of fixed assets has its own depreciation expense account and its own accumulated depreciation account.

CALCULATING DEPRECIATION

Various methods are used to calculate depreciation. Most of these methods base depreciation on three basic factors: the cost of a fixed asset, its estimated salvage value, and its estimated useful life.

- As noted previously, the cost of a fixed asset is the purchase price plus any amounts that must be spent to prepare the asset for use, such as shipping and installation costs.
- The **estimated salvage value** is the amount that a business expects a fixed asset to be worth at the end of its useful life. Salvage value is also known as *trade-in value*, *scrap value*, and *residual value*.
- The **estimated useful life** is the number of years that a business expects a fixed asset to be used in its operations.

Depreciation is calculated on a yearly basis. However, if a business owns a fixed asset for less than a year, it takes depreciation for only the amount of time that the asset was in service during the year. This situation often occurs in the year when a fixed asset was purchased and in the year when it is sold or scrapped.

For financial accounting purposes, the most commonly used depreciation methods are:
- The straight-line method
- The units-of-production method
- The double declining-balance method
- The sum-of-the-years'-digits method

THE STRAIGHT-LINE METHOD

The **straight-line method** of depreciation allocates an equal amount of depreciation to each year of an asset's useful life. For example, assume that a business buys a new machine for $42,000 on January 1, 2007. The machine has an estimated salvage value of $2,000 and an estimated useful life of four years. The annual depreciation for the machine is therefore $10,000.

Cost – Salvage Value = Depreciable Cost
$42,000 – $2,000 = $40,000

Depreciable Cost ÷ Useful Life = Annual Depreciation
$40,000 ÷ 4 (years) = $10,000

Table 12–1 shows the depreciation expense, accumulated depreciation, and book value of the machine throughout its life when the straight-line method is used. Notice that at the end of the fourth year (2010), the book value is equal to the estimated salvage value ($2,000). No fixed asset can be depreciated below its salvage value.

Table 12–1 An Example of the Straight-Line Depreciation Method

Year	Cost	Depreciation Expense	Accumulated Depreciation	Book Value End of Year
2007	$42,000	$10,000	$10,000	$32,000
2008	42,000	10,000	20,000	22,000
2009	42,000	10,000	30,000	12,000
2010	42,000	10,000	40,000	2,000

Keep in mind that the book value is simply the depreciated cost of a fixed asset. It does not necessarily represent the market value or even the replacement value of the asset.

THE UNITS-OF-PRODUCTION METHOD

The **units-of-production method** allocates depreciation on the basis of how much work the asset produces during each year of its useful life. For a factory machine, the work produced might be expressed in hours of operation. For an automobile or truck, it might be expressed in miles driven.

Consider again the machine purchased for $42,000 on January 1, 2007, which has an estimated salvage value of $2,000. Suppose that management expects the useful life of the machine to be 40,000 hours. The depreciation rate for the machine is $1 per hour.

Cost – Salvage Value = Depreciable Cost
$42,000 – $2,000 = $40,000

Depreciable Cost ÷ Useful Life = Depreciation Rate
$40,000 ÷ 40,000 (hours) = $1 per hour

Assume that the machine is used for 9,000 hours in the first year, 11,000 hours in the second year, 12,000 hours in the third year, and 8,000 hours in the fourth year. The amount of depreciation for the first year will be $9,000.

Usage x Depreciation Rate = Depreciation
9,000 hours x $1 per hour = $9,000

Table 12–2 shows the depreciation expense, accumulated depreciation, and book value for the machine through its life when the units-of-production method is used. Again, the book value at the end of the asset's life (40,000 hours) is $2,000, which is the salvage value.

Table 12–2 An Example of the Units-of-Production Depreciation Method

Year	Cost	Hours	Depreciation Expense	Accumulated Depreciation	Book Value End of Year
2007	$42,000	9,000	$ 9,000	$ 9,000	$33,000
2008	42,000	11,000	11,000	20,000	22,000
2009	42,000	12,000	12,000	32,000	10,000
2010	42,000	8,000	8,000	40,000	2,000

THE DOUBLE DECLINING-BALANCE METHOD

The **double declining-balance method** allocates depreciation at twice the straight-line rate. The doubled rate is applied to the book value of the asset each year. Because the book value decreases from year to year, more depreciation is taken in the early years of the asset's useful life and less depreciation is taken in the later years. Thus, the double declining-balance method is considered an **accelerated method** of depreciation.

Again, assume that a machine is purchased for $42,000 on January 1, 2007, and has an estimated useful life of four years and an estimated salvage value of $2,000. With the double declining-balance method, the salvage value is ignored. The first step in calculating depreciation is to find the straight-line rate and then double it. In this case, the doubled rate is 50%. (The straight-line rate for an asset with a four-year useful life is 25%.)

¼ = 0.25 x 2 = 0.50 or 50%

When the 50% rate is applied to the first year's book value, the depreciation is $21,000.

Book Value x Depreciation Rate = Depreciation
$42,000 x 0.50 = $21,000

In the second year, the book value is $21,000 and the depreciation is $10,500 ($21,000 x 0.50 = $10,500).

Table 12–3 shows the depreciation expense, accumulated depreciation, and book value for the machine throughout its life when the double declining-balance method is used. Notice that in the fourth year, the remaining book value is $2,625, slightly more than the estimated salvage value of $2,000. (Although salvage value is ignored when calculating depreciation with the double declining-balance method, the asset cannot be depreciated below its salvage value.)

Table 12–3 An Example of the Double Declining-Balance Depreciation Method

Year	Cost	Rate	Depreciation Expense	Accumulated Depreciation	Book Value End of Year
2007	$42,000	50%	$21,000	$21,000	$21,000
2008	42,000	50	10,500	31,500	10,500
2009	42,000	50	5,250	36,750	5,250
2010	42,000	50	2,625	39,375	2,625

THE SUM-OF-THE-YEARS'-DIGITS METHOD

sum-of-the-years'-digits method A method that allocates depreciation on the basis of a fraction that changes each year.

The **sum-of-the-years'-digits method** allocates depreciation on the basis of a fraction that changes for each year of an asset's useful life. This fraction is applied to the depreciable cost of the asset (the cost less the salvage value). Because the sum-of-the-years'-digits method produces more depreciation in the early years and less depreciation in the later years, it is also considered an accelerated method of depreciation.

The denominator of the fraction (the figure at the bottom of the fraction) remains constant. It is the sum of the digits of the years that make up the useful life of the asset. The numerator of the fraction (the figure at the top of the fraction) changes. It is the number of years that remain in the useful life of the asset.

For example, let us look again at the machine purchased for $42,000 on January 1, 2007. This machine has an estimated useful life of four years and an estimated salvage value of $2,000. The sum of the years' digits for the four years of its useful life is 10 (1 + 2 + 3 + 4 = 10). This is the denominator of the fraction that will be used to calculate depreciation for the asset.

The numerator for the first year will be 4 because there are four years remaining in the useful life of the asset. The numerator for the second year will be 3 because there are just three years remaining in its useful life at that point.

The fraction for the first year is 4/10 while the fraction for the second year is 3/10. Therefore, based on a depreciable cost of $40,000 ($42,000 – $2,000), the depreciation expense for the first two years is calculated as follows:

4/10 of $40,000 = $16,000
3/10 of $40,000 = $12,000

Table 12–4 shows the depreciation expense, accumulated depreciation, and book value for the machine throughout its life when the sum-of-the-years'-digits method is used. The book value remaining at the end of the fourth year is always equal to the estimated salvage value.

Table 12–4 An Example of the Sum-of-the-Years'-Digits Method

Year	Cost	Fraction	Depreciation Expense	Accumulated Depreciation	Book Value End of Year
2007	$42,000	4/10	$16,000	$16,000	$26,000
2008	42,000	3/10	12,000	28,000	14,000
2009	42,000	2/10	8,000	36,000	6,000
2010	42,000	1/10	4,000	40,000	2,000

ACCELERATED COST RECOVERY SYSTEMS

The four depreciation methods that we have discussed so far are used for financial accounting purposes. However, when preparing federal income tax returns, businesses must use either the **accelerated cost recovery system (ACRS)** or the **modified accelerated cost recovery system (MACRS)** to calculate depreciation. The federal government has mandated the use of these two methods to calculate depreciation for most types of fixed assets. ACRS applies to assets placed in service between 1981 and 1986. MACRS applies to assets placed in service after 1986.

The ACRS and MACRS apply to all types of fixed assets except real estate. These methods are intended to encourage businesses to purchase new fixed assets by providing quicker depreciation than the other accelerated methods. Both of these methods operate in a similar way, with just the details differing:

- Each method assigns different types of fixed assets to classes. The classes have specified cost recovery periods rather than useful lives. With the MACRS, the cost recovery periods are 3, 5, 7, 10, 15, and 20 years. For example, automobiles and light trucks have a cost recovery period of 5 years. Office equipment has a cost recovery period of 7 years.
- Each method ignores salvage value. The cost of the asset is fully depreciated.
- Each method uses accelerated depreciation in the early years of the cost recovery period and then switches to straight-line depreciation in the later years.
- Each method uses an approach called the **half-year convention** for the first year. No matter when the asset is placed in service during the first year, the rate for the first year assumes that the asset has been owned for half a year.
- The federal government publishes a table for each method that shows the year-by-year percentage of the cost of an asset that a business can take as depreciation. A portion of the MACRS table is shown in table 12–5. (The percentages after year 6 and for the 15-year and 20-year classes have been omitted.)

Table 12–5 MACRS Depreciation Percentages

Recovery Year	Recovery Period			
	3-Year	**5-Year**	**7-Year**	**10-Year**
1	33.33%	20.00%	14.29%	10.00%
2	44.45	32.00	24.49	18.00
3	14.81	19.20	17.49	14.40
4	7.41	11.52	12.49	11.52
5		11.52	8.93	9.22
6		5.76	8.92	7.37

To see how MACRS works, assume that the machine purchased for $42,000 on January 1, 2007, falls into the class that has a 5-year cost recovery period. Because of the half-year convention, the machine is actually depreciated for 6 years. The first and last years are considered half years. Table 12–6 provides an example of depreciation using the MACRS method.

Table 12–6 An Example of MACRS Depreciation

Year	Cost	Rate	Depreciation Expense	Accumulated Depreciation	Book Value End of Year
2007	$42,000	20.00%	$ 8,400	$ 8,400	$33,600
2008	42,000	32.00	13,440	21,840	20,160
2009	42,000	19.20	8,064	29,904	12,096
2010	42,000	11.52	4,838	34,742	7,258
2011	42,000	11.52	4,838	39,580	2,420
2012	42,000	5.76	2,420	42,000	—

PEACHTREE FIXED ASSETS ACCOUNTING

Peachtree makes it easy for you to set up and maintain fixed asset records, calculate depreciation, record entries for depreciation, and produce a variety of fixed asset reports. Peachtree supports the most common financial accounting methods for calculating depreciation, the tax accounting methods, and other types of methods.

Check POINT

1. What is depreciation?
2. Name the four most common financial accounting methods for calculating depreciation.

Answers
1. *Depreciation is the process of allocating the cost of a fixed asset to operations during its estimated useful life.*
2. *Four financial accounting methods for calculating depreciation are the straight-line method, the units-of-production method, the double declining-balance method, and the sum-of-the-years'-digits method.*

REMINDER

Peachtree 2007 Educational Version does not include the Fixed Assets module.

OBJECTIVE 2—CREATE SUBSIDIARY LEDGER RECORDS FOR INDIVIDUAL FIXED ASSETS

Woodward Construction Company currently owns one piece of equipment—a versatile machine that serves as an excavator, backhoe, and bulldozer. This machine was purchased for $112,000 and recorded in a general ledger account called Equipment. Woodward's general ledger also contains an Accumulated Depreciation–Equipment account and a Depreciation Expense–Equipment account. These two accounts are used to make adjusting entries for depreciation.

Because of its limited resources, Woodward currently leases any other fixed assets that it needs such as a pickup truck to transport materials to jobs. Later, as its finances improve, Woodward plans to purchase additional fixed assets.

As of the current accounting period, Feb 01, 2007 to Feb 28, 2007, Woodward has decided to use the Peachtree Fixed Assets module that comes with Peachtree Complete Accounting 2007 to maintain asset records and to calculate and record depreciation. Therefore, Woodward will no longer manually enter adjusting entries to account for depreciation expense. There are three major tasks to using the Peachtree Fixed Assets module:

1. Set up a new company in the Peachtree Fixed Assets module and map (link) it to Peachtree Accounting.
2. Create a new subsidiary ledger record for a fixed asset in the Fixed Assets module.
3. Calculate and record depreciation.

SETTING UP THE PEACHTREE FIXED ASSETS MODULE

Take the following steps to set up the Peachtree Fixed Assets module.

HINT

Double-click the *FAS for Peachtree* icon instead if it is on the desktop.

Step 1:

At the Windows desktop, click Start and then click All Programs.

Step 2:

Click FAS Solutions, FAS for Peachtree by Sage, and then click FAS for Peachtree by Sage.

Step 3:

Click File from the FAS for Peachtree window.

Step 4:

Click New Company from the drop-down list.

FIGURE 12-1

New Company Wizard

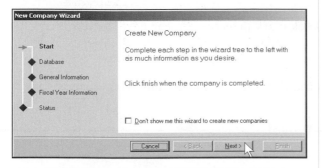

Step 5:

Click Next from the New Company Wizard window as shown in figure 12–1.

Step 6:

Click Next to accept the default database.

Step 7:

Key **Woodward Construction Company** in the Company Name box, accept the starting system number, and click Next.

FIGURE 12-2

Woodward Construction Company Selected

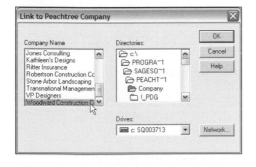

Step 8:

Enter 01/01/06 in the Start of Business Date box and click Next. (Accept December as the default for Month of Fiscal Year End.) Woodward began operations in January 2006; however, it switched from a manual accounting system to Peachtree in January 2007. Recall there were beginning balances when you set up Woodward.

Step 9:

Click Finish to complete the New Company Setup.

Step 10:

Open Woodward Construction Company in Peachtree Complete Accounting 2007 and minimize the screen.

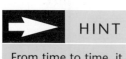

HINT

From time to time, it may be necessary to access Peachtree Complete Accounting while you are using Peachtree Fixed Assets. Both programs can be open at the same time.

Step 11:

Click *Map to Peachtree* at the bottom of the Edit Company window of the FAS for Peachtree module.

Step 12:

Select Woodward Construction Company from the Link to Peachtree Company window, as shown in figure 12–2.

Step 13:

Click OK to link Woodward Construction Company to FAS for Peachtree.

Step 14:

Minimize Peachtree Accounting, if necessary, and then click OK at the bottom of the FAS for Peachtree, Edit Company window to complete the New Company setup process.

CREATING A SUBSIDIARY LEDGER RECORD FOR AN EXISTING FIXED ASSET

Take the following steps to create a subsidiary ledger record for an existing fixed asset.

Step 1:

Click <u>F</u>ile and then Enable <u>W</u>izards from the FAS for Peachtree Main Menu bar.

Step 2:

Check New <u>A</u>sset Wizard if a check mark does not appear next to New Asset Wizard.

Step 3:

Click <u>A</u>sset and then <u>N</u>ew from the FAS for Peachtree Main Menu bar.

Step 4:

Click <u>N</u>ext from the New Asset Wizard.

Step 5:

Click <u>N</u>ext to accept none for the template.

Step 6:

Key **Excavator** in the *Description* field.

Step 7:

Key **001** in the *Co Asset No* field.

Step 8:

Key **EQ** in the *Class* field. (EQ represents Equipment.)

Step 9:

Key **Main Bldg** in the *Location* field.

Step 10:

Key **George Clark** in the *Custodian* field as shown in figure 12–3.

FIGURE 12-3
New Asset Wizard Completed General Information Window

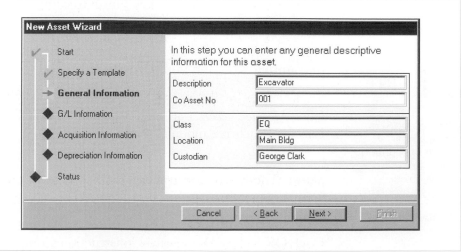

Step 11:
Click <u>N</u>ext.

Step 12:
At the *G/L Asset Acct No* field, click the arrow, and then click *108 Equipment*, as shown in figure 12–4.

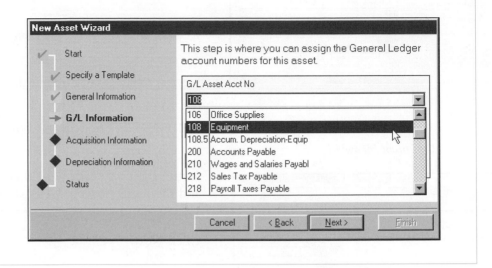

FIGURE 12-4
108 Equipment Selected

Step 13:
At the *G/L Expense Acct No* field, click the arrow, and then click *510 Depreciation Expense–Equipment*, as shown in figure 12–5.

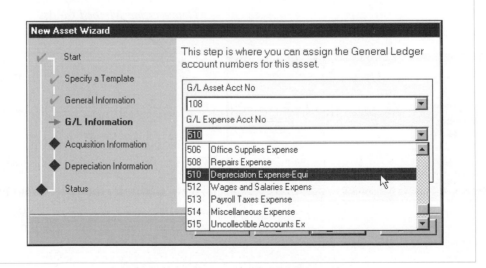

FIGURE 12-5

510 Depreciation Expense–Equipment Selected

Step 14:
At the *G/L Accum Acct No* field, click the arrow, and then click *108.5 Accum. Depr.–Equipment*, as shown in figure 12–6. Click <u>N</u>ext.

The FAS for Peachtree module automatically calculates depreciation for financial accounting purposes, federal income tax purposes, and other pur-poses. Woodward Construction Company wants to keep track of depreciation for financial accounting pur-poses at this time.

FIGURE 12-6

108.5 Accum. Depr.–Equipment Selected

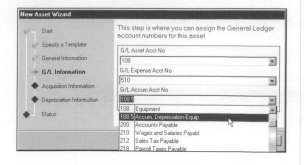

Step 15:

Key **112,000.00** in the *Acquisition Value* field.

Step 16:

At the *Acquisition Date* and the *Placed In Service Date* field click the pull-down arrow, and then select *01/01/06*.

Step 17:

Key **4323** in the *Purchase Order No* field.

Step 18:

Key **General Dynamics** in the *Vendor/Mfg* field.

Step 19:

Key **GHU7789965** in the *Mfg Serial No* field.

Step 20:

At the *Warranty Date* field click the pull-down arrow, and then select *01/01/11*, as shown in figure 12-7.

Step 21:

Click Next.

FIGURE 12-7

Completed Acquisition Information

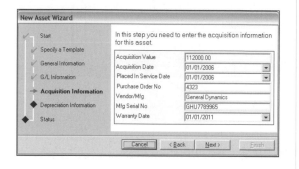

Step 22:

Click Personal, General from the *Property Type* drop-down list.

Step 23:

Click SF (Straight Line Full Month) from the *Depreciation Method* field.

Step 24:

Key **05 yrs 00 mos** in the *Estimated Life* field and **05 yrs 00 mos** in the *ADS Life* field, as shown in figure 12-8.

Step 25:

Click Next and then Finish.

Step 26:

Key **100** in the *Bus Use %* field if it is not already entered under the Internal Column. **Note:** Enter the data for the next four steps under the Internal Column.

FIGURE 12-8

Completed Depreciation Information

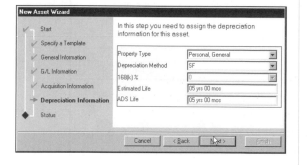

Step 27:

Key **52,000.00** in the *Salvage* field.

Step 28:

Key **01/2007** in the *Beg Date* field.

Step 29:

Key **1000** in the *Beg YTD* field. This amount represents the depreciation for January 2007. Remember that Woodward is going to use the Fixed Assets module beginning with February 2007.

Step 30:

Key **13,000** in the *Beg Accm* field. This amount represents the total accumulated depreciation through January 2007 ($12,000 for Fiscal Year 2006, and $1,000 for January 2007). Compare your work with figure 12-9.

FIGURE 12-9

Partially Completed Fixed Asset Information

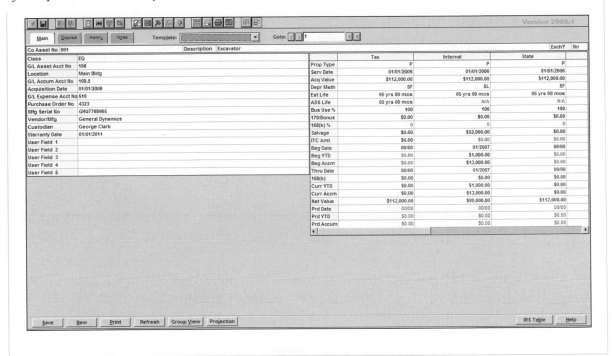

Step 31:

Click *Save* at the bottom of the Asset-[1] window.

Step 32:

E*x*it FAS for Peachtree.

CREATING A SUBSIDIARY LEDGER RECORD FOR A NEW FIXED ASSET

HINT

This is the purchase data information.

February 1, 2007, Woodward Construction Company purchased a new computer system for $4,500 on credit from Office Max (Invoice 33299). Woodward estimates that the computer system will have a useful life of four years and no salvage value. Record the purchase in Peachtree Complete Accounting.

Step 1:

Open Peachtree Complete Accounting.

Step 2:

Open Woodward Construction Company and close the Action Items log.

Step 3:

Create the following general ledger accounts:

Account ID:	**109**
Description:	**Computer**
Account Type:	**Fixed Assets**

Account ID:	109.5
Description:	Accum. Depr.–Computer
Account Type:	Accumulated Depreciation

Account ID:	511
Description:	Depr. Expense–Computer
Account Type:	Expenses

Step 4:

Record the purchase of the computer system using the Purchases/Receive Inventory window using 109 as the GL Account. Refer to the previous page for the purchase data information.

Step 5:

Minimize Peachtree Complete Accounting.

Step 6:

Open the FAS for Peachtree module. Click Asset and then click New.

Step 7:

Click *Don't show me this wizard to create new assets* from the New Wizard window and Cancel to close the wizard window.

Step 8:

Click the *New Asset* icon (the last icon on the left side of the toolbar). The New Asset worksheet appears, as shown in figure 12-10.

FIGURE 12-10
New Asset Worksheet

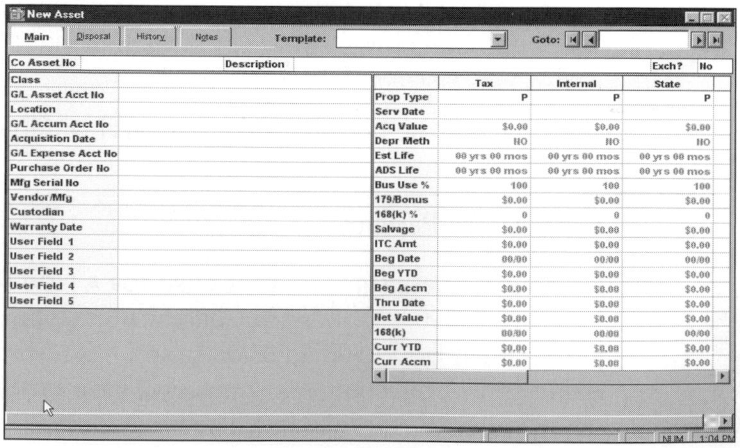

Step 9:

Use the following information to create the record for the new fixed asset:

Co Asset No	002
Description	Computer System
Class	EQ
G/L Asset Acct No	109
Location	Office
G/L Accum Acct No	109.5
Acquisition Date	02/01/07

G/L Expense Acct No	511
Purchase Order No	004569
Mfg Serial No	HHT334
Vendor/Mfg	Hewlett-Packard
Custodian	George Clark
Warranty Date	02/01/11
Prop Type	P (Use the Internal Column for the remaining entries.)
Service Date	02/01/07
Acq Value	$4,500
Depr Meth	SL
Est Life	04 years 00 mos
Bus Use %	100
Salvage Value	
Beg Date	
Beg YTD	
Beg Accm	

Step 10:

Click the *Save Asset* icon (2nd icon from left) on the Main Menu toolbar and Exit.

Check
POINT

1. For what tasks is the Fixed Assets module of Peachtree used?
2. What type of ledger is the fixed asset ledger?

Answers
1. *The Fixed Assets module of Peachtree is used to maintain asset records and to calculate and record depreciation.*
2. *The fixed asset ledger is a subsidiary ledger with records for individual fixed assets.*

PRACTICE *objective*   **2**

Bullfrog Maintenance Company, as of February 2007, wants to use the Fixed Assets module of Peachtree to maintain records of its fixed assets and calculate depreciation. Bullfrog currently owns only one fixed asset, a truck that appears in the Equipment account (108). This truck cost $42,000 and has accumulated depreciation of $10,750 through January 31, 2007. Recall that Bullfrog converted from a manual accounting system to Peachtree on January 1, 2007.

Step 1:

Open and minimize Bullfrog Maintenance Company in Peachtree Accounting.

Step 2:

Start FAS for Peachtree Accounting.

Step 3:

Create Bullfrog Maintenance Company as a new company in FAS for Peachtree. Use 01/01/06 as the start date. Remember to map (link) to Peachtree.

Step 4:

Use the following information to set up the asset account:

Co Asset No	001
Description	Maintenance Vehicle
Class	EQ
G/L Asset Acct No	112
Location	Garage
G/L Accum Acct No	112.5
Acquisition Date	01/01/06

G/L Expense Acct No	510
Purchase Order No	8569
Mfg Serial No	GM433234
Vendor/Mfg	General Motors
Custodian	Stanley Smith
Warranty Date	01/01/11
Prop Type	P (Use the Internal Column)
Service Date	01/01/06
Acq Value	$42,000
Depr Meth	SL
Est Life	05 yrs 00 mos
Bus Use %	100
Salvage Value	2000.00
Beg Date	01/2007
Beg YTD	666.67
Beg Accm	10,750

Step 5:

Click the _Save_ icon.

HINT

This is the purchase data information.

On February 23, 2007, Bullfrog Maintenance Company purchased a new computer system for $7,500 on credit from Office Depot (Invoice 23998). Bullfrog estimates that the computer system will have a salvage value of $500 and a useful life of five years.

Step 6:

Open Bullfrog Maintenance Company in Peachtree Complete Accounting.

Step 7:

Create the following general ledger accounts:

Account _ID_:	**111**
Description:	**Computer**
Account _Type_:	**Fixed Assets**

Account _ID_:	**111.5**
Description:	**Accum. Depr.–Computer**
Account _Type_:	**Accumulated Depreciation**

Account _ID_:	**511**
Description:	**Depreciation Expense–Computer**
Account _Type_:	**Expenses**

Step 8:

Record the purchase of the computer system using the Purchases/Receive Inventory window using 111 as the GL Account. Refer to the purchase data information above.

Step 9:

Use the following information to set up the asset record for the computer system in the FAS for Peachtree module:

Co Asset No	002
Description	Computer System
Class	EQ

G/L Asset Acct No	111
Location	Office
G/L Accum Acct No	111.5
Acquisition Date	02/23/07
G/L Expense Acct No	511
Purchase Order No	6985
Mfg Serial No	M6654
Vendor/Mfg	Motorola
Custodian	Stanley Smith
Warranty Date	02/23/12
Prop Type	P (Use the Internal Column for the remaining entries.)
Service Date	02/23/07
Acq Value	7,500
Depr Meth	SL
Est Life	05 yrs 00 mos
Bus Use %	100
Salvage Value	500.00
Beg Date	
Beg YTD	
Beg Accm	

Step 10:

Click the *Save Asset* (diskette) icon and E<u>x</u>it.

OBJECTIVE 3—CALCULATE AND RECORD THE DEPRECIATION OF FIXED ASSETS

Woodward Construction Company wants to calculate and record depreciation for the excavator and the computer system as of March 31, 2007. The FAS for Peachtree Fixed Assets module will make the necessary calculations automatically and transfer the information to the general journal and general ledger.

CALCULATING DEPRECIATION

Step 1:

Open Woodward Construction Company in both the Peachtree Fixed Assets module and Peachtree Complete Accounting.

Step 2:

In the FAS for Peachtree module, click Depre<u>c</u>iation and then <u>D</u>epreciate from the main menu toolbar.

Step 3:

Click Active Assets from the <u>G</u>roup drop-down list.

Step 4:

Select Internal from the Books list.

Step 5:

Key **03/31/07** in the *Calculate depreciation through:* field box.

Step 6:

Click *Update current reporting period for selected books*, from the Calculation field.

Step 7:
Click Send to *Window*, if needed, as shown in figure 12-11.

FIGURE 12-11
*Completed Depreciate
Window*

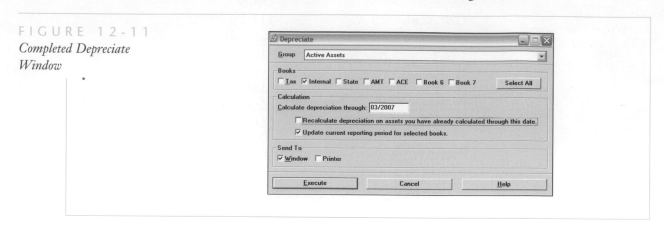

Step 8:
Click Execute and review the printout shown in figure 12-12.

FIGURE 12-12
Depreciation Expense Report Printout

Woodward Construction Company
Depreciation Expense Report
As of March 31, 2007

Book = Internal

FYE Month = December

Sys No	In Svc Date	Acquired Value	P T	Depr Meth	Est Life	Salv / 168(k) Sec 179	Depreciable Basis	Prior Thru	Prior Accum Depreciation	Depreciation This Run	Current YTD Depreciation	Current Accum Depreciation	Key Code
000001	01/01/06	112,000.00	P	SLMM	05 00	52,000.00	60,000.00	01/31/07	12,000.00	2,000.00	3,000.00	15,000.00	r
000002	02/01/07	4,500.00	P	SLMM	04 00	0.00	4,500.00			0.00	187.50	187.50	187.50	
	Grand Total	116,500.00				52,000.00	64,500.00		12,000.00	2,187.50	3,187.50	15,187.50	
	Less disposals and transfers Count = 0	0.00				0.00	0.00		0.00			0.00	
	Net Grand Total Count = 2	116,500.00				52,000.00	64,500.00		12,000.00	2,187.50	3,187.50	15,187.50	

Step 9:
Close the Depreciation Expense Report and Depreciate window.

TRANSFERRING DEPRECIATION TO THE GENERAL JOURNAL AND GENERAL LEDGER
You can use the FAS for Peachtree Fixed Assets module to automatically
record depreciation expense in the general journal and post it to the general
ledger.

Step 1:
Open Woodward Construction Company in Peachtree Accounting and minimize.

Step 2:
Open FAS for Peachtree.

Step 3:
Click Depreciation and Post Depreciation from the main menu toolbar.

Step 4:
Click *Active Assets* from the Group drop-down list.

Step 5:
Click *Internal* from the Book drop-down list.

Step 6:
Key **03/31/2007** in the *Period Posting Date* field.

Step 7:
Key **03/31/2007** in the *Journal Entry Date* field, as shown in figure 12-13.

FIGURE 12-13
Completed Post Depreciation Window

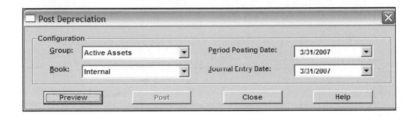

Step 8:
Click Preview from the Post Depreciation window and review the report.

Step 9:
Close Report.

Step 10:
Click Post to post the entries.

Step 11:
Maximize Woodward Construction Company in Peachtree Complete Accounting 2007.

Step 12:
Click Reports and then General Ledger from the main menu toolbar.

Step 13:
Select General Journal from the Report List and click Preview.

Step 14:
Select the period From: *Mar 1, 2007* To: *Mar 31, 2007* and click OK.

Step 15:
Review the preview as shown in figure 12-14 and close the General Journal window.

FIGURE 12-14
General Journal Entries for Depreciation Expense

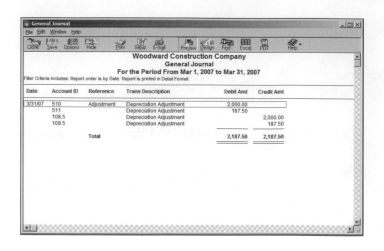

Close Woodward Construction Company.

Check POINT

1. What journal is used to record depreciation?
2. After the Peachtree Fixed Assets module is opened, what steps are needed to calculate the depreciation of an asset?

Answers
1. *The general journal is used to record depreciation.*
2. *The steps needed are click Depreciation, then Depreciate, complete the Depreciate window, and then click Execute.*

PRACTICE *objective* 3

Bullfrog Maintenance Company wants to calculate and record depreciation through June 30, 2007.

Step 1:
Open the Bullfrog Maintenance Company in the Peachtree Fixed Assets module and in Peachtree Complete Accounting.

Step 2:
Calculate the internal book depreciation as of June 30, 2007.

Step 3:
Print the *Depreciation Expense* report as of June 30, 2007. Your printout should look like figure 12–15.

Step 4:
Post depreciation to the general ledger as of June 30, 2007.

FIGURE 12-15

Depreciation Expense Report for Bullfrog Maintenance Company

Bullfrog Maintenance Company
Depreciation Expense Report
As of June 30, 2007

Book = Internal

FYE Month = December

Sys No	In Svc Date	Acquired Value	P T	Depr Meth	Est Life	Salv / 168(k) Sec 179	Depreciable Basis	Prior Thru	Prior Accum Depreciation	Depreciation This Run	Current YTD Depreciation	Current Accum Depreciation	Key Code
000001	01/01/06	42,000.00	P	SLMM	05 00	2,000.00	40,000.00	01/31/07	10,083.33	3,333.33	4,000.00	14,083.33	r
000002	02/23/07	7,500.00	P	SLMM	05 00	500.00	7,000.00		0.00	466.67	466.67	466.67	r
Grand Total		49,500.00				2,500.00	47,000.00		10,083.33	3,800.00	4,466.67	14,550.00	
Less disposals and transfers Count = 0		0.00				0.00	0.00		0.00			0.00	
Net Grand Total		49,500.00				2,500.00	47,000.00		10,083.33	3,800.00	4,466.67	14,550.00	
Count = 2													

Step 5:
Close Bullfrog Maintenance Company.

OBJECTIVE 4—MAKE ENTRIES TO RECORD THE DISPOSAL OF FIXED ASSETS

Remember that all fixed assets except land have limited lives. Eventually, they wear out or become obsolete, or their owners want to replace them with newer, more efficient models. When a fixed asset is no longer useful, a business will dispose of the asset by selling it, trading it in for a new asset, or scrapping it if it has no remaining value.

Suppose that Woodward Construction Company decides to sell the excavator that it owns. On March 31, 2007, it receives $120,000 for the excavator. Woodward must determine whether there is a gain or loss on this transaction and then record the disposal in its accounting records.

When a firm disposes of a fixed asset, it must bring depreciation on the asset up to date. Then it can find the book value of the asset and determine whether the sale produced a gain or loss.

In the case of the excavator sold by Woodward Construction Company, the depreciation entry made on March 31, 2007, results in accumulated depreciation of $15,000 and a book value of $97,000. Remember that the book value of a fixed asset is the difference between its cost and its accumulated depreciation. The cost of the excavator was $112,000. The book value is therefore $97,000 ($112,000 − $15,000 = $97,000).

If the selling price of a fixed asset is greater than its book value, there is a gain on the sale. If the selling price of a fixed asset is less than its book value, there is a loss on the sale. Because Woodward sold its excavator for $120,000 and the book value of the machine is $97,000, the firm has a gain of $23,000.

The gain on the sale of a fixed asset is considered other (nonoperating) income because it does not result from the normal operations of a business. It is therefore recorded in an account called Gain on Disposal of Fixed Assets. Similarly, the loss on the sale of a fixed asset is considered other (nonoperating) expense. It is recorded in an account called Loss on Disposal of Fixed Assets.

The sale of the excavator by Woodward Construction Company requires a debit of $120,000 to Cash, a debit of $15,000 to Accumulated Depreciation–Equipment, a credit of $112,000 to Equipment, and a credit of $23,000 to Gain on Disposal of Fixed Assets. The effects of this transaction are as follows:

- The debit to Cash records the amount received for the excavator.
- The debit to Accumulated Depreciation–Equipment removes the accumulated depreciation of the excavator from the accounting records.
- The credit to Equipment removes the cost of the excavator from the accounting records.
- The credit to Gain on Disposal of Fixed Assets records the income earned from the sale of the excavator.

RECORDING THE DISPOSAL OF A FIXED ASSET AT A GAIN

Woodward Construction Company does not yet have a Gain on Disposal of Fixed Assets account in its general ledger. Therefore, it must now create this account.

Step 1:
Open Woodward Construction Company in Peachtree Complete Accounting.

Step 2:
Create the following general ledger account:

Account ID:	**452**
Description:	**Gain on Disposal of Fxd Assets**
Account Type:	**Income**

Step 3:
Minimize the Peachtree window.

Step 4:
Open Woodward Construction Company in the FAS for Peachtree Fixed Assets module.

Step 5:
Double-click on Co Asset 001 and the Asset-[1] window appears.

Step 6:
Click the Disposal tab.

Step 7:

Key **03/31/07** in the *Disposal Date* field.

Step 8:

Click *Sale* from the Disposal Method drop-down list.

Step 9:

Key **120,000.00** in the *Cash Proceeds* field.

Step 10:

Click <u>S</u>ave and then review the disposal entries shown in figure 12-16 and make any needed corrections.

FIGURE 12-16
Completed Asset Disposal Window

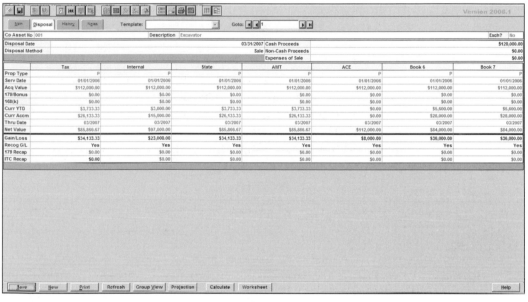

	Tax	Internal	State	AMT	ACE	Book 6	Book 7
Prop Type	P	P	P	P	P	P	P
Serv Date	01/01/2006	01/01/2006	01/01/2006	01/01/2006	01/01/2006	01/01/2006	01/01/2006
Acq Value	$112,000.00	$112,000.00	$112,000.00	$112,000.00	$112,000.00	$112,000.00	$112,000.00
179/Bonus	$0.00	$0.00	$0.00	$0.00	$0.00	$0.00	$0.00
168(k)	$0.00	$0.00	$0.00	$0.00	$0.00	$0.00	$0.00
Curr YTD	$3,733.33	$3,000.00	$3,733.33	$3,733.33	$0.00	$5,600.00	$5,600.00
Curr Accm	$26,133.33	$15,000.00	$26,133.33	$26,133.33	$0.00	$28,000.00	$28,000.00
Thru Date	03/2007	03/2007	03/2007	03/2007	03/2007	03/2007	03/2007
Net Value	$86,866.67	$97,000.00	$86,866.67	$85,866.67	$112,000.00	$84,000.00	$84,000.00
Gain/Loss	$34,133.33	$23,000.00	$34,133.33	$34,133.33	$8,000.00	$36,000.00	$36,000.00
Recog G/L	Yes	Yes	Yes	Yes	Yes	Yes	Yes
179 Recap	$0.00	$0.00	$0.00	$0.00	$0.00	$0.00	$0.00
ITC Recap	$0.00	$0.00	$0.00	$0.00	$0.00	$0.00	$0.00

Viewing the Disposed Assets Report

The *Disposed Assets* report shows detailed information about a fixed asset that has been sold, traded in, or scrapped. This information includes the cost, the accumulated depreciation, the net proceeds (the sum received for the asset), the book value, and the amount realized (the gain or loss on the disposal).

Step 1:

In the FAS for Peachtree Fixed Assets module, click <u>R</u>eports, click Standard Reports, and then click <u>D</u>isposal.

Step 2:

Click *Active Assets* from the <u>G</u>roup drop-down list.

Step 3:

Click *Internal* from the *Books* field. (Uncheck any other check marks.)

HINT

If you dispose of the wrong asset, you can reinstate it by selecting <u>R</u>eset Depreciation and then entering a date before the disposal date.

Step 4:

Click *Asset Count* and <u>D</u>*etail, subtotals and totals* from the *Configuration* field.

Step 5:

Click *Printer* from the *Sent To* field.

Step 6:

Click <u>R</u>*un Report* to view and print the report in figure 12-17.

FIGURE 12-17

Disposal Report

Woodward Construction Company
Disposal Report

Book = Internal
FYE Month = December

Sys No	Co Asset No	Description	Cl	In Svc Date	Disposal Date	D M	Acquired Value	Current Accum Depreciation	Net Proceeds	Gain/Loss Adjust Basis	Realized Gain (Loss)	G L
000001	001	Excavator	EQ	01/01/06	03/31/07	S	$ 112,000.00	$ 15,000.00	$ 120,000.00	$ 97,000.00	$ 23,000.00	Y
					Grand Total		$ 112,000.00	$ 15,000.00	$ 120,000.00	$ 97,000.00	$ 23,000.00	
					Count = 1							

	Gains	Losses	Net
Recognized	$ 23,000.00	$ 0.00	$ 23,000.00
Not Recognized	$ 0.00	$ 0.00	$ 0.00
Deferred	$ 0.00	$ 0.00	$ 0.00
Total	$ 23,000.00	$ 0.00	$ 23,000.00

Report Assumptions

Report Name: Disposal
Source Report: <Standard Report>

Calculation Assumptions:
    Include Sec 168(k) Allowance & Sec 179: No
    Adjustment Convention: None

Group/Sorting Criteria:
    Group = Active Assets
    Include Assets that meet the following conditions:
        Activity is currently A,D,F,J,K,L,M,N
    Sorted by: System No

Step 7:

Minimize or close the Asset window.

Entering the Disposal of a Fixed Asset in the General Journal

You must now enter the disposal of the excavator in Woodward Construction Company's general journal and post the information to its general ledger.

Step 1:

Open or restore Peachtree Complete Accounting.

Step 2:

Open Woodward Construction Company if it is not currently open.

Step 3:

Click Tas<u>k</u>s and then click <u>G</u>eneral Journal Entry.

Step 4:

At the General Journal Entry window, click the *calendar* icon and then select *Mar 31, 2007.*

Key **Asset 001 Disposal** in the *Reference* field.

Record the general journal entry shown in figure 12–18.

FIGURE 12-18

General Journal Entry for
Disposal of Asset 001

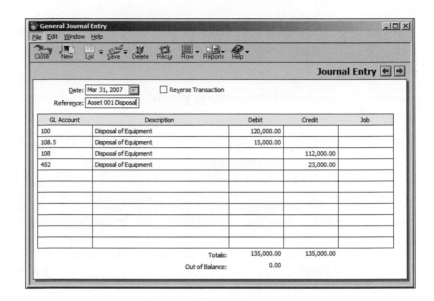

Step 7:
Click Save and then Close.

Check
P O I N T

1. What is the book value of a fixed asset?
2. What type of income is a gain on the disposal of a fixed asset?

Answers
1. *The book value of a fixed asset is the difference between its cost and its accumulated depreciation.*
2. *A gain on the disposal of a fixed asset is considered other (nonoperating) income.*

PRACTICE *objective* 4

On June 30, 2007, Bullfrog Maintenance Company decides to dispose of the truck that it owns in order to purchase a new model. Bullfrog sells the truck for $40,000 in cash. The current book value is $27,916.67.

Step 1:

Open Bullfrog Maintenance Company in both the Peachtree Fixed Assets module and Peachtree Complete Accounting.

Step 2:

Create the following general ledger account.

Account ID:	**452**
Description:	**Gain on Disposal of Fxd Assets**
Account Type:	**Income**

Step 3:

Enter the disposal in the Fixed Assets module for Asset 001.

Step 4:

Record the disposal of the truck in the general journal and post to the general ledger. Your General Journal Entry window should look like the one shown in figure 12–19.

FIGURE 12-19

Completed General Journal Entry for Disposal of Equipment

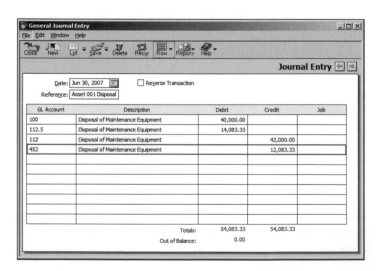

OBJECTIVE 5—PREPARE REPORTS SHOWING FIXED ASSETS AND DEPRECIATION

The Peachtree Fixed Assets module produces a variety of reports. Management can use these reports for many purposes. For example, management can periodically review the age of all fixed assets and develop plans to replace the older, less efficient ones. Because fixed assets are costly, many businesses set up long-term budgets for acquiring new fixed assets.

You have already viewed two of the reports available from the Peachtree Fixed Assets module: the *Depreciation Expense* report and the *Disposed Assets* report. You will now prepare the *Quarterly Acquisition* Report, which shows information about all fixed assets acquired during the period covered by the report.

On March 31, 2007, Woodward Construction Company wants to review the fixed assets that it acquired during the first three months of 2007. Follow the steps outlined below to prepare this report.

Step 1:

Open Woodward Construction Company in the FAS for Peachtree Fixed Assets module.

Step 2:

Click Reports and Standard Reports from the FAS for Peachtree main menu.

Step 3:

Click Quarterly Acquisition from the drop-down list.

Step 4:

Click *Active Assets* from the *Group* field selection list.

Step 5:

Click *Internal* from the *Books* field. (Remove any other checks.)

Step 6:

Select "Current reporting period 3/31/2007" from the Date field.

Step 7:

Select *Send to Window* and *Send to Printer* from the *Run Options* field.

Step 8:

Click Run Report and compare your report with figure 12-20.

FIGURE 12-20
Quarterly Acquisition Report

Woodward Construction Company
Quarterly Acquisition Report
For the fiscal year ended December 31, 2007

Book = Internal
FYE Month = December

	Acquisition Month/Period	Acquired Value	Percent
Quarter : 1			
	February 28, 2007	$ 4,500.00	
	Quarter : 1	$ 4,500.00	100.00%
	Grand Total	$ 4,500.00	100.00%

If no assets were acquired in a particular month, the month will not display.

Step 9:

Close the report window.

Check POINT

1. Name three of the reports produced by the Peachtree Fixed Assets module.
2. What report would management consult to review the cost of recently purchased fixed assets?

Answers

1. *Three reports are the Depreciation Expense report, the Disposed Assets report, and the Quarterly Acquisition report.*
2. *Management would consult the Quarterly Acquisition report.*

PRACTICE *objective* 5

Bullfrog Maintenance Company wants to prepare the Disposal Report.

Step 1:

Open Bullfrog Maintenance Company in the Peachtree Fixed Assets module and Peachtree Accounting.

Step 2:

Print the report. Your printout should look like figure 12–21.

FIGURE 12-21

Disposal Report for Bullfrog Maintenance Company

Bullfrog Maintenance Company
Disposal Report

Book = Internal
FYE Month = December

Sys No	Co Asset No	Description	Cl	In Svc Date	Disposal Date	D M	Acquired Value	Current Accum Depreciation	Net Proceeds	Gain/Loss Adjust Basis	Realized Gain (Loss)	G L
000001	001	Maintenance Vehicle	EQ	01/01/06	06/30/07	S	$ 42,000.00	$ 14,083.33	$ 40,000.00	$ 27,916.67	$ 12,083.33	Y
					Grand Total		$ 42,000.00	$ 14,083.33	$ 40,000.00	$ 27,916.67	$ 12,083.33	
					Count = 1							

	Gains	Losses	Net
Recognized	$ 12,083.33	$ 0.00	$ 12,083.33
Not Recognized	$ 0.00	$ 0.00	$ 0.00
Deferred	$ 0.00	$ 0.00	$ 0.00
Total	$ 12,083.33	$ 0.00	$ 12,083.33

The Internal Revenue Service maintains a Web site that people can visit to obtain federal tax forms and tax information. This site is located at www.irs.gov (see figure 12–22).

FIGURE 12-22
IRS Web Site

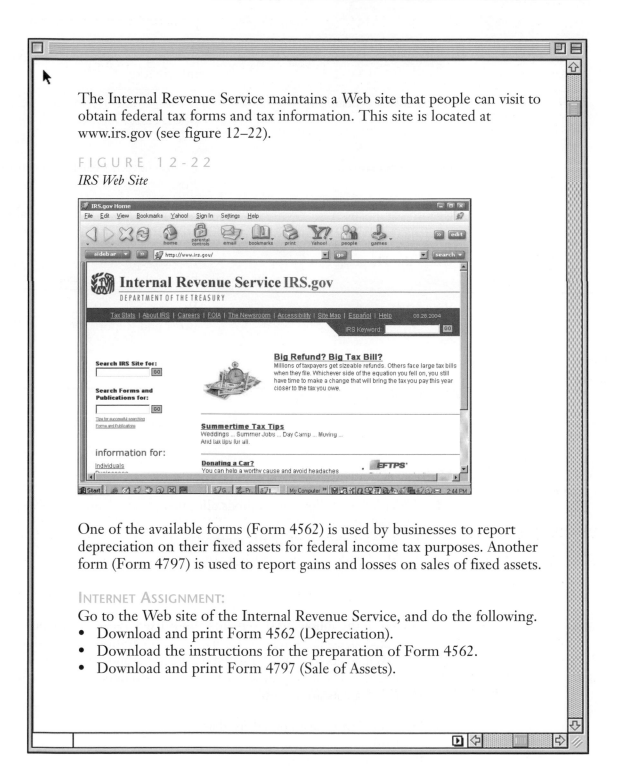

One of the available forms (Form 4562) is used by businesses to report depreciation on their fixed assets for federal income tax purposes. Another form (Form 4797) is used to report gains and losses on sales of fixed assets.

INTERNET ASSIGNMENT:
Go to the Web site of the Internal Revenue Service, and do the following.
- Download and print Form 4562 (Depreciation).
- Download the instructions for the preparation of Form 4562.
- Download and print Form 4797 (Sale of Assets).

SOFTWARE Command Summary

Create Subsidiary Ledger Records	Asset, New, enter the New Asset information
Calculate Depreciation	Depreciation, Depreciate, select Book, select Depreciation Period, Execute
Post Depreciation	Depreciation, Post Depreciation, Post
Record the Disposal of Fixed Assets	Select Co Asset No, Disposal tab, enter the disposal information
Undo the Disposal Entry	Reset Depreciation, enter a date before the disposal date
Prepare Reports	Reports, select Report Type, select Book and Report Date, Run Report

PROJECTS and Problems

CONTENT CHECK

Multiple Choice: Choose only one response for each question.

1. Which of the following methods allocates an equal amount of depreciation each year?
   A. Sum-of-the-years'-digits method
   B. Double declining-balance method
   C. Straight-line method
   D. Units-of-production method

2. Which of the following statements about fixed assets is *not* true?
   A. Fixed assets are intended for use in the operations of a business.
   B. Fixed assets have an estimated useful life of more than one year.
   C. Fixed assets are acquired for resale to customers.
   D. Fixed assets are tangible.

3. Depreciation is taken on all fixed assets except
   A. land.
   B. land improvements.
   C. buildings.
   D. equipment and machinery.

4. The difference between the cost of a fixed asset and its accumulated depreciation is the
   A. purchase price.
   B. book value.
   C. salvage value.
   D. selling price.

5. Depreciable cost is
   A. cost – depreciation expense.
   B. cost – accumulated depreciation.
   C. cost – salvage value.
   D. accumulated depreciation – salvage value.

Short-Essay Response: Provide a detailed answer for each question.

1. What is depreciation? Why must businesses record depreciation?
2. What is accelerated depreciation? Name two financial accounting methods for calculating depreciation that are accelerated.
3. What is the modified accelerated cost recovery system? When is this method used?
4. How is the sale of a fixed asset at a gain recorded? What general ledger accounts are debited and credited?
5. Why does the Fixed Assets Module of Peachtree provide for the use of both financial accounting and tax accounting methods of depreciation?

CASE PROBLEMS

PROBLEM 1A

On January 31, 2007, Robertson Construction Company decides to use the Fixed Assets Module of Peachtree (FAS for Peachtree) to keep records of its fixed assets. The only fixed asset currently on its books is construction equipment. This construction equipment cost $16,000, has an estimated salvage value of $1,000, and has an estimated useful life of four years. The equipment was purchased on January 1, 2007.

1. Create Robertson Construction Company in FAS for Peachtree. Remember to map to Peachtree. **Note:** Enter December as the fiscal year ending month and 01/01/07 as the business start date.

2. Use the following information to create a subsidiary ledger record for the construction equipment in FAS.

Co Asset No	001
Description	Construction Equipment
Class	EQ
G/L Asset Acct No	108
Location	Storage
G/L Accum Acct No	108.5
Acquisition Date	01/01/07
G/L Expense Acct No	510
Purchase Order No	1482
Mfg Serial No	MHS748392

Vendor/Mfg	Heavy Duty Solutions
Custodian	Michael Anderson
Warranty Date	01/01/11
Prop Type	P (Use the Internal Column)
Serv Date	01/01/07
Acq Value	$16,000
Depr Meth	SL
Est Life	04 yrs 00 mos
Bus Use %	100
Salvage Value	$1,000
Beg Date	
Beg YTD	
Beg Accum	

HINT

This is the purchase data information.

On January 31, 2007, Robertson Construction Company purchases landscaping equipment on credit from Steve's Supply Warehouse. The cost is $13,000, the estimated salvage value is $1,000, and the estimated useful life is four years. (Invoice 555.)

3. Create the following general ledger accounts.

Account ID	109
Description	Landscaping Equipment
Account Type	Fixed Assets

Account ID	109.5
Description	Accum. Depr.-Landscaping Eq.
Account Type	Accumulated Depreciation

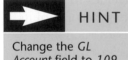

HINT

Change the *GL Account* field to *109*.

4. Use the Purchases/Receive Inventory window to record the purchase. Use the purchase data information above.

5. Use the following information to create a subsidiary ledger record for the landscaping equipment in FAS.

HINT

You may need to close and reopen FAS for Peachtree to synchronize the modules.

Co Asset No	002
Description	Landscaping Equipment
Class	EQ
G/L Asset Acct No	109
Location	Storage
G/L Accum Acct No	109.5
Acquisition Date	01/31/07
G/L Expense Acct No	510
Purchase Order No	1489
Mfg Serial No	THH652174
Vendor/Mfg	Heavy Duty Solutions
Custodian	Michael Anderson
Warranty Date	01/31/11
Prop Type	P (Use the Internal Column)
Serv Date	02/01/07
Acq Value	$13,000
Depr Meth	SL

Est Life	04 yrs 00 mos
Bus Use %	100
Salvage Value	$1,000
Beg Date	
Beg YTD	
Beg Accum	

6. Print the *Quarterly Acquisition* report for the Internal book as of 12/31/07.

PROBLEM 2A

On June 30, 2007, Robertson Construction Company updates the depreciation expense on its fixed assets. Use Peachtree Complete Accounting 2007 and its Fixed Assets module to do the following:

1. Calculate the depreciation expense as of June 30, 2007.
2. Print the *Depreciation Expense* report for June 30, 2007.
3. Post to the general ledger.
4. Print the general journal entries for June 30, 2007.

On July 1, 2007, Robertson decides to sell the landscaping equipment for $12,900 in cash. Robertson wants to purchase a more advanced model.

5. Create the following general ledger account.

Account ID:	452
Description:	Gain on Disposal of Fxd Assets
Account Type:	Income

6. Enter the disposal in the fixed asset record for Asset 002.
7. Print the *Disposal* report.
8. Record the disposal of the landscaping equipment in the general journal and post to the general ledger.
9. Print the general journal entries for July 1, 2007.

PROBLEM 1B

On January 31, 2007, Abelar Construction Company decides to use the Fixed Assets Module of Peachtree (FAS for Peachtree) to keep records of its fixed assets. The only fixed asset currently on its books is an excavator. This excavator cost $26,000, has an estimated salvage value of $5,000, and has an estimated useful life of seven years. The equipment was purchased on January 1, 2007.

1. Create Abelar Construction Company in FAS for Peachtree. Remember to map to Peachtree. **Note:** Enter December as the fiscal year ending month and 01/01/07 as the business start date.
2. Use the following information to create a subsidiary ledger record for the construction equipment in FAS.

Co Asset No	001
Description	Excavator
Class	EQ
G/L Asset Acct No	108
Location	Storage

G/L Accum Acct No	108.5
Acquisition Date	01/01/07
G/L Expense Acct No	510
Purchase Order No	5461
Mfg Serial No	WHS7125123
Vendor/Mfg	Heavy Duty Solutions
Custodian	Juan Abelar
Warranty Date	01/01/14
Prop Type	P (Use the Internal Column)
Serv Date	01/01/07
Acq Value	$26,000
Depr Meth	SL
Est Life	07 yrs 00 mos
Bus Use %	100
Salvage Value	$5,000
Beg Date	
Beg YTD	
Beg Accum	

HINT

This is the purchase data information.

On January 31, 2007, Abelar Construction Company purchases digging equipment on credit from Construction Supply Warehouse (Invoice 48537). The cost is $18,500, the estimated salvage value is $2,000, and the estimated useful life is five years.

3. Create the following general ledger accounts.

Account ID	109
Description	Digging Equipment
Account Type	Fixed Assets

Account ID	109.5
Description	Accum. Depr.-Digging Equipment
Account Type	Accumulated Depreciation

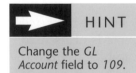

HINT

Change the GL Account field to 109.

4. Use the Purchases/Receive Inventory window to record the purchase. Use the purchase data information above.
5. Use the following information to create a subsidiary ledger record for the digging equipment in FAS.

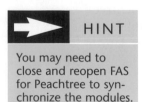

HINT

You may need to close and reopen FAS for Peachtree to synchronize the modules.

Co Asset No	002
Description	Digging Equipment
Class	EQ
G/L Asset Acct No	109
Location	Storage
G/L Accum Acct No	109.5
Acquisition Date	01/31/07
G/L Expense Acct No	510
Purchase Order No	1254
Mfg Serial No	SW84521
Vendor/Mfg	Heavy Duty Solutions

Custodian	Juan Abelar
Warranty Date	01/31/12
Prop Type	P (Use the Internal Column)
Serv Date	02/01/07
Acq Value	$18,500
Depr Meth	SL
Est Life	05 yrs 00 mos
Bus Use %	100
Salvage Value	$2,000
Beg Date	
Beg YTD	
Beg Accum	

6. Print the *Quarterly Acquisition* report for the Internal book.

PROBLEM 2B

On June 30, 2007, Abelar Construction Company updates the depreciation expense on its fixed assets. Use Peachtree Complete Accounting 2007 and its Fixed Assets module to do the following:

1. Calculate the depreciation expense as of June 30, 2007.
2. Print the *Depreciation Expense* report for June 30, 2007.
3. Post to the general ledger.
4. Print the general journal entries for June 30, 2007.

On July 1, 2007, Abelar decides to sell the digging equipment for $17,550 in cash. Abelar intends to lease a more powerful model.

5. Create the following general ledger account.

Account ID:	452
Description:	Gain on Disposal of Fxd Assets
Account Type:	Income

6. Enter the disposal in the fixed asset record for Asset 002.
7. Print the *Disposal* report.
8. Record the disposal of the digging equipment in the general journal and post to the general ledger.
9. Print the general journal entries for July 1, 2007.

Cooperative Learning

1. Form groups of three or four students, and prepare a list of four possible fixed assets that might be found in a doctor's office. Estimate the cost, salvage value, useful life, and depreciable cost for each of the six assets. Calculate the annual straight-line depreciation for each of the assets.
2. Survey a local CPA firm to determine what portion of the firm's clients use the straight-line method of depreciation for financial accounting purposes.

Writing and Decision Making

Gary Stevens, the newly hired manager of an engineering company, does not understand how the cost of the firm's equipment is expensed. In memo format, explain to him how depreciation provides a means of expensing the cost of the equipment.

CHAPTER

13

PARTNER-SHIPS AND CORPORATIONS

LEARNING OBJECTIVES

1. Understand partnerships and corporations

2. Create partnership accounts and enter partnership transactions

3. Close the fiscal year

4. Create corporate accounts and enter corporate transactions

5. Print partnership and corporate reports

SOFTWARE FEATURES

- Select or Change Organization Type

- Create General Ledger Accounts

- Edit General Ledger Accounts

- Print Financial Statements

sole proprietorship A business owned by one person.

partnership A business owned by two or more people.

corporation A business owned by stockholders or shareholders.

Remember that there are three basic types of business organization: the sole proprietorship, the partnership, and the corporation. A **sole proprietorship** is a business owned by one person. A **partnership** is a business owned by two or more people. A **corporation** is a business owned by stockholders or shareholders. A small corporation may have just a few stockholders, but large corporations have thousands of stockholders.

Up to now, the businesses that we have discussed in this book have all been sole proprietorships. Because sole proprietorships are simple to form and operate, they are the most common type of business organization in the United States. However, the vast majority of sole proprietorships are small firms with limited resources. Larger businesses are usually partnerships or corporations.

The accounting procedures of sole proprietorships, partnerships, and corporations are very similar. The main differences involve owners' equity accounts transactions and financial statements. You can use Peachtree to support all three types of business organization.

OBJECTIVE 1—UNDERSTAND PARTNERSHIPS AND CORPORATIONS

In this chapter, you will see how Peachtree is used to create owners' equity accounts, record owners' equity transactions, and prepare financial statements for partnerships and corporations. However, it is first necessary to understand the basic characteristics of partnerships and corporations.

CHARACTERISTICS OF PARTNERSHIPS

A partnership is formed when two or more people enter into a business arrangement for the purpose of making a profit.

Partnerships carry a variety of advantages. Like a sole proprietorship, a partnership is easy to form. In most areas, all that is required to form a partnership is to obtain a business license for the firm. No written contract between the partners is necessary. However, lawyers advise that such a contract, called a **partnership agreement**, be drawn up in order to avoid later disputes. The partnership agreement specifies the beginning investment of each partner, the responsibilities of the partners, the method of dividing profits and losses, the method of admitting new partners, the method of dissolving the partnership, and other important matters. If there is no partnership agreement, by law, all profits and losses are divided equally.

partnership agreement A written contract that specifies the terms of a partnership such as the division of profits and losses.

The management of a partnership usually has a greater amount of expertise than the management of a sole proprietorship. Each partner brings additional knowledge, skills, and experience to the business. For example, suppose that a software engineer, a sales manager, and an accountant become partners in a new software company. Each will be able to contribute expertise in a different area of the business: product development, marketing, and financial management. The management contributions of the different partners can have a synergistic effect. Together, the blend of talents may produce more successful results than the individual partners would be able to achieve on their own.

It is difficult to run a business successfully without sufficient capital. This is especially true for new businesses, which may have a weak cash flow in their early years. A partnership has a greater potential for obtaining capital than a sole proprietorship. In a partnership, two or more people are able to pool their resources. If they need additional capital, they may have a better chance of borrowing the required sum than a single individual does.

Partnerships are subject to less government regulation than corporations. Also, unlike corporations, partnerships do not pay an income tax on their earnings. Partnerships file information returns with federal and state tax agencies, but they are not liable for any income tax. Instead, each partner pays income tax on his or her share of the firm's earnings.

There are also disadvantages to organizing a business as a partnership. Like the owner of a sole proprietorship, partners have **unlimited liability** for the debts of the business. If the business is unable to pay its debts, the creditors can sue to obtain the personal assets of the partners in order to satisfy the outstanding debts.

Although the blend of management talent can be very beneficial to a partnership, disputes about management decisions can be harmful. If there are serious, ongoing disagreements about business policy, a partnership may eventually have to dissolve. Because of the divided management control, successful operation of a partnership requires a willingness to consider different viewpoints and make compromises.

Partnerships operate under the **mutual agency rule.** This means that any partner can enter into a contractual agreement on behalf of the partnership. All other partners must honor the agreement, even if they were not consulted in advance and they do not approve of the agreement. The mutual agency rule points out the need to select business partners wisely.

Partnerships have a **limited life.** A partnership ends whenever an existing partner dies or withdraws or when a new partner is admitted. In each of these cases, a new partnership must be formed in order to continue the business.

ACCOUNTING FOR PARTNERSHIPS

A partnership must have a separate capital account and a separate drawing account for each partner. When a partnership is formed, the investment of each partner is credited to his or her capital account. For example, suppose that Julie Smith and Anna Ramos form a partnership on January 1, 2007. Each invests $75,000 in cash.

January 1, 2007		
Cash	150,000	
J. Smith, Capital		75,000
A. Ramos, Capital		75,000

At the end of each accounting period, the profit or loss of the partnership for the period is calculated. If there was a profit during the period, each capital account is credited for the partner's share. If there was a loss, each capital account is debited for the partner's share. Remember that the division of profits and losses in a partnership is specified in the partnership agreement. If there is no partnership agreement, then, by law, profits and losses must be divided equally among the partners. The following entry is for a year-end profit of $60,000 divided equally.

December 31, 2007		
Income Summary	60,000	
J. Smith, Capital		30,000
A. Ramos, Capital		30,000

When a partner withdraws cash or other assets for personal use, the amounts are debited to the partner's drawing account. Many partners withdraw cash at regular intervals in order to have funds available to pay their personal living expenses. This amount is often referred to as a "salary," but it is actually a withdrawal of expected future profits and is therefore debited to the partner's drawing account rather than to the Salaries Expense account. In a sole proprietorship and a partnership, only the earnings of employees can be recorded in the Salaries Expense account. The following entry is for a monthly withdrawal of $2,000 in cash by each of two partners.

January 31, 2007		
J. Smith, Drawing	2,000	
A. Ramos, Drawing	2,000	
Cash		4,000

At the end of each accounting period, the balances of the partners' drawing accounts are closed into their capital accounts, as shown in the following year-end general journal entry.

December 31, 2007		
J. Smith, Capital	24,000	
A. Ramos, Capital	24,000	
J. Smith, Drawing		24,000
A. Ramos, Drawing		24,000

The balances of the partners' capital accounts are reported on the balance sheet. Some businesses also prepare a separate statement showing all changes in the partners' capital during the accounting period.

	J. Smith	A. Ramos	Total
Capital, Jan. 1, 2007	$ 75,000	$ 75,000	$150,000
Net income for year	30,000	30,000	60,000
Totals	$105,000	$105,000	$210,000
Less: Withdrawals	24,000	24,000	48,000
Capital, Dec. 31, 2007	$ 81,000	$ 81,000	$162,000

CHARACTERISTICS OF CORPORATIONS

The ownership of a corporation is divided into shares of stock. The owners are therefore known as **stockholders** or **shareholders**. Unlike a sole proprietorship or a partnership, a corporation is a legal entity that is separate from its owners.

A corporation may be small and have just a few stockholders, perhaps family members or a group of managers. This type of corporation is known as a **closely held corporation**. However, the corporations that most of us are familiar with—corporations such as IBM, Microsoft, Dell, Wal-Mart, and General Motors—are very large and have thousands of stockholders. A corporation of this kind is known as a **publicly held corporation** because the public, usually through a stock exchange, can purchase its stock.

Although there are more sole proprietorships and partnerships than corporations in the United States, corporations produce two-thirds of all business revenue. The reason for this disparity in revenue is that the largest businesses are most often organized as corporations.

stockholders or shareholders The owners of a corporation.

closely held corporation A corporation owned by just a few stockholders.

publicly held corporation A corporation with stock that can be purchased by the public.

Like a sole proprietorship and a partnership, a corporation has both advantages and disadvantages. The ability of a sole proprietorship or partnership to obtain capital depends mostly on the personal resources and personal credit reputation of the owners. A corporation, on the other hand, can raise funds by selling stock or issuing bonds. A corporation that has good prospects for growth can obtain funding from a large pool of potential investors.

Unlike the owners of sole proprietorships and partnerships, the stockholders of a corporation have **limited liability**. They are not personally liable for the debts of the business. If the corporation is unable to pay its debts, creditors cannot sue to obtain the personal assets of the stockholders. Therefore, the maximum amount that stockholders can lose in a failing corporation is the amount of their investment.

Because a corporation is a legal entity that is separate from its owners, it has a **continuous life**. Its life is not affected by changes in ownership, that is, by sales and purchases of shares by stockholders. A corporation can theoretically exist forever unless it is dissolved.

The mutual agency rule mentioned earlier does not apply to corporations. No contractual agreement made by an ordinary stockholder is legally binding on the firm. Only officers of the corporation are able to make binding commitments on its behalf.

When a corporation is formed, the stockholders elect a **board of directors** to look after their interests. The board of directors establishes policies for the firm and hires managers to carry out the policies. This separation of ownership and management allows the corporation to obtain the services of professional managers who have appropriate business training and experience.

Stockholders can vote in periodic elections for the board of directors but do not participate in the day-to-day operations of the corporation unless they are members of management.

The corporation structure has some disadvantages. Corporations require a **charter** from a state in order to operate. The state granting the charter is usually the one in which the corporation will have its headquarters. The process of applying for a charter, organizing the corporation, and issuing stock involves the work of lawyers and accountants. Therefore, the cost of forming a corporation can be substantial.

Organizing a corporation also involves much time and effort. For example, the organizers must establish a set of **bylaws**—the rules by which the corporation will operate. They must also establish corporate records such as the stockholders' ledger.

Corporations are more heavily regulated than sole proprietorships and partnerships. For example, the state and federal governments require that corporations file many different types of reports. Publicly held corporations must also meet accounting and financial reporting standards established by the Securities and Exchange Commission (a federal agency) and by the stock exchange (examples include NASDAQ and NYSE) on which their shares trade. These organizations require that publicly held corporations issue quarterly and annual financial statements.

Because a corporation is a legal entity that is separate from its owners, it pays an income tax on its earnings to the federal and state governments. When it distributes part of its earnings to stockholders in the form of dividends, the individual stockholders must pay income tax on the amounts they receive. This situation is referred to as **double taxation**.

limited liability The stockholders of a corporation are not personally liable for the debts of the business.

continuous life A corporation can exist forever. Its life is not affected by changes in ownership.

board of directors Individuals elected by stockholders to establish policies for a corporation and hire managers.

charter A legal document issued by a state that permits a corporation to operate.

bylaws A set of rules by which a corporation will operate.

double taxation As a legal entity, a corporation pays income tax on its earnings. When the stockholders receive part of the earnings in the form of dividends, they also pay income tax.

ACCOUNTING FOR CORPORATIONS

The corporate charter specifies the types of stock that can be issued and the maximum number of shares of each type. The two basic types of stock are common stock and preferred stock. **Common stock** provides various rights such as the right to vote for the board of directors and the right to receive dividends if the board of directors declares them. **Preferred stock** usually does not carry the right to vote but does provide a fixed dividend. Many corporations issue just one type of stock—common stock.

Some states require that stock be issued with a par value. The **par value** is an arbitrary amount that a corporation assigns to each share of its stock for legal and accounting purposes. This amount is printed on the stock certificate. Typical par values are $1, $10, and $100. The par value of a stock has nothing to do with its **market value**—the amount that a buyer is willing to pay for the stock at any given time.

The maximum number of shares of stock permitted by the corporate charter is known as the **authorized stock**. However, the number of shares actually issued is called **outstanding stock**. As the corporation sells more shares to investors, the amount of outstanding stock changes. Sometimes, a corporation will also buy back shares from investors.

Recording Paid-in Capital and Retained Earnings

When a corporation issues common stock at par value for cash, it debits the amount received to Cash and credits a stockholders' equity account called Common Stock. If the stock is issued above par value, the corporation still credits the par-value amount to the Common Stock account. However, it must credit the amount that is above par value to another stockholders' equity account called Paid-in Capital in Excess of Par—Common. For example, suppose that a corporation sells 1,000 shares of $10 par-value common stock at $15 per share. It receives $15,000 in cash. The journal entry appears below.

January 6, 2007		
Cash	15,000	
Common Stock		10,000
Paid-in Capital in Excess of Par—Common		5,000

If a corporation has par-value preferred stock, it will use stockholders' equity accounts called Preferred Stock and Paid-in Capital in Excess of Par—Preferred to record transactions involving the preferred stock.

At the end of each accounting period, the corporation's profit or loss for the period is transferred from the Income Summary account to a stockholders' equity account called Retained Earnings. This account shows the accumulated earnings of the corporation that have not been distributed to stockholders in the form of dividends. For example, suppose that a corporation has a profit (net income) of $130,000 for the year 2007. This amount is credited to Retained Earnings.

December 31, 2007		
Income Summary	130,000	
Retained Earnings		130,000

The Stockholders' Equity Section of the Balance Sheet

The balance sheet of a corporation has a Stockholders' Equity section, which contains the type of information shown below. Notice that the total stockholders' equity consists of paid-in capital and retained earnings. **Paid-in capital** is the amount of capital received from stockholders through their purchases of stock. **Retained earnings** are accumulated profits from past operations. The term **earned capital** is often used to describe retained earnings.

Stockholders' Equity

Paid-in Capital:		
Preferred Stock	$200,000	
Paid-in Capital in Excess of Par—Preferred	40,000	$240,000
Common Stock	$450,000	
Paid-in Capital in Excess of Par—Common	80,000	530,000
Total Paid-in Capital		$770,000
Retained Earnings		180,000
Total Stockholders' Equity		$950,000

Recording Dividends

Stockholders expect to receive a return on their investments. This return can come from an increase in the market value of their stock and/or from dividends paid by the corporation to its stockholders. When the market value of a stock increases, stockholders can sell their shares and realize the monetary gain if they wish.

A **dividend** is a distribution of part of a corporation's earnings to stockholders. Some corporations have a policy of paying dividends on a regular basis, such as every quarter. Other corporations, especially newer corporations in high-growth industries such as software and computers, might not pay dividends because they want to use their accumulated earnings to expand operations.

The board of directors is responsible for declaring dividends. For example, suppose that on January 31, 2007, the board of directors of a corporation declares a dividend of $1 per share to be paid on February 28 to "stockholders of record" (stockholders whose names appear in the corporation's records) as of February 15.

Dividends are usually paid in cash, but they may be paid in stock. On the date when a cash dividend is declared, the total amount is debited to Cash Dividends and credited to Cash Dividends Payable. Cash Dividends is a contra stockholders' equity account—a stockholders' equity account with a debit balance. Cash Dividends Payable is a liability account. On the date when the dividend is paid, Cash Dividends Payable is debited and Cash is credited. (Note that no journal entry is made on the date of record.)

January 31, 2007		
Cash Dividends	20,000	
Cash Dividends Payable		20,000
February 28, 2007		
Cash Dividends Payable	20,000	
Cash		20,000

Cash Dividends is a temporary account. When closing entries are made at the end of an accounting period, its balance is transferred to Retained Earnings. For example, suppose that the corporation discussed in this section pays only $20,000 in cash dividends during 2007. On December 31, it makes the entry shown below. The effects of this entry are to close the Cash Dividends account and to decrease the Retained Earnings account by $20,000, the amount paid out of retained earnings for the dividends.

December 31, 2007

Retained Earnings	20,000	
Cash Dividends		20,000

The Statement of Retained Earnings

statement of retained earnings A financial statement that shows the changes in a corporation's retained earnings during an accounting period.

Many corporations prepare a **statement of retained earnings** at the end of each accounting period. This statement shows the beginning balances of the Retained Earnings account, an addition for net income or a deduction for a net loss, a deduction for dividends paid, and the ending balance of the Retained Earnings account. An example is shown below.

Retained Earnings, Jan. 1, 2007	$ 70,000
Add: Net Income	130,000
	$200,000
Less: Dividends	20,000
Retained Earnings, Dec. 31, 2007	$180,000

Check POINT

1. What is a partnership?
2. Name five advantages of a corporation.

Answers
1. *A partnership is a business owned by two or more people.*
2. *Five advantages of a corporation are ease of raising capital, limited liability, continuous life, no mutual agency rule, and professional management.*

OBJECTIVE 2—CREATE PARTNERSHIP ACCOUNTS AND ENTER PARTNERSHIP TRANSACTIONS

When a partnership is formed, it is necessary to establish a capital account for each partner and a drawing account for each partner. All other general ledger accounts are the same as those used for a sole proprietorship.

Up to now, Woodward Construction Company has operated as a sole proprietorship. However, John Woodward, the owner, wants to expand operations and has decided to form a partnership with Molly Stone and Marjorie Brown. Both Stone and Brown have experience as managers in the construction industry and will provide additional capital.

According to the partnership agreement, Woodward will contribute the assets of his sole proprietorship business as of January 2, 2008. Stone will contribute $20,000 in cash. Brown will contribute $15,000 in cash and $5,000 in office supplies. The partnership will assume the liabilities of Woodward's sole proprietorship business. The starting date for the partnership is January 2, 2008.

Because Woodward is contributing more capital than the other partners and because they will benefit from his prior work in establishing the business, profits will be shared unequally. The partnership agreement they establish specifies that Woodward will receive 80% of the profits, Stone will receive 10%, and Brown will receive 10%. Losses will be shared in the same way.

Follow the steps outlined below to convert Woodward Construction Company from a sole proprietorship to a partnership and set up the necessary capital and drawing accounts. Note that the individual (monthly) fiscal year should be closed before converting Woodward Construction Company to a partnership.

CLOSING THE FISCAL YEAR

The closing process is similar to the process for changing the accounting period. However, when the fiscal year is closed, the records are generally purged and the company information must be backed up in order to save the data for future use. Once the fiscal year is closed, it is very difficult to access that information. Although it is not the end of Woodward's fiscal year, the closing process will be conducted in order to make a logical progression to the partnership formation.

Step 1:

Open Woodward Construction Company.

Step 2:

Click Tasks, System, and then Year-End Wizard.

Step 3:

At the Year-End Wizard-Welcome window, click Next, as shown in figure 13-1.

FIGURE 13-1

Year-End Wizard Welcome Window

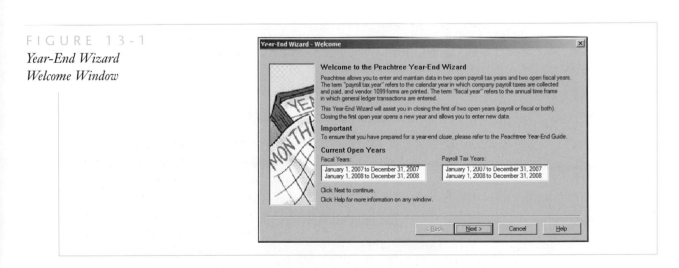

Step 4:

Click Next at the Year-End Wizard-Close Options dialog box to close the Fiscal and Payroll Tax Years as shown in figure 13-2.

FIGURE 13-2
*Year-End Wizard-Close
Options Box*

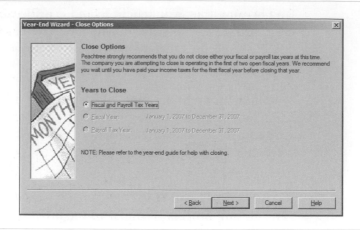

Step 5:

Click <u>N</u>ext at the Year-End Wizard-Unprinted Items Warning dialog box.

Step 6:

Click <u>N</u>ext at the Year-End Wizard-Reports dialog box to print fiscal year-end reports. All the year-end reports will be printed. Be aware that there are approximately 30 printouts. If you do not want to print any of the year-end reports, click Check None.

Step 7:

Click <u>N</u>ext on the Year-End Wizard-Internal Accounting Review dialog box.

Step 8:

Click the B<u>a</u>ck Up button on the Year-End Wizard-Back Up dialog box to back up company data.

Step 9:

Select *Include company name in the backup file name*, as shown in figure 13-3, then click <u>B</u>ack Up from the Back Up Company dialog box.

FIGURE 13-3

*Back Up Company
Window*

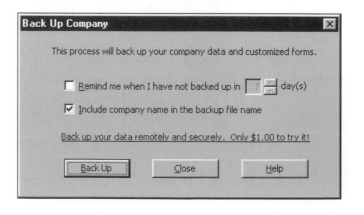

Step 10:

Click <u>S</u>ave and accept the default file name to save the backup file for Woodward Construction Company.

Step 11:

Click OK on the Peachtree Backup Size Warning window, and <u>N</u>ext to proceed past the Year-End Wizard Back Up window.

Step 12:

Click <u>N</u>ext at the Year-End Wizard-New Open Fiscal Years dialog box, as shown in figure 13-4.

FIGURE 13-4

*New Open Fiscal Years
Window*

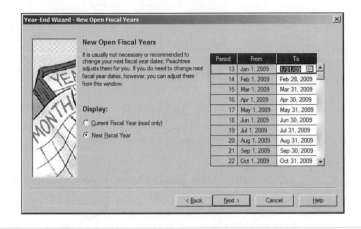

Step 13:

Click <u>N</u>ext to confirm the closing of fiscal year 2007 and the opening of fiscal years 2008 and 2009, as shown in figure 13-5.

FIGURE 13-5

*Year-End Wizard-Confirm
Close Window*

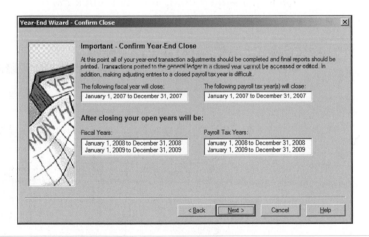

Step 14:

Click Begin <u>C</u>lose from the Year-End Wizard-Begin Close dialog box to begin the closing process.

Step 15:

Finally, click Finish from the Year-End Wizard-Congratulations! dialog box, as shown in figure 13-6.

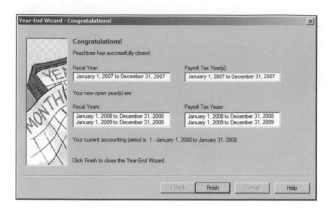

CONVERTING TO A PARTNERSHIP AND CREATING THE PARTNERSHIP ACCOUNTS

Step 1:

Open Woodward Construction Company, if needed.

Step 2:

Click Maintain and then Company Information.

Step 3:

At the Maintain Company Information window, click the down arrow at the *Form of Business* field, and then click *Partnership*, as shown in figure 13–7.

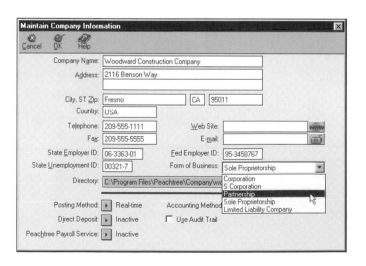

Step 4:

Click OK. The form of business has now been changed from a sole proprietorship to a partnership.

Step 5:
It is necessary to establish a capital account and a drawing account for each of the new partners. Create the following general ledger accounts:

Account ID:	**302**
Description:	**M. Stone, Capital**
Account Type:	**Equity–doesn't close**

Account ID:	**302.5**
Description:	**M. Stone, Drawing**
Account Type:	**Equity–gets closed**

Account ID:	**304**
Description:	**M. Brown, Capital**
Account Type:	**Equity–doesn't close**

Account ID:	**304.5**
Description:	**M. Brown, Drawing**
Account Type:	**Equity–gets closed**

Step 6:
Refer to the General Ledger Trial Balance to transfer any balance in the J. Woodward, Equity Account (301) to the J. Woodward, Capital Account (300), using the General Journal Entry feature.

The general journal entry should be:

January 2, 2008
    J. Woodward, Equity   16,546.34
        J. Woodward, Capital   16,546.34

Step 7:
Change the description of the following account:

Account ID:	**301**
Description:	**J. Woodward, Equity**
Account Type:	**Equity–Retained Earnings**

to—

Account ID:	**301**
Description:	**Partnership, Equity**
Account Type:	**Equity–Retained Earnings**

NOTE

If you used the Appendix to calculate depreciation for fixed assets, your number may be slightly off due to rounding. Therefore, if you have a different equity balance than the one given, transfer the amount you have.

RECORDING PARTNERSHIP TRANSACTIONS

The new partnership begins on January 2, 2008, when Molly Stone contributes $20,000 in cash and Marjorie Brown contributes $15,000 in cash and $5,000 in office supplies. Follow the steps outlined below to enter these partnership transactions.

Step 1:
Click Tasks and then Receipts.

Step 2:
At the Receipts window, key **Cash** in the *Name* field.

Step 3:
Key **Partner** in the *Reference* field.

Step 4:
At the *Date* field, click the *calendar* icon, and then select *Jan 2, 2008*.

Step 5:
Key **Partner Contribution** in the first row of the *Description* field.

Step 6:
Key **20,000.00** in the *Amount* field, as shown in figure 13–8.

FIGURE 13-8
Completed Receipts Window

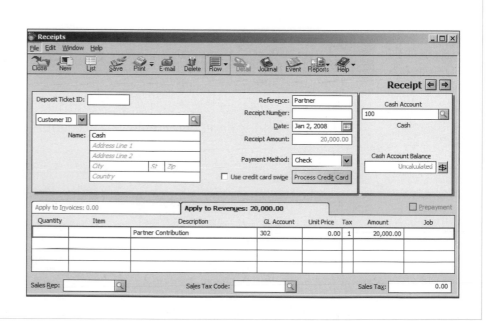

Step 7:
Click Journal on the Receipts toolbar.

Step 8:

The Accounting Behind the Screens window will appear. At the *Account No.* field in the first row, click the *magnifying glass* icon, and then click *302, M. Stone, Capital,* as shown in figure 13–9.

FIGURE 13-9
Accounting Behind the Screens Window

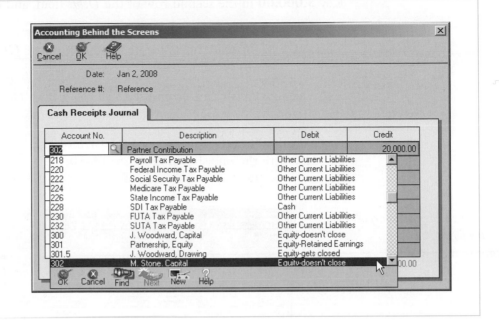

Step 9:

Click <u>O</u>K to close the Accounting Behind the Screens window.

Step 10:

Click <u>S</u>ave to save the entry, and then click Close.

Step 11:

Click Ta<u>s</u>ks, and then click <u>G</u>eneral Journal Entry.

Step 12:

At the General Journal Entry window in the <u>D</u>ate field, click the *calendar* icon, and then select *Jan 2, 2008.*

Step 13:

Key **Partner** in the *Refere<u>n</u>ce* field.

Step 14:

Click in the first row of the *GL Account* field, click the *magnifying glass* icon, and then click *100, Cash.*

Step 15:

Key **Partner Contribution** in the first row of the *Description* field.

Step 16:

Key **15,000.00** in the first row of the *Debit* field, and tab to the next line.

Step 17:

Click *106, Office Supplies* in the second row of the *GL Account* field.

Step 18:

Key **Partner Contribution** in the second row of the *Description* field, if needed.

Step 19:

Key **5,000.00** in the second row of the *Debit* field, and tab to the next line.

Step 20:

Click *304, M. Brown, Capital* in the third row of the *GL Account* field.

Step 21:

Key **Partner Contribution** in the third row of the *Description* field.

Step 22:

Key **20,000.00** in the third row of the *Credit* field. Compare your completed entry with the one shown in figure 13–10.

FIGURE 13-10

Completed General Journal Entry for Partner's Investment

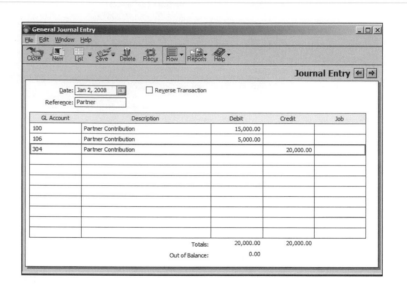

Step 23:

Click Save to save the entry, and then click Close.

ALLOCATING PARTNERSHIP PROFITS AND LOSSES

Woodward Construction Company will allocate profits and losses to the partners in the following way: 80% to Woodward, 10% to Stone, and 10% to Brown. Peachtree does not automatically distribute profits and losses to the capital accounts of partners. You must make the distribution prior to the closing process.

Before we can look at how profits and losses are allocated at Woodward Construction Company, we have to record the transactions for the month of January 2008.

Step 1:

Record the following transactions for January 2008 in the general journal. Then compare your completed entries with the ones shown on the General Journal report in figure 13–11.

Jan. 10   Had cash sales of $25,000 for services provided to customers. (Credit Account 400, Service Revenue.)

     12   Paid $1,400 for rent.

     14   Paid $2,600 for utilities.

     20   Molly Stone withdrew $1,500 for personal use.

     21   Marjorie Brown withdrew $1,600 for personal use.

FIGURE 13-11

Completed General Journal Entries January 2008

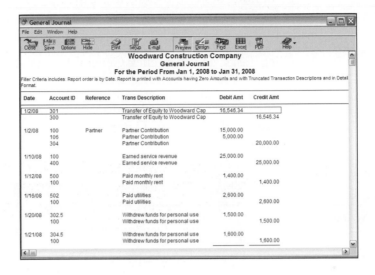

Step 2:

Use the Report feature to review the income statement for the month of January 2008. Your income statement should look like the one shown in figure 13–12.

FIGURE 13-12

Income Statement for January 2008

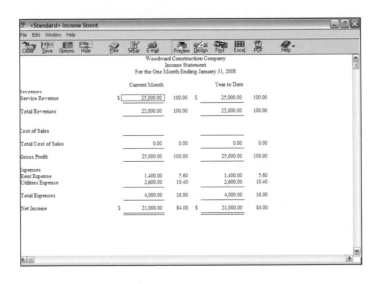

Notice that the income statement shows a net income (profit) of $21,000 for the month of January 2008. This net income must be distributed to the capital accounts of the partners as follows: $16,800 (80%) to Woodward, $2,100 (10%) to Stone, and $2,100 (10%) to Brown. The entry to distribute the net income involves a debit of $21,000 to Partnership Equity (Account 301) and a credit to each of the capital accounts for the appropriate amount. Partnership Equity takes the place of Income Summary in Woodward's accounting system. Its balance at the end of the accounting period represents the firm's net income or net loss for the period.

Step 3:

Click Tas<u>k</u>s, and then click <u>G</u>eneral Journal Entry.

Step 4:

Record the entry needed to distribute the net income to the capital accounts of each of the partners. Compare your completed entry with the one shown in figure 13–13.

FIGURE 13-13

Completed Entry for Distribution of Net Income to Partners

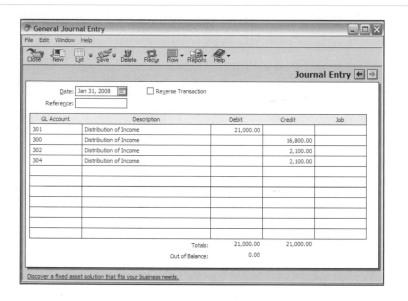

Step 5:

Click <u>S</u>ave and then Close.

Check
POINT

1. What two general ledger accounts are required for each partner?
2. What accounts are credited when net income is distributed to partners?

Answers
1. *A capital account and a drawing account are required for each partner.*
2. *The capital accounts of the partners are credited (increased) when net income is distributed.*

PRACTICE *objective* 2

On January 1, 2008, James Bull of Bullfrog Maintenance Company will form a partnership with Michael Green and Mitchell Norris. Bull will contribute the assets of his business, Green will contribute $30,000 in cash, and Norris will contribute $20,000 in cash and $10,000 in maintenance supplies. The partnership will assume the liabilities of Bull's business. Profits and losses will be allocated in the following way: 70% to Bull, 15% to Green, and 15% to Norris.

Step 1:

Open Bullfrog Maintenance Company.

Step 2:

Close the current fiscal year. (Print no reports, and ignore any messages about payroll or depreciation.) Change the form of business to a partnership.

Step 3:

Transfer the balance, $10,629.06, in the J. Bull, Equity account (301) to the J. Bull, Capital account (300) as of January 2, 2008.

Step 4:

Change the description of the J. Bull Equity Account (301) to the Partnership Equity Account.

Step 5:

Create the following accounts:

 NOTE

If you used the Appendix to calculate depreciation for fixed assets, your number may be slightly off due to rounding.

Account ID	**302**
Description	**M. Green, Capital**
Account Type	**Equity–doesn't close**
Account ID	**302.5**
Description	**M. Green, Drawing**
Account Type	**Equity–gets closed**
Account ID	**304**
Description	**M. Norris, Capital**
Account Type	**Equity–doesn't close**
Account ID	**304.5**
Description	**M. Norris, Drawing**
Account Type	**Equity–gets closed**

Step 6:

Journalize the contributions of Green and Norris as of January 2, 2008.

Step 7:

Journalize the following transactions that occurred in January 2008.

Jan. 10   Had cash sales of $50,000 for services provided to customers. (Credit Account 400, Service Revenue.)

    12   Paid $3,400 for rent.

    14   Paid $4,600 for utilities.

Step 8:

Review the Income Statement for the period.

Step 9:

Journalize the distribution of $42,000 of net income on January 31, 2008. Transfer the partnership equity balance to the capital accounts of the partners according to their agreed allocation of profits and losses.

OBJECTIVE 3—CREATE CORPORATE ACCOUNTS AND ENTER CORPORATE TRANSACTIONS

Legaleze Law Firm, Inc., has obtained a corporate charter from the state of California and is now ready to begin operations. It will do research and prepare documents for law firms and the legal departments of large companies.

The corporate charter authorizes Legaleze to issue 1,000,000 shares of $1 par-value common stock and 25,000 shares of $100 par value, 5% noncumulative preferred stock. The preferred stock pays an annual dividend of $5 per share (5% of $100). This stock is called "noncumulative" because unpaid dividends do not accumulate from year to year. If the corporation is not able to pay the dividend one year, it does not have to add the unpaid amount to the next year's dividend.

Legaleze plans to use Peachtree to keep its accounting records. Therefore, its first task is to complete the new company setup procedure of Peachtree.

SETTING UP A CORPORATION IN PEACHTREE

Step 1:

Set up a new company in Peachtree using the company information found in figure 13–14.

FIGURE 13-14

New Company Setup—Company Information Dialog Box

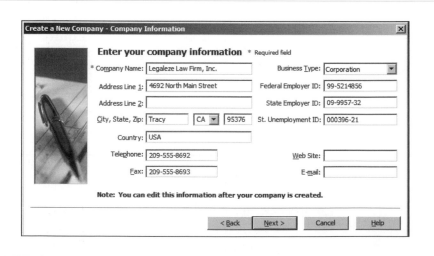

Step 2:

Select a Legal Firm from the extensive Chart of Accounts sample companies.

Step 3:

Select Accrual as the Accounting Method.

Step 4:

Select Real Time as the Posting Method.

Step 5:

Select 12 Monthly Accounting Periods.

Step 6:

Select January 2007 as the date of the first monthly accounting period.

Step 7:

Accept all other defaults.

CREATING CORPORATE ACCOUNTS

Legaleze will make use of a sample corporate chart of accounts provided by Peachtree. This chart of accounts includes general ledger accounts for common stock. However, because Legaleze plans to issue preferred stock as well as common stock, it must add the following accounts: Preferred Stock and Paid-in Capital in Excess of Par—Preferred.

Remember that when preferred stock is issued for more than its par value, two stockholders' equity accounts are affected. Preferred Stock is used to record the par-value amount of the shares issued. Paid-in Capital in Excess of Par—Preferred is used to record the amount received that is above par value.

Step 1:

Create the following general ledger accounts:

Account ID:	**39001**
Description:	**Preferred Stock**
Account Type:	**Equity–docsn't close**

Account ID:	**39002**
Description:	**Paid-In Capital-Preferred Stk**
Account Type:	**Equity–doesn't close**

Step 2:

Change the following general ledger account—

Account ID:	**39004**
Description:	**Paid-In Capital**
Account Type:	**Equity–doesn't close**

to—

Account ID:	**39004**
Description:	**Paid-In Capital-Common Stk**
Account Type:	**Equity–doesn't close**

Step 3:

View the new accounts on the firm's chart of accounts. Compare them with the stockholders' equity accounts shown in figure 13–15. Make any necessary corrections.

FIGURE 13-15
Chart of Accounts with Newly Created Accounts

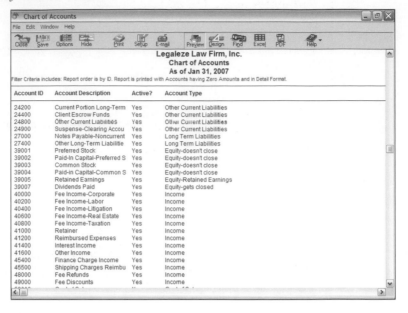

ENTERING CORPORATE TRANSACTIONS—ISSUING COMMON STOCK

On January 2, 2007, Legaleze issued 50,000 shares of its $1 par-value common stock for $10 per share. It received $500,000 in cash. The entry for this transaction requires a debit of $500,000 to Cash, a credit of $50,000 to Common Stock (50,000 shares x $1 par value), and a credit of $450,000 to Paid-in Capital in Excess of Par—Common Stock (50,000 shares x $9).

HINT

This entry can also be made in the cash receipts journal by using the Accounting Behind the Screens feature.

Step 1:
Click Tas**k**s, and then click **G**eneral Journal Entry.

Step 2:
At the General Journal Entry window, at the *D*ate field, click the *calendar* icon, and then select *Jan 2, 2007*.

Step 3:
At the *GL Account* field, click the *magnifying glass* icon, and then click *Regular Checking Account (10200)* as the account to be debited. (Legaleze uses Regular Checking Account as its main cash account.)

Step 4:
Key **Issued 50,000 shares of common stock** in the *Description* field.

Step 5:
Key **500,000.00** in the *Debit* field.

Step 6:
Tab to the next row, and click *Common Stock (39003)* as the first account to be credited.

Step 7:
Key **50,000.00** in the *Credit* field. This amount represents the par value of the 50,000 shares issued (50,000 x $1).

Step 8:
Tab to the next row, and click *Paid-In Capital-Common Stk (39004)* as the second account to be credited.

Step 9:
Key **450,000.00** in the *Credit* field. This amount represents the difference between the issue price and the par value of the 50,000 shares ($10 – $1 = $9 x 50,000 = $450,000). Compare your completed entry with the one that appears in figure 13–16.

FIGURE 13-16

Journal Entry for the Issuance of Common Stock

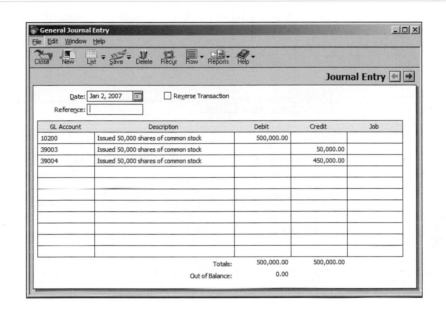

Step 10:
Click Save and Close to save the entry.

ENTERING CORPORATE TRANSACTIONS—RECEIVING DONATED CAPITAL

Sometimes a state, county, or city will donate an asset such as land or an unused building to a business. This donation is made for the purpose of economic development—so that the business will establish or expand operations in the area and create jobs for local residents.

For example, on January 5, 2007, the City of Tracy donated a parcel of land valued at $150,000 to Legaleze Law Firm, Inc. The firm will use this land to construct a building that will allow it to expand its staff. (The firm is currently renting an office with very limited space.)

To record this transaction, it is necessary to debit Land for $150,000 and credit a stockholders' equity account called Donated Capital for $150,000.

Donated capital will appear in the Stockholders' Equity section of the balance sheet along with paid-in capital (the capital supplied by investors through their purchases of stock) and retained earnings (the accumulated profits of the firm).

Step 1:

Create a general ledger account for donated capital. (Replace the account that is currently using 39005 as its ID.)

Account ID:	**39005**
Description:	**Donated Capital**
Account Type:	**Equity–doesn't close**

Create a new account for retained earnings, which was previously Account 39005:

Account ID:	**39006**
Description:	**Retained Earnings**
Account Type:	**Equity–Retained Earnings**

Step 2:

Click Save and Close.

Step 3:

Click Tasks, and then click General Journal Entry.

Step 4:

At the General Journal Entry window, in the *Date* field, click the *calendar* icon and then select *Jan 5, 2007*.

Step 5:

Click in the *GL Account* field, click the *magnifying glass* icon, and then click *Land (16900)*.

Step 6:

Key **Received donation of land** in the *Description* field.

Step 7:

Key **150,000.00** in the *Debit* field and tab down to the next row.

Step 8:

Click the *magnifying glass* icon and then *Donated Capital (39005)* in the *GL Account* field.

Step 9:

Key **150,000.00** in the *Credit* field. Compare your completed entry with the one that appears in figure 13–17.

FIGURE 13-17

Journal Entry for a Donation of Land

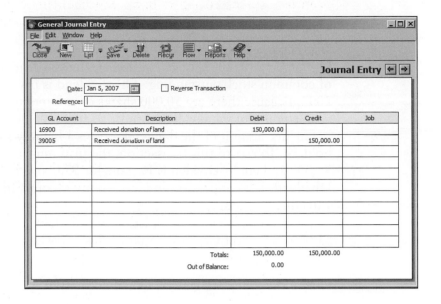

Step 10:

Click Save and Close to save the entry.

ENTERING CORPORATE TRANSACTIONS—GENERAL TRANSACTIONS

Legaleze had the following revenue and expense transactions during the month of January 2007.

Jan. 10   Received fees of $10,000 in cash for corporate legal services provided to a corporate client.

15   Paid $2,500 for rent.

16   Paid $565 for utilities.

20   Paid $1,200 for professional development costs.

Step 1:

Record the transactions in the general journal. Then compare your entries with figure 13–18.

FIGURE 13-18

Journal Entries for Revenue and Expense Transactions

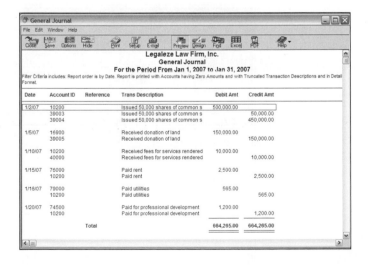

Step 2:

Click Close.

DECLARING A CASH DIVIDEND

On January 30, 2007, Legaleze declares a cash dividend of $0.10 per share of common stock outstanding. The dividend is payable on February 20, 2007. Because there are 50,000 shares of common stock outstanding, the total amount of the dividend will be $5,000 (50,000 x $0.10 = $5,000).

The declaration of the dividend creates a liability for Legaleze to its stockholders. To record this transaction, the firm must debit Cash Dividends for $5,000 and credit Dividends Payable for $5,000. Remember that Cash Dividends is a contra stockholders' equity account and Dividends Payable is a liability account.

When the dividend is paid, Legaleze will debit Dividends Payable for $5,000 and credit Cash for $5,000. This entry eliminates the liability.

Step 1:

Create the following general ledger account:

Account ID:	**24300**
Description:	**Dividends Payable**
Account Type:	**Other Current Liabilities**

Change the following general ledger account from—

Account ID:	**39007**
Description:	**Dividends Paid**
Account Type:	**Equity–gets closed**

to—

Account ID:	**39007**
Description:	**Cash Dividends**
Account Type:	**Equity–gets closed**

Step 2:

Record the declaration of the cash dividend in the general journal. Then compare your entry with figure 13–19.

FIGURE 13-19

Journal Entry for Declaration of a Cash Dividend

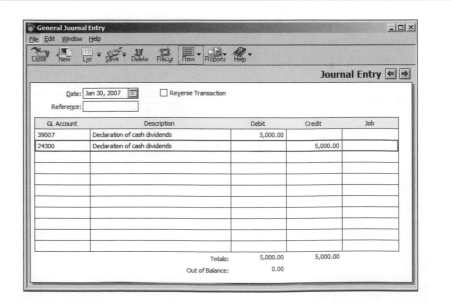

Step 3:

Click Save and Close to save the entry.

Check POINT

1. What two types of stock can a corporation issue?
2. What account is credited when a cash dividend is declared?

Answers
1. *A corporation can issue common stock and preferred stock.*
2. *The account credited is Cash Dividends Payable.*

PRACTICE *objective* 3

Abacus Executive Search, Inc., is a new corporation that will use Peachtree Complete Accounting 2007. On January 2, 2007, Abacus received its corporate charter. This charter authorizes the firm to issue 450,000 shares of $2 par-value common stock and 20,000 shares of $50 par value, 6% preferred stock.

Step 1:

Complete the new company setup procedure for Abacus. Use the information provided in figure 13–20.

FIGURE 13-20

New Company Setup—Company Information for Abacus Executive Search, Inc.

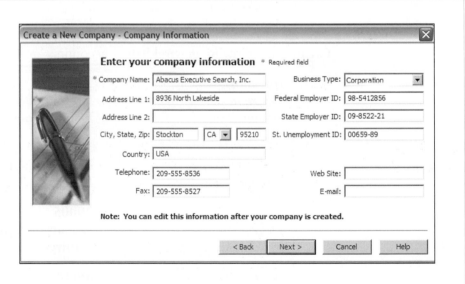

Step 2:

Use a sample company Chart of Accounts, and click *Employment Agency* as the type of business.

Use accrual accounting and real-time posting.

Use a fiscal year of 12 monthly accounting periods. Set up the monthly periods as shown in figure 13–21.

FIGURE 13-21

Create a New Company—
Fiscal Year

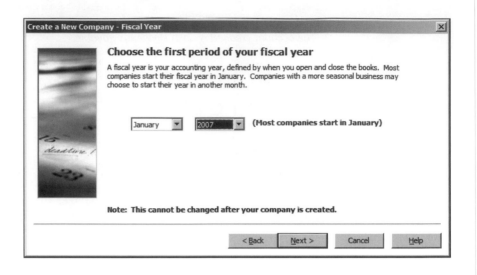

Step 5:

Accept all other defaults.

Step 6:

Create the following general ledger accounts:

Account ID:	**39001**
Description:	**Preferred Stock**
Account Type:	**Equity–doesn't close**
Account ID:	**39002**
Description:	**Paid-in Capital-Preferred Stk**
Account Type:	**Equity–doesn't close**
Account ID:	**39005**
Description:	**Donated Capital**
Account Type:	**Equity–doesn't close**
Account ID:	**39006**
Description:	**Retained Earnings**
Account Type:	**Equity–Retained Earnings**
Account ID:	**24300**
Description:	**Dividends Payable**
Account Type:	**Other Current Liabilities**

Change the following general ledger account from—

Account ID	**39004**
Description	**Paid-in Capital**
Account Type	**Equity–doesn't close**

to—

Account ID	**39004**
Description	**Paid-in Capital, Common Stk**
Account Type	**Equity–doesn't close**

Change the following general ledger account from—

Account ID:	**39007**
Description:	**Dividends Paid**
Account Type:	**Equity–gets closed**

to—

Account ID:	**39007**
Description:	**Cash Dividends**
Account Type:	**Equity–gets closed**

Step 7:

Abacus had the following transactions during the month of January 2007. Record these transactions in the general journal.

Jan. 3   Issued 45,000 shares of common stock for $300,000 in cash.
    4   Issued 3,000 shares of preferred stock for $200,000 in cash.
    5   Received land valued at $54,000 as a donation from the city of Stockton.
    10   Received fees of $20,000 in cash for placement services provided to a corporate client.
    15   Paid rent of $4,500.
    16   Paid utilities of $1,565.
    20   Paid professional dues of $1,200 (Account 64500, Dues and Subscriptions Exp).
    21   Paid license fees of $1,345.
    31   Declared a $4,500 cash dividend to all common stockholders. This dividend is payable on Feb. 15 at a rate of $0.10 per share. (The preferred stockholders do not receive a dividend until year-end.)

Step 8:

Review your work, and make any necessary corrections. Then save the entries.

OBJECTIVE 4—PRINT PARTNERSHIP AND CORPORATE REPORTS

income statement A report of a firm's revenue, expenses, and net income or net loss for an accounting period.

balance sheet A report of a firm's assets, liabilities, and owner's equity as of a specific date.

Every business—sole proprietorship, partnership, and corporation—prepares an income statement and a balance sheet at the end of the accounting period. Remember that the **income statement** reports the results of operations for the accounting period—the revenue, expenses, and net income or net loss. The **balance sheet** reports the financial condition of the business as of a specific day of the accounting period—the assets, liabilities, and owner's equity.

These statements are essentially the same for all types of business organization. The one major difference is the treatment of owner's equity on the balance sheet, as will be seen on the next few pages.

Partnerships and corporations may also prepare certain supplemental statements. For example, a corporation may prepare a statement of retained earnings that shows the changes in its retained earnings during the accounting period.

PREPARING PARTNERSHIP REPORTS

The balance sheet of a partnership shows the capital of each partner. A separate statement that explains the changes that took place in the partnership's equity during the accounting period may supplement this information. Such a statement usually includes the beginning balance of each partner's capital account, each partner's share of the net income or net loss for the period, each partner's withdrawals for this period, and the ending balance of each partner's capital account. This report is usually known as a statement of partners' equity. However, in Peachtree, a statement of retained earnings is used to provide information about the withdrawals of the partners.

Follow the steps outlined below to prepare a balance sheet and a statement of retained earnings for the partnership of Woodward, Stone, and Brown, which does business as Woodward Construction Company. (The income statement for this partnership appeared earlier in figure 13–12.)

Step 1:

Open Woodward Construction Company and close Action Items log.

Step 2:

Click Reports, and then click Financial Statements.

Step 3:

In the Report List section of the Select a Report dialog box, click *<Standard> Balance Sheet*. The date of the balance sheet is January 31, 2008.

Step 4:

Click Preview and examine the Capital section of the balance sheet, which shows the partners' equity. There is a separate capital account for each partner, as shown in figure 13–22.

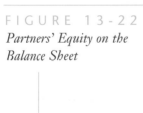

FIGURE 13-22

Partners' Equity on the Balance Sheet

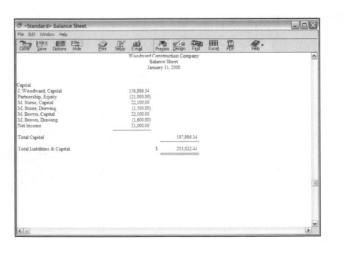

Step 5:

Print the report, if desired. Then close the preview window.

Step 6:

Click *<Standard> Retained Earnings.* The statement of retained earnings is for the month ending January 31, 2008.

Step 7:

Click Preview and examine the statement of retained earnings, as shown in figure 13–23. Note the separate drawing account for each partner.
J. Woodward does not appear listed because he had no withdrawals in this accounting period.

FIGURE 13-23

Statement of Retained Earnings for Woodward Construction Company

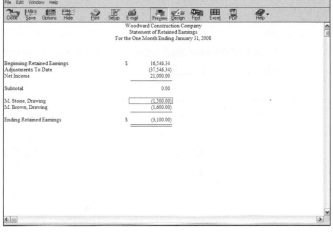

Step 8:

Print the report, if desired. Then close the preview window and the Select a Report dialog box.

PREPARING CORPORATE REPORTS

As noted previously, the balance sheet of a corporation contains a Stockholders' Equity section. This section shows the various types and amounts of capital that the corporation has as of a specific date, usually the last day of the accounting period. The three basic types of corporate capital are paid-in capital, earned capital, and donated capital.

Remember that paid-in capital is the capital received from stockholders through their purchases of common and preferred stock. Earned capital consists of accumulated earnings from the firm's operations. Donated capital comes from assets that are donated to a corporation by a state, county, or city.

The statement of retained earnings reports the changes that took place in retained earnings during the accounting period. It shows the beginning balance of the Retained Earnings account, an addition for net income or a deduction for a net loss, a deduction for dividends paid, and the ending balance of the Retained Earnings account.

Follow the steps outlined below to prepare a balance sheet and a statement of retained earnings for Legaleze Law Services, Inc.

Step 1:

Open Legaleze Law Services, Inc. and close the Action Items log.

Step 2:

Click Reports, and then click Financial Statements.

Step 3:

In the Report List section of the Select a Report dialog box, click <Standard> Balance Sheet. The date of the balance sheet is January 31, 2007.

Step 4:

Click Preview and examine the Capital section of the balance sheet, which shows the stockholders' equity. It should resemble figure 13–24.

FIGURE 13-24

Stockholders' Equity on the Balance Sheet

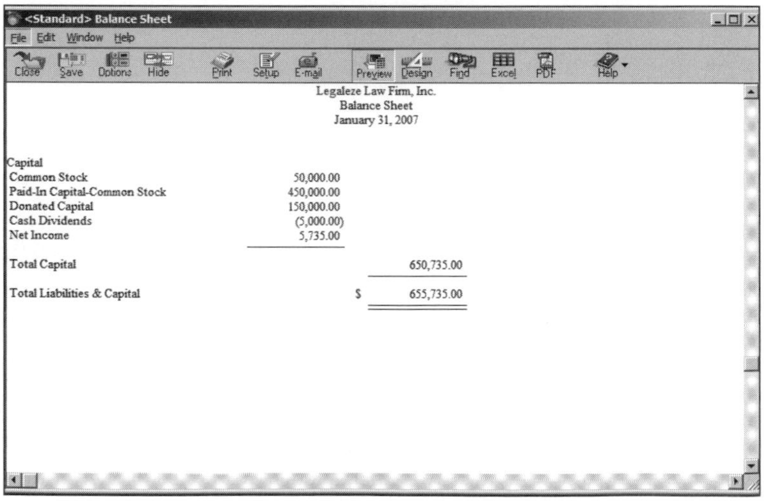

Step 5:
Close the preview window.

Step 6:

Click *<Standard> Retained Earnings*. The statement of retained earnings is for the month ending January 31, 2007.

Step 7:

Click Preview and examine the statement of retained earnings, which should look like figure 13–25. Note the reduction in retained earnings caused by the cash dividends.

FIGURE 13-25

Statement of Retained Earnings for Legaleze Law Firm, Inc.

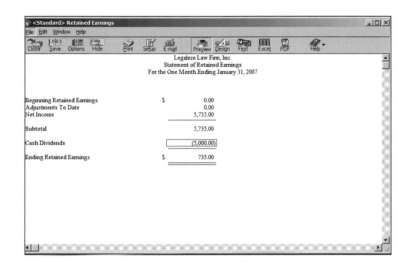

Step 8:

Close the preview window, then close the Select a Report dialog box.

POINT

1. What accounts appear in the equity section of the balance sheet for a partnership?
2. What are the three basic types of capital for a corporation?

Answers

1. *The accounts that appear in the equity section are the capital and drawing accounts of the partners.*
2. *The three basic types of capital for a corporation are paid-in capital, earned capital, and donated capital.*

PRACTICE *objective* 4

Step 1:

Open Abacus Executive Search, Inc.

Step 2:

Print the income statement, the balance sheet, and the statement of retained earnings for the month of January 2007. Your printouts should look like figures 13-26, 13-27, and 13-28, respectively.

FIGURE 13-26

Income Statement for Abacus Executive Search, Inc.

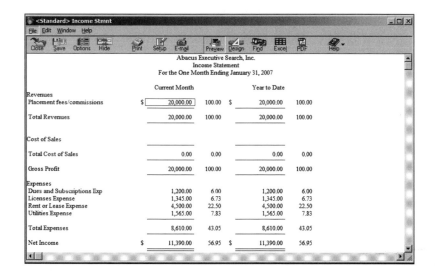

FIGURE 13-27
Partial Balance Sheet for Abacus Executive Search, Inc.

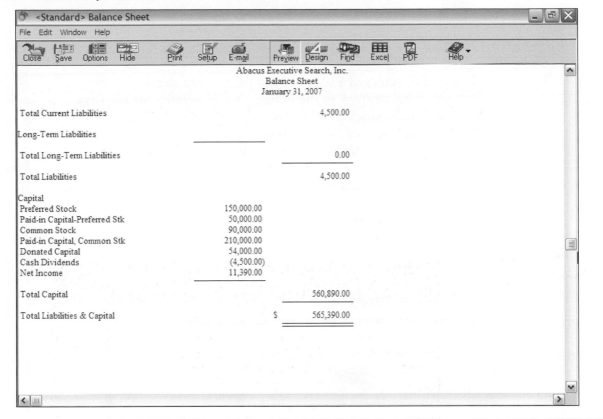

FIGURE 13-28
Statement of Retained Earnings for Abacus Executive Search, Inc.

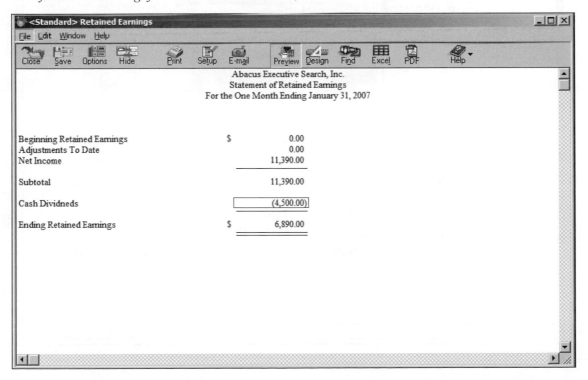

The board of directors of a software company wants to take the firm public—sell shares of stock to the public. One possibility for the firm might be to have its stock listed by the NASDAQ Stock Market, which trades the shares of many technology companies. Examples of firms that trade on the NASDAQ Stock Market are the computer companies Dell and Apple and the software companies Microsoft, Adobe Systems, and Oracle.

NASDAQ maintains a Web site at www.nasdaq.com. Its home page is shown in figure 13–29. This Web site can be used to find current price quotations (quotes) on NASDAQ stocks and many other types of information.

FIGURE 13-29

The Home Page of NASDAQ

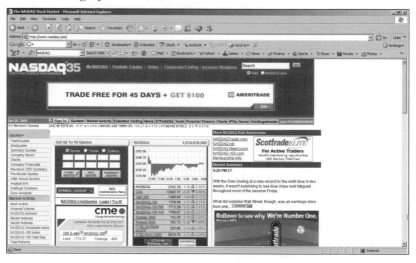

INTERNET ASSIGNMENT:

Go to the NASDAQ Web site, and do the following:

- Find the current price quotation for each of the technology stocks mentioned above.
- See if there is news about any of these five technology stocks.
- Look at the information about IPOs. These are initial public offerings—stocks that are being sold to the public for the first time.

SOFTWARE
Command Summary

Change Organization Type	<u>M</u>aintain, Company <u>I</u>nformation, change the business form
Edit Account Information	<u>M</u>aintain, Chart of <u>A</u>ccounts, enter the changes, <u>S</u>ave
Print Financial Statements	Reports, <u>F</u>inancial Statements, select the report type

PROJECTS
and Problems

CONTENT CHECK

Multiple Choice: Choose only one response for each question.

1. The equity section of the balance sheet for a partnership must show the
   A. liabilities.
   B. assets.
   C. capital of each partner.
   D. expenses.

2. Unless otherwise stated, partners share profits and losses
   A. according to their capital balances.
   B. according to the amount of time spent at the firm by each partner.
   C. based on the amount of business each partner generates.
   D. equally.

3. Which of the following is a disadvantage of the partnership form of organization?
   A. ease of formation
   B. greater management expertise than a sole proprietorship
   C. mutual agency rule
   D. less regulation and taxation than a corporation

4. Which of the following is a disadvantage of a corporation?
   A. limited liability
   B. ease of raising capital
   C. continuous life
   D. double taxation

5. Which of the following accounts would *not* be found in the equity section of a corporation's balance sheet?
   A. Common Stock
   B. Donated Capital
   C. Preferred Stock
   D. Dividends Payable

Short-Essay Response: Provide a detailed answer for each question.

1. What is the par value of stock? What is the market value?
2. What is a partnership? What are the advantages and disadvantages of this type of business organization?
3. What is the difference between authorized and outstanding stock?
4. What is a dividend?
5. What is the paid-in capital of a corporation? What is the earned capital?
6. What information appears on the statement of retained earnings for a corporation?

CASE PROBLEMS

PROBLEM 1A

On January 2, 2007, Jim Mathews and Gary Corbett formed a partnership. They will operate a business called the ABC Collection Service. Each will contribute $30,000 in cash. Profits and losses will be divided equally.

1. Use the information in figure 13–30 and the information given below to set up the business in Peachtree.

FIGURE 13-30

Setup Information for ABC Collection Service

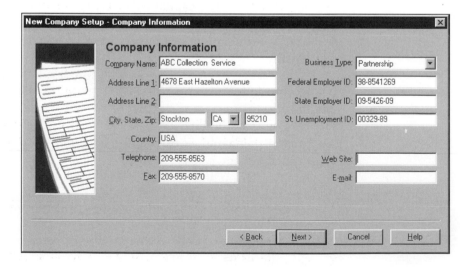

Chart of Accounts:	**Service Company**
Accounting Method:	**Accrual**
Posting Method:	**Real Time**
Accounting Periods:	**12 Monthly Accounting Periods**
Fiscal Year to Start:	**January 2007**
Defaults:	**Accept**

2. Establish the capital and drawing accounts needed by the partnership.

Create the following general ledger accounts:

Account ID:	**39008**
Description:	**Gary Corbett, Capital**
Account Type:	**Equity–doesn't close**

Account ID:	**39009**
Description:	**Gary Corbett, Drawing**
Account Type:	**Equity–gets closed**

Change the following general ledger account from—

Account ID:	**39006**
Description:	**Partners Contribution**
Account Type:	**Equity–doesn't close**

to—

Account ID:	**39006**
Description:	**Jim Mathews, Capital**
Account Type:	**Equity–doesn't close**

Change the following general ledger account from—

Account ID:	**39007**
Description:	**Partners Draw**
Account Type:	**Equity–gets closed**

to—

Account ID:	**39007**
Description:	**Jim Mathews, Drawing**
Account Type:	**Equity–gets closed**

3. Journalize the following transactions for the month of January 2007. (Use the general journal and Regular Checking Account.)

Jan.   2   Mathews contributed $30,000 in cash, and Corbett contributed $30,000 in cash.

10   Had cash sales of $23,000 for professional fees from customers.

11   Paid rent of $4,500.

15   Paid utilities of $1,500.

20   Mathews withdrew $1,000 in cash, and Corbett withdrew $1,000 in cash.

4. Print the following financial statements as of January 31, 2007: the income statement, balance sheet, and statement of retained earnings.

PROBLEM 2A

On January 2, 2007, General Consulting, Inc., received its corporate charter, which authorizes it to issue up to 2,000,000 shares of $1 par-value common stock and 50,000 shares of $100 par value, 6% cumulative preferred stock.

1. Use the information in figure 13–31 and the information given below to set up the business in Peachtree.

FIGURE 13-31

Setup Information for General Consulting, Inc.

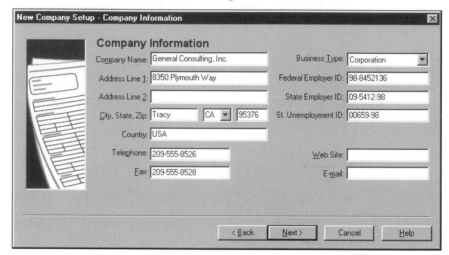

Chart of Accounts:	**Consulting Company**
Accounting Method:	**Accrual**
Posting Method:	**Real Time**
Accounting Periods:	**12 Monthly Accounting Periods**
Fiscal Year to Start:	**January 2007**
Defaults:	**Accept**

2. Journalize the following transactions for the month of January 2007. (Use the general journal and Regular Checking Account.)

Jan. 3 Issued 30,000 shares of common stock for $300,000 in cash.
10 Had cash sales of $43,000 for consulting services provided to customers.
11 Paid rent of $6,000.
15 Paid utilities of $1,600.
31 Declared a cash dividend of $0.20 for each share of common stock outstanding. (Create the Dividends Payable account. Change the Dividends Paid account into the Cash Dividends account.)

3. Print the following financial statements as of January 31, 2007: the income statement, balance sheet, and statement of retained earnings.

PROBLEM 1B

On January 2, 2007, Terry Jones and Carol Smith formed a partnership. They will operate a business called CBA Résumé Service. Each will contribute $25,000 in cash. Profits and losses will be divided equally.

1. Use the information in figure 13–32 and the information given below to set up the business in Peachtree.

FIGURE 13-32

Setup Information for CBA Résumé Service

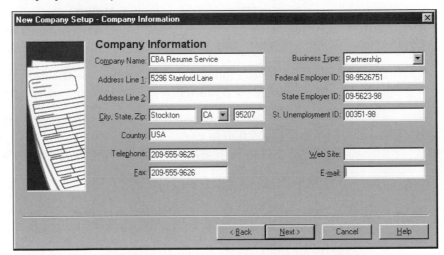

Chart of Accounts:	**Service Company**
Accounting Method:	**Accrual**
Posting Method:	**Real Time**
Accounting Periods:	**12 Monthly Accounting Periods**
Fiscal Year to Start:	**January 2007**
Defaults:	**Accept**

2. Establish the capital and drawing accounts needed by the partnership.

Create the following general ledger accounts:

Account ID:	**39008**
Description:	**Terry Jones, Capital**
Account Type:	**Equity–doesn't close**

Account ID:	**39009**
Description:	**Terry Jones, Drawing**
Account Type:	**Equity–gets closed**

Change the following general ledger account from—

Account ID:	**39006**
Description:	**Partners Contribution**
Account Type:	**Equity–doesn't close**

to—

Account ID:	**39006**
Description:	**Carol Smith, Capital**
Account Type:	**Equity–doesn't close**

Change the following general ledger account from—

Account ID:	**39007**
Description:	**Partners Draw**
Account Type:	**Equity–gets closed**

to—

Account ID:	**39007**
Description:	**Carol Smith, Drawing**
Account Type:	**Equity–gets closed**

3. Journalize the following transactions for the month of January 2007. (Use the general journal.)

Jan. 2 Jones contributed $25,000 in cash, and Smith contributed $25,000 in cash.

5 Had cash sales of $13,000 for professional services provided to customers.

11 Paid rent of $2,500.

15 Paid utilities of $1,500.

20 Jones withdrew $1,500 in cash, and Smith withdrew $1,500 in cash.

4. Print the following financial statements as of January 31, 2007: the income statement, balance sheet, and statement of retained earnings.

PROBLEM 2B

Barker Architectural Services, Inc. received its corporate charter, which authorizes it to issue up to 1,000,000 shares of $2 par-value common stock and 100,000 shares of $50 par value, 5% cumulative preferred stock.

1. Use the information in figure 13–33 and the information given below to set up the business in Peachtree.

Setup Information for Barker Architectural Services, Inc.

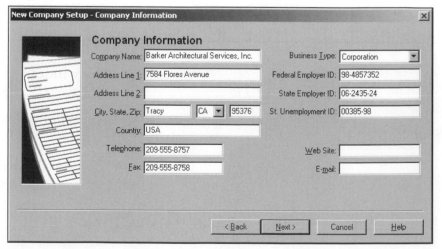

Chart of Accounts:	**Architectural Company**
Accounting Method:	**Accrual**
Posting Method:	**Real Time**
Accounting Periods:	**12 Monthly Accounting Periods**
Fiscal Year to Start:	**January 2007**
Defaults:	**Accept**

2. Journalize the following transactions for the month of January 2007. (Use the general journal and Regular Checking Account.)

Jan.   3   Issued 20,000 shares of common stock for $200,000 in cash.
10   Had cash sales of $56,000 for design services provided to customers.
11   Paid rent of $11,000.
15   Paid utilities of $4,700.
31   Declared a cash dividend of $0.60 for each share of common stock outstanding. (Create the Dividends Payable account. Change the Dividends Paid account into the Cash Dividends account.)

3. Print the following financial statements as of January 31, 2007: the income statement, balance sheet, and statement of retained earnings.

Cooperative Learning

1. In groups of three or four students, visit two different partnerships in your area. (Accounting and law firms are often partnerships.) Speak with a partner about the advantages and disadvantages of this type of organization. Ask how disagreements among partners are resolved. Prepare a brief report with your findings.
2. In groups of three or four students, research the requirements for obtaining a corporate charter in your state. Check the Web site of your state or the office of your Secretary of State. Prepare a list of the requirements.

Writing and Decision Making

Bruce Cho, the owner of a sole proprietorship software business would like to expand operations. He needs additional capital to develop new products. He is thinking of forming a corporation. In memo form, briefly explain the advantages and disadvantages of a corporation to Bruce Cho.

APPENDIX

FIXED
ASSETS
APPENDIX

1. Understand fixed assets and depreciation

2. Create accounts for new fixed assets

3. Calculate and record the depreciation of fixed assets

4. Make entries to record the disposal of fixed assets

5. Prepare and modify reports showing fixed assets and depreciation

The Fixed Assets (FAS for Peachtree) Module is not available on the Educational Version of Peachtree Complete Accounting 2007 that is distributed with this text. This appendix is to be used instead of Chapter 12, Fixed Assets, to learn computerized accounting procedures for fixed assets using Peachtree 2007.

SOFTWARE FEATURES

- Set Up Subsidiary Ledger Records for Fixed Assets

- Select a Depreciation Method

- Calculate and Record Depreciation

- Record the Disposal of Fixed Assets

- Prepare Fixed Asset Reports

Remember that assets are divided into several groups. One group consists of current assets: cash, assets that will be turned into cash within one year, and assets that will be used up within one year. Current assets include cash, petty cash, accounts receivable, merchandise inventory, supplies, and prepaid insurance.

current assets Cash, assets that will be turned into cash within one year, and assets that will be used up within one year.

Another group consists of fixed assets. These assets have the following characteristics:
- They have an expected life of more than one year.
- They are intended for use in the business and not for resale to customers.
- They are tangible, which means that they have a physical substance.

fixed assets Assets that have an expected life of more than one year, will be used in the business, and are tangible.

Examples of fixed assets are land, buildings, furniture, office equipment, factory machines, automobiles, and trucks. Fixed assets are also known as *plant assets*, *capital assets*, and *property, plant, and equipment*.

In addition to current assets and fixed assets, some businesses have intangible assets and natural resources. Intangible assets are long-term assets that have no physical substance, such as patents, trademarks, copyrights, and franchises. Natural resources are long-term assets that are removed from the ground, such as oil, natural gas, coal, and timber.

intangible assets Long-term assets that have no physical substance.

natural resources Long-term assets that are removed from the ground.

OBJECTIVE 1—UNDERSTAND FIXED ASSETS AND DEPRECIATION

A business must set up a general ledger account for each broad class of fixed assets that it owns. It might have general ledger accounts for land, land improvements, buildings, office furniture, office equipment, factory machines, and trucks. These accounts include all items in a class. For example, the Office Furniture account covers desks, chairs, sofas, file cabinets, and bookshelves. The Office Equipment account covers computers, printers, fax machines, copying machines, and telephone systems.

Because the general ledger accounts for fixed assets involve broad classes, most businesses also maintain records for the individual assets. These records form a subsidiary ledger called the fixed asset ledger.

fixed asset ledger A subsidiary ledger that contains records for individual fixed assets.

RECORDING THE COST OF FIXED ASSETS

When a fixed asset is purchased, the cost is debited to the appropriate general ledger account and entered in the appropriate subsidiary record. The cost of a fixed asset may be greater than the price paid for the asset. For example:

- The cost of land includes not only the price but also any amounts paid for real estate commissions, legal fees, taxes, removal of old structures, draining, and grading.
- Newly acquired land may require improvements such as sidewalks, fences, and outdoor lighting. (The cost of these items is debited to an account called Land Improvements rather than to the Land account.)
- The cost of a new building includes not only the amount paid for construction but also any fees paid for the planning work of architects and engineers, for permits and inspections, and for insurance during construction.
- The cost of machinery and equipment includes not only the price of the item but also any amounts paid for freight, taxes, installation, and insurance during delivery and installation.

RECORDING DEPRECIATION

Remember that **depreciation** is the process of allocating the cost of a fixed asset to operations during its estimated useful life. Because fixed assets help to produce revenue for a business, their cost must gradually be recorded as an expense while they are being used. This procedure allows the business to match its revenue and expenses.

All fixed assets except land are subject to depreciation. Land is not depreciated because it is considered to have an indefinite useful life. The other fixed assets have limited lives.

Because land is not subject to depreciation, when land and a building are purchased together for one price, this amount must be divided. One portion is debited to the Land account, and the other portion is debited to the Building account. Similarly, land improvements, which are subject to depreciation, are recorded in a separate account, not in the Land account.

Depreciation is an operating expense for a business. It is recorded as part of the adjusting entries for each accounting period. The adjustment for each class of fixed assets consists of a debit to a depreciation expense account and a credit to an accumulated depreciation account. For example, the depreciation for office equipment is recorded by debiting Depreciation Expense–Office Equipment and crediting Accumulated Depreciation–Office Equipment.

Notice that the account used for the credit part of the entry is not the asset account Office Equipment. Instead, it is Accumulated Depreciation–Office Equipment, a contra asset account. As long as the business owns the office equipment, the asset account shows the cost and the contra asset account shows all depreciation taken. On the balance sheet, both amounts are reported and the balance of the contra asset account is subtracted from the balance of the asset account. The difference between the two balances is the **book value** of the fixed asset.

Cost of Fixed Asset – Accumulated Depreciation = Book Value

Each class of fixed assets has its own depreciation expense account and its own accumulated depreciation account.

CALCULATING DEPRECIATION

Various methods are used to calculate depreciation. Most of these methods base depreciation on three basic factors: the cost of a fixed asset, its estimated salvage value, and its estimated useful life.

- As noted previously, the cost of a fixed asset is the purchase price plus any amounts that must be spent to prepare the asset for use, such as shipping and installation.
- The **estimated salvage value** is the amount that a business expects a fixed asset to be worth at the end of its useful life. Salvage value is also known as *trade-in value, scrap value,* and *residual value.*

- The **estimated useful life** is the number of years that a business expects a fixed asset to be used in its operations.

Depreciation is calculated on a yearly basis. However, if a business owns a fixed asset for less than a year, it takes depreciation for only the amount of time that the asset was in service during the year. This situation often occurs in the year when a fixed asset was purchased and in the year when it is sold or scrapped.

For financial accounting purposes, the four most commonly used depreciation methods are:

- The straight-line method
- The units-of-production method
- The double declining-balance method
- The sum-of-the-years'-digits method

THE STRAIGHT-LINE METHOD

The **straight-line method** of depreciation allocates an equal amount of depreciation to each year of an asset's useful life. For example, assume that a business buys a new machine for $42,000 on January 1, 2007. The machine has an estimated salvage value of $2,000 and an estimated useful life of four years. The annual depreciation for the machine is therefore $10,000.

Cost – Salvage Value = Depreciable Cost
$42,000 – $2,000 = $40,000

Depreciable Cost ÷ Useful Life = Annual Depreciation
$40,000 ÷ 4 (years) = $10,000

Table 12–1 shows the depreciation expense, accumulated depreciation, and book value of the machine throughout its life when the straight-line method is used. Notice that at the end of the fourth year (2010), the book value is equal to the estimated salvage value ($2,000). No fixed asset can be depreciated below its salvage value.

Table 12–1 An Example of the Straight-Line Depreciation Method

Year	Cost	Depreciation Expense	Accumulated Depreciation	Book Value End of Year
2007	$42,000	$10,000	$10,000	$32,000
2008	42,000	10,000	20,000	22,000
2009	42,000	10,000	30,000	12,000
2010	42,000	10,000	40,000	2,000

Keep in mind that the book value is simply the depreciated cost of a fixed asset. It does not necessarily represent the market value or even the replacement value of the asset.

THE UNITS-OF-PRODUCTION METHOD

The **units-of-production method** allocates depreciation on the basis of how much work the asset produces during each year of its useful life. For a factory machine, the work produced might be expressed in hours of operation. For an automobile or truck, it might be expressed in miles driven.

Consider again the machine purchased for $42,000 on January 1, 2007, which has an estimated salvage value of $2,000. Suppose that management expects the useful life of the machine to be 40,000 hours. The depreciation rate for the machine is $1 per hour.

Cost – Salvage Value = Depreciable Cost
$42,000 – $2,000 = $40,000

Depreciable Cost ÷ Useful Life = Depreciation Rate
$40,000 ÷ 40,000 (hours) = $1 per hour

Assume that the machine is used for 9,000 hours in the first year, 11,000 hours in the second year, 12,000 hours in the third year, and 8,000 hours in the fourth year. The amount of depreciation for the first year will be $9,000.

Usage x Depreciation Rate = Depreciation
9,000 hours x $1 per hour = $9,000

Table 12–2 shows the depreciation expense, accumulated depreciation, and book value for the machine through its life when the units-of-production method is used. Again, the book value at the end of the asset's life (40,000 hours) is $2,000, which is the salvage value.

Table 12–2 An Example of the Units-of-Production Depreciation Method

Year	Cost	Hours	Depreciation Expense	Accumulated Depreciation	Book Value End of Year
2007	$42,000	9,000	$ 9,000	$ 9,000	$33,000
2008	42,000	11,000	11,000	20,000	22,000
2009	42,000	12,000	12,000	32,000	10,000
2010	42,000	8,000	8,000	40,000	2,000

THE DOUBLE DECLINING-BALANCE METHOD

double declining-balance method A method that allocates depreciation at twice the straight-line rate.

The **double declining-balance method** allocates depreciation at twice the straight-line rate. The doubled rate is applied to the book value of the asset each year. Because the book value decreases from year to year, more depreciation is taken in the early years of the asset's useful life and less depreciation is taken in the later years. Thus, the double declining-balance method is considered an **accelerated method** of depreciation.

accelerated method A method in which more depreciation is taken in the early years of an asset's useful life and less in the later years.

Again, assume that a machine is purchased for $42,000 on January 1, 2007, and has an estimated useful life of four years and an estimated salvage value of $2,000. With the double declining-balance method, the salvage value is ignored. The first step in calculating depreciation is to find the straight-line rate and then double it. In this case, the doubled rate is 50%. (The straight-line rate for an asset with a four-year useful life is 25%.)

¼ = 0.25 x 2 = 0.50 or 50%

When the 50% rate is applied to the first year's book value, the depreciation is $21,000.

Book Value x Depreciation Rate = Depreciation
$42,000 x 0.50 = $21,000

In the second year, the book value is $21,000 and the depreciation is $10,500 ($21,000 x 0.50 = $10,500).

Table 12–3 shows the depreciation expense, accumulated depreciation, and book value for the machine throughout its life when the double declining-balance method is used. Notice that in the fourth year, the remaining book value is $2,625, slightly more than the estimated salvage value of $2,000. (Although salvage value is ignored when calculating depreciation with the double declining-balance method, the asset cannot be depreciated below its salvage value.)

Table 12–3 An Example of the Double Declining-Balance Depreciation Method

Year	Cost	Rate	Depreciation Expense	Accumulated Depreciation	Book Value End of Year
2007	$42,000	50%	$21,000	$21,000	$21,000
2008	42,000	50	10,500	31,500	10,500
2009	42,000	50	5,250	36,750	5,250
2010	42,000	50	2,625	39,375	2,625

THE SUM-OF-THE-YEARS'-DIGITS METHOD

sum-of-the-years'-digits method
A method that allocates depreciation on the basis of a fraction that changes each year.

The **sum-of-the-years'-digits method** allocates depreciation on the basis of a fraction that changes for each year of an asset's useful life. This fraction is applied to the depreciable cost of the asset (the cost less the salvage value). Because the sum-of-the-years'-digits method produces more depreciation in the early years and less depreciation in the later years, it is also considered an accelerated method of depreciation.

The denominator of the fraction (the figure at the bottom of the fraction) remains constant. It is the sum of the digits of the years that make up the useful life of the asset. The numerator of the fraction (the figure at the top of the fraction) changes. It is the number of years that remain in the useful life of the asset.

For example, let us look again at the machine purchased for $42,000 on January 1, 2007. This machine has an estimated useful life of four years and an estimated salvage value of $2,000. The sum of the years' digits for the four years of its useful life is 10 (1 + 2 + 3 + 4 = 10). This is the denominator of the fraction that will be used to calculate depreciation for the asset.

The numerator for the first year will be 4 because there are four years remaining in the useful life of the asset. The numerator for the second year will be 3 because there are only three years remaining in its useful life at that point.

The fraction for the first year is 4/10 while the fraction for the second year is 3/10. Therefore, based on a depreciable cost of $40,000 ($42,000 – $2,000), the depreciation expense for the first two years is calculated as follows:

4/10 of $40,000 = $16,000
3/10 of $40,000 = $12,000

Table 12–4 shows the depreciation expense, accumulated depreciation, and book value for the machine throughout its life when the sum-of-the-years'-digits method is used. The book value remaining at the end of the fourth year is always equal to the estimated salvage value.

Table 12–4 An Example of the Sum-of-the-Years'-Digits Method

Year	Cost	Fraction	Depreciation Expense	Accumulated Depreciation	Book Value End of Year
2007	$42,000	4/10	$16,000	$16,000	$26,000
2008	42,000	3/10	12,000	28,000	14,000
2009	42,000	2/10	8,000	36,000	6,000
2010	42,000	1/10	4,000	40,000	2,000

ACCELERATED COST RECOVERY SYSTEMS

The four depreciation methods that we have discussed so far are used for financial accounting purposes. However, when preparing federal income tax returns, businesses must use either the **accelerated cost recovery system (ACRS)** or the **modified accelerated cost recovery system (MACRS)** to calculate depreciation. The federal government has mandated the use of these two methods to calculate depreciation for most types of fixed assets. ACRS applies to assets placed in service between 1981 and 1986. MACRS applies to assets placed in service after 1986.

The ACRS and MACRS apply to all types of fixed assets except real estate. These methods are intended to encourage businesses to purchase new fixed assets by providing quicker depreciation than the other accelerated methods. Both of these methods operate in a similar way, with just the details differing:

- Each method assigns different types of fixed assets to classes. The classes have specified cost recovery periods rather than useful lives. With the MACRS, the cost recovery periods are 3, 5, 7, 10, 15, and 20 years. For example, automobiles and light trucks have a cost recovery period of 5 years. Office equipment has a cost recovery period of 7 years.
- Each method ignores salvage value. The cost of the asset is fully depreciated.
- Each method uses accelerated depreciation in the early years of the cost recovery period and then switches to straight-line depreciation in the later years.
- Each method uses an approach called the **half-year convention** for the first year. No matter when the asset is placed in service during the first year, the rate for the first year assumes that the asset has been owned for half a year.
- The federal government publishes a table for each method that shows the year-by-year percentage of the cost of an asset that a business can take as depreciation. A portion of the MACRS table is shown in table 12–5. (The percentages after year 6 and for the entire 15-year and 20-year classes have been omitted.)

Table 12–5 MACRS Depreciation Percentages

Recovery Year	Recovery Period			
	3-Year	**5-Year**	**7-Year**	**10-Year**
1	33.33%	20.00%	14.29%	10.00%
2	44.45	32.00	24.49	18.00
3	14.81	19.20	17.49	14.40
4	7.41	11.52	12.49	11.52
5		11.52	8.93	9.22
6		5.76	8.92	7.37

To see how MACRS works, assume that the machine purchased for $42,000 on January 1, 2007, falls into the class that has a 5-year cost recovery period. Because of the half-year convention, the machine is actually depreciated for 6 years. The first and last years are considered half years. Table 12–6 provides an example of depreciation using the MACRS method.

Table 12–6 An Example of MACRS Depreciation

Year	Cost	Rate	Depreciation Expense	Accumulated Depreciation	Book Value End of Year
2007	$42,000	20.00%	$ 8,400	$ 8,400	$33,600
2008	42,000	32.00	13,440	21,840	20,160
2009	42,000	19.20	8,064	29,904	12,096
2010	42,000	11.52	4,838	34,742	7,258
2011	42,000	11.52	4,838	39,580	2,420
2012	42,000	5.76	2,420	42,000	—

Check POINT

1. What is depreciation?
2. Name four financial accounting methods for calculating depreciation.

Answers
1. *Depreciation is the process of allocating the cost of a fixed asset to operations during its estimated useful life.*
2. *Four financial accounting methods for calculating depreciation are the straight-line method, the units-of-production method, the double declining-balance method, and the sum-of-the-years'-digits method.*

OBJECTIVE 2—CREATE SUBSIDIARY LEDGER RECORDS FOR INDIVIDUAL FIXED ASSETS

Woodward Construction Company currently owns one piece of equipment—a versatile machine that serves as an excavator, backhoe, and bulldozer. This machine was purchased for $112,000 and recorded in a general ledger account called Equipment. Woodward's general ledger also contains an Accumulated Depreciation–Equipment account and a Depreciation Expense–Equipment account. These two accounts are used to make adjusting entries for depreciation.

Because of its limited resources, Woodward currently leases any other fixed assets that it needs such as a pickup truck to transport materials to jobs. Later, as its finances improve, Woodward plans to purchase additional fixed assets.

Woodward Construction wants to use the general journal and the purchases journal to maintain its fixed assets, adjust depreciation expense, and accumulate depreciation for reporting purposes. Its only asset is the machine purchased at a cost of $112,000 and placed into service at the beginning of 2007, when the business was formed.

CREATING ACCOUNTS FOR NEW FIXED ASSETS

On February 1, 2007, Woodward Construction Company purchased a new computer system for $4,500 on account from Office Max (Invoice 33299). Woodward estimates that the computer system will have a useful life of four years and have no salvage value. Record the purchase in Peachtree Complete Accounting 2007.

Step 1:

Open Peachtree Complete Accounting

Step 2:

Open Woodward Construction Company and close the Action Items log.

Step 3:

Create the following ledger accounts:

Account ID:	**109**
Description:	**Computer**
Account Type:	**Fixed Assets**
Account ID:	**109.5**
Description:	**Accum. Depr.-Computer**
Account Type:	**Accumulated Depreciation**
Account ID:	**511**
Description:	**Depr. Expense-Computer**
Account Type:	**Expenses**

Step 4:

Record the purchase of the computer using the Purchases/Receive Inventory window using 109 as the GL Account.

FIGURE A-1

Computer Purchase Recorded

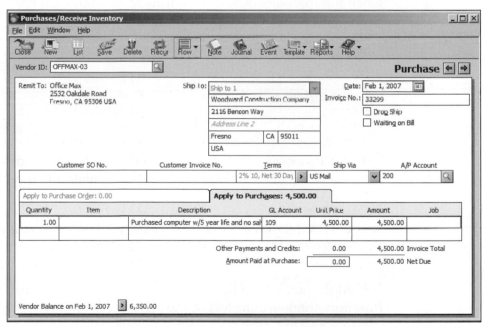

Step 5:

Key **Purchased computer w/5 year life and no salvage** in the *Description* field, as shown in figure A-1.

Step 6:

Click Save and then Close.

Check
POINT

1. What journal is used for fixed asset purchases on account?
2. What is a subsidiary ledger? How might it be used for fixed assets?

Answers
1. *The Purchase/Receive Inventory journal is used.*
2. *Subsidiary ledgers keep track of individual records—they can be used to keep track of individual fixed assets.*

PRACTICE *objective* 2

Bullfrog Maintenance Company wants to use Peachtree to maintain records of its fixed assets and calculate depreciation. Bullfrog currently owns only one fixed asset, a truck that appears in the Equipment account (108). This truck cost $42,000, has a salvage value of $2000, an expected life of 5 years, and has accumulated depreciation of $10,750 through January 31, 2007.

On February 23, 2007, Bullfrog Maintenance Company purchased a new computer system for $7,500 on credit from Office Depot (Invoice 23998). Bullfrog estimates that the computer system will have a salvage value of $500 and a useful life of five years.

Step 1:

Open Bullfrog Maintenance Company in Peachtree Complete Accounting.

Step 2:

Create the following general ledger accounts:

Account ID:	**111**
Description:	**Computer**
Account Type:	**Fixed Assets**
Account ID:	**111.5**
Description:	**Accum. Depr.–Computer**
Account Type:	**Accumulated Depreciation**
Account ID:	**511**
Description:	**Depr. Expense–Computer**
Account Type:	**Expenses**

Step 3:

Record the purchase of the computer system using the Purchases/Receive Inventory window using 111 as the GL Account and referring to the purchase data above.

Step 4:

Click the *Save* icon and Close.

OBJECTIVE 3—CALCULATE AND RECORD THE DEPRECIATION OF A FIXED ASSET

Woodward Construction Company wants to calculate and record depreciation for the excavator (Account 108) and the computer (Account 109), as of March 31, 2007. It will be necessary to manually calculate the depreciation and enter the amount into the accounting records.

Calculating Depreciation

Woodward Construction Company wants to calculate 2 months worth of depreciation for both assets, because no depreciation has been taken for February or March 2007. Follow the steps to manually calculate the total depreciation for the two-month period:

Excavating Equipment

The original cost of the excavator is $112,000, the salvage value is listed at $52,000, and its useful life is 5 years (60 months) and it was placed into service on Jan. 1, 2006. Note that depreciation of $13,000 has already been taken for the period January 1, 2006 to January 31, 2007.

COMPUTER EQUIPMENT

The original cost of the computer is $4,500, there is no salvage value, and its useful life is 4 years (48 months) and it was placed into service on Feb. 1, 2007.

Step 1:

Open Woodward Construction Company, if not already open.

Step 2:

Divide the cost of the excavator minus its salvage value by 60 (Total Life in Months) and multiply that amount by 2. The result is the depreciation for the period.

(($112,000 – $52,000)/60) = $1,000 per month.
$1,000 x 2 = $2,000, the depreciation for the two month period.

Step 3:

Divide the cost of the computer minus its salvage value by 48 (Total Life in Months) and multiply that amount by 2. The result is the depreciation for the period.

(($4,500 – $0)/48) = $93.75 per month.
$93.75 x 2 = $187.50, the depreciation for the two month period.

ENTERING DEPRECIATION IN THE GENERAL JOURNAL AND GENERAL LEDGER

Once the depreciation has been calculated, it is necessary to enter the amount as an adjusting entry in the general journal. Peachtree will automatically post the amounts from the general journal to the general ledger. The appropriate accounts have been created previously and are available for use in the general journal. The entries include the following:

March 31, 2007
    Depreciation Expense-Equipment   2,000
        Accumulated Depreciation-Equipment   2,000
           (To record depreciation through Mar 31, 2007)

March 31, 2007

Depreciation Expense-Computer	187.50	
Accumulated Depreciation-Computer		187.50

(To record depreciation through Mar 31, 2007)

Step 4:

Select Ta<u>s</u>ks and <u>G</u>eneral Journal Entry from the Main menu, as shown in figure A-2.

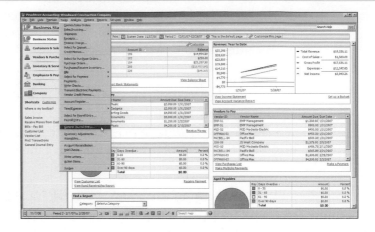

FIGURE A-2

Tasks and <u>G</u>eneral Journal Entry Selected from the Main Menu

Step 5:

In the General Journal Entry window, key **3/31/2007** in the *<u>D</u>ate* field.

Step 6:

Key **Adjustment** in the *Refere<u>n</u>ce* field.

Step 7:

Select **510** (Depreciation Expense-Equipment) as the GL Account.

Step 8:

Key **Depreciation Adjustment** in the *Description* field.

Step 9:

Key **2000.00** (Depreciation manually calculated) in the *Debit* field.

Step 10:

Select **108.5** (Accumulated Depreciation-Equipment) as the GL Account in the second row.

Step 11:

Key **Depreciation Adjustment** in the *Description* field, if needed.

Step 12:

Key **2000.00** (Depreciation manually calculated) in the *Credit* field.

Step 13:

Select **511** (Depreciation Expense-Computer) as the GL Account in the third row.

Step 14:

Key **Depreciation Adjustment** in the *Description* field.

Step 15:

Key **187.50** (Depreciation manually calculated) in the *Debit* field.

Step 16:

Select **109.5** (Accumulated Depreciation-Computer) as the GL Account in the fourth row.

Step 17:

Key **Depreciation Adjustment** in the *Description* field.

Step 18:

Key **187.50** (Depreciation manually calculated) in the *Credit* field.

Step 19:

Review your screen against figure A-3 for accuracy, making any necessary changes.

FIGURE A-3
Completed General Journal Entry for Fixed Asset Depreciation

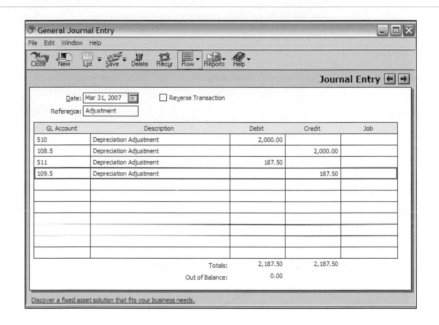

Step 20:

Save and close the General Journal Entry window.

Check POINT

1. What journal is used to record depreciation?
2. What accounts are affected when adjusting for fixed asset depreciation?

Answers
1. *The general journal is used to record depreciation.*
2. *Depreciation Expense & Accumulated Depreciation are affected.*

PRACTICE *objective* 3

Bullfrog Maintenance Company wants to calculate and record depreciation from February 1, 2007 through June 30, 2007.

Step 1:

Open the Bullfrog Maintenance Company in Peachtree Complete Accounting.

Step 2:

The manual calculation of the assets are as follows:

Equipment

($42,000 – $2,000)/60 = $666.67 per month.

$666.67 x 5 = $3333.35, the depreciation for the five-month period.

Computer

($7,500 – $500)/60 = $116.67 per month.

$116.67 x 4 = $466.68, the depreciation for the four-month period. Notice that the computer was put into service February 23, 2007. Therefore, there are only four full months of depreciation.

FIGURE A-4

Completed General Journal Depreciation Entry

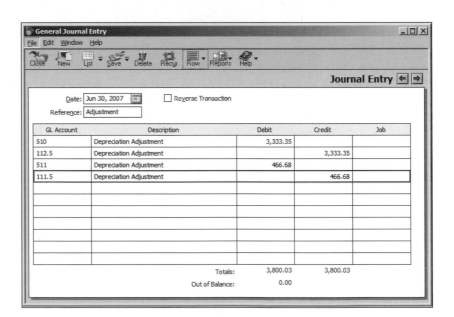

Step 3:

Record the depreciation expense in the general journal and post it to the general ledger. Refer to figure A-4 for comparison, making any necessary changes.

Step 4:

Close Bullfrog Maintenance Company.

Remember that all fixed assets except land have limited lives. Eventually, they wear out or become obsolete, or their owners want to replace them with newer, more efficient models. When a fixed asset is no longer useful, a business will dispose of the asset by selling it, trading it in for a new asset, or scrapping it if it has no remaining value.

Suppose that Woodward Construction Company decides to sell the excavator that it owns. On March 31, 2007, it receives $120,000 for the excavator. Woodward must determine whether there is a gain or loss on this transaction and then record the disposal in its accounting records.

When a firm disposes of a fixed asset, it must bring depreciation on the asset up to date. Then it can find the book value of the asset and determine whether the sale produced a gain or loss.

In the case of the excavator sold by Woodward Construction Company, the depreciation entry made on March 31, 2007, results in accumulated depreciation of $15,000 and a book value of $97,000. Remember that the book value of a fixed asset is the difference between its cost and its accumulated depreciation. The cost of the excavator was $112,000. The book value is therefore $97,000 ($112,000 – $15,000 = $97,000).

If the selling price of a fixed asset is greater than its book value, there is a gain on the sale. If the selling price of a fixed asset is less than its book value, there is a loss on the sale. Because Woodward sold its excavator for $120,000 and the book value of the machine is $97,000, the firm has a gain of $23,000.

The gain on the sale of a fixed asset is considered other (nonoperating) income because it does not result from the normal operations of a business. It is therefore recorded in an account called Gain on Disposal of Fixed Assets. Similarly, the loss on the sale of a fixed asset is considered other (nonoperating) expense. It is recorded in an account called Loss on Disposal of Fixed Assets.

The sale of the excavator by Woodward Construction Company requires a debit of $120,000 to Cash, a debit of $15,000 to Accumulated Depreciation–Equipment, a credit of $112,000 to Equipment, and a credit of $23,000 to Gain on Disposal of Fixed Assets. The effects of this transaction are as follows:

- The debit to Cash records the amount received for the excavator.
- The debit to Accumulated Depreciation–Equipment removes the accumulated depreciation of the excavator from the accounting records.
- The credit to Equipment removes the cost of the excavator from the accounting records.
- The credit to Gain on Disposal of Fixed Assets records the income earned from the sale of the excavator.

RECORDING THE DISPOSAL OF A FIXED ASSET AT A GAIN

Woodward Construction Company does not yet have a Gain on Disposal of Fixed Assets account in its general ledger. Therefore, it must now create this account.

Step 1:

Open Woodward Construction Company in Peachtree Complete Accounting.

Step 2:

Create the following general ledger account:

Account ID:	**452**
Description:	**Gain on Disposal of Fxd Assets**
Account Type:	**Income**

Step 3:

Select Tas<u>k</u>s and <u>G</u>eneral Journal Entry from the Main menu.

Step 4:

Key **3/31/07** in <u>*Date*</u> field.

Step 5:

Key **Disposal** in the *Refere<u>n</u>ce* field.

Step 6:

Select **100** (Cash) as the GL Account.

Step 7:

Key **Disposal of Excavator** in the *Description* field.

Step 8:

Enter **120,000.00** in the *Debit* field.

Step 9:

Go to next line and select **108.5** (Accumulated Depreciation-Equipment) for the GL Account.

Step 10:

Enter **15,000.00** in the *Debit* field.

Step 11:

Go to next line and select **108** (Equipment) for the GL Account.

Step 12:

Enter **112,000.00** in the *Credit* field.

Step 13:

Go to next line and select **452** (Gain on Disposal of Fixed Assets) for the GL Account.

Step 14:

Enter **23,000.00** in the *Credit* field.

Step 15:

Review figure A-5 for accuracy, making any necessary changes.

FIGURE A-5

General Journal Entry for Disposal of Fixed Asset

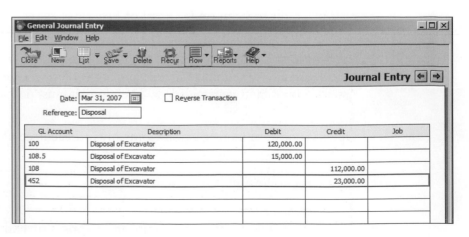

Step 16:

Click Save and then Close.

POINT

1. What is the book value of a fixed asset?
2. What type of income is a gain on the disposal of a fixed asset?

Answers
1. *The book value of a fixed asset is the difference between its cost and its accumulated depreciation.*
2. *A gain on the disposal of a fixed asset is considered other (nonoperating) income.*

P R A C T I C E *objective* 4

On June 30, 2007, Bullfrog Maintenance Company decides to dispose of the truck that it owns in order to purchase a new model. Bullfrog sells the truck for $40,000 in cash. The current book value is $27,916.65.

Step 1:

Open Bullfrog Maintenance Company in Peachtree Complete Accounting.

Step 2:

Create the following general ledger account.

Account ID:	**452**
Description:	**Gain on Disposal of Fxd Assets**
Account Type:	**Income**

Step 3:

Record the disposal of the truck in the general journal and post to the general ledger.

Step 4:

Review figure A-6 for accuracy, make any necessary changes, and then close.

FIGURE A-6

General Journal Entry for Disposal of a Fixed Asset

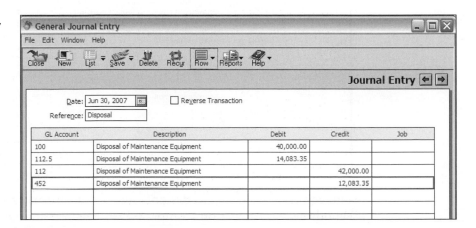

OBJECTIVE 5—PREPARE AND MODIFY REPORTS SHOWING FIXED ASSETS AND DEPRECIATION

Management needs to have information on the purchase, depreciation, and disposal of fixed assets so it can develop plans to replace older, less efficient ones. Many businesses set up long-term budgets for the replacement and acquisition of new fixed assets.

On March 31, 2007, Woodward Construction Company wants to review the depreciation and disposal of fixed assets since February 1, 2007. In addition, it would like to modify the default format of the report.

Step 1:

Open Woodward Construction Company, if not already open.

Step 2:

Click Reports and General Ledger from the drop-down list.

Step 3:

Select General Journal from the Select a Report, Report List.

Step 4:

Click Preview from the Main menu.

Step 5:

Deselect *Include Accounts with Zero Amounts*.

Step 6:

Select *Range* from the *Date* field.

Step 7:

Select from *Feb 1, 2007* to *Mar 31, 2007*.

Step 8:

Click OK. Compare your screen with figure A-7.

FIGURE A-7
General Journal Report

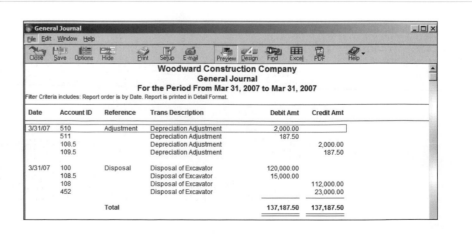

Management would like to design a new form for this printout to read "Woodward Construction Company Depreciation and Disposal" in bold-type centered on the report.

Step 9:
Select Design from the menu bar.

Step 10:
Select Fonts from the left toolbar.

Step 11:
Key **Depreciation and Disposal** in the *Title 1 Report Label* field, as shown in figure A-8.

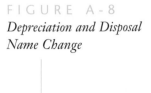
FIGURE A-8

Depreciation and Disposal Name Change

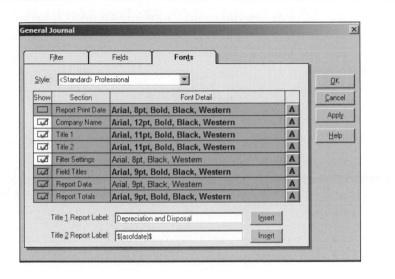

Step 12:
Click Insert, OK, and then OK again.

Step 13:
Click Save on the menu bar.

Step 14:
Key **Depreciation and Disposal, Mar** in the *Name* field, as shown in figure A-9.

FIGURE A-9

File Saved as Depreciation and Disposal, Mar

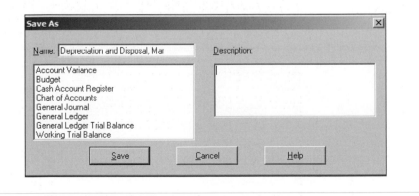

Step 15:
Click Save and then close or cancel all subsequent queries.

This report is available as a special report in the reports section.

1. Where can fixed asset depreciation & disposal transactions be found?
2. Can the General Journal Report be modified? If so, how?

Answers
1. In the General Journal.
2. Yes, by selecting Design from the menu.

Bullfrog Maintenance Company wants to prepare the following report for the period of February 1, 2007, to June 30, 2007.

Step 1:
Open Bullfrog Maintenance Company.

Step 2:
Prepare the report using the General Journal Report and modifying the report name to Depreciation and Disposal. Your printout should look like figure A-10.

FIGURE A-10

Depreciation and Disposal Report June 2007

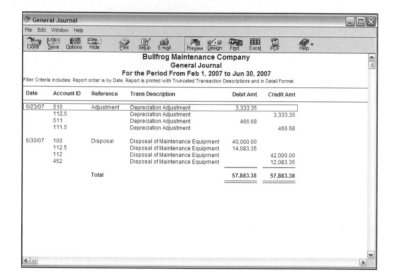

INTERNET *Access*

The Internal Revenue Service maintains a Web site that people can visit to obtain federal tax forms and tax information. This site is located at www.irs.gov (see figure A-11).

FIGURE A-11

IRS Web Site

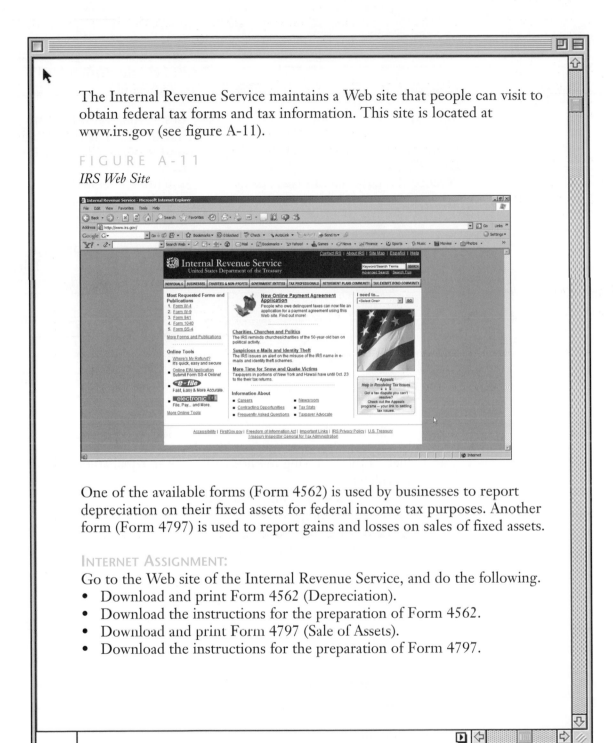

One of the available forms (Form 4562) is used by businesses to report depreciation on their fixed assets for federal income tax purposes. Another form (Form 4797) is used to report gains and losses on sales of fixed assets.

INTERNET ASSIGNMENT:

Go to the Web site of the Internal Revenue Service, and do the following.
- Download and print Form 4562 (Depreciation).
- Download the instructions for the preparation of Form 4562.
- Download and print Form 4797 (Sale of Assets).
- Download the instructions for the preparation of Form 4797.

S O F T W A R E
Command Summary

Create Subsidiary Ledger Records	<u>M</u>aintain, Chart of <u>A</u>ccounts, enter the asset information for Fixed Assets Account
Journalize Depreciation	<u>T</u>asks, <u>G</u>eneral Journal Entry, manually calculate depreciation for period
Record the Disposal of Fixed Assets	<u>M</u>aintain, <u>G</u>eneral Journal Entry, manually calculate gain or loss on disposal of asset
Prepare Reports	<u>R</u>eports, select Report Type, <u>D</u>esign, complete Report Filter

P R O J E C T S
and Problems

CONTENT CHECK
Multiple Choice: Choose only one response for each question.

1. Which of the following methods allocates an equal amount of depreciation each year?
   A. Sum-of-the-years'-digits method
   B. Double declining-balance method
   C. Straight-line method
   D. Units-of-production method

2. Which of the following statements about fixed assets is *not* true?
   A. Fixed assets are intended for use in the operations of a business.
   B. Fixed assets have an estimated useful life of more than one year.
   C. Fixed assets are acquired for resale to customers.
   D. Fixed assets are tangible.

3. Depreciation is taken on all fixed assets except
   A. land.
   B. land improvements.
   C. buildings.
   D. equipment and machinery.

4. The difference between the cost of a fixed asset and its accumulated depreciation is the
   A. purchase price.
   B. book value.
   C. salvage value.
   D. selling price.

5. Depreciable cost is
   A. Cost – depreciation expense.
   B. Cost – accumulated depreciation.
   C. Cost – salvage value.
   D. Accumulated depreciation – salvage value.

Short-Essay Response: Provide a detailed answer for each question.

1. What is depreciation? Why must businesses record depreciation?
2. What is accelerated depreciation? Name two financial accounting methods for calculating depreciation that are accelerated.
3. What is the modified accelerated cost recovery system? When is this method used?
4. How is the sale of a fixed asset at a gain recorded? What general ledger accounts are debited and credited?
5. Why does the Fixed Assets module of Peachtree provide for the use of both financial accounting and tax accounting methods of depreciation?

CASE PROBLEMS

PROBLEM 1A

On January 31, 2007, Robertson Construction Company's only fixed asset currently on its books is construction equipment. This construction equipment cost $16,000, has an estimated salvage value of $1,000, and has an estimated useful life of four years. The equipment was purchased on January 1, 2007.

On January 31, 2007, Robertson Construction Company purchases landscaping equipment on credit from Steve's Supply Warehouse. The cost is $13,000, the estimated salvage value is $1,000, and the estimated useful life is four years (Invoice 555).

1. Create the following general ledger accounts.

Account ID	109
Description	Landscaping Equipment
Account Type	Fixed Assets

Account ID	109.5
Description	Accum. Depr.-Landscaping Eq.
Account Type	Accumulated Depreciation

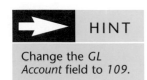

HINT

Change the *GL Account* field to *109*.

2. Use the Purchases/Receive Inventory window to record the purchase of the landscaping equipment.

3. Print the Chart of Accounts.

NOTE

Use Account 510 for both depreciation expenses.

PROBLEM 2A

On June 30, 2007, Robertson Construction Company updates the depreciation expense on its fixed assets. Use Peachtree Complete Accounting 2007 to do the following:

1. Calculate the depreciation expense of the construction equipment (6 months) and the landscaping equipment (5 months) as of June 30, 2007.
2. Post to the general ledger.
3. Print the general journal entries for June 30, 2007.

   On July 1, 2007, Robertson decides to sell the landscaping equipment for $12,900 in cash. Robertson wants to purchase a more advanced model.

4. Create the following general ledger account.

Account ID:	452
Description:	Gain on Disposal of Fxd Assets
Account Type:	Income

5. Record the disposal of the landscaping equipment in the general journal and post to the general ledger.
6. Print the general journal entries for July 1, 2007.

PROBLEM 1B

On January 31, 2007, Abelar Construction Company's only fixed asset currently on its books is an excavator. This excavator cost $26,000, has an estimated salvage value of $5,000, and has an estimated useful life of seven years. The equipment was purchased on January 1, 2007.

   On January 31, 2007, Abelar Construction Company purchases digging equipment on credit from Construction Supply Warehouse (Invoice 48537). The cost is $18,500, the estimated salvage value is $2,000, and the estimated useful life is five years.

HINT

Change the *GL Account* field to *109*.

1. Create the following general ledger accounts.

Account ID	109
Description	Digging Equipment
Account Type	Fixed Assets

Account ID	109.5
Description	Accum. Depr.-Digging Eq.
Account Type	Accumulated Depreciation

2. Use the Purchases/Receive Inventory window to record the purchase of the digging equipment.

3. Print the Chart of Accounts.

NOTE

Use Account 510 for both depreciation expenses.

PROBLEM 2B

On June 30, 2007, Abelar Construction Company updates the depreciation expense on its fixed assets. Use Peachtree Complete Accounting 2007 to do the following:

1. Calculate the depreciation expense of the excavator (6 months) and the digging equipment (5 months) as of June 30, 2007.
2. Post to the general ledger.
3. Print the general journal entries for June 30, 2007.

On July 1, 2007, Abelar decides to sell the digging equipment for $17,550 in cash. Abelar intends to lease a more powerful model.

4. Create the following general ledger account.

    Account ID: 452
    Description: Gain on Disposal of Fxd Assets
    Account Type: Income

5. Record the disposal of the digging equipment in the general journal and post to the general ledger.
6. Print the general journal entries for July 1, 2007.

Cooperative Learning

1. Form groups of three or four students, and prepare a list of four possible fixed assets that might be found in a doctor's office. Estimate the cost, salvage value, useful life, and depreciable cost for each of the four assets. Calculate the annual straight-line depreciation for each of the assets.
2. Survey a local CPA firm to determine what portion of the firm's clients use the straight-line method of depreciation for financial accounting purposes.

Writing and Decision Making

Gary Stevens, the newly hired manager of an engineering company, does not understand how the cost of the firm's equipment is expensed. In memo format, explain to him how depreciation provides a means of expensing the cost of the equipment.

INDEX

Accelerated cost recovery system (ACRS), 507, 587
Account # tab, Maintain Customers/Prospects window, 130
Account description, 51
Account ID
 description, 50
 new account setup, 50–51, 53–54, 83
 numeric ranges, 50
Account ID field, Maintain Chart of Accounts window, 53–55, 83, 335
Accounting
 definition, 4
 manual and computerized systems compared, 4–5
 purpose of, 4
 steps in process, 4
Accounting Behind the Screens window
 credit memos, 381–383
 debiting Uncollectible Accounts Expense, 162, 163–164
 discount application, 236, 255
 partnership transactions, 551
Accounting methods
 accrual basis, 43
 cash basis, 43
Accounting period
 changing, 321–323
 definition, 45
 setting for new company, 45–46
Account No. field
 General Journal Entry window, 294–296, 551–552, 558, 560
 GL Account field, 295
 Maintain Vendors window, 182, 348
Account Reconciliation command
 Reports menu, 270
 Tasks menu, 266
Account Reconciliation report, printing, 270–271, 274
Account Reconciliation window
 Account to Reconcile field, 266
 Adjust button, 267
 Deposits and Bank Credits section, 269
 Service Charges field, 269
 Statement Date field, 266
 Statement Ending Balance field, 266–267
 Status field, 266, 269

Account Rep field, Maintain Vendors window, 183
Accounts. *See also specific accounts*
 creating
  in accounts receivable ledger, 129–140
  corporation, 557–558
  new, 53–54, 83–85, 335–337, 372–373
  partnership, 548–549
  payroll, 421–430
 deleting, 55
 editing, 54–55
 uncollectible, 129, 158–164
 viewing with magnifying glass icon, 85
Accounts payable
 definition, 52, 180
 printing reports, 198–200, 211–215
 Vendor Ledgers report, 198–200
Accounts Payable account, general ledger, 52
 as controlling account, 180
 crediting purchases to, 180, 194
 debiting payments to, 180
Accounts Payable command, Reports menu, 198, 212
Accounts payable ledger
 definition, 180
 editing transactions, 197–198
 recording purchases on credit, 194–197
Accounts receivable
 definition, 51, 128
 Peachtree features for improving efficiency of, 128
 printing reports, 165–168
 uncollectible accounts, 129
Accounts Receivable account, general ledger, 51
 as controlling account, 129, 141
 crediting uncollectible account write-off to, 159
Accounts Receivable command, Reports menu, 147, 165, 262
Accounts receivable ledger
 creating accounts in, 129–140
 crediting uncollectible account write-off to, 159
 definition, 128
 recording sales on credit, 141–144
 recording sales on credit and partial collection, 144–147
Account to Reconcile field, 266
Account Type box, Maintain Chart of Accounts window, 54, 84, 335

Account types. *See also specific accounts*
 Accounts Payable, 52
 Accounts Receivable, 51
 Accumulated Depreciation, 52
 Cash, 51
 Cost of Sales, 52
 Equity-Doesn't Close, 52
 Equity-Gets Closed, 52
 Equity-Retained Earnings, 52
 Expenses, 52
 Fixed Assets, 52
 Income, 52
 Inventory, 51
 Long-Term Liabilities, 52
 Other Assets, 52
 Other Current Assets, 51
 Other Current Liabilities, 52
Accrual basis, accounting method, 43
Accumulated Depreciation account, 52
Accumulated Depreciation-Equipment account, 293
Acquisition Date field, New Asset Wizard, 512
Acquisition report, 527–528
Acquisition Value field, New Asset Wizard, 512
ACRS (accelerated cost recovery system), 507, 587
Action items
 adding events to action list, 153–155, 204–206
 defaults, setting up events as, 150–151, 201–202
 description, 149
 displaying, 155, 202, 206–207
 recording on the To Do list, 152–153, 203
 setting alerts, 156–157, 207–211
Action Items and Event Log Options
 accessing, 149, 150, 201
 Activities tab, 150, 201
  Event Type field, 202
  # of Days field, 202
 Start Up tab, 151, 202
 Transactions tab, 150–151, 201–202
Action Items command, Tasks menu, 150, 152, 155, 201, 203, 207
Action Items window
 Alert button, 156, 207
 Alerts tab, 156–157, 207–208, 211

Modified accelerated cost recovery system (MACRS), 507–508, 587–588
More Information section, New Company Setup-Chart of Accounts dialog box, 41–42
Multiple Price Levels window, 340–341
Multiple Sites field, Maintain Customers/Prospects window, 131
Mutual agency rule, 36, 539

Name field
   Maintain Customers/Prospects window, 129, 133
   Maintain Employees/Sales Reps window, 346
   Maintain Vendors window, 182, 185, 348
   Save As dialog box, 315
NASDAQ, 572
Natural resources, 502, 582
Navigating through Peachtree
   with custom toolbar, 12–13, 14–15
   with Menu bar, 13–14, 15
Navigation aids
   Company icon, 48–49
   General Journal Entry icon, 88, 104, 293–294
   General Ledger icon, 62, 104
   Pay Employees icon, 439
   Payroll Employees icon, 443, 444
   Payroll Setup Wizard icon, 422
   toolbar icons, 12
   viewing options, 13
Net income, definition, 107, 229
Net loss, definition, 107, 229
Net pay, 438
New accounts
   creating Cash account, 53–54, 83–84
   creating Inventory account, 335
   new company setup, 40–43, 48–50
   for vendors, 243–245, 373
New asset icon, 514
New Asset Wizard, 510–514
New button
   Chart of Accounts Beginning Balances window, 60–61
   Maintain Chart of Accounts window, 84
   Write Checks window, 242, 243
New command, Asset menu, 510, 514
New Company command, File menu, 509
   Company Information dialog box, 38–39, 49, 82

Defaults dialog box, 46
Finish dialog box, 46–47, 83
Introduction dialog box, 38, 49, 82
Posting Method dialog box, 44, 83
New Company Setup icon, Company folder, 48
New Company Wizard window, accessing, 509
New Name field, Copy Reports, Financial Statements & Letter Templates dialog box, 308
Note field, Create Event window, 154, 205
Notes field, To Do tab, Action Items window, 152, 203

Office Depot, 216–217
Office Manager field, Maintain Vendors window, 183
Office Max, 216–217
Office supply businesses, 216
1099 Type field, Maintain Vendors window, 182, 185, 348
Online banking, 175
Open an existing company command, 23
Open an Existing Company dialog box, 23–24
Open button
   General Journal Entry toolbar, 95, 97, 99
   Payments toolbar, 247
   Payroll Entry toolbar, 444
   Purchases/Receive Inventory window, 197
   Receipts toolbar, 256
   Select Invoice window, 379
Open Company command, File menu, 24
Open P.O. # field, Maintain Customers/Prospects window, 131
Opening
   files, 22–24
   Peachtree Complete Accounting 2007, 5–6
Opening window, 7, 9, 11, 12, 14
Opens the Internal Accounting Review icon, 12
Options button, Action Items toolbar, 150, 201
Options command, Menu bar, 12, 13
Options folder, Standard Income Stmnt, 109
Options menu, View Navigation Aid command, 293

Other Assets account, 52
Other Current Assets account, 51
Other Current Liabilities account, 52
Outstanding stock, 542
Overdue amounts, collecting, 149, 158
Overtime, preparing payroll with, 442–444
Overtime field, Payroll Entry window, 443

Paid-in capital, 543, 567
Paid-in Capital in Excess of Par-Common account, 542
Partnership, 35–36
   accounting for, 539–540
   accounts, creating, 548–549
   allocating profits and losses, 552–554
   characteristics of, 538–539
   converting to, 548–549
   definition, 538
   limited life, 539
   mutual agency rule, 539
   recording transactions, 550–552
   reports, 566–567
   unlimited liability, 539
Partnership agreement, 538, 544–545
Par value, 542
Paste command, 314, 439
Paycheck List window, 443–444, 480–482
Pay Employees, 439
Pay Employees icon, navigation aids, 439, 443, 444
Pay field
   Payments window, 236, 238, 355
   Receipts window, 254, 386
Pay Info tab, Maintain Employees/Sales Reps window, 432–435
Payment Defaults tab, Maintain Customers/Prospects window, 131
Payment List window, 248
Payment Method field
   Receipts window, 163, 254, 385
   Receive Payment window, 146
Payments
   paying bill for a purchase not previously recorded, 241–245
   paying invoice and previous balance, 238–241
   paying invoice with a discount, 232–238
   printing checks previously marked for payment, 247–248
   printing individual checks, 245